SOUTH-WESTERN College Publishing's

S0-BXT-790

1996 *edition*

PAYROLL ACCOUNTING

Bernard J. Bieg
Bucks County Community College

B. Lewis Keeling
Bucks County Community College

Contributing Editor
Dan W. Biagi
Walla Walla Community College

SOUTH-WESTERN College Publishing
An International Thomson Publishing Company

Senior Acquisitions Editor: Gary L. Bauer
Developmental Editor: Tom Bormann
Production Editor: Shelley Brewer
Production Editor—Software: Tim Butz
Technology Services Specialist: Lora Craver
Production House: Litten Editing and Production
Internal Design: Debbie Leffert, Jim DeSollar, Lotus Wittkopf
Cover Design: Michael Lindsay Design
Photo Research: Jennifer Mayhall
Marketing Manager: Dreis Van Landuyt

AH60FB
Copyright © 1996
by South-Western College Publishing
Cincinnati, Ohio

ISBN: 0-538-85723-4

1 2 3 4 5 6 7 8 9 DH 3 2 1 0 9 8 7 6 5
Printed in the United States of America

I(T)P
International Thomson Publishing
South-Western College Publishing is an ITP Company. The ITP trademark is
used under license.

PREFACE

GUIDE FOR STUDENTS AND INSTRUCTORS

Before you start reading PAYROLL ACCOUNTING, 1996 Edition, we invite you to spend a little time looking over the next few pages. They provide a quick guide to the features throughout the text that have made this the Number One selling payroll accounting book in the market. The 1996 Edition benefits from the helpful comments and suggestions contributed by many instructors and students who have taught and learned payroll accounting from previous editions. The new one-column format increases visual appeal and user friendliness.

NEED FOR PAYROLL ACCOUNTING

Payroll accounting has emerged as one of the most important components of the organization's total accounting system.

At the federal and state levels, frequent changes are being made in the laws that affect a company's payroll tax structure. Thus, payroll accounting requires a constant updating on the part of the persons charged with planning and organizing the payroll system. We update this book every year so that students are prepared as much as possible for their careers. Also, we focus on what you need to know to join the workforce and to be successful.

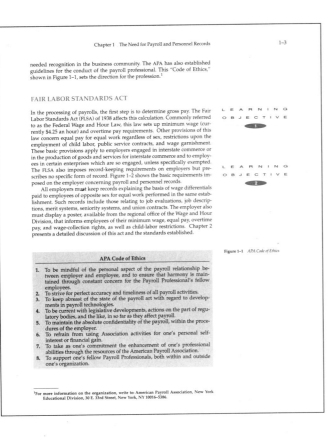

FEATURES OF 1996 PAYROLL ACCOUNTING

Integrated Learning Objectives

Each chapter begins with learning objectives, which are indicated in text where first discussed, and which are identified for end-of-chapter assignments.

This enables the instructor and students to find and focus on mastering specific learning objectives.

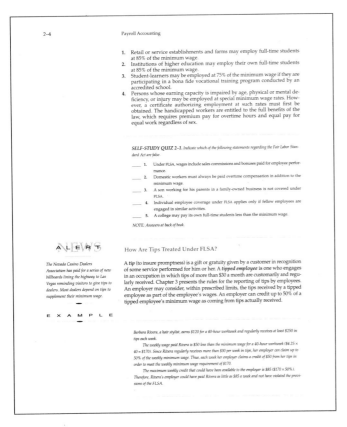

In-Text Self-Study Quizzes

Self-study quizzes appear in the text following major sections of material. Answers are given at the end of the book.

These self-study quizzes allow students to check their understanding of major concepts before moving on to new material.

Two-Page Chapter Openers

Each chapter opens with two pages that include Learning Objectives, That Was Then/This is Now vignette, and two photos to illustrate the vignette.

The photos enhance visual appeal, and the vignettes increase students' interest in payroll accounting.

Icons

Three icons in addition to learning objective numbers appear in the text margin: News Alert, IRS Connection, and On the Job.

"News Alerts" announce important information on current happenings in payroll accounting; "IRS Connections" provide information directly related to IRS procedures and laws; and "On the Job" gives realistic information to help payroll workers in the workplace.

Other Successful Features of 1996 PAYROLL ACCOUNTING

COMPUTERIZED PAYROLL ACCOUNTING
software by Klooster & Allen:

1. Models the DOS version of INTEGRATED ACCOUNTING software.
2. Prepares students for today's computerized payroll environment.
3. Includes pull-down menus that provide quick access to lists, reports, and help information.
4. Provides well-documented instructions in Appendix B that guide students through a computerized version of the Chapter 7 Payroll Project.
5. Helps students observe the differences and similarities between a manual and computerized payroll system.
6. Utilizes a totally seamless, integrated payroll system that automatically generates and posts journal entries for payroll and employer's payroll taxes.

- Unique, three-month simulated payroll project uses actual forms can be worked manually or electronically (with Payroll Accounting software).
- Most current federal and state tax laws.
- Newest required filled-in forms with line-by-line instructions.
- "As We Go To Press" section in front part of book summarizes the latest developments.
- **NEW** A Glossary of important terms at end of book.
- Tests for each of the first six chapters available in quantity, free of charge, from the publisher.
- Additional test questions, including ones for COMPUTERIZED PAYROLL ACCOUNTING, in the solutions manual.
- A list of Key Terms ends each of the first six chapters.

GOALS OF PAYROLL ACCOUNTING

1. To develop an understanding of the personnel and payroll records that provide the information required under the numerous laws affecting the operations of a payroll system.
2. To describe the payroll-record life of employees from their initial applications for employment to their applications for their first social security benefit checks.
3. To introduce the various aspects of the Fair Labor Standards Act and the other laws that affect payroll operations and employment practices.
4. To describe the basic payroll accounting systems and procedures used in computing wages and salaries and the timekeeping methods used to record time worked.
5. To explain the various phases of the Social Security Act, the federal income tax withholding law, and other laws relating to the payment of wages and salaries.
6. To provide practice in all payroll operations, the preparation of payroll registers, the recording of accounting entries involving payroll, and the preparation of payroll tax returns required of businesses.
7. To complete a payroll project manually or with a microcomputer. Students can use the optional diskette package to update employee files, to complete payroll reports, and to display quarterly reports and W-2 forms.

ACKNOWLEDGEMENTS

We express our appreciation to the many instructors and students who have contributed suggestions to make this textbook more interesting, understandable, and practical to those who pursue the study of payroll accounting. We greatly appreciate the time, experience, and expertise provided by the following reviewers:

Corinne Alesch
Western Iowa Tech Community
College

James Boyle
Heald College

Sherrie Dusch
Barnes Business College

Cynthia F. Gerber
Indiana Business College

Florence C. Godat
Northeast State Technical
Community College

Pompilio Gomez
Drake Business Schools

Harry E. Gray
Ivy Tech State College-Indianapolis

Gary Guinn
Skagit Valley College

Bill Huerter
Northeast Iowa Community College

Linda J. Jones
Neosho County Community
College

Frank A. Paliotta
Berkeley College

Alan Ransom
Cypress College

David L. Stone
Central Carolina Technical College

Jeffrey Wig
Central Lakes College

As a result of their very helpful recommendations, the 1996 Edition will better satisfy the learning needs of students and the teaching needs of instructors.

Bernard J. Bieg, Author
Dan W. Biagi, Contributing Editor

In 1994, we lost a great teacher, an acclaimed author, a perceptive editor, and a true friend. Many of the improvements made in this edition were ideas that began with Bill Keeling.

Not a page was written without reflecting on what Bill would suggest. His legacy is with us and this best edition ever is a tribute to him.

Bernard J. Bieg

As we go to press . . .

Chapter 1—Davis-Bacon Repeal

Proposals before both the House and Senate dealing with the possible repeal of the Davis-Bacon Act have been the subject of much debate during this session of Congress.

Chapter 2—Independent Contractor Status

The IRS has stepped up compliance checks on small business firms. The IRS feels that many misclassifications are deliberate, and they are attempting to clear up the definition of "independent contractors."

Chapter 3—Filing Electronically

The Treasury and the IRS have developed a program that will allow all employers to file reporting forms (940, 941, W-2's, etc.) electronically or on magnetic media. This program is expected to be in place by the end of 1996.

Chapter 3—Interest Rates

The IRS has changed interest rate charges for tax underpayments to 9% for most businesses and 11% for large corporations.

Chapter 3—Educational Assistance Proposal

The Employee Educational Assistance Act of 1995, being considered by the House of Representatives, would restore and make permanent the exclusion from employee income of employer-provided educational assistance of up to $5,250.

Chapter 3—OASDI Taxable Wage Base

Throughout this edition, an estimated OASDI taxable wage base of $63,000 has been used. In mid-October, the Social Security Administration set the actual taxable wage base at $62,700 for 1996.

Contents

THAT WAS THEN THIS IS NOW

Congress levied the first income tax in 1861 to raise funds for the Union Army, later abolishing the tax in 1872. Since then Congress has enacted numerous laws regulating payroll and personnel. Today the employer faces laws regulating income tax withholding, social security, unemployment, minimum wages, overtime, pay equity, and child labor.

THE NEED FOR PAYROLL AND PERSONNEL RECORDS

LEARNING OBJECTIVES

After studying this chapter, you should be able to:

1. Identify the various laws that affect employers in their payroll operations.

2. Explain the record-keeping requirements of these laws.

3. Explain the importance of a thorough record-keeping system.

4. Describe the employment procedures generally followed in a Human Resources Department.

5. Recognize the various personnel records used by businesses and know the type of information shown on each form.

6. Describe the procedures employed in a typical payroll accounting system.

7. Identify the *payroll register* and the *employee's earnings record*.

Payroll professionals are responsible for issuing over four billion paychecks each year to over a hundred million people in the workforce of the United States. The processing of payrolls allows no margin for error. Employees, employers, and government agencies monitor the work performed by payroll professionals. A payroll accounting system is the only operation in a business that is almost completely governed by various federal, state, and local laws and regulations. Rules establish who is an employee, when to pay an employee, when overtime is to be paid, what deductions are made, and when taxes are paid. Lack of compliance with these laws and regulations can result in both fines and back-pay awards.

With each new year, payroll administrators must keep abreast of the changes in legislation that affect their firms' payroll record keeping. An understanding of the various laws affecting payroll operations helps you know the required payroll and personnel records and procedures. This chapter examines briefly the various laws that affect employers in their payroll operations. You will be shown the payroll and personnel records that employers use to meet the requirements of the laws. First, however, let's take a brief look at payroll accounting as a profession.

THE PAYROLL PROFESSION

With the increased responsibilities of payroll specialists, the profession has seen a significant increase in salary compensation. In a survey done by the job placement agency, Robert Half International, the 1995 salary range for payroll clerks was $20,000 to $24,500. Typically, an entry-level payroll clerk collects, reviews, approves, and records time records. Also, the clerk updates attendance records, including vacation, sick, and personal days. Once a payroll is processed, the clerk reviews the information to ensure the accuracy of each employee's paycheck. As the clerk progresses in the Payroll Department, job responsibilities will include entering the following information into the payroll system:

1. Time-worked data.
2. Pay rate changes.
3. Tax rate changes.
4. Employee authorized payroll deductions.
5. New employee information.
6. Marital and employee allowance changes.

Providing information to the Finance Department concerning the amounts to be paid for taxes, health insurance premiums, retirement plans, etc., may also be part of the evolving duties of the advancing payroll professional. One of the final stages involves the completion of payroll tax returns, employee information returns, federal and state census returns, and fringe benefit and welfare plan returns.

Payroll professionals must keep abreast of the changes in their field so that they can remain technically proficient. This need has spurred the development of an association of payroll practitioners—the American Payroll Association (APA). Membership in the association is open to anyone interested in or engaged in the support of payroll accounting. The APA offers professional training seminars and various publications to its members. In addition, each year the APA administers an examination for the payroll accountant and awards a certificate to those who pass the exam (Certified Payroll Professional). This testing and certification process has helped the payroll profession to gain its needed recognition in the business community. The APA has also established guidelines for the conduct of the payroll professional. This "Code of Ethics," shown in Figure 1–1, sets the direction for the profession.[1]

FAIR LABOR STANDARDS ACT

In the processing of payrolls, the first step is to determine gross pay. The Fair Labor Standards Act (FLSA) of 1938 affects this calculation. Commonly referred to as the Federal Wage and Hour Law, this law sets up minimum wage (currently $4.25 an hour) and overtime pay requirements. Other provisions of this law concern equal pay for equal work regardless of sex, restrictions upon the employment of child labor, public service contracts, and wage garnishment. These basic provisions apply to employers engaged in interstate commerce or in the production of goods and services for interstate commerce and to employees in certain enterprises which are so engaged, unless specifically exempted. The FLSA also imposes record-keeping requirements on employers but prescribes no specific form of record. Figure 1–2 shows the basic requirements imposed on the employer concerning payroll and personnel records.

L E A R N I N G
O B J E C T I V E
1

All employers must keep records explaining the basis of wage differentials paid to employees of opposite sex for equal work performed in the same establishment. Such records include those relating to job evaluations, job descriptions, merit systems, seniority systems, and union contracts. The employer also must display a poster, available from the regional office of the Wage and Hour Division, that informs employees of their minimum wage, equal pay, overtime pay, and wage-collection rights, as well as child-labor restrictions. Chapter 2 presents a detailed discussion of this act and the standards established.

L E A R N I N G
O B J E C T I V E
2

Figure 1–1 *APA Code of Ethics*

APA Code of Ethics

1. To be mindful of the personal aspect of the payroll relationship between employer and employee, and to ensure that harmony is maintained through constant concern for the Payroll Professional's fellow employees.
2. To strive for perfect accuracy and timeliness of all payroll activities.
3. To keep abreast of the state of the payroll art with regard to developments in payroll technologies.
4. To be current with legislative developments, actions on the part of regulatory bodies, and the like, in so far as they affect payroll.
5. To maintain the absolute confidentiality of the payroll, within the procedures of the employer.
6. To refrain from using Association activities for one's personal self-interest or financial gain.
7. To take as one's commitment the enhancement of one's professional abilities through the resources of the American Payroll Association.
8. To support one's fellow Payroll Professionals, both within and outside one's organization.

---

[1]For more information on the organization, write to: American Payroll Association, New York Educational Division, 30 E. 33rd Street, New York, NY 10016–5386.

Figure 1–2 *Summary of Information Required by Major Federal Payroll Laws*

	Item	Fair Labor Standards Act	Social Security	Income Tax Withholding	Unemployment Tax
EMPLOYEE DATA	Name	Yes	Yes	Yes	Yes
	Address	Yes	Yes	Yes	Yes
	Sex	Yes	. . . .	. . . .	. . . .
	Date of birth	Yes	. . . .	. . . .	. . . .
	Social Security Number	Yes	Yes	Yes	Yes
	Withholding allowances claimed	. . . .	. . . .	Yes	. . . .
	Occupation	Yes	Yes	Yes	Yes
	Period employed	. . . .	Yes	Yes	Yes
	State where services rendered	. . . .	Yes	. . . .	Yes
EMPLOYMENT DATA	Day and time of day when workweek begins	Yes	. . . .	. . . .	. . . .
	Regular hourly rate of pay	Yes	. . . .	. . . .	. . . .
	Basis of wage payments; e.g., $5 per hour; $40 per day	Yes	. . . .	. . . .	. . . .
	Hours worked each day	Yes	. . . .	. . . .	. . . .
	Hours worked each week	Yes	. . . .	. . . .	. . . .
	Daily or weekly straight-time pay, exclusive of overtime pay	Yes	. . . .	. . . .	. . . .
	Amount and nature of exempt pay	Yes	. . . .	. . . .	. . . .
	Weekly overtime pay	Yes	. . . .	. . . .	. . . .
	Total additions to or deductions from wages	Yes	. . . .	. . . .	. . . .
	Total remuneration for payroll period	Yes	Yes	Yes	. . . .
	Total remuneration for calendar year	. . . .	Yes	. . . .	Yes
	Date of payment	Yes	Yes	Yes	Yes
	Payroll period	Yes	Yes	Yes	Yes
TAX DATA	Employee's wages subject to tax for payroll period	. . . .	Yes	Yes	. . . .
	Employee's wages subject to tax for calendar year	. . . .	Yes	. . . .	Yes
	Taxable remuneration—if different from total remuneration, reason for difference	. . . .	Yes	Yes	Yes
	Tax deductions from employee's wages	. . . .	Yes	Yes	Yes
	Date tax collected if other than date of payment	. . . .	Yes	Yes	. . . .
	Tax paid by employer but not deducted from employee's wages	. . . .	Yes	Yes	Yes
GEN'L	Specific form of records	No	No	No	No
	No. of years records must be kept	2–3	4	4	4

STATE MINIMUM WAGE AND MAXIMUM HOURS LAWS

Most states have established minimum wage rates for covered employees, either by legislation or by administrative order of the legislature whereby minimum wage rates are fixed for specific industries. As noted earlier, the Fair Labor Standards Act, a federal law, also applies minimum wage and maximum hour provisions to employers. Where both federal and state regulations cover the same employee, the higher of the two rates prevails. For example, the minimum hourly wage in Oregon is $4.75, or 50¢ greater than the federal minimum wage. All workers covered by that state's legislation would receive the higher state rate.

As payroll managers, you must be familiar with the administrative orders of your particular state, since the wage orders not only set minimum wages but also contain provisions affecting pay periods, pay for call-in time and waiting time, rest and meal periods, absences, meals and lodging, tips, uniforms, and other matters dealing with wages and hours. The state wage orders usually provide that the employer must keep records showing the wages paid, the hours worked, and such other information that will aid enforcement by state officials.

FAIR EMPLOYMENT LAWS

Federal and state legislation has been enacted to enforce fair employment practices. Many of these laws deal with discrimination on the basis of age, race, color, religion, sex, or national origin as a condition of employment.

Civil Rights Act of 1964

Title VII of the Civil Rights Act of 1964, entitled "Equal Employment Opportunity," provides for several fair employment practices. The act, as amended, forbids employers to discriminate in hiring, firing, promoting, compensating, or in any other condition of employment on the basis of race, color, religion, sex, or national origin. Guidelines, established by the Equal Employment Opportunity Commission (EEOC), also include physical characteristics in the definition of national origin discrimination. For example, unnecessary height or weight requirements could exclude some individuals on the basis of their national origin. The EEOC has also declared that sexual harassment violates the Civil Rights Act. Unwelcome sexual advances, requests for sexual favors, and other verbal or physical conduct of a sexual nature can constitute sexual harassment. The EEOC prohibits unions from including or segregating their members on these bases, and unions may not cause employers to discriminate on these bases. Employment agencies may not refer or refuse to refer applicants for employment on the basis of race, color, religion, sex, or national origin.

This act covers all employers who engage in an industry "affecting commerce" and who employ 15 or more workers for each working day in each of 20 or more weeks in the current or preceding calendar year. Employers specifically excluded from coverage of the fair employment practices legislation include: the United States government (state and local governments are covered), a corporation wholly owned by the United States, Indian tribes, private membership clubs (other than labor unions) exempt from federal income tax, and religious societies in the employment of members of a particular religion to work

Policies requiring employees to speak only English while working have created lawsuits. Unless the employer can show that this requirement is necessary for conducting business, the EEOC has stated that the English-only rule violates civil-rights laws.

on the societies' religious activities. Although the United States government is classed as an exempt employer, the act states that the policy of the United States government provides equal employment opportunities without discrimination and that the President should use his existing authority to implement this policy.

To accomplish the purpose of eliminating discrimination, the EEOC tries to obtain voluntary compliance with the law before filing a court action for an injunction. Where a state or local law forbids discriminatory practices, relief must first be sought under the state or local law before a complaint is filed with the Commission. The EEOC can institute court proceedings for an injunction if it believes that any person or group of persons is not complying with the law. In addition to federal fair employment legislation, more than half the states and some cities have laws that prohibit employers from discriminating on the basis of race, creed, color, or national origin. In most of the states a special commission or the state Department of Labor administers the laws and may authorize cease and desist orders that are enforceable in the courts.

Executive Orders

Employers not subject to Title VII coverage discussed above may come within the scope of the Civil Rights Act by reason of a contract or subcontract involving federal funds. In a series of *executive orders,* the federal government has banned, in employment on government contracts, discrimination based on race, color, religion, sex, or national origin. More significantly, the orders have been held to require that some contractors take affirmative action to ensure equal opportunity.

Affirmative Action. Affirmative action is designed to eliminate employment barriers to minorities, women, persons of various religious and ethnic groups, handicapped persons, and veterans. The concept of affirmative action was developed to clarify what firms seeking to conduct business with the federal government must do to be truly equal opportunity employers. An *affirmative action plan* prescribes a specific program to eliminate, limit, or prevent discriminatory treatment on the basis of race, ethnic group, and sex. Some plans are required by law, while others are developed voluntarily. Usually the plan involves an analysis of the work force utilization; the establishment of attainable results-oriented goals and time tables for recruiting, hiring, training, and promoting any underrepresented classes; an explanation of the methods to be used to eliminate discrimination; and the establishment of responsibility for implementing the program. A federal contractor or subcontractor with 50 or more employees and a contract of $50,000 or more must have a written affirmative action plan.

Executive Order 11246. This is the major antidiscrimination regulation for government contractors and subcontractors who perform work under a federal construction contract exceeding $10,000 and for the United States government itself. Examples of discrimination forbidden by Executive Order 11246 include a contractor's refusal to hire women for certain jobs because of overtime requirements or weightlifting requirements. In their affirmative action plans, covered contractors must scrutinize tests and other screening procedures and make all changes necessary to assure nondiscrimination. Contractors must post notices announcing their nondiscrimination responsibilities in places conspicuous to employees, applicants, and representatives of each labor union with which the contractors deal.

Age Discrimination in Employment Act (ADEA)

The Age Discrimination in Employment Act of 1967 (ADEA) prohibits employers, employment agencies, and labor unions from discriminating on the basis of age in their employment practices. The act covers only employers (who employ 20 or more workers), employment agencies, and labor unions engaged in an industry affecting interstate commerce. The act also covers federal, state, and local government employees, other than elected officials and certain aides not covered by civil service. The ADEA provides protection for virtually all workers over 40. A key exception involves executives who are 65 or over and who have held high policymaking positions during the two-year period before retirement. If such an employee is entitled to an annual retirement benefit from the employer of at least $44,000, the employee can be forcibly retired.

In order to prove compliance with the various fair employment laws, employers must keep accurate personnel and payroll records. All employment applications, along with notations as to their disposition and the reasons for the disposition, should be retained. All records pertaining to promotions, discharges, seniority plans, merit programs, incentive payment plans, etc., should also be retained.

Americans with Disabilities Act (ADA)

The Americans with Disabilities Act of 1990 (ADA) prohibits employers (with 15 or more employees), employment agencies, labor organizations, or joint labor-management committees from discriminating against qualified persons with disabilities because of their disability.

The prohibition of disability-based discrimination applies to job application procedures, hiring, advancement, termination, compensation, job training, and other conditions of employment. In addition, reasonable accommodations such as wheelchair accessible restrooms and ramps for qualified disabled job applicants and workers must be provided.

FEDERAL INSURANCE CONTRIBUTIONS ACT (FICA)

The Federal Insurance Contributions Act (FICA) is part of the social security program planned by the federal government to provide economic security for workers and their families. The act levies a tax on employers and employees in certain industries to be paid to the federal government and credited to the Federal Old-Age and Survivors' Trust Fund and the Federal Disability Insurance Trust Fund. The Old-Age, Survivors, and Disability Insurance (OASDI) tax levied on employees is a set percent of their gross wages, and it must be withheld from their pay. From these funds the federal government makes payments to persons who are entitled to benefits under the Social Security Act.

FICA also provides a two-part health insurance program, commonly known as Medicare, for the aged and the disabled. The Hospital Insurance (HI) plan is financed by a separate tax on both employers and employees. A Supplementary Medical Insurance plan to cover medical services not covered under the basic program is voluntary and is financed by those who desire coverage, with a matching payment by the federal government. Social security benefits are also available to the self-employed person under the provisions of the Self-Employment Contributions Act (SECA). This act imposes a tax on the net

NEWS ALERT

In January 1996, Martin Marietta Corporation is set to go on trial for age-discrimination in the termination of employees at one of their subsidiaries in Colorado. Between January 1990, and October 1992, 2,200 of 3,500 employees terminated at the facility were over 40 years of age. The EEOC seeks lost wages, potential reinstatement, and damages.

ON THE JOB

The United States Department of Justice has stated that the ADA covers people with AIDS (Acquired Immune Deficiency Syndrome) and AIDS-related conditions.

earnings from self-employment derived by an individual from any trade or business carried on by that person.

Chapter 3 gives detailed information about FICA and exemptions from its coverage, and Appendix A briefly covers the benefits available. Although FICA does not recommend a specific form for records, Figure 1–2 shows the specific information needed and the period of time to be retained.

INCOME TAX WITHHOLDING LAWS

With the passage of the 16th Amendment in 1913, taxation of income became constitutional. Today, an *income tax* is levied on the earnings of most employees and is deducted from their gross pay. In some cases, this may involve three separate deductions from the employee's gross pay—a federal income tax, a state income tax, and a local (city) income or wage tax. All of the acts that levy these various income taxes provide for the collection of taxes at the source of the wages paid (payroll withholding).

Federal Income Tax Withholding Law

The collection of federal income taxes at the source of wages paid came into being with the enactment of the Current Tax Payment Act of 1943, commonly referred to as a withholding tax law. A percentage formula is used in an attempt to collect the approximate tax on wages or salaries by requiring the employer to withhold a specified amount from each wage or salary payment. These withholdings are then turned over to the federal government for the employee's tax account. Over the years many changes have been made in the tax rates, exemptions, and allowable deductions. Chapter 4 covers the current requirements in detail. Employers must keep records showing the information referred to in Figure 1–2. However, the law does not prescribe any specific forms to be used for such record keeping.

State and Local Income Tax Withholding Laws

Most states impose *state* income taxes on individuals. The laws vary from state to state as to the amount to be withheld, exemptions from withholding, and the time for withholding reports to be filed. Employers may also be required by *local* income tax laws to deduct and withhold local income taxes on salaries or wages paid. Chapter 4 presents further discussion of the withholding of state and local income taxes.

UNEMPLOYMENT TAX ACTS

Unemployment insurance taxes provide funds at the state level for compensating unemployed workers. Taxes levied both by the federal government (Federal Unemployment Tax Act) and by the state government (State Unemployment Tax Acts) affect the employer.

Federal Unemployment Tax Act (FUTA)

Like the Federal Insurance Contributions Act, the Federal Unemployment Tax Act is incorporated in the Internal Revenue Code. If an employer employs one or more individuals in each of 20 or more weeks in occupations covered by FUTA or pays wages of $1,500 or more during any calendar quarter in the current or preceding calendar year, a federal unemployment insurance tax must be paid. The federal government uses the collected tax to pay state and federal administrative expenses of the unemployment program. Employers subject to FUTA receive credit against most of the FUTA tax when they contribute to their state unemployment compensation funds. Chapter 5 gives detailed information as to employers and employees who are subject to the requirements of the act. Employers subject to FUTA must keep permanent records that provide the information listed in Figure 1–2. FUTA prescribes no particular form for these records. However, each employer must use forms and accounting systems that will enable the District Director of the Internal Revenue Service to ascertain whether the tax is correctly computed and paid.

State Unemployment Tax Acts (SUTA)

All the states and the District of Columbia have enacted unemployment insurance laws. Each employer receives a credit against the FUTA tax because of the contribution (tax) to a state's unemployment compensation program. The taxes paid to the individual states by employers are used primarily for the payment of unemployment benefits.

The Social Security Act specifies certain standards that each state had to meet in passing an unemployment compensation law. These standards have resulted in a fairly high degree of uniformity in the requirements of state unemployment laws and in the records that must be kept by businesses. State laws do differ, however, making it necessary for employers to be familiar with the laws of the states in which they operate.

The state unemployment compensation laws require employers to keep payroll records similar to those required under the federal law. Penalties may be imposed for failure to keep the required records or for failure or delinquency in making the required returns or for default or delinquency in paying the contributions. The required period for retaining records varies in different states, but in no case should the records be kept for a period of less than four years because of the federal requirement. Chapter 5 covers state unemployment compensation and tax acts.

OTHER FEDERAL LAWS AFFECTING THE NEED FOR PAYROLL AND PERSONNEL RECORDS

Generally, the payroll and personnel records and reports that a business prepares and retains to meet the requirements of the laws already discussed provide sufficient information needed under the laws outlined in Figure 1–3 and discussed below.

Employee Retirement Income Security Act of 1974 (ERISA)

This act covers employee pension and welfare plans established or maintained (1) by any employer engaged in commerce or in any industry or activity affecting commerce and (2) by any employee organization representing employees engaged in commerce or in any industry or activity affecting commerce. The legislation insures that workers will earn pension rights, and safeguards those

Law	Coverage	Contract Dollar Minimum	Major Provisions
Davis-Bacon Act (1931)	Laborers for contractors or subcontractors on federal government contracts for construction, alteration, or repair of public buildings or works.	$2,000	Minimum wage set by Secretary of Labor (weight is given to union wage scale prevailing in the project area).
Walsh-Healey Public Contracts Act (1936)	Laborers for contractors who furnish materials, supplies, articles, and equipment to any agency of the United States.	$10,000	Single minimum wage determined by Secretary of Labor for all covered employees in a given industry.
McNamara-O'Hara Service Contract Act (1965)	Service employees on contracts with the United States or the District of Columbia for the furnishing of services.	$2,500	Minimum wage set by Secretary of Labor based on minimum wage found to be prevailing in that locality.
Occupational Safety and Health Act (OSHA) (1970)	Any business involved in interstate commerce.	-0-	Sets specific occupational and health standards for employers; requires that records be kept of work-related deaths, illnesses, and injuries.
Vocational Rehabilitation Act (1973)	Companies with federal agency contracts.	$2,500	Must include in the contract an affirmative action clause requiring that the handicapped applicant or employee will be given appropriate consideration.
Vietnam Era Veterans' Readjustment Act (1974)	Government contractors with federal contracts or subcontracts.	$10,000	Requires contractors to take affirmative action to employ and advance in employment qualified veterans of the Vietnam era and disabled veterans.

Figure 1–3 *Federal Laws Affecting the Need for Payroll and Personnel Records*

pension funds by regulating how the funds are to be raised and disbursed, who controls them, and what is to be done when funds are insufficient to pay promised benefits. However, the law *does not* require any employer to establish a pension plan.

ERISA was primarily designed to ensure that workers covered by private pension plans receive benefits from those plans in accordance with their credited years of service with their employers. *Vesting* conveys to employees the right to share in a retirement fund if they are terminated before the normal retirement age. The vesting process is linked to the number of years needed for workers to earn an equity in their retirement plans and to become entitled to full or partial benefits at some future date if they leave the company before retirement. Once vested, a worker has the right to receive a pension at retirement age, based on years of covered service, even though the worker may not be working for the firm at that time. Currently, the law provides for full vesting in five years or gradually over seven years (20% after three years and 20% a year for the next four). To protect against potential benefit losses because of a plan's termination, ERISA set up a government insurance program (The Pension Benefit Guaranty Corporation) to pay any benefits that could not be met with funds from the plan.

Individual Retirement Account (IRA). An *individual retirement account* (IRA) is a pension plan established and funded by an individual employee. The employee's contributions to an IRA may be made through the employer or a union or placed in an individual retirement savings account specified in the law. *Under certain conditions,* employees may put aside each year the lesser of $2,000 or 100% of their compensation without paying federal income taxes on their contributions. Chapter 4 presents a more detailed discussion of IRA accounts.

Simplified Employee Pension (SEP) Plan. By means of a *simplified employee pension (SEP) plan,* employers may make contributions to individual retirement accounts on behalf of their employees. Employers may make annual contributions of up to 15% of each employee's compensation (up to the first $150,000 of earnings). An employer places the contributions in an individual retirement account for the employee. The employee can also contribute to the plan. Employers must contribute for all employees who are 21 years of age or older and who have worked for the employer at least three of the past five years. The contributions made by the employer are fully and immediately vested.

Disclosure Requirements. The reporting and disclosure requirements set forth by ERISA have tremendous implications for the record-keeping requirements of employers. Informational reports must be filed with the U.S. Department of Labor, the IRS, and the government insurance program. In general, the reports consist of descriptions of the plans and the annual financial data. The plan descriptions include the eligibility requirements for participation and for benefits; provisions for nonforfeitable pension benefits; circumstances which may result in disqualification, loss, or denial of benefits; and procedures for presenting claims. The annual reports include financial statements and schedules showing the current value of plan assets and liabilities, receipts and disbursements, and employer contributions; the assets held for investment purposes; insurance data; and an opinion of an independent qualified public accountant. Upon written request from the participants, the administrator must also furnish a statement, not more than once in a 12-month period, of the total benefits accrued, accrued benefits that are vested, if any, or the earliest date on which accrued benefits will become vested.

Immigration Reform and Control Act of 1986 (IRCA)

This act bars employers from hiring and retaining aliens unauthorized to work in the United States. It also requires all employers to verify employment eligibility for all individuals hired after November 6, 1986. To do this, the employer must examine the employee's verification documents and have the employee complete Form I-9, Employment Eligibility Verification (not illustrated). Form I-9 lists the documents that the employee must furnish to the employer. These documents identify the employee and, if an alien, verify authorization to work in the United States. Form I-9 must be completed within three business days of the date the employee starts to work. The form must be retained for three years after the date of hiring or for one year after the date the employment is terminated, whichever is longer. The Immigration and Naturalization Service (INS) can levy fines if an audit uncovers record-keeping violations. Civil penalties range from $100 to $1,000 for each violation.

Family and Medical Leave Act of 1993 (FMLA)

This law requires employers that have 50 or more employees within a 75-mile radius to grant workers unpaid leave for a family or medical emergency. In cases of childbirth or adoption or serious illness of the employee or the employee's child, spouse, or parent, the employer must offer the worker as many as 12 weeks of unpaid leave. During the leave, employers must continue health-care coverage; and they must also guarantee that the employee will return to the same job or to a comparable position. The employer can substitute an employee's earned paid leave for any part of the 12-week family leave.

Employers can exempt the following:

1. The highest-paid 10% of their workforce.
2. Those who have not worked at least one year and at least 1,250 hours in the previous 12 months for the company.

OTHER STATE LAWS AFFECTING THE NEED FOR PAYROLL AND PERSONNEL RECORDS

States have enacted other laws which have a direct bearing on the payroll and personnel records that an employer must maintain and on the rights that must be extended to employees.

Workers' Compensation Laws

Workers' compensation insurance protects employees and their dependents against losses due to injury or death incurred during employment. Most states have passed laws that require employers to provide workers' compensation insurance by one of the following plans:

1. Contribution to a state compensation insurance fund administered by an insurance department of the state.
2. Purchase of workers' compensation insurance from a private insurance company authorized by the state to issue this type of policy.
3. Establishment of a self-insurance plan, approved by the state, under which the company bears all risk itself.

The employer bears the cost of the workers' compensation insurance premiums, except in Montana, New Mexico, Oregon, and Washington, where both the employer and the employee contribute to the workers' compensation fund. Benefits are paid to the injured worker, or to the survivors in the event of death, by the state, by the insurance company, or by the risk-assuming employer according to the adopted plan.

The insurance premiums are often based upon the total gross payroll of the business and may be stated in terms of an amount for each $100 of weekly wages paid to employees. The premium rates vary among types of jobs and vary in amount with the pay rate involved.

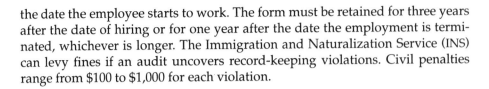

During the second half of 1994, 513 complaints were lodged under FMLA. Of these, the Department of Labor, Wage, and Hour Division found 302 violations.

Workers in California must now show that 51% of their stress comes from their jobs in order to win a workers' compensation claim. In the past, the threshold was only 10%. California is one of only eight states that allow stress-related compensation claims.

The rate for the office workers of the Volpe Parts Company is $0.60 per $100 of payroll, while the rate for machine-shop workers is $6 per $100 of payroll.

Because the premium rates vary according to the different degrees of danger in various classes of jobs, payroll records must indicate job classifications for rate purposes. If the employer has low accident experience, the rates may be reduced to a certain minimum.

State Disability Benefit Laws

California, Hawaii, New Jersey, New York, Rhode Island, and Puerto Rico have passed laws to provide *disability benefits* to employees absent from their jobs because of illness, accident, or disease *not arising out of their employment*. Chapter 5 presents further discussion of state disability benefit laws.

State Time-Off-To-Vote Laws

In many states employees may take time off from work to vote, and the United States Supreme Court has upheld the validity of time-off-to-vote laws. Although the laws of the states vary, generally the legislation provides that if employees entitled to vote in an election are absent from work for a specified period, they will not be penalized nor will there be a deduction from their wages. In most states the employee must have applied for the time off prior to the date of the election. Usually the law provides penalties if the employer refuses an employee the right-to-vote privileges that have been conferred by state law.

Legal Holidays

Payroll administration requires that we know what holidays are legally recognized by our state. For example, the due dates for returns and tax payments are extended by the federal government and many states when the scheduled due date falls on a Saturday, a Sunday, or a legal holiday. The federal government has declared New Year's Day (January 1), Independence Day (July 4), Veterans Day (November 11), Thanksgiving Day (fourth Thursday in November), and Christmas Day (December 25) to be legal public holidays. In addition, the following "Monday Holidays" are legal public holidays:

- Martin Luther King, Jr.'s Birthday, the third Monday in January.
- Presidents' Day, the third Monday in February.
- Memorial Day, the last Monday in May.
- Labor Day, the first Monday in September.
- Columbus Day, the second Monday in October.

Although almost all states have enacted legislation declaring most of the "Monday Holidays," we must be familiar with the legislation of our own state and those states wherein other employees of our firm may be working. The "Monday Holidays" affect only agencies under federal or state jurisdiction. Private firms are not required to observe these holidays.

HUMAN RESOURCES AND PAYROLL ACCOUNTING SYSTEMS

Up to this point, we have seen that a business must keep *human resources* (or *personnel*) and *payroll* records to meet the requirements of the various laws under which it operates. In addition, these records form an integral part of an effective business system. In developing its human resources system and payroll accounting system, a business should design basic forms and records that satisfy the requirements of all the laws applicable to that organization. Properly designed forms and records, as described in the closing pages of this chapter, not only supply the information required by the various laws but also provide management with information needed in its decision-making process. They also result in savings in both time and work because the necessary information is recorded, stored, retrieved, and distributed economically, efficiently, and quickly.

Before studying the employment process, it is important to examine the close relationship between the Payroll Department and the Human Resources Department. Some businesses consider payroll to be strictly an accounting function and, as such, place it under the direct control of the director of finance. However, because of the need for quick interchange of information between the Payroll and the Human Resources Departments, the recent trend has been to place payroll under the control of the Director of Human Resources. This movement toward centralization eliminates the duplication of many tasks, such as information reviews on both federal and state tax and census returns. With the required information in one department, the process of completing these forms is shortened. Further, questions from employees concerning sick pay, vacation pay, and other benefits can be answered from one source.

Individual computer programs have been developed for the combined needs of payroll and human resources. Information concerning such diverse activities as attendance, retirement benefits, health insurance coverages, and bonus pays is now available to designated employees in the Human Resources Department through a computer terminal. In the remainder of this chapter, we will assume that the two departments are operating separately.

HUMAN RESOURCES SYSTEM

In many medium-size and large companies, the **human resources system** embodies all those procedures and methods related to recruiting, selecting, orienting, training, and terminating personnel. Extensive record-keeping procedures are required in order to:

1. Provide data for considering promotions and changes in the status and earnings of workers.
2. Provide the information required by various federal, state, and local laws.
3. Justify company actions if investigated by national or state labor relations boards.
4. Justify company actions in discussions with local unions or plant committees.

Before the Payroll Department can pay newly hired employees, the Human Resources Department must process those employees. Figure 1–4 charts the procedure that the Human Resources Department follows in this hiring process.

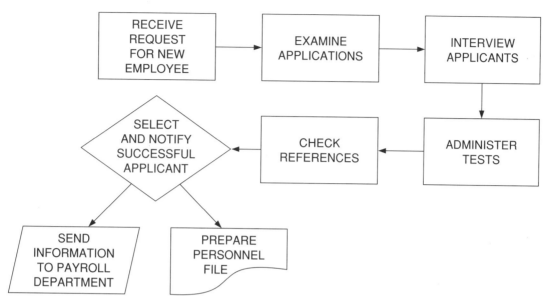

Figure 1–4 *Human Resources Department Procedure in the Hiring Process*

A number of companies that manufacture business forms have available standard personnel forms and records that may be successfully used if a business does not care to design its own special forms. In small companies it may not be necessary to keep such extensive personnel records. Frequently an application form or an employee history record may be the only document needed. Throughout the remainder of this chapter, several illustrations augment the discussion of the various human resources and payroll records. In the examples of these records, we shall follow Mary Louise Mosworth from her initial application for employment with the United Chemicals Company to her entry onto the company's payroll records.

Requisition for Personnel

The *requisition for personnel* form notifies the Human Resources Department of the need for additional or replacement employees. The requisition for new employees can be initiated in a number of ways. Some companies send a memo to the Human Resources Department stating the title of the position to be filled, a brief description of the duties of the job, and the salary range. Other companies may use preprinted forms. A preprinted form should indicate the type and number of persons needed, the position to be filled, the rate of pay for the job, the salary range, the date the employee is needed, a summary of any special qualifications, and whether the position is permanent or temporary.

Application for Employment

Every business, regardless of size, should have an application form to be filled out by a person seeking employment. The *application form* gives the applicant an opportunity to provide complete information as to personal qualifications, training, and experience. The form serves as a permanent record for the business and provides a means of obtaining information needed for various purposes. When the people who interview the applicant have the information before them, as requested on the application blank, they are reminded of questions that should be asked of the applicant and of facts that should be given the applicant.

The application form also provides information for the checking of references, serves as a guide to effective interviewing, and provides information for correlation with data obtained from employment tests. The basic information that should be provided by the application for employment form includes:

1. Personal information including the name, address, telephone number, and social security number of the applicant.
2. Educational background including a summary of the schools attended, whether the applicant graduated, and degrees conferred.
3. Employment and experience record.
4. Type of employment desired.
5. References.

Employers subject to fair employment laws must make certain that all aspects of the prehire inquiries are free of discrimination on the basis of race, color, religion, sex, national origin, or age. *Prehire inquiries* include questions asked in the employment interview and on application forms, resumes of experience or education required of an applicant, and any kind of written testing. None of the federal civil rights laws specifically outlaw questions concerning the race, color, religion, sex, national origin, or age of an applicant. However, if the employer can offer no logical explanation for asking such questions, the EEOC and the Wage and Hour Administrator view such questions as discriminatory. Of course, prehire questions pertaining to religion, sex, national origin, or age are allowed when these factors are bona fide occupational qualifications for a job.

Asking an applicant's age or date of birth may tend to deter the older worker. Thus, if an application form calls for such information, a statement should appear on that form notifying the applicant that the ADEA prohibits discrimination on the basis of age with respect to individuals who are at least 40. Some businesses have removed the "date of birth" and "year of graduation" questions from their application forms. Generally, an employer may not require information of a minority, a female, or an older applicant that would not be required of another applicant. It has also been held by the EEOC that asking a job applicant to list arrests on the job application violates the Civil Rights Act. An employer may seek or use information concerning criminal convictions of applicants or employees and may refuse to hire a convicted criminal only if a valid business need exists for doing so. The employer is also prohibited from making inquiries about an applicant's honorable discharge from the military service unless it can be proved that a proper business interest exists that justifies the asking of such information.

As Figure 1–5 shows, an application blank may provide space for an interview record. The interviewer completes this section of the form either while the interview is in process or after it has been completed. The comments appearing on the application blank in Figure 1–5 were those of Vernon T. Hansen, the Director of Human Resources. Often the potential supervisor interviews the applicant as well as a member of the Human Resources Department. In case an applicant is rejected, a notation on the application form enumerating the reasons for rejection will prove helpful in the future. This would simplify the restudy of the applicant's qualifications and provide a record in the event the company is accused of unfair labor practices.

Figure 1–5   *Application Blank (page 1)*

United Chemicals

PERSONAL

Name: *Mary Louise Mosworth*
Date: *June 18, 19--*

7 North Street
Phone Number: *555-5136*

City: *Huntington*   State: *WV*   Zip: *25703-2234*
Social Security Number: *293-77-1388*

In case of emergency, who would we notify?
Name: *Robert Mosworth*   Address: *7 North Street, Huntington*   Phone Number: *555-5136*

STATEMENT OF HEALTH

Is There Any Reason Why You Would Be Unable to Perform Any of the Duties of the Position for Which You Are Applying? *No*

If Yes, Explain:

EMPLOYMENT INFORMATION

Type Work Preferred: *Accounting - clerical*
When Available for Work: *at once*

Are You Now Employed? *No*   Reasons for Desiring Change:

Have You Ever Supervised People? *No*   How Many: Where:

List Special Skill and Office Equipment You Operate Efficiently: *video display terminal   typewriter, office copier,*

Present Typing Speed	No. Years in School?	In Experience?	Present Shorthand Speed	No. Years in School	In Experience?
65	*3*	*1*	—	—	—

PREVIOUS EMPLOYMENT

SHOW LAST POSITION FIRST. ANSWER ALL QUESTIONS

1   Name and Address of Company: *White Transfer Co., P.O. Box 801, Huntington, WV 25701-2231*

Date Employed	Date Terminated	Final Salary	Name of Supervisor
Feb 1, 19--	*Dec. 31, 19--*	*$5.80/hr.*	*Jean Sanning*

Reason for Termination: *To enter Business College*

Duties and Positions Held: *Clerk-typist — Verify extensions and prepare waybills*

2   Name and Address of Company: *Palmer Drugs, Broad & Center, Huntington, WV 25701-2232*

Date Employed	Date Terminated	Final Salary	Name of Supervisor
Aug. 10, 19--	*Jan. 31, 19--*	*$4.25/hr.*	*William Palmer*

Reason for Termination: *To accept full-time job at higher hourly rate*

Duties and Positions Held: *Cash register operator at check-out counter*

Figure 1–5 *Application Blank (page 2)*

		Name and Address of School	Years Attended	Average Grade	Major Course	Minor Course	Graduate?
EDUCATION	High School	Valley High School Huntington, WV	19__To 19__	B	Business	English	Yes
	College		19__To 19__				
			19__To 19__				
	Business School	Huntington College of Business–Huntington, WV	19__To 19__	A	Accounting	Office Procedures	Yes
	Other		19__To 19__				

Your Most Interesting Subjects in Last School Attended.
Accounting and Law

Your Most Difficult Subjects in Last School Attended.
Economics

Honors and Extracurricular Activities in Last School Attended.
Vice-President, Young Business Executives Club

PROFESSIONAL CERTIFICATES	Type	Issuing State	Date	No.
	None			
	Type	Issuing State	Date	No.
	Type	Issuing State	Date	No.

REFERENCES — List below three references not previously mentioned in application, and not related to you, who have known you at least three years.

Name	Address	Occupation or Profession
Rev. Stephen M. Keel	51 Parker Rd. Huntington, WV 25710-2237	Minister, Central Presbyterian Church
George P. Russell	163 21st Street Nitro, WV 25143-2139	Chemical Engineer
Mrs. Ethel Carson	416 Eighth Street Huntington, WV 25701-2236	Instructor

The above statements are true to the best of my knowledge and belief. I am willing to undergo a medical examination as a basis for further consideration of my application.

Signature __Mary L. Mosworth__

DO NOT WRITE IN SPACE BELOW

Employed? ☒ Yes ☐ No   Hold Application in Pending File ☐ Yes ☒ No

Date to Report to Work: *July 1, 19–*   Department: *Accounting*

Position: *Payroll Clerk*   Job Grade: *4*   Salary: *$1,500/mo.*

Remarks: *Very pleasing personality, well poised. Excellent scholastic background. Anxious to advance in accounting-related position.*

Interviewed By: ____ Interviewed By: ____ Interviewed By: *Vernon T. Hansen*

Reference Inquiry

Before employing an applicant, a company may check some of the references given on the application blank. Many businesses use a standard *reference inquiry form*, which is usually mailed to the person or company given as a reference. In some cases, businesses do not use a specially designed form for inquiring about references but instead write special letters. Other companies prefer a telephone reference check because they feel that a more frank opinion of the candidate is received over the telephone than in a letter. Some companies prefer not to check on personal references given by the job applicant since these tend to be less objective than business references. Today, any type of reference checking has taken on new meaning—expensive litigation. Because of this, many human resources departments give references only a cursory glance.

The Fair Credit Reporting Act of 1968 subjects employers to certain disclosure obligations when they seek an *investigative consumer report* from a consumer reporting agency on a job applicant or in certain instances on present employees. An investigative consumer report usually contains information about the individual's character, general reputation, and mode of living. Generally, the employer must notify the applicant or the employee in writing that such a report is being sought. Also, the employer must notify the applicant or employee that he or she may request information from the employer about the nature and scope of the information sought. In the event employment is denied because of the consumer report information, the employer must inform the individual that this was the reason or part of the reason for denying employment. Also, the employer must furnish the applicant with the name and address of the consumer reporting agency that made the report.

Hiring Notice

After the successful applicant is notified of employment and the starting date, time, and to whom to report, a *hiring notice* is sent to the Payroll Department so that the new employee can be added properly to the payroll. A hiring notice such as that shown in Figure 1–6 usually gives the name, address, and telephone number of the new employee, the department in which employed, the starting date, the rate of pay, the number of withholding allowances claimed, and any other information pertaining to deductions that are to be made from the employee's wages. Usually two copies of this form are prepared, with the original going to the Payroll Department and the duplicate being kept by the Human Resources Department.

Employee History Record

Although many businesses keep no personnel records other than the application blank, a need exists for a more detailed record such as the *employee history record*, which provides a continuous record of the relationship between the employer and the employee. The employee history record, in addition to providing personal and other information usually found on an application blank, provides space to record the employee's progress, attendance, promotions, performance appraisals, and salary increases.

Job applicants can now find out what previous employers are saying about them. A company, Documented Reference Check of Alto Loma, California, will for a fee check job references just as a prospective employer would, except that the reference check company reports back to the applicant.[2]

A poll conducted by the employment agency, Robert Half International indicated that only 56% of former employers were totally honest when giving references. The main reason given by these employers was the fear of lawsuits.

[2]Joseph Busler, "Employers Have to Be Careful When Employees Come and Go," *Camden Courier Post,* March 28, 1993, D–1.

```
┌──────────────────────────────────────────────────────────────────────────┐
│                           HIRING NOTICE                                    │
│                                                   NO. 220                  │
│                                                                            │
│  SOCIAL SECURITY NO. 293-77-1388                                           │
│                                         DATE _____ June 28, 19--          │
│  NAME Mary Louise Mosworth              CLOCK NO.  418                      │
│  ADDRESS 7 North St., Huntington, WV  ZIP 25703-2234  PHONE NO. 555-5136   │
│  OCCUPATION Payroll Clerk          DEPT. Accounting   GROUP NO. --         │
│  STARTING DATE July 1, 19--    TIME 8:00  A.M./P.M.   RATE $1,500 mo.      │
│  MARRIED            │ SINGLE    X      │ BIRTH DATE 8/1/--                 │
│  LAST        │ White Transfer Co.     │ LOCATION Huntington, WV           │
│  EMPLOYMENT  │ DATE LEFT 12/31/--     │ REASON Enrolled in college        │
│  NO. OF WITHHOLDING ALLOWANCES  1                                          │
│  IN EMERGENCY NOTIFY Robert Mosworth        PHONE NO.  555-5136            │
│  EMPLOYEE'S SIGNATURE IN FULL  Mary Louise Mosworth                        │
│  SUPERVISOR'S SIGNATURE  Margaret T. Johnson                               │
│  EMPLOYMENT DEPARTMENT                                                     │
│  ORIGINAL TO PAYROLL DEPT.                                                 │
│  DUPLICATE RETAINED BY HUMAN RESOURCES DEPT.                               │
└──────────────────────────────────────────────────────────────────────────┘
```

Figure 1–6 *Hiring Notice*

Change in Payroll Rate

The *change in payroll rate form* notifies the proper departments of a change in the employee's rate of remuneration. The change in rate may originate in the Human Resources Department or with the head of the department in which the employee works. In either event, the Payroll Department must be informed of the change for the employee so that the rate change is put into effect at the proper time and so that the records reflect the new rate. Figure 1–7 shows a form that may be used for this purpose. Ordinarily one copy is sent to the Payroll Department, one to the Human Resources Department, and one to the employee's department.

PAYROLL ACCOUNTING SYSTEM

L E A R N I N G
O B J E C T I V E
6

A *payroll accounting system* embodies all those procedures and methods related to the disbursement of pay to employees. A typical payroll accounting system includes the procedures shown in Figure 1–8. The nature of the payroll records depends to a great extent on the size of the work force and the degree to which the record keeping is automated. This course describes and illustrates manual payroll accounting systems. Appendix B describes computerized payroll accounting systems, along with operating instructions for using the software available with this text. In most payroll systems—manual or automated—two basic records include: the payroll register and the employee's earnings record.

CHANGE OF STATUS

Please enter the following change(s) as of   January 1, 19--

Name Mary L. Mosworth   Clock or Payroll No.   418   Soc. Sec. Number 293-77-1388

FROM

Job	Dept.	Shift	Rate
Payroll Clerk	Acct.	--	$1,500

TO

Job	Dept.	Shift	Rate
Accounting Clerk (A)	Acct.	--	$1,750

REASON FOR CHANGE:

- ☐ Hired
- ☐ Re-hired
- ☒ Promotion
- ☐ Demotion
- ☐ Transfer
- ☐ Merit Increase
- ☐ Leave of Absence to _____
- ☐ Length of Serv. Increase
- ☐ Re-eval. of Existing Job
- ☐ Resignation
- ☐ Retirement
- ☐ Layoff
- ☐ Discharge

Date

Other reason or explanation: _____
_____
_____

AUTHORIZED BY *Margaret T. Johnson* APPROVED BY *E. J. Dunn*

Prepare in triplicate: (1) Human Resources (2) Payroll (3) Employee's Department

---

Figure 1–7 *Change of Status Form*

Payroll Register

The *payroll register* is a multicolumn form used to assemble and summarize the data needed at the end of each payroll period. It provides a detailed listing of a company's complete payroll for that particular pay period. Thus, the payroll register lists all the employees who earned remuneration, the amount of remuneration, the deductions, and the net amount paid. The information provided in the payroll register is used primarily to meet the requirements of the Fair Labor Standards Act. However, the register also provides information for recording the payroll entries in the journal and for preparing reports required by other federal, state, and local laws. Figure 1–9 shows one form of payroll register. Another form, used in the Continuing Payroll Problem at the end of Chapters 2 through 6, is shown in the fold-out at the back of this book. Chapter 6 presents further discussion of the payroll register.

LEARNING OBJECTIVE

7

Employee's Earnings Record

In addition to the information contained in the payroll register, businesses must provide more complete information about the accumulated earnings of each employee. For that reason, it is necessary to keep a separate payroll record on each employee—the *employee's earnings record.* Each payday, after the information has been recorded in the payroll register, the information for each employee is transferred, or posted, to the employee's earnings record. The employee's earnings record provides the information needed to prepare

The retention requirements imposed on employers by various government agencies set a limit of seven years on payroll registers and eight years on employees' earnings records.

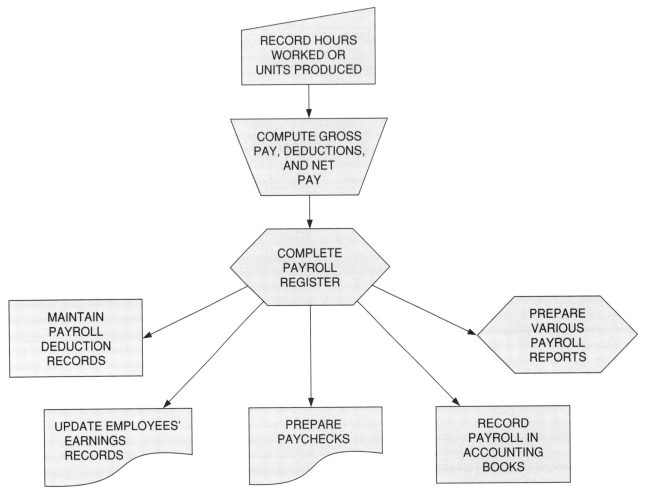

Figure 1–8   *Procedures in a Payroll Accounting System*

periodic reports required by the withholding tax laws, the FICA tax law, and state unemployment or disability laws. Employers also use the employee's earnings record in preparing *Form W-2, Wage and Tax Statement.* This form shows the amount of wages paid each worker in the course of the trade or business of the employer. Figure 1-10 shows an example of the employee's earnings record. Chapter 6 presents a more detailed discussion of the preparation and use of the earnings record.

Paycheck

When employees are paid by check, a check is written for each worker, using as the amount of net pay that figure appearing in the Net Paid column of the payroll register. Most paychecks, such as that depicted in Figure 1–11, carry a stub, or voucher, that shows the earnings and deductions. The following chapter covers paying workers in cash, by check, or by means of an electronic transfer of payroll funds.

PAYROLL REGISTER

FOR WEEK ENDING   **January 19**   19 - -

No.	Name	Total Hours Worked	Regular Earnings			Overtime Earnings			Total Earnings	Deductions				Net Paid	
			Hrs.	Rate	Amount	Hrs.	Rate	Amount		OASDI Tax	HI Tax	Fed. Income Tax	State Income Tax	Check No.	Amount
1 403	*Springs, Carl A.*	40	40	5.15	206.00				206.00	12.77	2.99	12.00	3.92	504	174.32
2 409	*Wiegand, Sue T.*	42	40	4.80	192.00	2	7.20	14.40	206.40	12.80	2.99	16.00	3.92	505	170.69
3 412	*O'Neill, John B.*	38	38	4.50	171.00				171.00	10.60	2.48	11.00	5.10	506	141.82
4 413	*Bass, Marie S.*	44	40	5.00	200.00	4	7.50	30.00	230.00	14.26	3.34	17.00	4.67	507	190.73
5 418	*Mosworth, M. L.*	41	40	S	403.85	1	15.15	15.15	419.00	25.98	6.08	48.00	13.15	508	325.79
47	*Totals*				3,895.75			317.20	4,212.95	261.20	61.09	808.00	124.24		2,958.42

Figure 1–9   *Payroll Register*

EMPLOYEE'S EARNINGS RECORD

Week	Week Ending	Total Hours Worked	Regular Earnings			Overtime Earnings			Total Earnings	Deductions				Net Paid		Cumulative Earnings
			Hrs.	Rate	Amount	Hrs.	Rate	Amount		OASDI Tax	HI Tax	Fed. Income Tax	State Income Tax	Check No.	Amount	
1	1/5	40	40	S	403.85				403.85	25.04	5.86	46.00	12.75	419	314.20	403.85
2	1/12	42	40	S	403.85	2	15.15	30.30	434.15	26.92	6.30	51.00	13.94	463	335.99	838.00
3	1/19	41	40	S	403.85	1	15.15	15.15	419.00	25.98	6.08	48.00	13.15	508	325.79	1,257.00

Sex	Department	Occupation	State Employed	S.S.No.	Name—Last First Middle	No. W/H Allow.
F M √	*Accounting*	*Accounting Clerk (A)*	*West Virginia*	*293–77–1388*	*Mosworth, Mary Louise*	*1*
						Marital Status *S*

Figure 1–10   *Employee's Earnings Record*

KEY TERMS

Affirmative action plan
Application form
Change in payroll rate form
Disability benefits
Employee history record
Employee's earnings record
Executive order
Fair employment legislation
Form W-2, Wage and Tax Statement
Hiring notice
Human resources system
Income tax

Individual retirement account (IRA)
Investigative consumer report
Payroll accounting system
Payroll register
Prehire inquiries
Reference inquiry form
Requisition for personnel
Simplified employee pension (SEP) plan
Unemployment insurance taxes
Vesting
Workers' compensation insurance

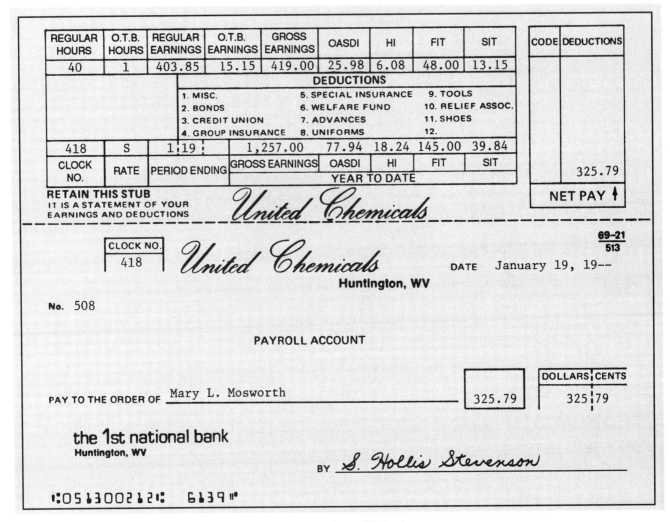

REGULAR HOURS	O.T.B. HOURS	REGULAR EARNINGS	O.T.B. EARNINGS	GROSS EARNINGS	OASDI	HI	FIT	SIT	CODE	DEDUCTIONS
40	1	403.85	15.15	419.00	25.98	6.08	48.00	13.15		

DEDUCTIONS

1. MISC.   5. SPECIAL INSURANCE   9. TOOLS
2. BONDS   6. WELFARE FUND   10. RELIEF ASSOC.
3. CREDIT UNION   7. ADVANCES   11. SHOES
4. GROUP INSURANCE   8. UNIFORMS   12.

CLOCK NO.	RATE	PERIOD ENDING	GROSS EARNINGS	OASDI	HI	FIT	SIT	
418	S	1 19	1,257.00	77.94	18.24	145.00	39.84	325.79

YEAR TO DATE

RETAIN THIS STUB IT IS A STATEMENT OF YOUR EARNINGS AND DEDUCTIONS

NET PAY ↑

United Chemicals

CLOCK NO. 418

United Chemicals
Huntington, WV

DATE January 19, 19--

No. 508

69-21 / 513

PAYROLL ACCOUNT

PAY TO THE ORDER OF Mary L. Mosworth   325.79   DOLLARS CENTS 325 79

the 1st national bank
Huntington, WV

BY *S. Hollis Stevenson*

⑆05⑈300212⑆ 6139⑈

Figure 1–11 *Paycheck with Stub Showing Current and Year-to-Date Earnings and Deductions*

QUESTIONS FOR REVIEW

1. Under the FLSA, what information concerning employees' wages earned must be maintained by the employer?
2. Which act sets the minimum wage and what is the current wage rate?
3. What types of unfair employment practices are prohibited by the Civil Rights Act of 1964 as amended?
4. What is the purpose of the Age Discrimination in Employment Act (ADEA)?
5. Who pays the social security taxes that are levied by the Federal Insurance Contributions Act?
6. How are the funds used which are provided by FUTA and SUTA?
7. Who is covered by the Walsh-Healey Public Contracts Act?
8. Explain the concept of vesting.
9. What is the maximum amount of tax-free contributions that an eligible employee can place in his or her IRA account each year?
10. Under the Family and Medical Leave Act, what is the maximum number of weeks of unpaid leave that a covered employer is required to offer an employee whose spouse is seriously ill?
11. Summarize the procedure that may be followed by the Human Resources Department in hiring new employees.

12. What kinds of information are commonly provided by the jobseeker on the application for employment form?
13. What is the significance of the Civil Rights Act of 1964 and the Age Discrimination in Employment Act in the employer's use of prehire inquiries?
14. What obligations are imposed upon the employer by the Fair Credit Reporting Act of 1968?
15. What procedures are usually included in a typical payroll accounting system?

QUESTIONS FOR DISCUSSION

1. What personnel records would you suggest for a small retailer with three employees?
2. What kind of problem can be encountered when requesting references from previous employers of job applicants?
3. In staffing their offices, some firms encourage in-house referrals (recommendations of their present employees). What are some possible objections to this practice as a means of obtaining job applicants? What advantages may be realized by the firm that uses in-house referrals?
4. The main office of a large bank has an annual turnover of 500 office workers. As an employment officer of this bank, discuss the sources you would use in obtaining replacement employees.
5. Among the questions asked on the application for employment form of Horner Company are the following:

   a. Have you ever worked for Horner Company under another name?
   b. Give the name of your church and list the religious holidays you observe.
   c. Indicate the name of your birthplace.
   d. Are you a citizen of the United States?
   e. Indicate the foreign languages you can read, write, or speak fluently. In view of federal and state civil rights laws, do you believe that Horner Company is acting legally or illegally in asking each of the questions listed above?

C1. **Paycheck Pickup.**

Jack works the night shift for Lemon Auto and sleeps during the day. Jack's wife customarily drops by on payday to pick up his check and take it to the bank. Lemon thought nothing of the practice since it had been going on for five years. One day Jack came bursting into the payroll department demanding to know where his paycheck was. It appears that he and his wife had separated the week before. Jack's wife cashed the check and took the money without his knowledge or permission. How do you think Lemon Auto settled this dispute?[3]

The Fair Labor Standards Act, passed in 1938, established the minimum wage at 25 cents per hour for the first year, to be increased to 30 cents for the next six years. Since then the minimum wage has been increased about 6 times. The current federal minimum wage, established in 1991 is $4.25 per hour. Proposals are currently underway to increase the minimum wage to $5.15 per hour.

COMPUTING AND PAYING WAGES AND SALARIES

LEARNING OBJECTIVES

After studying this chapter, you should be able to:

1. Explain the major provisions of the Fair Labor Standards Act.

2. Distinguish between the employees' *principal* activities and their *preliminary* and *postliminary* activities.

3. Describe the main types of records used to collect payroll data.

4. Perform the following computations:

    (a) Convert weekly wage rates to hourly wage rates.

    (b) Convert monthly and annual salary rates to hourly rates.

    (c) Compute regular earnings and overtime earnings to arrive at total gross earnings.

    (d) Compute overtime payments for pieceworkers using two different methods.

    (e) Compute earnings under incentive and commission plans.

5. Describe how wages are paid using (a) cash, (b) check, and (c) electronic transfer of funds.

This chapter examines the major provisions of the Fair Labor Standards Act, how to determine hours worked by employees, commonly used methods to record time worked, the major methods of computing salaries and wages, and the methods of paying employees.

WHAT IS THE FAIR LABOR STANDARDS ACT ?

The Fair Labor Standards Act (FLSA), commonly known as the Federal Wage and Hour Law, contains provisions and standards concerning minimum wages, equal pay for equal work regardless of sex, overtime pay, record keeping, and child labor. The Wage and Hour Division of the U.S. Department of Labor administers the act. Since its enactment in 1938, several amendments have broadened the law's definition of employees and enterprises.

Who Is Covered Under FLSA?

The FLSA provides for two bases of coverage—enterprise coverage and individual employee coverage.

Enterprise Coverage. *Enterprise coverage* includes all employees of an enterprise if:

1. At least two employees engage in interstate commerce or produce goods for interstate commerce. Interstate commerce refers to the trade, transportation, or communication among several states or between a state and any place outside that state. The law also covers employees if they handle, sell, or otherwise work on goods or materials that have been moved in or produced for interstate commerce, and
2. The business has annual gross sales of at least $500,000.

Coverage extends, *without regard to annual sales volume*, to those who operate:

1. A hospital.
2. A nursing home.
3. An institution for the mentally ill.
4. A school for mentally or physically handicapped or gifted children.
5. A preschool, elementary, or secondary school.
6. An institution of higher education.
7. A public agency.

The enterprise coverage under the FLSA does not apply to family establishments, often referred to as "mom and pop stores." Thus, if the only regular employees of an establishment include the owner, parent, spouse, child, or other immediate family member, the establishment is exempt from FLSA coverage.

Individual Employee Coverage. Under *individual employee coverage*, the FLSA covers a worker if the employee either engages in interstate commerce or produces goods for such commerce. Coverage also includes employment in a fringe occupation closely related and directly essential to the production of goods for interstate commerce. Coverage depends on the activities of the individual employee and not on the work of fellow employees, the nature of the employer's business, or the character of the industry as a whole. Thus, even though a business does not meet the enterprise coverage test, it must pay FLSA wages to those workers eligible for individual coverage.

James Rineheart works for a small manufacturing firm that has an annual sales volume of $370,000. Although the firm does not meet the $500,000 volume-of-sales requirement for enterprise coverage, Rineheart is individually covered since he operates machinery used to produce goods for interstate commerce.

Domestic workers also must be paid the minimum wage if:

1. They perform services in one or more homes for a total of more than 8 hours in any workweek, *or if*
2. They earn wages of at least $50 in any calendar quarter.

Domestic service consists of services of a household nature performed in or about a private home of the person who employs the domestic. Some typical domestics include cooks, butlers, maids, caretakers, gardeners, and chauffeurs. The term also includes a baby-sitter employed on other than a casual basis, such as a person who sits for a child five days a week. If the domestics do not live in the household, they must be paid overtime compensation as well as the minimum wage. However, live-in domestics do not have to be paid overtime. A casual baby-sitter (one employed on an irregular or intermittent basis) or a companion for the aged or infirm is completely exempt.

Independent contractors are not entitled to benefits under the Fair Labor Standards Act.

How Are Wages Defined Under FLSA?

Wages include the remuneration or compensation paid employees. The terms wages and salaries are commonly used interchangeably. However, *wage* usually refers to remuneration paid on an hourly, weekly, or piecework basis. *Salary* usually refers to the remuneration paid on a monthly, *biweekly* (every two weeks), *semimonthly* (twice a month), or yearly basis. Some examples include:

1. Salaries and Commissions
2. Vacation pay
3. Severance or dismissal pay
4. Earned bonuses
5. Other amounts agreed upon by the employer and the employee.
6. Fair market value of board lodging or other facilities ordinarily furnished to the employee.

What Is the Minimum Wage?

The FLSA of 1938 established a minimum wage of 25¢ an hour for a straight-time workweek of 44 hours. With the objective of improving the purchasing power of covered workers, succeeding amendments to the FLSA increased the minimum hourly rate and reduced the workweek. As of April 1, 1991, the minimum hourly wage was increased to its current rate of $4.25 and provides overtime pay for hours worked over 40 in a week.

Jacksonville, NC, having the lowest annual pay of 310 U.S. urban areas for four straight years, has been examined as a test case for the impact of raising the minimum wage on the economy. In Jacksonville, where the poverty rate is 9% and unemployment is just 5%, most people live on the minimum wage.

Who Can Be Paid Less Than the Minimum Wage Under FLSA?

Under certain conditions, wages lower than the minimum wage may be paid to some employees.

1. Retail or service establishments and farms may employ full-time students at 85% of the minimum wage.
2. Institutions of higher education may employ their own full-time students at 85% of the minimum wage.
3. Student-learners may be employed at 75% of the minimum wage if they are participating in a bona fide vocational training program conducted by an accredited school.
4. Persons whose earning capacity is impaired by age, physical or mental deficiency, or injury may be employed at special minimum wage rates. However, a certificate authorizing employment at such rates must first be obtained. The handicapped workers are entitled to the full benefits of the law, which requires premium pay for overtime hours and equal pay for equal work regardless of sex.

SELF-STUDY QUIZ 2–1. *Indicate which of the following statements regarding the Fair Labor Standard Act are false.*

_____ 1. Under FLSA, wages include sales commissions and bonuses paid for employee performance.

_____ 2. Domestic workers must always be paid overtime compensation in addition to the minimum wage.

_____ 3. A son working for his parents in a family-owned business is not covered under FLSA.

_____ 4. Individual employee coverage under FLSA applies only if fellow employees are engaged in similar activities.

_____ 5. A college may pay its own full-time students less than the minimum wage.

NOTE: Answers at back of book.

NEWS ALERT

The Nevada Casino Dealers Association has paid for a series of new billboards lining the highway to Las Vegas reminding visitors to give tips to dealers. Most dealers depend on tips to supplement their minimum wage.

How Are Tips Treated Under FLSA?

A *tip* (to insure promptness) is a gift or gratuity given by a customer in recognition of some service performed for him or her. A *tipped employee* is one who engages in an occupation in which tips of more than $30 a month are customarily and regularly received. Chapter 3 presents the rules for the reporting of tips by employees. An employer may consider, within prescribed limits, the tips received by a tipped employee as part of the employee's wages. An employer can credit up to 50% of a tipped employee's minimum wage as coming from tips actually received.

EXAMPLE

Barbara Rivera, a hair stylist, earns $120 for a 40-hour workweek and regularly receives at least $250 in tips each week.

The weekly wage paid Rivera is $50 less than the minimum wage for a 40-hour workweek ($4.25 × 40 = $170). Since Rivera regularly receives more than $30 per week in tips, her employer can claim up to 50% of the weekly minimum wage. Thus, each week her employer claims a credit of $50 from her tips in order to meet the weekly minimum wage requirement of $170.

The maximum weekly credit that could have been available to the employer is $85 ($170 × 50%). Therefore, Rivera's employer could have paid Rivera as little as $85 a week and not have violated the provisions of the FLSA.

If less than 50% of the minimum wage rate is received in tips, the amount received becomes the maximum permissible tip credit. In such a case, the employer must pay the balance so that a combination of the tips received and of the wages paid in cash (or in the form of board, lodging, or other facilities) equals the minimum wage.

E X A M P L E

Bill Hunt, a waiter, earns a weekly wage of $85 for a 40-hour workweek and receives tips totaling $80 each week. The weekly wage is $85 less than the minimum wage requirement for a 40-hour workweek ($170 – $85).

Each week Hunt's employer claims a credit for the tips that Hunt reports. However, the amount of tips received, $80, is less than the 50% tip credit taken ($170 × 50% = $85).

Thus, the maximum credit that the employer may take is $80, the tips received by Hunt. The employer must pay the balance, $5, along with the weekly wage of $85 so that the combined wages paid and the tip credit taken equal $170.

SELF-STUDY QUIZ 2–2. *Marion Yeld, a waitress, earns $90 a week for a 40-hour workweek. During one week Yeld received tips of $60.*

1.   What is the maximum amount of tip credit Yeld's employer may claim for that week?
      $ _____

2.   How much must the employer pay Yeld in addition to her $90 weekly wage?
      $ _____

What Is a Workweek Under FLSA?

The FLSA defines a *workweek* as a fixed and regularly recurring period of 168 hours—seven consecutive 24-hour periods. The individual employee's workweek is the statutory or contract number of hours to be worked regularly during that period. The workweek may begin on any day of the week and need not coincide with the calendar week. An employer may establish the same workweek for the business operations as a whole or assign different workweeks to individual workers or groups of workers.

An employer may change the day a workweek begins if intended to be a permanent change and not just to evade the overtime pay requirements of the FLSA. If, however, a union contract fixes the workweek, the employer's right to change the workweek depends upon the wording in the contract. Each workweek stands alone, and the overtime hours worked in one week may not be shifted to another workweek. Thus each workweek is a separate unit for the purpose of computing overtime pay.

How Is Overtime Computed?

Overtime Hours and Overtime Pay. The FLSA requires overtime pay for all hours worked in excess of 40 in a workweek. The FLSA requires no overtime pay for daily hours worked in excess of any given number or for work on Saturdays, Sundays, holidays, or other special days. The law requires overtime pay to be 1½ times the employee's regular hourly rate of pay, which must not be less than the statutory minimum.

E X A M P L E

If an employee's regular rate of pay is $4.40 an hour, the overtime rate must be at least $4.40 × 1.5, or $6.60 an hour.

If an hourly-rate employee works in pay periods of two weeks or longer, the employer can elect to give the employee 1.5 hours off for every overtime hour. However, the time off must be in the same pay period as the overtime hours worked.

Exceptions to Overtime Hours and Overtime Pay Provisions. An exception to overtime hours and overtime pay applies to *hospital employees.* Hospitals may enter into an agreement with their employees under which a 14-day period, rather than a workweek, becomes the basis for computing overtime pay. Employees entering such an agreement must receive overtime pay at not less than one and one-half times their regular hourly rate for hours worked in excess of 8 hours in any workday or in excess of 80 hours in a 14-day period, whichever is the greater number of overtime hours. Although employers have the option of using the normal workweek or the 14-day period, they cannot change from one method to the other arbitrarily.

E X A M P L E

Pam Valenti, a lab technician, agreed that a 14-day period would be used to figure her overtime pay. Valenti works 12 hours in one day during the period and 8 hours in each of the 9 other days during the period, a total of 84 hours.

Valenti is entitled to 80 hours of straight-time pay and 4 hours of overtime pay for the 14-day period.

If Valenti worked only 7 hours in each of the 9 other days during the period, or a total of 75 hours, she would be entitled to 71 hours of straight-time pay and 4 hours of overtime pay for the 14-day period.

An employer cannot pay an employee who works varying hours a flat or guaranteed monthly wage to compensate for all time worked, including overtime. However, a FLSA provision, referred to as the Belo plan, allows the employer to pay employees working irregular hours a guaranteed weekly wage, including payment for overtime hours up to a limited number. To be a valid plan, the contract must meet specific conditions.

Minimum wage legislation provides an exception for *employees receiving remedial education.* Under this law, employees who receive remedial education offered by their employers are permitted to work up to 10 hours overtime each week without receiving overtime compensation. The remedial training, which does not include training for a specific job, must be designed to provide reading and other basic skills at an eighth-grade level or below.

Compensatory Time Off. Employees of a state, a political subdivision of a state, or an interstate governmental agency may use compensatory time off in lieu of overtime compensation. Employees working in public safety, emergency response, or seasonal activities may accumulate compensatory time off up to 480 hours. (The 480-hour limit represents 320 hours of overtime actually worked at the 1½ overtime rate). Employees may "bank" their hours and use them later as time off at time and one-half during the course of their employment.

Employees whose work does not include the preceding activities may bank 240 hours for compensatory time off. The 240-hour limit represents 160 hours of overtime actually worked at the one and one-half overtime rate. Upon reaching the 480- or 240-hour limit, an employee must receive either cash for additional hours of overtime worked or use some compensatory time before receiving further overtime compensation in the form of compensatory time off. Note that not all 480 or 240 hours have to be accrued before compensatory time off may be used.

What Is the Equal Pay Act?

The Equal Pay Act amended the FLSA to require that men and women performing equal work receive equal pay. The Equal Pay Law applies to any employer having workers subject to the minimum pay provisions of the Wage and Hour Law. The law applies to *any establishment* wherein such workers are employed. The equal-pay requirements also apply to white-collar workers, including outside salespersons, exempt from the minimum wage standards.

The Equal Pay law prohibits an employer from discriminating by paying wages to employees of one sex at a lower rate than those paid the opposite sex for equal work on jobs that require equal skill, effort, and responsibility and that are performed under similar working conditions. However, wage differentials between sexes are allowable if based on a seniority system, a merit system, a payment plan that measures earnings by quantity or quality of production, or any factor other than sex. If an unlawful pay differential between men and women exists, the employer must raise the lower rate to equal the higher rate.

Who Is Exempt from FLSA Requirements?

Exempt employees are those workers exempt from some, or all, of the FLSA requirements such as minimum wages, equal pay, and overtime pay.

Executive, Administrative, and Professional Employees. The FLSA exempts some workers, such as executive, administrative, and professional employees from the minimum wage and overtime pay provisions if they satisfy certain tests. In order for an employee to be granted this exemption as an *executive,* all of the following requirements must be met:

1. The primary duty must be that of managing an enterprise or department or subdivision thereof.
2. The employee must customarily and regularly direct the work of two or more full-time employees.
3. The employee can hire and fire and suggest changes in the status of other employees.
4. The employee must customarily and regularly exercise discretionary powers.
5. The nonexempt work must be no more than 20% of the executive's weekly hours worked, or 40% in the case of executives of retail or service establishments.
6. The executive's salary must be at least $155 a week, exclusive of board, lodging, or other facilities. In Puerto Rico, the Virgin Islands, and American Samoa, the test is $130 a week; for the motion picture producing industry, a base rate of $250 a week applies.[1]

---

[1] The salary or fee for an *administrative* employee must also be at least $155 a week. The tests in Puerto Rico, the Virgin Islands, American Samoa, and for the motion picture producing industry are the same as for executives. However, for a *professional* employee, the salary or fee must be at least $170 a week, exclusive of board, lodging, or other facilities. In Puerto Rico, the Virgin Islands, and American Samoa, the amount is $150 a week; for the motion picture industry, the base rate is $250 a week.

A U.S. District court recently ruled that an employer cannot treat pregnancy leave differently from leave for other short-term disabilities when computing retirement pensions.

The court ruled in favor of an employee who applied for an early retirement plan offered by the company, but did not qualify for the necessary years of service with the company because she was given only one month's credit toward retirement for a pregnancy leave of more than eight months. The court ordered the company to pay back benefits plus interest and pay future benefits according to its retirement plan.

Employers are permitted to establish wage differentials based on seniority, merit, incentive, and variances other than sex.

Lawful differentials include: an employee, male or female, performing supervisory duties while in training for a supervisory position, a sales clerk authorized to approve customer's personal checks, and employees working the night shift requiring heavier physical work.

Unlawful differentials include: paying a newly hired female employee less than that paid to the male employee she replaced, turning out the lights at the end of the day, and employer-provided group benefits to one sex, but not to the opposite sex.

Employee Job Description	Minimum Wage Exemption	Equal Pay Exemption	Full Overtime Exemption
Agricultural employees.			X
Agricultural workers who are members of the employer's immediate family.	X	X	X
Air carrier employees if the carrier is subject to Title II of the Railway Labor Act.			X
Amusement or recreational establishment employees, provided the business has seasonal peaks.	X	X	X
Announcers, news editors, and chief engineers of radio or television stations in small communities.			X
Baby-sitters (casual) and companions to ill or aged persons unable to care for themselves.	X	X	X
Drivers and drivers' helpers who make local deliveries and are paid on a trip-rate or similar basis following a plan approved by the government.			X
Executive, administrative, and professional employees including teachers and academic administrative personnel in schools.	X		X
Fruit and vegetable employees who are engaged in the local transportation of these items or of workers employed or to be employed in the harvesting of fruits or vegetables.			X
Household domestic service employees who reside in the household.			X
Motion picture theater employees.			X
Motor carrier employees if the carrier is subject to regulation by the Secretary of Transportation.			X
Newspaper employees if the newspaper is published on a weekly, semiweekly, or daily basis and if the circulation is less than 4,000 copies, with the major circulation in the county of publication or contiguous counties.	X	X	X
Outside sales personnel.	X		X
Railroad, express company, and water carrier employees if the companies are subject to Part I of the Interstate Commerce Act.			X
Salespersons for automobile, truck, or farm implement dealers; parts stock clerks or mechanics; salespersons for boat, trailer, or aircraft dealers.			X
Taxicab drivers.			X

Figure 2–1 *Exemption Status of Workers Under FLSA*

Short Test of Exemption. A shorter test of exemption status may be applied to higher salaried employees who earn $250 or more each week. In this test, most highly paid employees need meet only the first two requirements listed above so long as their weekly salary (exclusive of board, lodging, or other facilities) equals $250 or more. Employees paid by the hour are not exempt from the minimum wage and overtime pay requirements and thus do not qualify for the salary test even if their total weekly compensation exceeds the limits specified.

Highly Skilled Computer Professionals. Employees highly skilled in computer systems analysis, programming, or related work in software functions may be exempt from the minimum wage and overtime requirements. Some of the job titles in this exemption include:

- computer programmer
- systems analyst
- applications programmer
- applications systems analyst
- software engineer
- software specialist
- systems engineer

The exemption does not apply to workers who operate computers or manufacture, repair, or maintain computer hardware and related equipment. To be exempt from the overtime requirements, the computer professional must be paid:

1. On an hourly basis.
2. At a rate greater than 6½ times the minimum wage, or more than $27.63 an hour ($4.25 × 6.5).

A *salaried* computer professional may qualify for exemption as a *professional* and thus also be exempt from the overtime requirements, provided the employee:

1. Earns at least $170 a week.
2. Meets the other requirements of a professional (work is primarily intellectual and nonstandard in character, uses discretion and independent judgment, and spends no more than 20% of the workweek on nonexempt work).

What Are the Child-Labor Restrictions Under FLSA?

The FLSA prohibits a business from the interstate shipment of its goods or services if it employs child labor unlawfully. Under the FLSA, the Secretary of Labor issues regulations that restrict the employment of individuals under the age of 18. The restrictions divide child employment into nonfarm occupations and agricultural occupations.

Nonfarm Occupations. The basic minimum age for most jobs is 16 years. This is the minimum age for work in manufacturing and processing jobs or in any other occupations except those declared by the Secretary of Labor as hazardous for minors under 18. Some of the jobs classified as hazardous include:

- motor-vehicle drivers and helpers.
- occupations in plants manufacturing or storing explosives.
- occupations in coal mines.
- occupations in slaughtering and meat-packing establishments.
- operating power-driven woodworking machines.
- doing excavation work.
- wrecking and demolishing buildings.

Children under 16 years of age may *not* be employed in manufacturing, mining, processing of goods; operating or tending power-driven machinery other than office machines; public messenger service; and jobs (other than office or sales work) connected with the transportation of persons or property by rail, highway, air, water, pipeline, or other means; warehousing and storage; communications and public utilities; construction, including demolition and repair.

Within certain limits 14- and 15-year-olds may be employed in retail, food service, and gasoline service establishments. For example, this age group may be employed in office and clerical work, including the operation of office machines; cashiering; selling; price marking and tagging by hand or by machine; errand and delivery work, kitchen work and other work involved in preparing

NEWS

and serving food and beverages; dispensing gasoline and oil; and car cleaning. The employment of minors between the ages of 14 and 16 cannot interfere with their schooling, health, and well-being. In addition, the following conditions must be met:

1. All work must be performed outside school hours.
2. There is a maximum 3-hour day and 18-hour week when school is in session (8 hours and 40 hours when not in session).
3. All work must be performed between 7 a.m. and 7 p.m. (9 p.m. during the summer).

Agricultural Occupations. The employment of children under age 12 is generally prohibited in agricultural occupations:

1. During hours when school is in session.
2. Outside school hours on farms, including conglomerates, that used more than 500 man-days of labor in any quarter of the preceding calendar year, and
3. Outside school hours on noncovered farms without parental consent.

However, children may work on farms owned or operated by their parents or guardians. Children 10 and 11 years old can work as hand harvest laborers outside school hours for up to eight weeks between June 1 and October 15, with a number of strict conditions on the employer. Children aged 12 and 13 may be employed only during hours when school is not in session provided there is parental consent or the employment is on a farm where the parents are employed. Children aged 14 and 15 may be employed, but only during hours when school is not in session. No child under the age of 16 may be employed in a hazardous farm occupation, such as operating large tractors, corn pickers, cotton pickers, grain combines, and feed grinders.

Certificate of Age. Employers cannot be charged with having violated the child-labor restrictions of the law if they have on file an officially executed *certificate of age* which shows that the minor has reached the stipulated minimum age. In most states a state employment or age certificate, issued by the Federal Wage and Hour Division or by a state agency, serves as proof of age. In some states a state or federal certificate of age, a state employment certificate, or a work permit may not be available. In such cases, the employer may rely on any one of the following documents as evidence of age for minor employees:

1. Birth certificate (or attested transcript thereof) or a signed statement of the recorded date and place of birth issued by a registrar of vital statistics or other officer charged with the duty of recording births.
2. Record of baptism (or attested transcript thereof) showing the date of birth of the minor.
3. Statement on the census records of the Bureau of Indian Affairs and signed by an administrative representative thereof showing the name and date and place of the minor's birth.

The employer should maintain a copy of the document or indicate in the payroll records which document verified the minor's age.

Penalties. The U.S. Government may bring civil or criminal actions against employers who violate the FLSA. Employers who willfully violate the wage and hour provisions of the law or the wage orders fixed by the Administrator of the Wage and Hour Division of the Department of Labor will be prosecuted and will be subject to a fine of not more than $10,000, or imprisonment for up to six months, or both. However, no person may be imprisoned for a first offense violation. If an imposed fine goes unpaid, however, the courts have the power to order imprisonment as an incident to the nonpayment. Violators of the child-labor provisions of the Act are subject to fines of $10,000 for each violation. Payroll managers should read the Fair Labor Standards Act and its amendments very carefully. They should consult a representative of the Wage and Hour Division regarding questions about how provisions of the law govern their companies.

Areas Not Covered by the FLSA. The FLSA does not require employers to pay extra wages for work on Saturday, Sunday, or holidays. It does not require vacation, holiday, or severance pay; nor does it limit the number of hours of work for persons 16 years of age or over, as long as the overtime pay provisions are met. In addition, the law does not require the employer to give employees the day off on holidays, nor to give them vacations. If the employee does work on a holiday, the employer need not pay the employee time and one-half. Thus, holidays, like Sundays, are treated the same as any other day. Whether time off is granted or overtime rates are paid depends on the employment agreement.

HOW IS EMPLOYEE'S WORK TIME DETERMINED?

To avoid paying for time not actually spent on the job and to eliminate payment for unnecessary overtime work, employers must know what types of employee activities count as working time under the law. Generally the hours counted as working time include all the time that employees actually work or must be on duty. A distinction must be made between an employee's principal activities and the preliminary and postliminary activities.

L E A R N I N G
O B J E C T I V E
2

Principal Activities

The *principal activities* of employees include those tasks employees must perform and include any work of consequence performed for the employer. Principal activities include those indispensable to the performance of productive work and those that are an integral part of a principal activity.

E X A M P L E

Ted Jambro is a lathe operator who oils and cleans his machines at the beginning of each workday and installs new cutting tools. These activities performed by Jambro are part of his principal activity.

The test of compensability with respect to principal activities requires that there be physical or mental exertion, controlled or required by the employer and performed for the employer's benefit.

Clothes-Changing Time and Wash-Up. Because of the nature of their work, some employees change clothes or wash on the employer's premises. Statutes or ordinances may require clothes changing or washing. Employees who spend time in changing clothes or washing on the employer's premises regard this time as part of their principal activities. However, even where the nature of the job or the law requires clothes changing or wash-up, it may be excluded from time worked either expressly or by custom and practice under a collective bargaining contract.

Travel Time. The time spent by employees in traveling to and from work need be counted as time worked only if contract, custom, or practice so requires. In some situations, however, travel time between home and work counts as time worked.

If an employee who regularly works at a fixed location is given a special one-day work assignment in another city, time worked includes the travel time. When performed during the workday as part of an employee's principal activities, the travel time counts as time worked.

E X A M P L E

Lisa Rubini receives an emergency call outside regular working hours and must travel substantial distance to perform a job away from Rubini's usual work site for one of the employer's customers. The travel time counts as time worked.

E X A M P L E

Reba Ferguson travels throughout the city to various job sites during regular working hours, 9 a.m. to 5 p.m., Mondays through Fridays. Such travel time counts as work time.

When Ferguson travels between workdays from one city to another, the travel time counts as working time when the hours correspond to regular working hours, even though the hours may occur on Saturday and Sunday.

For example, if Ferguson is sent on a trip requiring travel on Saturday and Sunday to be at a job the first thing Monday morning, the travel time on Saturday and Sunday between the hours of 9 a.m. and 5 p.m. counts as time worked, but travel time before 9 a.m. and after 5 p.m. does not count.

Rest Periods and Coffee Breaks. The FLSA does not require that an employer give employees a rest period or a coffee break. However, the employer may grant such rest periods voluntarily; or the union contract or municipal or state legislation may require them. In these cases, the time spent on a rest period 20 minutes or less counts as part of the hours worked. If longer than 20 minutes, the compensability for the time depends upon the employee's freedom during that time or upon the provisions of the union contract.

Meal Periods. Bona fide meal periods (not including coffee breaks or snack times) during which the employee is completely relieved from duty are not considered working time. Lunch periods during which the employee must perform some duties while eating are not bona fide meal periods.

E X A M P L E

Virginia Sherr, an office worker, must eat at her desk and operate the switchboard at lunch time. Sherr must be paid for the lunch period.

Training Sessions. Generally, working time includes the time spent by employees in attending lectures and meetings for training purposes.

The working time spent by postal clerks in learning mail distribution practices and the operation of letter sorting machines counts as compensable time because it is (a) controlled and required by the employer, (b) for the primary benefit of the employer, and (c) an integral and indispensable part of the employees' principal work activities.

However, time spent in training sessions need not be counted as working time if all the following conditions are met:

1. Attendance by the employee is voluntary.
2. The employee does not produce any goods or perform any other productive work during the meeting or lecture.
3. The meeting or lecture takes place outside regular working hours.
4. The meeting or lecture is not directly related to the employee's work.

Preliminary and Postliminary Activities

Activities regarded as *preliminary* and *postliminary* need not be counted as time worked unless required by contract or custom. Some examples of activities regarded as preliminary and postliminary include: walking, riding, or traveling to or from the actual place where employees engage in their principal activities; checking in and out at the plant or office and waiting in line to do so; changing clothes for the convenience of the employee, washing up and showering unless directly related to the specific type of work the employee is hired to perform; and waiting in line to receive paychecks.

Absences. The FLSA does not require an employer to pay an employee for hours not worked because of illness. For employees on an hourly wage basis, the time card shows the exact hours worked; and the time off does not count toward the 40 hours for overtime pay purposes even if the employee is paid for the absences. Employees on a salary basis are frequently paid for a certain number of days of excused absences after they have been employed by their company for a certain length of time. When the employee is absent from work, the department head usually must approve the time card for payment of salaries for hours not worked.

Tardiness. Employers may handle tardiness in many ways. Frequently when an employee is late or leaves early, causing the time clock to print in red, the supervisor must O.K. the time card. Some companies require the employee to sign a special slip indicating the reason for being late or leaving early. Some companies keep time according to the decimal system whereby each hour is divided into units of tens (6 minutes times 10 periods in each hour). An employee who is late **1 through 6 minutes** is penalized or "docked" one tenth of an hour. One who is **7 through 12 minutes** late is "docked" one fifth of an hour, etc. Many businesses following this procedure claim that when employees are "docked," there is a tendency to reduce tardiness.

WHAT RECORDS ARE USED FOR TIMEKEEPING?

The FLSA requires employers subject to the law to keep certain time and pay records. For example, employers must keep records that indicate the hours

Don't allow your nonexempt employees access to their workstations until it is time to begin regular work duties. Even if the early arrivals say they do not want to be paid for their catch-up work done prior to starting time, the employer must pay for the duties performed even though the work was done without the employer's permission.

A growing number of companies are establishing paid time-off banks, or PTO banks, in which a variety of paid time-off days, such as short-term sick leave, vacation, personal days, and funeral leave, are put into one "bank." Employees can withdraw days for whatever purpose they choose. A recent survey indicated that almost half of the companies using a PTO plan reported a drop in unscheduled absenteeism.

L E A R N I N G
O B J E C T I V E
3

each employee worked each workday and each workweek. Most of the information required by the FLSA, a company would usually keep in following ordinary business practices. Even though the 40-hour, 5-day workweek is the most common work schedule, the schedules of American workers have been changing and becoming increasingly diverse. To improve declining productivity, to decrease job dissatisfaction, and to reduce absenteeism, many firms have adopted alternative work schedules.

How the employer chooses the methods of keeping time records depends on the size of the company and whether employees are paid on an hourly, weekly, biweekly, semimonthly, or monthly basis. Employees on a salary basis usually work a given number of hours each day, generally on a definite schedule. Employees on an hourly wage basis may work a varying number of hours with some "down time" and layoffs and some overtime work. All of this time must be recorded in some way.

Time Sheets

A *time sheet*, illustrated in Figure 2–2, provides the information required by law and the data used to compute the payroll. Many small businesses that must

Figure 2–2 *Time Sheet*

WEEKLY TIME REPORT

EMPLOYEE NAME   *Alma Chapman*

DEPARTMENT   *Packing*

REPORT FOR WEEK ENDING SATURDAY   *June 12, 19--*

DAY	TIME IN	LUNCH PERIOD	TIME OUT	HOURS WORKED	EXCEPTIONS
Sunday	———	XXXXXXXXX	———	———	
Monday	8:00	– 45 minutes	10:05	2	S-6
Tuesday	7:50	– 45 minutes	4:40	8	
Wednesday	7:45	– 45 minutes	4:30	8	
Thursday	7:30	– 45 minutes	5:15	9	
Friday	8:00	– 45 minutes	4:45	8	
Saturday	———	XXXXXXXXX	———	———	
			WEEKLY TOTAL	35	6

Exception Code
S Sickness   H—Holiday
V—Vacation   E—Other
—

EMPLOYEE'S SIGNATURE: *Alma Chapman*

APPROVED BY: *James S. Malek*

keep a record of time worked by each employee require each person to sign a *time sheet*, indicating the times of arrival and departure from work. Time sheets may be used for each working day with employees signing their names on arrival and indicating the times they started and quit work. Some businesses have a timekeeper, who uses a similar form to record the hours worked by each person in the department. Some businesses require a record of the exact time an employee arrives and leaves, while others require only the total hours worked each day.

Time Cards

Under this timekeeping system, each employee receives a **time card** on which the time worked is recorded manually by the employee or automatically by a time clock. The time card is designed to fit various lengths of pay periods. Figure 2–3 shows one type of time card frequently used for a weekly pay period. The card provides space to record the hours worked, the rate of pay, deductions, and net pay. The payroll department inserts the handwritten figures to be used in computing total earnings, deductions, and net pay for the payroll period.

Some time clocks use the **continental system** of recording time, where each day consists of one 24-hour period, instead of two 12-hour periods. The time runs from 12 midnight to 12 midnight. Eight o'clock in the morning is recorded as 800; eight o'clock in the evening, as 2000. Figure 2–4 shows a time card that uses the continental system of recording time.

Most office workers use the time card which registers from 1 to 12 a.m. or p.m. with full minutes. However, for many manufacturing jobs, managers need additional information about how an employee spent time on a particular operation as the product passed along the line. In a job shop such as an auto or appliance repair shop, employees need to allocate their time to a single job. Where incentive plans are used, standards must be compared with actual time for the purposes of determining pay as well as for cost analysis of the individual parts produced.

For job costing, the continental time system, with minutes indicated in fractional equivalents, may be effectively used. Figure 2–5 shows the labor time or charge made against a specific job. The **job cost card**, prepared in advance by the scheduling or production control department, identifies the job and may accompany the job throughout the shop. Each employee who works on the job signs his or her name or clock number on the card in the space provided, together with the time registration on and off the job. Such a time record gives a complete summation of time spent on the job as soon as the job is completed and allows a study of the total time spent on a particular job.

Mechanical Time-Clock System

The number of time-clock stations used by an employer depends on the number of hourly employees, the number of employee entrances, etc. Usually each station has a centrally located time clock with an *In rack* on one side and an *Out rack* on the other. Before employees report for work on Monday morning, a card for each employee is placed in the rack. A clock number identifies each slot in the rack, and the cards are arranged chronologically by clock number. Each employee's card shows the clock number, name of employee, and a record of the hours worked.

No. **312**   Pay Ending _October 17, 19—_

NAME   GARY A. SCHNEIDER   262-09-7471

	Hours	Rate	Amount			DEDUCTIONS	OASDI	32	66
Reg.	40	10.75	430	00			HI	7	64
O/T	6	16.13	96	78			FIT	81	00
							SIT	10	54
							Group Life Ins.	1	60
							Hospital Ins.	3	15
Total Earnings			526	78			U.S. Sav. Bonds	5	00
Less Deductions			141	59			Other		
NET PAY			385	19			Total	141	59

Days	MORNING		AFTERNOON		OVERTIME		Daily
	IN	OUT	IN	OUT	IN	OUT	Totals
1	MO 7⁵⁹	MO 12⁰³	MO 1⁰⁰	MO 5⁰⁵			8
2	TU 7⁵⁰	TU 12⁰⁴	TU 12⁵⁹	TU 5⁰⁷			8
3	WE 7⁵¹	WE 12⁰¹	WE 12⁵⁰	WE 5⁰⁴	WE 5²⁹	WE 7³⁵	10
4	TH 8⁰⁰	TH 12⁰²	TH 12⁵⁸	TH 5⁰³			8
5	FR 8⁰⁰	FR 12⁰⁵	FR 1⁰¹	FR 5⁰⁶			8
6	SA 7⁵⁵	SA 12⁰⁴					4
7							

Signature _Gary A. Schneider_

Figure 2–3   *Time Card*

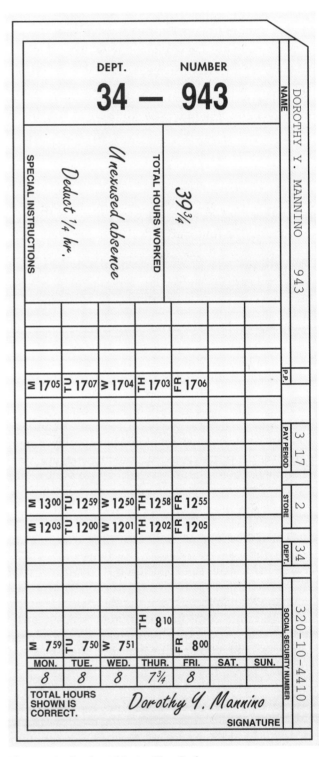

Figure 2–4   *Continental System Time Card*

1. When employees arrive for work, they remove their time cards from the Out rack and place them in the slot provided in the time clock, which actuates a device that prints the starting time for that day in the *Morning In* column of the card. The employees then place their cards in the proper place in the In rack.

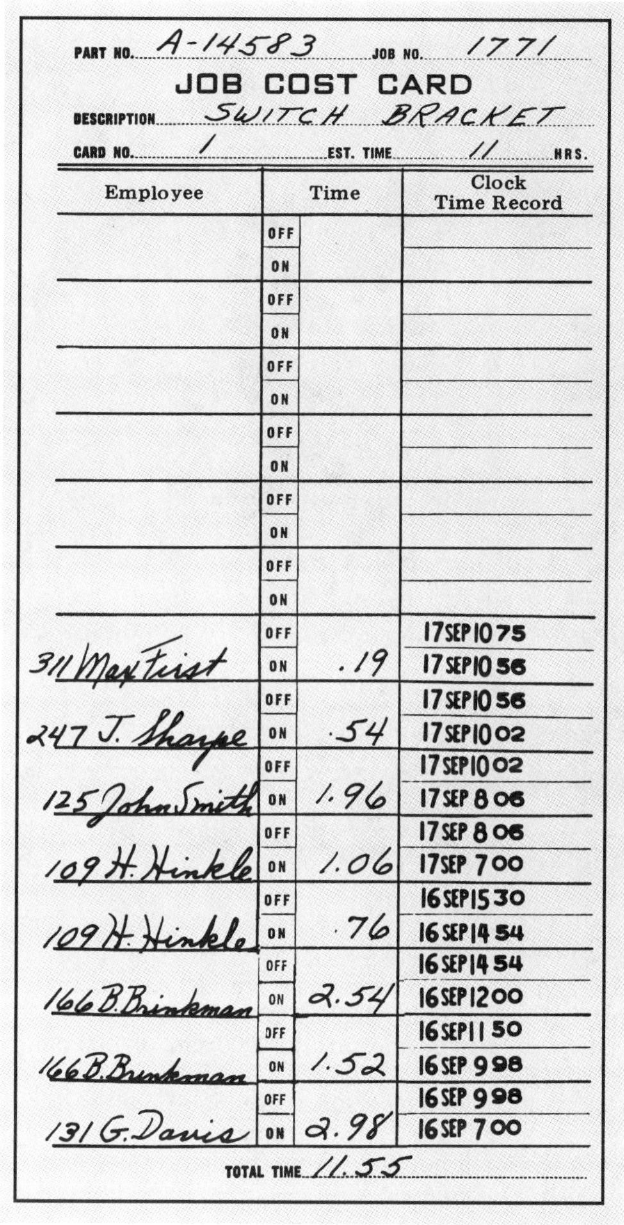

PART NO. A-14583 JOB NO. 1771

JOB COST CARD

DESCRIPTION SWITCH BRACKET

CARD NO. 1 EST. TIME 11 HRS.

Employee		Time	Clock Time Record
	OFF		
	ON		
	OFF		
	ON		
	OFF		
	ON		
	OFF		
	ON		
	OFF		
	ON		
	OFF		
	ON		
	OFF		17SEP1075
311 Max Feist	ON	.19	17SEP1056
	OFF		17SEP1056
247 J. Sharpe	ON	.54	17SEP1002
	OFF		17SEP1002
125 John Smith	ON	1.96	17SEP 806
	OFF		17SEP 806
109 H. Hinkle	ON	1.06	17SEP 700
	OFF		16SEP1530
109 H. Hinkle	ON	.76	16SEP1454
	OFF		16SEP1454
166 B. Brinkman	ON	2.54	16SEP1200
	OFF		16SEP1150
166 B. Brinkman	ON	1.52	16SEP 998
	OFF		16SEP 998
131 G. Davis	ON	2.98	16SEP 700

TOTAL TIME 11.55

Figure 2–5
Job Cost Card with Time Recorded in Hundredths of an Hour

2. When employees go to lunch, they remove their cards from the In rack, register the time, and place the cards in the Out rack. When they return they take the cards from the Out rack, register the *Afternoon In* time, and place the cards in the In rack. At closing time they take the cards from the In rack, register the *Afternoon Out* time, and place the cards in the Out rack.
3. On each succeeding day during the week, a similar procedure is followed. Each day an automatic adjustment in the time clock makes it print on the next lower line.
4. The time clock (see Figure 2–6) comes with a two-color ribbon. The clock prints all regular time in black, and irregular time in red. For example, if regular working hours were from 8.00 a.m. to 5:00 p.m., with an hour from noon to 1:00 p.m. for lunch, the regular working day would be eight hours. The clock would record as follows:

Figure 2–6 *Mechanical Time-Clock*

a. Black when the person rings in before 8:00 a.m. or 1:00 p.m.; also when the person rings out after 12:00 p.m. and 5:00 p.m.
b. Red when the person rings in after 8:00 a.m. or 1:00 p.m.; also when the person rings out before 12:00 p.m. and 5:00 p.m. In other words, when the clock prints red, the person arrived late or left early.
c. Red for both in and out for overtime work, so that special attention is called to the extra hours worked. (In Figures 2–4 and 2–5, red is indicated by the shaded areas.)

Blank spaces on the card indicate that the employee was absent or had neglected to "punch in" that day. For example, if the Morning In and Out columns were blank but time was recorded in the afternoon columns, it might indicate that the employee was absent in the morning. The payroll clerk collects the time cards at the end of the week and computes the total hours worked, including regular and overtime, during the week.

Computerized Time and Attendance Recording Systems

The main kinds of computerized time and attendance recording systems include:

1. *Card-generated systems*—employees use time cards similar to the traditional time cards illustrated earlier. Daily and weekly totals are calculated and printed on the time cards for data entry into the firm's computer system.

2. *Badge systems*—employees are issued plastic laminated badges containing punched holes or having magnetic strips or bar codes. The badges are used with electronic time clocks that collect and store data, which later become input to the computer system.
3. *Cardless and badgeless systems*—employees enter only their personal identification numbers (PIN) on a numerical or alphanumerical key pad. This system, like the badge system, uses time clocks to collect and store data for transmission to and processing by the firm's computer system.

For example, the Timekeeper, a self-contained, wall-mounted time clock, contains a computer system[2]. This time clock accepts time and attendance data from time cards and computes complex payroll and on-the-job information. Time-clock systems, such as the Timekeeper, eliminate most manual payroll processing operations. Employees receive their own time cards that show their daily attendance record, thus complying with federal, state, and union regulations. The Timekeeper also totals employee hours and rounds out employee time to fractions of an hour in accordance with the payroll practice of the firm.

The Timekeeper card, shown in Figure 2–7, is similar to the time cards illustrated previously. However, in addition to recording time in and time out, the card prints total hours worked each day and total hours worked from the beginning of the pay period indicated on the time card. The mark sense field at the bottom of the card identifies each employee or supervisor and authorizes access to and use of the Timekeeper. Prior to the use of the card, the mark sense field is marked with the employee's identification number, the shift, and the department. This marking may be done by the Timekeeper or with a pencil. The supervisors' time cards are used to activate the keyboard of the Timekeeper to enter data or to print summary reports on blank time cards. Some typical summary reports prepared by the Timekeeper include:

1. List of employee's daily and/or cumulative hours worked by shift and/or department.
2. Absentee list.
3. Tardy list.
4. List of employees on premises.
5. List of employees off premises.

When an employee places the card in the time clock, the computer scans the card, optically verifies the employee's number, and locates the last print line on the card. The time of entry is then printed on the next line. Simultaneously, the computer stores the punch-in time in the system's memory. When an employee punches out, the Timekeeper again verifies the employee's identification number and computes and rounds off the daily and cumulative payroll hours. Next, the actual punchout time and the computed cumulative hours are printed on the card and stored within the Timekeeper for transmission to a computer for payroll processing. Figure 2–8 charts a computerized time and attendance recording system.

Fractional Parts of an Hour

The FLSA requires that employees be paid for *all* time worked, including fractional parts of an hour. An employer cannot use an arbitrary formula or an estimate as a substitute for determining precisely the compensable working time

---

[2]Information supplied by Kronos, Incorporated.

Figure 2–7
*Mark-Sense Time Card Used in the
Timekeeper Computerized System*

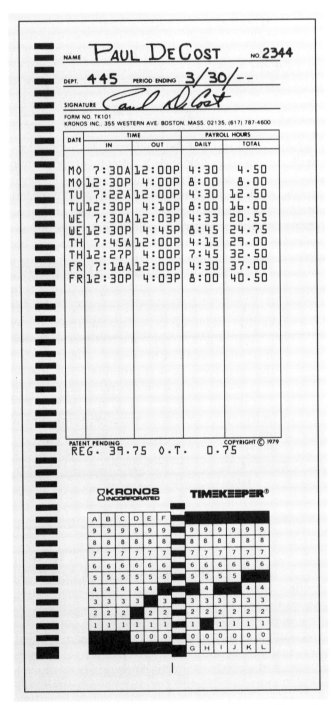

Kronos, Inc.

which is part of an employee's fixed or regular hours. However, an exception to
this rule involves the practice of recording an employee's starting and stopping
time to the nearest five minutes, or the nearest tenth of an hour, or the nearest
quarter of an hour. Employers must show that over a period of time the aver-
ages recorded in this manner result in the employees being paid for all the time
they actually worked.

Uncertain and indefinite working periods beyond the scheduled working
hours cannot be practicably determined. Therefore, a few seconds or minutes
may be disregarded since the law does not concern itself with trifles. Some

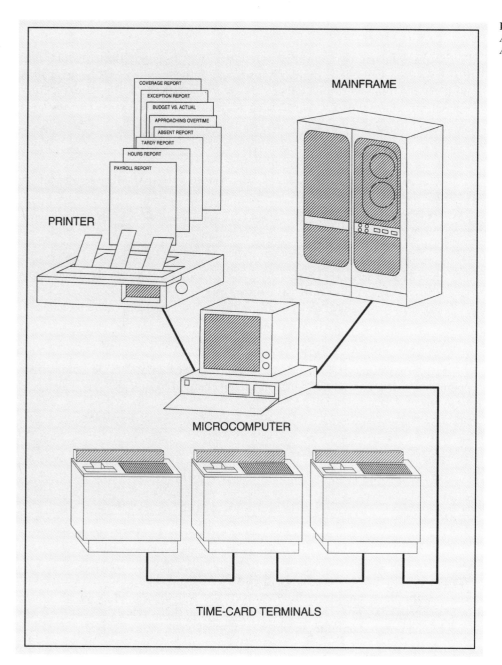

Figure 2–8
A Computerized Time and Attendance Recording System

courts have allowed from 10 to 20 minutes to be ignored, while other courts have refused to apply the law to periods as small as 10 minutes. Generally, a few minutes of time spent by employees on the company premises for their own convenience before or after their workday are not included in the hours worked.

HOW ARE WAGES AND SALARIES COMPUTED?

Employees are usually paid for time worked at a time rate, such as hourly, weekly, biweekly, semimonthly, or monthly. The employee may also be paid at a piece rate, incentive rate, commission basis, or a combination of these rates.

L E A R N I N G
O B J E C T I V E
4

Time Rate

To compute the wages of employees on an hourly basis, multiply the total regular hours worked by the regular hourly rate. If the employee works overtime, multiply the total overtime hours by the overtime rate. By adding the total regular earnings and the total overtime earnings, we obtain the ***gross earnings.***

E X A M P L E

Nick Sotakos works a 40-hour week at $6.20 an hour with overtime hours paid at 1½ times the regular rate.

Regular weekly earnings are	$248.00 (40 × $6.20)
The overtime rate is	$9.30 ($6.20 × 1.5)
If Sotakos works 4 hours overtime, additional earnings for the 4 hours are	$37.20 (4 × $9.30)
Sotakos' weekly gross earnings are	$285.20 ($248.00 + $37.20)
If paid only for time actually worked and he works only 36 hours during a week, Sotakos earns	$223.20 (36 × $6.20)

In the case of factory workers, many factories compute the actual time spent on a certain job so that amount can be charged to that job.

E X A M P L E

Sonla Butta spent 100 minutes on a certain job. The wages chargeable to that job at the regular hourly rate of $5.58 would be computed as follows:

$$\$5.58 \times \frac{100}{60} = \$9.30$$

Converting Weekly Wage Rates to Hourly Rates. When paying on a weekly basis, sometimes employers must convert the weekly wage rate to an hourly rate, especially to figure overtime earnings. To do this, divide the weekly wage rate by the number of hours in the regular workweek.

E X A M P L E

Joseph Gallo earns $212 a week for a workweek consisting of 40 hours. If Gallo worked 43 hours in a particular week, compute gross pay as follows:

$$\$212.00 \div 40 \text{ hours} = \$5.30 \text{ Hourly Wage Rate}$$

$$\$5.30 \text{ Hourly Wage Rate} \times 1.5 = \$7.95 \text{ Overtime Wage Rate}$$

$$\text{Gross Pay} = \$212 + (3 \text{ hours} \times \$7.95) = \$235.85$$

Figure 2–9 shows a table of weekly wage rates with corresponding hourly wage rates based on a 40-hour week and overtime wage rates at time and one-half for hours worked beyond 40. Practice varies as to the number of decimal

Weekly Wage Rate	Hourly Wage Rate (40-hr. week)	Overtime Wage Rate* (over 40 hrs.)
160	4.00	6.00
170	4.25	6.38
180	4.50	6.75
190	4.75	7.13
200	5.00	7.50
210	5.25	7.88
220	5.50	8.25
230	5.75	8.63
240	6.00	9.00
250	6.25	9.38
260	6.50	9.75
270	6.75	10.13
280	7.00	10.50
290	7.25	10.88
300	7.50	11.25

Figure 2–9
Table of Weekly Wage Rates Converted to Hourly Rates

*Rounded to two decimal places

places used in computing overtime wage rates. In Figure 2–10, the overtime wage rates have been rounded to two decimal places.

Converting Biweekly Wage Rates to Hourly Rates. If paying employees biweekly, divide the biweekly earnings by 2 to arrive at the weekly rate, and divide the weekly rate by the standard number of hours.

E X A M P L E

Patricia Mason earns $675 biweekly and works a standard 40-hour workweek. Compute Mason's hourly and overtime rates as follows:

$675.00 ÷ 2 = $337.50 Regular Weekly Earnings

$337.50 ÷ 40 = $8.44 Regular Hourly Rate

$8.44 × 1.5 = $12.66 Overtime Hourly Rate

Converting Monthly Salary Rates to Hourly Rates. If workers paid on a monthly basis earn overtime pay for work beyond a 40-hour week, compute the hourly overtime rate by converting the monthly salary rate to an hourly rate.

E X A M P L E

Greg Pruit earns $1,300 per month and works a standard 40-hour week. During one week Pruit earned 6 hours of overtime.

Step 1

Convert the monthly salary rate to a weekly rate by first annualizing the monthly salary. Divide the annual salary by 52 weeks.

$1,300 monthly salary × 12 months = $15,600 annual salary
$15,600 annual salary ÷ 52 weeks = $300 weekly salary

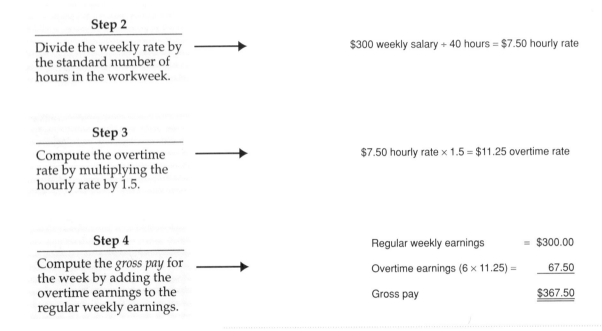

Step 2

Divide the weekly rate by the standard number of hours in the workweek. ⟶ $300 weekly salary ÷ 40 hours = $7.50 hourly rate

Step 3

Compute the overtime rate by multiplying the hourly rate by 1.5. ⟶ $7.50 hourly rate × 1.5 = $11.25 overtime rate

Step 4

Compute the *gross pay* for the week by adding the overtime earnings to the regular weekly earnings. ⟶

Regular weekly earnings	= $300.00
Overtime earnings (6 × 11.25) =	67.50
Gross pay	$367.50

Figure 2–10 shows a table of monthly salary rates with corresponding yearly rates, weekly rates, hourly rates based on a 40-hour week, and overtime rates at time and one-half for hours worked beyond 40.

Converting Semimonthly Salary Rates to Hourly Rates.   Semimonthly salary rates are converted the same as monthly rates except semimonthly earnings are multiplied by 24 instead of by 12 to compute the annual earnings.

Figure 2–10
Table of Monthly Salary Rates Converted to Yearly, Weekly, and Hourly Rates

Monthly Salary Rate	Yearly Salary Rate	Weekly Salary Rate	Hourly Salary Rate*	Overtime Salary Rate*
$ 725	8,700	167.31	4.18	6.27
750	9,000	173.08	4.33	6.50
775	9,300	178.85	4.47	6.71
800	9,600	184.62	4.62	6.93
825	9,900	190.38	4.76	7.14
850	10,200	196.15	4.90	7.35
875	10,500	201.92	5.05	7.58
900	10,800	207.69	5.19	7.79
925	11,100	213.46	5.34	8.01
950	11,400	219.23	5.48	8.22
975	11,700	225.00	5.63	8.45
1,000	12,000	230.77	5.77	8.66
1,025	12,300	236.54	5.91	8.87
1,050	12,600	242.31	6.06	9.09
1,075	12,900	248.08	6.20	9.30
1,100	13,200	253.85	6.35	9.53
1,125	13,500	259.62	6.49	9.74

*Based on 40-hour week, rounded to two decimal places

Margaret Johnson earns $1,175 semimonthly.

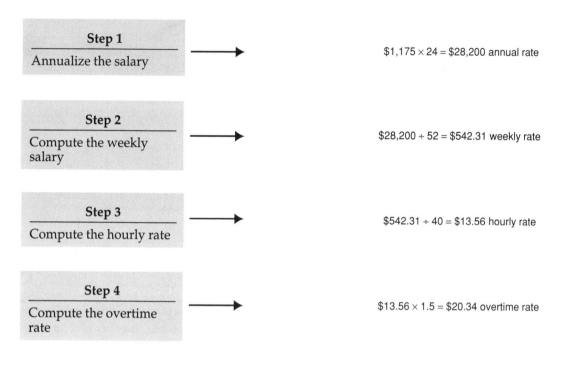

Step 1 Annualize the salary	→	$1,175 × 24 = $28,200 annual rate
Step 2 Compute the weekly salary	→	$28,200 ÷ 52 = $542.31 weekly rate
Step 3 Compute the hourly rate	→	$542.31 ÷ 40 = $13.56 hourly rate
Step 4 Compute the overtime rate	→	$13.56 × 1.5 = $20.34 overtime rate

Numerous tables of decimal equivalents, such as the one shown in Figure 2–11, and other time-saving devices obtained in stationery and office supply firms help in computing wages at the hourly rate.

Weekly salary $550:   *$550 × .025   = $13.75 hourly rate $550 × .0375 = $20.63 hourly overtime rate*
Monthly salary $1,800: $1,800 × .00577 = $10.39 hourly rate $1,800 × .00866 = $15.59 hourly overtime rate

Figure 2–11 *Table of Decimal Equivalents to Convert into Weekly, Hourly, and Hourly Overtime Salary Rates*

To convert into:	**Weekly Salary Rate**	**Hourly Salary Rate**	**Hourly Overtime Salary Rate**
Multiply the:			
Weekly salary rate by		.025	.0375
Semimonthly salary rate by	.4615	.01154	.0173
Monthly salary rate by	.2308	.00577	.00866
Yearly salary rate by	.01923	.00048	.000721

Fractional Cents. Practice in the treatment of fractions varies with different employers. In the case of union and other employment contracts, the method of computing regular and overtime hourly rates may be prescribed in the contracts. Using a table of decimal equivalents may yield weekly, hourly, and hourly overtime equivalents that differ by a cent or more from the amounts shown in Figures 2–9 and 2–10. Such differences occur due to the process of rounding at various stages in the calculations.

SELF-STUDY QUIZ 2–3. *Compute the hourly and overtime rates for a standard 40-hour workweek for the following amounts:*

		Hourly Rate	Overtime Rate
1.	$525.00 weekly	_____	_____
2.	$892.00 biweekly	_____	_____
3.	$1,450.00 semimonthly	_____	_____
4.	$1,600.00 monthly	_____	_____

Under FLSA, employers are required to pay pieceworkers for nonproductive time in addition to their productive time. If pieceworkers spend time on machinery maintenance or other tasks not related to production, that time must be included in computing overtime pay.

If, however, the employment contract provides that the piece-rate earnings cover nonproductive time, then extra pay at only half-time satisfies the FLSA requirement for overtime pay.

Piece Rate

Under the ***piece-rate system*** the employer pays workers according to their output, such as an amount for each unit or piece produced. Thus, the wages increase as production increases. The employer keeps production records for each employee so that these records will be available when computing the wages earned by each employee. The Fair Labor Standards Act specifies that under a piece-rate system, compute the regular hourly rate of pay as follows:

E X A M P L E

Peggy Zoe produced 12,500 items during a 40-hour workweek. Zoe is paid .015¢ per unit, and receives a bonus .005¢ for each unit over 12,000 in a week. Zoe's weekly earnings are:

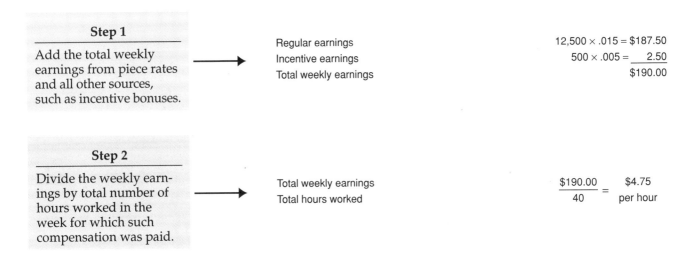

Step 1		
Add the total weekly earnings from piece rates and all other sources, such as incentive bonuses.	Regular earnings Incentive earnings Total weekly earnings	$12,500 \times .015 = \$187.50$ $500 \times .005 = \underline{\quad 2.50}$ $\$190.00$

Step 2		
Divide the weekly earnings by total number of hours worked in the week for which such compensation was paid.	Total weekly earnings Total hours worked	$\dfrac{\$190.00}{40} = \begin{array}{l}\$4.75\\ \text{per hour}\end{array}$

The piece rate must at least equal the statutory minimum wage rate. In some instances an employer may pay a worker an hourly rate for some hours and a piece rate for other hours during the week. In such cases, both the hourly rate and the piece-rate earnings must be at least the minimum rate.

Overtime Earnings for Pieceworkers—Method A. For overtime work, the pieceworker is entitled to be paid, in addition to piecework earnings for the entire period, a sum equal to one-half the regular hourly rate of pay multiplied by the number of hours worked in excess of 40 in the week.

E X A M P L E

Margo Adkins produced 3,073 pieces in a 44-hour workweek and is paid 14¾¢ for every unit produced.

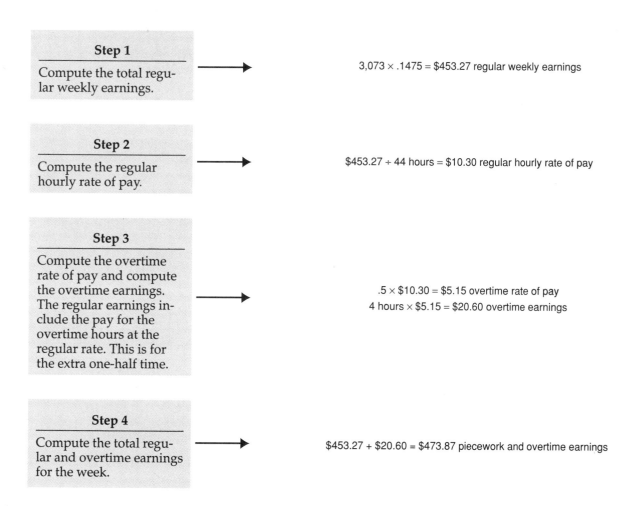

Step 1

Compute the total regular weekly earnings.

$3{,}073 \times .1475 = \$453.27$ regular weekly earnings

Step 2

Compute the regular hourly rate of pay.

$\$453.27 \div 44$ hours $= \$10.30$ regular hourly rate of pay

Step 3

Compute the overtime rate of pay and compute the overtime earnings. The regular earnings include the pay for the overtime hours at the regular rate. This is for the extra one-half time.

$.5 \times \$10.30 = \$5.15$ overtime rate of pay
4 hours $\times \$5.15 = \$20.60$ overtime earnings

Step 4

Compute the total regular and overtime earnings for the week.

$\$453.27 + \$20.60 = \$473.87$ piecework and overtime earnings

Overtime Earnings for Pieceworkers—Method B. Another method of computing overtime payment for pieceworkers complies with the requirements of the FLSA. Before doing the work, piece-rate employees may agree with their employer to be paid at a rate not less than one and one-half times the piece rate for each piece produced during the overtime hours. No additional overtime pay will be due the employees.

E X A M P L E

Assume that in the preceding example, Adkins earned overtime at a piece rate of one and one-half times the regular rate for all pieces produced during overtime hours. Of the total 3,073 pieces produced, 272 were produced in the 4 overtime hours. Adkins's total piecework and overtime earnings are as follows:

2,801 × .1475 = $413.15 Piecework Earnings
272 pieces × .2213 (.1475 × 1.5) = $60.19 Overtime Earnings
$413.15 + $60.19 = $473.34 Piecework and Overtime Earnings

SELF-STUDY QUIZ 2–4. *Bruce Eaton is paid 5¢ per unit under the piece-rate system. During one week Eaton worked 46 hours and produced 4,000 units. Compute the following:*

1. The piecework earnings $_____
2. The regular hourly rate $_____
3. The overtime hourly rate $_____
4. The overtime earnings $_____
5. The total earnings $_____

Special Incentive Plans

Most wage systems involving special incentives are modifications of the piece-rate system described previously.

E X A M P L E

Lo Tourneau pays its production workers according to the following incentive schedule:

Output	Rate
1st 100 units	$ 9.90 per C (hundred)
2nd 100 units	10.05 per C
3rd 100 units	10.25 per C
all units over 300	10.50 per C

On Monday, Adele Roche produced 410 pieces. Roche's daily earnings are calculated as follows:

1st 100	$ 9.90
2nd 100	10.05
3rd 100	10.25
110 units over 300	11.55
Total daily earnings	$41.75

Under many incentive plans, the company determines a standard for the quantity that an average worker can produce in a certain period of time. Workers failing to reach the standard earn a lower piece rate, while those who produce more than the standard receive a higher rate. With incentive plans, the computation of the payroll is usually more complicated than under the time-rate or piece-rate systems. Records of time worked as well as the production of each employee must be available in computing wages under most incentive plans.

Chu Wang, Inc., pays its blade polishers according to the following piece-rate incentive plan:

No. of Blades Polished Per 8-Hour Workday	Earnings Per Blade Polished
less than 1,850	.0150
1,850 to 1,999	.0165
2,000 (Daily Standard)	.0180
2,001 to 2,100	.0198
2,101 to 2,250	.0217
over 2,250	.0240

For one 5-day workweek, one of Wang's employees had the following production record. Gross earnings for the week are computed as follows:

	No. of Blades Polished Daily	Earnings Per Blade Polished	Daily Earnings
M	2,097	.0198	41.52
T	2,012	.0198	39.84
W	1,990	.0165	32.84
Th	2,253	.0240	54.07
F	1,992	.0165	32.87
Total weekly earnings			201.14

Commissions

The entire remuneration, or at least part of the remuneration, of certain employees may be on a commission basis. A *commission* is a stated percentage of revenue paid an employee who transacts a piece of business or performs a service. Thus, a salesperson working in a certain territory may have a fixed salary each year plus a bonus for sales in excess of a certain amount.

Maria Fontana receives an annual $22,500 base salary for working a certain territory. A sales quota of $800,000 has been set for that territory for the current year. Fontana will receive 6% commission on all sales in excess of $800,000. For the current year the sales in the territory are $830,000. The bonus paid Fontana would be:

$1,800 (6% of $30,000)

Fontana's total earnings for the year would be:

$24,300 ($22,500 + $1,800)

There are numerous variations of the commission method of remuneration. Some businesses offer special premiums or bonuses for selling certain merchandise. For example, to help move merchandise in a ready-to-wear department, a department store will frequently pay a premium or a bonus to the salesperson who sells specific items of merchandise. Commissions are considered to be payments for hours worked and must be included in determining the regular hourly rate. This applies regardless of whether the commission is the sole source of the employee's compensation or is paid in addition to a salary or hourly rate. It does not matter whether the commission earnings are computed daily, weekly, monthly, or at some other interval. However, in the case of outside salespeople who are exempt from the FLSA, commissions paid to them do not have to meet the minimum wage criteria. This also applies to all employees exempt because they are employed in establishments that meet the requirements for exemption.

Profit-Sharing Plans

Many businesses have developed *profit-sharing plans* whereby the employer shares with the employees a portion of the profits of the business. Generally, profit-sharing plans include three types:

1. Cash payments based upon the earnings of a specified period.
2. Profits placed in a special fund or account to be drawn upon by employees at some future time. This plan may be in the form of a savings account, a pension fund, or an annuity.
3. Profits distributed to employees in the form of capital stock.

The payments made pursuant to a bona fide profit-sharing plan that meets the standards fixed by the Secretary of Labor's regulations are not deemed wages in determining the employee's regular rate of pay for overtime purposes.

WHAT ARE THE METHODS OF PAYING WAGES AND SALARIES?

The three main methods used in paying wages and salaries include (1) cash, (2) check, and (3) electronic transfer. A small business may pay wages and salaries in cash, but most medium-size and large firms pay wages and salaries by check.

Paying Wages and Salaries in Cash

When a company pays wages and salaries in cash, a common procedure is used:

1. Compute the total wages earned, the deductions, and the net amount to be paid and record this information in the payroll register, as shown in Figure 1–9.
2. Prepare a supplementary payroll sheet showing the various denominations of bills and coins needed to pay the salary of each employee. The form in Figure 2–12 provides columns to list the names of the employees, the net amount to be paid, the denominations needed to pay each employee, the total amount needed to pay all employees, and the total number of each denomination needed to pay all employees.
3. Prepare a payroll slip by using the total amount of each denomination needed for the payroll. Figure 2–13 shows a payroll slip, similar to one that

HENDRIX, INC. SUPPLEMENTARY PAYROLL SHEET											June 30, 19
Name of Employee	**Net Amount to Be Paid**	**Bills**					**Coins**				
		$50	$20	$10	$5	$1	50¢	25¢	10¢	5¢	1¢
Brandon, Paul C.	$ 268.62	5		1	1	3	1		1		2
Connor, Rose T.	271.40	5	1			1		1	1	1	
Day, Joseph R.	297.28	5	2		1	2		1			3
Gee, Margaret F.	204.92	4				4	1	1	1	1	2
Hawke, Sidney O.	271.64	5	1			1	1		1		4
Kirk, Evelyn A.	288.24	5	1	1	1	3			2		4
Lerro, Doris B.	268.12	5		1	1	3			1		2
Pesiri, Armand G.	378.80	7	1		1	3	1	1		1	
Topkis, Christine W.	284.65	5	1	1		4	1		1	1	
Vogel, John C.	224.10	4	1			4			1		
Total	$2,757.77	50	8	4	5	28	5	4	9	4	17

Figure 2–12   *Supplementary Payroll Sheet*

many banks furnish, that lists the amount of each denomination needed for the payroll listed in Figure 2–12.

4. Write a check for the total amount of the payroll and present it to the bank with the payroll slip to obtain the proper denominations.
5. Place the amount due each employee in an envelope with a receipt showing the total earnings, the deductions, and the net amount paid. Distribute the prepared envelopes to the employees.

Paying Wages and Salaries by Check

When paying wages and salaries by check, the employer prepares and signs the checks in the usual way. The check preparer should ensure the accuracy of the names of the payees and the net amounts of the checks. Employers must give employees a periodic statement showing the deductions that have been made from their wages for tax purposes. The employer may distribute these statements each payday or give them out monthly, quarterly, or annually. Also, employees receive a statement at the time they leave the employ of the company. Most employers who pay wages and salaries by check indicate on each check issued or on the check stub or earnings statement the various deductions made. (See Figure 2–14.)

Many businesses maintain a payroll account at their bank in addition to their regular checking account. In such a case, all checks to pay wages and salaries are issued against the payroll account rather than against the regular checking account. When the company maintains a separate payroll account, its usual procedure is as follows:

1. Sets up a payroll account with a certain balance to be maintained at all times. A check against the regular checking account is issued and deposited in the payroll account. A small balance is desirable in the payroll account because it may be necessary to issue payroll checks before the regular payday. For example, if employees are leaving for vacation, they may receive their next payroll check before the regular payday.

Figure 2–13
Payroll Slip

Bank of Middleton		
PAYROLL WITHDRAWAL FROM THE ACCOUNT OF		
HENDRIX, INC.		

Date *June 30* 19——

Per *J. Stephens*

		DOLLARS	CENTS
BILLS:	100s		
	50s	*2* 500	00
	20s	160	00
	10s	40	00
	5s	25	00
	1s	28	00
HALF DOLLARS		2	50
QUARTERS		1	00
DIMES			90
NICKELS			20
PENNIES			17
TOTAL		*2* 757	77

2. Issues a check payable to Payroll, drawn on the regular checking account and deposited in the special payroll account at the bank.
3. Prepares individual checks, drawn against the special payroll account, and records the numbers of the payroll checks in the payroll register. Many companies having a large number of employees may use automatic means of signing the checks.

By maintaining a separate payroll account at the bank, the canceled payroll checks, accompanied by a statement of the payroll account balance, are returned separately from the canceled checks drawn upon the regular checking account, making it easier to reconcile both accounts. The payroll account bal-

EMPLOYEE'S NAME	ARTHUR T. COCO							PENLAND EQUIPMENT COMPANY, SAN MATEO, FL 32088-2279			
PAY PERIOD ENDING	HOURS	RATE	GROSS EARNINGS	OASDI TAX	HI TAX	FED. WITH. TAX	STATE WITH. TAX	UNION DUES		NET EARNINGS PAID
5/16/—	REG. T. 40 O.T. 12	5.50 8.25	319.00	19.78	4.63	20.00		3.00		271.59
EMPLOYEE: THIS IS A STATEMENT OF YOUR EARNINGS AND DEDUCTIONS FOR PERIOD INDICATED. KEEP THIS FOR YOUR PERMANENT RECORD.										

Figure 2–14   *Earnings Statement (Check Stub) Showing Payroll Deductions*

ance as shown on the bank statement should always be equal to the sum of the total of the outstanding payroll checks and any maintained balance, less any service charge.

Paying Wages and Salaries by Electronic Transfer

Under an *electronic funds transfer system (EFTS)*, employers do not have to issue a paycheck to each worker, although the worker is given a stub showing the amounts deducted. Instead, a computerized record is created for each employee that indicates:

1. The employee's bank
2. The account number at the bank
3. The net amount to be paid.

A day or two before payday the employer sends the information to the company's bank where the amounts due any employees who also keep their accounts at that bank are removed and deposited to the appropriate accounts. That bank sends the remaining names to an automated clearinghouse which sorts out the other bank names and prepares a computer tape for each bank to receive funds electronically. For banks unable to receive entries in electronic form, the clearinghouse creates a printed statement showing the customers' names and the amounts for which their accounts are to be credited. The actual crediting of accounts and the settlement occur on payday.

Under a "paperless" deposit and bill-paying system, employers may deposit wages in bank accounts designated by the employees if the deposits are voluntarily authorized by the employees. Thus, no paper paychecks ever pass hands. Millions of written checks may be eliminated each month, partly by electronically transferring some payroll dollars directly from the accounts of the employers to those of employees. After electronically transferring each employee's net pay directly into the worker's account, the employee may authorize the bank to automatically transfer funds from that account to the accounts of creditors such as the utility company and the department store.

Unclaimed Wages

Occasionally a worker may terminate employment or be terminated and not claim the final wage payment. The payroll manager is then faced with the question of what to do with the worker's unclaimed wages. Even though a uniform law exists on the subject of unclaimed or abandoned property, varying practices occur in those states that provide for the disposition of unclaimed property, such as unclaimed wages. The uniform law, followed by most states, provides that the holder of any unclaimed property must file a report after a specified statutory period and then surrender the property to the state. The length of the statutory period varies widely from state to state. In other states the holder of unclaimed property files a report with the state and the state then files suit for possession of the property. Because of the different practices among states, payroll managers must be well acquainted with the laws of their own states in the event they are faced with the difficult problem of disposing of unclaimed wages.

KEY TERMS

Biweekly

Commission

Continental system

Domestic service

Electronic funds transfer system (EFTS)

Enterprise coverage

Exempt employee

Gross earnings

Individual employee coverage

Job cost card

Piece-rate system

Principal activities

Profit-sharing plan

Salary

Semimonthly

Time card

Time sheet

Tip

Tipped employee

Wage

Wages

Workweek

QUESTIONS FOR REVIEW

1. Explain the two bases of coverage provided by the FLSA.
2. What kinds of establishments may employ full-time students at 85% of the minimum wage?
3. To what extent are tips considered wages under the FLSA?
4. Explain how a state employee working in the area of public safety may use compensatory time off in lieu of overtime compensation.
5. The following employees are exempt from various requirements of the FLSA. Indicate from which requirement or requirements each of the following employees is exempt:

   a. Amusement park employee
   b. Taxicab driver
   c. Casual baby-sitter
   d. Elementary school teacher
   e. Outside salesperson

6. In determining the working time of employees, how are the principal activities of employees defined?
7. Under what conditions is travel time counted as time worked?
8. A company grants its employees a 15-minute rest period twice each workday. Must the employees be paid for each rest period?
9. When is time spent by employees in attending lectures and meetings for training purposes not counted as working time?
10. Explain how to calculate the overtime hourly rate for employees who are paid biweekly.
11. Explain the two methods that may be used to calculate overtime wages for a pieceworker.
12. What is the uniform law on the subject of unclaimed or abandoned property?

QUESTIONS FOR DISCUSSION

1. At Struthers, Inc., factory employees work Monday through Friday at their regular hourly rates. On occasion they work on Saturdays, when they receive time and a half provided they worked 40 hours Monday through Friday.

   One week Sam Rico was absent Wednesday in order to attend a relative's funeral. Under the company's death-in-family policy, Rico's absence was paid for. Therefore, during the workweek Rico worked 32 hours and was paid for 40. That same week Struthers scheduled overtime for Saturday, and Rico worked 8 hours. He expected to be paid for 12 hours. However, the payroll manager informed him that he was entitled to only 8 hours' pay on Saturday because he had worked only 40 hours during the entire week. Do you agree that Rico is entitled to overtime pay for Saturday's hours? Explain.

2. Along with many other companies, Gomez Printers observes the Friday after Thanksgiving as a paid holiday. The company requires each employee to make up Friday's lost hours in the following workweek by working extra hours without pay. Is Gomez Printers proceeding legally by requiring its employees to work extra hours without compensation to make up for the hours lost on the Friday holiday? Explain.

3. The cashiers at a drugstore like to make a preliminary count of the $50 "cash bank" in their registers before they open the store for business. Is the time required to count the "cash bank' compensable under the overtime provisions of the FLSA?

4. The payroll department of DuMont has a policy of waiting one full week before correcting any paycheck errors of $30 or less. However, any pay shortages that exceed $30 are made up the same day. Also, any amounts less than $30 are made up the same day when the particular circumstances of the employees indicate that it would place an undue hardship on them to wait until the next pay one week later.

   Denise Harris, an order checker in DuMont's shipping department, discovered an error of $28.34 in her weekly check. When Harris reported the error, a payroll clerk informed her that she would have to wait until the next week's paycheck to recover the amount since the underpayment was less than $30.

   What is your reaction to DuMont's policy of providing for paycheck corrections? Assume that Harris protests the delay and in court argues that her earned wages should be paid on the date due. As the judge hearing the case, how would you decide?

5. It is 9:30 p.m. and while Hank Rodgers is watching the ball game on TV, the doorbell rings. When he opens the door, he finds Bobby, a neighbor, delivering the pizza he had ordered. The following conversation takes place:

   Hank: Hi, Bobby. You made it within the 30-minute time limit! I didn't know you were working at the pizza shop. Hey, are you old enough to be driving that jazzy delivery truck?
   Bobby: Yeah, no sweat! I'll be 16 in two months, just as soon as school is out.

   Is Bobby's employer violating any federal child-labor law? Explain.

6. In some companies employees are permitted to pick up the payroll check of another employee as a favor. What is your reaction to this practice?

PRACTICAL PROBLEMS

Special forms required to solve the Practical Problems are provided along with the problems in each chapter.

> NOTE: In this chapter and in all succeeding work throughout the course, *unless instructed otherwise*, calculate hourly rates and overtime rates as follows:
>
> 1. Carry the hourly rate and the overtime rate to 3 decimal places and then round off to 2 decimal places.
> 2. If the third decimal place is 5 or more, round to the next higher cent.
> 3. If the third decimal place is less than 5, simply drop the third decimal place.
>
> *Examples:* $4.765 should be rounded to $4.77.
> $4.764 should be rounded to $4.76.
>
> Also, use the minimum hourly wage of $4.25 in solving these problems and all that follow.

2–1. LO 4.

The hours worked and the hourly wage rates for five employees of the Cooley Company for the week ended September 10 follow.

a. For each employee, compute the gross earnings.
b. Compute the total gross earnings for all employees.

Employee	Hours Worked	Regular Hourly Wage Rate	(a) Gross Earnings
Dempski, R.	38	$8.40	$ _____
Floyd, B.	40	5.25	_____
Iskin, J.	37	6.30	_____
Macintyre, H.	40	6.95	_____
Serock, P.	32½	4.25	_____
		(b) Total gross earnings	$ _____

2–2. LO 4.

The wages and hours information for five employees of Serbu Enterprises for the week ended July 5 is given below. Employees work a standard 40-hour workweek and are paid time and one-half for all hours over 40 in each workweek.

a. For each employee, compute the regular earnings, overtime rate, overtime earnings, and total gross earnings.
b. Compute the total gross earnings for all employees.

(a)

Employee	Hours Worked	Regular Hourly Wage Rate	Regular Earnings	Overtime Rate	Overtime Earnings	Total Gross Earnings
Clay, T.	47	$6.45	$ _____	$ _____	$ _____	$ _____
DeMusis, G.	44	6.25	_____	_____	_____	_____
Kliny, A. . . .	42	5.90	_____	_____	_____	_____
Ostrow, B. .	48	4.85	_____	_____	_____	_____
Wax, W. . . .	45½	7.40	_____	_____	_____	_____

(b) Total gross earnings . . . . $ _____

2–3. LO 1.

Bruce Cabot is a waiter at the Towne House, where he receives a weekly wage of $80 plus tips for a 40-hour workweek. Cabot's weekly tips usually range from $180 to $200.

a. Under the Fair Labor Standards Act, the minimum amount of wages that Cabot must receive for a 40-hour workweek is . . . . $ _____
b. The maximum amount of tip credit that may be claimed that week by the Towne House is . . . . $ _____
c. In addition to the $80 weekly wage, the amount the Towne House must pay Cabot each week is . . . . $ _____

2–4. LO 1.

Tony Franco is a full-time student at Southern Junior College. After school hours he is employed by the college as a clerk at $3.50 per hour. One week he worked 18½ hours.

a. Franco's earnings for the week are . . . . $ _____
b. Is the hourly rate in violation of the FLSA? Explain.

c. If the hourly rate is in violation of the FLSA, the amount the college should pay Franco is . . . . $ _____

2–5. LO 1.

May Kim, a full-time student at Central University, is employed by Gifford's Dress Shop as a salesperson. Her hourly rate is $3.25. One week Kim worked 32¾ hours.

a. Kim's earnings for the week are .... $ _____

b. Is the hourly rate in violation of the FLSA? Explain.

c. If the hourly rate is in violation of the FLSA, the amount the dress shop should pay Kim is .... $ _____

2–6. LO 4.

Joe Vacca receives an hourly wage of $6.90 for a 40-hour week of 5 days, 8 hours daily. For Saturday work, he is paid one and one-half times the regular rate; for Sunday work, he is paid double the regular rate. During a certain week, he works the full 5-day week, plus 8 hours on Saturday and 4 hours on Sunday.

For this workweek, compute:

a. The regular earnings .... $ _____

b. The overtime earnings .... _____

c. The total earnings .... $ _____

2–7. LO 4.

Peter Romez receives $415 for a regular 40-hour week and time and one-half for overtime. For a workweek of 46 hours, compute:

a. The regular earnings .... $ _____

b. The overtime earnings .... _____

c. The total earnings .... $ _____

2–8. LO 4.

Chris Donato earns $1,475 each month and works 40 hours each week. Compute:

a. The hourly rate .... $ _____

b. The overtime rate at time and one-half .... $ _____

2–9. LO 4.

Kathleen Otto, a medical secretary, is paid $1,075 monthly for a 35-hour week. For overtime work she receives extra pay at the regular hourly rate up to 40 hours, and time and one-half beyond 40 hours in any week. During one semimonthly pay period, Otto worked 10 hours overtime. Only 2 hours of this overtime were beyond 40 hours in any one week. Compute:

a. The regular semimonthly earnings .... $ _____

b. The overtime earnings .... _____

c. The total earnings .... $ _____

2–10. LO 4.

Cynthia Porrini receives $4.90 per hour for a workweek of 5 days, 7½ hours daily. She is paid time and one-half for overtime, but the overtime rate is not effective until she works 40 hours during the week. Porrini is not paid for time off. During a certain week, she is absent 2 hours on Monday and works 8 hours on Saturday. Compute:

a. The regular earnings .... $ _____
b. The overtime earnings .... _____
c. The total earnings .... $ _____

2–11. LO 3, 4.

The time card below shows the time worked one week by Peter Van Horn. The employer disregards any time before 8:00 a.m. or 1:00 p.m. and after 5:00 p.m. Employees do not begin work until 8:00 a.m. or 1:00 p.m., and do not work beyond 5:00 p.m., unless they are asked to work overtime. Hours worked beyond the regular 8-hour day and on Saturday are paid at one and one-half times the regular rate. Hours worked on Sunday are paid double the regular rate.

No. 72						
Name Peter Van Horn						(a)
Day	Morning		Afternoon		Overtime		Hours Worked
	In	Out	In	Out	In	Out	
M	7:50	12:00	12:50	5:01			
T	7:56	12:01	12:49	5:02	5:30	7:31	
W	7:59	12:02	12:58	5:03			
T	7:45	12:00	12:55	5:00	5:29	8:02	
F	8:01	12:01	1:00	5:01	6:00	7:30	
S	7:48	12:02					
S			2:00	6:03			
(b)	Total Hours Worked						
Remarks_____							

Van Horn's regular wage rate is $4.78 per hour, and the regular workweek is 40 hours with five 8-hour days. Compute:

a. The hours worked each day. (Ignore the one-minute tardiness on Friday.)
b. The total hours worked.
c. The regular earnings .... $ _____
d. The overtime earnings .... _____
e. The total earnings .... $ _____

2–12. LO 3.

Under the decimal system of computing time worked at the Silverman Company, production workers who are tardy are "docked" according to the schedule shown below.

Minutes Late in Ringing In	Fractional Hour Deducted
1 through 6	1/10
7 through 12	2/10
13 through 18	3/10
19 through 24	4/10
etc.	

The regular hours of work, Monday through Friday, are from 7:30 to 11:30 a.m. and from 12:30 to 4:30 p.m. During one week Henry Vanderhoff, who earns $6.15 an hour, reports in and checks out as shown below. Employees are not paid for ringing in a few minutes before 7:30 and 12:30 nor for ringing out a few minutes after 11:30 and 4:30.

(a)

DAY	AM		PM		HRS WORKED
	In	Out	In	Out	
M	7:28	11:31	12:29	4:31	
T	7:35	11:30	12:30	4:30	
W	7:50	11:33	12:27	4:32	
Th	7:27	11:31	12:50	4:33	
F	7:28	11:32	12:40	4:30	

Refer to the partial time card above and compute:

a. The hours worked each day.
b. The total hours worked ....
c. The gross earnings for the week .... $ _____

2–13. LO 4.

The Toland Gear Company pays its employees according to the incentive schedule shown below.

Output	Rate per C (hundred)
1st 2,000 units	$1.95
next 100 units (2,001 to 2,100)	$2.00
all units over 2,100	$2.05

Using the following production data, compute:

a. The daily earnings for each employee.
b. The total daily earnings for all employees.

Employee	Units Produced		(a) Daily Earnings
Rocco D'Orazio	2,975		$
John Ervin	2,480		$
Kenneth Hicks	2,870		$
Joseph Mylotte	2,710		$
Thomas Wade	2,902		$
		(b) Total daily earnings	$

2–14. LO 4.

Zeller Parts, Inc., pays its employees according to the incentive schedule shown below.

Output	Rate per C (hundred)
1st 500 units	$6.15
next 100 units (501 to 600)	$6.25
all units over 600 ..	$6.45

Using the following production data, compute:

a. The daily earnings for each employee.
b. The total daily earnings for all employees.

Employee	Units Produced		(a) Daily Earnings
Pauline Bonovitz	560		$ _____
Jose DeLaRosa	570		$ _____
Harlan Girard	730		$ _____
Anna Mayne	800		$ _____
Betty Shore	835		$ _____
			$ _____
(b) Total daily earnings			$ _____

2–15. LO 4.

During the first week in November, Esther Coulter worked 45½ hours and produced 1,275 units under a piece-rate system. The regular piece rate is 18¢ a unit. Coulter is paid overtime according to the FLSA ruling for overtime work under a piece-rate system. Compute:

a. The piecework earnings .... $ _____
b. The regular hourly rate .... $ _____
    The overtime hourly rate .... $ _____

NOTE: In your computations, carry the regular hourly rate and the overtime rate each to 4 decimal places and then round off each rate to 3 decimal places.

c. The overtime earnings .... _____
d. The total earnings .... $ _____

2–16. LO 4.

Refer to Problem 2–15. Assume that Coulter had agreed with her employer prior to the performance of the work that she shall be paid one and one-half times the regular piece rate for all pieces produced during the overtime hours. Assume that her production totals for the week were: 1,075 pieces during regular hours and 200 pieces during overtime hours. Compute:

a. The piecework earnings . . . . $ _____
b. The overtime earnings . . . .   _____
c. The total earnings . . . . $ _____

2–17. LO 4.

The production record for Chu Wang, Inc., for the week ending April 16 is given on page 2–29. This record shows the weekly output for six of the firm's blade polishers. The company's piece-rate incentive plan is described on page 2–28.

For overtime work a premium is paid the employees. The premium rate for each piece produced during the overtime hours is one and one-half times the piece rate the employee earned that day for the total pieces produced. The production record shows that of the six blade polishers, only Correro worked overtime during the week. Of the total 2,757 blades polished by Correro on Wednesday, 584 were produced in two overtime hours.

On the production record, compute:

a. The earnings per blade polished for each employee.
b. The daily earnings for each employee.
c. The weekly earnings for each employee.

CHU WANG, INC.
Production Record for the Week Ending April 16, 19—

Employee	Day	No. of Blades Polished	(a) Earnings Per Blade Polished	(b) Daily Earnings
Luis Agosto	M	2,000	$ _____	$ _____
	T	2,170	_____	_____
	W	Absent	_____	_____
	T	2,116	_____	_____
	F	2,009	_____	_____
			(c) Total	$ _____
Ana Correro	M	2,240	$ _____	$ _____
	T	2,298	_____	_____
	W	2,173 (Regular)	_____	_____
		584 (Overtime)		
	T	2,284	_____	_____
	F	2,069	_____	_____
			(c) Total	$ _____
Pearl Gaines	M	1,900	$ _____	$ _____
	T	1,950	_____	_____
	W	2,005	_____	_____
	T	2,107	_____	_____
	F	2,003	_____	_____
			(c) Total	$ _____
Thomas Kelman	M	1,980	$ _____	$ _____
	T	2,050	_____	_____
	W	2,010	_____	_____
	T	2,000	_____	_____
	F	2,007	_____	_____
			(c) Total	$ _____
Eloise Miller	M	2,217	$ _____	$ _____
	T	2,130	_____	_____
	W	2,020	_____	_____
	T	960	_____	_____
	F	2,010	_____	_____
			(c) Total	$ _____
David Rotberg	M	2,200	$ _____	$ _____
	T	2,195	_____	_____
	W	1,998	_____	_____
	T	2,090	_____	_____
	F	2,000	_____	_____
			(c) Total	$ _____

2–18. LO 4.

Refer to Problem 2–17. On the form given below, compute:

a. The average earnings per blade polished by each of the six workers during the week.
b. The average earnings per blade polished for all six workers during the week.
c. How the average earnings per blade polished for all six workers during the week compare with the daily standard earnings of $.0180 per blade.

Employee	Weekly Earnings	+	No. Blades Polished	=	(a) Average Earnings Per Blade
Luis Agosto	$ _____		_____		$ _____
Ana Correro	_____		_____		_____
Pearl Gaines	_____		_____		_____
Thomas Kelman	_____		_____		_____
Eloise Miller	_____		_____		_____
David Rotberg	_____		_____		_____
Total	$ _____		_____		

(b) $ _____ ÷ _____ = $ _____
    (Total weekly earnings)   (Total blades polished)   (Average earnings per blade
                                                               polished by all six workers)

(c) Average earnings per blade polished by all six workers: .... $ _____
    Daily standard earnings per blade polished: .... .0180
    The actual average for the week is (less than or greater than) the daily
    standard earnings by .... $ _____

2–19. LO 4.

Joan Sullivan, a sales representative, earns an annual salary of $17,750 and receives a commission on that portion of her annual sales that exceeds $60,000. The commission is 8.5% on all sales up to $45,000 above the quota. Beyond that amount, she receives a commission of 10%. Her total sales for the past year were $128,000. Compute:

a. The regular annual salary .... $ _____
b. The commission ....
c. The total annual earnings .... $ _____

2–20. LO 4.

Joyce Sand is employed as a salesperson in the men's department of Lukens Fashions. In addition to her weekly base salary of $240, Sand is paid a commission of 1% on her total net sales for the week (total gross sales less any customer returns). During the past week, to promote the sale of its fine cashmere sweaters, Lukens agreed to pay Sand an additional PM (push money) of 2% of the total net sales of cashmere sweaters. Sand's weekly sales tally is given below.

Item	Gross Sales	Customer Returns
Regular sweaters	$400	$48
Cashmere sweaters	995	75
Ties	190	-0-
Dress shirts	445	39
Sports shirts	185	25

Compute Sand's total weekly earnings, showing her (a) Weekly base salary, (b) commission, (c) PM, and (d) total weekly earnings.

a. Weekly base salary .... $ 240.00
    Weekly gross sales .... $ _____
      Less customer returns .... _____
    Weekly net sales .... $ _____
b. Commission: $ _____ × 1% .... _____
    Weekly gross sales of cashmere sweaters .... $ _____
      Less customer returns .... _____
    Weekly net sales of cashmere sweaters .... $ _____
c. PM: $ _____ × 2% .... _____
d. Total weekly earnings .... $ _____

2–21. LO 3, 4.

Potts, Inc., recently converted from a 5-day, 40-hour workweek to a 4-day, 40-hour workweek, with overtime continuing to be paid at one and one-half times the regular hourly rate for all hours worked beyond 40 in the week. In this company, time is recorded under the continental system, as shown on the time card at the right.

Sue Ellen Boggs is part of the Group B employees whose regular workweek is Tuesday through Friday. The working hours each day are 800 to 1200; 1230 to 1630; and 1800 to 2000. The company disregards any time before 800, 1230, and 1800, and permits employees to ring in up to 10 minutes late before any deduction is made for tardiness. Deductions are made to the nearest 1/4 of an hour for workers who are more than 10 minutes late in ringing in.

Refer to the time card and compute:

No. 160					Hr. Rate $4.45		
Name Sue Ellen Boggs					O.T. Rate $6.675		
Time	Mon	Tues	Wed	Thurs	Fri	Sat	
Evening — Out		2002	2001	2005	2000		
Evening — In		1801	1809	1802	1800		
Afternoon — Out		1630	1631	1630	1635		
Afternoon — In		1230	1231	1230	1238		
Morning — Out		1200	1202	1200	1203	1201	
Morning — In		755	750	813	759	800	Total for Week
Daily Totals	(a)						(b)

Remarks *13 minutes late Thursday – deduct ¼ hr.*

a. The daily total hours.
b. The total hours for the week.
c. The regular weekly earnings .... $ _____
d. The overtime earnings ....
e. The total weekly earnings .... $ _____

The job cost card used by Gamma Manufacturing Company to record the time spent in assembling its micro relays follows.

```
┌─────────────────────────────────────────────┐
│              JOB COST CARD                    │
│   Part No. B-640      Job No. 12              │
│   Description MICRO RELAY 640                 │
│   Card No. 1    Estimated Time 6 Hrs.        │
├────┬──────────┬──────┬──────────────────────┤
│ No.│ Employee │ Time │ Time Clock Record     │
├────┼──────────┼──────┼──────────────────────┤
│    │          │ OFF  │                       │
│    │          │ ON   │                       │
│    │          │ OFF  │                       │
│    │          │ ON   │                       │
│    │          │ OFF  │                       │
│    │          │ ON   │                       │
│    │          │ OFF  │                       │
│    │          │ ON   │                       │
│    │          │ OFF  │                       │
│    │          │ ON   │                       │
│ 64 │ Bill     │ OFF  │ 4 JUN 15¹²            │
│    │ Fleming  │ ON   │ 4 JUN 15⁰⁰            │
│ 31 │ Laura    │ OFF  │ 4 JUN 14⁷⁴            │
│    │ Packard  │ ON   │ 4 JUN 13⁰⁰            │
│ 44 │ HARRY    │ OFF  │ 4 JUN 11⁸²            │
│    │ O'NEILL  │ ON   │ 4 JUN 10⁰⁰            │
│ 27 │ Ella     │ OFF  │ 4 JUN 09⁷⁵            │
│    │ Poole    │ ON   │ 4 JUN 08⁵⁰            │
│ 47 │ Martha   │ OFF  │ 4 JUN 08⁴⁸            │
│    │ Ayers    │ ON   │ 4 JUN 08²⁵            │
│ 19 │ Peter    │ OFF  │ 4 JUN 08²⁰            │
│    │ Wilson   │ ON   │ 4 JUN 07³⁰            │
├────┴──────────┴──────┴──────────────────────┤
│              TOTAL TIME_____               │
└─────────────────────────────────────────────┘
```

On the form given below:

a. Compute the time spent on the job by each employee and the total time spent by all employees. *Note that the time is recorded in hundredths of an hour.*

b. Use the hourly wage rates given to compute the total labor cost for producing the one relay. In your computations, carry out the labor cost for each employee and the total labor cost to 4 decimal places.

No.	Employee	(a) Time	Hourly Wage Rate	(b) Labor Cost
64	Bill Fleming	_____	$5.75	$_____
31	Laura Packard	_____	6.10	_____
44	Harry O'Neill	_____	6.30	_____
27	Ella Poole	_____	5.25	_____
47	Martha Ayers	_____	6.75	_____
19	Peter Wilson	_____	6.50	_____
	Totals	_____		$_____

c. The company's time study engineer has determined that the standard labor cost for producing one micro relay is $36.5025. Compute by what percentage (plus or minus) the actual labor cost on June 4 varied from the predetermined standard. .... _____

2–23. LO 5.

Hendrix, Inc., pays its employees' weekly wages in cash. A supplementary payroll sheet that lists the employees' names and their earnings for a certain week is shown below. Complete the payroll sheet by calculating the total amount of payroll and indicating the least possible number of denominations that can be used in paying each employee. However, no employees are to be given bills in denominations greater than $20.

HENDRIX, INC.

Supplementary Payroll Sheet

For Period Ending August 15, 19—

Name of Employee	Net Amount Paid	Bills				Coins				
		$20	$10	$5	$1	50¢	25¢	10¢	5¢	1¢
Chad T. Biskis	$251.75									
Nicole A. Cibik	256.52									
Domingo M. Diaz	184.94									
Laura B. Elias	202.59									
Ari M. Fleischer	253.64									
Diane Y. Germano	296.50									
Arnold B. Herst	194.26									
Edward C. Kenner	199.89									
Kathleen J. Marfia	234.01									
Kimberly A. Picket	195.80									
Total										

2–24. LO 5.

Refer to Problem 2–23. After you have completed the supplementary payroll sheet, prepare the payroll slip and check below. Sign your name on the "Per" line of the payroll slip. The check should be made payable to *Payroll* and signed with your signature below the company name.

a

Bank of Middleton

PAYROLL WITHDRAWAL FROM THE ACCOUNT OF

HENDRIX, INC.

Date _____ 19____

Per _____

		DOLLARS	CENTS
BILLS:	100s		
	50s		
	20s		
	10s		
	5s		
	1s		
HALF DOLLARS			
QUARTERS			
DIMES			
NICKELS			
PENNIES			
	TOTAL		

⑈0⑆204563⑆ 121 ⑆63229⑈

b

No. 1915

56—456
422

19 ____

HENDRIX, INC.
PAYROLL ACCOUNT

PAY TO
THE ORDER OF _____

$ _____

_____ DOLLARS

HENDRIX, INC.

Bank of Middleton

⑈0204563⑆ 121 ⑆63229⑈

CONTINUING PAYROLL PROBLEM

In the Continuing Payroll Problem, presented at the end of succeeding chapters, you will gain experience in computing wages and salaries and preparing a payroll register for the Steimer Company, Inc., a newly formed corporation. At the end of subsequent chapters, information will be presented so that the payroll register can be completed step by step as you proceed through the discussion material relating to that particular section of the payroll register.

The Steimer Company is a small manufacturing firm located in Philadelphia, PA. The company has a work force of both hourly and salaried employees. Each employee is paid for hours actually worked during each week, with the time worked being recorded in quarter-hour increments. The standard workweek consists of 40 hours, with all employees being paid time and one-half for any hours worked beyond the 40 regular hours.

Wages are paid every Friday, with one week's pay being held back by the company. Thus, the first payday for the Steimer Company is January 14 for the workweek ending January 7.

The information below will be used in preparing the payroll for the pay period ending January 7.

Time Card No.	Employee Name	Hourly Wage or Salary
11	Mary L. Lopenski	$4.50 per hour
12	Anthony P. Wren	$4.25 per hour
13	Leroy A. Young	$5.10 per hour
21	Lester D. Hayes	$4.90 per hour
22	Meredith O. McGarry	$5.75 per hour
31	Nancy B. Costello	$215 per week
32	Gloria D. Hopstein	$1,700 per month
33	Vernon U. Porth	$1,350 per month
51	Marsha T. Stone	$1,510 per month
99	Harold Y. Steimer	$52,000 per year

Ms. Nancy B. Costello prepares the time clerk's report for each pay period. Her report for the first week of operations is given below.

TIME CLERK'S REPORT NO. 1

For Period Ending January 7, 19--

Time Card No.	Employee	Time Record						Time Worked	Time Lost
		M	T	W	T	F	S		
11	Mary L. Lopenski	8	8	8	8	8	—	40	
12	Anthony P. Wren	8	8	8	8	8	8	48	
13	Leroy A. Young	8	5½	8	8	8	—	37½	2½ hrs. tardy
21	Lester D. Hayes	10	10	8	8	10	—	46	
22	Meredith O. McGarry	8	8	8	8	8	—	40	
31	Nancy B. Costello	9	8	8	8	8	1¼	41¼	
32	Gloria D. Hopstein	8	8	8	8	8	—	40	
33	Vernon U. Porth	8	8	8	8	8	—	40	
51	Marsha T. Stone	8	8	8	8	8	4	44	
99	Harold Y. Steimer	8	8	8	8	8	—	40	

Using the payroll register for the Steimer Company, which is reproduced on a fold-out at the back of the book, proceed as follows:

1. Enter each employee's time card number and name in the appropriate columns.
2. Record the regular hours and the overtime hours worked for each employee, using the time clerk's report as your reference.
3. Complete the Regular Earnings columns (Rate Per Hour and Amount) and the Overtime Earnings columns (Rate Per Hour and Amount) for each employee.
4. Record the Total Earnings for each employee by adding the Regular Earnings and the Overtime Earnings.

Note: Retain your partially completed payroll register for use at the end of Chapter 3.

CASE PROBLEMS

C1. **Reducing the Cost of Compensated Leave Time. LO 1.**

For the past several weeks, Adele Delgado, payroll manager for the Petrillo Packing Company, has been studying the mounting costs of accrued vacations and sick leave. Most of her firm's employees are entitled to two weeks' vacation each year and the privilege of accruing their vacation time for future use. Also, the workers have a generous sick-leave plan that reimburses them while they are ill at home or in the hospital.

Scanning the employees' accrued vacation times on the computer printout, Delgado notes the line entry for John Mannick. Mannick recently retired and cashed in 14 weeks of accrued vacation–all paid at his current wage, which was much more than when he originally earned the vacations. And, of course, the firm's payroll taxes for the accrued vacation payout were significantly increased.

Delgado also knows that some workers feel shortchanged if they do not use their sick leave each year. They realize that if the leave is not used, they lose it for that year. Probably, she thinks, this accounts for those who regularly become ill on Mondays or Fridays.

What solutions can you offer to limit the cost of and more effectively manage the firm's policies for compensated leave time?

C2. **Selecting A Computerized Time and Attendance Recording System. LO 3.**

Assume you are the payroll clerk for Yours Truly, Inc., which employs 23 full-time workers. At the present time all of the company's employees record their time and attendance on one electromechanical time clock, which is adequate for the number of workers in your firm. As part of a feasibility study, you have been given the responsibility to investigate which kind of automated equipment will enable your company to process its payroll more efficiently and economically.

During your study you accumulate the following information:

1. Cost of the electromechanical time clock now in use, $1,000.
2. Cost of one calculating time clock that prints in and out times and automatically figures daily and weekly totals, $1,500.
3. Cost of one calculating time clock that will interface with your company's computer, $2,500. This system feeds all payroll data directly to the computer, thus eliminating the step of data entry from hard-copy time cards.
4. Cost of a badge-based system, for firms employing 50 or more employees, $5,000; for businesses with 1,000 employees or more, $50,000.
   This system, depending on the use of an employee's coded identification badge, eliminates time cards. The data are collected at a terminal, where the time is automatically recorded and sent to a central computer.
5. Estimated time required for you to process manually one time card, 7 minutes.
6. Your present hourly wage, $8.50.
7. Cost of an outside part-time bookkeeper to do the payroll work, $10 an hour.

Based upon the information you have obtained, prepare a report in which you recommend the type of equipment that should be installed to automate the payroll accounting operations, along with the estimated savings your company will realize during the first year.

THAT WAS THEN THIS IS NOW

The first social security checks went out on January 30, 1940 and totaled $75,844. The first check went to a Vermont widow, who received $22.54. In 1994, monthly beneficiaries of social security benefits totaled 42,518,000 with total monthly benefits paid of $25,869,000,000.

SOCIAL SECURITY TAXES

LEARNING OBJECTIVES

After studying this chapter, you should be able to:

1. Identify, for social security purposes, those persons covered under the law and those services that make up employment.

2. Identify the types of compensation that are defined as wages.

3. Apply the current tax rates and wage base for FICA and SECA purposes.

4. Explain the importance of obtaining and correctly using the Employer's Identification Number and the Employee's Social Security Number.

5. Complete Form 941, Employer's Quarterly Federal Tax Return, and Form 8109, Federal Tax Deposit Coupon.

6. Describe the different requirements and procedures for depositing FICA taxes and income taxes withheld from employees' wages.

7. Recognize that, as collection agents for the government, employers may be subject to civil and criminal penalties if they fail to carry out their duties.

This chapter presents the old-age, survivors, disability and health insurance program (OASDHI), which provides monthly benefits to workers who qualify under the provisions of the Social Security Act. To cover the cost of this program, the act imposes taxes on employers and their employees. The statutes that provide the taxes include:

1. **Federal Insurance Contributions Act (FICA),** which imposes two taxes on employers and two taxes on employees. One of the taxes finances the federal old-age, survivors, and disability insurance program (OASDI).The other finances the hospital insurance (HI), or Medicare, program.
2. **Self-Employment Contributions Act (SECA),** which levies a tax upon the net earnings of the self-employed.

L E A R N I N G
O B J E C T I V E

WHO IS COVERED UNDER FICA?

The retirement and disability parts of the social security program cover most workers in the United States. By identifying a "covered" employee and "covered" employment, it can then be determined who pays the tax and who receives benefits. Before an individual is considered to be "covered" for social security purposes, the following must be determined:

1. If the individual is an "employee", defined by the common law relationship of employer and employee.
2. If the service the individual renders is "employment" as defined by FICA tax law.
3. If the compensation the individual receives is "taxable wages" as defined by FICA tax law.

Who Is an Employee?

An individual is an *employee* if they perform services in a covered employment. As long as the common-law relationship of employer and employee exists and the employment is not exempt from the provisions of the law, both are covered and must observe its provisions.

A *common-law relationship* of employer and employee exists when the employer has the right to control both what work will be done and how it will be done. To determine if a worker may be classified as an employee and if the employer has the right to control, the Internal Revenue Service uses the 20-factor common-law test shown in Figure 3–1. If workers do not meet these tests, generally they are classified as independent contractors, as discussed later.

Employees of a Corporation. Managers, superintendents, supervisors, department heads, and other executives of a corporation are considered employees under the FICA tax law. All officers, such as the president, vice-presidents, secretary, and the treasurer, are also employees of the corporation. Their salaries are taxable the same as the wages paid to other employees. If, however, the corporation officers perform no services as such and receive no compensation in any form, they are not considered employees of the corporation. Also, a director of a corporation who performs no services other than attending and participating in meetings of the board of directors is not an employee.

Partnerships. Partners generally are not employees of the partnership. In some cases, however, a partnership may operate as an association that may be classified as a corporation. In such situations, any partner who renders services similar to those of corporate officers would be an employee.

The Common-Law Test

1. **Instructions.** Must comply with the employer's instructions about when, where, and how to work.
2. **Training.** Receive training from or at the direction of the employer. This may include working along with an experienced employee or attending meetings.
3. **Integration.** Provide services that are integrated into the business. That is, the success or continuation of the employer's business depends significantly on the performance of certain services provided by the worker.
4. **Services rendered personally.** Perform the work personally.
5. **Hiring Assistants.** Hire, supervise, and pay assistants for the employer.
6. **Continuing relationship.** Have a continuing relationship with the employer. May exist where the work is performed at frequently recurring, although irregular, intervals.
7. **Set hours of work.** Must follow set hours of work.
8. **Full-time required.** Work full-time for the employer.
9. **Work done on premises.** Do their work on the employer's premises.
10. **Order or sequence set.** Must do their work in a sequence set by the employer.
11. **Reports.** Must submit regular oral or written reports to the employer.
12. **Payments.** Receive payments of regular amounts at set intervals.
13. **Expenses.** Receive payments for business and/or traveling expenses.
14. **Tools and materials.** Rely on the employer to furnish tools and materials.
15. **Investment.** Lack a significant investment in facilities used to perform the service.
16. **Profit or loss.** Cannot make a profit or suffer a loss from their services.
17. **Works for one person or firm.** Work for one employer at a time.
18. **Offers services to general public.** An employee does not offer their services to the general public.
19. **Right to fire.** An employee can be fired by the employer.
20. **Right to quit.** May quit their job at any time without liability.

Figure 3–1
The Common-Law Test

Occupations Specifically Covered by FICA. In addition to the Common Law test, FICA law also provides specific coverage for the four occupations listed below. However, such persons are not covered by FICA if they have a substantial interest in the facilities used in connection with their jobs, or if the services consist of a single transaction.

1. Agent-drivers and commission-drivers who distribute food and beverage products, or handle laundry or dry cleaning.
2. Full-time life insurance salespersons.
3. Full-time traveling or city salespersons.
4. An individual who works at home on materials or goods that you supply and that must be returned to you or to a person you name, if you also furnish specifications for the work to be done.

Employees of the Federal Government. FICA covers all federal government employees hired on or after April 1, 1986. In 1983, all federal employees became subject to the hospital insurance (HI) portion of the FICA tax, with the following exceptions:

- Medical interns.
- Student nurses.
- Inmates of U.S. penal institutions.

C O N N E C T I O N

If you want the IRS to determine whether a worker is an employee, file **Form SS-8, Determination of Employee Work Status** *for Purposes of Federal Employment Taxes and Income Tax Withholding.*

- Those serving temporarily in case of fire, storm, earthquake, flood, and similar emergency.

Certain federal employees became subject to both OASDI and HI taxes on or after January 1, 1984. As of that date, these groups included:

- All newly hired employees.
- Legislative Branch employees and those not covered by the civil service retirement system.
- Members of Congress, the President, and the Vice President.
- Sitting federal judges and political appointees at the executive level and senior executive service.

Employees of State and Local Governments. State and local government employees hired after March 31, 1986, became subject only to the HI portion of the FICA tax. Beginning July 1, 1991, full OASDHI coverage was extended to all state and local government employees who were not currently covered by a public employee retirement program.

Government Payments and Employer Payments. OASDHI covers members of the uniformed services on active duty, with their contributions and benefits computed on their basic pay. However, amounts paid in excess of their basic pay (such as for sea or foreign duty, hazardous duty, etc.) are not subject to FICA.

Some employers pay their workers the difference between the workers' salaries and the amounts they receive from the federal or state government while on duty with the armed forces or the state National Guard. If the worker is temporarily serving with the state National Guard, the payments are treated as wages and are subject to FICA. If the employment relationship is terminated, as when the employee enlists or is drafted into the U.S. Armed Forces or is called to active duty in the state National Guard, the payments are *not* considered wages for employment.

Who Is an Independent Contractor?

The FICA tax law identifies *independent contractors* as persons who follow an independent trade, business, or profession where they offer their services to the public. The Small Business Administration estimates that nearly 5 million workers are independent contractors, hired each year by 31% of all employers.[1] The test in Figure 3–2 determines independent contractor status.

Figure 3–2
Test for Independent Contractor Status

Test for Independent Contractor Status

Workers *may* be classified as independent contractors if they:

1. Hire, supervise, and pay assistants.
2. Determine the sequence of their work.
3. Set their own hours of work.
4. Work for as many employers as they wish.
5. Are paid by the job.
6. Make their services available to the public.
7. Have an opportunity for profit or loss.
8. Furnish their own tools.
9. Have a substantial investment in their trade.
10. May be dismissed only under terms of contract.

[1]Virginia N. Gibson, "Unraveling the Mystery of Independent Contractors," *HR Focus*, May 1992, p. 23

Employers do not pay payroll taxes on payments made to independent contractors. If the IRS determines that an employer has misclassified a worker as an independent contractor, the employer faces substantial fines and penalties. Typical examples of independent contractors include:

- Lawyers.
- Public accountants.
- Consultants.
- Advertising agencies.
- Building contractors.
- Real estate agents.

Who Is a Household Employee?

If a worker performs household services in or around your home subject to your will and control, as to both what must be done and how it will be done, that worker is your household employee. It does not matter whether you exercise this control as long as you have the legal right to control the method and result of the work. Some examples of workers who *may* be household employees include:

- Baby-sitters
- Caretakers
- Cooks
- Drivers
- Gardeners
- Governesses
- Housekeepers
- Maids

Household employees do not include people (a) who work for you in your business, (b) who follow an independent trade, business, or profession in which they offer services to the general public.

Exempt Employees. Employees of not-for-profit organizations became subject to FICA taxes on January 1, 1984. Some services, such as those performed by duly ordained ministers of churches, remain exempt from FICA taxes. Ministers, certain members of religious orders, and Christian Science practitioners previously electing exemption from social security coverage may now be covered by filing a waiver form with the IRS. Once an election to be covered by social security is made, it is irrevocable.

Voluntary Coverage. Coverage under FICA can be extended to certain classes of services that otherwise would be excluded. For example, service in the employ of a state or local government that began prior to April 1, 1986 is still exempt for the OASDI portion of the FICA tax. However, coverage can be extended to these employees by means of a voluntary agreement entered into by the state and Secretary of Health and Human Services. When a state elects voluntary coverage, it becomes responsible for the collection and payment of the FICA tax as if it were covered employment.

Who Is an Employer?

Every *person* is an *employer* if the person employs one or more individuals for the performances of services in the United States, unless such services or employment are specifically excepted by the law. The term "person" as defined in the law means an individual, a trust or estate, a partnership, or a corporation.

An employer who classifies an employee as an independent contractor and had no reasonable basis for doing so can be held liable for employment taxes not withheld from that worker, and may be held personally liable for a penalty equal to the taxes that should have been paid.

The IRS decided that a temporary employment agency hiring out legal secretaries was the employer of those workers for FICA, FUTA, and federal income tax withholding purposes. The workers were not, as the agency claimed, independent contractors.

HR 4278—October 22, 1994 Under this new law: (1) The social security tax threshold for Household Employees is increased to $1,000 in annual earnings, (2) Employers are still required to file W-2 forms for workers earning less than $1,000, (3) Domestic workers under the age of 18 are exempt unless their principle occupation is household employment, (4) Household employers are required to report social security obligations annually on their 1040 tax returns after 1994, (5) Farm employers are required to comply with the domestic tax threshold and filing procedures for household workers, and (6) The threshold will be indexed in future years, not exceeding $100 increments per year.

The term *employment* means any service performed by employees for their employer, regardless of the citizenship or residence of either. FICA covers most types of employment, but there are specific exclusions. Some types of employment are wholly exempt from coverage. Others are exempt only if the cash wages received are less than a stipulated dollar amount as shown in Figure 3–3.

Partially Exempt Employment. If an employee's services performed during one-half or more of any period constitute covered employment, then all the employee's services for that pay period must be counted as covered employment. On the other hand, if the employee's services during more than one-half of a pay period do not constitute covered employment, then none of the services for that pay period are counted as covered employment. A pay period cannot exceed 31 consecutive days.

Figure 3–3
Exempt Employment

Employment Type	Conditions of Exclusion
Agricultural services	Compensation of all farms workers is less than $2,500 in any calendar year, or compensation is less than $150 for each worker in a calendar year. Remuneration other than cash is not taxed.
Domestic service	Performed in a local college club, chapter of a college fraternity or sorority, or service performed in the employ of a school, college, or university by a student who is *enrolled* and *regularly attending classes* at the school, college, or university.
Service performed by children under the age of 18, in parental business	This exclusion applies to children employed by a father or mother whose business is a sole proprietorship or a partnership. This exclusion does *not* apply to children under age 18 employed by a family-owned corporation.
Services performed by civilians for the U.S. government	Of any of its agencies if such agencies are specifically exempt from the employer portion of the FICA tax, or if such services are covered by a retirement system established by law.
Service performed by railroad workers	For employers covered by the Railroad Retirement Tax Act.
Services performed in the employment of foreign governments	Ambassadors, ministers, and other diplomatic officers and employees.
Services performed by an individual under the age of 18, as newspaper distributor	Delivery or distribution of newspapers or shopping news, excluding delivery or distribution to a point for subsequent delivery or distribution.
Services performed by student nurses	In the employ of a hospital or a nurses' training school chartered or approved under state law, and the nurses are *enrolled* and *regularly attending classes* in that school. FICA only exempts the pay received by student nurses if the pay is nominal and their work is part-time and an integral part of the curriculum.

SELF-STUDY QUIZ 3–1. FICA covers which of the following (indicate Yes or No):

_____ 1. Andrian Mitchell, a full-time life insurance salesperson.

_____ 2. Martha Hoyas, a computer programmer, who designs software for various clients bid by her company.

_____ 3. Martin Hernandez, the president and chief executive officer of a corporation.

_____ 4. Sarah Bennett, an office assistant employed by her parents, who operate a family-owned corporation.

_____ 5. Stuart Schuck, who offers his lawn care service to homeowners in the neighborhood.

What Are Taxable Wages?

LEARNING OBJECTIVE 2

The amount of wages paid by employers to their employees during the calendar year determines the amount of OASDHI taxes. The basis of payment may be hourly, daily, weekly, biweekly, semimonthly, monthly, annually, piece rate, or percentage of profits. Wages include the following:

1. Actual money received by employees, whether called wages or salaries.
2. Cash value of meals and lodging provided for the convenience of the employees.
3. Bonuses and commissions paid by the employer with respect to employment.

Tips. FICA considers cash tips of $20 or more in a calendar month as taxable wages. Employees must report their tips in writing to their employers by the 10th of the month following the month in which the tips were received. Rules for reporting tips by employees and employers are summarized below:

1. Employees report tips on *Form 4070, Employee's Report of Tips to Employer*, shown in Figure 3–5. This form also provides a place to record an employee's daily record of tips (not illustrated) for retention in their personal files.
2. Employees who fail to report tips received of $20 or more in any month must complete *Form 4137, Social Security and Medicare Tax on Unreported Tip Income* (not shown). On this form, the employees compute the amount of FICA tax due on their unreported tip income. Later the employees report the amount of FICA tax due on their personal income tax return.
3. Employees failing to report tips to their employers may be penalized 50% of the FICA tax due on the tips. Employees should attach a statement to their income tax returns explaining why they did not initially report the tips to their employers. The Tax Court may rule that the non-reporting of tip income constitutes fraud.
4. Employers must collect the employee's FICA tax on the tips that each employee reports. The employer deducts the employee's FICA tax from the wages due the employee or from other funds the employee makes available. The employer collects the employee's OASDI tax throughout the year until the employee's combined wages and tips total the taxable wage base for that year. The employer collects HI tax on all wages and tips for the year.
5. Employers are also liable for their share of the FICA tax on any tips subject to the employee's FICA tax. However, businesses that provide food or beverages for consumption on their premises receive a business tax credit equal to the amount of the employer's portion of the FICA tax paid on tips.

Figure 3–4
Other Types of Taxable Wages

Type of Wage	Conditions
Advance payments	For future work to be done by the individual receiving the advance where the employer considers the work satisfaction for the advance.
Cash and non-cash prizes and awards	For outstanding work, exceeding sales quotas, contributing suggestions that increase productivity or efficiency.
Back pay awards	Pay received in one period for employment in an earlier period, unless it is a settlement for failure to employ workers.
Bonuses	For services rendered by employees for an employer.
Christmas gifts	Except gifts of nominal value (such as a turkey or a ham).
Commissions	On sales or insurance premiums paid as compensation for services performed.
Death benefits	Wage payments (not gratuity) to an employee's dependents after the employee's death. Payments made after the calendar year in which the employee died and employer-provided death-benefit plans are not taxed
Dismissal pay	Payments by employer for involuntary separation of an employee from the employer's service.
Guaranteed annual wage payments	Union contract agreements whereby an employer guarantees certain employees will either work during or be paid for each normal workweek in a calendar year.
Idle time or standby payments	Amounts paid workers who are at the beck and call of an employer but who are performing no work.
Jury duty pay	The difference between the employee's regular wages and the amount received for jury duty, paid by employers.
Moving expense reimbursements	Unless the employee will be entitled to deduct these moving expenses in determining taxable income for federal income tax purposes.
Retroactive wage increases	
Stock payments	The fair market value of stock transferred by employers to employees as remuneration for services.
Vacation pay	
Employees' federal income and social security taxes paid for by the employer	Payment of the employee portion of the FICA tax by the employer for domestics working in the employer's home and for agricultural laborers is an exception to this rule.
The first six months of sick pay	For sickness or accident disability. Payments under a state temporary disability law are also subject to FICA taxes.
Non-cash fringe benefits	Personal use of company car, employer-provided vehicles for commuting, flights on employer-provided airplanes, and free or discounted flights on commercial airlines.
Employer-paid premiums for an employee's group-term life insurance coverage	Exceeding $50,000. For retired workers, their group-term life insurance that exceeds $50,000 is also subject to FICA.

This credit does not apply to the part of tips used to satisfy minimum wage requirement.

6. Large food and beverage establishments (11 or more employees where tipping is customary) are required to allocate to their tipped employees the excess of 8% of the establishments' gross receipts over the tips reported by their employees. However, employers withhold FICA taxes only from the tips reported by employees, not from tips that are allocated. The amount of allocated tip income is shown separately on the employee's *Wage and Tax Statement (Form W-2)*, explained in Chapter 4.

Every large food or beverage establishment must report the amount of its receipts from food and beverage operations annually to the IRS and the amount of tips reported by its employees. In some cases, as noted before, the establishment must allocate amounts as tips to its employees. *Form 8027, Employer's Annual Information Return of Tip Income and Allocated Tips* (not illustrated), is used.

Tax Savings for the Employer and the Employee. FICA tax only applies to types of compensation considered taxable under the law. If a company applies the tax to exempt payments, the company and the employee both suffer. Examples of compensation that the law excludes follow.

Meals and Lodging. FICA exempts the value of meals or lodging furnished employees for the convenience of the employer. The value of meals or lodging not meeting this test will be subject to FICA tax. The IRS places no specific value on meals or lodging furnished by employers to employees. Instead, the IRS relies on state valuations. Where a state has no law or regulation on the subject, fair value is defined as the reasonable prevailing value of the meals or lodging. To determine fair value, some of the factors used include:

1. The value employers charge in their accounting records for meals or lodging.
2. Agreements on the value between employer and employees.
3. The specific type of meal or lodging.

Sick Pay. FICA defines **sick pay** as any payment made to individuals due to personal injury or sickness, that does not constitute wages. Sick pay payments must be part of a plan to which the employer is a party. Sick pay must not include amounts paid to individuals who are permanently disabled. The first six

Employers and employees of large food or beverage establishments where the tips average less than 8% of the gross receipts may petition the IRS to reduce the tip allocation. The tip allocation may be set as low as 2%. The IRS Revenue Procedure that provides the guidelines for petitioning states that more than one-half of the directly tipped employees must consent to the petition.

Figure 3–5 *Form 4070, Employee's Report of Tips to Employer*

Form **4070** Department of the Treasury Internal Revenue Service	**Employee's Report of Tips to Employer** ▶ For Paperwork Reduction Act Notice, see back of the form.	OMB No. 1545-0065
Employee's name and address Morton O. Tanenbaum 1704 Elm St., San Diego, CA 92121-8837		Social security number 269 21 7220
Employer's name and address (include establishment name, if different.) Holland House Inn 9 Fairway, San Diego, CA 92123-1369		
Month or shorter period in which tips were received from July 1, 19___, to July 31, 19___		Tips $ 389.10
Signature *Morton O. Tanenbaum*		Date August 10, 19___

months of sick pay an employee receives are considered wages and subject to FICA tax. The period off the job must be continuous for six months. A relapse after a return to work starts a new six-month period. Payments made after the expiration of six calendar months following the last month in which the employee worked for the employer are not taxed.

Sick pay payments may also be made by a third party, including insurance companies, trusts providing sick and accident benefits, and employers' associations funded to pay sickness and accident benefits. The third party is treated as a separate employer and must withhold and deposit the FICA taxes. However, the third party may be relieved of the liability for the employer's share of the FICA taxes if the third party fulfills each of these requirements:

1. Withholds and deposits the employee portion of the FICA tax.
2. Notifies the employer of the amount of wages or compensation involved.

For convenience, an employer may contract to have the third party deposit the employer portion of the tax as well as the employee portion. Generally payments made to employees or their dependents for medical or hospital expenses in connection with sickness or accident disability are not considered wages. However, these payments must be part of a plan established by the employer for all employees or for a particular class of employees.

Simplified Employee Pension (SEP) Plans. Employers may contribute to individual retirement accounts and annuities set up by or on behalf of employees. As indicated in Chapter 1, such contribution arrangements are called *simplified employee pension (SEP) plans*. Employer contributions to SEP plans are exempt from FICA taxes if there is reason to believe that employees will be entitled to deduct the employer contributions for federal income tax purposes.

Payments for Educational Assistance. *Educational assistance* refers to the expenses that an employer pays for an employee's education, such as tuition, fees, and payments for books, supplies, and equipment. Also, educational assistance includes the cost of employer-provided courses of instruction (books, supplies, and equipment). Educational assistance excludes payment for tools or supplies that employees keep after they complete a course of instruction. Payments for job-related educational expenses are not subject to FICA taxes if the education maintains or improves skills required by the individual's employment. Prior to 1995, non-job related educational expenses were also excluded up to $5,250 annually. This provision expired at the end of 1994.

The Internal Revenue Code specifies that an employer's nondiscriminatory educational assistance plan must be in writing and designed for the exclusive purpose of providing employees with educational assistance. Further, the plan must not discriminate in favor of company officers, shareholders, owners, or highly compensated employees.

SELF-STUDY QUIZ 3–2. Which of the following are subject to FICA tax (indicate Yes or No)?

_____ 1. A $15 gift certificate for a local grocery store given to employees as a Christmas gift.
_____ 2. Sales representatives using their company cars for personal use on weeknights and weekends.
_____ 3. Employer's contributions to a Simplified Employee Pension Plan for its employees.
_____ 4. A tuition reimbursement plan that pays tuition for employees successfully completing job-related courses.
_____ 5. Severance pay made to an employee discharged for theft.

What Is the Taxable Wage Base?

The employer must consider the *taxable wage base* when computing the OASDI portion of the FICA tax. The law exempts wages that exceed this base during the calendar year (**$63,000** estimated for **1996**).The actual OASDI taxable wage base is not released until November each year. Once the OASDI taxable wage base has been reached, all payments made to the employee during the remainder of the year are not taxable. The wage base applies to amounts *paid* employees in a calendar year and not to the time when the services were performed by the employees. The HI portion of the FICA tax does not have a ceiling, thus employers compute this tax on the total wages and salaries paid during the year. As social security benefits increase each year based on changes in the Consumer Price Index, the taxable wage base is increased too.

Renee Riley receives pay on January 3, 1997, for work done during the last week of December, 1996. The wages would be taxed as income in the calendar year 1997, using 1997 tax rates.

	Rate	Wage Base
OASDI	6.2 %	$63,000 (estimated)
HI	1.45%	None

Tax Rates. The Social Security Act as amended imposes a separate tax on employers and employees for old-age, survivors, and disability insurance (OASDI) benefits and for hospital insurance (HI) benefits. The 1996 tax rates for both the employer and the employee portions of the tax follow:

Determining OASDI Tax:

If

Cumulative Wages	+	Current Wage Payment	< OASDI Wage Base, then
$52,400	+	$3,000	= $55,400

Compute the OASDI Tax on the entire wage payment. ($3,000 × .062 = $186.00)

If:

Cumulative Wages	+	Current Wage Payment	> OASDI Wage Base, then
$60,500	+	$3,000	= $63,500

Compute the OASDI Tax on the difference between the Wage Base and the Cumulative Wages:

$63,000	–	$60,500	= ($2,500 × .062 = $155.00)
Wage Base	–	Cumulative Wages	

Employees' FICA (OASDHI) Taxes and Withholdings. FICA requires employers to collect the OASDHI taxes from their employees and pay the taxes to the IRS at the same time they pay their own tax. The employer deducts the tax from the wages at the time of payment. The amount of each tax to be withheld is computed by applying to the employee's taxable wages the tax rate in effect at the time that the wages are received. The liability for the tax extends to both the employee and the employer; but after the employer has collected the tax, the employee's liability ceases. The examples below illustrate the computation of the FICA taxes to be withheld.

ON THE JOB

If you acquire substantially all of the business property of another employer, or a unit of that employer's business, you are considered a successor employer and can use the wages the prior employer paid to your new employees against the taxable wage base.

1. *Maria Schwant, employed by the Gobel Company, earned $460 during the week ended February 3, 1996. Prior to February 3, Schwant's cumulative gross earnings for the year were $2,765.70. FICA taxes to be withheld on $460 are computed as follows:*

OASDI		HI	
Taxable Wages	$ 460	Taxable Wages	$460
Tax Rate	×6.2%	Tax Rate	×1.45%
OASDI Tax to be Withheld . . .	$28.52	HI Tax to be Withheld	$6.67

2. *Anne Fergo, a salaried employee of the Lafayette Advertising Agency, is paid $1,475 every Friday. Prior to the pay of October 27, 1996 (the 43rd pay of the year), she had earned $61,950. The FICA taxes to be withheld from Fergo's pay on October 27 are computed as follows:*

OASDI		HI	
Taxable Wage Limit	$63,000	Taxable Wage Limit	NONE
Wages Paid to Date	61,950	Wages Paid to Date	$61,950
Taxable Wages this Pay	$ 1,050	Taxable Wage this Pay . . .	1,475
Tax Rate	×6.2%	Tax Rate	×1.45%
OASDI Tax to be Withheld . . .	$ 65.10	HI Tax to be Withheld	$ 21.39

3. *Marc Todd, president of Uni-Sight, Inc., is paid $2,885 semimonthly. Prior to his last pay on December 29, 1996, Todd had earned $66,355. The FICA taxes to be withheld from Todd's pay on December 29 are computed as follows:*

OASDI		HI	
Taxable Wage Limit	$63,000	Taxable Wage Limit	NONE
Wages Paid to Date	66,355	Wages Paid to Date	$66,355
Taxable Wages This Pay	-0-	Taxable Wage this Pay . . .	2,885
OASDI Tax to be Withheld . . .	-0-	Tax Rate	×1.45%
		HI Tax to be Withheld	$ 41.83

Employer's FICA (OASDI Taxes). In addition to withholding the correct amount of FICA tax from the employees' taxable earnings, the employer must make contributions to the program. The employer's portion of the tax is based on the wages paid to the employees. The employer's taxes, however, are not computed on the wages paid each employee, but on the total wages paid all employees. As with employee withholdings, once the OASDI taxable wage base is reached, the employer no longer contributes for that particular employee. The OASDI tax is 6.2% of each employee's wages paid and the HI tax is 1.45% of each employee's wages paid.

The Bradford Company has 100 employees, each earning $375.25 a week.

OASDI		
Amount of OASDI tax withheld from each employee's paycheck each week:	$23.27	(6.2% × $375.25)
Total tax withheld from the 100 employees' wages:	$2,327.00	($23.27 × 100)
Tax on employer:	$2,326.55	(6.2% × $37,525)

HI
—

Amount of HI tax withheld from each employee's paycheck each week:	$5.44	(1.45% × $375.25)
Total tax withheld from the 100 employees' wages is:	$544.00	($5.44 × 100)
Tax on employer:	$544.11	(1.45% × $37,525)

SELF-STUDY QUIZ 3–3. McDuff's Fine Foods employs five people. For each person, compute the amount of OASDI and HI tax for the first week in January.

Employee	Weekly Wage	OASDI	HI
Mary Britton	$ 225.00		
Bob Yold	300.00		
Martin Rold	175.00		
Maria Aldo	1,000.00		
Gil Hammerstien	2,200.00		

Compute the Employer's portion of the FICA taxes, based on the payroll data above.

*Will any of the employees exceed the **Taxable Wage Base** during the year? If yes, on which payday will it occur?*

WHO IS A SELF-EMPLOYED PERSON?

The Self-Employment Contributions Act (SEC) extended coverage under the social security system to the self-employed in 1951. Over the years, most self-employed persons have become covered by the law.

Self-Employment Income

SECA uses an individual's *self-employment income* as the basis for levying taxes and for determining the amount of income to credit toward OASDI insurance benefits or HI coverage. Self-employment income generally consists of the net earnings derived by individuals from a business or profession carried on as a sole proprietorship or as a partnership. Self-employed persons determine their net earnings by finding the sum of the following:

1. The **gross income** derived by an individual from any business or profession carried on, less allowable deductions attributable to such business or profession, and
2. The **individual's distributive share** (whether or not distributed) of the ordinary net income or loss from any business or profession carried on by a partnership of which the individual is a member.

Usually the net business income of individuals as shown in their income tax returns makes up their net earnings from self-employment for the purpose of the Social Security Act. Earnings of less than $400 from self-employment are ignored. For computing the OASDI taxes, the maximum self-employment taxable income of any individual for 1996 is $63,000 (estimated). For the HI taxes, however, the total self-employment income is taxable. If any wages are received, the individual can reduce the maximum amount of taxable self-employment income by the amount of such wages.

E X A M P L E

Beth Rolland receives wages of $65,000 from her job in 1996. She also earned $15,000 in self-employment income during the year. In computing her OASDI taxes, none of her self-employment income is considered, since her wages exceed the taxable wage base of $63,000. However, in computing her HI taxes, all of her earnings from self-employment are taxed.

If the wages received in 1996 amount to less than $63,000, any self-employment earnings amounting to $400 or more must be counted as self-employment income up to an aggregate amount of $63,000 for OASDI taxes.

E X A M P L E

George Talbot receives wages in 1996 amounting to $52,700. His net earnings from self-employment amount to $14,600. Talbot must count $10,300 of his earnings in determining taxable self-employment income for OASDI taxes.

FICA Taxable Wage Base	−	Wages Rec'd in 1996	=	Taxable Self-Employment Income
$63,000	−	$52,700	=	$10,300

Taxable Year. In computing the taxes on self-employment income, sole proprietors use the same taxable year as that used for income tax purposes. In the case of a partnership, the taxable year of the partners may not correspond with that of the partnership. In such instances the partners are required to include in computing net earnings from self-employment their distributive share of the income or loss from the partnership for any taxable year ending with or within their taxable year.

Reporting Self-Employment Income. Sole proprietors report their self-employment income by transferring certain data from *SCHEDULE C (Form 1040), Profit or Loss from Business.* SECA requires self-employed persons to include SECA taxes in their quarterly payment of estimated income taxes. The taxpayer's estimated income tax is the sum of the estimated income taxes and SECA taxes less any credits against the tax. Thus, each quarter the self-employed person currently pays SECA taxes into the social security and Medicare funds.

Self-Employment OASDHI Taxes. The 1996 social security tax rates for self-employed persons are: OASDI—12.4% and HI—2.9%. However, self-employed persons can reduce their taxable self-employment income in order to lessen the impact of the higher tax rates. This deduction is computed according to the instructions that accompany *SCHEDULE SE (Form 1040), Self-Employment Tax.*

SELF-STUDY QUIZ 3–4. Lori Kinmark works as a jeweler for a local company. She earns $900.00 per week, plus a year-end bonus of $2,000. Kinmark also earns an additional net self-employment income of $18,000 per year.

$____ **1.** Compute Kinmark's annual earnings from employment.

$____ **2.** Compute Kinmark's total earnings from job and from self-employment income.

<u>$</u>   **3.**   How much self-employment income should Kinmark include in computing taxable self-employment income for OASDI taxes?

APPLICATION FOR EMPLOYER IDENTIFICATION NUMBER (FORM SS-4)

Every employer of one or more persons must file an application for an identification number, *Form SS-4,* available from any IRS or social security office. Figure 3–6 shows a filled-in copy of Form SS-4. The employer should file this form early enough to allow for processing, preferably four to five weeks before the identification number (EIN) is needed. The employer files the application with the IRS service center where the federal tax returns are filed. If the employer has no legal residence, or principal place of business, or principal office in any IRS district, the application should be sent to: Internal Revenue Service, Philadelphia, PA 19255-0005.

    The employer must enter the EIN on all returns, forms, and correspondence sent to the District Director of Internal Revenue that relate to the taxes imposed under FICA. The employer uses the EIN in any correspondence with the Social Security Administration (SSA) and enters the number on forms issued by the SSA. The penalty for failing to supply the identification number is discussed later in this chapter. Regardless of how many different business locations are operated, the employer receives only one EIN. If the owner sells or otherwise transfers a business, the new owner must file an application for a new identification number.

Employee's Application for Social Security Card (Form SS-5)

Under the Social Security Act every employee and every self-employed person must have a social security number (SSN). The application for a SSN is available at any social security or IRS office. The *Application for a Social Security Card (Form SS-5)* can be filed with any field office of the SSA. Figure 3–7 shows a filled-in copy of Form SS-5.

    The application should be filed far enough in advance of its first required use to allow for the processing of the application. The Social Security Act requires applicants for a social security card to furnish evidence of their age, identity, and U.S. citizenship or lawful alien status. Applicants may apply either by mailing the required documents and forms to their nearest Social Security office or apply in person if they are age 18 or older and have never had a Social Security card, or if they are aliens whose immigration documents should not be sent through the mail. After filing Form SS-5, the employee will receive from the SSA a card showing the assigned social security number.

    Upon receipt of their SSN, employees should inform their employers of the number assigned them. If employees change positions, they must notify the new employer of their SSN when they begin employment. If an employee changes his or her name by court order or by marriage, the individual should request a new social security card by completing Form SS-5. Employees may have their SSN changed at any time by applying to the SSA and showing good reasons for a change. Otherwise, only one number is assigned to an employee and the employee will continue to use that number regardless of the changes in positions or employers for whom service is rendered.

    The Secretary of Health and Human Services is authorized to assure that SSNs are issued to or on behalf of children who are below school age at the

L E A R N I N G
O B J E C T I V E

4

I R S
CONNECTION

Employers can receive their EINs immediately by calling the Tele-TIN phone number for their IRS service center. The instructions for Form SS-4 list the Tele-TIN phone numbers, as well as complete directions for applying by phone.

JOB
ON THE

The employer must obtain each employee's SSN to enter on Form W-2 (discussed in Chapter 4). If the employer does not provide the correct name and SSN, he or she may owe a penalty.

    If the employee's name is not correct as shown on the card, including a name change due to marriage or divorce, the employee should request a new card.

Figure 3–6　*Form SS-4, Application for Employer Identification Number*

Form **SS-4**	**Application for Employer Identification Number**	EIN
Department of the Treasury Internal Revenue Service	(For use by employers and others. Please read the attached instructions before completing this form.)	OMB No. 1545-0003

Please type or print clearly.

1 Name of applicant (True legal name) (See instructions.)
Montana Mining, Inc.

2 Trade name of business, if different from name in line 1

3 Executor, trustee, "care of" name
Care of Carla P. Ortiz

4a Mailing address (street address) (room, apt., or suite no.)
P.O. Box 447

5a Address of business (See instructions.)
1200 High Gap

4b City, state, and ZIP code
Butte, MT 59701-0210

5b City, state, and ZIP code
Butte, MT 59701-1200

6 County and state where principal business is located
Silver Bow, MT

7 Name of principal officer, grantor, or general partner (See instructions.) ▶ Grant X. Bilton, President–379-39-3280

8a Type of entity (Check only one box.) (See instructions.)
☐ Individual SSN ____ ☐ Estate ☐ Plan administrator SSN ____ ☐ Trust
☐ REMIC ☐ Personal service corp. ☒ Other corporation (specify) Extraction ☐ Partnership ☐ Farmers' cooperative
☐ State/local government ☐ National guard ☐ Federal government/military ☐ Church or church controlled organization
☐ Other nonprofit organization (specify) ____ If nonprofit organization enter GEN (if applicable) ____
☐ Other (specify) ▶ ____

8b If a corporation, give name of foreign country (if applicable) or state in the U.S. where incorporated ▶
Foreign country ____ | State Montana

9 Reason for applying (Check only one box.)
☒ Started new business
☐ Hired employees
☐ Created a pension plan (specify type) ▶
☐ Banking purpose (specify) ▶
☐ Changed type of organization (specify) ▶ ____
☐ Purchased going business
☐ Created a trust (specify) ▶ ____
☐ Other (specify) ▶

10 Date business started or acquired (Mo., day, year) (See instructions.)
July 3, 19—

11 Enter closing month of accounting year. (See instructions.)
June

12 First date wages or annuities were paid or will be paid (Mo., day, year). **Note:** *If applicant is a withholding agent, enter date income will first be paid to nonresident alien. (Mo., day, year)* . . . . ▶ July 12, 19—

13 Enter highest number of employees expected in the next 12 months. **Note:** *If the applicant does not expect to have any employees during the period, enter "0."* . . . . ▶

Nonagricultural	Agricultural	Household
450		

14 Principal activity (See instructions.) ▶ Copper Extraction

15 Is the principal business activity manufacturing? . . . . ☐ Yes ☒ No
If "Yes," principal product and raw material used ▶

16 To whom are most of the products or services sold? Please check the appropriate box. ☒ Business (wholesale)
☐ Public (retail) ☐ Other (specify) ▶ ☐ N/A

17a Has the applicant ever applied for an identification number for this or any other business? . . . . ☐ Yes ☒ No
Note: *If "Yes," please complete lines 17b and 17c.*

17b If you checked the "Yes" box in line 17a, give applicant's true name and trade name, if different than name shown on prior application.
True name ▶　　　　　　　　　Trade name ▶

17c Enter approximate date, city, and state where the application was filed and the previous employer identification number if known.

Approximate date when filed (Mo., day, year)	City and state where filed	Previous EIN

Under penalties of perjury, I declare that I have examined this application, and to the best of my knowledge and belief, it is true, correct, and complete.

Telephone number (include area code)
406-555-2400

Name and title (Please type or print clearly.) ▶ Carla P. Ortiz, V.P., Finance

Signature ▶ *Carla P. Ortiz*　　　　　Date ▶ 7/3/—

Note: *Do not write below this line.　For official use only.*

Please leave blank ▶	Geo.	Ind.	Class	Size	Reason for applying

Form **SS-4**

Figure 3–7 *Form SS-5, Application for a Social Security Card*

SOCIAL SECURITY ADMINISTRATION
Application for a Social Security Card

Form Approved
OMB No. 0960-0066

INSTRUCTIONS

- Please read "How To Complete This Form" on page 2.
- Print or type using black or blue ink. DO NOT USE PENCIL.
- After you complete this form, take or mail it along with the required documents to your nearest Social Security office.
- If you are completing this form for someone else, answer the questions as they apply to that person. Then, sign your name in question 16.

1 NAME To Be Shown On Card

▶ Bertha   Mary   Davis
FIRST   FULL MIDDLE NAME   LAST

FULL NAME AT BIRTH IF OTHER THAN ABOVE
FIRST   FULL MIDDLE NAME   LAST

OTHER NAMES USED

2 MAILING ADDRESS Do Not Abbreviate

▶ 18 Dundee Avenue
STREET ADDRESS, APT. NO., PO BOX, RURAL ROUTE NO.

Akron   Ohio   44320-2968
CITY   STATE   ZIP CODE

3 CITIZENSHIP (Check One)

[X] U.S. Citizen [ ] Legal Alien Allowed To Work [ ] Legal Alien Not Allowed To Work [ ] Foreign Student Allowed Restricted Employment [ ] Conditionally Legalized Alien Allowed To Work [ ] Other (See Instructions On Page 2)

4 SEX

[ ] Male [X] Female

5 RACE/ETHNIC DESCRIPTION (Check One Only—Voluntary)

[ ] Asian, Asian-American Or Pacific Islander [ ] Hispanic [X] Black (Not Hispanic) [ ] North American Indian Or Alaskan Native [ ] White (Not Hispanic)

6 DATE OF BIRTH 8 1 77
MONTH DAY YEAR

7 PLACE OF BIRTH (Do Not Abbreviate) Lima   Ohio
CITY   STATE OR FOREIGN COUNTRY   FCI

Office Use Only

8 MOTHER'S MAIDEN NAME Ruth   Ann   Archer
FIRST   FULL MIDDLE NAME   LAST NAME AT HER BIRTH

9 FATHER'S NAME Roger   Paul   Davis
FIRST   FULL MIDDLE NAME   LAST

10 Has the person in item 1 ever applied for or received a Social Security number before?

[ ] Yes (If "yes", answer questions 11-13.) [X] No (If "no", go on to question 14.) [ ] Don't Know (If "don't know", go on to question 14.)

11 Enter the Social Security number previously assigned to the person listed in item 1.

[ ][ ][ ] – [ ][ ] – [ ][ ][ ][ ]

12 Enter the name shown on the most recent Social Security card issued for the person listed in item 1.

FIRST   MIDDLE   LAST

13 Enter any different date of birth if used on an earlier application for a card.
MONTH   DAY   YEAR

14 TODAY'S DATE ▶ 1 12 --
MONTH DAY YEAR

15 DAYTIME PHONE NUMBER ▶ (419) 555-4321
AREA CODE

DELIBERATELY FURNISHING (OR CAUSING TO BE FURNISHED) FALSE INFORMATION ON THIS APPLICATION IS A CRIME PUNISHABLE BY FINE OR IMPRISONMENT, OR BOTH.

16 YOUR SIGNATURE

▶ *Bertha M. Davis*

17 YOUR RELATIONSHIP TO THE PERSON IN ITEM 1 IS:

[X] Self [ ] Natural Or Adoptive Parent [ ] Legal Guardian [ ] Other (Specify)

DO NOT WRITE BELOW THIS LINE (FOR SSA USE ONLY)					
NPN		DOC	NTI	CAN	ITV
PBC	EVI	EVA	EVC	NWR	DNR	UNIT

EVIDENCE SUBMITTED

SIGNATURE AND TITLE OF EMPLOYER(S) REVIEWING EVIDENCE AND/OR CONDUCTING INTERVIEW

DATE

DCL   DATE

Form **SS-5** (5/88)

request of their parents or guardians and to children of school age when they first enroll in school. Further, SSNs must be obtained for children age one or over who are claimed as dependents on federal income tax returns. To thwart cheaters who claim dogs, cats, and nonexistent people as dependents, taxpayers must list on their tax returns the taxpayer identification numbers of any claimed dependents age one or over. The Secretary also ensures that SSNs are assigned to aliens when they are admitted to the United States under conditions that permit them to work.

Criminal penalties (of up to $5,000 or imprisonment of up to 5 years, or both) exist for persons involved in the following situations:

1. Knowingly and willfully using a SSN obtained with false information.
2. Using someone else's SSN.
3. Altering a social security card.
4. Buying or selling a card claimed to be issued by the Secretary.
5. Possessing a card or counterfeit card with the intent to sell or alter it.

Request for Earnings and Benefit Estimate Statement. Each employee who has received taxable wages under the Social Security Act has an account with the SSA. This account shows the amount of wages credited to the employee's account. When employees or their dependents claim benefits, the wage credits in the employee's account are used to compute the amount of benefits payable, as discussed in Appendix A. Employees can use *Form SSA-7004-SM* (not illustrated) to request a statement of wages credited to their account. Copies of this form are available by contacting the district office of the SSA or by calling 1-800-772-1213. The worker will receive a statement showing the yearly earnings, the social security taxes paid each year, and a projection of the benefits the worker or the survivors will receive if the worker retires, dies, or is disabled. If workers find any discrepancies between their records and the accounts kept by the SSA, claims can be made for adjustment. Errors will be corrected if they are reported within 3 years, 3 months, and 15 days following the close of any taxable year.

Employers may verify employees' social security numbers through the SSA's Enumeration Verification System (EVS). To use the system, you must use round tapes, 3480 cartridges, or paper; and there is a limit of 300 employees per paper submission. For information, call the EVS service at 410-965-7140.

What Returns Are Required For Social Security Purposes?

Employers covered under FICA are liable for their own FICA taxes and their employees' FICA and income taxes withheld from employees' wages. Withholding of income taxes is discussed in Chapter 4. Every employer, except those employing agricultural workers, who is required to withhold income taxes from wages or who is liable for social security taxes must file:

1. A *quarterly* tax and information return. This return shows the total FICA wage paid and the total FICA taxes (employer and employee contributions) and federal income taxes withheld.
2. An *annual* return of withheld federal income taxes. This return covers *nonpayroll* items such as backup withholding, withholding on gambling winnings, pensions, annuities, IRAs, and military retirement.
3. An *annual* record of federal tax liability. Certain depositors, discussed later, are required to report on a *daily* basis their liability for backup withholding and income taxes withheld on gambling winnings, pensions, annuities, IRAs, and military retirement.

Generally an employer must deposit the income taxes and social security taxes withheld and the employer's FICA taxes in an authorized depository or a Federal Reserve bank that serves the employer's geographic area. In other instances, the employer is not required to deposit the taxes but, instead, may remit them with the quarterly return.

Any employer who fails to pay the withheld income taxes and FICA taxes, or fails to make deposits and payments, or does not file the tax returns as required by law, may be required to deposit such taxes in a special trust account for the U.S. government and file monthly tax returns. Figure 3–8 lists and briefly describes the major forms used to prepare FICA tax returns and deposits.

What Are the Deposit Requirements? (Nonagricultural Workers)

L E A R N I N G
O B J E C T I V E
6

The requirements for depositing FICA taxes and income taxes withheld from employees' wages vary according to the amount of such taxes reported during a *"lookback period,"* explained below. Depending on the total amount of taxes involved (federal income tax and FICA tax withheld from employees' earnings plus the employer's portion of the FICA tax), employers may have to deposit their taxes several times a month or monthly. Some employers may not have to make any deposits but, instead, may pay their taxes at the time of filing their

Figure 3–8
Major Forms for Preparing FICA Tax Returns and Deposits

Form 941, Employer's Quarterly Federal Tax Return	Required of all covered employers, except employers of household and agricultural employees, who withhold income tax and social security taxes. (See Figure 3–11.)
Form 941c, Supporting Statement to Correct Information	Used to correct income and social security tax information previously reported on Forms 941, 941-M, 941-SS, 943, 945.
Form 941-V, Form 941 Payment Voucher	Filled in by employers with a total tax liability of less than $500 for the quarter who are making payment with Form 941.
Form 941-M, Employer's Monthly Federal Tax Return	Required of employers who have not complied with the requirements for filing returns or paying or depositing all taxes reported on quarterly returns. Notification to file Form 941-M is received from the District Director, and preaddressed forms are mailed the employer monthly.
Form-941-PR, Employer's Quarterly Federal Tax Return	Required of employers to report social security taxes for workers in Puerto Rico.
Form 941-SS, Employer's Quarterly Federal Tax Return	Required of employers to report social security taxes for workers in American Samoa, Guam, the Northern Mariana Islands, and the Virgin Islands.
Form 943, Employer's Annual Tax Return for Agricultural Employees	Used by employers of agricultural workers for reporting FICA and income taxes on wages paid.
Form 8109, Federal Tax Deposit	Completed at the time of depositing various types of taxes such as withheld income and FICA (Form 941), agricultural withheld income and FICA (Form 943), and federal unemployment (Form 940, as discussed in Chapter 5).

quarterly return, Form 941, discussed later in this chapter. Most employers, however, are either monthly or semiweekly depositors.

The amount of employment taxes that the employer reports on the quarterly returns for the four quarters in the lookback period determines if the employer is a monthly or a semiweekly depositor. A lookback period consists of four quarters beginning July 1 of the second preceding year and ending June 30 of the prior year. These four quarters are the employer's lookback period even if no taxes were reported for any of the quarters. Figure 3–9 shows the lookback period for 1996. Each November the IRS notifies employers whether they will be a monthly or a semiweekly depositor for the next calendar year.

Figure 3–9
Lookback Period for Calendar Year 1996

1994		1995	
July–Sept.	Oct.–Dec.	Jan.–Mar.	Apr.–June

Monthly Depositors. A *monthly depositor* is one who reported employment taxes of *$50,000* or *less* for the four quarters in the lookback period. Monthly depositors are required to deposit their taxes in a Federal Reserve bank or an authorized financial institution by the 15th day of the following month. If a deposit is required to be made on a day that is not a banking day, the deposit is considered timely if it is made by the close of the next banking day.

A new employer becomes a monthly depositor until a lookback period that can be used to determine deposit frequency is established. However, if an unsatisfied deposit of $100,000 or more triggers the $100,000 One-Day Rule (discussed below) at any time during the year, the new employer becomes a semiweekly depositor for the remainder of the current calendar year and the subsequent calendar year.

E X A M P L E

1. *The Robart Company's deposit status for 1996 was determined by using the lookback period shown in Figure 3–9. During the two quarters of 1994, Robart reported employment taxes (FICA & Employees' Income Tax) of $16,000. For each of the two quarters in 1995, the company reported taxes of $10,000. Since the taxes reported by Robart during the lookback period do not exceed $50,000, the company is classed as a monthly depositor and follows the monthly rule for the current year, 1996.*

2. *Valencia, Inc., is a monthly depositor. For August taxes, Valencia must deposit the $11,000 on or before September 15, 1996. Since September 15 is Sunday, a nonbanking day, Valencia must deposit the taxes by the close of the next banking day, Monday, September 16.*

Semiweekly Depositors. A *semiweekly depositor* is one who reported employment taxes of more than $50,000 for the four quarters in the lookback period. Depending upon what day of the week the employer makes wage payments, deposits must be made as follows:

Payment Days	Deposit by
Wednesday, Thursday, and/or Friday	Following Wednesday
Saturday, Sunday, Monday, and/or Tuesday	Following Friday

If a semiweekly deposit period spans two quarters, the liability that applies to one quarter is separate from the liability that applies to the other quarter. Even though the deposits are made on the same day, two separate deposits must be made.

1. *The Meyer Company's deposit status for 1996 was determined by using the lookback period shown in Figure 3–9. In the two quarters of 1994, Meyer reported taxes of $35,000. The taxes reported in the two quarters of 1995 totaled $30,000.* **Since the total taxes reported during the four quarters of the lookback period exceeded $50,000, Meyer is subject to the semiweekly rule for the current year, 1996.**

2. *The employees of DeVeau, a semiweekly depositor, are paid every Monday. On October 7, 1996, DeVeau has accumulated taxes totaling $24,000. DeVeau is required to deposit the $24,000 on or before the following Friday, October 11.*

3. *Yeltz Inc., a semiweekly depositor, has accumulated taxes on Saturday, March 30, 1996, and on Tuesday, April 2, 1996. The company needs to make two separate deposits on Friday, April 5, even though they are part of the same semiweekly deposit period.*

One-Day Rule. If on any day during a deposit period, an employer has accumulated $100,000 or more in employment taxes, the taxes must be deposited by the close of the next banking day. When determining whether the $100,000 threshold is met, a monthly depositor takes into account only those taxes accumulated in the calendar month in which the day occurs. A semiweekly depositor takes into account only those taxes accumulated in the Wednesday-Friday or Saturday-Tuesday semiweekly periods in which the day occurs.

1. *On Tuesday, January 16, 1996, Parker Company accumulated $105,000 in employment taxes for wages paid on that day. Regardless of Parker's deposit status, the firm is required to deposit the $105,000 by the next banking day, Wednesday, January 17. Note that if Parker was not subject to the semiweekly rule on January 16, 1996, the company would become subject to that rule as of January 17, 1996.*

2. *The Quincy Company is subject to the semiweekly rule. On Monday, February 5, 1996, Quincy accumulated $120,000 in employment taxes. The firm is required to deposit the $120,000 by the next banking day, Tuesday, February 6.*

On Tuesday, February 6, Quincy accumulates $30,000 more in employment taxes. Even though Quincy had a previous $120,000 deposit obligation that occurred earlier in the semiweekly period, Quincy now has an additional and separate deposit obligation that must be met by the following Friday, February 9.

Accumulated Employment Taxes Less Than $500 at the End of a Calendar Quarter. If during a calendar quarter the accumulated employment taxes are less than $500, no deposits are required. The taxes may be paid to the IRS at the time of filing the quarterly return, Form 941, discussed later in this chapter. However, if the employer wishes, the taxes may be fully deposited by the end of the next month.

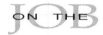

*If an employer does not deposit social security, Medicare, and withheld income taxes on time with an authorized financial institution or Federal Reserve bank, the IRS can require the employer to file monthly returns for these taxes on **Form 941-M, Employer's Monthly Federal Tax Return.***

The Safe Harbor Rule (98% Rule). The amount deposited by an employer may be affected by the *safe harbor rule.* Under this rule, an employer satisfies the deposit obligations provided:

1. The amount of any shortfall does not exceed the greater of $100 or 2% of the amount of employment taxes required to be deposited.
2. The employer deposits the shortfall on or before the shortfall make-up date.

A *shortfall* is the excess of the amount of employment taxes required to be deposited over the amount deposited on or before the last date prescribed for the deposit. The shortfall make-up rules follow:

1. *Monthly depositors:* The shortfall must be deposited or remitted by the due date for the quarterly return, in accordance with the applicable form and instruction.
2. *Semiweekly depositors and those subject to the $100,000 one-day rule:* The shortfall must be deposited on or before the first Wednesday or Friday, whichever is earlier, falling on or after the 15th day of the month following the month in which the deposit was required to be made.

E X A M P L E

1. *On Friday, June 7, 1996, Rogers, Ltd., a semiweekly depositor, pays wages and accumulates employment taxes. Rogers makes a deposit on Wednesday, June 12, in the amount of $4,000. Later, it was determined that Rogers was actually required to deposit $4,080 by Wednesday.*

   Rogers has a shortfall of $80. The shortfall is less than the greater of $100 or 2% of the amount required to be deposited. Therefore, Rogers satisfies the safe harbor rule so long as the $80 shortfall is deposited by Wednesday, July 17.

2. *On Friday, November 1, 1996, Stacy Company, a semiweekly depositor, pays wages and accumulates employment taxes. Stacy makes a deposit of $30,000 but later finds that the amount of the deposit should have been $32,000.*

   The $2,000 shortfall ($32,000 – $30,000) exceeds the greater of $100 or 2% of the amount required to be deposited (2% × $32,000 = $640). Thus, the safe harbor rule was not met. As a result, Stacy is subject to a failure-to-deposit penalty, as described later in this chapter.

Deposit Requirements for Employers of Agricultural Workers. The deposit-making rules that apply to employers of agricultural laborers resemble those for employers of nonagricultural workers (Figure 3–10). However, there are exceptions, explained in the instructions accompanying *Form 943, Employer's Annual Tax Return for Agricultural Employees.* In making deposits all employers must use the Federal Tax Deposit Coupon (Form 8109), discussed in a later section.

Deposit Requirements for Employers of Household Employees. Household or domestic employees are usually not subject to federal income tax withholding, but they may voluntarily request that federal income taxes be withheld from their wages. Even though federal income taxes are not withheld from their wages, they are subject to FICA taxes if each worker has been paid cash wages of $1,000 more in a calendar year. Non-cash items given to household employees are not subject to FICA tax.

Employers who withhold and pay FICA taxes and federal income taxes for household services must report these taxes on Form 1040, *Federal Individual*

Accumulated Unpaid Liability	Deposit Requirement
1. $50,000 or less in the lookback period—	1. Monthly taxes must be deposited on or before the 15th of the following month.
2. More than $50,000 in the lookback period—	2. (a) Payday on Wednesday, Thursday, and/or Friday—must be deposited on or before following Wednesday. (b) Payday on Saturday, Sunday, Monday, and/or Tuesday—must be deposited on or before following Friday.
3. $100,000 or more on any day—	3. Must be deposited by the close of the next business day.
4. Less than $500 at end of calendar quarter—	4. Must be paid by end of following month, either as a deposit or with the quarterly tax return (Form 941).

Figure 3–10
Summary of Deposit Rules for Nonagricultural Employers

Income Tax Return. However, if the employer is a sole proprietor and files *Form 941, Employer's Quarterly Federal Tax Return for Business Employees,* the taxes for the household employees must be included on Form 941.

Deposit Requirements for State and Local Government Employers. As indicated earlier, coverage may extend to employees of state and local governments by means of a voluntary agreement entered into between the state and the Secretary of Health and Human Services. Each state and local government employer covered under a voluntary agreement must file its return on Form 941 with the IRS and deposit its FICA taxes through the federal deposit system. State and local government employers must make their tax deposits according to the same deposit schedule used by private employers.

Procedures for Making Deposits. Deposits of FICA and employees' federal income taxes withheld are made using preprinted *Federal Tax Deposit Coupons, Form 8109.* Employers indicate on the coupon the type of tax being deposited. Figure 3–11 shows a sample coupon and part of the instructions for completion.

Employers who make their deposits at a Federal Reserve bank must make them at the Federal Reserve bank that serves their geographic area. They must make payment with an *"immediate credit item."* An *immediate credit item* is a check or other instrument of payment the receiving bank gives immediate credit in accordance with its check-collection schedule. If a deposit is not made with an immediate credit item, the bank stamps the coupon to reflect the name of the bank and the date on which the proceeds of the accompanying payment instrument are collected by the Federal Reserve bank. This date determines the timeliness of the payment.

IRS CONNECTION

Under a program called Autogen, the IRS automatically supplies employers with new coupon books when needed. If the resupply of FTD coupons has not been received, the employer should contact the local IRS office. The coupons can be sent to a branch office, tax preparer, or service bureau making the employer's deposit by showing the appropriate address on the change form provided in the coupon book.

SELF-STUDY QUIZ 3–5.

_____ **1.** Braxton Industries, a semiweekly depositor, pays its employees every Friday. When should the company deposit the employment taxes for each weekly payday?

_____ **2.** What rule should Jackson Repair, a new company, follow in making its deposits for accumulated employment taxes?

_____   **3.**   Quincy Motors (a semiweekly depositor) accumulates taxes of $105,000 on Monday and must deposit this amount on Tuesday, the next banking day. On Tuesday, the company accumulates additional taxes of $20,000. What deposit rule should Quincy follow for depositing the additional $20,000?

Figure 3–11   *Form 8109-B, Federal Tax Deposit Coupon, and a Portion of the Accompanying Instructions*

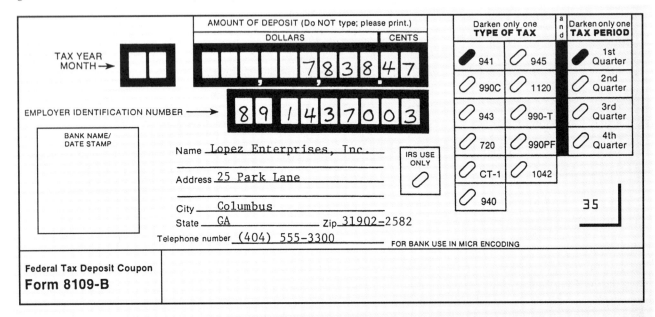

IMPORTANT

OMB NO. 1545-0257

Read instructions carefully before completing Form 8109-B, Federal Tax Deposit Coupon.

Note: *Except for the name, address, and telephone number, entries are processed by optical scanning equipment and must be made in pencil. Please use a soft lead (for example, a #2 pencil) so that the entries can be read more accurately by the optical scanning equipment. The name, address, and telephone number may be completed other than by hand. You CANNOT use photocopies of the coupons to make your deposits. DO NOT staple, tape or fold the coupons.*

Schedule A, Form 941 Filers (4th quarter 1993 ONLY).—If you are making a deposit for the 4th quarter 1993 during January 1994, darken the **945** box under TYPE OF TAX and the 4th quarter box under TAX PERIOD.

Paperwork Reduction Act Notice.—We ask for the information on this form to carry out the Internal Revenue laws of the United States. You are required to give us the information. We need it to ensure that you are complying with these laws and to allow us to figure and collect the right amount of tax.

The time needed to complete and file this form will vary depending on individual circumstances. The estimated average time is 3 min. If you have comments concerning the accuracy of this time estimate or suggestions for making this form more simple, we would be happy to hear from you. You can write to both the **Internal Revenue Service,** Attention: Reports Clearance Officer, PC:FP, Washington, DC 20224; and the **Office of Management and Budget,** Paperwork Reduction Project (1545-0257), Washington, DC 20503. DO NOT send this form to either of these offices. Instead, see the instructions on the back of this page.

Purpose of Form.—Use Form 8109-B deposit coupons to make tax deposits only in the following two situations:

1. You have not yet received your resupply of preprinted deposit coupons (Form 8109); or

2. You are a new entity and have already been assigned an employer identification number (EIN), but have not yet received your initial supply of preprinted deposit coupons (Form 8109).

Note: *If you do not receive your resupply of deposit coupons and a deposit is due or you do not receive your initial supply within 5–6 weeks of receipt of your EIN, please contact your local IRS office.*

If you have applied for an EIN, have not received it, and a deposit must be made, send your payment to your Internal Revenue Service Center. Make your check or money order payable to the Internal Revenue Service and show on it your name (as shown on Form **SS-4,** Application for Employer Identification Number), address, kind of tax, period covered, and date you applied for an EIN. Also attach an explanation to the deposit. Do NOT use Form 8109-B in this situation. DO NOT use Form 8109-B to deposit delinquent taxes assessed by the IRS. Pay those taxes directly to the IRS.

How To Complete the Form.—Enter your name exactly as shown on your return or other IRS correspondence, address, and EIN in the spaces provided. If you are required to file a Form 1120, 990-C, 990-PF (with net investment income), 990-T, or 2438, enter the month in which your tax year ends in the **TAX YEAR MONTH** boxes. For example, if your tax years ends in January, enter 01; if it ends in June, enter 06; if it ends in December, enter 12. Please make your entries for EIN and tax year month (if applicable) in the manner specified in *Amount of Deposit* below. Darken one box each in the *Type of Tax* and *Tax Period* columns as explained below.

Amount of Deposit.—Enter the amount of the deposit in the space provided. Enter the amount legibly, forming the characters as shown below:

Hand-print money amounts without using dollar signs, commas, a decimal point, or leading zeros. The commas and the decimal point are already shown in the entry area. For example, a deposit of $7,635.22 would be entered like this:

DOLLARS								CENTS	
					7	6	3	5	22

If the deposit is for whole dollars only, enter "00" in the CENTS boxes.

The timeliness of deposits is determined by the date received by the commercial bank depository or the Federal Reserve bank. A deposit will be considered timely if the employer establishes that it was mailed at least two days before the due date. Deposits of $20,000 by an employer required to deposit tax more than once a month must be received by the due date to be timely.

When making a deposit, the employer enters the amount of the payment and the check or money order number in the accounting records. The check or money order serves as a source document for the entry. Each FTD coupon has a stub that the employer keeps as a record of payment. The canceled check, bank receipt, or money order is the employer's receipt. The FTD coupon itself is not returned to the employer but is used to credit the employers' tax account, identified by the employer's identification number entered on the coupon. The bank stamps the date and bank name on the coupon and forwards the tax deposit to the IRS for posting to the taxpayer's account. The IRS reconciles the tax deposits with the payments claimed by the employer on each quarterly return. At this point, settlement of the employer's tax liability is made.

HOW DO YOU PREPARE FORM 941? (EMPLOYER'S QUARTERLY FEDERAL TAX RETURN)

L E A R N I N G
O B J E C T I V E
5

Generally the employer must make a quarterly return of FICA taxes and withheld income taxes for the three months of each calendar quarter, using *Form 941, Employers' Quarterly Federal Tax Return*. Figure 3–12 shows a completed copy of Form 941. Once the form has been filed, the employer receives pre-addressed forms every three months. If the employer has not received the form, the employer should request one from an IRS office in time to file the return when due.

Beginning with the first quarter of 1994, all non-payroll items (backup withholding and withholding from pensions, annuities, IRAs, military retirement and gambling winnings) were removed from Form 941. These items are reported on *Form 945, Annual Return of Withheld Federal Income Tax* (Chapter 4).

IRS CONNECTION

Completing the Return

Fill in the State Code box in the upper left corner as follows:

1. Use the Postal Service two-letter state abbreviation as the State Code.
2. If you made your deposits in a state other than that shown in the address on the form, enter the state code for that state.
3. Enter the code "MU" in the box if you deposit in more than one state.
4. If you deposit in the same state as shown in your address, don't make an entry in this box.
5. In addition, semiweekly and next-day depositors must complete Schedule B of *Form 941, Employer's Record of Federal Tax Liability*, instead of Form 941, line 17. The employer's tax liability is listed by each payday. See Figure 3–13.

To complete Form 941, lines 1–17, the employer obtains the information from various sources, such as those listed in Figure 3–14.

Signing Form 941

The form must be signed by the employer or other person who is required to withhold and pay the tax. If the employer is:

Beginning in 1995, employers whose employment tax liabilities exceeded $78 million during the 1993 calendar year must make deposits by Electronic Funds Transfer, using TAXLINK. Employers not required to make deposits in this manner may enroll in the program by calling 1-800-829-5469.

The new deposit system will be phased in over a period of years, based on the following schedule:

47 million: calendar year 1993– Jan. 1, 1996

47 million: calendar year 1994– Jan. 1, 1996

$50,000: calendar year 1995– Jan. 1, 1997

$50,000: calendar year 1996– Jan. 1, 1998

$20,000: calendar year 1997– Jan. 1, 1999

Figure 3–12 *Form 941, Employer's Quarterly Federal Tax Return*

Form **941**

Department of the Treasury
Internal Revenue Service

4141

Employer's Quarterly Federal Tax Return

▶ See separate instructions for information on completing this return.

Please type or print.

OMB No. 1545-0029

Enter state code for state in which deposits made . ▶ ☐ (see page 2 of instructions).

Name (as distinguished from trade name)

Trade name, if any
LOPEZ ENTERPRISES, INC.

Address (number and street)
25 PARK LANE

Date quarter ended
MAR 31, 1996

Employer identification number
89-1437003

City, state, and ZIP code
COLUMBUS, GA
31902-2582

T	
FF	
FD	
FP	
I	
T	

If address is different from prior return, check here ▶ ☐

IRS Use

1 1 1 1 1 1 1 1 1 1   2   3 3 3 3 3   4 4 4

5 5 5   6   7   8 8 8 8 8   9 9 9   10 10 10 10 10 10 10 10 10 10

If you do not have to file returns in the future, check here ▶ ☐ and enter date final wages paid ▶

If you are a seasonal employer, see **Seasonal employers** on page 2 and check here (see instructions) ▶ ☐

1	Number of employees (except household) employed in the pay period that includes March 12th ▶		24	
2	Total wages and tips subject to withholding, plus other compensation	2	74895	92
3	Total income tax withheld from wages, tips, and sick pay	3	12372	13
4	Adjustment of withheld income tax for preceding quarters of calendar year	4	-0-	
5	Adjusted total of income tax withheld (line 3 as adjusted by line 4—see instructions)	5	12372	13
6a	Taxable social security wages . . . . \$ 74895 | 92 × 12.4% (.124) =	6a	9287	09
b	Taxable social security tips . . . . \$ -0- × 12.4% (.124) =	6b	-0-	
7	Taxable Medicare wages and tips . . . . . . \$ 74895 | 92 × 2.9% (.029) =	7	2171	98
8	Total social security and Medicare taxes (add lines 6a, 6b, and 7). Check here if wages are not subject to social security and/or Medicare tax . . . . ▶ ☐	8	11459	07
9	Adjustment of social security and Medicare taxes (see instructions for required explanation) Sick Pay \$ _____ ± Fractions of Cents \$ .41 ± Other \$ _____ =	9		41
10	Adjusted total of social security and Medicare taxes (line 8 as adjusted by line 9—see instructions)	10	11459	48
11	**Total taxes** (add lines 5 and 10)	11	23831	61
12	Advance earned income credit (EIC) payments made to employees, if any	12	-0-	
13	Net taxes (subtract line 12 from line 11). **This should equal line 17, column (d) below** (or line D of Schedule B (Form 941))	13	23831	61
14	Total deposits for quarter, including overpayment applied from a prior quarter	14	23831	61
15	**Balance due** (subtract line 14 from line 13). Pay to Internal Revenue Service	15	-0-	
16	**Overpayment,** if line 14 is more than line 13, enter excess here ▶ \$ _____ and check if to be: ☐ Applied to next return OR ☐ Refunded.			

• **All filers:** If line 13 is less than \$500, you need not complete line 17 or Schedule B.

• **Semiweekly depositors:** Complete Schedule B and check here . . . . ▶ ☒

• **Monthly depositors:** Complete line 17, columns (a) through (d) and check here . . . . ▶ ☐

17	Monthly Summary of Federal Tax Liability.			
	(a) First month liability	(b) Second month liability	(c) Third month liability	(d) Total liability for quarter

Sign Here

Under penalties of perjury, I declare that I have examined this return, including accompanying schedules and statements, and to the best of my knowledge and belief, it is true, correct, and complete.

Signature ▶ *David S. Lopez*

Print Your Name and Title ▶ David S. Lopez   President

Date ▶ 4/30/96

For Paperwork Reduction Act Notice, see page 1 of separate instructions.   Cat. No. 17001Z   Form **941**

Figure 3–13 *Employer's Record of Federal Tax Liability*

SCHEDULE B (FORM 941) (Rev. January 1994) Department of the Treasury Internal Revenue Service 5151	**Employer's Record of Federal Tax Liability** ▶ See Circular E for more information about employment tax returns. ▶ Attach to Form 941 or Form 941-SS.	OMB No. 1545-0029 Expires 1-31-96

Name as shown on Form 941 (Form 941-SS) *Lopez Enterprises*	Employer identification number 89-1437003	Date quarter ended 3/31/96

You must complete this schedule if you are required to deposit on a semiweekly basis, or if your tax liability on any day is $100,000 or more. Show tax liability here, not deposits. (The IRS gets deposit data from FTD coupons.)

A. Daily Tax Liability—First Month of Quarter

1		8		15		22		29	
2		9		16		23		30	
3		10		17		24		31	
4		11		18		25			
5		12	4019 12	19		26	3819 35		
6		13		20		27			
7		14		21		28			

A Total tax liability for first month of quarter . . . . ▶ | **A** | 7838 47

B. Daily Tax Liability—Second Month of Quarter

1		8		15		22		29	
2		9	4026 82	16		23	3913 96	30	
3		10		17		24		31	
4		11		18		25			
5		12		19		26			
6		13		20		27			
7		14		21		28			

B Total tax liability for second month of quarter . . . . ▶ | **B** | 7940 78

C. Daily Tax Liability—Third Month of Quarter

1		8	4107 19	15		22	3945 17	29	
2		9		16		23		30	
3		10		17		24		31	
4		11		18		25			
5		12		19		26			
6		13		20		27			
7		14		21		28			

C Total tax liability for third month of quarter . . . . ▶ | **C** | 8052 36

D Total for quarter (add lines **A**, **B**, and **C**). This should equal line 13 of Form 941 . . . . . ▶ | **D** | 23831 61

For Paperwork Reduction Act Notice, see page 2.   Cat. No. 11967Q   Schedule B (Form 941) (Rev. 1-94)

1. An *individual*, the return should be signed by that person.
2. A *corporation*, the return should be signed by its president, vice-president, or other principal officer authorized to sign the return. Corporate officers or duly authorized agents may use facsimile signatures under certain conditions. Each group of returns must be accompanied by a letter signed by the person authorized to sign the returns declaring that (a) the facsimile signature appearing on the returns is the signature adopted by him/her, and (b) the signature was affixed to the returns by the officer or agent or at his/her direction.
3. A *partnership* or *other unincorporated organization*, a responsible and duly authorized partner or officer having knowledge of the firms affairs should sign the return.
4. A *trust* or *estate*, the return should be signed by the fiduciary of the trust or estate.
5. A *political body*, such as a state or territory, the return should be signed by the officer or employee having control of the wage payments or officer properly designated for that purpose.

Paying the FICA Taxes

Employers may pay FICA taxes directly to the IRS by check or money order, which should be made payable to the "Internal Revenue Service." Cash payments made in person are permissible, but employers should not send cash through the mail.

Privately Printed Forms

Under certain conditions, Form 941 may be privately printed. The forms must be exact facsimile reproductions of the officially printed Form 941 and meet other requirements contained in the Revenue Procedures, available from the IRS. In addition to providing specifications for substitute forms, the IRS provides reproduction proofs of its own forms at a prescribed per-page charge.

Filing Form 941

The law requires employers to file Form 941 on or before the last day of the month following the close of the calendar quarter for which the return applies. If an employer makes timely tax deposits for the quarter, the employer may file Form 941 on or before the 10th day of the second month following the close of the calendar quarter. If an employer has not made any deposits during the quarter, the ten-day extension for filing the form is still available if the employer makes a deposit of any taxes due on or before the last day of the first calendar month following the close of the quarter. In other words, the ten-day extension only applies to Form 941 but not to any deposits due with Form 941.

E X A M P L E

1. An employer files a return by April 30 for the calendar quarter ending March 31.
2. An employer makes timely deposits for the quarter ending March 31. The form can be filed on or before May 10.
3. The Pruit Company was not required to make any deposits for FICA taxes during the quarter ending March 31. The company makes its deposit for the first quarter taxes on April 25 for taxes due. Pruit can still file Form 941 on or before May 10 for the first quarter return.

Figure 3–14   *Sources of Information for Completing Form 941*

Line Number	Source of Information
1	Payroll register.
2	General ledger accounts for wages and salaries; Forms 4070, or employees' written statements reporting cash tips.
3	General ledger accounts.
4	Forms 941 previously filed and general ledger accounts—to determine amount of errors made in income tax withheld from wages paid in earlier quarters of the calendar year.
5	Add lines 4 and 3 if additional income tax withheld is being reported; subtract line 4 from line 3 if the amount of income tax withheld is being reduced.
6a	Payroll register; include any social security taxes (OASDI) paid for employees, sick pay, and taxable fringe benefits subject to OASDI. Do not include any tips. Do not report any employees' wages that exceed $63,000, the taxable wage base for 1996.
6b	Forms 4070, or employees' written statements to report cash tips. Enter all tips reported until tips and wages for each employee reach $63,000. Report this information even if you are unable to withhold the employee OASDI tax. Do not include allocated tips, which should be reported on Form 8027.
7	Payroll register; Forms 4070, or employees' written statements to report cash tips. Report amounts paid to certain federal, state, and local government employees who are subject only to the HI portion of the FICA tax.
8	Add lines 6a, 6b, and 7.
9	Forms 941 previously filed. Correct errors in social security taxes reported on earlier return or correct errors in credits for overpayments of penalty or interest paid on tax for an earlier quarter. If you report both an underpayment and an overpayment, show only the difference. Use Form 941c to explain any amount on line 9, other than adjustments for fractions of cents or third-party sick pay. Or, you may attach a statement that shows the nature of error(s) being corrected. Use form W-2c, Statement of Corrected Income and Tax Amounts, to adjust an employee's social security, wages, tips, or tax withheld for a prior year. Also, complete Form W-3c, Transmittal of Corrected Income and Tax Statements. To adjust for the tax on tips: Include the total uncollected employee social security tax for lines 6b and 7. To adjust for the tax on third-party sick pay: Deduct the social security tax on third-party sick pay for which you are not responsible. Enter the amount of the adjustment in the space for "Sick Pay." To adjust for fractions of cents: If there is a difference between the total tax on line 8 and the total deducted from your employees' wages or tips plus the employer's tax on those wages or tips (general ledger accounts) because of fractions of cents added or dropped in collecting the tax, report the difference. Enter this difference in the space for "Fractions of Cents."
10	Add line 9 to line 8 if you are reporting additional taxes for an earlier quarter. Subtract line 9 from line 8 if you are deducting the amount of taxes reported for an earlier quarter or claiming credit for overpayments of penalty or interest paid on tax for an earlier quarter.
11	Record total taxes by adding lines 5 and 10.
12	If applicable, show the amount of any advance earned income credit (EIC) payments made (discussed in Chapter 4). The amount of the advance EIC payments does not change the amount deducted and withheld from employees' pay for income tax and employee FICA taxes. Advance EIC payments that you make are treated as made from the amounts withheld as income tax and employee FICA taxes and your FICA tax contributions.
13	Determine net taxes by subtracting line 12 from line 11.
14	General ledger accounts, previous Form 941; record the total deposits for the quarter, including any overpayment applied from previous quarter.
15	Compute balance due by subtracting line 14 from line 13. Pay the balance due IRS.
16	Compute overpayment by subtracting line 13 from line 14 and indicate if amount is to be applied to the next return or refunded.
17	General ledger accounts; to be completed only by monthly depositors.

If the last day for filing a quarterly return falls on Saturday, Sunday, or a legal holiday, the employer may file the return on the next business day. If the return is filed by mailing, the employer should mail the return in sufficient time for it to reach the IRS Center no later than the next business day under ordinary handling of the mail.

Individual employers file quarterly returns with the IRS Center of the region in which the employer's principal place of business or office or agency is located. The return may still be filed at the local office of the district director of the IRS if the taxpayer hand delivers the return.

Reporting FICA Information on Magnetic Media

The IRS permits reporting agents for groups of employers to furnish the information required for Form 941 on magnetic tape instead of paper documents. Agents who wish to file returns in this manner must first file a letter of application or submit Form 8655, Reporting Agent Authorization. Also, at the option of the employer, the IRS may permit the use of a composite employment tax return in lieu of Form 941. A single form, together with magnetic tapes or other approved media, is used for the returns of more than one employer. Some states that require employers to file detailed quarterly wage reports authorize the combined reporting on magnetic tape of social security and state unemployment compensation data. By means of the combined tape format, employers forward one tape or diskette to the SSA and a copy to the appropriate participating state unemployment agency.

WHAT ARE THE PENALTIES? (FAILURE TO COMPLY)

Employers act as collection agents for the government by collecting employment taxes and paying them to the appropriate government agency. Employers who fail to carry out their duties as collection agents are subject to civil and criminal penalties. The penalties may be additions to the tax, interest, and fines and imprisonment. Penalties are imposed on employers who fail to do the following:

1. File employment tax returns.
2. Pay over employment taxes when due.
3. Make timely deposits.
4. Furnish wage and tax statements.
5. File or provide information returns.
6. Supply identification numbers.

The penalty depends on the degree of willfulness present in the employer's conduct. Persons other than the employer who have the duty or responsibility for collecting, accounting for, and paying over any taxes may also be assessed penalties. Passing bad checks in payment of any employment tax also carries a penalty.

Failure to File Employment Tax Returns

If an employer fails to file an employment tax return on the date prescribed for filing, a certain percentage of the amount of tax required to be reported will be added to the tax. Employers may avoid this addition if they show to the satisfaction of the IRS that failure to file was due to reasonable cause and not willful conduct.

Additions to the Tax	5% of the net amount of tax that should have been reported; an additional 5% for each additional month or fraction of a month during which failure continues, not to exceed 25%.
	15% per month, not to exceed 75% for fraudulent failure to file.
Criminal Penalties	Not more than $25,000 ($100,000 for corporations), imprisonment of not more than 1 year, or both.
	Not more than $100,000, imprisonment of not more than 3 years, or both for willfully signing a return not true and correct as to every material statement.

Source: Bradford McKee, "Shifting the Burdens of Payroll Paperwork," *Nation's Business*, January 1993: 9.

E X A M P L E

Ned Fromton, an employer, files his employment tax return 20 days after the due date of the return. The amount of tax that should have been reported is $6,000. Fromton's penalty is:

Failure to file (5% × $6,000) = $300   Note—any fraction of a month counts as a whole month.

Failure to Pay Over Employment Taxes

Employers who fail to pay over the required amount of employment taxes when due are faced with the following civil and criminal penalties.

Additions to the Tax	½ % of the net amount due if the failure to pay lasts no longer than one month; ½% for each additional month the failure continues, not to exceed 25%. In addition, any taxes due will bear interest at the rate of 10% per year. Large corporate underpayments ($100,000) will carry the rate of 12%.[1]
	20% of the underpayment for negligence (*failure to make a reasonable attempt to comply*) or intentional disregard (*careless, reckless, or intentional disregard of the law*) of the payment rules.
	75% of the underpayment if underpayment is due to fraud with the intent to evade the tax.
The 100% Penalty	100% of the tax due for willfully failing to collect, account for, or pay over employment taxes or willfully attempting to evade or defeat the taxes.
Tax Levies	Levy on and seize any property and property rights held by the employer at the time of levy for failure of the employer to pay any taxes, 10 days after notice and demand for payment.
Criminal Penalties	Not more than $10,000, imprisonment of not more than 5 years, or both, for willful failure to pay the tax. These penalties are in addition to the 75% fraud penalty.

IRS CONNECTION

The IRS has estimated that 30% of all employers incur penalties for insufficient or late deposits of payroll taxes.

[1]The IRS sets the interest rate each calendar quarter, based on the short-term Treasury bill rate for the first month in each calendar quarter, plus 3 percentage points, and applies it for the following calendar quarter.

E X A M P L E

The Yeld Company failed to pay their employment taxes of $5,000 for March (due May 1) until May 20. The failure to pay penalty assessed against the Yeld Company is:

Failure to Pay Tax ($5,000 × ½%)	=	$25.00
Interest on Taxes Due ($5,000 × .10 × 19/365)	=	<u>26.03</u>
Total Penalty		$51.03

Note—In addition, a penalty for failure to make a timely deposit will also be assessed. If it was determined that Yeld's failure was due to negligence, the penalty would be:

Negligence Penalty ($5,000 × 20%)	=	$1,000

Failure to Make Timely Deposits

Penalties may apply if employers do not make required deposits on time in an authorized government depository.

Deposits made 1 to 5 days late	2% of the undeposited taxes
Deposits made 6 to 15 days late	5% of the undeposited taxes
Deposits made 16 or more days late	10% of the undeposited taxes
Deposits made at unauthorized financial institutions or directly to IRS	10% of the undeposited taxes
Amounts unpaid more than 10 days after IRS notice	15% of the undeposited taxes

E X A M P L E

1. *Greerson Inc. must make a deposit of $1,800 on June 15. The deposit was made 12 days late. The penalty assessed against Greerson is:*

   Failure to make timely deposit ($1,800 × 5%) = $90

2. *Holt Enterprises fails to make a required deposit of $1,500 on November 15. On December 15, the company incurs an additional liability of $2,000. The company makes a deposit on December 15 of $2,200, assuming that the December deposit is paid in full and that $200 will be applied to the late November deposit.*

   However, since deposits are applied first to past due underdeposits in order of due date, the December deposit will be applied as follows:
   $1,500 to the November liability
   $700 to the December liability
   The company will be penalized on both underdeposits based on the number of late days.

Failure to Furnish Wage and Tax Statements

If employers willfully fail to furnish their employees with properly executed wage and tax statements, or willfully furnish false or fraudulent statements, the civil penalty is $50 for each statement.

Maximum Penalty	$100,000 in any calendar year.
Intentional Disregard	$100 per statement or, if greater, 10% of the amount required to be shown on the statement. No limit on the maximum penalty for the calendar year.
Criminal Penalties	$1,000 fine, imprisonment for not more than one year, or both, for each offense.

Failure to Furnish Information Returns

Employers who fail to timely file their information returns are subject to $50 for each failure.

Maximum Penalty	$250,000 in any calendar year.
Correction within 30 days	$15 per failure, maximum fine $75,000.
Correction after 30 days, before August 1st	$30 per failure, maximum fine $150,000.
Intentional Disregard	$100 per statement, or, if greater, 10% of the amount to be shown on the statement. No limit on the maximum penalty for the calendar year.

Failure to Supply Identification Numbers

Failure to include ID number on tax return	$5 per failure.
Failure to provide ID to another person, as required	$50 per failure, maximum fine $100,000.
Failure to provide another's ID, as required	$50 per failure, maximum fine $100,000.

Bad Checks

Checks or money orders not tendered in good faith	2% of the amount. If the check is less than $750, penalty is $15 or the amount of the check, whichever is less.

KEY TERMS

Common-law relationship
Educational assistance
Employee
Employer
Employment
Immediate credit item
Independent contractor
Lookback period

Monthly depositor
Person
Safe harbor rule
Self-employment income
Semiweekly depositor
Shortfall
Sick pay
Taxable wage base

QUESTIONS FOR REVIEW

1. For social security purposes, what conditions must an individual meet to be classified as a "covered" employee?
2. Under what conditions does a common-law relationship exist between an employee and an employer?
3. Summarize the test conditions under which a worker is classified as an independent contractor.
4. For social security purposes, what conditions must an individual meet to be classified as a "covered" employer?
5. What are an employer's responsibilities for FICA taxes on:

   a. Tips reported by employees?
   b. Wages paid tipped employees?

6. Explain how the value of meals and lodging furnished by the employer may or may not represent taxable wages under FICA.
7. What conditions exclude sick pay from the definition of wages for FICA tax purposes?
8. John Luis receives wages from 3 employers during 1996. Is he entitled to a refund on the OASDI taxes paid on wages in excess of limit? If so, how can he receive a refund?
9. What are the Self-Employment tax rates for 1996? Explain how the tax is computed.
10. How does an employer file an application for an employer identification number?
11. Summarize the deposit rules for nonagricultural employees.
12. What is the purpose of Form 8109?
13. Explain how the timeliness of a deposit of employment taxes is determined.
14. How often must an employer file Form 941?
15. What are the penalties imposed on the employer for the following:

    a. Form 941 not filed by the due date.
    b. Seven days late making a deposit.
    c. Gives the IRS a bad check.

QUESTIONS FOR DISCUSSION

1. In order to improve the cash flow of the company, Ned Nash decided to postpone depositing all employment taxes a few months ago. He told his sales manager, "I'll pay up before the IRS catches up with me." What risks does Nash face by not upholding his responsibility for the collection and payment of employment taxes?
2. On Wednesday, June 15, Lapoint Company had employment taxes of $25,000 that were required to be deposited on or before Wednesday, June 22. The deposit was mailed and postmarked Wednesday, June 22, and delivered on Thursday, June 23. What deposit rules is Lapoint following? Was the deposit made in a timely manner?

3. During a recent strike at the Ultima Hotel, union members were paid strike benefits by their union. Don Volmer, a union representative, participates in negotiations with the hotel.

    a. Are the strike benefits paid to union members taxable under FICA?

    b. Are the payments Volmer receives for his services as a union negotiator subject to FICA taxes?

4. When employees of the County Bank are summoned to serve on jury duty, the firm pays its workers the difference between their regular wages and the amount received for jury duty. One such employee has been receiving $365 per week. She just completed a five-day week of jury duty, for which she was paid $65 ($9 per day plus 20 cents per mile from her house to the courthouse, a 20-mile trip). How much of the employee's earnings are subject to FICA tax?

PRACTICAL PROBLEMS

3–1. LO 4.

The biweekly taxable wages for the employees of Stork Foods follow. Compute the FICA taxes for each employee and the employer's FICA taxes.

Employee No.	Employee Name	Biweekly Taxable Wages	FICA Taxes OASDI	FICA Taxes HI
711	Burke, Mark	$479.68	$ _____	$ _____
512	Celeo, Mary	495.00	_____	_____
624	Filmore, Juanita	385.25	_____	_____
325	Harrison, Bob	397.25	_____	_____
422	Lang, Will	785.00	_____	_____
210	Pagat, Mel	775.50	_____	_____
111	Troy, Sheila	495.25		
		Totals	$ _____	$ _____

Employer's OASDI $ _____ $ _____
          Total Taxable   Employer's OASDI
          Wages   Tax

Employer's HI Tax $ _____ $ _____
          Total Taxable   Employer's HI
          Wages   Tax

3–2. LO 4.

During 1996, Sharon Gilmore, president of the Perkins Company, was paid a semimonthly salary of $6,800. Compute the amount of FICA taxes that should be withheld from her:

		OASDI	HI
a.	9th paycheck	$ _____	$ _____
b.	10th paycheck	$ _____	$ _____
c.	24th paycheck	$ _____	$ _____

3–3. LO 4, 5.

Artis Norton began working as a part-time waiter on June 1, 1996, at Sporthouse Restaurant. The cash tips of $160 that he received during June were reported on Form 4070, which he submitted to his employer on July 1. During July, he was paid wages of $525 by the restaurant. Compute:

		OASDI	HI
a.	The amount of FICA taxes that the employer should withhold from Norton's wages during July.	$ _____	$ _____
b.	The amount of the employer's FICA taxes on Norton's wages and tips during July.	$ _____	$ _____

3–4. LO 4, 5.

The annual salary paid each of the officers of Groton, Inc., follows. The officers are paid semimonthly on the 15th and the last day of the month. Compute the FICA taxes to be withheld from each officer's pay on (a) July 31 and (b) December 31.

July 31

Name and Title	Annual Salary	OASDI Taxable Earnings	OASDI Tax	HI Taxable Earnings	HI Tax
Learner, Jake, President	$110,400				
Oldman, Clara, VP Finance	75,000				
Burke, Sarah, VP Sales	64,800				
Aneson, Max, VP Manufact.	54,000				
White, Beth, VP Personnel	51,600				
Jackson, Bart, VP Secretary	49,200				

December 31

Name and Title	Annual Salary	OASDI Taxable Earnings	OASDI Tax	HI Taxable Earnings	HI Tax
Learner, Jake, President	$110,400				
Oldman, Clara, VP Finance	75,000				
Burke, Sarah, VP Sales	64,800				
Aneson, Max, VP Manufact.	54,000				
White, Beth, VP Personnel	51,600				
Jackson, Bart, VP Secretary	49,200				

3–5. LO 4, 5.

Audrey Martin and Beth James are partners in the Country Gift Shop, which employs the individuals listed below. Paychecks are distributed every Friday to all employees. Based on the information given, compute the amounts listed below.

Name and Position	Salary	OASDI Taxable Earnings	OASDI Tax	HI Taxable Earnings	HI Tax
Zena Vertin, Office	$ 335 per week				
Nicole Norge, Sales	1,980 per month				
Bob Mert, Delivery	285 per week				
Audrey Martin, Partner	650 per week				
Beth James, Partner	650 per week				
Totals		$	$	$	$

Employer's OASDI Tax $ _____
Employer's HI Tax $ _____

3–6. LO 6.

Hugh Crandal was paid a salary of $39,800 during 1996 by the Pope Company. In addition, during the year Crandal started his own business as a public accountant and reported a net business income of $28,000 on his income tax return for 1996. Compute the following:

a. The amount of FICA taxes that was withheld from his earnings during 1966 by the Pope Company.

OASDI $ _____

HI $ _____

b. Crandal's self-employment taxes on the income derived from the public accounting business for 1996.

$ _____

3–7. LO 4.

The Tyler Spa Company pays its salaried employees monthly on the last day of each month. The annual salary payroll for 1996 follows. Compute the following for the payroll of December 31.

Employee	Annual Salary	OASDI Taxable Wages	OASDI Tax	HI Tax
Darton, Carla	$22,150			
Drake, Neville	18,900			
Ferrins, Margaret	24,000			
Guild, Ben	68,040			
Hart, Nora	20,900			
Kyle, Jacob	19,500			
Lorenzo, Maria	18,540			
Quinn, Susan	56,900			
Roper, Hugh	17,850			
Washington, Ted	51,200			
Totals		$	$	$

Employer's OASDI Tax _____   Employer's HI Tax _____

3–8. LO 4.

The weekly and hourly wage schedule for the employees of Quirk, Inc. follows. All employees work a full 40-hour week. Compute the following:

a. OASDI and HI taxable wages for each employee for a full week in February, 1996.
b. FICA taxes to be withheld from each employee's wages.
c. Net Wages for each employee.
d. Totals for each column on the form.
e. The employer's FICA taxes.

Employee	Wage		OASDI Taxable Wages	HI Taxable Wages	OASDI Tax	HI Tax	Net Wages
Amy Burnhart	$290.00	Weekly	$	$	$	$	$
Greg Clooney	385.00	Weekly					
Bart Eaton	435.00	Weekly					
Jan Gilmore	550.00	Weekly					
Derek Krest	5.70	Per Hour					
Jim Pratt	5.85	Per Hour					
Paul Stalk	6.25	Per Hour					
Vi Ulk	7.10	Per Hour					
Totals			$	$	$	$	$

Employer's FICA Taxes $ _____ $ _____
                                OASDI   HI

3–9. **LO 4.**

The monthly and hourly wage schedule for the employees of Quirk, Inc. follows. All employees work a full 40-hour week. Compute the following:

a. The total wages of each part-time employee for December 1996.
b. The OASDI and HI taxable wages for each employee.
c. The FICA taxes withheld from each employee's wages for December.
d. Totals of columns.
e. The employer's FICA taxes for the month.

Employees	Total Monthly Payroll	OASDI Taxable Wages	HI Taxable Wages	OASDI Tax	HI Tax
Full-Time Office					
Adaiar, Gene	$1,400.00				
Crup, Jason	1,300.00				
Essex, Joan	1,975.00				
Garza, Irma	1,985.00				
Leason, Mel	1,900.00				
Pruit, Marne	5,600.00				
Rubble, Deanne	2,400.00				
Simpson, Dick	3,985.00				
Truap, Ann	5,000.00				
Wilson, Trudy	1,500.00				

	Hours Worked	Hourly Rate	Total Part-Time Wages				
Part-Time Office							
Kyle, Judy	170	$5.05					
Laird, Sharon	170	4.85					
Maxwell, Sara	140	6.10					
Nelson, Donna	145	5.00					
Scott, Kim	162	5.65					
Totals							

Employer's FICA taxes OASDI $_____ HI $_____

3–10. **LO 8.**

Stan Barker opened Quik-Stop Market on January 2, 1996. The business is subject to FICA taxes. At the end of the first quarter of 1996, Barker must file Form 941, Employer's Quarterly Federal Tax Return. Using Form 941, reproduced on the next page, prepare the return on the basis of the information shown below.

Employer's address: **234 Oak, Seattle, WA 98006**
Employer's ID number: **61-1325874**

Each employee is paid semimonthly on the 15th and last day of each month. Shown below is the payroll information for each of the six pay periods in the first quarter of 1996. All pay periods were the same.

PAYROLL INFORMATION FOR EACH OF THE 6 PAY PERIODS FROM JANUARY–MARCH

Employee	SSN	Semimonthly Wage	OASDI Tax	HI Tax	Federal Income Tax	Total Deductions	Net Pay
Albert Greer	384-10-7233	$ 580	$ 35.96	$ 8.41	$ 44	$ 88.37	$ 491.63
Patty Dilts	345-90-8451	585	36.27	8.48	88	132.75	452.25
Jerod Hughs	528-09-3668	1,290	79.98	18.71	202	300.69	989.31
Denise Eaton	766-43-6527	650	40.30	9.43	92	141.73	508.27
Totals		$3,105	$192.51	$45.03	$426	$663.54	$2,441.46

Employer's FICA taxes $192.51 $45.02
                          OASDI   HI

None of the employees reported tips during the quarter. No advance earned income credit (EIC) payments were made to the workers.

Note: Lines 6a and 7 of Form 941, total taxable wages, are computed by multiplying by the combined tax rate for both employer and employee. Small differences due to rounding may occur between this total and the total taxes withheld from employees each pay period and the amount of the employer's taxes calculated each pay period. This difference is reported on line 9 as deduction or addition as "Fractions of Cents."

3–10.

Form 941

Employer's Quarterly Federal Tax Return

4141

Department of the Treasury
Internal Revenue Service

▶ See separate instructions for Information on completing this return.

Please type or print.

OMB No. 1545-0029

Enter state code for state in which deposits made . ▶ ⬚⋮⬚ (see page 2 of instructions).

Name (as distinguished from trade name)	Date quarter ended
Trade name, if any	Employer identification number
Address (number and street)	City, state, and ZIP code

T	
FF	
FD	
FP	
I	
T	

If address is different from prior return, check here ▶ ⬚

IRS Use

| 1 1 1 1 1 1 1 1 1 1 | 2 | 3 3 3 3 3 3 | 4 4 4 |
| 5 5 5 | 6 | 7 | 8 8 8 8 8 | 9 9 9 | 10 10 10 10 10 10 10 10 10 |

If you do not have to file returns in the future, check here ▶ ⬚ and enter date final wages paid ▶

If you are a seasonal employer, see **Seasonal employers** on page 2 and check here (see instructions) ▶ ⬚

1 Number of employees (except household) employed in the pay period that includes March 12th ▶

2 Total wages and tips subject to withholding, plus other compensation	2	
3 Total income tax withheld from wages, tips, and sick pay	3	
4 Adjustment of withheld income tax for preceding quarters of calendar year	4	
5 Adjusted total of income tax withheld (line 3 as adjusted by line 4—see instructions)	5	
6a Taxable social security wages . . . $_____ × 12.4% (.124) =	6a	
b Taxable social security tips . . . $_____ × 12.4% (.124) =	6b	
7 Taxable Medicare wages and tips . . . $_____ × 2.9% (.029) =	7	
8 Total social security and Medicare taxes (add lines 6a, 6b, and 7). Check here if wages are not subject to social security and/or Medicare tax . . . . ▶ ⬚	8	
9 Adjustment of social security and Medicare taxes (see instructions for required explanation) Sick Pay $_____ ± Fractions of Cents $_____ ± Other $_____ =	9	
10 Adjusted total of social security and Medicare taxes (line 8 as adjusted by line 9—see instructions) .	10	
11 **Total taxes** (add lines 5 and 10) .	11	
12 Advance earned income credit (EIC) payments made to employees, if any	12	
13 Net taxes (subtract line 12 from line 11). **This should equal line 17, column (d) below** (or line D of Schedule B (Form 941)) .	13	
14 Total deposits for quarter, including overpayment applied from a prior quarter .	14	
15 **Balance due** (subtract line 14 from line 13). Pay to Internal Revenue Service .	15	

16 Overpayment, if line 14 is more than line 13, enter excess here ▶ $_____
and check if to be: ⬚ Applied to next return **OR** ⬚ Refunded.

- **All filers:** If line 13 is less than $500, you need not complete line 17 or Schedule B.
- **Semiweekly depositors:** Complete Schedule B and check here . . . . ▶ ⬚
- **Monthly depositors:** Complete line 17, columns (a) through (d) and check here . . . . . ▶ ⬚

17	Monthly Summary of Federal Tax Liability.		
(a) First month liability	(b) Second month liability	(c) Third month liability	(d) Total liability for quarter

Sign Here

Under penalties of perjury, I declare that I have examined this return, including accompanying schedules and statements, and to the best of my knowledge and belief, it is true, correct, and complete.

Signature ▶   Print Your Name and Title ▶   Date ▶

Form **941**

3–42

3–11. **LO 8.**

During the fourth calendar quarter of 1996, the Bayview Inn employed the persons listed below. Also given are the employee's salaries or wages and the amount of tips reported to the owner. The tips were reported by the 10th of each month. The Federal Income Tax and FICA tax to be withheld from the tips were estimated by the owner and withheld equally over the 13 weekly pay periods. The employer's portion of FICA tax on the tips was estimated as the same amount.

Employee	Salary or Wage	Tips Reported
Grant Frazier	$25,000/year	
Joseph LaVanga	18,000/year	
Susanne Ayers	250/week	$2,240.90
Howard Cohen	225/week	2,493.10
Lee Soong	250/week	2,640.30
Mary Yee	250/week	2,704.00
Helen Woods	325/week	
Koo Shin	325/week	
Aaron Abalis	400/week	
David Harad	170/week	

Employees are paid weekly on Friday. The following paydays occurred during this quarter:

October	November	December
4 weekly paydays	4 weekly paydays	5 weekly paydays

Taxes withheld for the 13 paydays in the fourth quarter follow:

Federal Income Tax	Employer's and Employees' FICA taxes on Tips
$5,720	$118.61 + $118.61 per week

Based on the information given, complete Form 941 on the following page.

3–11.

Form 941

Department of the Treasury
Internal Revenue Service

4141

Employer's Quarterly Federal Tax Return

▶ See separate instructions for information on completing this return.

Please type or print.

OMB No. 1545-0029

Enter state code for state in which deposits made . ▶ ☐☐ (see page 2 of instructions).

Name (as distinguished from trade name)

Date quarter ended
DEC 31, 1996

| T | |
| FF | |

Trade name, if any
BAYVIEW INN

Employer identification number
65-4263607

| FD | |
| FP | |

Address (number and street)
404 UNION AVE.

City, state, and ZIP code
MEMPHIS, TN
38112-1404

| I | |
| T | |

If address is different from prior return, check here ▶ ☐

IRS Use

1 1 1 1 1 1 1 1 1 1 2 3 3 3 3 3 3 4 4 4

5 5 5 6 7 8 8 8 8 8 9 9 10 10 10 10 10 10 10 10 10

If you do not have to file returns in the future, check here ▶ ☐ and enter date final wages paid ▶

If you are a seasonal employer, see **Seasonal employers** on page 2 and check here (see instructions) ▶ ☐

1	Number of employees (except household) employed in the pay period that includes March 12th ▶	
2	Total wages and tips subject to withholding, plus other compensation	**2**
3	Total income tax withheld from wages, tips, and sick pay	**3**
4	Adjustment of withheld income tax for preceding quarters of calendar year	**4**
5	Adjusted total of income tax withheld (line 3 as adjusted by line 4—see instructions) . . .	**5**
6a	Taxable social security wages . . . . $ _____ × 12.4% (.124) =	**6a**
b	Taxable social security tips . . . . $ _____ × 12.4% (.124) =	**6b**
7	Taxable Medicare wages and tips . . . . . $ _____ × 2.9% (.029) =	**7**
8	Total social security and Medicare taxes (add lines 6a, 6b, and 7). Check here if wages are not subject to social security and/or Medicare tax . . . . ▶ ☐	**8**
9	Adjustment of social security and Medicare taxes (see instructions for required explanation) Sick Pay $ _____ ± Fractions of Cents $ _____ ± Other $ _____ =	**9**
10	Adjusted total of social security and Medicare taxes (line 8 as adjusted by line 9—see instructions)	**10**
11	**Total taxes** (add lines 5 and 10)	**11**
12	Advance earned income credit (EIC) payments made to employees, if any	**12**
13	Net taxes (subtract line 12 from line 11). **This should equal line 17, column (d) below** (or line D of Schedule B (Form 941))	**13**
14	Total deposits for quarter, including overpayment applied from a prior quarter	**14**
15	Balance due (subtract line 14 from line 13). Pay to Internal Revenue Service	**15**

16 Overpayment, if line 14 is more than line 13, enter excess here ▶ $ _____
and check if to be: ☐ Applied to next return **OR** ☐ Refunded.

- **All filers:** If line 13 is less than $500, you need not complete line 17 or Schedule B.
- **Semiweekly depositors:** Complete Schedule B and check here . . . . ▶ ☐
- **Monthly depositors:** Complete line 17, columns (a) through (d) and check here . . . . ▶ ☐

17	**Monthly Summary of Federal Tax Liability.**			
	(a) First month liability	(b) Second month liability	(c) Third month liability	(d) Total liability for quarter

Sign Here

Under penalties of perjury, I declare that I have examined this return, including accompanying schedules and statements, and to the best of my knowledge and belief, it is true, correct, and complete.

Signature ▶

Print Your Name and Title ▶

Date ▶

Form **941**

3–12. LO 8, 9.

The taxable wages and withheld taxes for the Stafford Company (EIN 25-7901462), semiweekly depositor, for the first quarter of 1996 follow.

Semimonthly Paydays	Gross and Taxable Wages	FICA With-held OASDI	FICA With-held HI	Federal Income Tax Withheld
1/15	$ 24,500	$1,519.00	$ 355.25	$ 3,185.00
1/31	23,985	1,487.07	347.78	3,090.00
2/15	25,190	1,561.78	365.26	3,410.00
2/29	25,530	1,582.86	370.19	3,497.00
3/15	24,950	1,546.90	361.78	3,385.00
3/29	25,100	1,556.20	363.95	3,400.00
	$149,255	$9,253.81	$2,164.21	$19,967.00

a. Complete Schedule B of Form 941 on page 46 for the first quarter for the Stafford Company.
b. List the due dates of each deposit in the first quarter.

Paydays	Deposit Due Dates
January 15	_____
January 31	_____
February 15	_____
February 29	_____
March 15	_____
March 29	_____

3–12.

<table>
<tr><td colspan="2">SCHEDULE B
(FORM 941)
(Rev. January 1994)
Department of the Treasury
Internal Revenue Service</td><td colspan="3">Employer's Record of Federal Tax Liability
▶ See Circular E for more information about employment tax returns.

▶ Attach to Form 941 or Form 941-SS.</td><td>OMB No. 1545-0029
Expires 1-31-96</td></tr>
</table>

5151

Name as shown on Form 941 (Form 941-SS)	Employer identification number	Date quarter ended

You must complete this schedule if you are required to deposit on a semiweekly basis, or if your tax liability on any day is $100,000 or more. Show tax liability here, not deposits. (The IRS gets deposit data from FTD coupons.)

A. Daily Tax Liability—First Month of Quarter

1		8		15		22		29	
2		9		16		23		30	
3		10		17		24		31	
4		11		18		25			
5		12		19		26			
6		13		20		27			
7		14		21		28			

A Total tax liability for first month of quarter . . . . ▶ | **A** |

B. Daily Tax Liability—Second Month of Quarter

1		8		15		22		29	
2		9		16		23		30	
3		10		17		24		31	
4		11		18		25			
5		12		19		26			
6		13		20		27			
7		14		21		28			

B Total tax liability for second month of quarter . . . . ▶ | **B** |

C. Daily Tax Liability—Third Month of Quarter

1		8		15		22		29	
2		9		16		23		30	
3		10		17		24		31	
4		11		18		25			
5		12		19		26			
6		13		20		27			
7		14		21		28			

C Total tax liability for third month of quarter . . . . ▶ | **C** |

D Total for quarter (add lines **A**, **B**, and **C**). This should equal line 13 of Form 941 . . . . ▶ | **D** |

For Paperwork Reduction Act Notice, see page 2.	Cat. No. 11967Q	Schedule B (Form 941) (Rev. 1-94)

3–13. LO 9, 10.

The Trainer Company is a monthly depositor whose tax liability for March 1996 is $205.

1. Complete the Federal Tax Deposit Coupon for the March taxes.

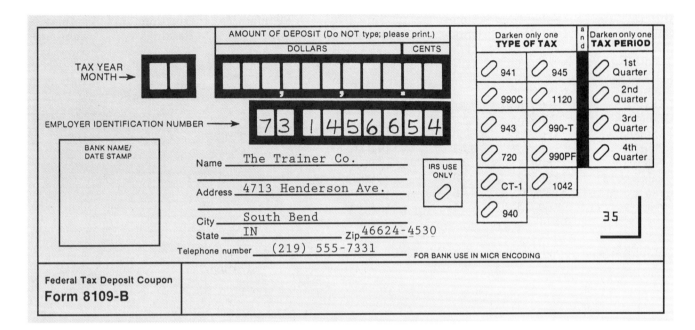

2. What is the due date for the deposit of these taxes?   _____
3. Assume that no deposit was made until May 20. Compute the following penalties:

   a. Penalty for failure to make timely deposit. $ _____
   b. Penalty for failure to pay tax when due. $ _____
   c. Interest on taxes due and unpaid. $ _____
   d. Total penalty imposed. $ _____

3–14. LO 5.

At the Payne Die Company, office workers are employed for a 40-hour workweek on either an annual or a monthly salary basis. In the plant, most workers are paid on a piece-rate basis under a plan in which overtime is equal to one-half the regular hourly pay.

   Given on the form on the following page are the current annual and monthly salary rates for five office workers and the number of units produced by six plant workers for the week ended November 1, 1996.

   For each worker compute:

a. Regular earnings for the weekly payroll ended November 1, 1996.
b. Overtime earning (if applicable).
c. Total regular and overtime earnings.
d. FICA taxable wages for this pay period.
e. FICA taxes to be withheld for this pay period.
f. Net pay for this pay period.

3–14.

PAYNE DIE COMPANY

Employee	Salary/ Unit Rate	Hours Worked	Units Produced	Regular Earnings	Overtime Earnings	Total Earnings
Lentz, R.	16,900 /yr.	40				
Steyer, C.	28,080 /yr.	40				
Long, S.	6,000 /mo.	40				
Richey, S.	1,400 /mo.	48				
Taveau, G.	900 /mo.	40				
Manella, V.	8.50 /M	30	18,000			
Platt, R.	12.50 /M	46	19,000			
Flora, L.	11.80 /M	48	17,000			
Valadez, M.	12.50 /M	40	16,000			
Yau, C.	12.50 /M	48	19,500			
Katz, B.	8.50 /M	33	16,500			
	Totals					

Employer's FICA taxes for week ended November 1, 1996: $ _____ OASDI $ _____ HI

CONTINUING PAYROLL PROBLEM

Refer to the partially completed payroll register you started at the end of Chapter 2. You will now determine the amount of FICA taxes to be withheld from each employee's pay for the pay period ending January 7.

1. In the Taxable Earnings columns, record the amount of each employee's weekly earnings that is subject to FICA taxes.
2. Using the amount recorded in step(1), compute the taxes for each employee and record in the appropriate column.

Note: Keep your partially completed payroll register for use at the end of Chapter 4.

CASE PROBLEMS

C1. **Auditing Form 941. LO 8, 9.**

Your assistant has just completed a rough draft of Form 941, shown on page 51, for the quarter ending March 31, 19–. As the supervisor and authorized signer, you are auditing the form before it is mailed to ensure its accuracy.

Four of the company's general ledger accounts are shown below and on the next page. Employees are paid on the 15th and last day of each month. The company is a monthly depositor. Indicate any changes that should be made on the form before it is signed and mailed.

PAYNE DIE COMPANY (Concluded)

Cumulative Earnings as of Last Pay Period	FICA Taxable Wages This Pay Period		FICA Taxes to Be Withheld		Net Pay
	OASDI	HI	OASDI	HI	
14,950.00	_____	_____	_____	_____	_____
25,380.00	_____	_____	_____	_____	_____
61,900.00	_____	_____	_____	_____	_____
17,600.02	_____	_____	_____	_____	_____
9,553.74	_____	_____	_____	_____	_____
8,380.00	_____	_____	_____	_____	_____
17,570.10	_____	_____	_____	_____	_____
10,418.13	_____	_____	_____	_____	_____
11,603.90	_____	_____	_____	_____	_____
16,145.67	_____	_____	_____	_____	_____
6,513.50	_____	_____	_____	_____	_____
	_____	_____	_____	_____	_____

FICA TAXES PAYABLE—OASDI   Account No. 214

Date		Debit	Credit	Balance Debit	Balance Credit
19—					
Jan.	15		773.96		773.96
	15		773.94		1,547.90
	19	1,547.90			—
	31		843.78		843.78
	31		843.78		1,687.56
Feb.	2	1,687.56			—
	15		833.74		833.74
	15		833.72		1,667.46
	22	1,667.46			—
	28		803.79		803.79
	28		803.79		1,607.58
Mar.	3	1,607.58			—
	15		786.72		786.72
	15		786.72		1,573.45
	20	1,573.45			—
	31		787.88		787.88
	31		787.87		1,575.75
Apr.	5	1,575.75			—

FICA TAXES PAYABLE—HI
Account No. 215

Date		Debit	Credit	Balance Debit	Balance Credit
19—					
Jan.	15		181.01		181.01
	15		181.01		362.02
	19	362.02			—
	31		197.34		197.34
	31		197.32		394.66
Feb.	2	394.66			—
	15		194.98		194.98
	15		194.98		389.96
	22	389.96			—
	28		187.98		187.98
	28		187.98		375.96
Mar.	3	375.96			—
	15		184.01		184.01
	15		183.99		368.00
	20	368.00			—
	31		184.26		184.26
	31		184.24		368.50
Apr.	5	368.50			—

EMPLOYEES FEDERAL INCOME TAX PAYABLE
Account No. 216

Date		Debit	Credit	Balance Debit	Balance Credit
19—					
Jan.	15		1,980.00		1,980.00
	19	1,980.00			—
	31		2,217.00		2,217.00
Feb.	2	2,217.00			—
	15		2,016.00		2,016.00
	22	2,016.00			—
	28		2,007.00		2,007.00
Mar.	3	2,007.00			—
	15		1,970.00		1,970.00
	20	1,970.00			—
	31		1,887.00		1,887.00
Apr.	5	1,887.00			—

WAGES AND SALARIES
Account No. 511

Date		Debit	Credit	Balance Debit	Balance Credit
19—					
Jan.	15	12,483.16		12,483.16	
	31	13,609.40		26,092.56	
Feb.	15	13,447.13		39,539.69	
	28	12,964.43		52,504.12	
Mar.	15	12,689.02		65,193.14	
	31	12,707.69		77,900.83	

Form **941**		**Employer's Quarterly Federal Tax Return**	

Department of the Treasury
Internal Revenue Service

4141

▶ See separate instructions for information on completing this return.
Please type or print.

Enter state code for state in which deposits made . ▶ ☐:☐ (see page 2 of instructions).

Name (as distinguished from trade name)

Trade name, if any
COASTAL COMPANY
Address (number and street)
77 CASTRO

Date quarter ended
MAR 31, 1996
Employer identification number
77-2267142
City, state, and ZIP code
SAN FRANCISCO, CA 94117-6903

OMB No. 1545-0029

T	
FF	
FD	
FP	
I	
T	

If address is different from prior return, check here ▶ ☐

IRS Use

1 1 1 1 1 1 1 1 1 2 3 3 3 3 3 4 4 4

5 5 5 6 7 8 8 8 8 8 9 9 9 10 10 10 10 10 10 10 10 10 10

If you do not have to file returns in the future, check here ▶ ☐ and enter date final wages paid ▶
If you are a seasonal employer, see **Seasonal employers** on page 2 and check here (see instructions) ▶ ☐

1	Number of employees (except household) employed in the pay period that includes March 12th ▶			*19*
2	Total wages and tips subject to withholding, plus other compensation	**2**	*77900*	*38*
3	Total income tax withheld from wages, tips, and sick pay	**3**	*12077*	*00*
4	Adjustment of withheld income tax for preceding quarters of calendar year	**4**	*−0−*	
5	Adjusted total of income tax withheld (line 3 as adjusted by line 4—see instructions)	**5**	*12077*	*00*
6a	Taxable social security wages . . . . $ *77900* *38* × 12.4% (.124) =	**6a**	*9659*	*65*
b	Taxable social security tips . . . . $ *−0−* × 12.4% (.124) =	**6b**	*−0−*	
7	Taxable Medicare wages and tips . . . . . $ *77900* *38* × 2.9% (.029) =	**7**	*2259*	*11*
8	Total social security and Medicare taxes (add lines 6a, 6b, and 7). Check here if wages are not subject to social security and/or Medicare tax . . . . ▶ ☐	**8**	*11918*	*76*
9	Adjustment of social security and Medicare taxes (see instructions for required explanation) Sick Pay $ _____ ± Fractions of Cents $ *.04* ± Other $ _____ =	**9**		*04*
10	Adjusted total of social security and Medicare taxes (line 8 as adjusted by line 9—see instructions)	**10**	*11918*	*80*
11	**Total taxes** (add lines 5 and 10)	**11**	*23995*	*80*
12	Advance earned income credit (EIC) payments made to employees, if any	**12**	*−0−*	
13	Net taxes (subtract line 12 from line 11). **This should equal line 17, column (d) below** (or line D of Schedule B (Form 941))	**13**	*23995*	*80*
14	Total deposits for quarter, including overpayment applied from a prior quarter	**14**	*23977*	*80*
15	**Balance due** (subtract line 14 from line 13). Pay to Internal Revenue Service	**15**	*18*	*00*

16 **Overpayment,** if line 14 is more than line 13, enter excess here ▶ $ _____
and check if to be: ☐ Applied to next return   OR   ☐ Refunded.
• **All filers:** If line 13 is less than $500, you need not complete line 17 or Schedule B.
• **Semiweekly depositors:** Complete Schedule B and check here . . . . ▶ ☐
• **Monthly depositors:** Complete line 17, columns (a) through (d) and check here . . . . ▶ ☐

17	**Monthly Summary of Federal Tax Liability.**			
	(a) First month liability	(b) Second month liability	(c) Third month liability	(d) Total liability for quarter
	8189.14	*8063.96*	*7742.70*	*23995.80*

Sign Here

Under penalties of perjury, I declare that I have examined this return, including accompanying schedules and statements, and to the best of my knowledge and belief, it is true, correct, and complete.

Signature ▶   Print Your Name and Title ▶   Date ▶

Form **941**

C2. **Employee or Independent Contractor? LO 1, 2.**

Martin Urich rents a cab from Weldman Cab Company for $175 per day. Urich pays for all maintenance and gas on the cab. He keeps all fares. The cab company provides advertising, two way radio communication, and dispatching. Is Urich an employee of the cab company? Explain.

C3. **Household Employee? LO 3.**

Nelson operates a placement service for companion-sitting for the elderly. He placed Martha Jackson with Mrs. Mock, an elderly woman who needed a person to assist with her personal needs, household care, and companionship. Jackson is paid directly from Mrs. Mock. Jackson had to pay a placement fee of $50 to Nelson. Is Jackson an employee of Nelson, or a household employee of Mrs. Mock? Explain.

C4. **Hiring a Former Employee for the Summer. LO 1.**

To provide coverage for a programmer who will be on vacation during July and August, Software Systems has decided to contact a former employee, Hank Green. The following discussion took place between the payroll supervisor of the company and Green.

Supervisor: It will be good having you back with us tomorrow. In fact, you can use your old office. Your former assistant can help you get settled in. We are in a rush to get the bugs out of this new program, and I know you are just the one who can help.

Green: Sounds fine to me. It will be good to see all the old familiar faces again. It's going to be a challenge working on your new payroll program. Will I be able to use one of your new notebook computers?

Supervisor: I've already requisitioned one for you and it will be on your desk tomorrow morning. By the way, we are now "flexing" our department, so you should plan to be here between 9:00 and 9:30. That way you can leave any time after 4:00.

Green: Good. Oh, is the company still paying every other week?

Supervisor: Yes. But we will carry you as an independent contractor, doing seasonal work for us. This means we will pay you a weekly flat fee, with no deductions.

Is the supervisor proceeding correctly by classifying Green as an independent contractor? Explain.

When the Revenue Act of 1913 was signed into law, the top rate was 6% on incomes that exceeded $500,000. Today, the top tax rate is 39.6% on incomes that exceed $256,500.

INCOME TAX WITHHOLDING

LEARNING OBJECTIVES

After studying this chapter, you should be able to:

1. Explain coverage under the federal income tax withholding law by determining: (a) the employer/employee relationship, (b) the kinds of payments defined as wages, and (c) the kinds of employment excluded under the law.

2. Explain the types of withholding allowances that may be claimed by employees for income tax withholding purposes.

3. Explain the purpose of Form W-4 and list the proper procedures for using the information contained on the form.

4. Compute the amount of federal income tax to be withheld using: (a) the percentage method, (b) the wage-bracket method.

5. Compute the amount of federal income tax to be withheld using alternative methods such as: (a) quarterly averaging, (b) annualizing of wages, (c) cumulative withholding.

6. Compute the withholding of federal income taxes on supplementary wage payments.

7. Explain how employees may receive Advance Earned Income Credit, and how the employer computes the amount of the advance.

8. Complete Form W-2 and become familiar with other wage and tax statements.

9. Review completion of *Form 941, Employer's Quarterly Federal Tax Return*, and *Form 8109, Federal Tax Deposit Coupon*.

10. Describe the major types of information returns.

11. Explain the impact of state and local income taxes on the payroll accounting process.

This chapter describes the employer's responsibility for withholding income taxes from employees' wages and paying these taxes to the federal government. In addition, many employers must also comply with state, city, and county income tax withholding laws. Employers must be aware of these laws to avoid possible penalties.

L E A R N I N G
O B J E C T I V E
1

WHO IS COVERED UNDER FEDERAL INCOME TAX WITHHOLDING LAWS?

Before an individual withholds any tax under the tax law, the following conditions must exist:

1. There must be, or have been, an employer-employee relationship.
2. The payments received by the employee must be defined as wages under the law.
3. The employment must not be exempted by the law.

Employer-Employee Relationship

Since the Income Tax Reform Act of 1986, it has been estimated that the Internal Revenue Code has been amended some four thousand times. The original Income Tax Code of 1914 contained fourteen pages of law and the forms consisted of four pages, including the instructions to complete the forms. There were 4,000 employees of the IRS in 1914. Today there are 9,400 pages of laws, 4,000 pages of IRS forms and 115,000 employees.

As discussed in Chapter 3, establishing the correct relationship between the employer and employee is a very important factor in complying with the Social Security Tax Law. The same rules apply to this relationship for Federal Income Tax Withholding. Figure 4–1 summarizes the employer-employee relationship.

What Are Taxable Wages?

For withholding purposes, the term *wages* includes the total compensation paid to employees for services. Employers withhold federal income taxes on the *gross amount* of wages before deductions such as state and local taxes, insurance premiums, savings bonds, profit-sharing contributions, and union dues. Examples of employee compensation subject to withholding include:

- Wages and Salaries
- Vacation Allowances
- Supplemental Payments

Figure 4–1
Employee-Employer Relationship

An individual is an *employee* if they perform services in a covered employment. As long as the common-law relationship of employer and employee exists and the employment is not exempt from the provisions of the law, both are covered and must observe its provisions. There are no distinctions made between classes or grades of employees. Superintendents, managers, and other administrative and executive personnel are employees. Partners are not considered employees. Directors of a corporation are not employees unless they perform services other than participating in board of director meetings. Government employees include both officers and elected officials.

An *employer* is any person or organization for whom an individual performs any service as an employee. The 20-factor common law test (Figure 3–1) is used to determine if a worker is an employee and if the employer has the right to control the employee. The definition of employer includes any of the following, regardless of the number of individuals that may be employed: sole proprietors, partners, corporations, not-for-profit corporations, federal and state governments (including Puerto Rico and District of Columbia).

- Bonuses and Commissions
- Fringe Benefits
- Tips

Employees may receive compensation in ways other than their regular wage payments. Figure 4–2 shows some special types of payments that are also subject to federal income tax withholding.

Fringe Benefits

Unless the law says otherwise, fringe benefits are subject to federal income tax withholding. In general, the amount to include is the amount by which the fair market value of the benefits exceed what the employee paid, plus any amount the law excludes. Fringe benefits include employer provided items such as:

- Cars
- Free or discounted flights
- Discounts on property or services
- Vacations
- Memberships in social or country clubs
- Tickets for entertainment and sporting events

Meals and Lodging	Unless furnished for the employer's convenience and on the employer's premises, as a condition of employment. Cash allowances for meals and lodging are taxable.
Travel and Business Expenses (non-accountable plans)	If (1) employee is not required to or does not substantiate expenses with receipts, or (2) if employee receives travel advances and the employee does not or is not required to return any unused amount of the advance.
Disabled Worker's Wages	Withhold for wages paid after the year in which worker became entitled to disability insurance under the Social Security Act.
Supplemental Unemployment Compensation	To the extent they are includible in employee's gross income. It does not include separation due to disciplinary problems or age.
Moving Expenses	Non-qualified reimbursed and employer-paid expenses are subject to withholding. Non-qualified expenses include: cost of sale of old residence, purchase of new residence, house hunting, temporary living expenses, and meals.
Employee Stock Options	Nonstatutory stock options are subject to withholding when the employee exercises the stock option.
Partially Exempt Employment	If the employee spends half or more time in a pay period performing services subject to employment taxes, all pay in that pay period is taxable.
Sick Pay	Subject to withholding whether paid by the employer or third party.
Payments to Nonresident Aliens	Subject to withholding (unless excepted by regulations).

Figure 4–2
Taxable Payments to Employees

Nontaxable Fringe Benefits

- Services provided at no additional cost
- Qualified employee discounts
- Working condition fringes
- Minimal value fringes
- Meals at employer's eating establishment
- Qualified transportation fringes
- Use of on-premises athletic facilities
- Reduced tuition for education

Services the employer provides at no additional cost, qualified employee discounts, meals at employer-run eating establishments, and reduced tuition provided to officers, owners, or highly paid employees are excluded from their income only if the benefits are given to employees on a nondiscriminatory basis.

Withholding on Fringe Benefits. The employer may add the value of fringe benefits to regular wages for a payroll period and figure withholding taxes on the total, or they may withhold the tax on the value of the benefits at the flat 28% supplemental wage rate. The employer may choose not to withhold income tax on the value of an employee's personal use of a vehicle. The employer must, however, withhold social security, Medicare, or railroad retirement taxes on the use of the vehicle. The employer may make a reasonable estimate of the value of the fringe benefits on the dates the employer chooses for the purpose of making deposits. In general, the employer must figure the value of fringe benefits no later than January 31 of the next year.

E X A M P L E

Employers may treat the value of a single fringe benefit as paid on one or more dates in the same calendar year even if the employee receives the entire benefit at one time.

A one-time receipt of a $1,000 fringe benefit in 1996 can be treated as four payments of $250, each in a different pay period of 1996.

*If you need to determine if a certain type of payment or individual is subject to income tax withholding, check **Circular E, Employer' Tax Guide**. Special classes of employment and payments are listed, along with their treatment under employment tax laws.*

Traveling Expenses

Accountable Plan. Employee expense reimbursement amounts paid under an accountable plan are not subject to income tax withholding. An accountable plan requires the employer's reimbursement or allowance arrangement to meet all three of the following rules:

1. They must have paid or incurred deductible expenses while performing services as your employee.
2. They must adequately account to the employer for these expenses within a reasonable period of time.
3. They must return any excess reimbursement or allowance within a reasonable period of time.

Nonaccountable Plan. A nonaccountable plan is an arrangement that does not meet the requirements for an accountable plan. All amounts paid under this plan are wages and subject to income tax withholding.

Cafeteria Plans

Cafeteria plans, including flexible spending arrangements, are tax-favored benefit plans where all participants are employees who choose among cash payment and certain qualified benefits. The deductions from the employee's pay for these benefits are made on a pre-tax basis, so that they lower the employee's taxable earnings.

Taxable Tips

Employees must report cash tips to the employer by the 10th of the month following the month they receive the tips. This report includes tips paid by the employer for charge customers and tips the employee receives directly from the customers. Employees can use a special IRS form. Tips of less than $20 in a month are not reported.

Withholding from Tips. The employer collects income tax, as well as social security taxes, on reported tips. The following procedures apply to withholding income tax on reported tips:

1. The employer collects the tax from the employee's wages, or from other funds the employee makes available.
2. When tips are reported in connection with employment where the employee also receives a regular wage, compute the withholding tax on the tips as a supplemental wage payment.
3. If the withholding tax exceeds the amount of wages paid to the employee, the employee must pay the uncollected portion of the taxes directly to the IRS when filing the annual income tax return.
4. The employer is not required to audit or verify the accuracy of the tip income reported.

Allocated Tips. Large food and beverage establishments that have customary tipping and normally had more than 10 employees on a typical business day in the preceding year may be required to allocate tips among employees if:

> *The total tips reported by the employees during any payroll period are less than 8% of the establishment's gross receipts for that period.*

The amount of allocated tips to employees equals:

> *8% of gross receipts minus carryout sales and sales with at least a 10% service charge added less tips reported by the employees.*

The tip allocation may be made using one of three methods: hours worked, gross receipts, good faith agreement.

What Payments Are Exempt from Withholding?

The law excludes certain payments and payments to certain individuals, as shown in Figure 4–3. The law does not require persons making such payments to withhold federal income taxes.

Flexible spending arrangements now offered by some employers let you pay medical and dependent care benefits with before-tax dollars. A $5,000 FSA for dependent care (the maximum permitted) equals $1,550 in federal income tax savings for an individual in the 31% tax bracket.

Employers who allocate tips must file Form 8027, Employer's Annual Information Return of Tip Income and Allocated Tips. The employer does not withhold income tax on allocated tips. Regardless of whether the employee receives an allocation, they are required to report all tip income on their personal income tax return. Employees who fail to report the full amount of the allocation must substantiate the lesser amount reported.

SELF-STUDY QUIZ 4–1. Check any item of employee compensation not subject to withholding:

_____ **a.** Company-provided lunches at the plant to reduce tardiness by keeping employees on the premises.

_____ **b.** Year-end bonuses to managers and supervisors.

_____ **c.** Work-out room for employee use during lunch hours.

_____ **d.** Travel advances to salespersons for overnight sales calls out of town.

Figure 4–3
Exempt Payments

Type of Payment or Individual	Conditions
Advances	For travel and other business expenses reasonably expected to be incurred.
Accident and Health Insurance Payments	Exempt except 2% shareholder-employees of S corporations.
Educational Assistance	If education maintains or improves employee's skills required by the job.
De Minimus Fringe Benefits	Benefits of so little value as to make accounting for the benefit unreasonable and administratively impractical.
Dependent Care Assistance	To the extent it is reasonable to believe the amounts will be excludable from gross income.
Domestic Service	Private home, local college club, or local chapter of college fraternity or sorority.
Employee Business Expense Reimbursements	Accountable plans for amounts not exceeding specified government rates for mileage, lodging, meals, and incidental expenses.
Foreign Service by U.S. Citizens	As employees for affiliates of American employers if entitled to exclusion under section 911 or required by law of foreign country to withhold income tax on such payment.
Ministers of Churches, Members of Religious Orders	Performing services for the order, agency of the supervising church, or associated institution.
Public Officials	For fees only, not salaries.
Individuals Under 18	For delivery of or distribution of newspapers, shopping news and vendors of newspapers and magazines where payment is the difference between the purchase and sales price.
Deceased Person's Wages	Paid to the person's beneficiary or estate.
Sickness or Injury Payments	Payments made under worker's compensation law or contract of insurance.
Moving Expense Reimbursements	For qualified expenses, if the employee is entitled to a deduction for these expenses on the individual's federal income tax return.
Group-Term Life Insurance Costs	The employer's cost of group-term life insurance less than $50,000.
Retirement and Pension Plans	• Employer contributions to a qualified plan. • Employer contributions to IRA accounts under a SEP (see section 402(g) for salary reduction limitation. • Employer contributions to section 403(b) annuity contract [see section 402(g) for limitation]. • Elective contributions and deferrals to plans containing a qualified cash or deferred compensation arrangement, such as 410(k).

_____ **e.**   Employer-paid sick pay.
_____ **f.**   Memberships in the local country club for department managers.
_____ **g.**   Meals provided by a local restaurant for its employees.

HOW ARE WITHHOLDING ALLOWANCES DETERMINED?

The law entitles employees to exempt a portion of their earnings from with-holding by claiming a *personal allowance* and allowances for their dependents if they furnish their employers with a claim for the allowances. Employees may also claim special allowances and allowances for itemized deductions and tax credits. However, employees can not claim the same withholding allowances with more than one employer at the same time.

Personal Allowances

Employees can claim a *personal allowance* for themselves and each qualified dependent, provided they are not claimed on another person's tax return. In 1995, the amount of the personal allowance was $2,500. A married employee may claim one personal allowance for his or her spouse if the spouse is not claimed as a dependent on another person's tax return.

Allowances for Dependents

Employees may claim one allowance for each dependent (other than a spouse) who will be claimed on their federal income tax returns. To qualify as a depen-dent, the person must meet specific requirements that are listed in the instruc-tions accompanying the individual's federal income tax return.

Additional Withholding Allowance

Employees can reduce the amount of withholding by claiming a *special with-holding allowance,* whether or not they plan to itemize deductions on their tax return. An additional withholding allowance can be claimed by a person under any one of the following situations:

1.   Single person who has only one job.
2.   Married person who has only one job with nonworking spouse.
3.   Person's wages from a second job or the spouse's wages (or both) equal $1,000 or less.

This allowance is only used to compute the employee's income tax with-holding. The employee does not claim this allowance on his or her income tax return.

Other Withholding Allowances

Withholding allowances reduce the overwithholding of income taxes on em-ployees' wages. In addition to the allowances already discussed, employees may be entitled to withholding allowances based on estimated tax credits, such as child care, and itemized deductions for medical expenses, mortgage interest, and charitable contributions. Employees take these credits on their federal income tax returns. The number of withholding allowances is determined on the worksheet that accompanies Form W-4, *Employee's Withholding Allowance Certificate*, and is then reported on that form.

How Do You Complete Form W-4? (Employee's Withholding Allowance Certificate)

Employers who pay providers for dependent care may be asked by their employees for help in completing Form W-10, Dependent Care Provider's Identification and Certification. *Employees may not claim an exclusion for employer-provided dependent care assistance benefits unless the dependent care provider is identified by name, address and taxpayer identification number.*

The employer uses *Form W-4, Employee's Withholding Allowance Certificate,* to compute how much income tax to withhold from employees' wages. The employer must have Form W-4 on file for each employee. This form contains the withholding allowance certificate (shown in Figure 4–4), detailed instructions, and worksheets for employees to use in completing the certificate.

Completing Form W-4. The employee completes Form W-4 when they begin work for an employer. Employers must retain the withholding certificate as a supporting record of the withholding allowances used in deducting income taxes from the employees' salaries and wages. Once filed, the certificate remains in effect until an amended certificate takes effect. Withholding certificates should be retained as long as they are in effect and for four years thereafter. If the employee does not complete the W-4, the employer withholds taxes as if the employee is single, with no withholding allowances.

Withholding Allowances. The number of withholding allowances claimed on Form W-4 may differ from the number of exemptions claimed on the employee's tax return. The process of determining the correct number of withholding allowances begins with the number of personal exemptions the employee expects to claim on his tax return. The employee then increases or decreases this number based on the employee's personal financial situation. The

Figure 4–4   *W-4 Employee's Withholding Allowance Certificate*

Form **W-4** Department of the Treasury Internal Revenue Service	**Employee's Withholding Allowance Certificate** ▶ For Privacy Act and Paperwork Reduction Act Notice, see reverse.	OMB No. 1545-0010 **1995**
1 Type or print your first name and middle initial **Albert J.**	Last name **Cox**	2 Your social security number 542 : 13 : 6921
Home address (number and street or rural route) **421 Eastmont**	3 ☒ Single ☐ Married ☐ Married, but withhold at higher Single rate. Note: *If married, but legally separated, or spouse is a nonresident alien, check the Single box.*	
City or town, state, and ZIP code **Richland, WA 99352**	4 If your last name differs from that on your social security card, check here and call 1-800-772-1213 for a new card . . . . . ▶ ☐	

5	Total number of allowances you are claiming (from line G above or from the worksheets on page 2 if they apply) .	5	4
6	Additional amount, if any, you want withheld from each paycheck	6	$ 0
7	I claim exemption from withholding for 1995 and I certify that I meet **BOTH** of the following conditions for exemption: • Last year I had a right to a refund of **ALL** Federal income tax withheld because I had **NO** tax liability; **AND** • This year I expect a refund of **ALL** Federal income tax withheld because I expect to have **NO** tax liability. If you meet both conditions, enter "EXEMPT" here . . . . ▶	7	

Under penalties of perjury, I certify that I am entitled to the number of withholding allowances claimed on this certificate or entitled to claim exempt status.

Employee's signature ▶ *Albert J. Cox*   Date ▶ *January 2* , 19 *95*

8 Employer's name and address (Employer: Complete 8 and 10 only if sending to the IRS)	9 Office code (optional)	10 Employer identification number

worksheets provided with Form W-4 enable the employee to determine the exact number of allowances to enter on the certificate.

Changing Form W-4. If the status of an employee changes with respect to the number of withholding allowances or marital status, the employee files an amended W-4. If there is a *decrease* in the number of allowances, the employee should furnish the employer with a new certificate within 10 days, unless the decrease is due to the death of the dependent or spouse. In these cases, the employee files an amended certificate on December 1 since the allowance is not lost during the current tax year. If the employee has an *increase* in the number of allowances, the employee does not have to file a new certificate. The employer makes the certificate effective no later than the start of the first payroll period ending on or after the 30th day from the date the replacement Form W-4 is received. The employer may not repay or reimburse the employee for income taxes overwithheld before the effective date of the new certificate, but may reimburse the employee after that date if the employer failed to implement the new certificate.

Exemption from Income Tax Withholding. Employees may claim exemption from income tax withholding if they had no income tax liability last year and expect none in the current year. The exemption is valid for one year and must be claimed on a new Form W-4 filed by February 15 of each year. If a new certificate is not filed, taxes are withheld at the single rate with zero withholding allowances.

*Pub. 505, Tax Withholding and Estimated Tax, contains detailed instructions for completing Form W-4. When ordering Forms W-4, you may also wish to order **Pub. 505** and **Pub. 919,** Is my Withholding Correct for 1996?*

E X A M P L E

Single persons who made less than $6,400 in 1995 owed no federal income tax. Married couples filing jointly with combined wages up to $11,550 incurred no tax liability. Part-time, summer, and student employees will not incur a tax liability.

Employees may not claim exemption from withholding if (1) income exceeds $650 and includes unearned income (interest, dividends) *and* (2) another person claims the employee as a dependent on their tax return.

Additional and Voluntary Withholding Agreements. In some instances, employees want additional federal income taxes withheld from their wages, such as a person with two or more jobs, or a married couple where both work. If claiming zero allowances is not satisfactory, the employee may request an amount of additional tax to be withheld on Line 6 of Form W-4.

If an employee receives payments not classified as wages, or an employer-employee relationship does not exist, individuals can voluntarily request that the employer or the one making the payments withhold federal income taxes from their payments. These individuals need only furnish a Form W-4. Requests for additional and voluntary withholding become effective when the employer accepts them and begins to withhold tax. The agreements remain in effect until the specified termination date or until the termination is mutually agreed upon. Either party may terminate an agreement prior to a specified date or mutual agreement by furnishing the other party with a signed, written notice of termination.

Employers must send copies of certain Forms W-4 received during the quarter for employees still employed at the end of the quarter. The employer sends copies when the employee: (1) Claims more than 10 withholding allowances, and (2) Claims exemption from withholding and wages normally more than $200 per week.[1]

---

[1]Until notified by the IRS, the employer must withhold based on the W-4's filed by the employees.

Figure 4–5 *Procedures for Submitting Forms W-4*

- Send Forms W-4 that meet the prescribed conditions each quarter with Form 941, unless you file Form 941 on magnetic media. In such cases, submit paper forms to the appropriate service center with a cover letter. Complete boxes 8 and 10 on any Forms W-4 you send in.
- Send copies of any written statements from employees in support of the claims made on the form, even if the Forms W-4 are not in effect at the end of the quarter.
- In certain cases, the IRS may notify you in writing that you must submit specified forms more frequently to your district director separate from Form 941.
- Unless notified, base withholding on the Forms W-4 that you send to IRS.
- If notified by IRS, base withholding on the number of allowances shown in the IRS notice. The employee will also receive a similar notice.
- If the employee later files a new Form W-4, follow it only if exempt status is not claimed or the number of withholding allowances does not exceed the IRS notice.
- If the employee later files a new Form W-4 that does not follow the IRS notice, disregard it and continue to withhold based on the IRS notice.
- If the employee prepares a new Form W-4, explaining any difference with the IRS notice, and submits it to you, send the Form W-4 and explanation to the IRS office shown in the notice. Continue to withhold according to the IRS notice until notified.

E X A M P L E

Individuals who may wish to request additional withholding or a voluntary agreement to withhold include:

- *Clergy*
- *Two wage-earner married couples*
- *Domestic workers in a private home*
- *Individuals receiving interest and dividends*
- *Individuals receiving self-employment income*

NEWS
A L E R T

Employers can allow employees to make changes electronically to their W-4s. Their participation must be voluntary, and they must file their initial W-4 on paper.

Withholding on Nonresident Aliens. To avoid underwithholding, nonresident aliens should (1) not claim exemption from income tax withholding; (2) request withholding as single, regardless of actual status; (3) claim only one allowance. Residents of Canada, Mexico, Japan, or Korea may claim more than one allowance.

Other Withholdings

Federal income taxes are also withheld from other kinds of payments made to current and former employees, described below.

Withholding for Pension or Annuity Payments. Payments made from pension, profit-sharing, stock bonus, annuity and certain deferred compensation plans and individual retirement arrangements are generally treated as wages for the purpose of withholding, unless recipients elect not to have federal income taxes withheld. Payers must withhold on monthly pension and annuity payments exceeding $1,150 ($13,800 a year) unless the payees elect otherwise.

Withholding is done as if the recipients were married and claiming three withholding allowances. By completing *Form W-4P, Withholding Certificate for Pension or Annuity Payments,* or a substitute form, an employee can elect to have no income tax withheld from payments received, or change the amount of tax that would ordinarily be withheld. Form W-4P remains in effect until the recipient changes or revokes the certificate.

Withholding from Sick Pay. *Form W-4S, Request for Federal Income Tax Withholding from Sick Pay* must be filed with the payer of sick pay if the employee wants federal income taxes withheld from the payments. Form W-4S is filed only if the payer is a third party, such as an insurance company. The form should not be filed with the worker's employer who makes such payments since employers already must withhold income taxes from sick pay.

Withholding for Child Support. The Family Support Act of 1988 requires the immediate withholding for child-support payments for all cases supported by a court order. The amount withheld is equal to the amount of the delinquency, subject to the limits prescribed in the federal garnishment law, discussed in Chapter 6. Employers may withhold a fee, set by each state, for administrative costs.

Withholding to Collect Delinquent Taxes. Collecting delinquent federal taxes by means of payroll deduction has been authorized by the IRS. Under this procedure, employees use the *Payroll Deduction Agreement, Form 2159,* to authorize their employer to deduct specified amounts from their salaries or wages each payday. The employer remits the amounts withheld to the IRS at regular, agreed-upon intervals.

Invalid Forms

Any unauthorized change or addition to Form W-4 makes it invalid. This includes the employee taking out any language certifying that the form is correct. A Form W-4 is also invalid if, by the date an employee gives it to you, he or she indicates in any way that it is false. The employer should not use an invalid form to figure withholding. The employee should be told that the form is invalid, and another should be submitted. If the employee does not give the employer a valid one, the employer withholds as if the employee were single and claiming no withholding allowances. If an earlier form is available for the employee, the employer may withhold using that form.

Form W-4 information may be filed with the IRS on magnetic media. If you wish to file on magnetic media, submit Form 4419, Application for Filing Information Returns Magnetically/Electronically, to request authorization. See Pub. 1245 Specifications for Filing Form W-4, Employee's Withholding Allowance Certificate, on Magnetic Tape 5¼ and 3½-Inch Magnetic Diskettes. To obtain additional information about magnetic media, call the IRS Martisburg Computing Center at (304) 263-8700.

SELF-STUDY QUIZ 4–2

1. Grace Kyle submitted a new Form W-4 claiming one additional withholding allowance. Kyle also requested to be reimbursed for the overwithholding prior to the change. How should the payroll manager respond to Kyle?

2. Bob Bradley is upset because his paycheck on February 28, 1996, has federal income tax withheld, even though he filed a W-4 in 1995 claiming exemption from withholding. What should the payroll manager say to Bradley?

3. Greg Volmer, married with a nonemployed spouse, has three dependent children. The couple also plans to incur $1,800 in dependent care expenses. How many personal allowances can Volmer claim on his W-4?

HOW IS FEDERAL INCOME TAX WITHHOLDING DETERMINED?

After the employer learns the number of withholding allowances for an employee from Form W-4, the employer selects a withholding method. Employers usually choose either the *percentage method* or the *wage-bracket method.* Both distinguish between married and unmarried persons, and both methods provide the full benefit of the allowances claimed by the employee on Form W-4.

Both methods take into account a *standard deduction,* an amount of money used to reduce an individual's adjusted gross income in arriving at the taxable income. For 1995, the following standard deductions apply:

Joint return filers and surviving spouses	$6,550
Married persons filing separately	3,275
Head of household filers	5,750
Single filers	3,900

These amounts are increased for single and married individuals or surviving spouses age 65 or older or blind.

Each year the standard deductions are adjusted for inflation. The adjustment also applies to the additional standard deductions available to elderly or blind persons.

The choice of methods is usually based on the number of employees and the payroll accounting system used. The employer can change from one method to another at any time, and different methods may be used for different groups of employees.

Percentage Method

To compute the tax using this method, follow these steps:

Step 1

Determine the amount of gross wages earned. If the wage ends in a fractional dollar amount, round the gross pay to the nearest dollar.

Nick Volente, single, claims two allowances, and earns $802.63 semimonthly.

Round Gross Wages to $803.00

Step 2

Multiply the number of allowances claimed by the amount of one allowance for the appropriate payroll period, as shown in the Table of Allowance Values in Figure 4–6.

Table of Allowance Values for semimonthly payroll period shows $104.17

Multiply $104.17 × 2 = $208.34

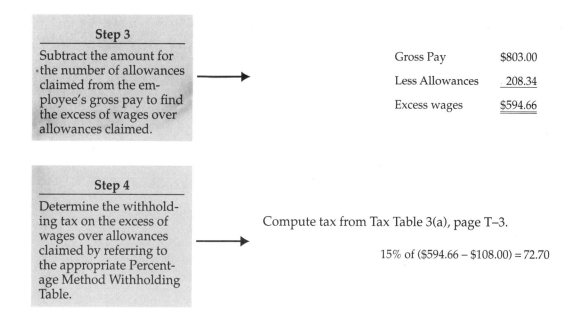

Step 3
Subtract the amount for the number of allowances claimed from the employee's gross pay to find the excess of wages over allowances claimed.

Gross Pay	$803.00
Less Allowances	208.34
Excess wages	$594.66

Step 4
Determine the withholding tax on the excess of wages over allowances claimed by referring to the appropriate Percentage Method Withholding Table.

Compute tax from Tax Table 3(a), page T–3.

15% of ($594.66 – $108.00) = 72.70

Figure 4–6   *Table of Allowance Values for 1995*

Weekly	48.08	Biweekly	96.15	Semimonthly	104.17	Monthly	208.33
Quarterly	625.00	Semiannual	1,250.00	Annual	2,500.00	Daily/Misc.	9.62

To compute more easily an employee's excess of wages over allowances claimed, you may use the table shown in Figure 4–7. To use this table:

1. Locate the total number of withholding allowances claimed by the employee in the far-left column.
2. Determine the total dollar amount of the employee's withholding allowances in the corresponding line in the appropriate payroll period column.
3. Subtract the amount obtained in Step 2 from the total wages earned by the employee for the payroll period to find the excess wages.
4. Compute the withholding tax on the excess of wages over allowances claimed by referring to the appropriate Percentage Method Withholding Table in Tax Table A.

SELF-STUDY QUIZ 4–3. Gina Swant, married and claims 3 allowances, receives a salary of $1,100.25 each week. Compute the amount to withhold for federal income tax using the percentage method and Figure 4–7. Show the results of each step, as described for figuring withholding using the percentage method.

Step 1 Result _____   Step 2 Result _____

Step 3 Result _____   Step 4 Result _____

Wage-Bracket Method

The IRS provides statutory wage-bracket tables for weekly, biweekly, semi-monthly, monthly, and daily or miscellaneous pay periods. Copies may be

Figure 4–7

If the number of allowances is	And wages are paid							
	Weekly	Biweekly	Semi-monthly	Monthly	Quarterly	Semi-Annually	Annually	Daily or Misc.
	The total amount of withholding allowances for that payroll period is—							
0	$ 0	$ 0	$ 0	$ 0	$ 0	$ 0	$ 0	$ 0
1	48.08	96.15	104.17	208.33	625.00	1,250.00	2,500.00	9.62
2	96.16	192.30	208.34	416.66	1,250.00	2,500.00	5,000.00	19.24
3	144.24	288.45	312.51	624.99	1,875.00	3,750.00	7,500.00	28.86
4	192.32	384.60	416.68	833.32	2,500.00	5,000.00	10,000.00	38.48
5	240.40	480.75	520.85	1,041.65	3,125.00	6,250.00	12,500.00	48.10
6	288.48	576.90	625.02	1,249.98	3,750.00	7,500.00	15,000.00	57.72
7	336.56	673.05	729.19	1,458.31	4,375.00	8,750.00	17,500.00	67.34
8	384.64	769.20	833.36	1,666.64	5,000.00	10,000.00	20,000.00	76.96
9	432.72	865.35	937.53	1,874.97	5,625.00	11,250.00	22,500.00	86.58
10	480.80	961.50	1,041.70	2,083.30	6,250.00	12,500.00	25,000.00	96.20
11 or more	Multiply the amount of one withholding allowance for the specific payroll period by the number of allowances claimed.							

obtained from the District Director of Internal Revenue. Tax Table B at the end of the textbook provides tables for weekly, biweekly, semimonthly, monthly and daily pay periods for single and married persons effective January 1, 1995. To use the wage-bracket method, follow these steps:

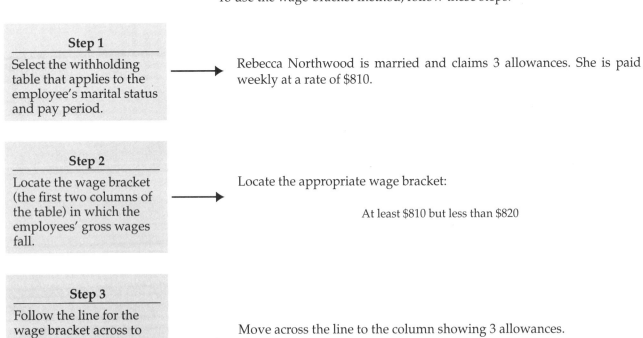

Step 1

Select the withholding table that applies to the employee's marital status and pay period.

→ Rebecca Northwood is married and claims 3 allowances. She is paid weekly at a rate of $810.

Step 2

Locate the wage bracket (the first two columns of the table) in which the employees' gross wages fall.

→ Locate the appropriate wage bracket:

At least $810 but less than $820

Step 3

Follow the line for the wage bracket across to the right to the column showing the appropriate number of allowances. Withhold this amount of tax.

→ Move across the line to the column showing 3 allowances.

The tax to withhold is $82.

Figure 4–8   *Married Persons—Weekly Payroll Period*   *Partial Wage-Bracket Table*

| If the wages are | | And the number of withholding allowances claimed is | | | | | | | | | | |
At least	But less than	0	1	2	3	4	5	6	7	8	9	10
		The amount of income tax to be withheld is										
$740	$750	$ 93	$ 86	$79	$72	$64	$57	$50	$43	$36	$28	$21
750	760	95	88	80	73	66	59	52	44	37	30	23
760	770	96	89	82	75	67	60	53	46	39	31	24
770	780	98	91	83	76	69	62	55	47	40	33	26
780	790	99	92	85	78	70	63	56	49	42	34	27
790	800	101	94	86	79	72	65	58	50	43	36	29
800	810	102	95	88	81	73	66	59	52	45	37	30
810	820	104	97	89	82	75	68	61	53	46	39	32
820	830	105	98	91	84	76	69	62	55	48	40	33
830	840	108	100	92	85	78	71	64	56	49	42	35

Note: If the amount of an employee's wages exceeds the amount shown in the last bracket of the table, use the percentage method of withholding.

SELF-STUDY QUIZ 4–4. Quirk Motors uses the wage-bracket method to withhold from the semimonthly earnings of its employees. For each employee, compute the amount to withhold from their earnings for the payroll period ending March 15.

Employee	Marital Status	No. of Allowances	Salary	Federal Income Tax Withheld
Kyle Lamb	S	1	$1,100	_____
Zed Nurin	S	0	850	_____
Carol Hogan	M	4	975	_____
Marla Vick	M	2	3,000	_____
Al Marks	S	3	1,200	_____

WHAT ARE OTHER METHODS OF WITHHOLDING?

In addition to the two principal methods of withholding previously described, employers may use other methods such as *Quarterly Averaging, Annualizing Wages,* and *Cumulative Withholding.*

QUARTERLY AVERAGING. Turner, Inc. estimates that Carl Moyer will be paid $6,000 during the second quarter of the year. Moyer is married and claims six withholding allowances.

Step 1—Divide the estimated quarterly wages by 6 (the number of semimonthly pay periods in the quarter).

$6,000 ÷ 6 = $1,000

Step 2—Find the amount of federal income tax to withhold from each semimonthly payment.

MARRIED Persons—SEMIMONTHLY Payroll Period

Wages at least $1,000 but not more than $1,020 for 6 allowances = $18

E X A M P L E

ANNUALIZING WAGES. *Marc Field, married with 3 allowances, receives $1,050 semimonthly. Under the annualizing method, do the following:*

Step 1—Multiply the semimonthly wage by 24 pay periods to compute his annual wage.

$$\$1,050 \times 24 = \$25,200$$

Step 2—Subtract withholding allowances of $7,500 (3 × $2,500).

$$\$25,200 - 7,500 = \$17,700$$

Step 3—Use Tax Table 7(b) and apply the Percentage Method *to the taxable wages.*

$17,700 \times 15\%$ of the excess over $6,400. ($17,700 - 6,400) \times .15 = \$1,695$

$1,695 \div 24$ semimonthly payroll = $70.63 per paycheck

E X A M P L E

CUMULATIVE WITHHOLDING. *Erin Burg, single with 1 allowance, is a salesperson and has been paid $28,000 in commissions during the first three quarters of the year (19 biweekly pay periods). At the beginning of the next quarter she will receive a commission check for $3,700. To use cumulative withholding:*

Step 1—Add the total of all wages

$$\$28,000 + \$3,700 = \$31,700$$

Step 2—Divide the total by the number of pay periods

$31,700 \div 20 = \$1,585$ average biweekly wage

Step 3—Using the Percentage Method from Table 2(a) the income taxes on $1,585 are $278.12.

Total income taxes for 20 pay periods is ($278.12 \times 20) = \$5,562.40$

Step 4—Subtract taxes already withheld from the total computed above.

$$\$5,562.40 - \$5,105.56 = \$456.84$$

Step 5—Withhold $456.84 from the commission check on the 20th biweekly pay day.

If the employer had computed withholding using the percentage method on the $3,700, the tax would be $918.49.

WHAT ARE SUPPLEMENTAL WAGE PAYMENTS?

L E A R N I N G
O B J E C T I V E
6

Supplemental wage payments include items such as vacation pay, bonuses, commissions, and dismissal pay. Since these types of payments may be paid at a different time than the regular payroll and not related to a particular payroll, the employer must decide whether to lump the regular wages and supplemental wages together or withhold from the supplemental wages separately. The IRS has issued rules that indicate which method the employer should use.

Vacation Pay

Vacation pay is subject to withholding as though it were a regular payment made for the payroll period or periods occurring during the vacation. If the vacation pay is for a time longer than your usual payroll period, spread it over the pay period(s) for which you pay it. When vacation pay is in lieu of taking vacation time, treat it as a supplemental wage payment. A lump-sum vacation payment on termination of employment is also treated as a supplemental wage payment.

Supplemental Wages Paid with Regular Wages

If the employer pays supplemental wages with regular wages but does not specify the amount of each type of wage, the employer withholds as if the total were a single payment for a regular payroll period.

E X A M P L E

Ashley Watson, married with 3 allowances, earns a monthly salary of $1,800. She also receives a bonus on sales that exceed her quota for the year. For this year, her bonus amounts to $4,600. Watson's employer pays her the regular salary and the bonus together on her December paycheck. The withholding for the December pay is computed on the total amount of $6,400 ($1,800 + $4,600). Using the percentage Tax Table 4(b), the amount to withhold is $1,070.61.

Supplemental Wages Paid Separately from Regular Wages

If the supplemental wages are paid separately, or combined with regular wages and the amount of each is specified, the income tax withholding method depends on whether or not you withhold income tax from the employee's regular wages. If you withhold income tax from the employee's regular wages, you can use either of the following methods for supplemental wages.

Method A. Withhold a flat 28%.

E X A M P L E

Referring to the preceding example, you may indicate separately on Watson's paycheck stub the amount of each payment. The amount of federal income tax to be withheld is computed as follows:

		Taxes Withheld	
Regular monthly earnings	$1,800	$ 99.00	(from wage-bracket tax tables)
Annual bonus	4,600	1,288.00	(4,600 × 28%)
Totals	$6,400	$1,387.00	

Method B. Add the supplemental wages and regular wages for the most recent payroll period. Then figure the income tax as if the total were a single payment. Subtract the tax already withheld from the regular wage. Withhold the remaining tax from the supplemental wage.

E X A M P L E

Brian Early, married with two allowances, is paid $985 semimonthly. The tax to be withheld under the wage-bracket method on each semimonthly pay is $77. Early is paid his regular wage on June 15. On June 18 he receives a bonus of $500. The tax on the bonus is computed as follows:

Regular wage payment . . .	$ 985
Bonus	500
Total	$1,485

Tax on total from the wage-bracket table in Tax Table B	$152
Less tax already withheld on $985	77
Tax to be withheld from $500 bonus	$ 75

If you did not withhold income tax from the employee's regular wages, use Method B. This would occur when the value of the employee's withholding allowances claimed on the W-4 exceeds the wages.

SELF-STUDY QUIZ 4–5. Milton Stewart, married with 2 allowances, received his regular semimonthly wage of $1,450 on June 15. On June 20 he received a semiannual bonus of $500. Compute the amount of federal income tax to withhold on the bonus using each method for computing supplemental wage payments.

Method A   _____

Method B   _____

WHAT IS ADVANCE EARNED INCOME CREDIT?

L E A R N I N G
O B J E C T I V E
7

The *earned income credit* (EIC) reduces federal income taxes for an eligible employee (see Figure 4–9) who has a qualifying child, and for the low-income taxpayers who have no qualifying children. The credit can be claimed at the time

Figure 4–9
Employees Eligible for Advance EIC

Only eligible employees can receive advance EIC payments. The eligibility requirements are summarized below.

1. The employee must have a qualifying child as defined on Form W-5.
2. The employee's expected 1995 earned income and adjusted gross income (including spouse if filing jointly) must each be less than $24,396.

Note: Certain employees who do not have a qualifying child may be able to claim the EIC on their tax return, but are not eligible to get advance EIC payments.

of filing their individual income tax returns. However, to get these payments with his or her pay, the employee must give the employer a properly completed *Form W-5, Earned Income Credit Advance Payment Certificate.* The employer must make advance EIC payments to employees who complete and sign Form W-5. For 1995, the maximum advance payment is $1,257.

Form W-5

Eligible employees who want to receive advance EIC payments must file Form W-5 with their employer. On this form the employee shows the following:

- Expected eligibility for the credit in 1995.
- If they have a qualifying child.
- If they are married.
- If married, whether their spouse has a certificate in effect with any other employer.
- If another W-5 is on file with another current employer.

An employee can have only one certificate in effect with a current employer. If the employee is married and the employee's spouse works, each spouse files a separate Form W-5. This form remains in effect until the end of the calendar year or the employee revokes the certificate or files another one. A new certificate must be filed by December 31 in order to continue receiving payment in the new year. Figure 4–10 shows an example of a filled in Form W-5.

Employee's Change of Status

After an employee has submitted a signed Form W-5, if circumstances change that make the employee ineligible for the credit, they must revoke the certificate within 10 days after learning of the change. The employee then gives the employer a new Form W-5 stating that he or she is no longer eligible for advance EIC payments. If the employee's situation changes because his or her spouse files a Form W-5, the employee must file a new certificate showing that his or her spouse has a certificate in effect with an employer. If the employee's spouse has a Form W-5 no longer in effect, the employee may file a new Form W-5.

Figure 4–10   *Earned Income Credit Advance Payment Certificate*

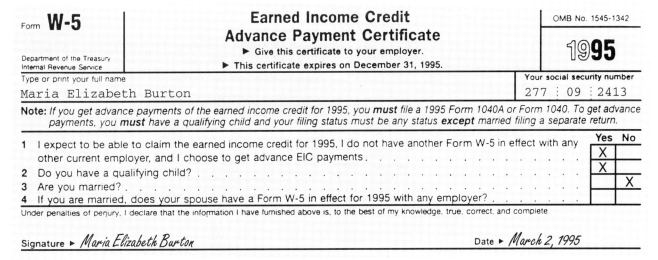

For 1995, you should notify the follow-ing employees that they may be able to claim the EIC on their 1995 returns: (1) employees with one qualifying child and wages less than $24,396, (2) employees with two or more qualifying children and wages less than $26,673, and (3) employees without qualifying children and wages less than $9,230.

Employer Responsibilities

Employers must notify employees who have no income tax withheld that they may be eligible for EIC payments. The employer may use any of the following methods to notify employees.

1. The IRS Form W-2, which has the required statement about the EIC on the back of Copy C.
2. A substitute Form W-2 with the same EIC statement on the back of the employee's copy.
3. Notice 797, Possible Federal Refund Due to the Earned Income Credit (EIC).
4. Your written statement with the same wording as Notice 797.

Computing the Advance EIC

Employers must include the advance EIC payment with wages paid to their eligible employees who have filed Form W-5. In determining the advance payment, the employer considers the following factors:

1. Wages and reported tips for the pay period.
2. Whether the employee is married or single.
3. Whether a married employee's spouse has a Form W-5 in effect with an employer.

To figure the amount of the advance payment, the employer uses either the *Tables for Percentage Method of Advance EIC Payments* or *Tables for Wage Bracket Method of Advance EIC Payments*. There are separate tables for employees whose spouses have a certificate in effect.

E X A M P L E

Renee Riley is paid $150 per week. She has filed Form W-5 showing that she is married and that her husband has given his employer Form W-5. Using the "Married With Both Spouses Filing Certificate" in Figure 4–11, the advance EIC payment is $8.

Paying the Advance EIC

The advance EIC payments do not affect the amount of income taxes or FICA taxes withheld from employees' wages. Since the EIC payments are not compensation for services rendered, they are not subject to payroll taxes. Generally the employer pays the amount of the advance EIC payment from withheld income taxes and FICA taxes. It is possible that for a payroll period the advance EIC payments may be more than the withheld income taxes and the FICA taxes. In such cases, the employer can:

1. Reduce each advance EIC payment proportionately, or
2. Elect to make full payment of the advance EIC amount and treat such full amounts as an advance payment of the company's employment tax liability.

The amount of the advance EIC payments does not change the amount that employers must withhold from their employee's wages for income taxes and FICA. Advance EIC payments made by the employer are treated as having been

Figure 4–11   *MARRIED With Both Spouses Filing Certificate*

Wages		Payment	Wages		Payment	Wages		Payment	Wages		Payment
At Least	But less than	to be made	At Least	But less than	to be made	At Least	But less than	to be made	At Least	But less than	to be made
$ 0	$ 5	$0	$ 35	$ 40	$ 7	$125	$135	$10	$195	$205	$3
5	10	1	40	45	8	135	145	9	205	215	2
10	15	2	45	50	9	145	155	8	215	225	1
15	20	3	50	55	10	155	165	7	225	—	0
20	25	4	55	105	11	165	175	6			
25	30	5	105	115	11	175	185	5			
30	35	6	115	125	11	185	195	4			

made from amounts withheld as income tax, employee FICA taxes, and from the employer's FICA taxes. The amount of advance EIC payments is considered to have been paid over to the IRS on the day the wages are paid to employees.

E X A M P L E

Nolan Inc. has 10 employees each entitled to advance EIC payments of $12. The total advance payments made by Nolan for the payroll period is $120. The total income tax withheld for the payroll period is $110. The total FICA taxes for employees and employer are $128.

Nolan is considered to have made a deposit of $120 advance EIC payment on the day the wages are paid. The $120 is treated as if the company has paid the total $110 in income tax withholding and $10 of the employee FICA taxes. The company is liable only for $118 of the FICA taxes.

Employer's Returns and Records

The employer takes into account the amount of the advance EIC payments when completing Form 941. The amount of the advance EIC payments is subtracted from the total amount of income taxes and FICA taxes in order to determine the net taxes due for the quarter. All records of advance EIC payments should be retained four years and be available for review by the IRS. These records include:

1. Copies of employees' Forms W-5.
2. Amounts and dates of all wage payments and advance EIC payments.
3. Dates of each employee's employment.
4. Dates and amounts of tax deposits made.
5. Copies of returns filed.

NEWS
ALERT

By 1996, when the expansion is complete, nearly 19 million households will be getting $25 billion a year through the Earned Income Tax Credit. In 1996, a taxpayer with two or more children will get back 40 cents for every dollar earned up to $8,900, for a maximum credit of $3,560.

SELF-STUDY QUIZ 4–6.

1. During one week Georgia Brewer earned $155. She and her spouse have both filed Form W-5. Using the information presented in Figure 4–11, compute the amount of advance EIC payment Brewer is entitled to receive.
   $ _____
2. On a certain payday, the Gregory Company made advance EIC payments to its employees that amounted to more than the federal income taxes withheld. Does the company have to make a tax deposit for this payday? Explain.

WHAT ARE INDIVIDUAL RETIREMENT ACCOUNTS?

Individual Retirement Accounts

Under certain conditions, an employee may put aside each year the lesser of $2,000 (or $2,250 for spousal IRA with at least $250 placed in spouse's account) or 100% of their compensation without paying federal income taxes on their contributions. To be eligible for such deductible (tax-free) contributions, either of the following two conditions must be met:

1. The individual does not belong to a company-funded retirement plan. (In the case of a married employee, neither spouse can belong to an employer's retirement plan.)
2. The individual has adjusted gross income less than $25,000. (In the case of a married employee, the combined adjusted gross income must be less than $40,000.)

If the employee or spouse belongs to another qualified plan, partial tax-free deductions are allowed if:

1. The employee is single or head of household and has adjusted gross income less than $35,000.
2. The employee is married, filing a joint return and has adjusted gross income less than $50,000.
3. The employee is married, filing separately and has adjusted gross income less than $10,000.

Nondeductible IRA Contributions

A person who is ineligible to make a deductible contribution is permitted to make nondeductible contributions to a separate IRA account. The earnings on the nondeductible contributions are not subject to federal income tax until withdrawn. The limit on nondeductible contributions for a taxable year are the lesser of $2,000 or 100% of the employee's compensation.

WHAT ARE WAGE AND TAX STATEMENTS?

Employers must furnish *wage and tax statements* to employees informing them of the wages paid during the calendar year and the amount of taxes withheld from those wages. The employer sends copies of these statements to the federal government and, in many cases, to state, city, and local governments.

Form W-2

Form W-2, Wage and Tax Statement, shown in Figure 4–12, is prepared if any of the following items apply to an employee during the calendar year:

1. Income tax or social security tax taxes were withheld.
2. Income tax would have been withheld if the employee had not claimed more than one withholding allowance or had not claimed exemption from withholding on Form W-4.
3. Any amount was paid for services, if the employer is in a trade or business. The cash value of any noncash payments made should be included.
4. Any advance EIC payments were made.

Figure 4–12 *W-2 Wage and Tax Statement*

a Control number	22222	Void ☐	For Official Use Only ▶ OMB No. 1545-0008		
b Employer's identification number 13-5407221				1 Wages, tips, other compensation 29360.18	2 Federal income tax withheld 4610.00
c Employer's name, address, and ZIP code				3 Social security wages 29360.18	4 Social security tax withheld 1820.33
Stone Metal Products 600 Third Avenue Philadelphia, PA 19103-5600				5 Medicare wages and tips 29360.18	6 Medicare tax withheld 425.72
				7 Social security tips	8 Allocated tips
d Employee's social security number 382-13-7478				9 Advance EIC payment	10 Dependent care benefits
e Employee's name (first, middle initial, last) Henry T. Tate				11 Nonqualified plans	12 Benefits included in box 1
483 Monroe Street Philadelphia, PA 19119-4821				13 See Instrs. for box 13 C 78.00	14 Other BC/BS Premium w/h 296.00

15 Statutory employee ☐	Deceased ☒	Pension plan ☒	Legal rep. ☐	Hshld. emp. ☐	Subtotal ☐	Deferred compensation ☐

f Employee's address and ZIP code

16 State	Employer's state I.D. No.	17 State wages, tips, etc.	18 State income tax	19 Locality name	20 Local wages, tips, etc.	21 Local income tax
PA	46-8-0013	29360.18	822.09	Phila.	29360.18	1456.26

Cat. No. 10134D   Department of the Treasury—Internal Revenue Service

Form **W-2** Wage and Tax Statement **1995**

Copy A For Social Security Administration

For Paperwork Reduction Act Notice, see separate Instructions.

Figure 4–13 summarizes the instructions for completing each of the boxes on Form W-2. If an entry does not apply to the firm or employee, leave the box blank. Employers must give employees Form W-2 on or before January 31 following the close of the calendar year. When employees leave the service of the employer, you may give them Form W-2 any time after employment ends. If employees ask for Form W-2, the employer should give it to them within 30 days of their request or the final wage payment, whichever is later. In instances where terminated workers may be re-hired at some time before the year ends, the employer may delay furnishing the form until January 31 following the close of the calendar year. Employers distribute Form W-2 copies as follows:

Copy A—To the Social Security Administration by the end of February following the year for which Form W-2 is applicable.
Copy 1—To the state, city, or local tax department.
Copy B—To employees for filing with their federal income tax return.
Copy C—To employees for their personal records.
Copy 2—To employees for filing with their state, city, or local income tax returns.
Copy D—Retained by the employer.

If Form W-2 has been lost or destroyed, employers are authorized to furnish substitute copies to the employee. The substitute form should be clearly marked **REISSUED STATEMENT.** Do not send Copy A of the substitute

TIB-4, Magnetic Media Reporting, Submitting Annual W-2 Copy A Information to the Social Security Administration contains the reporting specifications and procedures for magnetic media filing of Copy A of Forms W-2.

You can get magnetic media reporting specifications by calling 1-800-772-1213.

Figure 4–13 *How to Complete Form W-2*

Box A—Control number: For the employer to identify the individual Forms W-2. Up to 7 digits may be used to assign the number, which the employer uses when writing the Social Security Administration about the form. The employer does not have to use this box.

Void: Put an X in this box when an error has been made. Amounts shown on void forms should not be included in your subtotal Form W-2.

Box B—Employer's identification number (EIN): Enter the number assigned to you by the IRS. Do not use a prior owner's EIN. If you do not have an EIN when filing Forms W-2, enter "Applied For". You can get an EIN by filing Form SS-4.

Box C—Employer's name, address, and Zip code: This entry should be the same as shown on your Form 941 or 943.

Box D—Employee's social security number: An employee who does not have an SSN should apply for one by completing Form SS-5.

Box F— Employee's address and Zip code: This box is combined with Box E on all copies except Copy A to allow you to mail employee's copies in a window envelope or as a self-mailer.

Box 1—Wages, tips, other compensation: Record, before any payroll deductions, the total of (1) wages, prizes, and awards paid; (2) noncash payments (including certain fringe benefits); (3) tips reported by employee to employer (not allocated tips); (4) certain employee business expense reimbursements; (5) cost of accident and health insurance premiums paid on behalf of 2% or more shareholder employees by an S corporation; (6) taxable benefits made from a Section 125 (cafeteria plan); and (7) all other compensation including scholarships and fellowship grants and payments for moving expenses. Other compensation is an amount you pay your employee from which federal income tax is not withheld. You may show other compensation on a separate Form W-2.

Box 2—Federal income tax withheld: Record the amount of federal income tax withheld from the employee's wages for the year.

Box 3—Social security wages: Enter the total wages paid (before payroll deductions) subject to employee social security (OASDI) tax. Do not include social security tips and allocated tips. Generally, noncash payments are considered wages. Include employee business expenses reported in box 1. Include employer contributions to qualified cash or deferred compensation plans and to retirement arrangements described in Box 13 (Codes D, E, F, and G), even though the deferrals are not includible in Box 1 as wages, tips, and other compensation. Include any employee OASDI and HI taxes and employee state unemployment compensation taxes you paid for your employee rather than deducting it from wages. Report in this box the cost of group-term life insurance coverage over $50,000 that is taxable to former employees. Report the cost of accident and health insurance premiums paid on behalf of 2% or more shareholder-employees by an S corporation only if the exclusion under Section 312(a)(2)(B) is not satisfied. Do not enter more than the maximum OASDI taxable wage base for the year.

Box 4—Employee social security tax withheld: Record the total social security (OASDI) tax (not your share) withheld or paid by you for the employee. Include only taxes withheld for the year's wages.

Box 5—Medicare wages and tips: Enter the Medicare (HI) wages and tips. Be sure to enter tips the employee reported even if you did not have enough employee funds to collect the HI tax for those tips. Report in this box the cost of group-term life insurance coverage over $50,000 that is taxable to former employees.

Box 6—Medicare tax withheld: Enter the total employee Medicare (HI) tax (not your share) withheld or paid by you for your employee. Include only taxes withheld for the year's wages.

Box 7—Social security tips: Record the amount the employee reported even if you did not have enough employee funds to collect the social security (OASDI) tax for the tips. The total of Boxes 3 and 7 should not be more than the maximum OASDI wage base for the year. But report all tips in box 1 along with wages and other compensation.

Box 8—Allocated tips: If you are a large food or beverage establishment, record the amount of tips allocated to the employee. Do not include this amount in Boxes 1, 5, or 7.

Box 9—Advance EIC payment: Record the total amount paid to the employee as advance earned income credit payments.

Box 10—Dependent care benefits: Record the total amount of dependent care benefits paid or incurred by you for your employee. This total should include any amount in excess of the exclusion.

Box 11—Nonqualified plans: Enter the amount from a Nonqualified deferred compensation plan or Section 457 plan that was distributed or became taxable because the substantial risk of forfeiture lapsed. Include this amount in Box 11 only if it is also includible in Boxes 1, 3, and 5. Report distributions to beneficiaries of deceased employees on Form 1099-R.

Box 12—Benefits included in Box 1: Record the total value of the taxable fringe benefits included in Box 1 as other compensation. Do not include amounts reported in Boxes 10 and/or 13. You may use a separate statement, Box 14, or multiple Forms W-2, if necessary, to report all Box 12 entries. If you use multiple Forms W-2, do not report the same federal wage and tax data to SSA on more than one Copy A.

Box 13—: Complete and code this box for all applicable items listed below in the Reference Guide. Additional information about any coded item may be found in the IRS's Instructions for Form W-2. Do not report in Box 13 any items not listed as Codes A through Q. Do not enter more than three codes in this box. If you are reporting more than three items, use a separate Form W-2 or a substitute Form W-2 to report the additional items.

Use a capital letter when entering each code. Leave one space blank after the code and enter the dollar amount on the same line. Use decimal points but not dollar signs or commas, such as J 358.00.

Box 14—Other: Use this box for any other information you want to give your employee. Label each item. Examples are union dues, health insurance premiums deducted, moving expenses paid, nontaxable income, or educational assistance payments.

Box 15—: Mark the boxes that apply.

Statutory employee: Mark this box for statutory employees whose earnings are subject to social security (OASDI) and Medicare (HI) taxes but not subject to federal income tax withholding.

Deceased: Mark this box if the employee is now deceased. If an employee is deceased, you must report wages or other compensation for services performed and paid in the year of death to the estate or beneficiary. Report wages paid after the date of death that are not subject to federal income tax withholding on Form 1099-Misc., Miscellaneous Income.

Pension plan: Mark this box if the employee was an active participant (for any part of the year) in a retirement plan such as 401(k) and SEP.

Legal representative: Mark this box when the employee's name is the only name shown but is shown as a trust account, or another name is shown in addition to the employee's name and the other person or business is acting on behalf of the employee.

942 employee: For household employers only. Mark this box if you are a household employer filing a single Form W-2. See Form 942 instructions.

Subtotal: Do not subtotal if you are submitting 41 or fewer Forms W-2. If you are submitting 42 or more Forms W-2, give subtotal figures for every 41 individual forms and the last group of forms. Mark the Subtotal box on the form that shows the subtotal dollar amount for the preceding 41 forms and for the last group of forms, even if less than 41 forms. Show subtotal amounts for Boxes 1 through 11, and 13.

Deferred compensation: Mark this box if the employee has made an elective deferral to a section 401(k), 403(b),408(k)(6), or 501(c)(18)(D) retirement plan. Also, mark this box if an elective or nonelective deferral was made to a section 457(b) plan.

Boxes 16 through 21—State or local income tax information: You do not have to complete these boxes, but you may want to if you use copies of this form for your state and local returns. The ID number is assigned by each individual state. The state and local information boxes can be used to report wages and taxes on two states and two localities. Keep each state's and locality's information separated by the dotted line.

Reference Guide for Box 13 Codes

A—Uncollected social security (OASDI) tax on tips

B—Uncollected Medicare (HI) tax on tips

C—Group-term life insurance over $50,000

D—Elective deferrals to a Section 401(k) cash or deferred arrangement

E—Elective deferrals to a Section 403(b) salary reduction agreement

F—Elective deferrals to a section 408(k)(6) salary reduction SEP

G—Elective and nonelective deferrals to a Section 457(b) deferred compensation plan (state and local government and tax-exempt employers).

H—Elective deferrals to a Section 501(c)(18)(D) tax-exempt organization plan.

J—Nontaxable sick pay

K—20% excise tax on excess golden parachute payments

L—Substantiated Employee Business Expense (federal rate)

M—Uncollected social security (OASDI) tax on group-term life insurance coverage

N—Uncollected Medicare (HI) tax on group-term life insurance coverage

P—Excludable reimbursed moving expenses

Q—Military employee basic quarters and subsistence

statement to the Social Security Administration. If, after a reasonable effort, the employer cannot deliver a Form W-2, the employer retains the employees' copies of the form for a four-year period. A "reasonable effort" means the forms were mailed to the last known address of the employee.

Form W-2c

To correct errors in previously filed Forms W-2, employers file *Form W-2c, Statement of Corrected Income and Tax Amounts*, shown in Figure 4–14. File Copy A with the Social Security Administration and the remaining copies as noted on the bottom of each form. Form W-3c should accompany all corrected wage and tax statements unless the correction is for only one employee, or to correct employees' names, addresses, or social security numbers.

Form W-3

Form W-3, Transmittal of Wage and Tax Statements, must be filed with the Social Security Administration by employers and other payers as a transmittal for Forms W-2. On Form W-3, the employer indicates the number of documents

Figure 4–14   *Form W-2c, Statement of Corrected Income and Tax Amounts*

a Year/Form corrected **19 95 / W-2**	Void ☐	OMB No. 1545-0008	For Official Use Only ▶		
b Employee's name, address, and ZIP code ☐ Corrected			c Employer's name, address, and ZIP code ☐ Corrected		
Henry T. Tate 483 Monroe Street Philadelphia, PA 19119-4821			Stone Metal Products 600 Third Avenue Philadelphia, PA 19103-5600		

d Employee's correct SSN 382-13-7478	e Employer's SSA number **69-**	f Employer's Federal EIN 13-5407221	g Employer's state I.D. number 46-8-0013

h Previously reported ▶	Stat. emp. ☐	De-ceased ☐	Pension plan ☐	Legal rep. ☐	Def'd. comp. ☐	IRA/SEP ☐	i Corrected ▶	Stat. emp. ☐	De-ceased ☐	Pension plan ☐	Legal rep. ☐	Def'd. comp. ☐	IRA/SEP ☐	j Employer's use

Complete k and/or l only if incorrect on the last form you filed. Show incorrect item here. ▶	k Employee's incorrect SSN	l Employee's name (as **incorrectly** shown on previous form)	

	Form W-2 box	(a) As previously reported	(b) Correct information	(c) Increase (decrease)
	1 Wages, tips, other comp.			
	2 Federal income tax withheld	4610.00	4160.00	(450.00)
	3 Social security wages			
	4 Social security tax withheld			
	5 Medicare wages and tips			
CHANGES	6 Medicare tax withheld			
	7 Social security tips			
	8 Allocated tips			
	17 State wages, tips, etc.			
	18 State income tax			
	20 Local wages, tips, etc.			
	21 Local income tax			

See back of Copy D for Instructions and the Paperwork Reduction Act Notice.   Copy A   For Social Security Administration

Form **W-2c** (Rev. 10-94)   **Statement of Corrected Income and Tax Amounts**   Department of the Treasury Internal Revenue Service

being transmitted. Form W-3 and the accompanying documents enable the Social Security Administration and the IRS to compare the totals to the taxes withheld as reported on the employers' 941. Figure 4–15 shows a completed Form W-3. The employer files all Forms W-2 with one W-3. When an employer has a large number of forms to be transmitted, the employer can forward the forms in separate packages clearly identified with the payer's name and identifying number. Forms W-3 and the related documents are filed with the Social Security Administration by the end of February each year.

Form W-3c

The *Transmittal of Corrected Income and Tax Statements, Form W-3c,* is used to accompany copies of Form W-2c, sent to the Social Security Administration. This form can also be used to correct a previously filed Form W-3.

Privately Printed Forms

Employers may use their own forms by obtaining specifications for the private printing of Forms W-2 from any IRS center or district office. To the extent that

Figure 4–15 *Form W-3, Transmittal of Wage and Tax Statements*

a Control number	For Official Use Only ▶ OMB No. 1545-0008		
b **Kind of Payer** 941 [X] Military [ ] 943 [ ] CT-1 [ ] Hshld. [ ] Medicare govt. emp. [ ]	1 Wages, tips, other compensation 2620736.40	2 Federal income tax withheld 330317.19	
	3 Social security wages 2066400.00	4 Social security tax withheld 128116.80	
c Total number of statements 132	d Establishment number	5 Medicare wages and tips 2620736.40	6 Medicare tax withheld 38000.68
e Employer's identification number 88-1936281	7 Social security tips	8 Allocated tips	
f Employer's name Grove Electronics	9 Advance EIC payments 778.00	10 Dependent care benefits	
33 Vista Road Vallejo, CA 94590-0033	11 Nonqualified plans	12 Deferred compensation 319530.00	
	13 Adjusted total social security wages and tips 2066400.00		
	14 Adjusted total Medicare wages and tips 2620736.40		
g Employer's address and ZIP code			
h Other EIN used this year	15 Income tax withheld by third-party payer		
i Employer's state I.D. No.			

Under penalties of perjury, I declare that I have examined this return and accompanying documents, and, to the best of my knowledge and belief, they are true, correct, and complete.

Signature ▶ *Carl W. Tolan*   Title ▶ President   Date ▶ 2/28/96

Telephone number (415) 555-3200

Form **W-3 Transmittal of Wage and Tax Statements 1995**   Department of the Treasury Internal Revenue Service

the privately printed forms meet the specifications, the employer may use them without prior approval of the IRS.

SELF-STUDY QUIZ 4–7.

1. The Marquat Company deducts unions dues from its employees' paychecks monthly during the year and sends them to the local union office. How should the company report this deduction on the employees' Form W-2?

2. Gringle's terminated 10 of its employees on July 15. The company informed each employee that it may rehire them again during their peak season in September. When should the company furnish each employee with a W-2 statement?

3. While preparing her 1996 personal income tax return, Connie Becker, an employee of Trident Mills, discovered that she had lost her Form W-2. What procedures should the company follow to prepare a new Form W-2 for Becker?

WHAT RETURNS MUST EMPLOYERS COMPLETE?

LEARNING OBJECTIVE 9

Employers must file returns reporting the amount of wages paid and the amount of taxes withheld at designated times, beginning with the first quarter in which taxable wages are paid. Rules that require different returns for different types of employees further complicate the accounting tasks and payroll procedures. Figure 4–16 briefly summarizes the major returns completed by employers.

Figure 4–16 *Major Returns Filed by Employers*

Form 941, Employer's Quarterly Federal Tax Return	For reporting federal income taxes withheld during the calendar quarter and the employer and employee portions of the FICA taxes. Form 941 is illustrated in Chapter 3.
Form 941-M, Employer's Monthly Federal Tax Return	For reporting federal income taxes withheld and FICA taxes on a monthly basis. IRS may require monthly returns and payments of taxes from employers who have not complied with the requirements for filing returns or the paying or depositing of taxes reported on quarterly returns. You are not required to file this return unless notified by the IRS.
Form 942, Employer's Quarterly Tax Return for Household Employees	For reporting federal income taxes withheld as a result of voluntary withholding agreements between employers and their domestic employees. Form 942 is also completed by employers who are liable for FICA taxes on wages paid to domestic workers.
Form 943, Employer's Annual Tax Return for Agricultural Employees	For reporting the withholding of federal income taxes and FICA taxes on wages paid to agricultural workers. Form 943 is used for agricultural employees even though the employer may employ nonagricultural workers.
Form 945, Annual Return of Withheld Federal Income Tax (See Figure 4–17)	Used to report tax liability for nonpayroll items such as backup withholding and withholding on gambling winnings, pensions, and annuities, and deposits made for the year. Backup withholding occurs when an individual receives taxable interest, dividends, and certain other payments and fails to furnish the payer with their correct taxpayer identification numbers. Payers are then required to withhold 31% of those payments. Backup withholding does not apply to wages, pensions, annuities, or IRAs.
Form 945-A, Annual Record of Federal Tax Liability	Completed by all semiweekly depositors and monthly depositors who accumulate $100,000 or more on any day to report on a daily basis their backup withholding and income taxes withheld from gambling winnings, pensions, and annuities.

Figure 4–17   *Form 945, Annual Return of Withheld Federal Income Tax*

Form 945 — Annual Return of Withheld Federal Income Tax

► For withholding reported on Forms 1099 and W-2G.

► See separate Instructions. For more information on income tax withholding, see Circular E.

4545   Please type or print.

Department of the Treasury
Internal Revenue Service

OMB No. 1545-1430

19

IRS USE ONLY

T	
FF	
FD	
FP	
I	
T	

Enter state code for state in which deposits made (see page 3 of instructions).

Name (as distinguished from trade name)

Employer identification number
31-7207411

Trade name, if any
LICITRA'S

Address (number and street)
1410 MAIN STREET

City, state, and ZIP code
WIMAUMA, FL
33598-0527

If address is different from prior return, check here ►

IRS Use

1 1 1 1 1 1 1 1 1 1   2   3 3 3 3 3 3   4 4 4

5 5 5   6   7   8 8 8 8 8 8   9 9   10 10 10 10 10 10 10 10 10 10

If you do not have to file returns in the future, check here ► ☐ and enter date final payments paid ► _____

1	Federal income tax withheld from pensions, annuities, IRAs, gambling winnings, etc.	1	470 00
2	Backup withholding	2	
3	**Total taxes** (add lines 1 and 2). This must equal line 7M below or line M of Form 945-A	3	470 00
4	Total deposits for 1994 from your records	4	470 00
5	**Balance due** (subtract line 4 from line 3). Pay to the Internal Revenue Service (See instructions.)	5	-0-

6   **Overpayment,** if line 3 is less than line 4, enter overpayment here ► $ _____ and check if to be:

☐ Applied to next return   OR   ☐ Refunded

- **All filers:** If line 3 is less than $500, you need not complete line 7 or Form 945-A.
- **Semiweekly depositors:** Complete Form 945-A and check here .... ► ☐
- **Monthly depositors:** Complete line 7, entries **A** through **M** and check here .... ► ☐

7   Monthly Summary of Federal Tax Liability

	Tax liability for month		Tax liability for month		Tax liability for month
A January		F June		K November	
B February		G July		L December	
C March		H August		M Total liability for year (add lines A through L)	
D April		I September			
E May		J October			

Sign Here

Under penalties of perjury, I declare that I have examined this return, including accompanying schedules and statements, and to the best of my knowledge and belief, it is true, correct, and complete.

Signature ► *Pauline V. Licitra*

Print Your Name and Title ► Pauline V. Licitra
Owner/Manager

Date ► 1/31/97

Form **945**

WHAT ARE INFORMATION RETURNS?

L E A R N I N G
O B J E C T I V E
10

The IRS requires employers to file *information returns* to report compensation paid to certain individuals who are not employees. These returns allow the IRS to determine if taxpayers are reporting their true income. Figure 4–18 briefly summarizes the major information returns required by the IRS. The employer sends copies of the returns to the IRS and the payee of the amount involved by the end of January.

To transmit each type of Form 1099, the employer uses *Form 1096, Annual Summary and Transmittal of U.S. Information Returns.* Employers use a separate 1096 Form to transmit each type of information return. For example, one Form 1096 is used to transmit all Forms 1099-Misc., and another Form 1096 is used to transmit all Forms 1099-INT. The employer files Form 1096 and all accompanying forms on or before the last day of February of the year following the payment.

Figure 4–18 *Major Information Returns*

Form 1099-Misc., Miscellaneous Income (See Figure 4–19)	For reporting miscellaneous income, such as rents, royalties, commissions, fees, prizes and awards of at least $600 paid to nonemployees, and any backup withholding. Gross royalty payments of $10 or more must also be reported on this form. Life insurance companies may use either 1099-Misc. or Form W-2 to report payments to full-time life insurance sales agents.
Form 1099-INT, Interest Income	For reporting payments of (a) interest of $10 or more paid or credited on earnings from savings and loans, credit unions, bank deposits, corporate bonds, etc. (b) interest of $600 or more from other sources; (c) forfeited interest due on premature withdrawals of time deposits: (d) foreign tax eligible for the recipient's foreign tax credit withheld and paid on interest; (e) payments of any interest on bearer certificates of deposit.
Form 1099-DIV, Dividends and Distributions	For reporting dividends totaling $10 or more to any person; foreign tax withheld and paid on dividends and other distributions on stock for a person; distributions made by corporations and regulated investment companies (including money market funds) as part of liquidation.
Form 1099-PATR, Taxable Distributions Received from Cooperatives	For cooperatives to report patronage dividends paid and other distributions made that total $10 or more during the year.
Form 1099-R, Distributions From Pensions, Annuities, Retirement or Profit-Sharing Plans, IRAs, Insurance Contracts, etc.	For reporting all distributions from pensions, annuities, profit-sharing and retirement plans, and individual retirement arrangements made by employees' trusts or funds; federal, state or local government retirement system; life insurance companies.
Form 1099-G, Certain Government Payments	For reporting unemployment compensation payments, state and local income tax refunds of $10 or more, taxable grants, income tax refunds, and agricultural subsidy payments.
Form 5498, Individual Retirement Arrangement Information	For reporting contributions received from each person to an IRA or simplified employee pension plan (SEP) and qualified deductible voluntary employee contributions to a plan maintained by the employer.
Form 8027, Employer's Annual Information Return of Tip Income and Allocated Tips	For large food or beverage establishments to report the amount of receipts from food or beverage operations, the amount of tips reported by employees, and the amounts allocated as tips to employees.

Figure 4–19 *Form 1099-MISC, Miscellaneous Income*

9595	☐ VOID	☐ CORRECTED		
PAYER'S name, street address, city, state, and ZIP code	**1** Rents $	OMB No. 1545-0115		
Worldwide Publishing Co. 40 Fifth Avenue New York, NY 10011-4000	**2** Royalties $34970.65	**19**95	**Miscellaneous Income**	
	3 Other income $	Form **1099-MISC**		
PAYER'S Federal identification number 75-4013736	RECIPIENT'S identification number 461-91-4821	**4** Federal income tax withheld $	**5** Fishing boat proceeds $	**Copy A** **For**
RECIPIENT'S name Laurie T. Musberger		**6** Medical and health care payments $	**7** Nonemployee compensation $	**Internal Revenue Service Center**
		8 Substitute payments in lieu of dividends or interest $	**9** Payer made direct sales of $5,000 or more of consumer products to a buyer (recipient) for resale ▶ ☐	**File with Form 1096.**
Street address (including apt. no.) 1043 Maple Drive				For Paperwork Reduction Act Notice and
City, state, and ZIP code Chicago, IL 60615-3443		**10** Crop insurance proceeds $	**11** State income tax withheld $	instructions for completing this form, see **Instructions for**
Account number (optional)	2nd TIN Not. ☐	**12** State/Payer's state number 85-33378		**Forms 1099, 1098, 5498, and W-2G.**

Form **1099-MISC**   Department of the Treasury - Internal Revenue Service

MAGNETIC FILING FORM W-2 AND INFORMATION RETURNS

If employers file 250 or more Forms W-2 or other information returns (for each type of information return), they must use magnetic media instead of paper forms. Filing Forms W-2 does not require approval of the medium by the Social Security Administration. However, the employer must use *Form 6559, Transmitter Report and Summary of Magnetic Media*, to identify themselves when submitting magnetic media files. For other information returns, the employer obtains prior approval of the medium. The employer must complete *Form 4419, Application for Filing Information Returns Magnetically/Electronically*, and file it with the IRS. If employers can prove that filing Forms W-2 or other information returns magnetically would be an undue hardship, they may request a waiver by submitting *Form 8508, Request for Waiver From Filing Information Returns on Magnetic Media*, to the IRS 45 days prior to the due date of the return.

HOW DO YOU WITHHOLD FOR STATE INCOME TAX?

In addition to federal income taxes, many states also have income tax withholding requirements. The situation is further complicated if an employer has employees in several states. This requires employers to know how much tax to withhold, what types of employees and payments are exempt, and how to pay the tax. Employers must also be informed about each state's regulations regarding:

LEARNING OBJECTIVE **11**

1. The required frequency of making wage payments.
2. The acceptable media of payment.
3. The maximum interval between the end of a pay period and the payday for that period.
4. The time limits for making final wage payments to employees who are discharged, laid off, quit, or go on strike.

5. How often to inform employees of the deductions made from their wages.
6. The maximum amount of unpaid wages to pay the surviving spouse or family of a deceased worker.

Employers in most states use wage-bracket tables and percentage method formulas to determine the amount of state income taxes to withhold from their employees' wages. However, when the size of wage payments and the frequency of such payments are irregular, overwithholding may result. Thus, employees become dissatisfied with the amount of their take-home pay. Although the federal income tax law and regulations provide for the use of alternative withholding methods in such situations, the methods are not automatically adopted by the states. Therefore, employers must decide for their individually affected states, which, if any, of the federal alternative withholding methods may be used to compute the amount of state income tax withholding. In states imposing personal income taxes, the laws vary as to the withholding of taxes from wages paid. Most states having income tax laws require employers to withhold tax from both nonresidents and residents, unless a *reciprocal agreement* exists with one or more states to the contrary. For example, a reciprocal agreement may exist between two states where both states grant an exemption to nonresidents who work in each of those states.

State Income Tax Returns and Reports

Payroll managers should be familiar with four main types of state income tax returns or reports:

1. **Periodic withholding returns** on which you report the wages paid and the state tax withheld during the reporting period. Figure 4–20 shows the employer *Deposit Statement of Income Tax Withheld* used by employers in Pennsylvania. Depending on the amount of state income taxes withheld for each quarterly period, employers may be required to pay the taxes semimonthly, monthly, or quarterly. Some states require employers to deposit their withheld income taxes through electronic funds transfer (EFT).

Figure 4–20 *Form PA-501R, Pennsylvania Employer Deposit Statement of Income Tax Withheld*

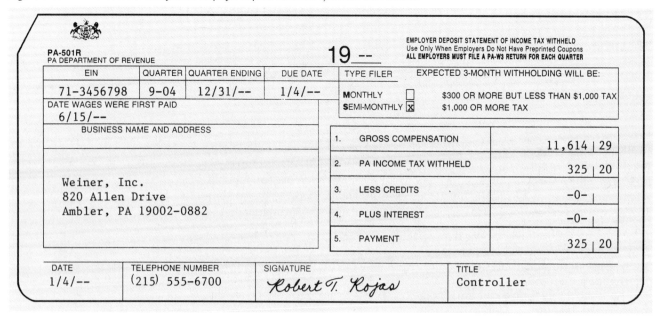

2. **Reconciliation returns** that compare the total amount of state tax paid as shown on the periodic returns with the amounts of state tax declared to have been withheld from employees' wages. Figure 4–21 shows *The Employer Quarterly Reconciliation Return of Income Tax Withheld* for use by employers in Pennsylvania. Employers who have computer systems may submit their information on magnetic media.
3. **Annual statements** to employees showing the amount of wages paid during the year and the state tax withheld from those wages.
4. **Information returns** used to report payments to individuals that are not subject to withholding and/or are not reported on the annual employee wage and tax statements. See figure 4-18 for a listing of the major information returns.

Since the requirements for transmitting returns and reports vary from state to state, employers should become familiar with the tax regulations of the state in which their business is located and of the state or states in which their employees reside. Because federal regulations require filing of information returns on magnetic media, many states permit employers to submit wage information on magnetic disk or tape. Also, many states take part in the Combined Federal/State Filing Program, which enables employers to file information returns with the federal government and authorize release of the information to the applicable state. To participate in this program, employers must first obtain permission from the IRS.

Withholding Local Income Taxes

In addition to state income tax laws, many cities and counties have passed local income tax legislation requiring employers to deduct and withhold income taxes or license fees on salaries or wages paid. In Alabama, several cities have license fee ordinances that require the withholding of the fees from employee's wages. Certain employees in Denver, Colorado, are subject to the withholding

Figure 4–21 *Form PA-W3R, Pennsylvania Employer Quarterly Reconciliation Return of Income Tax Withheld*

PA-W3R
PA DEPARTMENT OF REVENUE

19--

EMPLOYER QUARTERLY RECONCILIATION RETURN OF INCOME TAX WITHHELD
For Use ONLY When Employers Do Not Have Preprinted Coupons

EIN	QUARTER	QUARTER ENDING	DUE DATE
71-3456798	9-04	12/31/--	1/31/--

BUSINESS NAME AND ADDRESS
Weiner, Inc.
820 Allen Drive
Ambler, PA 19002-0882

RECORD OF PA WITHHOLDING TAX BY PERIOD

PERIOD	SEMI-MONTHLY AMOUNTS WITHHELD	PERIOD	MONTHLY AMOUNTS WITHHELD
1ST HALF OF MONTH	331.34	1ST MONTH	
2ND HALF OF MONTH	310.17	2ND MONTH	
1ST HALF OF MONTH	325.39	3RD MONTH	
2ND HALF OF MONTH	365.74		
1ST HALF OF MONTH	304.51		
2ND HALF OF MONTH	325.20		
TOTAL (ENTER TOTAL ON LINE 2.)	1,962.35	TOTAL (ENTER TOTAL ON LINE 2.)	

QUARTERLY FILERS COMPLETE LINES 1-5 ONLY.

1. TOTAL COMPENSATION SUBJECT TO PA TAX	70,083.81
2. TOTAL PA WITHHOLDING TAX (FROM LEFT)	1,962.35
3. TOTAL DEPOSITS FOR QUARTER (INCLUDING VERIFIED OVERPAYMENTS)	1,962.35
4. OVERPAYMENT (IF LINE 3 IS GREATER THAN LINE 2)	-0-
5. TAX DUE/PAYMENT (IF LINE 2 IS GREATER THAN LINE 3)	-0-

Under penalties of perjury, I declare that I have examined this return and to the best of my knowledge and belief, it is true, correct and complete.

Date	Telephone Number	Signature	Title
1/31/--	(215) 555-6700	Robert T. Rojas	Controller

of the Denver Occupational Privilege Tax from their compensation. In Kentucky, a number of cities and counties impose a license fee (payroll tax).

Figure 4–22 shows the return that must be completed by employers in Philadelphia. All must withhold the city income tax from compensation paid their employees. Depending upon the amount of taxes withheld, employers may be required to make deposits weekly, monthly, or quarterly. For any late payments of the tax, the city imposes a penalty on the underpayment. Employers must file annual reconciliation returns by the end of February, reporting the amount of taxes deducted during the preceding calendar year.

Figure 4–22 *Form W-1-5, The City of Philadelphia Employer's Return of Tax Withheld*

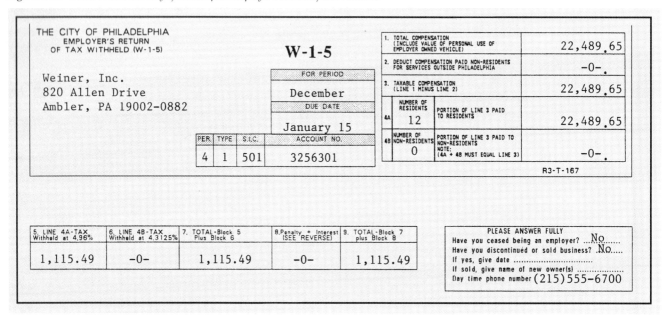

KEY TERMS

Annualizing wages	Quarterly averaging of wages
Backup withholding	Reciprocal agreement
Cumulative withholding	Special withholding allowance
Earned income credit (EIC)	Standard deduction
Employee	Supplemental wage payments
Employer	Wage and tax statement
Information return	Wage-bracket method
Percentage method	Wages
Personal allowance	

QUESTIONS FOR REVIEW

NOTE: Use the Tax Tables A and B at the back of this textbook and the tax regulations presented in this chapter to answer all questions and solve all problems.

1. To what extent are cash tips treated as remuneration subject to federal income tax withholding?

2. Under what conditions must a large food establishment allocate tips to its tipped employees?
3. For each of the following kinds of wage payments, indicate whether or not the wages are exempt from the withholding of federal income taxes:

   a. Three weeks' vacation pay.
   b. Weekly advance to a sales representative for traveling expenses to be incurred.
   c. Weekly wages paid the housekeeper in a college fraternity.
   d. Monthly salary received by Rev. Cole Carpenter.
   e. Benefits paid by a union to its members who are on strike.

4. What is a personal allowance? What was the amount of a personal allowance for 1995?
5. On July 15, William Mitchell amended his Form W-4 to increase the number of withholding allowances from four to seven. Mitchell asked for a refund of the amount of overwithheld income taxes from January 1 to July 15 when the number of allowances was only four. Should Mitchell be reimbursed for the income taxes overwithheld before the effective date of the amended Form W-4?
6. Under what conditions may employees be exempt from the withholding of federal income taxes during 1996? How do such employees indicate their no-tax-liability status?
7. Employers must submit copies of Form W-4 to the IRS under what conditions?
8. Commencing in June, Slade Exon is eligible to receive monthly payments from a pension fund. What procedure should Exon follow if he does not wish to have federal income taxes withheld from his periodic pension payments?
9. Rhonda Gramm is single and her wages are paid weekly. What is the amount of Gramm's one withholding allowance? Howard Heinz, married, claims two withholding allowances and his wages are paid semi-monthly. What is the total amount of his withholding allowance?
10. Max Lieberman, a married employee, fails to furnish his employer with a withholding allowance certificate. His weekly wages amounts to $445. Under the percentage method, will any portion of his wages be subject to withholding? If so, indicate what portion.
11. The Baucus Company has just completed the processing of its year-end payroll and distributed all the weekly paychecks. The payroll department is now computing the amount of the annual bonus to be given each worker. What methods may be used by the company in determining the amount of federal income taxes to be withheld from the annual bonus payments?
12. From what source do employers obtain the funds needed to make advance EIC payments to their eligible employees?
13. Orrin D'Amato, single, participates in his firm's pension retirement plan. This year his adjusted gross income will be about $42,000. How much of his compensation may D'Amato contribute to an IRA this year without paying federal income taxes on the contribution?
14. The employer completes Form W-3 for what purpose?
15. Why must some employers file Form 1096?

QUESTIONS FOR DISCUSSION

1. Alex Oberstar, a cook in the Lagomarsino company cafeteria, is furnished two meals each day during his eight-hour shift. Oberstar's duties require him to have his meals on the company's premises. Should the cash value of Oberstar's meals be included as part of his taxable wages? Explain.
2. The Solomon Company ordinarily pays its employees on a weekly basis. Recently one of the employees, Bernard Nagle, was sent from the home office on a three-week trip. Nagle has now returned to the office and you are preparing a single check covering his three-weeks' services. Should you withhold federal income taxes on the total gross earnings for the three-week period or should you compute the federal income taxes as if Nagle were receiving three separate weekly wage payments?
3. Investigate your state's income tax withholding law (or that of some other state assigned by your instructor) and find the answers to the following questions:

   a. Who must withhold the tax?
   b. How are covered employers and covered employees defined?
   c. Are there any reciprocal agreements the state has entered into? If so, describe them.
   d. How is the withholding rate determined?
   e. What payments are subject to withholding?

    f. What payments are not subject to withholding?

    g. Are there any employee withholding exemptions?

    h. What methods of withholding are permitted?

    i. Describe each of the returns required by the state.

    j. What kinds of information must be retained by employers in their withholding tax records?

    k. What penalties are imposed for failure to comply with the withholding law?

    l. Are any employers required to deposit their withheld income taxes through electronic funds transfer (EFT)? If so, what requirements does the state impose?

4. Janice Sikorski, one of your firms workers, has just come into the payroll Department and says to you: "I am thinking of amending my Form W-4 so that an additional $10 is withheld each week. That way I will get a fat refund next year. What do you think of my idea?" How would you reply to Sikorski?

5. Anita Leland, a waitress in the Atlantis Casino, reported tips of $467 to her employer last year. Two months after she filed her federal income tax return, Leland received a letter from the IRS informing her that she had earned $5,260 in tips rather than the $467 reported and that she owed the government $1,872.94 in back taxes.

    a. How is the IRS able to determine the amount of tips received by a waitress in a casino?

    b. If the IRS is correct in its determination of the tips received, is Atlantis subject to a penalty for not having withheld payroll taxes on all the tips Leland received during the year?

PRACTICAL PROBLEMS

4–1. LO 4.

Use the percentage method to compute the federal income taxes to withhold from the wages or salaries of each employee.

Employee No.	Employee Name	Marital Status	No. of Withholding Allowances	Gross Wage or Salary	Amount to Be Withheld
1	Amoroso, A.	M	4	$610 weekly	_____
2	Finley, R.	S	0	$825 biweekly	_____
3	Gluck, E.	S	5	$9,630 quarterly	_____
4	Quinn, S.	M	8	$925 semimonthly	_____
5	Treave, Y.	M	3	$1,975 monthly	_____

4–2. LO 4.

Use (a) the percentage method and (b) the wage-bracket method to compute the federal income taxes to withhold from the wages or salaries of each employee.

Employee	Marital Status	No. of Withholding Allowances	Gross Wage or Salary	Amount to Be Withheld Percentage Method	Amount to Be Withheld Wage-Bracket Method
Astin, N.	S	2	$475 weekly	_____	_____
Copeland, S.	S	1	$960 weekly	_____	_____
Jensen, R.	M	6	$1,775 biweekly	_____	_____
Schaffer, H.	M	4	$1,480 semimonthly	_____	_____
Yelm, T.	M	9	$5,380 monthly	_____	_____

4–3. LO 4.

Eaton Enterprises uses the wage-bracket method to determine federal income tax withholding on its employees. Compute the amount to withhold from the wages paid each employee.

Employee	Marital Status	No. of Withholding Allowances	Payroll Period W=Weekly S=Semimonthly M=Monthly D=Daily	Wage	Amount to Be Withheld
Hal Bower	M	1	W	$1,350	_____
Ruth Cramden	S	1	W	$590	_____
Gil Jones	S	3	W	$675	_____
Teresa Kern	M	6	M	$4,090	_____
Ruby Long	M	2	M	$2,730	_____
Katie Luis	M	8	S	$955	_____
Susan Martin	S	1	D	$96	_____
Jim Singer	S	4	S	$2,010	_____
Martin Torres	M	4	M	$3,215	_____

4-4. LO 4.

The names of the employees of the Western Music Shop are listed on the following payroll register. Employees are paid weekly. The marital status and the number of allowances claimed are shown on the payroll register, along with each employee's weekly salary. Complete the payroll register for the payroll period ending October 6, the 40th weekly payday. The state income tax rate is 2% of total earnings and the city income tax rate is 1.5% of the total gross earnings.

FOR PERIOD ENDING _____ 19___

EMPLOYEE'S NAME	MARITAL STATUS	NO. OF W/H ALLOW.	TOTAL EARNINGS	DEDUCTIONS (a) FICA OASDI	DEDUCTIONS (a) FICA HI	(b) FIT	(c) SIT	(d) CIT	(e) NET PAY
Bennet, Marvin	M	3	1 6 0 0 00						
Green, Robert	S	1	2 8 5 00						
Herd, Ben	M	0	1 5 5 00						
Larson, Beverly	S	3	3 2 4 25						
Maston, Roberta	S	1	3 7 5 00						
Nash, Tim	S	2	5 5 8 50						
Stelt, Harold	S	1	4 7 0 50						
Zelder, Nadine	M	3	3 8 0 00						
Totals									

Compute the employer's FICA taxes for the pay ending October 6.

OASDI Taxes

   OASDI taxable earnings $ _____

   OASDI taxes $ _____

HI Taxes

   HI taxable earnings $ _____

   HI taxes $ _____

The names of the employees of Cox Security Systems and their regular salaries are shown in the following payroll register. Note that Hill and Van Dyne are paid monthly on the last day, while all others are paid weekly.

In addition to the regular salaries, the company pays an annual bonus based on the amount of earnings for the year. For the current year, the bonus amounts to 8% of the annual salary paid to each employee. The bonus is to be paid along with the regular salaries on December 31, but the amount of the bonus and the amount of the regular salary will be shown separately on each employee's earnings statement. Assume that all employees received their regular salary during the entire year.

Prepare the payroll for the pay period ending December 31, showing the following for each employee:

Use the wage-bracket method to withhold federal income tax from the regular salaries.
Withhold a flat 28% on the annual bonus.
Total salaries and bonuses are subject to a 2% state income tax and a 1% city income tax.

FOR PERIOD ENDING _____ 19____

EMPLOYEE'S NAME	MARITAL STATUS	NO. OF W/H ALLOW.	EARNINGS REGULAR	EARNINGS (a) SUPP'L.	(b) TOTAL	DEDUCTIONS (c) FICA OASDI	DEDUCTIONS (c) FICA HI	(d) FIT	(e) SIT	(f) CIT	(e) NET PAY
Hill, J. Harvey	M	5	5 0 0 0 00								
Van Dyne, Joyce S.	M	2	2 8 5 0 00								
Abbott, Leslie N.	S	1	5 2 0 00								
Bunger, Russel L.	M	4	4 6 5 00								
Noblet, Thomas D.	M	2	3 8 0 00								
Short, Frank C.	S	1	3 5 0 00								
Toban, Harriette O.	M	2	5 7 5 00								
Wyeth, Amy R.	S	0	4 2 5 00								
Totals											

Compute the employer's FICA taxes for the pay ending December 31.

OASDI Taxes

    OASDI taxable earnings $ _____

    OASDI taxes $ _____

HI Taxes

    HI taxable earnings $ _____

    HI taxes $ _____

4-6. LO 4, 6.

During the quarter ending December 31 of the current year, Cox Security Systems had 13 weekly paydays and three monthly paydays. Using the data given in Problem 4–5, complete the following form to show:

a. Total earnings paid during the quarter, including both the regular and the supplemental earnings.
b. Total amount of FICA taxes withheld during the quarter.
c. Total amount of federal income taxes withheld during the quarter.
d. Total amount of state income taxes withheld during the quarter.
e. Total amount of city income taxes withheld during the quarter.
f. Total net amount paid each employee during the quarter.

EMPLOYEE'S NAME	(a) TOTAL EARNINGS	(b) FICA OASDI	(b) FICA HI	(c) FIT	(d) SIT	(e) CIT	(f) NET PAY
Hill, J. Harvey							
Van Dyne, Joyce S.							
Abbott, Leslie N.							
Bunger, Russel L.							
Noblet, Thomas D.							
Short, Frank C.							
Toban, Harriette O.							
Wyeth, Amy R.							
Totals							

DEDUCTIONS

4–7. **LO 7.**

The employees of Evergreen Garden Center are paid weekly. The names of five employees of the company are given on the following payroll register. The payroll register also shows the marital status and number of withholding allowances claimed, and the total weekly earnings for each worker. Assume that each employee is paid the same weekly wage on each payday in 1996. Also shown below is the wage-bracket table for Advance Earned Income Credit (EIC) Payments for a weekly payroll period. Each employee listed on the payroll register has completed a Form W-5 indicating that the worker is not married. Complete the payroll register for the weekly period ending December 1, 1996. The state income tax rate is 1.5% on total earnings.

EMPLOYEE'S NAME	MARITAL STATUS	NO. OF W/H ALLOW.	TOTAL EARNINGS	(a) FICA OASDI	(a) FICA HI	(b) FIT	(c) SIT	(d) ADVANCE EIC PAYMENT	(e) NET PAY
Allen, R.	S	4	$229 00						
Dilts, Y.	S	1	412 00						
Martin, E.	S	2	215 00						
Roselli, T.	S	3	376 00						
Whitman, Q.	S	1	125 00						
Totals									

WEEKLY Payroll Period

SINGLE or MARRIED Without Spouse Filing Certificate

Wages— At least	But less than	Payment to be made	Wages— At least	But less than	Payment to be made	Wages— At least	But less than	Payment to be made	Wages— At least	But less than	Payment to be made
0	5	0	70	75	14	255	265	20	395	405	6
5	10	1	75	80	15	265	275	19	405	415	5
10	15	2	80	85	16	275	285	18	415	425	4
15	20	3	85	90	17	285	295	17	425	435	3
20	25	4	90	95	18	295	305	16	435	445	2
25	30	5	95	100	19	305	315	15	445	455	1
30	35	6	100	105	20	315	325	14	455	—	0
35	40	7	105	110	21	325	335	13			
40	45	8	110	115	22	335	345	12			
45	50	9	115	215	23	345	355	11			
50	55	10	215	225	23	355	365	10			
55	60	11	225	235	22	365	375	9			
60	65	12	235	245	21	375	385	8			
65	70	13	245	255	21	385	395	7			

4-8. LO 9.

During the fourth quarter of 1996 there were seven biweekly paydays on Friday (October 4, 18; November 1, 15, 29; December 13, 27) for Emerald City Repair. Assume that each of the seven biweekly payrolls was the same as the one shown below. Using the forms supplied below and on pages 42–45, complete the following for the fourth quarter:

a. Federal Tax Deposit Coupons, Forms 8109. The employer's phone number is (501) 555-7331.
b. Employer's Quarterly Federal Tax Return, Form 941. The form is signed by you.
c. Employer's Report of State Income Tax Withheld for the quarter, due on or before January 31, 1997.

Biweekly Payroll Data

Total Earnings	OASDI	HI	FIT	SIT	EIC Payments
$2,675.00	$165.85	$38.79	$243.00	187.25	$251.00

Employer's OASDI	$165.85
Employer's HI	$38.79

EMPLOYER'S REPORT OF STATE INCOME TAX WITHHELD

(DO NOT WRITE IN THIS SPACE)

IMPORTANT: PLEASE REFER TO THIS NUMBER IN ANY CORRESPONDENCE →

WITHHOLDING IDENTIFICATION NUMBER	MONTH OF OR QUARTER ENDING
42-7-3301	DEC. 96

IF YOU ARE A SEASONAL EMPLOYER AND THIS IS YOUR FINAL REPORT FOR THIS SEASON, CHECK HERE ☐ AND SHOW THE NEXT MONTH IN WHICH YOU WILL PAY WAGES.

EMERALD CITY REPAIR
10 SUMMIT SQUARE
CITY, STATE 00000-0000

IF NAME OR ADDRESS IS INCORRECT, PLEASE MAKE CORRECTIONS.

THIS REPORT MUST BE RETURNED EVEN IF NO AMOUNT HAS BEEN WITHHELD

Under penalties prescribed by law, I hereby affirm that to the best of my knowledge and belief this return, including any accompanying schedules and statements, is true and complete. If prepared by a person other than taxpayer, his affirmation is based on all information of which he has any knowledge.

SIGNATURE: TITLE: DATE:

1. GROSS PAYROLL THIS PERIOD . . . . $
2. STATE INCOME TAX WITHHELD . . . . $
3. ADJUSTMENT FOR PREVIOUS PERIOD(S). (ATTACH STATEMENT) $
4. TOTAL ADJUSTED TAX (LINE 2 PLUS OR MINUS LINE 3) $
5. PENALTY (25% OF LINE 4)
6. INTEREST . . . .
7. TOTAL AMOUNT DUE AND PAYABLE . . . . $

MAIL THIS REPORT WITH CHECK OR MONEY ORDER PAYABLE TO THE DEPT. OF REVENUE ON OR BEFORE DUE DATE TO AVOID PENALTY.

Date _____   Name _____

4–8.

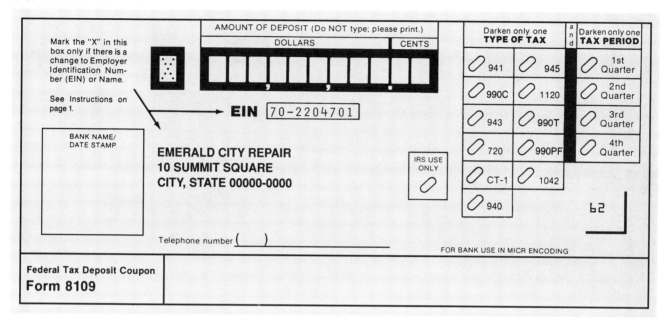

To be deposited on or before _____

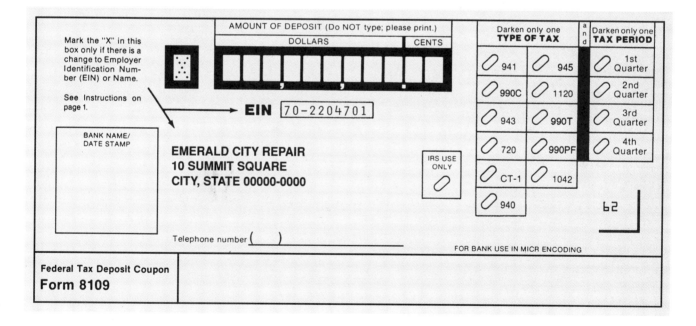

To be deposited on or before _____

4–8.

	AMOUNT OF DEPOSIT (Do NOT type; please print.)			Darken only one **TYPE OF TAX**		a n d	Darken only one **TAX PERIOD**

Mark the "X" in this box only if there is a change to Employer Identification Number (EIN) or Name.

See Instructions on page 1.

DOLLARS　　　　CENTS

EIN 70-2204701

BANK NAME/ DATE STAMP

EMERALD CITY REPAIR
10 SUMMIT SQUARE
CITY, STATE 00000-0000

IRS USE ONLY

TYPE OF TAX		TAX PERIOD
941	945	1st Quarter
990C	1120	2nd Quarter
943	990T	3rd Quarter
720	990PF	4th Quarter
CT-1	1042	
940		62

Telephone number ( )

FOR BANK USE IN MICR ENCODING

Federal Tax Deposit Coupon
Form 8109

To be deposited on or before _____

4–8.

Form 941

Department of the Treasury
Internal Revenue Service

4141

Employer's Quarterly Federal Tax Return

▶ See separate Instructions for information on completing this return.

Please type or print.

Enter state code for state in which deposits made . ▶ ⊡ (see page 2 of instructions).

Name (as distinguished from trade name)

Trade name, if any
EMERALD CITY REPAIR

Address (number and street)
10 SUMMIT SQUARE

Date quarter ended
DEC 31, 1996

Employer identification number
70-2204701

City, state, and ZIP code
CITY, STATE
00000-0000

OMB No. 1545-0029

| T |
| FF |
| FD |
| FP |
| I |
| T |

If address is different from prior return, check here ▶ ☐

IRS Use

| 1 | 1 | 1 | 1 | 1 | 1 | 1 | 1 | 1 | 1 | 2 | 3 | 3 | 3 | 3 | 3 | 3 | 4 | 4 | 4 |
| 5 | 5 | 5 | 6 | 7 | 8 | 8 | 8 | 8 | 8 | 9 | 9 | 9 | 10 | 10 | 10 | 10 | 10 | 10 | 10 | 10 | 10 | 10 |

If you do not have to file returns in the future, check here ▶ ☐ and enter date final wages paid ▶

If you are a seasonal employer, see **Seasonal employers** on page 2 and check here (see instructions) ▶ ☐

1	Number of employees (except household) employed in the pay period that includes March 12th ▶		
2	Total wages and tips subject to withholding, plus other compensation	**2**	
3	Total income tax withheld from wages, tips, and sick pay	**3**	
4	Adjustment of withheld income tax for preceding quarters of calendar year	**4**	
5	Adjusted total of income tax withheld (line 3 as adjusted by line 4—see instructions) . . .	**5**	
6a	Taxable social security wages . . . . $ _____ × 12.4% (.124) =	**6a**	
b	Taxable social security tips . . . . $ _____ × 12.4% (.124) =	**6b**	
7	Taxable Medicare wages and tips . . . . . $ _____ × 2.9% (.029) =	**7**	
8	Total social security and Medicare taxes (add lines 6a, 6b, and 7). Check here if wages are not subject to social security and/or Medicare tax . . . . ▶ ☐	**8**	
9	Adjustment of social security and Medicare taxes (see instructions for required explanation) Sick Pay $ _____ ± Fractions of Cents $ _____ ± Other $ _____ =	**9**	
10	Adjusted total of social security and Medicare taxes (line 8 as adjusted by line 9—see instructions)	**10**	
11	**Total taxes** (add lines 5 and 10)	**11**	
12	Advance earned income credit (EIC) payments made to employees, if any	**12**	
13	Net taxes (subtract line 12 from line 11). **This should equal line 17, column (d) below** (or line D of Schedule B (Form 941))	**13**	
14	Total deposits for quarter, including overpayment applied from a prior quarter	**14**	
15	**Balance due** (subtract line 14 from line 13). Pay to Internal Revenue Service	**15**	
16	**Overpayment,** if line 14 is more than line 13, enter excess here ▶ $ _____		

and check if to be: ☐ Applied to next return **OR** ☐ Refunded.

• **All filers:** If line 13 is less than $500, you need not complete line 17 or Schedule B.

• **Semiweekly depositors:** Complete Schedule B and check here . . . . ▶ ☐

• **Monthly depositors:** Complete line 17, columns (a) through (d) and check here . . . . ▶ ☐

17	Monthly Summary of Federal Tax Liability.			
	(a) First month liability	(b) Second month liability	(c) Third month liability	(d) Total liability for quarter

Sign Here

Under penalties of perjury, I declare that I have examined this return, including accompanying schedules and statements, and to the best of my knowledge and belief, it is true, correct, and complete.

Signature ▶ _____   Print Your Name and Title ▶ _____   Date ▶ _____

Form **941**

4–9. **LO 8.**

During the first week of 1997 the payroll department of the Figley Corporation is preparing the Forms W-2 for distribution to its workers along with their payroll checks on January 5. In this problem you will complete six of the forms in order to gain some experience in recording the different kinds of information required.

Assume each worker earned the same weekly salary for each of the 52 paydays in 1996.

Using the following information obtained from the personnel and payroll records of the firm, complete Copy A of the six Forms W-2 reproduced on the following pages.

Company Information:

Address: 4800 River Road
                    Philadelphia, PA 19113-5548
Federal identification number: 13-7490972
State identification number: 46-3-1066

Income Tax Information:

The wage-bracket method is used to determine federal income tax withholding.
The Pennsylvania tax rate is 2.8% of the worker's weekly gross wages.
The city tax rate for residents of Philadelphia is 4.96% of the worker's weekly gross wages.

Employee Data	Payroll Data
Patricia A. Grimes 54 Gradison Place Philadelphia, PA 19113-4054	Single 1 allowance $415 per week SS#: 376-72-4310
Roberta P. Kurtz 56 Andrews Court, Apt. 7 Philadelphia, PA 19103-3356	Married 1 allowance $485 per week SS#: 272-33-8804
David P. Markle 770 Camac Street Philadelphia, PA 19101-3770	Single 0 allowances $365 per week SS#: 178-92-3316 Union dues withheld: $102
Harold W. Rasul 338 North Side Avenue Philadelphia, PA 19130-6638	Married 7 allowances $1,250 SS#: 269-01-6839 Cost of group-term life insurance exceeding $50,000: $262.75 No income tax withheld on insurance cost.
Christine A. Shoemaker 4900 Gladwynne Terrace Philadelphia, PA 19127-0049	Married 2 allowances $320 per week SS#: 368-14-5771 Advance EIC payments $12 per week Union dues withheld: $102
Angelo Zickar 480-A Hopkinson Tower Philadelphia, PA 19101-3301	Single 1 allowance $390 per week SS#: 337-99-8703 Educational assistance payments (job-required): $675

Date _____   Name _____

4–9.

<table>
<tr><td colspan="2">a Control number</td><td>22222</td><td>Void ☐</td><td colspan="2">For Official Use Only ▶
OMB No. 1545-0008</td></tr>
<tr><td colspan="3">b Employer's identification number</td><td></td><td>1 Wages, tips, other compensation</td><td>2 Federal income tax withheld</td></tr>
<tr><td colspan="3" rowspan="3">c Employer's name, address, and ZIP code</td><td rowspan="3"></td><td>3 Social security wages</td><td>4 Social security tax withheld</td></tr>
<tr><td>5 Medicare wages and tips</td><td>6 Medicare tax withheld</td></tr>
<tr><td>7 Social security tips</td><td>8 Allocated tips</td></tr>
<tr><td colspan="3">d Employee's social security number</td><td></td><td>9 Advance EIC payment</td><td>10 Dependent care benefits</td></tr>
<tr><td colspan="3">e Employee's name (first, middle initial, last)</td><td></td><td>11 Nonqualified plans</td><td>12 Benefits included in box 1</td></tr>
<tr><td colspan="3"></td><td></td><td>13 See Instrs. for box 13</td><td>14 Other</td></tr>
<tr><td colspan="4">f Employee's address and ZIP code</td><td colspan="2">15 Statutory employee ☐ Deceased ☐ Pension plan ☐ Legal rep ☐ 942 emp ☐ Subtotal ☐ Deferred compensation ☐</td></tr>
<tr><td>16 State</td><td>Employer's state I.D. No.</td><td>17 State wages, tips, etc.</td><td>18 State income tax</td><td>19 Locality name 20 Local wages, tips, etc</td><td>21 Local income tax</td></tr>
</table>

Department of the Treasury—Internal Revenue Service

Form **W-2** **Wage and Tax Statement** **1996**

Copy A For Social Security Administration

<table>
<tr><td colspan="2">a Control number</td><td>22222</td><td>Void ☐</td><td colspan="2">For Official Use Only ▶
OMB No. 1545-0008</td></tr>
<tr><td colspan="3">b Employer's identification number</td><td></td><td>1 Wages, tips, other compensation</td><td>2 Federal income tax withheld</td></tr>
<tr><td colspan="3" rowspan="3">c Employer's name, address, and ZIP code</td><td rowspan="3"></td><td>3 Social security wages</td><td>4 Social security tax withheld</td></tr>
<tr><td>5 Medicare wages and tips</td><td>6 Medicare tax withheld</td></tr>
<tr><td>7 Social security tips</td><td>8 Allocated tips</td></tr>
<tr><td colspan="3">d Employee's social security number</td><td></td><td>9 Advance EIC payment</td><td>10 Dependent care benefits</td></tr>
<tr><td colspan="3">e Employee's name (first, middle initial, last)</td><td></td><td>11 Nonqualified plans</td><td>12 Benefits included in box 1</td></tr>
<tr><td colspan="3"></td><td></td><td>13 See Instrs. for box 13</td><td>14 Other</td></tr>
<tr><td colspan="4">f Employee's address and ZIP code</td><td colspan="2">15 Statutory employee ☐ Deceased ☐ Pension plan ☐ Legal rep ☐ 942 emp ☐ Subtotal ☐ Deferred compensation ☐</td></tr>
<tr><td>16 State</td><td>Employer's state I.D. No.</td><td>17 State wages, tips, etc.</td><td>18 State income tax</td><td>19 Locality name 20 Local wages, tips, etc</td><td>21 Local income tax</td></tr>
</table>

Department of the Treasury—Internal Revenue Service

Form **W-2** **Wage and Tax Statement** **1996**

Copy A For Social Security Administration

a Control number	22222	Void ☐	For Official Use Only ▶ OMB No. 1545-0008	

b Employer's identification number	**1** Wages, tips, other compensation	**2** Federal income tax withheld
c Employer's name, address, and ZIP code	**3** Social security wages	**4** Social security tax withheld
	5 Medicare wages and tips	**6** Medicare tax withheld
	7 Social security tips	**8** Allocated tips
d Employee's social security number	**9** Advance EIC payment	**10** Dependent care benefits
e Employee's name (first, middle initial, last)	**11** Nonqualified plans	**12** Benefits included in box 1
	13 See Instrs. for box 13	**14** Other

15 Statutory employee ☐	Deceased ☐	Pension plan ☐	Legal rep ☐	942 emp ☐	Subtotal ☐	Deferred compensation ☐

f Employee's address and ZIP code

16 State Employer's state I.D. No.	**17** State wages, tips, etc.	**18** State income tax	**19** Locality name	**20** Local wages, tips, etc.	**21** Local income tax

Department of the Treasury—Internal Revenue Service

Form **W-2** Wage and Tax Statement **1996**

Copy A For Social Security Administration

a Control number	22222	Void ☐	For Official Use Only ▶ OMB No. 1545-0008	

b Employer's identification number	**1** Wages, tips, other compensation	**2** Federal income tax withheld
c Employer's name, address, and ZIP code	**3** Social security wages	**4** Social security tax withheld
	5 Medicare wages and tips	**6** Medicare tax withheld
	7 Social security tips	**8** Allocated tips
d Employee's social security number	**9** Advance EIC payment	**10** Dependent care benefits
e Employee's name (first, middle initial, last)	**11** Nonqualified plans	**12** Benefits included in box 1
	13 See Instrs. for box 13	**14** Other

15 Statutory employee ☐	Deceased ☐	Pension plan ☐	Legal rep ☐	942 emp ☐	Subtotal ☐	Deferred compensation ☐

f Employee's address and ZIP code

16 State Employer's state I.D. No.	**17** State wages, tips, etc.	**18** State income tax	**19** Locality name	**20** Local wages, tips, etc.	**21** Local income tax

Department of the Treasury—Internal Revenue Service

Form **W-2** Wage and Tax Statement **1996**

Copy A For Social Security Administration

4–9.

a Control number	22222	Void ☐	For Official Use Only ▶ OMB No. 1545-0008	

b Employer's identification number	1 Wages, tips, other compensation	2 Federal income tax withheld
c Employer's name, address, and ZIP code	3 Social security wages	4 Social security tax withheld
	5 Medicare wages and tips	6 Medicare tax withheld
	7 Social security tips	8 Allocated tips
d Employee's social security number	9 Advance EIC payment	10 Dependent care benefits
e Employee's name (first, middle initial, last)	11 Nonqualified plans	12 Benefits included in box 1
	13 See Instrs. for box 13	14 Other

15 Statutory employee ☐	Deceased ☐	Pension plan ☐	Legal rep ☐	942 emp ☐	Subtotal ☐	Deferred compensation ☐

f Employee's address and ZIP code

16 State Employer's state I.D. No.	17 State wages, tips, etc.	18 State income tax	19 Locality name	20 Local wages, tips, etc.	21 Local income tax

Department of the Treasury—Internal Revenue Service

Form **W-2** Wage and Tax Statement **1996**

Copy A For Social Security Administration

---

a Control number	22222	Void ☐	For Official Use Only ▶ OMB No. 1545-0008	

b Employer's identification number	1 Wages, tips, other compensation	2 Federal income tax withheld
c Employer's name, address, and ZIP code	3 Social security wages	4 Social security tax withheld
	5 Medicare wages and tips	6 Medicare tax withheld
	7 Social security tips	8 Allocated tips
d Employee's social security number	9 Advance EIC payment	10 Dependent care benefits
e Employee's name (first, middle initial, last)	11 Nonqualified plans	12 Benefits included in box 1
	13 See Instrs. for box 13	14 Other

15 Statutory employee ☐	Deceased ☐	Pension plan ☐	Legal rep ☐	942 emp ☐	Subtotal ☐	Deferred compensation ☐

f Employee's address and ZIP code

16 State Employer's state I.D. No.	17 State wages, tips, etc.	18 State income tax	19 Locality name	20 Local wages, tips, etc.	21 Local income tax

Department of the Treasury—Internal Revenue Service

Form **W-2** Wage and Tax Statement **1996**

Copy A For Social Security Administration

CONTINUING PAYROLL PROBLEM

Refer to the partially completed payroll register which you worked on at the end of Chapter 3. You will now determine the amount of income tax to withhold for each employee, proceeding as follows:

1. In the appropriate columns of your payroll register, record the marital status and number of withholding allowances claimed for each employee, using the information provided.
2. Record the amount of federal income taxes, using the wage-bracket method.
3. Record the state income taxes on the gross weekly earnings for each employee. The rate is 2.8% for the state of Pennsylvania.
4. Record the city income taxes on the gross weekly earnings of each employee. The rate is 4.96% for the city of Philadelphia residents.

Time Card No.	Marital Status	No. of Allowances
11	S	1
12	S	0
13	M	2
21	M	4
22	S	2
31	M	3
32	M	6
33	S	1
51	M	5
99	M	7

CASE PROBLEMS

C1. **Answering Employees' Questions About Wage Reporting.**

During the past week, one of your newly employed payroll associates dropped into your office to ask several questions regarding wage reporting for federal income and social security tax purposes. If you were the payroll supervisor, how would you answer each of the following questions raised by your associate?

1. I just noticed that the social security number is wrong on three of the worker's W-2 forms. How do I go about correcting the forms? Will the workers be penalized for filing incorrect forms?
2. Eileen Huang informed me today that I had withheld too much Medicare tax from her pay last year. She is right! What forms do I use to make the correction?
3. You asked me last week to locate one of our former employees, Warren Bucks. I can't seem to track him down. What should I do with his Form W-2?
4. Is it okay to use titles like "M.D." and "Esq." when I keyboard data in the W-2 forms?

THAT WAS
THEN
THIS IS
NOW

U.S. unemployment reached between 15 and 17 million by the end of 1932. Americans who did work averaged little more than $16 per week. The jobless rate for fiscal year 1993 was 6.8%, with 21.9 billion in benefits paid. The average weekly unemployment benefit payment was $178.58.

UNEMPLOYMENT COMPENSATION TAXES

LEARNING OBJECTIVES

After studying this chapter, you should be able to:

1. Describe the basic requirements for an individual to be classified as an employer or an employee under the Federal Unemployment Tax Act.

2. Describe the factors considered in determining the coverage of interstate employees.

3. Identify generally what is defined as taxable wages by the Federal Unemployment Tax Act.

4. Compute the federal unemployment tax and the credit against this tax.

5. Describe how an experience rating system is used in determining employers' contributions to state unemployment compensation funds.

6. Complete the reports required by the Federal Unemployment Tax Act.

7. Describe the types of information reports under the various state unemployment compensation laws.

8. Describe the factors that determine eligibility for unemployment compensation benefits.

The Social Security Act of 1935 ordered every state to set up an unemployment compensation program in order to provide payments to workers during periods of temporary unemployment. Payroll taxes at both the federal and state levels fund this unemployment insurance program. The Federal Unemployment Tax Act (FUTA) imposes a tax on employers based on wages paid for covered employment. It is *not* collected or deducted from employees' wages. The funds collected by the federal government as a result of this tax pay the cost of administering both the federal and the state unemployment insurance programs. The FUTA tax is *not* used for the payment of weekly benefits to unemployed workers. Such benefits are paid by the states in accordance with each state's unemployment tax law (SUTA). These unemployment benefits are paid out of each state's trust fund, which is financed by state unemployment taxes. Because all states conform to standards specified in FUTA, considerable uniformity exists in the provisions of the state unemployment compensation laws. However, many variations in eligibility requirements, rates of contributions, benefits paid, and duration of benefits exist. All the states, Puerto Rico, the Virgin Islands, and the District of Columbia have enacted unemployment compensation laws that have been approved by the Social Security Administration.

You can realize the extent of the federal-state unemployment insurance program in terms of the people involved by the fact that in July, 1995, the number of unemployed persons was 7.6 million out of a civilian labor force of about 132.5 million. At that time the jobless rate was 5.7%. *Unemployed persons* include young people seeking positions for the first time, seasonal workers unemployed a part of each year, and workers who lost their jobs through various causes and cannot find other suitable employment.

COVERAGE UNDER FUTA AND SUTA

Other than a few significant exceptions as explained in this section, the coverage under FUTA is similar to that under FICA, as described in Chapter 3.

Employers—FUTA

The federal law levies a payroll tax on employers for the purpose of providing more uniform administration of the various state unemployment compensation laws. The federal law considers a person or a business an employer if *either* of the following two tests applies:

1. Pays wages of $1,500 or more during any calendar quarter in the current or preceding calendar year, or
2. Employs one or more persons, on at least some portion of one day, in each of 20 or more calendar weeks during the current or preceding taxable year.

A number of points serve to clarify the meaning of the two alternative tests: (a) a calendar week is defined as seven successive days beginning with Sunday; (b) the 20 weeks need not be consecutive; (c) the employees need not be the same employees; (d) regular, part-time, and temporary workers are considered employees; (e) in determining the employer's status, employees include individuals on vacation or sick leave; and (f) members of a partnership are not considered to be employees. As soon as an employer meets either test, the employer becomes liable for the FUTA tax for the entire calendar year.

E X A M P L E

In the Vemor Company, the 20th week of having one or more employees does not occur until November of 1996. The company becomes liable for FUTA tax on all taxable wages paid beginning with January 1, 1996.

Once attained, the employer status continues for two calendar years. Thus, an employer may be covered in the second calendar year even though the employer does not meet the coverage requirements for that year. Once the second calendar year has ended, the employer's FUTA liability terminates until the coverage requirements are once again met. Generally the nature of the business organization has no relevance in determining employer status. Thus, the employer may be an individual, corporation, partnership, company, association, trust, or estate. There may be instances where it is difficult to determine which of two entities is the employer for purposes of FUTA. As under FICA, the question is answered by determining which entity has the ultimate right to direct and control the employees' activities. It is not necessary that the employer actually direct or control the manner in which the services are performed; it is sufficient if the employer has the right to do so. Other factors characteristic of an employer include the right to discharge and the furnishing of tools and a place to work.

Employers—SUTA

In general, employers specifically excluded under the federal law are also excluded under the state laws. However, as a result of variations found in state unemployment compensation laws, not all employers covered by the unemployment compensation laws of one or more states are covered by FUTA. For example, the services performed by some charitable organizations may be covered by a state's unemployment compensation act, but these same services may be exempt from FUTA coverage. In order to have their state unemployment insurance laws approved by the federal government, the states must provide coverage for most state and local government workers, including employees in nonprofit elementary and secondary schools. In addition, coverage is extended to employers of domestic workers who pay $1,000 or more for such services in any calendar quarter of the current or preceding year.

Employees—FUTA

Every individual is considered an employee if the relationship between the worker and the person for whom the services are performed is the legal common-law relationship of employer and employee. This individual would then be counted in determining whether the employer is subject to FUTA. Chapter 3 covers the nature of this common-law relationship. No distinction is made between classes or grades of employees. Thus, superintendents, managers, and other supervisory personnel are employees. An officer of a corporation is an employee of the corporation, but a director, as such, is not.

For the purpose of the FUTA tax, the term "employee" also means any of the following who perform service for remuneration:

Domestic service is not to be considered when determining employer status under FUTA for the wage test or the "1-in-20" test.

1. An agent-driver or a commission-driver who distributes food or beverages (other than milk) or laundry or dry-cleaning services for the principal.
2. A traveling or a city salesperson engaged in full-time soliciting and transmitting to the principal orders for merchandise for resale or supplies for use in business operations.

If a person in one of these categories has a substantial investment in facilities used to perform the services (not including transportation facilities), the individual is an independent contractor and not a covered employee. Also, individuals are not covered if their services are a single transaction that is not part of a continuing relationship with the persons for whom they are performed. The work performed by the employee for the employer includes any services of whatever nature performed within the United States, regardless of the citizenship or residence of either. FUTA coverage also includes service of any nature performed outside the United States by a citizen of the United States for an American employer. The major exception is that service performed in Canada or in any other adjoining country with which the United States has an agreement relating to unemployment does not constitute covered employment.

An employee may perform both included and excluded employment for the same employer during a pay period. In such a case, the services which predominate in the pay period determine the employee's status with that employer for the period. FUTA wholly exempts some services from coverage. Among those *excluded* from coverage in 1996 include:

1. Independent contractors, such as physicians, lawyers, dentists, veterinarians, contractors, subcontractors, public stenographers, auctioneers, and others who follow an independent trade, business, or profession in which they offer their services to the public.
2. Directors of corporations, unless they perform services for the corporation other than those required by attending and participating in meetings of the board of directors.
3. Members of partnerships.
4. Insurance agents or solicitors paid solely on a commission basis.
5. Agricultural laborers; however, if the employer employs 10 or more during any 20 different weeks in a year or pays $20,000 or more in a quarter during the current or preceding year, the exemption is lost.
6. Casual laborers, unless cash remuneration paid for such service is $50 or more in a calendar quarter, and the person to whom it is paid is regularly employed by the one for whom the services were performed during that period.
7. Domestic workers, students or nonstudents, rendering service in a private home, local college club, or local chapter of a college fraternity or sorority. If the work is performed for an employer who paid $1,000 or more for such services in any calendar quarter of the current or preceding year, the exemption is lost.
8. Foreign students and exchange visitors who are carrying out the purposes for which they are admitted into the United States, such as studying, teaching, or conducting research. If employed for other purposes, they would not be excluded.
9. Students enrolled full-time in a work-study or internship program, for work that is an integral part of the student's academic program.
10. Service performed by an individual for a son, daughter, or spouse, or by a child under the age of 21 for a parent.
11. Services performed by individuals in fishing and related activities if the vessel is less than ten net tons.
12. Service performed in the employ of foreign, federal, state, or local governments and certain of their instrumentalities. However, taxes imposed by

FUTA apply to these federal instrumentalities: federal reserve banks, federal loan banks, and federal credit unions.

13. Government employees of international organizations, such as the United Nations.
14. Individuals under 18 years of age who deliver or distribute newspapers or shopping news (other than delivery or distribution to any point for subsequent delivery and distribution) and retail vendors of any age who sell and distribute newspapers and magazines to the ultimate consumer.
15. Services performed by employees or employee representatives for employers covered by either the Railroad Retirement Tax Act or the Railroad Unemployment Insurance Act.
16. Services performed by a student who is enrolled and regularly attending classes at a school, college, or university, if service is performed for school, college, or university.
17. Student nurses and hospital interns.
18. Services performed in the employ of a religious, educational, or charitable organization that is exempt from federal income tax. This exemption includes service in church-sponsored elementary and secondary schools.

Employees—SUTA

The definition of "employee" as established by FUTA applies to a majority of the states, although minor variations exist in the state laws. One variation involves firms that employ persons who work in more than one state. In these cases, we must determine which state covers the workers for unemployment compensation purposes.

Coverage of Interstate Employees. An *interstate employee* is an individual who works in more than one state. To prevent duplicate contributions on the services of interstate employees, all states have adopted a uniform definition of employment in terms of where the work is localized. This definition covers the entire services of an interstate worker in one state only—that state in which the worker will most likely look for a job if he or she becomes unemployed. The several factors that must be considered in determining coverage of interstate employees, in their order of application, include:

L E A R N I N G

O B J E C T I V E

2

1. Place where the work is *localized*.
2. Location of *base of operations*.
3. Location of place from which operations are *directed or controlled*.
4. Location of *employee's residence*.

Place Where the Work is Localized. Under this main criterion of coverage adopted by the states, if all the work is performed within one state, it is clearly "localized" in that state and constitutes "employment" under the law of that state. In some cases, however, part of the person's work may be performed outside the state. In such instances the entire work may be treated as localized within the state if the services performed in other states are temporary or transitory in nature.

E X A M P L E

Carson Thomson is a sales representative whose regular sales territory lies within Arizona. Thomson is covered by the laws of Arizona, with respect to his total employment, even though he makes frequent trips to the firm's showrooms in Los Angeles to attend sales meetings and to look over new lines of goods.

Location of Base of Operations. Often a worker may perform services continually in two or more states. In such situations the employment in one state is not incidental to the employment in the other state. Thus, the test of localization does not apply, and the base of operations test must be considered. Under this test, the employee's services may be covered by the laws of a single state even though the services are not localized within that state. The base of operation is the place of a more or less permanent nature from which the employee starts work and to which the employee customarily returns. It could be a particular place where his or her (a) instructions are received, (b) business records are maintained, (c) supplies are sent, or (d) office is maintained (may be in the employee's home).

E X A M P L E

Mitch Goldman travels through four southern states for the Irwin Company, which is headquartered in Georgia. His work is equally divided among the four states. When working in Georgia, he reports to the main office for instructions. The location of his base of operations is clearly Georgia, and his services are subject to the Georgia laws.

Location of Place from Which Operations Are Directed or Controlled. Often an employee's services are not localized in any state. Or it may be impossible to determine any base of operations. If the place of control can be fixed in a particular state in which some service is performed, that will be the state in which the individual is covered.

E X A M P L E

Joyce Mendes is a sales representative whose sales territory is so widespread that she does not retain any fixed business address or office. She receives all orders or instructions by mail or wire wherever she may happen to be. Clearly the work is not localized in any state, and no fixed base of operations exists. However, the services performed by Mendes may still come under the provisions of a single state law—the law of that state in which is located the place of direction or control, provided that some of Mendes's work is also performed in that state.

Location of Employee's Residence. If an employee's coverage cannot be determined by any of the three tests described, a final test, that of the employee's residence, is used. Thus, the worker's service is covered in its entirety in the state in which the employee lives, provided some of the service is performed in that state.

E X A M P L E

Robert Donald is employed by the Prang Company of Indiana. He lives in Iowa, and his work territory includes Iowa, Minnesota, and Wisconsin. Since neither the base of operations nor the place from which his work is directed is in a state in which he works, he is covered in his state of residence (Iowa).

Reciprocal Arrangements and Transfers of Employment. The states have entered into several types of interstate agreements, known as *reciprocal arrangements,* to provide unemployment insurance coverage and payment of benefits to interstate workers. The most widely accepted type of interstate coverage arrangement is the Interstate Reciprocal Coverage Arrangement. Under this arrangement, an employer can elect to cover all of the services of a worker in any one state in which (a) the employee performs any work, or (b) the employee maintains a residence, or (c) the employer maintains the place of business.

E X A M P L E

Morris Davidson is a salesperson for the Tannenbaum Company. His sales territory includes parts of Connecticut and Massachusetts, and his services can be considered localized in both states. Under the Interstate Reciprocal Coverage Arrangement, the company elects to cover Davidson under the law of Massachusetts.

Once the employer chooses the state in which all the services of the interstate workers are to be covered, this state approves the election of coverage. Then, the appropriate agencies of the other states in which services are performed are notified so that they can agree to the coverage in the state of election. Another aspect of reciprocal arrangements concerns the transfer of an employee from one state to another during the same calendar year. In all the states, an employer can include, for purposes of determining the taxable wage base in the second state, wages paid an employee with respect to employment covered by the unemployment compensation law of the previous state.

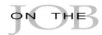

The only states that do not participate in reciprocal arrangements are Alaska, Kentucky, Mississippi, New Jersey, and New York, plus Puerto Rico.

E X A M P L E

The Karlson Company has paid wages of $4,000 to an employee in State A. During the year the employee is transferred to State B, which has a $7,000 taxable salary limitation for its state unemployment tax. The company has a credit of $4,000 against this $7,000 limit. Thus, the company has to pay State B's unemployment tax on only the next $3,000 of wages earned by that worker in State B during the remainder of the calendar year.

Coverage of Americans Working Overseas. As mentioned before, coverage extends to U.S. citizens working abroad for American employers. The state of the employer's principal place of business would provide the coverage. If the principal place of business cannot be determined, the state of incorporation or the state of residence of the individual owners would be the state of coverage.

Wages—FUTA

Generally *wages* means all remuneration for employment, including the cash value of all remuneration paid in any medium other than cash, with certain exceptions.

L E A R N I N G
O B J E C T I V E
3

E X A M P L E

An exemption from FUTA exists for commissions paid to insurance agents and solicitors who are paid solely by commission.

During 1996 taxable wages include only the first $7,000 of remuneration paid by an employer to an employee with respect to employment during any calendar year. The basis upon which the remuneration is paid is immaterial. It may be paid on a piece-work basis or it may be a percentage of profits; it may be paid hourly, daily, weekly, biweekly, semimonthly, monthly, or annually. Some of the more common types of payments made to employees and the taxability status of these payments include:

Taxable Wages for Unemployment Purposes

1. Advance payment for work to be done in the future.
2. Cash and noncash prizes and awards for doing outstanding work, for exceeding sales quotas, or for contributing suggestions that increase productivity or efficiency.
3. Bonuses as remuneration for services.
4. Christmas gifts, excluding noncash gifts of nominal value.
5. Commissions as compensation for covered employment.
6. Payments representing compensation for services by an employee paid to the dependents after an employee's death. Payments in the nature of a gratuity rather than compensation for services are nontaxable. Any payments made by an employer to an employee's estate or to the employee's survivors after the calendar year in which the employee died are excluded from the definition of wages and thus may not be taxed.
7. Dismissal payments.
8. Idle time and standby payments.
9. Retroactive wage increases.
10. Transfer of stock by an employer to the employees as remuneration for services. (The fair market value of the stock at the time of payment is the taxable base.)
11. Payments under a guaranteed annual wage plan.
12. Contributions by an employer to a supplemental unemployment individual-account plan, to which the employee has a fully vested and nonforfeitable right.
13. All tips, including charged tips, reported by the employee to the employer.
14. Vacation pay.
15. Payment by the employer of the employee's FICA tax or the employee's share of any state unemployment compensation tax without deduction from the employee's wages.
16. Payments to employees or their dependents on account of sickness or accident disability. These payments are *not* taxable after the expiration of six months following the last calendar month in which the employee worked. Payments for work missed due to pregnancy are not classified as taxable wages during the first six months of absence.
17. Employer contributions to cash or deferred arrangements to the extent that the contributions are not included in the employees' gross income.

Nontaxable Wages for Unemployment Purposes

1. Advances or reimbursement of ordinary and necessary business expenses incurred in the business of the employer.
2. Bonuses under a supplemental compensation plan paid upon retirement, death, or disability of an employee.

3. Caddy fees.
4. Commissions paid to insurance agents and solicitors who are paid solely by commission. Such persons are classified as independent contractors, not employees.
5. Courtesy discounts to employees and their families.
6. Payments made by an employer under a plan established by the employer for health, accident, or life insurance, or retirement benefits on behalf of the employees or their dependents.
7. Reimbursement of an employee's moving expenses if at the time of payment, it is reasonable to believe that the employee will be entitled to a deduction for those expenses at the time of filing his or her federal income tax return.
8. Allowances made to an individual by a prospective employer for expenses incurred in connection with interviews for possible employment.
9. Retirement pay.
10. Strike benefits paid by a union to its members.
11. Workers' compensation payments.
12. Educational assistance payments to workers, if the education maintains or improves skills required by the individual's employment.
13. Value of meals and lodging furnished employees for the convenience of the employer.

Wages—SUTA

The definition of taxable wages is fairly uniform under the various state unemployment compensation laws. However, some variations exist among the states as to the status of particular kinds of payments. For example, about one sixth of the states have ruled that Christmas bonuses or gifts are "wages" when substantial, contractual, or based on a percentage of the employee's wages or length of service. New Hampshire, however, does not include gifts or gratuities of $25 or less as wages, unless paid under a contract related to past or future employment. A further variation in defining taxable wages among the states arises in the treatment of *dismissal payments,* sometimes called payments in lieu of notice, separation pay, or terminal leave pay. Generally such payments are considered wages whether or not the employer must legally make the payments. However, in some states dismissal payments do not constitute wages unless the employer must legally make them. Puerto Rico does not consider any type of dismissal payment to be wages.

UNEMPLOYMENT COMPENSATION TAXES AND CREDITS

The base of the unemployment compensation tax is wages *paid* rather than *wages payable.* Thus, an employer is liable for the unemployment compensation tax in the year in which wages are paid employees, not necessarily in the year in which the services are rendered. Thus, if an employee performs services in 1995 but is not paid for them until 1996, the employer is liable for the tax in 1996 and the 1996 tax rates apply. Wages are considered paid when actually paid or when *constructively paid.* Wages are considered constructively paid when credited to the account of, or set apart for, an employee so that they may be drawn upon at any time, even though they are not actually possessed by the employee.

Tax Rate—FUTA

Under FUTA, all employers, as defined earlier, are subject to a tax with respect to having individuals in their employ. For 1996, the employer's tax rate is 6.2% of the first $7,000 wages paid each employee during the calendar year. Thus, an employer is liable for the FUTA tax on wages paid each employee until the employee's wages reach the $7,000 level. If an employee has more than one employer during the current year, the taxable wage base applies separately to each of those employers, unless one employer has transferred the business to the second.

E X A M P L E

Assume that in 1996 an employer had charged the wages account for $63,910. Of this amount, $720 will not be paid until the first payday in 1997. Further, the wages actually paid to employees in 1996 in excess of $7,000 each amounted to $19,840. The gross FUTA tax imposed on the employer is computed as follows:

Total amount charged to wages during 1996		$63,910.00
Less:		
Wages not to be paid until 1997	$ 720	
Wages paid in excess of $7,000 limit	19,840	20,560.00
Total taxable wages		$43,350.00
Rate of tax		6.2%
Amount of gross FUTA tax		$ 2,687.70

L E A R N I N G
O B J E C T I V E
4

Credits Against FUTA Tax. The actual FUTA tax paid is usually only 0.8%, since employers are entitled to a credit against their FUTA tax liability for contributions made under approved state unemployment compensation laws. The maximum credit permitted is 5.4% (90% of 6%). Thus, in the preceding example where the *gross* FUTA tax rate is 6.2%, the *net* FUTA rate would be .8% if the full 5.4% credit applied. Employers that pay state unemployment taxes of less than 5.4% get an additional credit against the FUTA tax for the difference between the amount actually paid to the state and the amount they would have paid if their rate were 5.4%.

The net FUTA tax may be computed in two ways:

E X A M P L E

1. Total taxable earnings (above example)		$43,350.00
Net rate of tax (6.2% – 5.4%)		.8%
Amount of net FUTA tax		$ 346.80
2. Amount of gross FUTA tax (6.2%)		$ 2,687.70
Total taxable wages	$43,350	
Credit against tax	5.4%	
Total credit		2,340.90
Amount of net FUTA tax		$ 346.80

To obtain the maximum credit of 5.4% against the federal tax, the employer must make the state contributions on or before the due date for filing the annual return under FUTA (see page 5–21). If the employer is late in paying the state contributions, the credit is limited to 90% of the amount that would have been allowed as a credit if the late contributions had been paid on or before January 31, 1997.

E X A M P L E

The Sutcliffe Company had taxable wages totaling $87,500 in 1996. During the year the company was late in paying some of its state contributions. The penalty for tardiness is shown in the following calculation of the firm's net FUTA tax for 1996:

Amount of gross FUTA tax ($87,500 × 6.2%)		$ 5,425.00
State taxable wages	$87,500	
Sutcliffe's SUTA tax rate	5.4%	
Sutcliffe's SUTA tax	$ 4,725	

Breakdown of Sutcliffe's SUTA tax payments:
Before 1/31/97—$3,000 × 100% credit		(3,000.00)
After 1/31/97—$1,725 × 90% credit		(1,552.50)
Amount of net FUTA tax		$ 872.50

If the company had made timely payments of its state contributions, the amount of its net FUTA tax would have been reduced to $700, for a savings of $172.50, as follows:

Amount of gross FUTA tax ($87,500 × 6.2%)		$ 5,425.00
Total taxable wages	$87,500	
Credit against tax	5.4%	
Total credit		4,725.00
Amount of net FUTA tax ($87,500 × .8%)		$ 700.00

$872.50 – $700.00 = $172.50, savings

Experience Rating. In some cases, employers may pay contributions into their state unemployment fund at a rate lower than 5.4%. The method by which the employer contributions may be adjusted because of a favorable employment record is referred to as *experience rating* or *merit rating*. Thus, an employer's favorable experience rate (employment record) qualifies the employer for a SUTA rate lower than 5.4%. As noted before, FUTA provides for a credit equal to the employer's SUTA rate plus an additional credit so that the *full 5.4% credit* still applies. In this way, employers who have steady employment histories and, therefore, lower SUTA tax rates, are not penalized when the FUTA tax is paid.

SELF-STUDY QUIZ 5–1. Garo Company pays taxable wages (FUTA and SUTA) of $188,000 during 1996. Garo Company has a state unemployment tax rate of 4.1% for 1996 because of its past employment record. Compute Garo Company's 1996 FUTA and SUTA taxes.

$_____   FUTA
$_____   SUTA

If an employer receives an additional credit against the FUTA tax because the state experience rate is less than 5.4%, the additional credit is not subject to the 90% FUTA credit limitation for late SUTA payments. The credit reduction applies only to actual SUTA tax payments made after January 31, 1997.

E   X   A   M   P   L   E

Rudder Company has a $70,000 federal and state taxable payroll and has earned a reduced state tax rate of 4%. If their state tax payments are not timely, the FUTA tax calculation is as follows:

Basic FUTA tax ($70,000 × .062)		$4,340
Less 90% credit for state taxes ($70,000 × .04 × 90%)	$2,520	
Less additional credit for state tax if rate were 5.4%		
[$70,000 × (.054 – .04)]	980	
Total credit		3,500
Net FUTA tax		$ 840

If Rudder Company had made their SUTA payments before the due date of Form 940, the credit for the payments (4%) and the additional credit (1.4%) would have provided a total credit of $3,780, and a FUTA tax savings of $280.

Where contributions are paid into more than one state unemployment compensation fund, the credit against the federal tax is still limited to 5.4%.

E   X   A   M   P   L   E

The contribution rate of Domski Supply in Kansas is 5.5% and in Missouri, 2%. The credit against the gross FUTA tax on the wages paid is 5.4% in each state.

The unemployment compensation laws of certain states set the taxable wage base at a figure higher than the first $7,000 paid to each employee. For example, in Arkansas, the wage base for 1996 was the first $9,000. In such states, the total contributions that the employer must pay into the state fund may exceed 5.4% of the taxable wages as established by FUTA (first $7,000 of each employee's earnings). However, the maximum credit that can be claimed against the gross FUTA tax for the state contributions is 5.4% of the first $7,000 of each individual employee's earnings.

Title XII Advances. States, who due to financial difficulties cannot pay their unemployment compensation benefits, may borrow funds from the federal government under Title XII of the Social Security Act. The states use these funds, called **Title XII advances,** to pay their regular unemployment benefits. Under the repayment provisions established by the federal government, if a state defaults in its payments, the credit against the gross FUTA tax is reduced by 0.3% beginning the *second taxable year after the advance.* This penalty increases by an additional 0.3% for each succeeding year in which there is a balance due the federal government. Thus, employers in those states have their gross FUTA tax rate increased by 0.3% the second year after the advance, then by 0.6%, 0.9%, etc. The credit reductions for the affected states will appear in the Employer's Annual Federal Unemployment (FUTA) Tax Return, Form 940 (see Figure 5–2), which is filed by each employer.

However, a cap—a limitation on the amount the federal credit may be reduced—has been established for states that meet certain solvency requirements as determined by the Secretary of Labor. The credit reduction (cap) applicable to employers in the affected states is limited to either 0.6% of wages paid, or the percentage credit reduction in effect in the state for the preceding taxable year if greater than 0.6%. The determination of the credit reduction is made on or before November 10 of each year. Michigan was the last state to be penalized for nonpayment of Title XII advances. In 1992, Michigan employers had their credit reduced by 1.1%, which resulted in a net FUTA tax of 1.9%. Connecticut, Massachusetts, and Michigan had outstanding loan balances at the beginning of 1993. However, they satisfied these obligations by November 10, 1993; and none of the states had a credit reduction in 1993.

Tax Rates—SUTA

Figure 5–1 presents a summary of each state's 1995 unemployment compensation laws, including the tax rates and the wage limitations. The tax rate applied to each employer within a particular state yields the funds used by that state in paying benefits to its unemployed workers. Currently, all states have enacted *pooled-fund laws* as a basis for their unemployment insurance systems. By means of pooled funds, the cost of unemployment benefits is spread among all the employers in a particular state.

Employer Contributions. Every state has its own unemployment compensation law with varying tax rates and taxable wage bases. To minimize the impact of unemployment insurance taxes on newly covered employers, each state sets an initial contributions rate for new employers that will apply for a specific period of time. During this period of time the new employer's employment record can be developed and an experience rating later established. A state may assign a contributions rate of not less than 1% to newly covered employers on some "reasonable basis" other than employment experience. Once the new employer has accumulated the experience required under the provisions of the state law, a new rate will be assigned. For example, North Carolina applies 1.8% to new employers.

Employee Contributions. Some states, as shown in Figure 5–1, impose a contributions requirement on employees in addition to the contributions made by the employer.

The grace period for payment of loans has been extended by one year if the state amended its unemployment law in 1993 to increase estimated revenues by at least 25% in the first year after enactment of the state legislation.

EXAMPLE

1. *Fay Nannen earns $320 during the first week of February while working for Dango, Inc. Since the company is located in New Jersey, Nannen would have $3.60 deducted from her pay (1.125% of $320). This 1.125% tax would be deducted on the first $17,600 paid to her during the year. (In New Jersey, 0.5% of the employees' contributions is for the disability benefit plan and 0.625% for the unemployment insurance fund.)*
2. *John Garrison works in Puerto Rico, and earns $450 each week. He would contribute $1.35 (0.3% of $450) of each pay to a disability fund. This 0.3% deduction would continue until his cumulative pay for the year reached $9,000.*

Figure 5–1   *Summary of State Unemployment Compensation Laws (1995)*

Warning: The provisions of the state laws are subject to change at any time.

State	Size of Firm (1 employee in specified time and/or size of payroll[1])	Contributions (On first $7,000 unless otherwise indicated)		Benefits (Excluding dependency allowances)			
		Employer Min.-Max.	Employee	Waiting Period (weeks)	Max. per Week	Min. per Week	Max. Duration (weeks)
ALABAMA	20 weeks	0.2%–5.4% on first $8,000		none	$180	$22	26
ALASKA	any time	1.0%–5.4% on first $23,900	0.5% on first $23,900	1	212	44	26
ARIZONA	20 weeks	0.1%–5.46%		1	185	40	26
ARKANSAS	10 days	0.5%–6.4% on first $9,000		1	254	45	26
CALIFORNIA	over $100 in any calendar quarter	1.1%–5.4%	1.30% on first $31,767 (disability ins.)	1	230	40	26
COLORADO	any time	0.0%–5.4% on first $10,000		1	267	25	26
CONNECTICUT	20 weeks	2.0%–6.9% on first $10,000		none	335	15	26
DELAWARE	20 weeks	1.0%–9.5% on first $8,500		none	265	20	26
DISTRICT OF COLUMBIA	any time	1.9%–7.4% on first $10,000		1	347	50	26
FLORIDA	20 weeks	0.2%–5.4%		1	250	10	26
GEORGIA	20 weeks	0.06%–8.64% on first $8,500		1	185	37	26
HAWAII	any time	0.2%–5.4% on first $25,500	0.5% of maximum weekly wages of $593.94, not to exceed $2.97 per week (disability ins.)	1	344	5	26
IDAHO	20 weeks or $300 in any calendar quarter	0.1%–5.4% on first $21,000		1	240	44	26
ILLINOIS	20 weeks	0.6%–8.2% on first $9,000		1	242	51	26
INDIANA	20 weeks	0.2%–5.5%		1	202	50	26
IOWA	20 weeks	0.05%–7.05% on first $14,200		1	216	30	26
KANSAS	20 weeks	0.05%–6.4% on first $8,000		1	255	63	26
KENTUCKY	20 weeks	0.3%–9.0% on first $8,000		none	232	22	26
LOUISIANA	20 weeks	0.3%–6.05% on first $8,500		1	181	10	26
MAINE	20 weeks	2.4%–7.5%		1	192	35	26
MARYLAND	any time	1.8%–8.3% on first $8,500		none	223	25	26
MASSACHUSETTS	13 weeks	2.2%–8.1% on first $10,800		1	325	21	30
MICHIGAN	20 weeks or $1,000 in calendar year	0.05%–13.0% on first $9,500		none	293	43	26
MINNESOTA	20 weeks	0.4%–9.15% on first $15,300		1	304	38	26
MISSISSIPPI	20 weeks	1.1%–5.4%		1	165	30	26
MISSOURI	20 weeks	0.0%–7.8% on first $8,500		1	175	45	26
MONTANA	over $1,000 in current or preceding year	0.3%–6.4% on first $15,500		1	223	54	26
NEBRASKA	20 weeks	0.1%–5.4%		1	170	20	26

[1]**$1,500 in any calendar quarter in current or preceding calendar year unless otherwise specified.**

Figure 5–1 (Concluded)   *Summary of State Unemployment Compensation Laws (1995)*

Warning: The provisions of the state laws are subject to change at any time.

State	Size of Firm (1 employee in specified time and/or size of payroll[1])	Contributions (On first $7,000 unless otherwise indicated)		Benefits (Excluding dependency allowances)			
		Employer Min.-Max.	Employee	Waiting Period (weeks)	Max. per Week	Min. per Week	Max. Duration (weeks)
NEVADA	$225 in any quarter	0.25%–5.4% on first $16,400		none	$230	$16	26
NEW HAMPSHIRE	20 weeks	0.05%–6.5% on first $8,000		none	204	32	26
NEW JERSEY	$1,000 in any year	0.5%–5.8% on first $17,600	1.125% (.5% for disability ins.; .625% for unempl. comp.)	1	347	69	26
NEW MEXICO	20 weeks or $450 in any quarter	0.3%–5.4% on first $13,500		1	207	39	26
NEW YORK	$300 in any quarter	2.6%–7.1%	0.5% of weekly wages, not to exceed 60¢ per week (disability ins.)	1	300	40	26
NORTH CAROLINA	20 weeks	0.00%–5.7% on first $11,300		1	282	22	26
NORTH DAKOTA	20 weeks	0.2%–5.4% on first $13,400		1	237	43	26
OHIO	20 weeks	0.7%–8.5% on first $9,000		1	245	68	26
OKLAHOMA	20 weeks	0.1%–5.5% on first $10,700		1	245	16	26
OREGON	18 weeks or $225 in any quarter	0.7%–5.43% on first $19,000		1	292	67	26
PENNSYLVANIA	any time	1.8895%–10.3056% on first $8,000	0.11% on all wages	1	340	35	26
PUERTO RICO	any time	1.0%–5.4%	0.3% on first $9,000 (disability ins.)	1	133	7	26
RHODE ISLAND	any time	2.3%–8.4% on first $16,800	1.1% on first $38,000 (disability ins.)	1	317	42	26
SOUTH CAROLINA	20 weeks	1.3%–5.4%		1	207	20	26
SOUTH DAKOTA	20 weeks	0.0%–7.7%		1	168	28	26
TENNESSEE	20 weeks	0.10%–10.0%		1	200	30	26
TEXAS	20 weeks	0.31%–6.31% on first $9,000		1	252	42	26
UTAH	$140 in calendar quarter in current or preceding calendar year	0.3%–8.0% on first $16,500		1	253	16	26
VERMONT	20 weeks	0.6%–5.9% on first $8,000		1	210	36	26
VIRGIN ISLANDS	any time	0.1%–9.5% on first $13,900		1	211	15	26
VIRGINIA	20 weeks	0.18%–6.28% on first $8,000		1	208	65	26
WASHINGTON	any time	0.5%–5.42% on first $19,900		1	343	73	30
WEST VIRGINIA	20 weeks	1.5%–8.5% on first $8,000		1	282	24	28
WISCONSIN	20 weeks	0.02%–9.75 on first $10,500		none	266	50	26
WYOMING	$500 in current or preceding calendar year	0.27%–8.77% on first $11,900		1	220	16	26

---

[1]$1,500 in any calendar quarter in current or preceding calendar year unless otherwise specified.

SELF-STUDY QUIZ 5–2. Moss Company paid wages of $6,000 to John Castellano in Arizona. During the year, Castellano transferred to the company's office in Colorado, and received $26,000 for the rest of the year. The company's unemployment tax rate for Colorado is 2.9%. What would the Moss Company pay to Colorado for unemployment taxes on John's wages?

$ _____

Experience Rating. As indicated earlier, the concept of experience rating is based upon the payment of state unemployment taxes according to the employer's stability of employment. As an employer experiences a lower employee turnover, generally the state unemployment tax rate is lower. Similarly, a high employee turnover generally leads to a higher tax rate. By qualifying for reduced state unemployment contributions, an employer can realize substantial tax savings.

In all states, some type of experience-rating plan provides for a reduction in the employer's tax contributions based on the employer's experience with the risk of unemployment. Of the several formulas used to determine the contribution rates, the most commonly used is the *reserve-ratio formula:*

$$\text{Reserve Ratio} = \frac{\text{Contributions less Benefits Paid}}{\text{Average Payroll}}$$

The amount of the unemployment compensation contributions (taxes paid), the benefits paid by the state, and the employer's payroll are entered by the state on each employer's record. The benefits paid are subtracted from the contributions, and the balance of the employer's account is divided by the average payroll for a stated period of time to determine the reserve ratio. Under this plan, the balance carried forward each year equals the difference between the employer's total contributions and the total benefits paid to former employees by the state. Employers must accumulate and maintain a specified reserve before their contribution rate can be reduced. The contribution rates are established according to a schedule under which the higher the reserve ratio, the lower the tax rate. The formula assures that no employers are granted a rate reduction unless during the year they contribute more to the fund than has been withdrawn.

Employers who have built up a balance in their reserve account (contributions paid in less benefits charged) are sometimes referred to as *positive-balance employers.* The larger the positive balance in a company's reserve account, the lower will be its tax rate. Employers whose reserve accounts have been charged for more benefits paid out than contributions paid in are referred to as *negative-balance employers,* and their high tax rates reflect this fact.

Computing the Contribution Rate. In an experience-rating system, the rate of contributions for employers is based on the employment experience of the employer. The rate is determined by computing the total of the reserve built up by employer contributions over a certain period of time and by computing the ratio of the amount in the reserve account to the employer's average annual payroll as determined under the state's formula.

EXAMPLE

The Parson Company is an employer located in a state with an unemployment compensation law containing merit-rating provisions for employers who meet certain requirements. Below is a summary of the total wages for the years 1992 to 1995, inclusive. For the purpose of the illustration, assume that the total wages and taxable wages are the same amount.

Quarter	1992	1993	1994	1995
1st	$11,000	$10,000	$ 8,500	$10,500
2nd	10,000	9,000	9,500	11,000
3rd	10,000	9,500	10,000	11,000
4th	10,500	9,750	9,500	9,500
Total	$41,500	$38,250	$37,500	$42,000

The State Unemployment Compensation Commission maintains a separate account for each employer. The account is credited with contributions paid into the unemployment compensation fund by the employer and is charged with unemployment benefits paid from the fund.

For 1996, the state law set up the following contribution rate schedule for employers:

Reserve Ratio	Rate
Negative reserve balance	6.7%
0.0% to less than 8%	5.9%
8% to less than 10%	5.0%
10% to less than 12%	4.1%
12% to less than 15%	3.2%
15% and over	2.5%

The state law under discussion defines "annual payroll" as the wages paid during a 12-month period ending with the last day of the third quarter of any calendar year. The average annual payroll is the average of the last three annual payrolls.

The following computations show the state contributions made by the Parson Company for the calendar years 1992 to 1995, inclusive, the federal tax imposed under FUTA, and the method of arriving at the contribution rate for the calendar year 1996:

1992

Taxable wages	$41,500	
Rate (SUTA)	× 2.7%	
State contributions:		$1,120.50
Federal tax: .8% of $41,500		332.00
Total unemployment tax		$1,452.50

1993

Taxable wages	$38,250	
Rate (SUTA)	× 2.7%	
State contributions:		$1,032.75
Federal tax: .8% of $38,250		306.00
Total unemployment tax		$1,338.75

1994

Taxable wages	$37,500	
Rate (SUTA)	× 3.4%	
State contributions:		$1,275.00
Federal tax: .8% of $37,500		300.00
Total unemployment tax		$1,575.00

1995

Taxable wages		$42,000
Rate (SUTA)		× 3.7%
State contributions:		$1,554.00
Federal tax: .8% of $42,000		336.00
Total unemployment tax		$1,890.00

In computing the average annual payroll and the ratio of the balance in the reserve account to the average annual payroll, you must remember that the average annual payroll is the average of the last three annual payrolls, with each annual payroll period running from October 1 to September 30.

Assume that the Parson Company paid state contributions of $960 in 1990 and $1,010 in 1991 and that $1,850 was charged to the employer's account for unemployment compensation benefits during 1994 and 1995. The contribution rate for 1996 is computed as follows:

Computation of rate for 1996:

Annual payroll period ending 9/30/93	$ 39,000
Annual payroll period ending 9/30/94	37,750
Annual payroll period ending 9/30/95	42,000
Total of last 3 annual payroll periods	$ 118,750

Average annual payroll:

$118,750 divided by 3 = $39,583

Contributions for 1990	$ 960.00
Contributions for 1991	1,010.00
Contributions for 1992	1,120.50
Contributions for 1993	1,032.75
Contributions for 1994	1,275.00
Contributions for 1995 (first nine months)	1,202.50
Total contributions	$6,600.75
Less amount of benefits paid	1,850.00
Balance in reserve account 9/30/95	$4,750.75

$4,750.75, divided by average annual payroll, $39,583 = 12%

Since the reserve is 12% of the average annual payroll, the tax rate for 1996 is 3.2% (the ratio is between 12% and 15%).

Voluntary Contributions. In some states, employers may obtain reduced unemployment compensation rates by making *voluntary contributions* to the state fund. Employers deliberately make these contributions in addition to their regularly required payments of state unemployment taxes. The voluntary contributions increase the balance in the employer's reserve account so that a lower contributions rate may be assigned for the following year. Thus, the new lower tax rate will save the employer more in future state unemployment tax payments than the amount of the voluntary contribution itself.

E X A M P L E

To illustrate the tax saving that may be realized as a result of making voluntary contributions, consider the following case of the Werner Company, which is subject to the unemployment compensation law of a state that uses the reserve-ratio formula to determine experience ratings. The following contribution rate schedule applies for 1997:

Reserve Ratio	Rate
0.0% to less than 1%	6.2%
1.0% to less than 1.4%	5.6%
1.4% to less than 1.8%	5.0%
1.8% to less than 2.2%	4.4%
2.2% to less than 2.6%	3.8%
2.6% to less than 3.0%	3.2%
3.0% and over	2.6%

For the three 12-month periods ending on June 30, 1996, the company had an average annual taxable payroll of $330,000. This is the base that the state uses as the average payroll. As of June 30, 1996, the credits to the employer's account exceeded the benefits paid by $6,800. Thus, the 1997 reserve ratio is 2.06% ($6,800 ÷ $330,000), which would result in the assignment of a 4.4% tax rate, as shown in the preceding table. If the employer's 1997 total taxable payroll were $390,000, the SUTA contribution would amount to $17,160.

If the Werner Company makes a voluntary contribution into the state fund within the time period specified by the state law, the tax for 1997 will be less. For example, if the company contributes $460, the reserve ratio will be 2.2% ($7,260 ÷ $330,000). As a result, the tax rate will be reduced to 3.8%, with the following savings realized in 1997:

Tax Payment with No Voluntary Contribution (4.4% × $390,000) = ...		$17,160
Tax Payment with Voluntary Contribution	$ 460	
(3.8% × $390,000) =	14,820	15,280
Tax Savings		$ 1,880

An employer who desires to make a voluntary contribution usually must determine without the aid of the state administrative agency the amount of the contribution needed in order to obtain a lower contribution rate. In some states, the agencies provide worksheets that aid employers in determining the amount of voluntary contributions required. If the amount of voluntary contribution does not reduce the employer's contribution rate, the contribution ordinarily will not be refunded. Instead, the state may give the employer credit against any future SUTA taxes due. As with the regular contributions, the state must receive the voluntary contributions by a certain date before they can be credited to the employer's account and be used in computing a new tax rate. In some states, the employer may have a certain number of days following the mailing of the tax rate notice to make the voluntary contributions. For instance, in Arizona, the voluntary contributions must be paid by January 31. In West Virginia, the contribution must be sent in within 30 days of the mailing of the rate notice.

Voluntary contributions are allowed in 23 states, and each state requires that a voluntary contribution be identified as such.

UNEMPLOYMENT COMPENSATION REPORTS REQUIRED OF THE EMPLOYER

Employers liable for both the FUTA and the SUTA tax must file periodic reports with both the federal and the state governments. For FUTA tax reporting, employers file an annual return (either Form 940 or 940-EZ) and a tax deposit form (Form 8109). Also, employers covered by state unemployment compensation laws generally submit two major kinds of reports. One is a tax return, on which the employer reports the tax due the state. The other is a wage report, which reflects the amount of taxable wages paid to each of the employer's covered employees.

Form **940** Department of the Treasury Internal Revenue Service	**Employer's Annual Federal** **Unemployment (FUTA) Tax Return** ▶ For Paperwork Reduction Act Notice, see separate instructions.	OMB No. 1545-0028 **1996**

		T	
		FF	
	Name (as distinguished from trade name) Calendar year 1996	FD	
If incorrect, make any necessary change. ▶	Trade name, if any SHANNON HEATING COMPANY	FP	
		I	
	Address and ZIP code Employer identification number P.O. BOX 1803 LANSDOWNE, PA 19019-3636 79:2360320	T	

A Are you required to pay unemployment contributions to only one state? (If no, skip questions B through D.) . ☐ Yes ☒ No

B Did you pay all state unemployment contributions by **January 31, 1996?** (If a 0% experience rate is granted, check "Yes.") (If no, skip questions C and D.) . . . . ☐ Yes ☐ No

C Were all wages that were taxable for FUTA tax also taxable for your state's unemployment tax? (If no, skip D.) ☐ Yes ☐ No

D Did you pay all wages in states or territories other than the U.S. Virgin Islands? . . . . ☐ Yes ☐ No

If you answered "No" to any of these questions, you must file Form 940. If you answered "Yes" to all the questions, you may file Form 940-EZ, which is a simplified version of Form 940. You can get Form 940-EZ by calling 1-800-TAX-FORM (1-800-829-3676).

E If you will not have to file returns in the future, check here, complete, and sign the return . . . . ▶ ☐

F If this is an Amended Return, check here . . . . ▶ ☐

Part I Computation of Taxable Wages

1	Total payments (including exempt payments) during the calendar year for services of employees .	1	85730	42
2	Exempt payments. (Explain each exemption shown, attach additional sheets if necessary.) ▶	2		
3	Payments of more than $7,000 for services. Enter only amounts over the first $7,000 paid to each employee. Do not include payments from line 2. The $7,000 amount is the Federal wage base. Your state wage base may be different. **Do not use the state wage limitation**	3	25317	62
4	Total exempt payments (add lines 2 and 3)	4	25317	62
5	**Total taxable wages** (subtract line 4 from line 1, enter result, and go to Part II). . . . . . ▶	5	60412	80

Form **940**

Figure 5–2 *Form 940, Employer's Annual Federal Unemployment (FUTA) Tax Return (page 1)*

Annual FUTA Return—Form 940

Form 940, Employer's Annual Federal Unemployment (FUTA) Tax Return, is the prescribed form for making the return required of employers in reporting the tax imposed under FUTA. Figure 5–2 shows a filled-in copy of this form.

Completing the Return. Employers complete Questions A, B, and C. If all of these questions are answered "YES," the employer can file the simplified annual tax return, Form 940-EZ, shown in Figure 5–4. If the employer answers "NO" to any of the questions, Form 940 must be completed. The information needed to complete Form 940 may be obtained from the sources listed in Figure 5–3.

Payment of Balance Due. After computing the final net FUTA tax (Part II, Line 7), the employer compares the net tax with the total deposits for the year in

| Form 940 | | | | | | | | | | | Page **2** |

Part II   Tax Due or Refund

1	Gross FUTA tax. Multiply the wages in Part I, line 5, by .062						**1**		3745	59
2	Maximum credit. Multiply the wages in Part I, line 5, by .054 . . .	**2**		3262 |29						

3   Computation of tentative credit (Note: *All taxpayers must complete the applicable columns.*)

Note: *The additional credit shown in column (h) is limited to 3% of the taxable payroll for the U.S. Virgin Islands. Use 3% (.03) in column (f). See Part II, line 3, columns (f) and (h), on page 4 of the separate instructions.*

(a) Name of state	(b) State reporting number(s) as shown on employer's state contribution returns	(c) Taxable payroll (as defined in state act)	(d) State experience rate period		(e) State experience rate	(f) Contributions if rate had been 5.4% (col. (c) x .054)	(g) Contributions payable at experience rate (col. (c) x col. (e))	(h) Additional credit (col. (f) minus col.(g)). If 0 or less, enter 0.	(i) Contributions actually paid to state
			From	To					
PA	20747	40000.00	1/1	12/31	2.4	2160.00	960.00	1200.00	960.00
IN	83-48032	7040.58	1/1	12/31	2.2	380.19	154.89	225.30	154.89
KY	7321	13372.22	1/1	12/31	2.0	722.10	267.44	454.66	267.44
3a	Totals . . . ▶	60412.80						1879.96	1382.33

3b	Total tentative credit (add line 3a, columns (h) and (i) only—see instructions for limitations on late payments) ▶		3262	29
4				
5				
6	**Credit:** Enter the smaller of the amount in Part II, line 2, or line 3b.	**6**	3262	29
7	**Total FUTA tax** (subtract line 6 from line 1)	**7**	483	30
8	Total FUTA tax deposited for the year, including any overpayment applied from a prior year . .	**8**	483	30
9	**Balance due** (subtract line 8 from line 7). This should be $100 or less. Pay to the Internal Revenue Service. See page 2 of the separate instructions for details . . . . ▶	**9**	–0–	
10	**Overpayment** (subtract line 7 from line 8). Check if it is to be: ☐ **Applied to next return,** or ☐ Refunded . . . . ▶	**10**		

Part III   Record of Quarterly Federal Unemployment Tax Liability *(Do not include state liability)*

Quarter	First	Second	Third	Fourth	Total for year
Liability for quarter	203.42	159.95	98.83	21.10	483.30

Under penalties of perjury, I declare that I have examined this return, including accompanying schedules and statements, and to the best of my knowledge and belief, it is true, correct, and complete, and that no part of any payment made to a state unemployment fund claimed as a credit was or is to be deducted from the payments to employees.

Signature ▶ *J. D. Shannon*   Title (Owner, etc.) ▶ Owner   Date ▶ 1/31/97

Figure 5–2   *Form 940, Employer's Annual Federal Unemployment (FUTA) Tax Return (page 2)*

order to determine the balance due. Depending on the amount of the liability, the employer either deposits the balance due or remits it directly to the IRS with Form 940.

Signing Form 940. Form 940 must be signed by:

1. The individual, if a sole proprietorship.
2. The president, vice-president, or other principal officer, if a corporation.
3. A responsible and duly authorized member, if a partnership or other unincorporated organization.
4. A fiduciary, if a trust or estate.

Filing the Return. The employer must file the annual return not later than January 31 following the close of the calendar year. If, however, the employer has made timely deposits that pay the FUTA tax liability in full, as discussed below, we may delay the filing of Form 940 until February 10. We must file the return on a calendar-year basis even though our company operates on a fiscal-year basis different from the calendar year. If January 31 falls on Saturday, Sunday, or a legal holiday, we may file the return on the following business day. A mailed return bearing a postmark indicating it was mailed on or before the due date will be considered to have been timely filed even though received after the due date.

Line No.	Source of Information
A	State unemployment tax forms
B	General ledger account for SUTA Taxes Payable
C	State unemployment tax forms

Part I—Computation of Taxable Wages

1	General ledger account(s) for wages and salaries
2	Personnel records, time sheets, and employee earnings records
3	Employee earnings records
4	Follow directions for addition.
5	Follow directions for subtraction.

Part II—Tax Due or Refund

1 and 2	Follow directions for multiplication.
3	From the appropriate states' unemployment tax returns
6	Determine the smaller of Part II, line 2, or line 3b.
7	Follow the directions for subtraction.
8	General ledger account for FUTA Taxes Payable
9 and 10	Compare the net tax with the total deposits for the year.

Part III—Record of Quarterly Federal Unemployment Tax Liability

1	From the quarterly balances in the FUTA Taxes Payable account in the general ledger

Figure 5–3 *Sources of Information for Completing Form 940*

Upon application of the employer, the district director or the director of a service center may grant a reasonable extension of time in which to file the return, but not for payment of the tax. However, no extension will be granted for a period longer than 90 days. Generally, we must file the application for an extension in writing on or before the due date for filing the return. We must file the return with the IRS center for the district in which our employer's principal place of business or office or agency is located. The instructions for Form 940 list the addresses of the IRS centers. If Form 940 is not available, the employer may make a statement disclosing the amount of wages paid and the amount of tax due. This statement will be accepted as a tentative return until the return is made on the proper form. A privately designed and printed or a computer-prepared substitute Form 940 is permitted if certain IRS specifications are met. For specific approval, a sample of the new form must be sent to the IRS.

Revenue Procedures have been issued for magnetic media filing of Form 940 by reporting agents. A letter of application must first be filed with the appropriate Internal Revenue Service Center if the agents desire to use this method of filing. Once an employer has filed Form 940, the IRS will send the employer a preaddressed Form 940 near the close of each subsequent calendar year. In addition, a Federal Tax Deposit Coupon Book, Form 8109, will be mailed to the employer.

Amending the Return. When filing a corrected return, the employer must complete a new Form 940 for the year being amended. The "Amended Return" box on Form 940 should be checked, and the correct figures should be completed on the form. The return must be signed, and an explanation of the reasons for filing an amended return should be attached.

Final Return. If a company has ceased doing business, a final Form 940 must be completed (check box on Form 940 to indicate a final return), and the balance of the tax paid. In addition, a statement giving the name and address of the person(s) in charge of the required payroll records must be included with Form 940.

Annual FUTA Return—Form 940-EZ

Employers who have uncomplicated tax situations may use a streamlined Form 940. In order to use *Form 940-EZ, Employer's Annual Federal Unemployment (FUTA) Tax Return*, an employer must satisfy four simple tests:

1. Must have paid state unemployment taxes to only one state.
2. Must have made the state unemployment tax payments by the due date of Form 940-EZ.
3. All wages that were taxable for FUTA purposes were also taxable for state unemployment tax purposes.
4. Must not be located in a state that is subject to a FUTA credit reduction due to nonpayment of Title XII advances.

As Figure 5–4 shows, Form 940-EZ is easier to complete than Form 940. This is also apparent when you compare the IRS's estimates of the average time spent in completing the two forms:

	940	940-EZ
Recordkeeping	12 hours, 55 minutes	5 hours, 55 minutes
Learning about the law or the form	18 minutes	7 minutes
Preparing and sending the form to the IRS	31 minutes	28 minutes

Quarterly Deposit Form—FUTA

We compute the net FUTA tax on a quarterly basis during the month following the end of each calendar quarter. We compute the tax by multiplying .8% by that part of the first $7,000 of each of the employee's annual wages that the employer paid during the quarter. If the employer's tax liability exceeds $100, we must deposit it with a Federal Reserve bank or an authorized commercial bank on or before the last day of the month following the end of the quarter. The deposit is considered timely if the bank receives it by the due date or if the employer can establish that it was mailed two days before the due date. We make a similar computation and deposit for each of the first three quarters of the year. Each quarterly deposit is to be accompanied by a preinscribed *Federal Tax Deposit Coupon (Form 8109)*. Figure 5–5 shows a filled-in copy of this deposit form. If the tax liability for the first quarter is $100 or less, a deposit is not required; however, we must add the amount of the liability to the amount subject to deposit for the next quarter, in order to compare the total tax due with the $100 minimum for that quarter.

E X A M P L E

As shown in Figure 5–2, the tax liability of the Shannon Heating Company for the 1st quarter of 1996 was $203.42; since the liability exceeded $100, a deposit was made on April 30, 1996. The tax liability for the 2nd quarter was $159.95, and a deposit was made on July 31, 1996. The tax liability for the 3rd quarter was $98.83, but since this amount was less than the $100 limit, no deposit was required. The tax liability for the 4th quarter was $21.10. Since the accumulated liability of $119.93 exceeded the $100 limit, a deposit of $119.93 was made on January 31, 1997, as shown on Form 8109 in Figure 5–5.

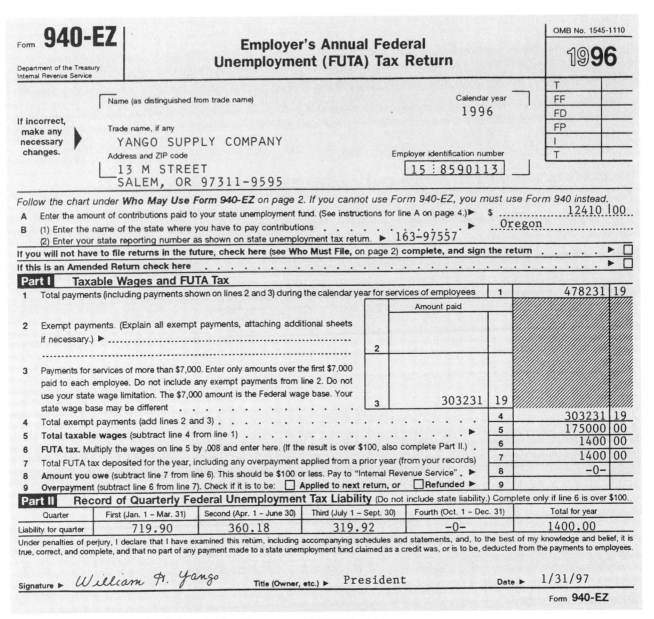

Figure 5–4 *Form 940-EZ, Employer's Annual Federal Unemployment (FUTA) Tax Return*

At the time of filing the annual return on Form 940, the employer pays the balance of tax owed for the prior year and not yet deposited. If the amount of tax reportable on Form 940 exceeds by more than $100 the sum of amounts deposited each quarter, the employer must deposit the total amount owed and undeposited (Form 8109) on or before January 31 following the year for which Form 940 is filed. If the amount owed is $100 or less, the employer may remit it with the annual form. A voucher (Form 940-V), attached to the bottom of Form 940, should be filled in if payment accompanies the filing.

In the case of an employer in a state subject to the FUTA credit reduction because of Title XII advances, we compute the deposits by multiplying the taxable wages by .8% during each of the first three quarters of the year. Since the penalty rate cannot be known with certainty until November of the current year, the procedure for the first three quarters is the same as that used by an

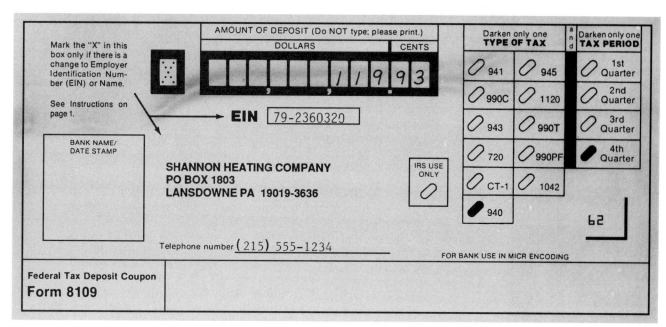

Figure 5–5   *Form 8109, Federal Tax Deposit Coupon*

employer in any state. However, since the amount of the penalty imposed for the year will be known during the fourth quarter, the deposit for the last quarter of the year will include the penalty for the entire year. This deposit is due by January 31 of the next year.

SELF-STUDY QUIZ 5–3. The FUTA taxable wages of Davies Company during 1996 follows. List the amount and the due date of each deposit of FUTA taxes for the year.

	Amount	Due Date
1st Quarter—$22,000	$ _____	_____
2nd Quarter—$24,000	$ _____	_____
3rd Quarter—$12,000	$ _____	_____
4th Quarter—$10,000	$ _____	_____

Penalties—FUTA

As indicated in Chapter 3, the Internal Revenue Code subjects employers to civil and criminal penalties for failing to file returns, pay the employment taxes when due, and make timely deposits. These penalties apply, generally, without regard to the type of tax or return involved. Figure 3–15 presents all of the penalties.

Information Reports—SUTA

A wide variation exists in the official forms that the states provide for filing the reports required under the unemployment compensation laws. Therefore, we must become familiar with the law and regulations of each state in which liability might be incurred.

L E A R N I N G
O B J E C T I V E
7

The reports required of the employers by the individual states determine: (1) the employer's liability for the contributions, (2) the amount of the contribution due on a quarterly basis, and (3) the amount of benefits to which employees will be entitled if they become unemployed. The most important of the required reports follow:

1. Status reports
2. Contribution reports
3. Wage information reports
4. Separation reports
5. Partial unemployment notices

Status Reports. Under the unemployment compensation laws of most states, new employers must register or file an initial statement or *status report.* This report determines the employer's liability to make contributions into the state unemployment compensation fund. A status report may be required of employers regardless of whether they are liable for contributions under the state law.

Contribution Reports. All employers liable for contributions under the unemployment compensation law of any state must submit a quarterly *contribution report* or tax return. This report provides a summary of the wages paid during the period and shows the computation of the tax or contribution. Usually, we must file this report on or before the last day of the month following the close of the calendar quarter, and the tax or contribution must be paid at the same time.

Wage Information Reports. In most states we must make *wage information reports* concerning individual employees. Usually we file these reports with the quarterly contribution reports. Figure 5–6 shows an example of a quarterly wage information report. On the report we may list all employee names, SSNs, taxable wages, taxable tips, state in which worker was employed during the reported quarter, and employer's federal account number. We may also be required to list for each employee the number of credit weeks earned during the quarter. (A *credit week* is defined by the state's unemployment compensation law; for example, Pennsylvania defines a credit week as any calendar week in the quarter during which the person earned remuneration of not less than $50).

About three fourths of the states permit the use of the same magnetic tape for reporting state wage information that is used for federal social security reporting purposes. By using the same magnetic tape and reporting specifications to satisfy both state and federal requirements, we eliminate the need to transcribe information from the tape prepared for the federal government for submission to the state. The payroll manager should contact the state agency to determine whether federal-state combined magnetic tape reporting is acceptable.

Separation Reports. Whenever a worker becomes separated from employment, we may be required to furnish a *separation report* providing a wage and employment record of the separated employee and the reason for leaving. Usually we must give a copy of the report to the worker in order that the individual may be informed of any entitlement to unemployment insurance benefits.

Partial Unemployment Notices. Most states require employers to give *partial unemployment notices* to those workers who become "partially unemployed" so that they are informed of their potential eligibility for partial unemployment benefits. *Partial unemployment* refers to employment by the individual's regular employer but on a reduced scale because of lack of work. In most states the notice must be given to the worker immediately after a week of partial employment

Figure 5–6   *Pennsylvania Form UC-2, Employer's Report for Unemployment Compensation*

EMPLOYER'S REPORT FOR UNEMPLOYMENT COMPENSATION

UC-2A'S

READ INSTRUCTIONS ON REVERSE SIDE OF EMPLOYER'S COPY
ANSWER EACH ITEM. TYPE OR PRINT IN INK

PA FORM UC-2   REV. 11-89

QTR. 1ST   YEAR 19--

| INV. OR R.D. CLEARANCE | EMPL. ALPHA INDEX | CASHIER'S TRANSMITTAL NUMBER | 1. TOTAL NUMBER OF COVERED EMPLOYES IN PAY PERIOD INCL. 12TH OF MONTH — INCLUDE EMPLOYES WHOSE WAGES EXCEED TAXABLE LIMIT. IF NONE ENTER "0." | FIRST MONTH 6 | SECOND MONTH 6 | THIRD MONTH 7 |

I CERTIFY THAT THE INFORMATION ON FORMS UC-2/2A/2B IS TRUE AND CORRECT TO THE BEST OF MY KNOWLEDGE AND BELIEF. NO PART OF THE AMOUNT OF EMPLOYER CONTRIBUTIONS REPORTED ON TAXABLE WAGES WAS DEDUCTED OR IS TO BE DEDUCTED FROM THE EMPLOYE'S WAGES.

SIGN HERE DO NOT PRINT   *Jack B. Kiel*
SIGNATURE OF OWNER, PARTNER, RESPONSIBLE OFFICER OR AUTHORIZED AGENT

TITLE President   DATE 5-1-95
GIVE EXACT TITLE

EMPLOYER'S CONTRIBUTION RATE ▶ .041   EMPLOYER'S ACCT. NO. 79-16093-0

2. GROSS WAGES	31,790 00
2A. EMPLOYE CONTRIBUTIONS WITHHELD. WITHHOLDING RATE IS .0011	34 97
3. TAXABLE WAGES FOR EMPLOYER CONTRIBUTIONS	29,290 00
4. EMPLOYER CONTRIBUTIONS DUE (RATE X ITEM 3)	1,200 89
4A. TOTAL CONTRIBUTIONS DUE (ITEM 2A + 4)	1,235 86
5. INTEREST DUE SEE INSTRUCTIONS	-0-
6. PENALTY DUE SEE INSTRUCTIONS	-0-
7. TOTAL REMITTANCE (ITEM 4A + 5 + 6)	1,235 86

FOR DEPT. USE

DO NOT WRITE IN THIS SPACE

MAKE CHECKS PAYABLE TO: PA UC FUND

KIELSO COMPANY
8101 ARCHER LANE
NORRISTOWN, PA 19401-1936

SUBJECTIVITY DATE

DATE PAYMENT RECEIVED
REPORT TIMELY
REPORT DELINQUENT DATE

POST CASH CREDIT
WE $
C $
I $
P $
EXAMINED BY

IF ADDRESS HAS CHANGED, PLEASE CORRECT UC-2B PORTION OF THIS FORM

EMPLOYER'S QUARTERLY REPORT OF WAGES PAID TO EACH EMPLOYE

PA FORM UC-2A   REV. 11-89

QTR. 1ST   YEAR 19--

7A. TEL. NO. OF PREPARER 215-555-8210

8. TOTAL NUMBER OF PAGES IN THIS REPORT	1
9. GROSS WAGES (MUST AGREE WITH ITEM 2 ABOVE AND TOTALS OF ITEM 14)	31,790 00
10. TOTAL NUMBER OF EMPLOYES LISTED IN ITEM 13 ON ALL PAGES	7
11. PLANT NUMBER	N/A

FOR DEPT. USE

12. EMPLOYE'S SOC. SEC. ACCT. NO.	13. NAME OF EMPLOYE (TYPE OR PRINT IN INK) FIRST NAME	INITIAL	LAST NAME	14. GR. WAGES PD. THIS QTR.	15. CREDIT WEEKS
111 09 8271	Janet	L	Carroll	6,300 00	13
095 19 1918	Carson	H	Long	1,900 00	5
212 16 3790	Heidi	M	Dorsey	2,990 00	13
091 78 6510	Mary	F	Ernst	2,100 00	13
109 05 0093	Jack	B	Kiel	10,500 00	13
170 91 9008	Alan	W	Pinkett	4,100 00	13
089 87 1792	Lawrence	B	Golic	3,900 00	13

LIST ANY ADDITIONAL EMPLOYES ON FORM UC-2A SUPPLEMENT OR ON CONTINUATION SHEETS APPROVED BY THE DEPARTMENT.

TOTAL FOR THIS PAGE _____   31,790 00

has been completed. After that, the employer ordinarily furnishes the worker with some kind of low-earnings report during each week of partial employment so that the worker will be assured of the receipt of supplemental or partial benefits.

Penalties—SUTA

All states have some form of penalty for failure to pay, or for the late payment of contributions, and also for failure to file reports. Some states impose a 10% penalty if the failure to pay the tax is due to negligence, and in a few states, a 50% penalty is imposed if the failure to pay is due to fraud. Many states also deny experience rates to employers who are delinquent in filing reports or paying contributions. In some states employers who have been delinquent in paying their contributions may be required to pay the contributions monthly rather than quarterly.

UNEMPLOYMENT COMPENSATION BENEFITS

Unemployment compensation benefits, payments made to workers temporarily unemployed, are provided primarily under the unemployment compensation law of each state. Each state specifies the qualifications to be met by the unemployed worker in order to be eligible for benefits, the amount of the benefits to be paid each individual, and the duration of the period for which benefits will be paid.

As discussed in Chapter 4, payers of unemployment compensation benefits must send copies of Form 1099-G to the Internal Revenue Service and to the person receiving the benefits. This form is used only when the total benefits paid are $10 or more. These benefits are includable in the recipient's gross income for federal income tax purposes.

Employee Benefits—SUTA

There is no uniform rate of unemployment benefits payable by all states. The amount of the benefits that an unemployed worker is entitled to receive usually is about 50% of the regular weekly wages subject to minimum and maximum amounts specified by law. Maximum weekly benefits vary widely among states, from 50% to 70% of average weekly wages. Figure 5–1 shows the minimum and maximum amounts of benefits (excluding dependency allowances) provided under the laws of each state.

The states limit the total amount of benefits an unemployed worker may receive in any year. Usually the limit is expressed in the terms of amounts rather than weeks. Thus, the maximum amount of benefits allowed under the various state laws ranges from 26 to 30 times the individual's weekly benefit amount. Therefore, if a certain employee should qualify for weekly benefits of $150 and the maximum benefits payable during the year are $4,500, the employee would be entitled to receive benefits during a period of 30 weeks.

Dependency Allowances. The state unemployment compensation laws often provide for payment of a *dependency allowance,* which is an additional weekly benefit to unemployed workers with dependents. For example, Connecticut provides for a weekly dependency allowance of $10 each for the claimant's nonworking spouse and each child and stepchild (but for no more than five dependents). However, the total dependency allowance cannot exceed 50% of the benefit otherwise payable to the claimant. In those states that provide dependency allowances, the allowances are sometimes made only to workers with dependent children of a stipulated age.

Eligibility for Benefits. The unemployment compensation laws of all the states require that a claimant meet certain conditions before becoming eligible to receive benefits. An analysis of the required qualifications in most states reveals that the claimant must:

1. File a claim for benefits.
2. Be able to work.
3. Be available for work.
4. Be actively seeking work or make a reasonable effort to obtain work.
5. Have earned a certain amount of wages or worked a certain number of weeks in covered employment.
6. Have registered at the local state employment office.
7. Have served the required waiting period.
8. Not be disqualified under any of the other provisions of the law.

Disqualification of Benefits. Certain disqualifications are set up in the state laws to conserve the funds and to ensure the intended purpose of *unemployment insurance*, which is to compensate for involuntary unemployment. While wide variation occurs in the state laws, some of the more common reasons for disqualification include the following:

1. Discharge for misconduct.
2. Voluntarily leaving work without good cause.
3. Unemployment due to a labor dispute.[1]
4. Leaving work to attend school.
5. Commitment to penal institution.
6. False or fraudulent representation to obtain benefits.
7. Refusal of suitable employment.
8. Receipt of certain kinds of remuneration.

Most state laws provide that an unemployed individual shall not be entitled to unemployment compensation benefits during any week in which the person receives remuneration from other sources, such as workers' compensation for temporary partial disability, old-age benefits under the Social Security Act, vacation allowances, dismissal wages, earnings from self-employment, or unemployment compensation benefits from another state. In some cases, however, if such remuneration is less than the benefits due the individual, the person shall receive the amount of the benefits less such remuneration. An individual otherwise qualified may receive unemployment compensation benefits regardless of age. Thus, minors and persons over the age of 65 may qualify for unemployment compensation benefits.

Benefits for the Unemployed as a Result of Major Disaster. The *Disaster Relief Act* provides unemployment benefits to persons who become unemployed as a result of a major disaster. The benefits will be available so long as the individual's unemployment caused by a major disaster continues or until the individual is reemployed in a suitable position. In no event, however, will the benefits be paid for longer than one year after the disaster has been declared.

LEARNING OBJECTIVE

8

In Maine, applicants for benefits who quit to follow their spouses to a new area are not disqualified.

---

[1]**Most states provide benefits to strikers who have been replaced by nonstriking employees, and many states allow strikers to collect benefits in cases where their employers continue to operate.**

Benefits for Federal Employees. The *Federal Employee Unemployment Compensation* program of the Social Security Act provides unemployment insurance for federal civilian employees. If a federal civilian worker becomes unemployed, eligibility for benefits is determined under the unemployment law of the state in which the person last worked in federal civilian employment. If eligible, the person is entitled to unemployment benefits in the amounts and under the conditions provided by the state unemployment insurance law. Upon request by the state, the federal employing agencies make available their findings pertaining to federal civilian employment, wages, and reasons for job separation.

Benefits for Ex-Service Personnel. The *Federal Unemployment Compensation for Ex-Servicemen* program of the Social Security Act provides unemployment compensation benefits for ex-service personnel. The benefits are determined by the unemployment insurance law of the state in which the person first files a claim that establishes a benefit year as the most recent separation from active military service.

Disability Benefits. Five states—California, Hawaii, New Jersey, New York, and Rhode Island—and Puerto Rico provide for the payment of ***disability benefits*** to workers who suffer wage losses through unemployment due to nonoccupational disease or injury. The programs in these states have developed in response to the need for protecting workers not eligible for either workers' compensation or unemployment insurance. The programs are not health insurance as such, for benefits are paid only to offset the wage loss of an employee who becomes sick or suffers an accident not connected with work.

Payment of disability benefits under the state laws are, for the most part, financed by employee contributions. In Hawaii, New Jersey, New York, and Puerto Rico, however, employers are required to contribute. In California, New Jersey, and Puerto Rico, the benefits are provided under a state-administered plan; but employers may substitute their own plans if they so wish. However, such "private" or "voluntary" plans must provide benefits at least as favorable as those payable under the state plan.

Supplemental Unemployment Benefits (SUB). Many union contracts provide for the private supplementation of state unemployment compensation benefits to provide payments to employees during periods of layoff. In nearly all of the states that have investigated the ***Supplemental Unemployment Benefits (SUB)*** plan benefits in relation to state unemployment compensation benefits, it has been ruled that workers who receive SUB may also simultaneously be paid unemployment compensation benefits. A SUB plan is usually one of two types: (a) the pooled-fund plan or (b) the individual-account plan.

Pooled-Fund Plan. This plan, also known as the "auto" or "Ford-type" plan, is the most common type of SUB plan. Under this plan employers contribute to a general fund a certain number of cents for each hour worked by employees currently on the job. Employees usually have a right to benefits from the fund only upon layoff and only after meeting stipulated eligibility requirements.

Individual-Account Plan. Under this plan, found mainly in the plate glass industry, contributions are paid to separate trusts for each employee and the employee has a vested and nonforfeitable right to the amount in the fund. Workers are entitled to the fund upon layoff and have a right to the fund when their employment is terminated. In the event the worker dies, the designated beneficiary receives the content of the trust.

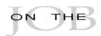

In Europe, jobless benefits are commonly paid to employees of companies that reduce the hours of all employees rather than lay off individual employees. In this country, seventeen states offer this pro-rata program, but few employers opt to participate.

Weeks of Unemployment	Source of Benefits	Starting Point	Life of Program
1st to 26th	Regular state program (funded entirely from state unemployment accounts)	Operates continuously	Permanent
27th up to 52nd	Emergency Unemployment Compensation Act (funded entirely with federal funds)	Nation's seasonally adjusted unemployment rate 7% or higher. State's adjusted insured unemployemnt rate determines whether extension is for 20 or 26 weeks	Expired April 30, 1994

Figure 5–7   *Sources and Duration of Benefits*

FUTA Funds

As indicated earlier, the net FUTA tax the employer pays to the federal government primarily pays the state and federal administrative expenses of the total unemployment insurance program. However, there was a program of *federal emergency benefits* for employees who exhausted their regular state unemployment insurance benefits. Generally, under this program, unemployment benefits were provided for an extra 20 or 26 weeks to jobless workers. This program of extended benefits expired on April 30, 1994.

As indicated earlier, the FUTA provides that when a state's unemployment compensation fund does not meet its benefit obligations, the state may obtain an advance from its federal account in the unemployment trust fund. Such advances constitute loans that must be repaid. If the loans (Title XII advances) are not repaid within the specified period, the net FUTA tax on employers in the *affected state* is increased until the loan has been recaptured through the increased taxes (see page 5–12).

Summary of Sources and Duration of Benefits

The chart in Figure 5–7 shows how the federal-state unemployment insurance system operates in a state in which the basic duration of benefits is 26 weeks. In addition to the kinds of benefits listed in the chart, legislation may be enacted that extends the federal-state benefits program.

KEY TERMS

Constructively paid wages
Contribution report
Dependency allowance
Disability benefits
Dismissal payments
Experience rating
Individual-account plan
Interstate employee

Merit rating
Negative-balance employers
Partial unemployment
Partial unemployment notice
Pooled-fund laws
Pooled-fund plan
Positive-balance employers
Reciprocal arrangements

Reserve-ratio formula
Separation report
Status report
Supplemental unemployment benefits
Title XII advances

Unemployment compensation benefits
Unemployment insurance
Voluntary contributions
Wage information report

QUESTIONS FOR REVIEW

1. How are the employer's contributions to FUTA used by the federal government?
2. What two alternative tests are applied to a business in order to judge whether it is an "employer" and, therefore, subject to the FUTA tax?
3. To what extent does FUTA coverage extend to services that a citizen of the United States performs for an American employer outside the United States?
4. As far as SUTA is concerned in most states, how does an employer account for the wages that are paid to an employee who is transferred to another plant location in a different state during the same calendar year?
5. Which of the following types of payments are taxable under FUTA:

   a. Commissions as compensation for covered employment.
   b. Christmas gifts of nominal value.
   c. Courtesy discounts to employees.
   d. Reimbursement of ordinary and necessary business expenses.
   e. Dismissal payments.

6. An employer, because of a favorable experience rating, is permitted to pay a state contribution at a reduced rate of 1.5%. What percentage of taxable wages must be paid in the aggregate to the federal and state governments?
7. What are two situations in which an employer could be liable for a net FUTA tax greater than .8%?
8. What is the purpose of Title XII advances?
9. How is the SUTA tax rate determined for a new employer?
10. In 1995:

    a. Which state(s) had the widest range of SUTA tax rates for employers?
    b. Which state(s) paid the highest weekly maximum benefit (excluding dependency allowances) to qualified unemployed workers?
    c. Which state(s) had the highest taxable wage base for the SUTA tax?

11. a. For an employer who is subject to FUTA, what are the basic forms that must be filed with the federal government?
    b. When must these forms be filed?
    c. How are taxable wages computed on the annual return?

12. What special steps must be taken when completing Form 940 for a company that has ceased operations during the year?
13. Which employers can file Form 940-EZ?
14. For 1996, the Baxter Company paid a 2.2% state unemployment tax to Arizona. What percentage of taxable wages would be paid in the aggregate to the federal and state governments for unemployment?
15. What is a separation report?

QUESTIONS FOR DISCUSSION

1. Can the owner of a small business receive unemployment compensation? Explain.
2. What arguments could be made for raising the upper limits of the SUTA tax rates?

3. Check the unemployment compensation law of your state and determine the answers to the following questions:

   a. How do nonprofit organizations, subject to coverage, make payments to the unemployment compensation fund?
   b. Can part-time teachers collect unemployment compensation between school terms?
   c. Can professional athletes receive unemployment compensation?
   d. Are aliens covered by the unemployment compensation law?
   e. How do employers protest or appeal benefit determinations and charges against their accounts?
   f. Briefly describe how a person's weekly benefit rate and maximum benefit amount are determined.
   g. Can an unemployed worker collect additional benefits if he or she has dependents? If so, how much is paid for each dependent?
   h. Does the state provide payment of partial benefits?
   i. Are benefits payable to a female during pregnancy?
   j. Can employers make voluntary contributions to their state unemployment reserve accounts?
   k. For what reasons may an unemployed worker be disqualified from receiving unemployment benefits?
   l. What steps are taken by the state unemployment agency to prevent the improper payment of claims?

4. As a way of curbing the unemployment rate, California has instituted a "shared-work compensation" program. Under this program, a company faced with a layoff of its workers may place its entire work force on a four-day workweek during the period of hardship. During this period of reduced workweeks, the employees collect partial unemployment benefits. When business rebounds, the firm returns to its normal five-day workweek, and the unemployment compensation benefits cease. Participation in the program must be approved by both the employer and the unions. If, however, the firm is not unionized, management has the discretion of putting the plan into effect.

   a. What are the benefits of such a shared-work compensation program to (1) the employer and (2) the employees?
   b. What disadvantages do you see in the operation of a shared-work compensation program, especially from the viewpoint of organized labor?

PRACTICAL PROBLEMS

5–1. **LO 4, 5.**

During the year, Nanchez Company has a SUTA tax rate of 5.9%. The taxable payroll for the year for FUTA and SUTA is $67,000. Compute:

a. Net FUTA tax .... $ _____
b. Net SUTA tax ....   _____
c. Total unemployment taxes .... $ _____

5–2. **LO 4, 5.**

Parrett Company's payroll for the year is $737,910. Of this amount, $472,120 is for wages paid in excess of $7,000 to each individual employee. The SUTA rate in Parrett Company's state is 2.9% on the first $7,000 of each employee's earnings. Compute:

a. Net FUTA tax .... $ _____
b. Net SUTA tax ....   _____
c. Total unemployment taxes .... $ _____

5–3. **LO 4, 5.**

Garrison Shops had a SUTA tax rate of 3.7%. The state's taxable limit was $8,000 of each employee's earnings. For the year, the Garrison Shops had FUTA taxable wages of $67,900 and SUTA taxable wages of $83,900. Compute:

a. Net FUTA tax .... $ _____
b. Net SUTA tax .... $ _____

5–4. **LO 4, 5.**

Due to its experience rating, Ianelli, Inc., is required to pay unemployment taxes on its payroll as follows:

1. Under SUTA for Illinois on taxable wages of $18,000, the contribution rate is 4%.
2. Under SUTA for Indiana on taxable wages of $24,000, the contribution rate is 2.65%.
3. Under SUTA for Ohio on taxable wages of $79,000, the contribution rate is 2.9%.
4. Under FUTA, the taxable wages are $103,500.

Compute:

a. SUTA taxes paid to Illinois .... $ _____
b. SUTA taxes paid to Indiana .... $ _____
c. SUTA taxes paid to Ohio .... $ _____
d. FUTA taxes paid .... $ _____

5–5. **LO 1, 4.**

The Brooks Company began its operations in August of the current year. During August and September, the company paid wages of $6,950. For the last quarter of the year, the taxable wages paid amounted to $12,910. None of the employees were paid more than $7,000 this year.

a. Is the Brooks Company liable for FUTA tax this year? Explain.

b. If so, what is the amount of the *gross* FUTA tax before any credit is granted for the SUTA tax? .... $_____

5–6. **LO 1, 3, 4.**

In September, 1996, the Haley Paint Corporation began operations in a state that requires new employers of one or more individuals to pay a state unemployment tax of 3.5% of the first $7,000 of wages paid each employee.

An analysis of the company's payroll for the year shows total wages paid of $177,610. The salaries of the president and the vice-president of the company were $20,000 and $15,000, respectively, for the four-month period; but there were no other employees who received wages in excess of $7,000 for the four months. Included in the total wages were $900 paid to a director who only attended director meetings during the year, and $6,300 paid to the factory superintendent.

Besides the total wages of $177,610, a payment of $2,430 was made to the O'Hara Accounting Company for an audit they performed on the company's books in December, 1996. Compute:

a. Net FUTA tax .... $_____
b. SUTA tax .... $_____

5–7. **LO 2, 3, 4, 5.**

In April of the current year, Korn Steel Company transferred Harry Marsh from its factory in Tennessee to its plant in South Carolina. The company's SUTA tax rates based on its experience ratings are 3.2% in Tennessee and 3.8% in South Carolina. Both states base the tax on the first $7,000 of each employee's earnings. This year the Korn Steel Company paid Harry Marsh wages of $9,900; $2,800 were paid in Tennessee and the remainder in South Carolina. Compute:

a. Amount of SUTA tax the company must pay to Tennessee on Marsh's wages .... $_____
b. Amount of SUTA tax the company must pay to South Carolina on Marsh's wages ..... $_____
c. Amount of the net FUTA tax on Marsh's wages .... $_____

5–8. LO 3, 4.

The partnership of Edward and Farnam paid the following wages during this year:

M. Edward (partner)	$21,000
S. Farnam (partner)	19,000
N. Pearson (supervisor)	12,500
T. Grunhart (factory worker)	9,700
R. Rice (factory worker)	9,200
D. Brown (factory worker)	7,900
S. Koenig (bookkeeper)	10,900
C. Chang (maintenance)	4,500

In addition, the partnership owed $200 to Chang for work he performed during December. However, payment for this work will not be made until January of the following year. Compute:

a. *Gross* FUTA tax for the partnership for this year .... $ _____
b. *Net* FUTA tax for this year .... $ _____

5–9. LO 4, 5.

Demigold Company paid wages of $170,900 this year. Of this amount, $114,000 was taxable for net FUTA and SUTA purposes. The state's contribution tax rate is 3.1% for the Demigold Company. Due to cash flow problems, the company did not make any SUTA payments until after the Form 940 filing date. Compute:

a. Amount of credit the company would receive against the FUTA tax for its SUTA contributions .... $ _____
b. Amount that the Demigold Company would pay to the federal government for their FUTA tax .... $ _____
c. Amount that the company lost because of their late payments .... $ _____

5–10. LO 4, 5.

During 1996, the Jordan Company was subject to the Alaska state unemployment tax of 4.2%. The company's taxable earnings for FUTA were $86,700 and for SUTA, $171,000. Compute:

a. SUTA tax that the Jordan Company would pay to the State of Alaska .... $ _____
b. Net FUTA tax for 1996 .... $ _____
c. Amount of the employees' disability insurance tax for 1996 (use the employee's tax rate that is shown in Figure 5–1 on pages 5–14 and 5–15) .... $ _____

5–11. LO 5.

The following unemployment tax-rate schedule is in effect during the calendar year 1996 in State A, which uses the reserve-ratio formula in determining employer contributions:

Reserve Ratio	Contributions Rate
0.0% or more, but less than 1%	6.7%
1.0% or more, but less than 1.2%	6.4%
1.2% or more, but less than 1.4%	6.1%
1.4% or more, but less than 1.6%	5.8%
1.6% or more, but less than 1.8%	5.5%
1.8% or more, but less than 2.0%	5.2%
2.0% or more, but less than 2.2%	4.9%
2.2% or more, but less than 2.4%	4.6%
2.4% or more, but less than 2.6%	4.3%
2.6% or more, but less than 2.8%	4.0%
2.8% or more, but less than 3.0%	3.7%
3.0% or more, but less than 3.2%	3.4%
3.2% or more	3.1%

The Grant Company, which is located in State A, had an average annual payroll of $850,000 for the three 12-month periods ending on June 30, 1995 (the computation date for the tax year 1996). As of June 30, 1995, the total contributions that had been made to the Grant Company's reserve account, in excess of the benefits charged, amounted to $17,440. Compute:

a. Grant Company's reserve ratio for 1996 .... _____ %
b. 1996 contributions rate for the company .... _____ %
c. Smallest contribution that the company can make in order to reduce its tax rate if State A permits voluntary contributions .... $ _____
d. Tax savings realized by the company, taking into consideration the voluntary contribution made in "c" if the taxable payroll in 1996 is $980,000 .... $ _____

5–12. LO 5.

As of June 30, 1995 (the computation date for the 1996 tax rate), the Zimfer Company had a negative balance of $867 in its unemployment reserve account in State A. The company's average payroll over the last three 12-month periods amounted to $360,000. The unemployment compensation law of State A provides that the tax rate of an employer who has a negative balance on the computation date shall be 7.2% during the following calendar year. Using the tax-rate schedule presented in Problem 5–11, compute:

a. The smallest voluntary contribution that the Zimfer Company should make in order to effect a change in its tax rate .... $ _____
b. The amount of the tax savings as a result of the voluntary contribution if the Zimfer Company's taxable payroll for 1996 is $420,000 .... $ _____

5–13.LO 3, 4, 5.

Marlene Grady and Pauline Monroe are partners engaged in operating the MGM Doll Shop, which has employed the following persons since the beginning of the year:

V. Hoffman (general office worker)	$1,700 per month
A. Drugan (saleswoman)	$15,000 per year
G. Beiter (stock clerk)	$180 per week
S. Egan (deliveryman)	$220 per week
B. Lin (cleaning and maintenance, part-time)	$160 per week

Grady and Monroe are each paid a weekly salary allowance of $450.

The doll shop is located in a state that requires unemployment compensation contributions of employers of one or more individuals. The company is subject to state contributions at a rate of 3.1% for wages not in excess of $8,100. Compute each of the following amounts based upon the 41st weekly payroll period for the week ending October 11, 1996:

a.   Amount of FICA taxes (OASDI and HI) to be withheld from the earnings of each person.

	OASDI	HI
M. Grady	$	$
P. Monroe		
V. Hoffman		
A. Drugan		
G. Beiter		
S. Egan		
B. Lin		

b.   Amount of the employer's FICA taxes for the weekly payroll ....

c.   Amount of state unemployment contributions for the weekly payroll .... $

d.   Amount of the net FUTA tax on the payroll .... $

e.   Total amount of the employer's payroll taxes for the weekly payroll .... $

5–14. **LO 5.**

Glavine Steel Company is located in State H, which enables employers to reduce their contribution rates under the experience-rating system. During 1982 to 1991, inclusive, the company's total contributions to state unemployment compensation amounted to $14,695. For the calendar years 1992 to 1995, inclusive, the contribution rate for employers was 2.7%.

The contributions of each employer are credited to an account maintained by the State Unemployment Compensation Commission. This account is credited with contributions paid into the account by the employer and is charged with unemployment benefits that are paid from the account. Starting January 1, 1996, the contributions rate for all employers in State H will be based on the following tax-rate schedule:

Reserve Ratio	Contributions Rate
Contributions falling below benefits paid	7.0%
0.0% to 7.9%	5.5%
8.0% to 9.9%	4.5%
10.0% to 11.9%	3.5%
12.0% to 14.9%	2.5%
15.0% or more	1.5%

The annual payroll is the total wages payable during a 12-month period ending with the last day of the third quarter of any calendar year. The average annual payroll is the average of the last three annual payrolls. The SUTA tax rate for the year is computed using the information available as of September 30 of the preceding year.

The schedule below shows the total payroll and the taxable payroll for the calendar years 1992 to 1995.

Calendar Year	1992		1993		1994		1995	
	Total Payroll	Taxable Payroll	Total Payroll	Taxable Payroll	Total Payroll	Taxable Payroll	Total Payroll	Taxable Payroll
First Quarter	$12,000	$12,000	$11,000	$11,000	$13,000	$13,000	$10,000	$10,000
Second Quarter	11,750	11,750	11,500	11,400	12,750	12,700	9,300	9,300
Third Quarter	12,500	12,250	12,750	12,400	12,200	12,000	9,350	9,350
Fourth Quarter	13,000	12,500	12,500	12,200	14,000	13,750	—	—

Unemployment benefits became payable to the company's qualified unemployed workers on January 1, 1983. Between that time and September 30, 1995, total benefits amounting to $15,100.90 were charged against the employer's account. Compute:

a. Contribution rate for 1996 . . . . _____ %

b. Rate for 1996 if $2,000 additional benefits had been charged by mistake to the account of the Glavine Steel Company by the State Unemployment Compensation Commission . . . . _____ %

5–15. LO 6.

As the accountant for the Monroe Trucking Company, you are preparing the company's annual return, Form 940. Use the following information to complete Form 940 on pages 5–42 and 5–43.

The net FUTA tax liability for each quarter of 1996 was as follows: 1st, $97; 2nd, $87; 3rd, $69.70; and 4th, $59.50. Since the net FUTA tax liability did not exceed $100 until the end of the 2nd quarter, the company was not required to make its first deposit of FUTA taxes until July 31, 1996. The second deposit was not required until January 31, 1997. Assume that the federal tax deposit coupons (Form 8109) were completed and the deposits made on these dates.

a.   State F's reporting number: 73902.
b.   The Monroe Trucking Company has one employee who performs all of his duties in another state—State P. The employer's identification number for this state is 7-115180.
c.   Total payments made to employees during calendar year 1996:

State F	$53,450
State P	9,100
Total	$62,550

d.   Payments made to employees in excess of $7,000: $23,400.
e.   Amount contributed to unemployment compensation fund of State F under merit rating, 1.8% of $32,150, or $578.70, for calendar year 1996. For State P, the contribution was 3.6% of $7,000 (the taxable salary limit), or $252.
f.   Form is to be signed by Elmer P. Lear, Vice-President.

5–15 (Continued).

Form **940**	**Employer's Annual Federal Unemployment (FUTA) Tax Return**	OMB No. 1545-0028
Department of the Treasury Internal Revenue Service	▶ For Paperwork Reduction Act Notice, see separate instructions.	**1996**

If incorrect, make any necessary change. ▶	Name (as distinguished from trade name)	Calendar year 1996	T	
			FF	
	Trade name, if any		FD	
	MONROE TRUCKING COMPANY		FP	
	Address and ZIP code	Employer identification number	I	
	423 BRISTOL PIKE	54 0663793	T	
	NEWTOWN, STATE F 18940-4523			

A Are you required to pay unemployment contributions to only one state? (If no, skip questions B through D.) . ☐ Yes ☐ No

B Did you pay all state unemployment contributions by January 31, 1996? (If a 0% experience rate is granted, check "Yes.") (If no, skip questions C and D.) . . . . ☐ Yes ☐ No

C Were all wages that were taxable for FUTA tax also taxable for your state's unemployment tax? (If no, skip D.) ☐ Yes ☐ No

D Did you pay all wages in states or territories other than the U.S. Virgin Islands? . . . . ☐ Yes ☐ No

If you answered "No" to any of these questions, you must file Form 940. If you answered "Yes" to all the questions, you may file Form 940-EZ, which is a simplified version of Form 940. You can get Form 940-EZ by calling 1-800-TAX-FORM (1-800-829-3676).

E If you will not have to file returns in the future, check here, complete, and sign the return . . . . ▶ ☐

F If this is an Amended Return, check here . . . . ▶ ☐

Part I   Computation of Taxable Wages

		Amount paid		
1	Total payments (including exempt payments) during the calendar year for services of employees .		1	
2	Exempt payments. (Explain each exemption shown, attach additional sheets if necessary.) ▶	2		
3	Payments of more than $7,000 for services. Enter only amounts over the first $7,000 paid to each employee. Do not include payments from line 2. The $7,000 amount is the Federal wage base. Your state wage base may be different. **Do not use the state wage limitation**	3		
4	Total exempt payments (add lines 2 and 3)		4	
5	**Total taxable wages** (subtract line 4 from line 1, enter result, and go to Part II) . . . . . . ▶		5	

Form **940**

5–15 (Concluded).

Form 940   Page **2**

Part II	Tax Due or Refund

1 Gross FUTA tax. Multiply the wages in Part I, line 5, by .062 . . . . **1**

2 Maximum credit. Multiply the wages in Part I, line 5, by .054 . . . | **2** |

3 **Computation of tentative credit** (Note: *All taxpayers must complete the applicable columns.*)

Note: *The additional credit shown in column (h) is limited to 3% of the taxable payroll for the U.S. Virgin Islands. Use 3% (.03) in column (f). See Part II, line 3, columns (f) and (h), on page 4 of the separate instructions.*

(a) Name of state	(b) State reporting number(s) as shown on employer's state contribution returns	(c) Taxable payroll (as defined in state act)	(d) State experience rate period		(e) State experience rate	(f) Contributions if rate had been 5.4% (col. (c) x .054)	(g) Contributions payable at experience rate (col. (c) x col. (e))	(h) Additional credit (col. (f) minus col.(g)). If 0 or less, enter 0.	(i) Contributions actually paid to state
			From	To					

3a Totals . . . ▶

3b Total tentative credit (add line 3a, columns (h) and (i) only—see instructions for limitations on late payments) ▶

4

5

6 **Credit:** Enter the smaller of the amount in Part II, line 2, or line 3b **6**

7 **Total FUTA tax** (subtract line 6 from line 1) **7**

8 Total FUTA tax deposited for the year, including any overpayment applied from a prior year . . **8**

9 **Balance due** (subtract line 8 from line 7). This should be $100 or less. Pay to the Internal Revenue Service. See page 2 of the separate instructions for details . . . . ▶ **9**

10 **Overpayment** (subtract line 7 from line 8). Check if it is to be: ☐ Applied to next return, or ☐ Refunded . . . . ▶ **10**

Part III	Record of Quarterly Federal Unemployment Tax Liability (*Do not include state liability*)

Quarter	First	Second	Third	Fourth	Total for year
Liability for quarter					

Under penalties of perjury, I declare that I have examined this return, including accompanying schedules and statements, and to the best of my knowledge and belief, it is true, correct, and complete, and that no part of any payment made to a state unemployment fund claimed as a credit was or is to be deducted from the payments to employees.

Signature ▶   Title (Owner, etc.) ▶   Date ▶

The information listed below refers to the employees of the Dumas Company for the year ended December 31, 1996. The wages are separated into the quarters in which they were paid to the individual employees.

Name	Social Security #	1st Qtr.	2nd Qtr.	3rd Qtr.	4th Qtr.	Total
Robert G. Cramer	173-68-0001	$ 1,800	$ 2,000	$ 2,000	$ 2,200	$ 8,000
Daniel M. English (Foreman)	168-95-0003	3,000	3,400	3,400	3,400	13,200
Ruth A. Small	199-99-1998	2,000	2,300	2,300	2,400	9,000
Harry B. Klaus	168-75-7413	1,600	1,700	1,700	1,700	6,700
Kenneth N. George (Mgr.)	179-18-6523	3,600	4,000	4,500	5,000	17,100
Mavis R. Jones	123-45-6789	1,600	1,700	1,700	-0-	5,000
Marshall T. McCoy	131-35-3334	1,400	1,400	-0-	-0-	2,800
Bertram A. Gompers (President)	153-00-1014	4,500	5,000	5,500	6,300	21,300
Arthur S. Rooks	171-71-7277	-0-	700	1,700	1,700	4,100
Mary R. Bastian	186-83-8111	3,000	3,200	3,200	3,200	12,600
Klaus C. Werner	143-21-2623	2,300	2,500	2,500	2,500	9,800
Kathy T. Tyler	137-36-3534	-0-	-0-	1,300	1,700	3,000
Totals		$24,800	$27,900	$29,800	$30,100	$112,600

For 1996, State D's contributions rate for the Dumas Company, based on the experience rating system of the state, was 2.8% of the first $7,000 of each employee's earnings. The state tax returns are due one month after the end of each calendar quarter. During 1996, the company paid $1,976.80 of contributions to State D's unemployment fund.

Employer's phone number: (613) 555-0029. Employer's State D reporting number: 80596.

Using the forms supplied on pages 5–45 to 5–48, complete the following for 1996:

a. Federal Tax Deposit Coupons—Form 8109
b. Employer's Report for Unemployment Compensation, State D—4th Quarter only
c. Employer's Annual Federal Unemployment (FUTA) Tax Return—Form 940-EZ

Indicate on each form the date that the form should be submitted and the amount of money that must be paid.

The president of the company signs all tax forms.

5–16 (Continued).

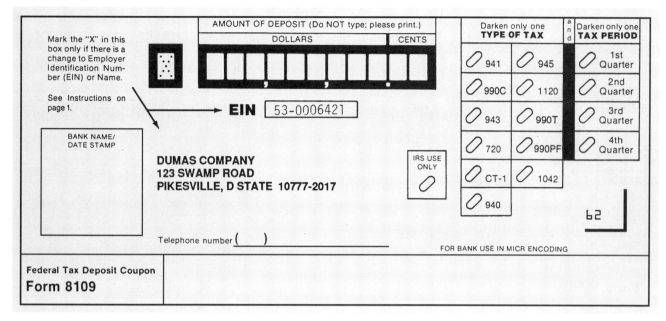

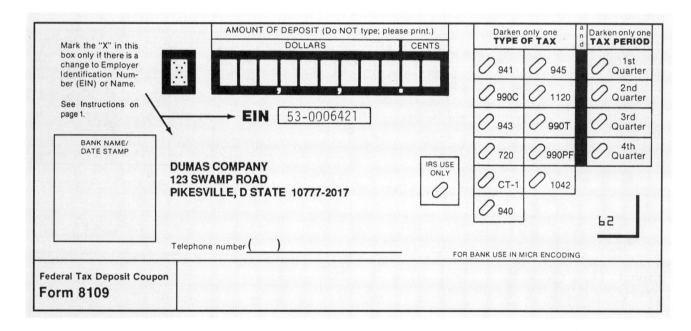

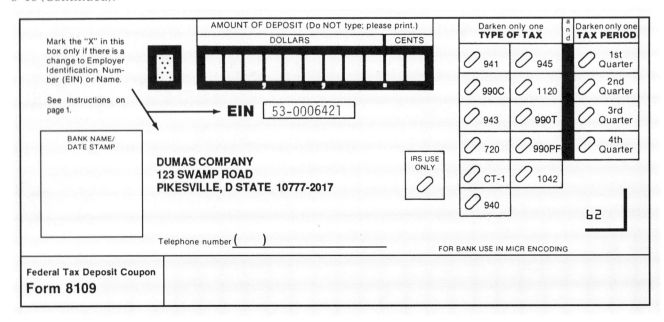

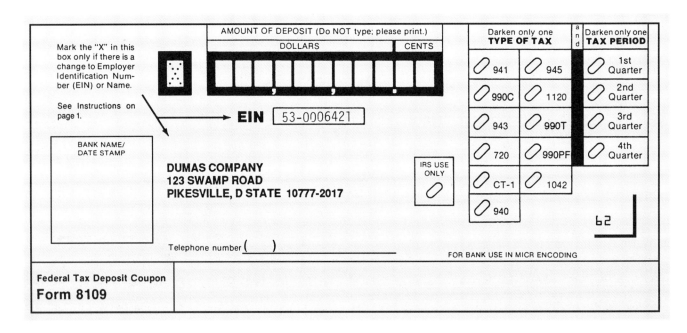

5–16 (Continued).

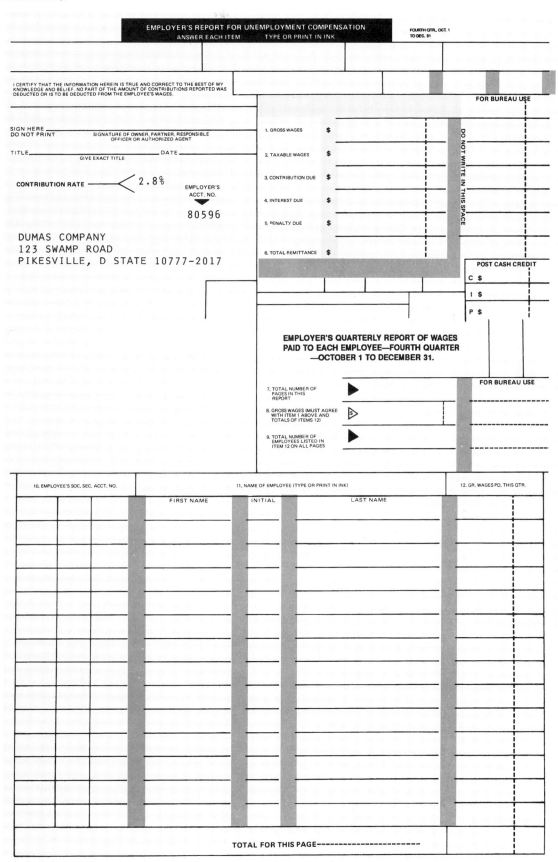

Form **940-EZ**	**Employer's Annual Federal Unemployment (FUTA) Tax Return**	OMB No. 1545-1110
Department of the Treasury Internal Revenue Service		**1996**

				T	
If incorrect, make any necessary changes. ▶	Name (as distinguished from trade name)	Calendar year **1996**		FF	
				FD	
	Trade name, if any **DUMAS COMPANY**			FP	
				I	
	Address and ZIP code **123 SWAMP ROAD** **PIKESVILLE, D STATE 10777-2017**	Employer identification number **53 : 0006421**		T	

*Follow the chart under **Who May Use Form 940-EZ** on page 2. If you cannot use Form 940-EZ, you must use Form 940 instead.*

A Enter the amount of contributions paid to your state unemployment fund. (See instructions for line A on page 4.) ▶ $ ....

B (1) Enter the name of the state where you have to pay contributions . . . . ▶ ....
   (2) Enter your state reporting number as shown on state unemployment tax return. ▶

If you will not have to file returns in the future, check here (see **Who Must File**, on page 2) complete, and sign the return . . . . . . ▶ ☐

If this is an Amended Return check here . . . . ▶ ☐

Part I	**Taxable Wages and FUTA Tax**

#	Description		Amount paid		
1	Total payments (including payments shown on lines 2 and 3) during the calendar year for services of employees	1			
2	Exempt payments. (Explain all exempt payments, attaching additional sheets if necessary.) ▶	2			
3	Payments for services of more than $7,000. Enter only amounts over the first $7,000 paid to each employee. Do not include any exempt payments from line 2. Do not use your state wage limitation. The $7,000 amount is the Federal wage base. Your state wage base may be different	3			
4	Total exempt payments (add lines 2 and 3)		4		
5	**Total taxable wages** (subtract line 4 from line 1) . . . . ▶		5		
6	**FUTA tax.** Multiply the wages on line 5 by .008 and enter here. (If the result is over $100, also complete Part II.) ▶		6		
7	Total FUTA tax deposited for the year, including any overpayment applied from a prior year (from your records)		7		
8	**Amount you owe** (subtract line 7 from line 6). This should be $100 or less. Pay to "Internal Revenue Service". ▶		8		
9	**Overpayment** (subtract line 6 from line 7). Check if it is to be: ☐ **Applied to next return, or** ☐ **Refunded** ▶		9		

Part II	**Record of Quarterly Federal Unemployment Tax Liability** (Do not include state liability.) Complete only if line 6 is over $100.

Quarter	First (Jan. 1 – Mar. 31)	Second (Apr. 1 – June 30)	Third (July 1 – Sept. 30)	Fourth (Oct. 1 – Dec. 31)	Total for year
Liability for quarter					

Under penalties of perjury, I declare that I have examined this return, including accompanying schedules and statements, and, to the best of my knowledge and belief, it is true, correct, and complete, and that no part of any payment made to a state unemployment fund claimed as a credit was, or is to be, deducted from the payments to employees.

Signature ▶   Title (Owner, etc.) ▶   Date ▶

Form **940-EZ**

CONTINUING PAYROLL PROBLEM

Refer to the partially completed payroll register that you worked on at the end of Chapter 4. You will now compute the employees' SUTA contributions and the employer's liability for unemployment taxes (FUTA and SUTA) for the pay of January 14. These computations will be used at the end of Chapter 6 in recording the payroll tax entries.

The employee's SUTA tax rate is 0.15% on all wages paid during the year. Record each employee's SUTA contribution in the SUTA Deductions column.

To compute the employer's liability for unemployment taxes, proceed as follows:

1. Enter each employee's gross earnings in the Taxable Earnings—FUTA and SUTA columns.
2. Total the Taxable Earnings—FUTA and SUTA columns.
3. At the bottom of your payroll register, compute the following for the total payroll:

   a. Net FUTA tax. Since this is the first pay period of the year, none of the employees are near the $7,000 ceiling; therefore, each employee's gross earnings is subject to the FUTA tax.
   b. Since the Steimer Company is a new employer, Pennsylvania has assigned the company a contribution rate of 3.5% on the first $8,000 of each employee's earnings.

NOTE: Retain your partially completed payroll register for use at the end of Chapter 6.

CASE PROBLEMS

C1. **Reducing a High Unemployment Tax Rate.**

Over the past two years, Kermit Stone, the controller of the Hilton Company, has been concerned that the company has been paying a large amount of money for state unemployment taxes. On reviewing the "unemployment file" with the head accountant, Deborah Murtha, he learns that the company's tax rate is near the top of the range of the state's experience-rating system.

After calling the local unemployment office, Stone realizes that the turnover of employees at the Hilton Company has had an adverse effect on the company's tax rates. In addition, after consulting with Murtha, he discovers that the eligibility reports that come from the state unemployment office are just signed and sent back to the state without any review.

The eligibility reports are notices that an ex-employee has filed a claim for unemployment benefits. By signing these reports "blindly," the company, in effect, tells the state that the employee is eligible for the benefits. Any benefits paid are charged by the state against the Hilton Company's account.

Stone is convinced that the rates the company is paying are too high, and he feels that part of the reason is the "blind" signing of the eligibility reports. Besides this, he wonders what other steps the company can take to lower its contribution rate and taxes.

Submit recommendations that might help Stone reduce the "unfair" burden that the unemployment compensation taxes are leveling on the Hilton Company.

THAT WAS
THEN
THIS IS
NOW

The first recorded labor strike occurred in Egypt in 1170 B.C., when sharp inflation brought an organized protest by men working on a new pyramid. Men refused to work because the payroll was delayed. Union membership in 1994 totaled almost 17 million, requiring many employers to comply with union contracts in computing employee salaries and benefits.

Analyzing and Journalizing Payroll Transactions

Learning Objectives

After studying this chapter, you should be able to:

1 Record payrolls in payroll registers and post to employees' earnings records.

2 Journalize the entries to record the payroll, payroll taxes, and payment of payroll-related liabilities.

3 Post to the various general ledger accounts that are used to accumulate information from the payroll entries.

4 Explain the payment and the recording of the payroll tax deposits.

5 Understand the need for end-of-period adjustments.

6 Identify the general ledger accounts used to record payroll transactions.

This chapter presents the procedures for recording the payroll in a payroll register and for transferring information from the payroll register to the employees' earnings records. Also, we shall analyze typical transactions pertaining to a company's payroll, record these transactions in the company's book of original entry, and post them to the proper ledger accounts.

THE PAYROLL REGISTER

As you have seen in Figure 1–9 and in completing the Continuing Payroll Problem, the payroll register gives detailed information about the payroll for each pay period. To summarize, the payroll register may provide the following types of information:

1. The title of the form.
2. The period covered by the payroll and the date on which the pay period ends.
3. Department or branch. Some large businesses with many departments or branches prepare a separate sheet in the payroll register for each department or branch on each payday. Other firms provide "distribution" columns such as "Sales Salaries," "Office Salaries," and "Plant Wages" for classifying the gross wages and salaries according to the nature of the wage and salary expense. The total of each distribution column shows the total amount for that particular operating expense.
4. A column to record the name of each employee. Many businesses provide a column to record an identifying number such as the time clock number for each employee.
5. Marital status and number of withholding allowances. This information determines the income tax deductions.
6. A record of time worked. Many companies show detailed information in the payroll register as to hours worked each day by each employee.
7. Some companies provide separate columns to show a total of regular hours worked and a total of overtime hours worked during the pay period. This information helps a business that schedules much overtime work.

Figure 6–1 *Payroll Register (left side)*

FOR WEEK ENDING **January 17**																			19 —			
					TIME RECORD						REGULAR EARNINGS						OVERTIME EARNINGS					
	NO.	NAME	MARITAL STATUS	NO. W/H ALLOW.	M	T	W	T	F	S	HOURS	RATE PER HOUR	AMOUNT			HOURS	RATE PER HOUR	AMOUNT				
1	10	*Amand, Jorge L.*	M	2	8	8	8	8	8	4	40	5 20	2	0	8 00	4	7 80	3	1	20		
2	12	*Basile, Carole O.*	M	4	8	8	8	8	10		40	7 10	2	8	4 00	2	10 65	2	1	30		
3	13	*Darnell, Robert T.*	S	1	8	8	8	8	8		40	6 30	2	5	2 00							
4	23	*Gorbus, Glen A.*	M	2	8	8	8	8	8	8	40	5 90	2	3	6 00	8	8 85	7	0	80		
5	24	*Granger, Mary I.*	S	1	8	8	8	0	8		32	5 10	1	6	3 20							
36		**Totals**											24	9	7 20			2	6	5	50	

8. The regular rate of pay and the amount earned at the regular rate.
9. A space to record the overtime rate and the total earnings at the overtime rate.
10. A column to record the total earnings.
11. Information about deductions from total earnings. A separate column may be provided for each type of deduction. The various deductions will be discussed later in this chapter.
12. A column to show the net amount paid (total earnings less deductions). When paying by check, a company usually provides a column for the number of each employee's check.
13. Some firms provide special columns in the payroll register to indicate that portion of the employee's wages taxable under the Federal Insurance Contributions Act (OASDI and HI) and other laws that require payment of taxes only on wages up to the taxable limits.

The partial payroll register shown in Figure 6–1 contains most of the information outlined above. This register is used to compute the pay for hourly workers for a weekly pay period. The layout of the section devoted to time or hours worked will vary, depending on the payroll period and the work schedules of each individual business. Many companies that manufacture business forms design and produce payroll registers sold through stationery stores and office supply houses. Although some small businesses still prepare the payroll manually, most businesses use computers to process their payrolls.

Proving the Totals of the Payroll Register

As shown later in this chapter, the payroll register provides the information needed in preparing the *journal entries* to record (1) the wages earned, deductions from wages, and net amount paid each payday and (2) the employer's payroll taxes. Prior to making the journal entry to record the payroll, check the accuracy of the amounts entered in the payroll register by proving the totals of the money columns. Prove the partial payroll register shown in Figure 6–1 as follows:

Figure 6–1 *Payroll Register (right side)*

DEPT. ACCOUNTING—10

TOTAL EARNINGS	FICA OASDI	FICA HI	FED. INCOME TAX	STATE INCOME TAX	GROUP INS.	CHECK NO.	NET PAID AMOUNT	FICA OASDI	FICA HI	FUTA & SUTA	
2 3 9 20	1 4 83	3 47	2 00	4 78	9 00	898	2 0 5 12	2 3 9 20	2 3 9 20	2 3 9 20	1
3 0 5 30	1 8 93	4 43	——	6 11	9 00	899	2 6 6 83	3 0 5 30	3 0 5 30	3 0 5 30	2
2 5 2 00	1 5 62	3 65	2 4 00	5 04	3 90	900	1 9 9 79	2 5 2 00	2 5 2 00	2 5 2 00	3
3 0 6 80	1 9 02	4 45	1 3 00	6 14	9 00	901	2 5 5 19	3 0 6 80	3 0 6 80	3 0 6 80	4
1 6 3 20	1 0 12	2 37	1 0 00	3 26	3 90	902	1 3 3 55	1 6 3 20	1 6 3 20	1 6 3 20	5
27 6 2 70	17 1 29	4 0 06	21 5 00	5 5 25	5 4 70		22 2 6 40	27 6 2 70	27 6 2 70	27 6 2 70	36

Proof:

Regular earnings	$2,497.20	
Overtime earnings	265.50	
Total earnings		$2,762.70
FICA tax withheld—OASDI	$ 171.29	
FICA tax withheld—HI	40.06	
Federal income taxes withheld	215.00	
State income taxes withheld	55.25	
Group insurance withheld	54.70	
Total deductions		$ 536.30
Total net pay		2,226.40
Total earnings		$2,762.70

In preparing the journal entry to record a payroll, you make an entry each payday to record the aggregate amount of wages earned, deductions made, and net payments to all employees, as determined from the Totals line of the payroll register. After making the journal entry, you must transfer, or post, the information from the journal to the appropriate general ledger accounts.

Some companies use a formal **payroll journal** instead of a payroll register to record each payroll. When you record the payroll originally in a payroll journal, you post from the payroll journal to the general ledger accounts.

In most companies having computer-driven payroll systems, the payroll programs are interfaced with the general ledger programs. In these systems, computers generate the payroll entries into a printed journal-entry format and post to the various general ledger accounts automatically from these entries.

Using the Information in the Payroll Register

In addition to serving as the source of authority for preparing journal entries to record the payroll and the employer's payroll taxes, the payroll register provides information that meets the record-keeping requirements of the Fair Labor Standards Act. Also, the payroll register provides data used in preparing periodic reports required by various laws.

Besides the information contained in the payroll register, businesses must provide information about the accumulated earnings of each employee. Therefore, companies keep a separate payroll record on each employee—the employee's earnings record. This record, introduced in Figure 1–10, is discussed in the following section.

THE EMPLOYEE'S EARNINGS RECORD

The employee's earnings record, a supplementary record, provides information for:

1. *Preparing the payroll register.* The earnings record contains information such as the hourly rate, marital status, and number of withholding allowances claimed, needed to compute gross earnings and to determine the amount to withhold for income tax purposes.
2. *Preparing reports* required by state unemployment compensation or disability laws.
3. *Determining when the accumulated wages of an employee reach the cutoff level* for purposes of FICA (OASDI), FUTA, or SUTA. As shown in Figure 6–2, a special "Cumulative Earnings" column is provided so that the total amount of

accumulated wages can be recorded each pay period. Thus, when the FICA (OASDI), FUTA, or SUTA cutoff has been reached, the record shows that the employee or the employer no longer has a liability for that particular tax during the rest of the calendar year. (In Figure 6–1, the FUTA and SUTA taxable wage cutoffs are the same [$7,000]. However, another separate column would be needed in the payroll register if there were a different cutoff for the SUTA tax.)

4. *Preparing payroll analyses* for governmental agencies and for internal management control. Information such as the department in which the employee works and the job title serves as the basis for such analyses.

5. *Settling employee grievances* regarding regular pay and overtime pay calculations and the withholding of amounts for income taxes and other purposes.

6. *Completing Forms W-2*, which show for each employee the annual gross earnings, income taxes withheld, wages subject to FICA taxes, and FICA taxes withheld.

A business keeps an employee's earnings record for each employee whose wages are recorded in the payroll register. Each payday, after the information has been recorded in the payroll register, the information for each employee is posted to the employee's earnings record. The columns are arranged so that the information can be transferred easily. The earnings record shown in Figure 6–2 is arranged for weekly pay periods. You will note that totals are provided for each quarter so that you can enter information easily on the quarterly tax returns. The bottom of page 1 of the earnings record shows a line for semiannual totals. The bottom of page 2 of the form, which is not illustrated, shows a line for annual totals that you will need in preparing Form 940 or Form 940-EZ and other year-end reports.

RECORDING THE GROSS PAYROLL AND WITHHOLDINGS

After you have recorded the payroll in the payroll register and posted to the employees' earnings records, you must enter the information in the employer's accounting system. An entry for the totals of each payroll period should be made in the general journal and posted to the general ledger. You can obtain the amounts needed for this entry from the Totals line at the bottom of the last payroll register sheet.

The following journal entry to record the payroll includes a debit to the appropriate expense account(s) for the gross payroll and credits to the various liability accounts for the withholdings from the pay and for the net amount to be paid employees:

	Debit	Credit
Salary Expense	XXX	
Liabilities (Withholdings)		XXX
Cash or Salaries Payable (Net Pay)		XXX
To record the payment of salaries and the liabilities for the employees' taxes withheld.		

Gross Payroll

You should record the total gross payroll (regular earnings and overtime earnings) as the debit portion of the payroll entry. The account has a title such as

Figure 6–2 Employee's Earnings Record (page 1)

WEEK	19— WEEK ENDING	TOTAL WORKED DAYS	TOTAL WORKED HRS.	REGULAR EARNINGS HRS.	REGULAR EARNINGS RATE	REGULAR EARNINGS AMOUNT	OVERTIME EARNINGS HRS.	OVERTIME EARNINGS RATE	OVERTIME EARNINGS AMOUNT	FICA OASDI	FICA HI	FEDERAL INCOME TAX	STATE INCOME TAX	GROUP INSURANCE	NET PAID CK. NO.	NET PAID AMOUNT	CUMULATIVE EARNINGS	TIME LOST
1	1/3	5	44	40	5 20	208 00	4	7 80	31 20	14 83	3 47	2 00	4 78	9 00	510	205 12	239 20	
2	1/10	5	42	40	5 20	208 00	2	7 80	15 60	13 86	3 24	1 00	4 47	9 00	706	192 03	462 80	
3	1/17	6	44	40	5 20	208 00	4	7 80	31 20	14 83	3 47	2 00	4 78	9 00	898	205 12	702 00	
4																		
5																		
6																		
7																		
8																		
9																		
10																		
11																		
12																		
13																		
QUARTER TOTAL																		
1																		
2																		
13																		
QUARTER TOTAL																		
SEMIANNUAL TOTAL																		

SEX F	SEX M	DEPARTMENT	OCCUPATION	WORKS IN (STATE)	S.S. ACCOUNT NO.	NAME—LAST	FIRST	MIDDLE	NO. W/H ALLOW.	MARITAL STATUS
	X	A-10	Clerk-Typist	XXX	204-43-1186	Amand	Jorge	Luis	2	M

Wages Expense or *Salaries Expense.* In the case of a company with many departments or cost centers, the accounts would have titles such as *Wages Expense— Department A, Wages Expense—Maintenance,* and *Wages Expense—Residential Services.* These accounts show the total gross earnings that the employer incurs as an *expense* each payday.

FICA Taxes—Employee

The employer must withhold FICA taxes for each employee. Since the employer has withheld these taxes from the pay of the employees and now owes this amount to the IRS, the taxes withheld represent a *liability* of the employer. When recording the payroll, you should credit accounts entitled *FICA Taxes Payable—OASDI* and *FICA Taxes Payable—HI* for the amounts withheld.

Federal Income Taxes

Employers must withhold a percentage of their employees' wages for income tax purposes. Chapter 4 presented the methods of ascertaining the amounts to be withheld from wages for income tax purposes. As with FICA taxes withheld, the employer also owes to the IRS the federal income taxes withheld from the employees' pay. You should keep a separate account in the general ledger for recording the employer's *liability* for the amount of federal income taxes withheld. A suitable title for this account, *Employees Federal Income Taxes Payable,* may be abbreviated to read *Employees FIT Payable.* The account is credited for the total amount of federal income taxes withheld each payday and is subsequently debited for the amounts paid to a depositary or to the IRS.

State and City Income Taxes

Employers may be required to withhold state and city income taxes in addition to the federal income taxes. You should keep a separate account in the general ledger for recording the employer's *liability* for the amount of each kind of income tax withheld. Account titles that may be used include: *Employees State Income Taxes (SIT) Payable* and *Employees City Income Taxes (CIT) Payable.*

Employees' Contributions to State Funds

A few states require employees to contribute to state unemployment compensation or disability funds. In states requiring employee contributions, the employer deducts the amount of the contributions from the employees' wages at the time the wages are paid. The *liability* for employees' contributions may be recorded in the same account as the employer's contributions; namely, *SUTA Taxes Payable.* Or, a separate ledger account, such as *SUTA Taxes Payable—State A* and *SUTA Taxes Payable—State B,* may be opened for each state. If employees make contributions to a disability benefit fund, this amount is usually reported separately to the state and should be recorded in a separate liability account such as *Employees Disability Contributions Payable.*

Net Pay

The total of the net amount paid to the employees each payday is credited to either the *Cash* account or the *Salaries Payable* account.

SELF-STUDY QUIZ 6–1. The totals from the payroll register of the Olt Company for the week of January 22 show:

Gross Earnings	95,190.00
Withholdings:	
FICA taxes—OASDI	5,901.78
FICA taxes—HI	1,380.26
Federal Income Tax	14,270.00
State Income Tax	1,427.85
State Unemployment Tax	951.90
Net Pay	71,258.21

Journalize the entry to record the payroll of January 22.

RECORDING PAYROLL TAXES

In this section we shall analyze the journal entries that record the *employer's* payroll taxes, each of which has been discussed in preceding chapters:

1. *FICA*—taxes imposed under the Federal Insurance Contributions Act for old-age, survivors, and disability insurance (OASDI) and hospital insurance (HI) benefits.
2. *FUTA*—taxes imposed under the Federal Unemployment Tax Act.
3. *SUTA*—contributions to the unemployment compensation funds of one or more states.

The following accounts will be needed in the general ledger if the employer is subject to FICA taxes, FUTA taxes, and SUTA taxes:

1. *Payroll Taxes*—an expense account for the FICA, FUTA, and SUTA taxes on the employer.
2. *FICA Taxes Payable—OASDI*—a liability account for the tax withheld from employees' wages plus the employer's portion of the tax.
3. *FICA Taxes Payable—HI*—a liability account for the tax withheld from employees' wages plus the employer's portion of the tax.
4. *FUTA Taxes Payable*—a liability account for the accumulation of the employer's federal unemployment taxes payable to the federal government.
5. *SUTA Taxes Payable*—a liability account for the amount payable to state unemployment compensation fund(s).

The following journal entry to record the payroll taxes includes a debit to the tax expense account for the total of the employer's payroll taxes and credits to the various tax liability accounts:

	Debit	Credit
Payroll Taxes	XXX	
Liabilities (Various Taxes)		XXX
To record the payroll taxes and liabilities of the employer.		

FICA Taxes—Employer

The law states specifically that deductions made from the wages of employees under FICA should be recorded immediately as liabilities on the books of the company. The law does not require that employers record their part of the FICA taxes at the time the *wages are paid*. However, in order to place the tax expense in the proper accounting period, the common practice is to record the employer's FICA tax liabilities each payday.

The taxes withheld from the employees' wages represent liabilities of the employer. They do not constitute expenses of the employer since the employer simply withholds the amount of the taxes. However, the taxes on the employer represent both business expenses and liabilities of the employer. The employer may deduct the employer's FICA contributions as a *business expense* for federal income tax purposes (and the costs of all other payroll taxes).

SUTA Taxes

Under the state unemployment compensation laws, employers must pay contributions into one or more state unemployment compensation funds. When an employer must make contributions to the state unemployment compensation funds of more than one state, it may be advisable to keep a separate liability account for the contributions payable to each state.

FUTA Tax

An employer subject to the gross FUTA tax of 6.2% may be able to claim credit in paying the federal tax because of contributions made to state unemployment compensation funds. As discussed in Chapter 5, the maximum credit is 5.4%, even though the amount of state contributions is more than or less than 5.4%. Thus, the net FUTA tax (6.2% − 5.4%) is .8%. Although you do not actually claim the credit against the FUTA tax until Form 940 or Form 940-EZ is filed with the Internal Revenue Service, you may record the FUTA tax at the net amount (.8%) at the time you make the entry to record the employer's payroll taxes.

E X A M P L E

The employees of the Absicon Company earn wages during the year amounting to $26,400, all of which is subject to the gross FUTA tax of 6.2%. The company must make contributions to the unemployment compensation fund of the state in which the business is located at the rate of 2.8% of the wages paid each employee. Absicon computes the federal and state unemployment taxes as follows:

SUTA tax, 2.8% of $26,400 = ...		$739.20	
Gross FUTA tax, 6.2% of $26,400 = ...	$1,636.80		
Less credit for SUTA tax, 5.4% of $26,400 = ...	−1,425.60	211.20	(net FUTA tax)
Total unemployment taxes		$950.40	

More simply, the net FUTA tax is computed by multiplying the taxable wages, $26,400, by the net FUTA tax rate, 0.8%, yielding $211.20.

The recording of the employer's FUTA tax for each pay period at .8% also applies to employers who, due to their state's liability for Title XII advances, have a net FUTA tax in excess of .8%. Since the exact rate is not known until November and the payment of the penalty is not made until the last deposit of the year, the FUTA tax expense for each payroll during the year is computed at .8%. The extra FUTA tax, due to the penalty charge, can be recorded as a single *adjusting entry* at the end of the year:

	Debit	Credit
Dec. 31 Payroll Taxes	XXX	
FUTA Taxes Payable		XXX
To record the employer's penalty for the year for the state's nonpayment of Title XII advances.		

The FUTA tax, like the FICA taxes and the contributions to the state for unemployment compensation purposes, is a social security tax. Thus, the FUTA tax can be charged to the same expense account as the other payroll taxes on the employer, the Payroll Taxes account. However, since employers may be required to pay the net FUTA tax quarterly, and to pay the FICA taxes more frequently, an employer should keep separate liability accounts for recording these two taxes.

SELF-STUDY QUIZ 6–2. The Olt Company's gross payroll for the week of January 22 was $95,190.00. This total pay was taxable for federal (.8%) and state (3.15%) unemployment taxes. Journalize the entry to record the Olt Company's payroll taxes for this pay.

Entries to Record Wages and Payroll Taxes

In the following illustrations of recording (or journalizing) wages and the payroll taxes imposed under both the federal and state laws, the employer is responsible for the following taxes:

1. FICA tax—OASDI on employees: 6.2%.
2. FICA tax—HI on employees: 1.45%.
3. FIT withheld from employees.
4. FICA tax—OASDI on employers: 6.2%.
5. FICA tax—HI on employers: 1.45%.
6. Net FUTA tax: .8%.
7. SUTA tax: 2.4%.

The weekly payroll amounts to $3,200, and the entire amount is subject to all social security and unemployment taxes. You may record this information in two separate journal entries. In the first entry, you might record the wages expense of the employer and the liabilities for the FICA taxes and FIT withheld in a two-column general journal as follows:

	Debit	Credit
Wages Expense	3,200.00	
FICA Taxes Payable—OASDI		198.40
FICA Taxes Payable—HI		46.40
Employees FIT Payable		230.00
Cash		2,725.20
To record the payment of wages and the liability for the employees' FICA taxes and FIT withheld.		

LEARNING OBJECTIVE 3

We can analyze this entry in T-accounts as follows:

WAGES EXPENSE

3,200.00	

This debit represents the employees' gross earnings for the pay period. This results in an increase in the operating expenses of the employer.

FICA TAXES PAYABLE—HI

	46.40

This credit results in an increase in a liability of the employer.

The amount credited to FICA Taxes Payable—HI is computed as follows:

1.45% of $3,200 = $46.40,   amount deducted from employees' wages

CASH

	2,725.20

This credit results in a decrease in an asset.

The amount credited to Cash is computed as follows:

$3,200.00, gross wages earned
−474.80, employees' taxes withheld
$2,725.20, net amount paid employees

In the second entry, you can record the employer's payroll taxes as follows:

	Debit	Credit
Payroll Taxes	347.20	
FICA Taxes Payable—OASDI		198.40
FICA Taxes Payable—HI		46.40
FUTA Taxes Payable		25.60
SUTA Taxes Payable		76.80

To record the payroll taxes and the employer's liability for the taxes.

FICA TAXES PAYABLE—OASDI

	198.40

This credit results in an increase in a liability of the employer.

The amount credited to FICA Taxes Payable—OASDI is computed as follows:

6.2% of $3,200 = $198.40,   amount deducted from employees' wages

EMPLOYEES FIT PAYABLE

	230.00

This credit results in an increase in a liability of the employer.

The amount credited to Employees FIT Payable is obtained by using one of the withholding methods explained in Chapter 4.

Let's analyze this entry by means of T-accounts as shown below:

PAYROLL TAXES

347.20	

This debit results in an increase in the operating expenses.

The amount debited to Payroll Taxes is computed as follows:

6.2% of $3,200 = $198.40, employer's OASDI tax
1.45% of $3,200 =   46.40, employer's HI tax
.8% of $3,200 =   25.60, employer's net FUTA tax
2.4% of $3,200 =   76.80, employer's SUTA tax
Total payroll taxes $347.20

FICA TAXES PAYABLE—OASDI		FICA TAXES PAYABLE—HI	
	198.40		46.40
	198.40		46.40
	The second credit amount, representing the employer's OASDI tax, also increases the employer's liability. The amount is determined as shown in the computation of the payroll taxes.		The second credit amount, representing the employer's HI tax, also increases the employer's liability. The amount is determined as shown in the computation of the payroll taxes.

FUTA TAXES PAYABLE		SUTA TAXES PAYABLE	
	25.60		76.80
	This credit results in an increase in a liability of the employer. The amount is determined as shown in the computation of the payroll taxes.		This credit results in an increase in a liability of the employer. The amount is determined as shown in the computation of the payroll taxes.

In the preceding illustration no contributions were required of employees for state unemployment compensation purposes. Assume that the employees had been required to make contributions of 1% to state unemployment compensation funds. The payroll entry would then appear as follows:

	Debit	Credit
Wages Expense	3,200.00	
FICA Taxes Payable—OASDI		198.40
FICA Taxes Payable—HI		46.40
Employees FIT Payable		230.00
SUTA Taxes Payable		32.00
Cash		2,693.20

To record the payment of wages and the liability for the employees' FICA, FIT, and SUTA taxes withheld.

In a small company with few employees, you can compute the hours worked, determine net pay, and prepare the paychecks or pay envelopes in a relatively short period of time. For such companies, a journal entry wherein you directly credit the cash account for the total net pay is a logical, efficient procedure.

In larger companies, however, the calculation of hours worked, the determination of net pay, and the preparation of paychecks may extend over the greater part of a workday, or even longer. In such companies because of the workload involved in meeting each payroll, especially when the paychecks must be mailed to far-flung branch offices, the paychecks may be prepared several days in advance of their actual distribution to the workers. Further, the preparation of the workers' paychecks may occur in one accounting period, although the actual payment is made in the following accounting period. Thus, to show an accurate picture of the firm's liability for the payroll, at the time of recording the payroll the net pay is accrued and credited to a liability account such as Salaries Payable or Accrued Salaries Payable, instead of to the Cash account. Later, when the paychecks are given to the workers, an entry is made to record the payment of the payroll. In this entry the liability account Salaries Payable is debited and the Cash account is credited.

RECORDING WORKERS' COMPENSATION INSURANCE EXPENSE

As indicated in Chapter 1, most states have passed laws that require employers to provide workers' compensation insurance to protect their employees against losses due to injury or death incurred during employment. The expense account, *Workers' Compensation Insurance Expense*, can be used to record the premiums paid by the company to provide this coverage. Usually the employer estimates and pays the premium in advance. The insurance premium, often based upon the total gross payroll of the business, may be stated in terms of an amount for each $100 of weekly wages paid to employees. At the end of the year, all the payrolls are audited and the company pays an additional premium or receives credit for an overpayment. Since the premium rate varies with the hazard involved in the work performed, your personnel and payroll records should provide for a careful classification of employees by kind or grade of work and a summary of labor costs according to the insurance premium classifications.

E X A M P L E

The McMahon Company has only two different grades of work—office clerical and machine shop. The premium rates for 1996 are $.18 per $100 of payroll for the office clerical workers, and $2.90 per $100 of payroll for the machine-shop workers. Based upon past experience and budgetary projections for 1996, the company estimates its annual premium to be $8,900 and sends a check for that amount to the insurance carrier at the beginning of the year. The entry to record this transaction:

Workers' Compensation Insurance Expense	8,900.00	
Cash		8,900.00

The effect of this entry, when posted to the ledger accounts, increases the operating expenses of the company and decreases the assets.

At the end of 1996 the payrolls for the year are audited and analyzed and the current rates are applied to determine the actual premium as follows:

Work Grade	Total Payroll	Rate per $100	Premium
Office clerical	$ 81,000	$ .18	$ 145.80
Machine shop	312,000	2.90	9,048.00
Total	$393,000		$9,193.80
Less estimated premium paid in January			8,900.00
Balance due			$ 293.80

A check is written for the balance due the insurance company, and the following entry is made in the journal:

Workers' Compensation Insurance Expense	293.80	
Cash		293.80

ON THE

An effective way to reduce workers' compensation costs is for employers to assist their disabled workers in finding jobs which they are capable of performing despite a work-related injury. As long as the job offer is made in good faith (and not just to avoid payment of benefits), the employee must accept the job offer.

RECORDING THE DEPOSIT OR PAYMENT OF PAYROLL TAXES

The journal entries required to record the deposit or payment of FICA taxes and income taxes withheld and the payment of FUTA and SUTA taxes are explained below.

Depositing FICA Taxes and Federal Income Taxes Withheld

As explained in Chapter 3, the requirements for depositing FICA taxes and federal income taxes withheld from employees' wages vary in relation to the total volume of such taxes.

E   X   A   M   P   L   E

On April 15, the ledger accounts FICA Taxes Payable—OASDI, FICA Taxes Payable—HI, and Employees FIT Payable of the Nannan Company appear as follows:

FICA TAXES PAYABLE—OASDI

		4/15	697.07
		4/15	697.07
			1,394.14

FICA TAXES PAYABLE—HI

		4/15	163.02
		4/15	163.02
			326.04

EMPLOYEES FIT PAYABLE

		4/15	1,601.19

The company must complete Form 8109 and deposit the FICA and the federal income taxes. The following journal entry records this deposit:

FICA Taxes Payable—OASDI	1,394.14	
FICA Taxes Payable—HI	326.04	
Employees FIT Payable	1,601.19	
Cash		3,321.37

When posted, the debits of $1,394.14 and $326.04 to FICA Taxes Payable—OASDI and FICA Taxes Payable—HI remove the liabilities for the employer's share, as well as the employees' share, of the FICA taxes imposed. The debit to Employees FIT Payable removes the liability for the total amount of federal income taxes withheld from the employees' wages during the period. The credit to Cash reduces the assets of the company.

Paying State or City Income Taxes

When the employer turns over to the state or city the amount of income taxes withheld from employees' wages, the appropriate journal entry would be recorded as follows:

	Debit	Credit
Employees SIT Payable	XXX	
or		
Employees CIT Payable	XXX	
Cash		XXX

Paying FUTA and SUTA Taxes

At the time of completing Form 8109 and depositing the FUTA taxes that have accumulated during the preceding calendar quarter, an entry is made as follows:

	Debit	Credit
FUTA Taxes Payable	XXX	
Cash		XXX

Employers subject to the net FUTA tax plus a penalty for Title XII advances (see Chapter 5, page 5–12) must make an adjusting entry prior to the last payment of the FUTA tax for the year. Since the amount of the penalty is not known until the fourth quarter, the penalty has not yet been recorded as a payroll tax expense. Therefore, an adjusting entry is made on December 31 to record the expense and the liability. This liability will be paid in January, in addition to the payment for the fourth quarter net FUTA tax.

The quarterly payment of state unemployment contributions is recorded as follows:

	Debit	Credit
SUTA Taxes Payable	XXX	
Cash		XXX

RECORDING END-OF-PERIOD ADJUSTMENTS

In most cases, the end of the fiscal (accounting) period does not coincide with the end of the payroll period. Therefore, adjustments are commonly made to record the end-of-period wages and accrued vacation pay.

LEARNING OBJECTIVE

5

Wages

To record the adjustment for end-of-period wages, the wages for this last payroll period must be split between the fiscal period just ending (accrued wages) and the fiscal period just beginning. For instance, if the fiscal period ends on Wednesday and payday takes place every Friday, the wages earned by the employees on Monday, Tuesday, and Wednesday are an expense of the fiscal period just ended. However, the wages earned on Thursday and Friday (payday) apply to the new fiscal period.

In order to record the wage expense properly for the fiscal period ended, an adjusting entry must be made on the last day of the fiscal period. However, since there is no actual wage payment, there is no need to credit any withholding accounts. The credit part of the entry involves a single liability account for the total wage expense. In the case above, the wage expenses of Monday, Tuesday, and Wednesday would be recorded in the following *adjusting entry:*

	Debit	Credit
Wages Expense	XXX	
Wages Payable		XXX

         To record wages incurred but unpaid as of the end of
         the fiscal period.

In a situation where the employer holds back one week's pay (earnings for the current week are not paid until the following Friday), the adjusting entry for the example shown above would accrue eight days of expense (one full week plus Monday, Tuesday, and Wednesday).

Vacation Pay

Another adjustment required at the end of the accounting period concerns vacation pay. If a company has a vacation policy, the employees earn the right for paid future absences during the current period. Therefore, a liability should be accrued at the end of the current period. Whether making the adjustment each payday, each month, or each year, the expense must be recorded when the liability is created, not necessarily in the period in which it is paid.

E X A M P L E

The employees of the Dansly Company are entitled to one day's vacation for each month worked. The average daily pay for each of the 50 employees is $130. The adjusting entry to record the vacation expense of $6,500 ($130 × 50) at the end of each month is:

Vacation Benefits Expense...................................	6,500.00	
Vacation Benefits Payable		6,500.00

When employees eventually use their vacation time, the payment entry debits Vacation Benefits Payable, not Wages Expense. This expense was previously recorded in the adjusting entry, as shown above. Postretirement benefits such as health care and pension also require adjusting entries of this type. These benefits must be reported as expenses during the employees' working years when they earn the entitlements.

RECORDING TRANSACTIONS PERTAINING TO OTHER PAYROLL DEDUCTIONS

Up to this point in our discussion of deductions made from wages and salaries, we have been limited to FICA taxes, state unemployment contributions, and income taxes. However, most companies have other deductions that must be taken into consideration when preparing the payroll. Regardless of the number of deductions or the types of deductions made from employees' wages, we must provide a systematic means of keeping a record of the total wages for each employee, the deductions for each purpose, and the net amount paid. It is impossible to say that a certain type of record is satisfactory for every organization or even for each company doing a certain kind of business. Each business organization has its own problems and peculiarities that will affect the type of record needed. It is important, therefore, that we keep all the records required by law, as well as those needed for other purposes.

Although you should have a separate column in the payroll register for each deduction, the payroll register may become too cumbersome if there are too many columns for deductions. Many businesses, therefore, use a payroll register with a separate column for each of the major deductions and lump all other deductions together in one column headed "Other Deductions." Some companies use only one column for deductions and place the entire total in that column. If this practice is followed, it is usually necessary to have a supplementary record of deductions showing a detailed breakdown of the total for each employee. This supplementary record serves as the basis for obtaining the figure for total deductions shown in the payroll register.

The deductions for FICA taxes, income taxes, disability benefits, and state unemployment benefits are required by law. Most other payroll deductions result from company policies, collective bargaining agreements, court orders, or employee authorizations. Some of the purposes for making deductions include:

1. Group insurance.
2. Health insurance.
3. Purchase of government bonds.
4. Union dues.
5. Garnishment of wages.
6. Pension and retirement benefits.

Group Insurance

Many companies have a *group insurance* program for employees. Such programs usually permit employees to obtain life insurance at a much lower rate than would be possible if the employee purchased the insurance as an individual. Under some group insurance plans, the employer and the employee share the cost of the insurance premium. The employees' share may be deducted from their wages every payday, every month, or every quarter.

When recording a payroll which makes deductions from employees' wages for group insurance, the amount withheld from their wages is applied toward the payment of their share of the premium. The total amount withheld is credited to a *liability* account with a title such as *Group Insurance Premiums Collected* or *Group Insurance Payments Withheld*. This general ledger account serves the same purpose as the accounts used to record payroll taxes withheld from employees' wages.

Health Insurance

Many companies have developed their own health insurance plans for employees, or are members of private insurance groups that provide coverage for employees of companies that are members of the group. If employees bear the cost or a portion of the cost of such insurance, the portion paid by the employees is usually deducted every payday from the wages of the employees. (This voluntary form of insurance protection should not be confused with the health insurance program for the aged. The latter program, Medicare, is discussed in Appendix A.)

The amounts withheld from the employees' wages for health insurance are credited to a *liability* account such as *Health Insurance Premiums Collected.*

Employers often pay the premium for health insurance in advance to the insurance carrier. At the time of paying the premium, a prepaid expense account such as *Prepaid Health Insurance* is debited for the amount paid the carrier. Periodically this account is adjusted through the health insurance or fringe benefit expense account, and if applicable, the employees' withholding account.

Purchase of Government Savings Bonds

Employees are encouraged to invest a certain amount of their wages in government savings bonds. Such plans or similar savings plans encourage employees to save a certain amount of each salary payment. The theory behind such deductions is that most employees will not miss a small amount that is set aside each payday, and over a period of time the deductions accumulate into a sizable amount.

Employees authorize their employer to make payroll deductions for the purchase of savings bonds by completing authorization forms that indicate the amount to be withheld and how frequently. The amounts withheld from the paychecks are set aside by the employer, acting in a trustee position, until a sufficient amount has been accumulated for the purchase of savings bonds for the employees. The minimum denomination for Series EE savings bonds for new participants in a payroll savings plan is $100. A $100 bond can be purchased as soon as the participant has accumulated the $50 purchase price in his or her withholding account.

E X A M P L E

Wayne Richards has authorized his employer to withhold $10 from his pay every two weeks toward the purchase of a Series EE U.S. savings bond, which has a maturity value of $100. At the time of preparing each biweekly payroll, the employer credits the liability account U.S. Savings Bonds Deductions Payable for $10. After the employer has recorded five similar entries, the balance of the liability account will be $50, the amount required for the purchase of one $100 Series EE U.S. savings bond. At this time the employer purchases the bond, which is later delivered to the employee. The journal entry to record this transaction includes a debit of $50 to the liability account U.S. Savings Bonds Deductions Payable and a corresponding credit to the Cash account.

Union Dues

In companies in which employees are members of unions that require employees to pay dues to the union, many employees pay their dues, assessments, and initiation fees through deductions from wages, known as a **check-off system.** Amounts withheld from union members' wages are credited to a *liability* account such as *Union Dues Payable.* Monthly, or as agreed upon by the union and the employer, the amounts withheld are turned over to the treasurer of the union. At this time a journal entry is made in which the payment of union dues is recorded by debiting the liability account and crediting the cash account.

Garnishment of Wages

Garnishment refers to the legal or equitable procedure by means of which a portion of the wages of any person must be withheld for payment of a debt.

Through the garnishment process, a creditor, with the aid of the courts, may require the employer to hold back a portion of the debtor's wages and pay that amount to the court or to the creditor. In some companies the amounts to be held back are deducted each payday from the employee's wages.

The Consumer Credit Protection Act limits the amount of wages subject to garnishment, in general, to 25% of a worker's disposable earnings. ***Disposable earnings*** are the earnings remaining after withholding for income taxes and for other amounts required by law. (In cases of support orders, the limits on the amounts that can be taken from an employee's pay range from 50% to 65% of weekly disposable wages, depending on the employee's number of dependents.)

The provisions of the Consumer Credit Protection Act also prohibit an employer from discharging an employee simply because the employee's wages are subject to garnishment for one indebtedness. If another garnishment for a second indebtedness should arise, the worker could be discharged, provided a considerable amount of time had *not* elapsed between the two occasions of indebtedness. It is possible that the lapse of time could make the first garnishment immaterial. The payroll manager should also be aware that state garnishment laws that are more favorable to employees have priority over the federal law.

Federal Tax Levy

In satisfying a tax levy for unpaid back taxes, the employer must compute the amount that is exempt from levy. This part is paid to the employee and the remainder of the pay is sent to the IRS to cover the debt. The IRS issues tables to help in computing the exempt amount. The IRS uses Form 668-W (not illustrated) to notify an employer of a tax levy. Copies of the form must then be forwarded to the employee for completion of a statement of filing status and exemptions. This information will then allow the employer to compute the actual levy. If the employee fails to return the signed statement within three working days to the employer, the exempt amount is based on married-filing-separately status with one personal exemption.

Pension and Retirement Benefits

Since in many instances social security benefits are inadequate for retired employees and their dependents, many firms provide pension and retirement plans that will supplement the government benefits. Although the benefit formulas and eligibility rules vary, the coverage is about the same for production workers, office employees, and managers. Many pension plans are financed solely by employer contributions, but other plans involve employee contributions. Once these contributions are deducted from the employees' pay, they become a liability for the employer and are recorded as such in the payroll entry.

Some employers also provide their employees with the opportunity to set up their own Individual Retirement Accounts (IRA) through a payroll deduction plan (see page 1–11). These voluntary contributions are deducted from the paychecks of the employees who set up their own retirement accounts. These deductions are recorded as a liability in the payroll entry. This liability account will be cleared as the employer pays the contributions to the financial institution that is in charge of each employee's retirement account.

Under the Family Support Act, all states must permit child-support garnishment from the beginning of the support payments. In the past, some states garnished wages for child support only after the parent had fallen behind in payments.

The IRS also collects support payments by withholding from income tax refunds due delinquent payers. In 1993, the IRS collected $703 million in delinquent child support payments from tax refunds.

SUMMARY OF ACCOUNTS USED IN RECORDING PAYROLL TRANSACTIONS

L E A R N I N G
O B J E C T I V E
6

The following listing summarizes some of the general ledger accounts that may be used to record payroll transactions:

1. *Wages and Salaries*—an operating expense account in which the gross payroll is recorded.
2. *Payroll Taxes*—an operating expense account in which are recorded all payroll taxes on the employer under FICA, FUTA, and the various state unemployment compensation laws.
3. *Workers' Compensation Insurance Expense*—an operating expense account in which are recorded the premiums paid by the company to provide coverage for employees against employment-related injury or death.
4. *Vacation Benefits Expense*—an operating expense account in which are recorded the costs of the vacation time that has been earned by employees.
5. *FICA Taxes Payable—OASDI*—a current liability account in which are recorded deductions made from employees' wages and the employer's portion of the OASDI tax.
6. *FICA Taxes Payable—HI*—a current liability account in which are recorded deductions made from employees' wages and the employer's portion of the HI tax.
7. *FUTA Taxes Payable*—a current liability account in which is recorded the employer's federal unemployment taxes.
8. *SUTA Taxes Payable*—a current liability account in which are recorded the amounts due the states for the employer's unemployment compensation contributions. This account may also be credited for amounts deducted from employees' wages, if employees must contribute to state unemployment compensation funds.
9. *Employees FIT Payable*—a current liability account in which are recorded deductions made from employees' wages for federal income taxes.
10. *Employees SIT Payable*—a current liability account in which are recorded deductions made from employees' wages for state income taxes.
11. *Health Insurance Premiums Collected*—a current liability account in which are recorded deductions made from employees' wages for their share of the premiums paid for health insurance coverage.
12. *Union Dues Payable*—a current liability account in which are recorded the deductions made from union members' wages for their union dues, assessments, or initiation fees.
13. *Wages Payable*—a current liability account in which are recorded the wages that have been earned by employees but not yet paid to them.
14. *Vacation Benefits Payable*—a current liability account in which are recorded the costs of vacation time that has been earned by employees but not yet used.

ILLUSTRATIVE CASE

The following illustrative case shows the accounting procedures used by the Brookins Company in recording payroll transactions during the third quarter of its fiscal year. The fiscal year of the company ends on June 30, 19—. Brookins pays employees semimonthly on the 15th and the last day of the month. When the 15th or the last day of the month falls on Saturday or Sunday, employees are paid on the preceding Friday.

On January 1, 19—, the balances of the accounts used in recording payroll transactions follow. These account balances are shown in the general ledger on pages 6–26 and 6–28.

Acct. No.	Account Title	Account Balance
11	Cash	$85,000.00
20	FICA Taxes Payable—OASDI	734.29
21	FICA Taxes Payable—HI	171.73
22	FUTA Taxes Payable	122.00
23	SUTA Taxes Payable	40.50
25	Employees FIT Payable	1,472.00
26	Employees SIT Payable	474.42
28	Union Dues Payable	80.00
51	Wages and Salaries	46,500.00
55	Payroll Taxes	4,254.50

The first $63,000 in wages and salaries paid is subject to the OASDI tax on both the employer (6.2%) and the employees (6.2%). The total wages and salaries paid are subject to the HI tax on both the employer (1.45%) and the employees (1.45%). The employer is also subject to a net FUTA tax of .8%, based on the first $7,000 in earnings paid each employee during a calendar year; and a SUTA tax of 2.3%, based on the first $7,000 in earnings paid during a calendar year. The state does not require contributions of employees for unemployment compensation or disability insurance.

The wage-bracket method is used to determine the amount of federal income taxes to be withheld from the employees' earnings. The state income tax law requires that a graduated percentage of the gross earnings of each employee be withheld each payday. Under the check-off system, union dues are withheld each payday from the union workers who are employed in the plant. On or before the fourth of each month the dues collected during the preceding month are turned over to the treasurer of the union.

In the following narrative of transactions, the January 14 (Friday) payroll transaction is explained in detail on page 6–22. All other transactions are stated briefly. Adjacent to the narrative are the journal entries to record the transactions. The ledger accounts showing the transactions posted are on pages 6–26 and 6–28.

Narrative of Transactions	Journal			Page 15
		P.R.	Debit	Credit
	19—			
Jan. 4. Paid the treasurer of the union $80, representing the union dues withheld from the workers' earnings during the month of December.	Jan. 4 Union Dues Payable .... Cash .... To record the payment of the union dues withheld during December.	28 11	80.00	80.00
Jan. 14. Paid total wages and salaries of all employees, $3,890. All the earnings are taxable under FICA. In addition to the social security taxes, the company withheld $455 from the employees' earnings for federal income taxes, $85.58 for state income taxes, and $45 for union dues. (See the explanation of the January 14 payroll transaction given on the following page.)	14 Wages and Salaries .... FICA Taxes Payable—OASDI . FICA Taxes Payable—HI ..... Employees FIT Payable ...... Employees SIT Payable ...... Union Dues Payable .... Cash .... To record the payment of wages and the liabilities for the employees' taxes withheld.	51 20 21 25 26 28 11	3,890.00	241.18 56.41 455.00 85.58 45.00 3,006.83

Narrative of Transactions	Journal	P.R.	Debit	Credit
Jan. 14. Recorded the employer's payroll taxes for the first pay in January. All the earnings are taxable under FICA, FUTA, and SUTA.	Jan. 14 Payroll Taxes	55	418.18	
	FICA Taxes Payable—OASDI .	20		241.18
	FICA Taxes Payable—HI	21		56.41
	FUTA Taxes Payable	22		31.12
	SUTA Taxes Payable	23		89.47
	To record the payroll taxes and liabilities of the employer.			
Jan. 18. Completed Form 8109 and deposited with a Federal Reserve bank the FICA taxes and employees' federal income taxes withheld on the two December payrolls. At the end of December the total liability for FICA taxes and federal income taxes withheld was $2,378.02. (January 17 is Martin Luther King, Jr.'s birthday, which is a bank holiday.)	18 FICA Taxes Payable—OASDI	20	734.29	
	FICA Taxes Payable—HI	21	171.73	
	Employees FIT Payable	25	1,472.00	
	Cash	11		2,378.02
	To record the deposit of FICA taxes and federal income taxes withheld for the December 15 and 31 payrolls.			
	18 Employees SIT Payable	26	474.42	
	Cash	11		474.42
	To record the payment of the state income taxes withheld during the fourth quarter.			

The analysis of the January 14 payroll transaction follows:

1. Wages and Salaries is debited for $3,890, the total of the employees' gross earnings.
2. FICA Taxes Payable—OASDI is credited for $241.18, the amount withheld from the employees' earnings for OASDI taxes.
3. FICA Taxes Payable—HI is credited for $56.41, the amount withheld from the employees' earnings for HI taxes.
4. Employees FIT Payable is credited for $455, the amount withheld from employees' earnings for federal income tax purposes.
5. Employees SIT Payable is credited for $85.58, the amount withheld from employees' earnings for state income taxes.
6. Union Dues Payable is credited for $45, the amount withheld from union members' earnings.
7. Cash is credited for $3,006.83, the net amount paid the employees ($3,890 gross earnings − $241.18 OASDI − $56.41 HI − $455 FIT − $85.58 SIT − $45 union dues).

8. Payroll Taxes is debited for $418.18, the amount of taxes imposed on the employer under FICA, FUTA, and SUTA. The computation of the total payroll taxes is:

FICA—OASDI:	6.2% of $3,890 =	$241.18
FICA—HI:	1.45% of $3,890 =	56.41
FUTA:	.8% of $3,890 =	31.12
SUTA:	2.3% of $3,890 =	89.47
Total payroll taxes		$418.18

9. FICA Taxes Payable—OASDI is credited for the amount of tax on the employer, which is 6.2% of $3,890, or $241.18.
10. FICA Taxes Payable—HI is credited for the amount of tax on the employer, which is 1.45% of $3,890, or $56.41.
11. FUTA Taxes Payable is credited for $31.12, the liability incurred because of the taxes imposed on the employer under FUTA.
12. SUTA Taxes Payable is credited for $89.47, the amount of the contributions payable to the state.

Narrative of Transactions	Journal	P.R.	Debit	Page 16 Credit
Jan. 31. Paid total wages and salaries, $4,100. All of this amount constitutes taxable earnings under FICA. Withheld $483 for federal income taxes, $90.20 for state income taxes, and $45 for union dues.	Jan. 31 Wages and Salaries . . . . FICA Taxes Payable—OASDI . FICA Taxes Payable—HI . . . . . Employees FIT Payable . . . . Employees SIT Payable . . . . Union Dues Payable . . . . Cash . . . . To record the payment of wages and the liabilities for the employees' taxes withheld.	51 20 21 25 26 28 11	4,100.00	 254.20 59.45 483.00 90.20 45.00 3,168.15
Jan. 31. Recorded the employer's payroll taxes for this payroll. All the earnings are taxable under FICA, FUTA, and SUTA.	31 Payroll Taxes . . . . FICA Taxes Payable—OASDI . FICA Taxes Payable—HI . . . . . FUTA Taxes Payable . . . . SUTA Taxes Payable . . . . To record the payroll taxes and liabilities of the employer.	55 20 21 22 23	440.75	 254.20 59.45 32.80 94.30
Jan. 31. Completed Form 8109 and deposited $122 with a Federal Reserve bank to remove the liability for FUTA taxes for the fourth quarter of the previous year.	31 FUTA Taxes Payable . . . . Cash . . . . To record the deposit of FUTA taxes for the fourth quarter.	22 11	122.00	 122.00
Jan. 31. Filed the state unemployment contributions return for the quarter ending December 31, and paid $40.50 to the state unemployment compensation fund.	31 SUTA Taxes Payable . . . . Cash . . . . To record payment of contributions to state unemployment compensation fund for the fourth quarter.	23 11	40.50	 40.50
Jan. 31. Filed the Employer's Annual Federal Unemployment (FUTA) Tax Return, Form 940-EZ, for the preceding calendar year. No journal entry is required since the liability for FUTA taxes was removed by the timely deposit on January 31, 19—. No taxes were paid at the time of filing the annual return.				
Jan. 31. Filed the quarterly return (Form 941) with the IRS Center for the period ended December 31. No journal entry is required since the liability for FICA taxes and employees' federal income taxes withheld was removed by the timely deposit on January 18, 19—. No taxes were paid or deposited at the time of filing Form 941.				
Feb. 4. Paid the treasurer of the union $90, representing the union dues withheld from the workers' earnings during the month of January.	Feb. 4 Union Dues Payable . . . . Cash . . . . To record the payment of the union dues withheld during January.	28 11	90.00	 90.00

Narrative of Transactions	Journal	P.R.	Debit	Page 17 Credit

Feb. 15. Paid total wages and salaries, $4,000. All of this amount is taxable under FICA. Withheld $470 for federal income taxes, $88 for state income taxes, and $45 for union dues.	Feb. 15 Wages and Salaries . . . .
	FICA Taxes Payable—OASDI .
	FICA Taxes Payable—HI . . . . .
	Employees FIT Payable . . . . . .
	Employees SIT Payable . . . .
	Union Dues Payable . . . .
	Cash . . . .
	   To record the payment of
	   wages and the liabilities for
	   the employees' taxes with-
	   held.
		51
		20
		21
		25
		26
		28
		11
			4,000.00	
				248.00
				58.00
				470.00
				88.00
				45.00
				3,091.00

Feb. 15. Recorded the employer's payroll taxes. All the earnings are taxable under FICA, FUTA, and SUTA.	15 Payroll Taxes . . . .
	FICA Taxes Payable—OASDI .
	FICA Taxes Payable—HI . . . . .
	FUTA Taxes Payable . . . .
	SUTA Taxes Payable . . . .
	   To record the payroll taxes
	   and liabilities of the employer.
		55
		20
		21
		22
		23
			430.00	
				248.00
				58.00
				32.00
				92.00

Feb. 15. Completed Form 8109 and deposited $2,160.48 with a Federal Reserve bank to remove the liability for the FICA taxes and the employees' federal income taxes withheld on the January 14 and January 31 payrolls.	15 FICA Taxes Payable—OASDI . . . .
	FICA Taxes Payable—HI . . . .
	Employees FIT Payable . . . .
	Cash . . . .
	   To record the deposit of
	   FICA taxes and federal in-
	   come taxes withheld for the
	   January 14 and January 31
	   payrolls.
		20
		21
		25
		11
			990.76
			231.72
			938.00
				
				2,160.48

Feb. 28. Paid total wages and salaries, $4,250. All of this amount is taxable under FICA. Withheld $502 for federal income taxes, $93.50 for state income taxes, and $50 for union dues.	28 Wages and Salaries . . . .
	FICA Taxes Payable—OASDI .
	FICA Taxes Payable—HI . . . . .
	Employees FIT Payable . . . .
	Employees SIT Payable . . . .
	Union Dues Payable . . . .
	Cash . . . .
	   To record the payment of
	   wages and the liabilities for
	   the employees' taxes with-
	   held.
		51
		20
		21
		25
		26
		28
		11
			4,250.00	
				263.50
				61.63
				502.00
				93.50
				50.00
				3,279.37

Feb. 28. Recorded the employer's payroll taxes. All the earnings are taxable under FICA, FUTA, and SUTA.	28 Payroll Taxes . . . .
	FICA Taxes Payable—OASDI .
	FICA Taxes Payable—HI . . . . .
	FUTA Taxes Payable . . . .
	SUTA Taxes Payable . . . .
	   To record the payroll taxes
	   and liabilities of the em-
	   ployer.
		55
		20
		21
		22
		23
			456.88	
				263.50
				61.63
				34.00
				97.75

Mar. 4. Paid the treasurer of the union $95, representing the union dues withheld from the workers' earnings during the month of February.	Mar. 4 Union Dues Payable . . . .
	Cash . . . .
	   To record the payment of the
	   union dues withheld during
	   February.
		28
		11
			95.00	
				95.00

Narrative of Transactions	Journal	P.R.	Debit	Page 18 Credit

Mar. 15. Paid total wages and salaries, $4,300. All of this amount is taxable under FICA. Withheld $554 for federal income taxes, $94.60 for state income taxes, and $50 for union dues.	Mar. 15 Wages and Salaries . . . .
	 FICA Taxes Payable—OASDI
	 FICA Taxes Payable—HI . . . .
	 Employees FIT Payable . . . . .
	 Employees SIT Payable . . . . .
	 Union Dues Payable . . . .
	 Cash . . . .
	   To record the payment of
	   wages and the liabilities for
	   the employees' taxes with-
	   held.
		51
		 20
		 21
		 25
		 26
		 28
		 11
			4,300.00	
				 266.60
				 62.35
				 554.00
				 94.60
				 50.00
				 3,272.45

Mar. 15. Recorded the employer's payroll taxes. All the earnings are taxable under FICA, FUTA, and SUTA.	15 Payroll Taxes . . . .
	 FICA Taxes Payable—OASDI
	 FICA Taxes Payable—HI . . . .
	 FUTA Taxes Payable . . . .
	 SUTA Taxes Payable . . . .
	   To record the payroll taxes
	   and liabilities of the em-
	   ployer.
		55
		 20
		 21
		 22
		 23
			462.25	
				 266.60
				 62.35
				 34.40
				 98.90

Mar. 15. Completed Form 8109 and deposited $2,234.26 with a Federal Reserve bank to remove the liability for FICA taxes and the employees' federal income taxes withheld on the February 15 and February 28 payrolls.	15 FICA Taxes Payable—OASDI . . .
	 FICA Taxes Payable—HI . . . .
	 Employees FIT Payable . . . .
	 Cash . . . .
	   To record the deposit of
	   FICA taxes and federal in-
	   come taxes withheld for the
	   February 15 and February
	   28 payrolls.
		20
		 21
		 25
		 11
			1,023.00
			 239.26
			 972.00
				
				 2,234.26

Mar. 31. Paid total wages and salaries, $4,320. All of this amount is taxable under FICA. Withheld $570 for federal income taxes, $95.04 for state income taxes, and $50 for union dues.	31 Wages and Salaries . . . .
	 FICA Taxes Payable—OASDI
	 FICA Taxes Payable—HI . . . .
	 Employees FIT Payable . . . . .
	 Employees SIT Payable . . . . .
	 Union Dues Payable . . . .
	 Cash . . . .
	   To record the payment of
	   wages and the liabilities for
	   the employees' taxes with-
	   held.
		51
		 20
		 21
		 25
		 26
		 28
		 11
			4,320.00	
				 267.84
				 62.64
				 570.00
				 95.04
				 50.00
				 3,274.48

Mar. 31. Recorded the employer's payroll taxes. All of the earnings are taxable under FICA, FUTA, and SUTA.	31 Payroll Taxes . . . .
	 FICA Taxes Payable—OASDI
	 FICA Taxes Payable—HI . . . .
	 FUTA Taxes Payable . . . .
	 SUTA Taxes Payable . . . .
	   To record the payroll taxes
	   and liabilities of the em-
	   ployer.
		55
		 20
		 21
		 22
		 23
			464.40	
				 267.84
				 62.64
				 34.56
				 99.36

After journalizing and posting the transactions for January through March, the general ledger payroll accounts as shown on the next two pages carry the following balances:

1. *FICA Taxes Payable—OASDI:* $1,068.88, the amount of the liability for the taxes imposed on both the employer and the employees with respect to wages and salaries paid on March 15 and March 31. The FICA taxes, along with the employees' federal income taxes withheld, must be deposited in a Federal Reserve bank by April 15.

2. *FICA Taxes Payable—HI:* $249.98, the amount of the liability for the taxes imposed on both the employer and the employees with respect to wages and salaries paid on March 15 and March 31. The FICA taxes, along with the employees' federal income taxes withheld, must be deposited in a Federal Reserve bank by April 15.

3. *FUTA Taxes Payable:* $198.88, the accumulation of the amounts credited to this account each payday during the first three months of the calendar year. The balance of the account on March 31 must be deposited in a Federal Reserve bank by May 2.

4. *SUTA Taxes Payable:* $571.78, the amount due to the state unemployment compensation fund. This liability must be paid on or before May 2.

5. *Employees FIT Payable:* $1,124, the amount due for federal income taxes withheld from employees' earnings on March 15 and March 31. This amount, along with the balances of the FICA Taxes Payable accounts, represents a liability that must be deposited in a Federal Reserve bank by April 15.

6. *Employees SIT Payable:* $546.92, the amount due for state income taxes withheld from employees' earnings during the first three months of the calendar year. This amount must be paid to the treasurer of the state on the date specified in the state's income tax law.

7. *Union Dues Payable:* $100, amount due the treasurer of the union on or before April 4.

8. *Wages and Salaries:* $71,360, the total gross earnings for the three quarters of the company's fiscal year. The entire amount is an operating expense of the business.

9. *Payroll Taxes:* $6,926.96, the total payroll taxes for the three quarters imposed on the employer under FICA, FUTA, and SUTA. The entire amount is an operating expense of the business.

GENERAL LEDGER

CASH   11

Date	Item	P.R.	Dr.	Cr.	Balance Dr.	Balance Cr.
19—						
Jan. 1	Bal.	√			85,000.00	
4		J15		80.00	84,920.00	
14		J15		3,006.83	81,913.17	
18		J15		2,378.02	79,535.15	
18		J15		474.42	79,060.73	
31		J16		3,168.15	75,892.58	
31		J16		122.00	75,770.58	
31		J16		40.50	75,730.08	
Feb. 4		J16		90.00	75,640.08	
15		J17		3,091.00	72,549.08	
15		J17		2,160.48	70,388.60	
28		J17		3,279.37	67,109.23	
Mar. 4		J17		95.00	67,014.23	
15		J18		3,272.45	63,741.78	
15		J18		2,234.26	61,507.52	
31		J18		3,274.48	58,233.04	

FICA TAXES PAYABLE—OASDI   20

Date	Item	P.R.	Dr.	Cr.	Balance Dr.	Balance Cr.
19—						
Jan. 1	Bal.	√				734.29
14		J15		241.18		975.47
14		J15		241.18		1,216.65
18		J15	734.29			482.36
31		J16		254.20		736.56
31		J16		254.20		990.76
Feb. 15		J17		248.00		1,238.76
15		J17		248.00		1,486.76
15		J17	990.76			496.00
28		J17		263.50		759.50
28		J17		263.50		1,023.00
Mar. 15		J18		266.60		1,289.60
15		J18		266.60		1,556.20
15		J18	1,023.00			533.20
31		J18		267.84		801.04
31		J18		267.84		1,068.88

FICA TAXES PAYABLE—HI   21

Date	Item	P.R.	Dr.	Cr.	Balance Dr.	Balance Cr.
19—						
Jan. 1	Bal.	√				171.73
14		J15		56.41		228.14
14		J15		56.41		284.55
18		J15	171.73			112.82
31		J16		59.45		172.27
31		J16		59.45		231.72
Feb. 15		J17		58.00		289.72
15		J17		58.00		347.72
15		J17	231.72			116.00
28		J17		61.63		177.63
28		J17		61.63		239.26
Mar. 15		J18		62.35		301.61
15		J18		62.35		363.96
15		J18	239.26			124.70
31		J18		62.64		187.34
31		J18		62.64		249.98

EMPLOYEES FIT PAYABLE   25

Date	Item	P.R.	Dr.	Cr.	Balance Dr.	Balance Cr.
19—						
Jan. 1	Bal.	√				1,472.00
14		J15		455.00		1,927.00
18		J15	1,472.00			455.00
31		J16		483.00		938.00
Feb. 15		J17		470.00		1,408.00
15		J17	938.00			470.00
28		J17		502.00		972.00
Mar. 15		J18		554.00		1,526.00
15		J18	972.00			554.00
31		J18		570.00		1,124.00

EMPLOYEES SIT PAYABLE   26

Date	Item	P.R.	Dr.	Cr.	Balance Dr.	Balance Cr.
19—						
Jan. 1	Bal.	√				474.42
14		J15		85.58		560.00
18		J15	474.42			85.58
31		J16		90.20		175.78
Feb. 15		J17		88.00		263.78
28		J17		93.50		357.28
Mar. 15		J18		94.60		451.88
31		J18		95.04		546.92

FUTA TAXES PAYABLE   22

Date	Item	P.R.	Dr.	Cr.	Balance Dr.	Balance Cr.
19—						
Jan. 1	Bal.	√				122.00
14		J15		31.12		153.12
31		J16		32.80		185.92
31		J16	122.00			63.92
Feb. 15		J17		32.00		95.92
28		J17		34.00		129.92
Mar. 15		J18		34.40		164.32
31		J18		34.56		198.88

UNION DUES PAYABLE   28

Date	Item	P.R.	Dr.	Cr.	Balance Dr.	Balance Cr.
19—						
Jan. 1	Bal.	√				80.00
4		J15	80.00			——
14		J15		45.00		45.00
31		J16		45.00		90.00
Feb. 4		J16	90.00			——
15		J17		45.00		45.00
28		J17		50.00		95.00
Mar. 4		J17	95.00			——
15		J18		50.00		50.00
31		J18		50.00		100.00

SUTA TAXES PAYABLE   23

Date	Item	P.R.	Dr.	Cr.	Balance Dr.	Balance Cr.
19—						
Jan. 1	Bal.	√				40.50
14		J15		89.47		129.97
31		J16		94.30		224.27
31		J16	40.50			183.77
Feb. 15		J17		92.00		275.77
28		J17		97.75		373.52
Mar. 15		J18		98.90		472.42
31		J18		99.36		571.78

WAGES AND SALARIES							**51**	

Date	Item	P.R.	Dr.	Cr.	Balance Dr.	Balance Cr.
19—						
Jan. 1	Bal.	√			46,500.00	
14		J15	3,890.00		50,390.00	
31		J16	4,100.00		54,490.00	
Feb. 15		J17	4,000.00		58,490.00	
28		J17	4,250.00		62,740.00	
Mar. 15		J18	4,300.00		67,040.00	
31		J18	4,320.00		71,360.00	

PAYROLL TAXES							**55**	

Date	Item	P.R.	Dr.	Cr.	Balance Dr.	Balance Cr.
19—						
Jan. 1	Bal.	√			4,254.50	
14		J15	418.18		4,672.68	
31		J16	440.75		5,113.43	
Feb. 15		J17	430.00		5,543.43	
28		J17	456.88		6,000.31	
Mar. 15		J18	462.25		6,462.56	
31		J18	464.40		6,926.96	

KEY TERMS

Business expense
Check-off system
Disposable earnings
Garnishment

Group insurance
Journal entry
Payroll journal

QUESTIONS FOR REVIEW

1. What are the main kinds of information contained in a payroll register?
2. For what reason are "distribution" columns sometimes provided in the payroll register?
3. Explain how to prove the accuracy of the totals of the payroll register.
4. Which payroll record is used by the employer in completing Forms W-2?
5. Explain the use of the "Cumulative" column in the employee's earnings record.
6. In Philadelphia, Pennsylvania, most workers are subject to three income taxes upon their earnings—federal, state, and city. Should an employer in Philadelphia record the liability for the withholding of all three income taxes in one liability account such as Income Taxes Payable?
7. What special accounts must usually be opened in the general ledger to record payroll tax entries?
8. Is it necessary for an employer who is subject to FICA and FUTA taxes to keep a separate expense account for the taxes under each act?
9. What is the effect of each of the following postings upon the assets, liabilities, and owner's equity of a company?

   a. A debit to Wages.
   b. A credit to FICA Taxes Payable—HI.
   c. A debit to SUTA Taxes Payable.
   d. A credit to Cash.

10. Why is it necessary to classify employees by kind of work performed when computing the cost of workers' compensation insurance?
11. What accounts are debited and credited when an employer records the deposit of FICA taxes and federal income taxes that have been withheld?
12. When are expenses of benefits such as vacation pay and retirement pay recorded? Explain.
13. What is meant by the *garnishment* of wages?

QUESTIONS FOR DISCUSSION

1. In what respect does an employee's earnings record resemble a ledger?
2. The Golic Corporation has undertaken a cost study of its operations. One area of concern to the company is the total cost of labor, particularly the cost of employee benefits. Prepare a list of the different kinds of costs that a company might incur as part of its "total package" salary cost.
3. Along with five payroll deductions required by law (FICA—OASDI and HI, Employees FIT, Employees SIT, and Employees CIT), five other deductions are typically made from the employees' earnings in the Cranston Company. What methods are available to the company in recording these ten deductions in the payroll register?

PRACTICAL PROBLEMS

Omit the writing of explanations for the journal entries.

6–1. LO 2, 4.

    a. An employer, Gail Winters, is subject to FICA taxes but exempt from FUTA and SUTA taxes. During the last quarter of the year, her employees earned monthly wages of $8,500, all of which is taxable. The amount of federal income taxes withheld each month is $1,040. Journalize the payment of wages and record the payroll tax on November 30.

JOURNAL

	DATE	DESCRIPTION	POST. REF.	DEBIT	CREDIT	
1						1
2						2
3						3
4						4
5						5
6						6
7						7
8						8
9						9
10						10

    b. Prior to posting the November 30 payroll transaction, the FICA Taxes Payable—OASDI, the FICA Taxes Payable—HI, and the Employees FIT Payable accounts had zero balances. Winters must deposit with a Federal Reserve bank the FICA taxes and income taxes withheld on the November 30 payroll. Journalize the deposit of the payroll taxes on December 15.

JOURNAL

	DATE	DESCRIPTION	POST. REF.	DEBIT	CREDIT	
1						1
2						2
3						3
4						4
5						5
6						6

6–2. **LO 2.**

The employees of the Morton Music Company earn total wages of $4,690 during January. The total amount is taxable under FICA, FUTA, and SUTA. The state contribution rate for the company is 3.6%. The amount withheld for federal income taxes is $685. Journalize the payment of the monthly wages and record the payroll taxes.

JOURNAL

	DATE	DESCRIPTION	POST. REF.	DEBIT	CREDIT	
1						1
2						2
3						3
4						4
5						5
6						6
7						7
8						8
9						9
10						10
11						11

6–3. LO 2.

Tex, Inc., has a semimonthly payroll of $38,000 on May 15. The total payroll is taxable under FICA Taxes—HI, $32,850 is taxable under FICA Taxes—OASDI, and $29,300 is taxable under FUTA and SUTA. The state contribution rate for the company is 3.1%. The amount withheld for federal income taxes is $5,780. The amount withheld for state income taxes is $809. Journalize the payment of the wages and record the payroll taxes on May 15.

JOURNAL

	DATE	DESCRIPTION	POST. REF.	DEBIT	CREDIT	
1						1
2						2
3						3
4						4
5						5
6						6
7						7
8						8
9						9
10						10
11						11
12						12

6–4. **LO 2.**

Refer to Problem 6–3. Assume that the employees of Tex, Inc., must also pay state contributions (disability insurance) of 1% on the taxable payroll of $29,300, and that the employees' contributions are to be deducted by the employer. Journalize the May 15 payment of wages, assuming that the state contributions of the employees are kept in a separate account.

JOURNAL

	DATE	DESCRIPTION	POST. REF.	DEBIT	CREDIT	
1						1
2						2
3						3
4						4
5						5
6						6
7						7
8						8
9						9
10						10
11						11
12						12
13						13
14						14
15						15

6–5. LO 2.

The employees of the Pelter Company earn wages of $12,000 for the two weeks ending April 20. The entire amount of wages is subject to the FICA taxes, but only $9,800 is taxable under the federal and state unemployment compensation laws. The state contribution rate of the employer is 2.9%. All employees are subject to state unemployment contributions of .5% on the taxable wages of $9,800, and the employees' contributions are to be deducted by the employer. Journalize the payment of the wages and record the payroll taxes, assuming that the contributions of the employer and the employees are recorded in one account, SUTA Taxes Payable. (Ignore employee income tax in this problem.)

JOURNAL

	DATE	DESCRIPTION	POST. REF.	DEBIT	CREDIT	
1						1
2						2
3						3
4						4
5						5
6						6
7						7
8						8
9						9
10						10
11						11
12						12
13						13
14						14
15						15
16						16
17						17
18						18
19						19
20						20
21						21
22						22
23						23
24						24
25						25
26						26
27						27

6–6. **LO 2.**

The following information pertains to the payroll of the Furphy Textile Company on June 1:

a. The total wages earned by employees are $2,180.
b. The state unemployment insurance contribution rate is 2.5%.
c. The entire amount of wages is taxable under FICA, FUTA, and SUTA.
d. The amount withheld from the employees' wages for federal income taxes is $309; for state income taxes, $43.10; and for group insurance, $16.80.

Journalize the payment of wages and record the payroll taxes on June 1.

JOURNAL

	DATE	DESCRIPTION	POST. REF.	DEBIT	CREDIT	
1						1
2						2
3						3
4						4
5						5
6						6
7						7
8						8
9						9
10						10
11						11
12						12
13						13
14						14
15						15

6–7. LO 4.

On December 31, 1996, the Reuter Company has a balance of $98.75 in the FUTA Taxes Payable account. This represents the employer's liability for the fourth quarter taxes. Journalize the entry the Reuter Company should make in January, 1997, to record the last deposit of FUTA taxes for 1996.

JOURNAL

	DATE	DESCRIPTION	POST. REF.	DEBIT	CREDIT	
1						1
2						2
3						3
4						4
5						5
6						6

6–8. LO 4, 6.

On December 31, 1996, the Mayes Company has a balance of $134.95 in the FUTA Taxes Payable account, which represents their liability for the fourth quarter taxes. However, the Mayes Company is an employer in a state where employers are liable for a penalty of .6% for Title XII advances. The company has not recorded any of the penalty during the year.

Journalize the adjusting entry to be made on December 31 (the total taxable payroll for FUTA for the year was $212,500), and also the entry to deposit the FUTA taxes on January 31, 1997.

JOURNAL

	DATE	DESCRIPTION	POST. REF.	DEBIT	CREDIT	
1						1
2						2
3						3
4						4
5						5
6						6

6–9. **LO 6.**

In Oregon, employers who are covered by the state Workers' Compensation Law must withhold employee contributions from the wages of covered employees at the rate of 1.7¢ for each hour or part of an hour that the worker is employed. Every covered employer is assessed 1.7¢ per hour for each worker employed for each hour or part of an hour. The employer-employee contributions for workers' compensation are collected monthly, quarterly, or annually by the employer's insurance carrier, according to a schedule agreed upon by the employer and the carrier. The insurance carrier remits the contributions to the state's Workers' Compensation Department.

The Brunansky Company, a covered employer in Oregon, turns over the employer-employee workers' compensation contributions to its insurance carrier by the 15th of each month for the preceding month. During the month of July the number of full employee-hours worked by the company's employees was 24,190; the number of part-time employee-hours was 2,440.

a. The amount the company should have withheld from its full-time and part-time em-employees during the month of July for workers' compensation insurance is . . . . $ _____

b. The title you would give to the general ledger account to which the amount withheld from the employees' earnings would be credited is:

c. Journalize the entry on July 31 to record the employer's liability for workers' compensation insurance for the month.

JOURNAL

	DATE	DESCRIPTION	POST. REF.	DEBIT	CREDIT	
1						1
2						2
3						3
4						4
5						5

d. Journalize the entry on August 15 to record payment to the insurance carrier of the amount withheld from the employees' earnings for workers' compensation insurance and the amount of the employer's liability.

JOURNAL

	DATE	DESCRIPTION	POST. REF.	DEBIT	CREDIT	
1						1
2						2
3						3
4						4
5						5

6–10. **LO 1.**

The form on page 6–40 shows the amounts that appear in the Earnings to Date column of the employees' earnings records for 10 workers in the Unger Company. These amounts represent the cumulative taxable earnings for each worker as of October 18, the company's last payday. The form also gives the gross amount of earnings to be paid each worker on the next payday, October 25.

In the state where the Unger Company is located, the tax rates and bases are as follows:

Tax on Employees:

FICA—OASDI	6.2% on first $63,000
FICA—HI	1.45% on *total earnings*
SUTA	.5% on first $8,000

Tax on Employer:

FICA—OASDI	6.2% on first $63,000
FICA—HI	1.45% on *total earnings*
FUTA	.8% on first $7,000
SUTA	1.8% on first $8,000

In the appropriate columns of the form on page 6–40, do the following:

1. Compute the amount to be withheld from each employee's earnings on October 25 for (a) FICA—OASDI, (b) FICA—HI, and (c) SUTA, and determine the total employee taxes.
2. Record the portion of each employee's earnings that is taxable under FICA, FUTA, and SUTA and calculate the total employer's payroll taxes on the October 25 payroll.

THE UNGER COMPANY

Employee	Earnings to Date	Gross Earnings Oct. 25	Taxes to Be Withheld from Employees' Earnings Under			Employer Taxes Portion of Employees' Earnings Taxable Under			
			FICA		SUTA	FICA		FUTA	SUTA
			OASDI	HI		OASDI	HI		
1. Weiser, Robert A.	$62,290	$790							
2. Stankard, Laurie C.	14,950	295							
3. Grow, Joan L.	4,060	240							
4. Rowe, Paul C.	8,190	235							
5. McNamara, Joyce M.	7,460	195							
6. O'Connor, Roger T.	62,710	810							
7. Carson, Ronald B.	8,905	280							
8. Kenny, Ginni C.	4,325	175							
9. Devery, Virginia S.	57,010	590							
10. Wilson, Joe W.	3,615	205							
Total Employee Taxes			$	$	$	$	$	$	$
			1.(a)	1.(b)	1.(c)				

Total Taxable Earnings .... $

× Applicable Tax Rate ....

Totals .... $

Total Payroll Taxes .... $

2.

6–11. LO 2, 3, 4, 5 and 6.

In the Illustrative Case in this chapter, payroll transactions for the Brookins Company were analyzed, journalized, and posted for the third quarter of the fiscal year. In this problem you are to record the payroll transactions for the last quarter of the firm's fiscal year. The last quarter begins on April 1.

Refer to the Illustrative Case on pages 6–20 to 6–28 and proceed as follows:

a. Analyze and journalize the transactions described in the following narrative. Use the two-column journal paper provided on pages 6–43 to 6–46. Omit the writing of explanations in the journal entries.
b. Post the journal entries to the general ledger accounts on pages 6–47 to 6–52.

Narrative of Transactions:

April 1. Paid the treasurer of the union the amount of union dues withheld from workers' earnings during March.
15. Payroll: $6,105. All wages and salaries taxable. Withheld $565 for federal income taxes, $107.32 for state income taxes, and $50 for union dues.
15. Paid the treasurer of the state the amount of state income taxes withheld from workers' earnings during the first quarter.
15. Completed Form 8109 and deposited funds in a Federal Reserve bank to remove the liability for FICA taxes and employees' federal income taxes withheld on the March payrolls.
29. Payroll: $5,850. All wages and salaries taxable. Withheld $509 for federal income taxes, $128.90 for state income taxes, and $55 for union dues.
29. Filed the Employer's Quarterly Federal Tax Return (Form 941) for the period ended March 31. No journal entry is required since the FICA taxes and federal income taxes withheld have been timely deposited in a Federal Reserve bank.
29. Completed the quarterly deposit (Form 8109) for the period ended March 31 and deposited the FUTA taxes in a Federal Reserve bank.
29. Filed the state contribution return for the quarter ended March 31 and paid the amount to the state unemployment compensation fund.
May 2. Paid the treasurer of the union the amount of union dues withheld from workers' earnings during April.
13. Payroll: $5,810. All wages and salaries taxable. Withheld $507 for federal income taxes, $125.05 for state income taxes, and $55 for union dues.
16. Completed Form 8109 and deposited funds with a Federal Reserve bank to remove the liability for FICA taxes and federal income taxes withheld on the April payrolls.
31. Payroll: $6,060. All wages and salaries taxable. Withheld $533 for federal income taxes, $119.00 for state income taxes, and $50 for union dues.
June 3. Paid the treasurer of the union the amount of union dues withheld from workers' earnings during May.
15. Payroll: $6,380. All wages and salaries taxable, except only $5,000 is taxable under FUTA and SUTA. Withheld $549 for federal income taxes, $128.70 for state income taxes, and $50 for union dues.
15. Completed Form 8109 and deposited funds with a Federal Reserve bank to remove the liability for FICA taxes and federal income taxes withheld on the May payrolls.
30. Payroll: $6,250. All wages and salaries taxable, except only $4,770 is taxable under FUTA and SUTA. Withheld $538 for federal income taxes, $127.60 for state income taxes, and $50 for union dues.

6–11 (Continued).

   c. Answer the following questions:

1. The total amount of the liability for FICA taxes and federal income taxes withheld as of June 30 is .... $ _____

2. The total amount of the liability for state income taxes withheld as of June 30 is .... $ _____

3. The amount of FUTA taxes that must be paid to the federal government on or before August 1 (July 31 is a Sunday) is .... $ _____

4. The amount of contributions that must be paid into the state unemployment compensation fund on or before August 1 is .... $ _____

5. The total amount due the treasurer of the union is .... $ _____

6. The total amount of wages and salaries expense since the beginning of the fiscal year is .... $ _____

7. The total amount of payroll taxes expense since the beginning of the fiscal year is .... $ _____

8. Using the partial journal below, journalize the entry to record the vacation accrual at the end of the company's fiscal year. The amount of the Brookins Company's vacation accrual for the fiscal year is $15,000.

JOURNAL

	DATE	DESCRIPTION	POST. REF.	DEBIT	CREDIT	
1						1
2						2
3						3
4						4
5						5
6						6

Date _____   Name _____

6–11 (Continued).

JOURNAL

	DATE	DESCRIPTION	POST. REF.	DEBIT	CREDIT	
1						1
2						2
3						3
4						4
5						5
6						6
7						7
8						8
9						9
10						10
11						11
12						12
13						13
14						14
15						15
16						16
17						17
18						18
19						19
20						20
21						21
22						22
23						23
24						24
25						25
26						26
27						27
28						28
29						29
30						30
31						31
32						32
33						33
34						34

6–43

6–11 (Continued).

JOURNAL

	DATE	DESCRIPTION	POST. REF.	DEBIT	CREDIT	
1						1
2						2
3						3
4						4
5						5
6						6
7						7
8						8
9						9
10						10
11						11
12						12
13						13
14						14
15						15
16						16
17						17
18						18
19						19
20						20
21						21
22						22
23						23
24						24
25						25
26						26
27						27
28						28
29						29
30						30
31						31
32						32
33						33
34						34

Date _____   Name _____

6–11 (Continued).

JOURNAL

	DATE		DESCRIPTION	POST. REF.	DEBIT	CREDIT	
1							1
2							2
3							3
4							4
5							5
6							6
7							7
8							8
9							9
10							10
11							11
12							12
13							13
14							14
15							15
16							16
17							17
18							18
19							19
20							20
21							21
22							22
23							23
24							24
25							25
26							26
27							27
28							28
29							29
30							30
31							31
32							32
33							33
34							34

6–11 (Continued).

JOURNAL

	DATE	DESCRIPTION	POST. REF.	DEBIT	CREDIT	
1						1
2						2
3						3
4						4
5						5
6						6
7						7
8						8
9						9
10						10
11						11
12						12
13						13
14						14
15						15
16						16
17						17
18						18
19						19
20						20
21						21
22						22
23						23
24						24
25						25
26						26
27						27
28						28
29						29
30						30
31						31
32						32
33						33
34						34

6–11 (Continued).

ACCOUNT   **CASH**   ACCOUNT NO.   11

DATE		ITEM	POST. REF.	DEBIT	CREDIT	BALANCE	
						DEBIT	CREDIT
19— Apr.	1	Balance	√			5 8 2 3 3 04	

6–11 (Continued).

FICA TAXES PAYABLE—OASDI ACCOUNT NO. 20

DATE		ITEM	POST. REF.	DEBIT	CREDIT	BALANCE	
						DEBIT	CREDIT
19—Apr.	1	*Balance*	√				1 0 6 8 88

Date _____   Name _____

6–11 (Continued).

ACCOUNT   **FICA TAXES PAYABLE—HI**   ACCOUNT NO. 21

DATE		ITEM	POST. REF.	DEBIT	CREDIT	BALANCE	
						DEBIT	CREDIT
19— Apr.	1	*Balance*	√				2 4 9 98

6–11 (Continued).

ACCOUNT   **FUTA TAXES PAYABLE**   ACCOUNT NO. 22

DATE		ITEM	POST. REF.	DEBIT	CREDIT	BALANCE	
						DEBIT	CREDIT
19— Apr.	1	Balance	√				1 9 8 88

ACCOUNT   **SUTA TAXES PAYABLE**   ACCOUNT NO. 23

DATE		ITEM	POST. REF.	DEBIT	CREDIT	BALANCE	
						DEBIT	CREDIT
19— Apr.	1	Balance	√				5 7 1 78

Date _____   Name _____

6–11 (Continued).

ACCOUNT **EMPLOYEES FIT PAYABLE** ACCOUNT NO. 25

DATE	ITEM	POST. REF.	DEBIT	CREDIT	BALANCE	
					DEBIT	CREDIT
19— Apr. 1	Balance	√				1 1 2 4 00

ACCOUNT **EMPLOYEES SIT PAYABLE** ACCOUNT NO. 26

DATE	ITEM	POST. REF.	DEBIT	CREDIT	BALANCE	
					DEBIT	CREDIT
19— Apr. 1	Balance	√				5 4 6 92

6–51

6–11 (Continued).

ACCOUNT **UNION DUES PAYABLE** ACCOUNT NO. 28

DATE		ITEM	POST. REF.	DEBIT	CREDIT	BALANCE	
						DEBIT	CREDIT
19— Apr.	1	Balance	√				1 0 0 00

ACCOUNT **WAGES AND SALARIES** ACCOUNT NO. 51

DATE		ITEM	POST. REF.	DEBIT	CREDIT	BALANCE	
						DEBIT	CREDIT
19— Apr.	1	Balance	√			7 1 3 6 0 00	

ACCOUNT **PAYROLL TAXES** ACCOUNT NO. 55

DATE		ITEM	POST. REF.	DEBIT	CREDIT	BALANCE	
						DEBIT	CREDIT
19— Apr.	1	Balance	√			6 9 2 6 96	

CONTINUING PAYROLL PROBLEM

In this last phase of your work on the Continuing Payroll Problem, you will record the amounts withheld for group insurance and health insurance and calculate the net pay for each employee. Refer to the partially completed payroll register upon which you were working at the end of Chapter 5 and proceed as follows:

1. In the appropriate column of the payroll register, record the amount to be withheld for group life insurance. Each employee contributes 85¢ each week toward the cost of group insurance coverage, with the exception of McGarry and Porth, who are not yet eligible for coverage under the company plan.
2. Record the amount to be withheld for health insurance. Each employee contributes $1.65 each week toward the cost of health insurance.
3. Record the net pay for each employee. The net pay for each employee is obtained by subtracting the total amount of all deductions from the total earnings.
4. Each worker is to be paid by check. Assign check numbers commencing with No. 313.
5. Foot all money columns of the payroll register and prove the accuracy of the column totals.
6. On a separate sheet of paper:
    a. Prepare the journal entries as of January 12 to record the payroll and the payroll taxes for the week ending January 7. Credit Salaries Payable for the total net pay.
        Use the following tax rates and bases: employer's FICA—OASDI, 6.2% on the first $63,000; employer's FICA—HI, 1.45% on total earnings; FUTA, .8% on the first $7,000; and SUTA, 3.5% on the first $8,000.
    b. Prepare the journal entry to record the payment of the payroll on January 14, when the paychecks are distributed to all workers.

Your work on the Continuing Payroll Problem is now completed and you may be asked to submit your payroll register to your instructor. The experience you have gained in working on each of the succeeding phases of the Continuing Payroll Problem will aid you in undertaking the payroll work involved in Chapter 7. In Chapter 7, the Comprehensive Payroll Project, you will be responsible for all aspects of payroll operations for a company for an entire calendar quarter.

CASE PROBLEM

C1. **Budgeting for Fringe Benefits.**

Frank Flynn is the payroll manager for the Powlus Supply Company. During the budgeting process, Sam Kinder, the Director of Finance, asked Flynn to arrive at a set percentage that could be applied to each budgeted salary figure to cover the fringe benefits cost that will be incurred by the Powlus Company for each employee. After some discussion, it was determined that the best way to compute this percentage would be to base the fringe benefits cost on the average salary paid by the company.

Kinder wants this fringe benefits percentage to cover payroll taxes (FICA, FUTA, and SUTA) and other benefits costs covered by the company (workers' compensation expense, health insurance costs, and vacation pay).

Flynn gathers the following information in order to complete the analysis:

Average annual salary	$24,000
FICA rates	6.2% and 1.45%
FUTA	0.8% on 1st $7,000
SUTA	3.3% on 1st $10,400
Workers' compensation costs	$.97 per $100 of payroll
Health insurance costs	$75.15 per month
Vacation pay earned	2 weeks' pay earned each year to be used in following year.

Compute the percentage that can be used in the budget.

THAT WAS THEN THIS IS NOW

In 1891, Brink's Express, later to become the leading U.S. armored truck money transport company, began moving bank funds and payroll money with a horse and wagon. In today's "paperless" banking system, over 35% of American workers receive their payroll payments by direct deposit through electronic funds transfer systems.

PAYROLL PROJECT

LEARNING OBJECTIVES

Chapter 7 consists of a simulation, or practice set, for payroll accounting. You will apply the knowledge acquired in this course to practical payroll situations. This simulation is a culmination of the information presented in the textbook.

After completing the simulation, you should be able to:

1. Prepare payroll registers.

2. Maintain employees' earnings records.

3. Journalize and post payroll and payroll tax entries.

4. Complete federal, state, and city tax deposit forms and journalize the transactions.

5. Prepare various quarter-end and year-end payroll tax forms.

6. Make the accrual entries for the payroll at the end of a year.

The Payroll Project will provide you with extended practice in keeping payroll records and accounting for payroll transactions. Your completion of this project involves an application of the information learned in the preceding chapters. The work provided resembles that prevailing in the office of every employer in the United States subject to the provisions of the federal wage and hour law, income tax withholding laws, the social security laws, and the unemployment compensation laws.

In this project you are employed by the Glo-Brite Paint Company. As the payroll clerk in the accounting department, you have been in charge of the payroll records since the company first began operations on January 5 of the current year. The company employs about 800 individuals; but for the purpose of this project, payroll records will be kept for only a dozen or so employees. By understanding the principles of payroll accounting for a few employees, you should be able to keep similar records for several hundred employees.

For purposes of this project, you will assume that the payroll records, tax reports, and deposits have been completed and filed for the first three quarters of this year. Your work will involve the processing of the payrolls for the last quarter of the year and the completion of the last quarterly and annual tax reports and forms.

BOOKS OF ACCOUNT AND PAYROLL RECORDS

The books of account and payroll records that you will use in this project are described below.

Journal

You will use a two-column general journal to record all transactions affecting the accounts in the general ledger. This book of original entry serves as a posting medium for transactions affecting the payroll accounts.

General Ledger

A general ledger is used in keeping the payroll accounts. The ledger is ruled with balance-column ruling, which makes it possible to keep a continuous record of each account balance. Some of the ledger accounts will have beginning balances carried over from the first three quarters of the year.

The chart of accounts in Figure 7–1 has been used in opening the general ledger accounts (pages 7–35 to 7–42). The Glo-Brite Paint Company has other accounts in its general ledger, but those listed in the partial chart of accounts are the only accounts required in completing this project.

Payroll Register

The payroll register provides the information needed for journalizing each payroll and for posting to the employees' earnings records.

Employee's Earnings Record

The employee's earnings record provides a summary of each employee's earnings, deductions, and taxable wages. The information recorded in this record is posted from the payroll register.

Account Title	Account No.
Cash	11
Payroll Cash	12
FICA Taxes Payable—OASDI	20.1
FICA Taxes Payable—HI	20.2
FUTA Taxes Payable	21
SUTA Taxes Payable	22
Employees SUTA Payable	23
Employees FIT Payable	24
Employees SIT Payable	25
Employees CIT Payable	26
Group Insurance Premiums Collected	27
Union Dues Payable	28
Administrative Salaries	51
Office Salaries	52
Sales Salaries	53
Plant Wages	54
Payroll Taxes	56

Figure 7–1   *Partial Chart of Accounts*

From the personnel data given in Figure 7–2, an employee's earnings record has been maintained for each employee (pages 7–43 to 7–50). The first line of each of these records shows the employee's cumulative figures for the first three quarters of the year. Note that only one-half page has been used for each employee's earnings record. In actual practice, however, both sides of a complete sheet would be used for the same employee.

GENERAL INFORMATION

The home office and the manufacturing plant of the Glo-Brite Paint Company are located at 2215 Salvador Street, Philadelphia, PA 19175-0682. The company's federal identification number is 31-0450660; the state identifying number, 46-3-3300; the city identifying number, 501-6791855.

Regular Hours of Work

The workweek for all employees is 40 hours. The office is open from 8:00 a.m. to 5:00 p.m. each day, except weekends. Glo-Brite allows one hour for lunch, 12:00 p.m. to 1:00 p.m. The plant operates on a five-day workweek of eight hours per day, with normal working hours from 7:00 a.m. to 11:00 a.m. and 12:00 p.m. to 4:00 p.m.

Overtime

All employees except the president, the sales manager, sales representatives, and supervisors are paid *time and a half* for any overtime exceeding 40 hours a week. Workers in the plant are paid *time and a half* for any hours worked over eight each workday. The overtime rate for any work scheduled on Saturdays, Sundays, or holidays is *twice* the regular hourly rate of pay.

Figure 7–2 *Glo-Brite Employees*

Personnel Data—October 1, 19—

BONNO, Anthony Victor, 694 Bristol Avenue, Philadelphia, PA 19135-0617. Married, claiming 4 withholding allowances. Telephone, 555-9827. Social Security No. 537-10-3481. Position, mixer operator in Plant. Wages, $7.65 per hour. Group insurance, $24,000.

FERGUSON, James Claude, 808 Sixth Street, Philadelphia, PA 19106-0995. Married, claiming 5 withholding allowances. Telephone, 555-8065. Social Security No. 486-03-8645. Position, sales manager. Salary, $32,500 per year. Group insurance, $49,000. Department: Sales.

FORD, Catherine Louise, 18 Dundee Avenue, Philadelphia, PA 19151-1919. Divorced, claiming 2 withholding allowances. Telephone, 555-0235. Social Security No. 213-09-4567. Position, executive secretary. Salary, $975 per month. Group insurance, $18,000. Department: Office.

MANN, Dewey Wilson, 3007 Bisque Drive, Philadelphia, PA 19199-0718. Married, claiming 4 withholding allowances. Telephone, 555-0774. Social Security No. 282-37-9352. Position, sales representative. Salary, $1,950 per month. Group insurance, $35,000. Department: Sales.

O'NEILL, Joseph Tyler, 2100 Broad Street, Philadelphia, PA 19121-7189. Married, claiming 3 withholding allowances. Telephone, 555-2332. Social Security No. 897-04-1534. Position, president. Salary, $60,000 per year. Group insurance, $90,000. Department: Administrative.

RUSSELL, Virginia Aloise, 8004 Dowling Road, Philadelphia, PA 19135-9001. Single, claiming 1 withholding allowance. Telephone, 555-3681. Social Security No. 314-21-6337. Position, time clerk. Salary, $845 per month. Group insurance, $15,000. Department: Office.

RYAN, Norman Allen, 7300 Harrison Street, Philadelphia, PA 19124-6699. Married, claiming 4 withholding allowances. Telephone, 555-6660. Social Security No. 526-23-1223. Position, electrician in Plant. Wages, $9.80 per hour. Group insurance, $31,000.

SOKOWSKI, Thomas James, 133 Cornwells Street, Philadelphia, PA 19171-5718. Married, claiming 2 withholding allowances. Telephone, 555-5136. Social Security No. 662-04-8832. Position, supervisor in Plant. Salary, $450 per week. Group insurance, $35,000.

STUDENT, 7018 Erdrick Street, Philadelphia, PA 19135-8517. Single, claiming 1 withholding allowance. Position, accounting trainee. Salary, $650 per month. Group insurance, $12,000. Department: Office.

WILLIAMS, Ruth Virginia, 9433 State Street, Philadelphia, PA 19149-0819. Single, claiming 0 withholding allowances. Telephone, 555-5845. Social Security No. 518-30-6741. Position, programmer. Salary, $1,235 per month. Group insurance, $22,000. Department: Office.

Timekeeping

All office and plant employees, except the president, the sales manager, sales representatives, and supervisors, must ring in and out daily on a time clock. Also, those employees who ring in and out must notify the time clerk of the reason for lost time. (The unemployment compensation laws of some states require this information.) The time clerk prepares a weekly report of the hours worked by each employee.

The calendar for the last quarter of the year is presented below:

October

S	M	T	W	T	F	S
				1	2	3
4	5	6	7	8	9	10
11	12	13	14	15	16	17
18	19	20	21	22	23	24
25	26	27	28	29	30	31

November

S	M	T	W	T	F	S
1	2	3	4	5	6	7
8	9	10	11	12	13	14
15	16	17	18	19	20	21
22	23	24	25	26	27	28
29	30					

December

S	M	T	W	T	F	S
		1	2	3	4	5
6	7	8	9	10	11	12
13	14	15	16	17	18	19
20	21	22	23	24	25	26
27	28	29	30	31		

Payday

Employees are paid biweekly on Friday. The first payday in the fourth quarter is Friday, October 9. Since the weekly time clerk's report is not finished until the Monday following the end of each week, the first pay (October 9) will be for the two weeks, September 20—26 and September 27—October 3. The company, in effect, holds back one week's pay. This policy applies to all employees. The next payday (October 23) will cover the days worked in the weeks ending October 10 and October 17.

Payroll Taxes—Contributions and Withholdings

Payroll taxes are levied upon the Glo-Brite Paint Company and its employees as shown in Figure 7–3.

Depositing Taxes

The company must deposit federal, state, and city taxes during this quarter. The deposit rules that affect the company appear in Figure 7–4.

Group Insurance

The company carries group life insurance on all its employees in an amount equal to one and one-half times the annual salary or wages paid each

Figure 7–3 *Glo-Brite Payroll Taxes*

Payroll Taxes Levied Upon the Glo-Brite Paint Company and Its Employees		
Federal Income Taxes (FIT)	Withheld from each employee's gross earnings in accordance with information given on Form W-4 and employee's earnings record. Wage-bracket method is used to determine FIT withholding.*	
Pennsylvania State Income Taxes (SIT)	2.8% withheld from each employee's gross earnings during the fourth quarter.*	
Philadelphia City Income Taxes (CIT)	4.96% withheld from gross earnings of each employee.*	
Pennsylvania State Unemployment Taxes (SUTA)	*Employer:*	3.5% on first $8,000 gross earnings paid each employee during the calendar year.
	Employee:	0.15% on all wages paid.**
Federal Unemployment Taxes (FUTA)	Net tax rate of .8% on first $7,000 gross earnings paid each worker in the calendar year.	
Federal Insurance Contributions Act (FICA)	*OASDI— Employer and Employee:*	6.2% on first $63,000 gross earnings paid each worker in the calendar year.
	HI— Employer and Employee:	1.45% on total gross earnings paid each worker in the calendar year.

*Tax withholdings for FIT, SIT, CIT, and SUTA are based on rates used in 1995. Rates for 1996 were not available at the time of publishing.
**1994 rate.

employee. The group insurance program fully covers full-time employees. A notation has been made on each employee's earnings record to show that each month 30¢ for each $1,000 of insurance coverage is deducted from the employee's earnings to pay a portion of the premium cost. This deduction is made only on the *last payday of each month*. The amount withheld is credited to a liability account entitled Group Insurance Premiums Collected.

The employer pays any additional premium, which varies each year depending upon the average age of the employees and other factors. The employer must pay an estimated premium in advance at the beginning of the year. This amount is recorded as a debit to Prepaid Group Insurance in the general ledger. Prepaid Group Insurance, an asset account, will be adjusted at the end of the year by crediting it for the employees' share of the premium collected by withholding from their earnings during the year (the balance in Account No. 27, Group Insurance Premiums Collected). The prepaid account is also credited for the company's share of the premium. At the same time, this amount will be charged to an appropriate expense account, after which the prepaid group insurance account will balance, provided the insurance year is the same as the company's fiscal year. Otherwise, the balance of the account at the end of the fiscal year will represent a prepaid expense (asset).

Union Dues

Both workers in the plant (Bonno and Ryan) are union members. Under the check-off system, $8 is deducted *each payday* from the plant workers' earnings

Figure 7–4 *Deposit Rules*

Deposit Rules for the Glo-Brite Paint Company	
Federal	The FICA taxes and FIT taxes must be deposited on or before the 15th of the month following the month in which the taxes were withheld. Since Glo-Brite is a new employer and has no tax liabilities during the lookback period, the company is subject to the monthly deposit rule.
Pennsylvania	Since the state income taxes withheld total $1,000 or more each quarter, the company must remit the withheld taxes semimonthly. The taxes must be remitted within three banking days after the semimonthly periods ending on the 15th and the last day of the month.
Philadelphia	Since the city income taxes withheld are more than $350 but less than $16,000 each month, the company is subject to the monthly rule. The city income taxes withheld during the month must be remitted by the 15th day of the following month.

for union dues, assessments, and initiation fees. A notation to this effect has been made on each plant worker's earnings record. On or before the tenth of each month, the amounts withheld during the preceding month are turned over to the treasurer of the union.

Distribution of Labor Costs

Figure 7–5 shows how the salaries and wages are to be charged to the labor cost accounts.

NARRATIVE OF PAYROLL TRANSACTIONS

October 9, 19—

No. 1   The first payroll in October covered the two workweeks that ended on September 26 and October 3. This payroll transaction has been entered for you in the payroll register, the employees' earnings records, the general journal, and the general ledger. By reviewing the calculations of the wages and deductions in the payroll register and the posting of the information to the employees' earnings records, you can see the procedure to be followed each payday.

Wages and salaries are paid by issuing special payroll checks. When the bank on which they are drawn receives such checks, they will be charged against the payroll cash account.

Observe the following rules in computing earnings each pay period:

1. Do not make any deduction from an employee's earnings if the employee loses less than 15 minutes of time in any day. Time lost that exceeds 15 minutes is rounded to the nearest quarter-hour and deducted. If the time lost by an employee is not to be deducted, the time clerk will make a notation to that effect on the Time Clerk's Report.
2. In completing the time record columns of the payroll register for all workers, you should place an 8 in the day column for each full day worked. If an employee works less than a full day, show the actual hours for which the employee will be paid.

TIME CLERK'S REPORT NO. 38
For the Week Ending September 26, 19—

Employee	Time Record							Time Worked	Time Lost
	S	M	T	W	T	F	S		
Bonno, A. V.		8	8	8	8	8		40 hrs.	. . .
Ford, C. L.		8	8	8	8	8		40 hrs.	. . .
Russell, V. A. . . .		8	8	8	8	8		40 hrs.	. . .
Ryan, N. A.		8	8	8	8	8		40 hrs.	. . .
Student		8	8	8	8	8		40 hrs.	. . .
Williams, R. V. . . .		8	8	D	8	8		32 hrs.	8 hrs.*

*Time lost because of personal business; charged to personal leave; no deduction for this time lost.
D = lost full day

3. In the case of an employee who begins work during a pay period, compute the earnings by multiplying *one full week* worked, if any, by the weekly rate. For any *partial week,* compute the earnings for that week by multiplying the hours worked by the hourly rate of pay.

4. If time lost is to be deducted from a salaried employee's pay, determine the employee's pay by multiplying the actual hours worked for that week by the hourly rate. The following schedule shows the weekly and hourly wage rates of the salaried employees:

Employee	Weekly Rate	Hourly Rate
Ferguson, James C.	$ 625.00	$15.63
Ford, Catherine L.	225.00	5.63
Mann, Dewey W.	450.00	11.25
O'Neill, Joseph T.	1,153.85	28.85
Russell, Virginia A.	195.00	4.88
Sokowski, Thomas J.	450.00	11.25
Student	150.00	3.75
Williams, Ruth V.	285.00	7.13

5. Plant workers (Bonno and Ryan), other than supervisors, are employed on an hourly basis. Compute the wages by multiplying the number of hours worked during the pay period by the employee's hourly rate.

Figure 7–5 *Glo-Brite Labor Cost Accounts*

Personnel	Account to Be Charged
President (O'Neill)	Administrative Salaries
Executive Secretary (Ford) Programmer (Williams) Time Clerk (Russell) Student (Accounting Trainee)	Office Salaries
Sales Manager (Ferguson) Sales Representative (Mann)	Sales Salaries
Workers (Bonno and Ryan) Supervisor (Sokowski)	Plant Wages

The information needed and the sequence of steps that are completed for the payroll are presented in the following discussion.

The time clerk prepared Time Clerk's Reports Nos. 38 and 39 from the time cards used by the employees for these workweeks. Inasmuch as the president, sales manager, the sales representatives, and the supervisors do not ring in and out on the time clock, their records are not included in the time clerk's report; but their salaries must be included in the payroll.

Employee	Time Record							Time Worked	Time Lost
	S	M	T	W	T	F	S		
Bonno, A. V.		8	8	8	8	8		40 hrs.	. . .
Ford, C. L.		8	8	8	8	8		40 hrs.	. . .
Russell, V. A. . . .		8	8	8	8	8		40 hrs.	. . .
Ryan, N. A.		8	8	8	8	8		40 hrs.	. . .
Student		8	8	8	8	8		40 hrs.	. . .
Williams, R. V. . .		8	8	8	8	8		40 hrs.	. . .

TIME CLERK'S REPORT NO. 39
For the Week Ending October 3, 19—

① The following schedule shows the hourly wage rates of the two hourly employees used in preparing the payroll register for the payday on October 9.

Employee	Hourly Rate
Bonno, Anthony V.	$7.65
Ryan, Norman A.	9.80

② The entry required for each employee is recorded in the payroll register (see page 7–66). The names of all employees are listed in alphabetical order, including yours as "Student." The fold-out payroll register forms needed to complete this project are bound at the back of the book (pages 7–65 to 7–68).

No deduction has been made for the time lost by Williams. Thus, the total number of hours (80) for which payment was made is recorded in the Regular Earnings Hours column of the payroll register. However, a notation of the time lost (D) was made in the Time Record column. When posting to Williams' earnings record, 80 hours is recorded in the Regular Earnings Hours column (no deduction for the time lost).

In computing the federal income taxes to be withheld, the wage-bracket tables in Tax Table B at the back of the book were used. Each payroll in the project requires the use of the tax tables for a *biweekly payroll period*.

Each payday $8 was deducted from the earnings of the two plant workers, for union dues.

Payroll check numbers were assigned beginning with check No. 672.

In the Labor Cost Distribution columns at the extreme right of the payroll register, each employee's gross earnings were recorded in that column that identifies the department in which the employee regularly works. The totals of the Labor Cost Distribution columns provide the amounts to be charged to the appropriate salary and wage expense accounts and aid department managers and supervisors in comparing the actual labor costs with the budgeted amounts.

Once the net pay of each employee was computed, all the amount columns in the payroll register were footed, proved, and ruled.

③ An entry was made in the journal (page 7–26) transferring from the regular cash account to the payroll cash account the amount of the check issued to Payroll to cover the net amount of the payroll; next, the entry was posted.

④ Information from the payroll register was posted to the employees' earnings records (see pages 7–44 to 7–48).

Note that when posting the deductions for each employee, a column has been provided in the earnings record for recording each deduction for FICA (OASDI and HI), SUTA, FIT, SIT, and CIT. All other deductions for each employee are to be totaled and recorded as one amount in the Other Deductions column. Subsidiary ledgers are maintained for Group Insurance Premiums Collected and Union Dues Withheld. Thus, any question about the amounts withheld from an employee's earnings may be answered by referring to the appropriate subsidiary ledger. In this project your work will not involve any recording in or reference to the subsidiary ledgers.

⑤ The proper journal entry recorded salaries, wages, taxes, and the net amount of cash paid. The journal entry to record the payroll for the first pay in the fourth quarter appears below and in the general journal (page 7–26).

Administrative Salaries	2,307.69	
Office Salaries	1,710.00	
Sales Salaries	2,150.00	
Plant Wages	2,296.00	
FICA Taxes Payable—OASDI		524.75
FICA Taxes Payable—HI		122.74
Employees SUTA Payable		12.72
Employees FIT Payable		670.00
Employees SIT Payable		236.99
Employees CIT Payable		419.80
Union Dues Payable		16.00
Payroll Cash		6,460.69

The amounts charged the salary and wage expense accounts were obtained from the totals of the Labor Cost Distribution columns in the payroll register. As shown in the listing of the labor cost accounts, Figure 7–5, the salaries and wages were charged as follows:

Administrative Salaries

Joseph T. O'Neill (President)

Office Salaries

Catherine L. Ford (Executive Secretary)
Virginia A. Russell (Time Clerk)
Student (Accounting Trainee)
Ruth V. Williams (Programmer)

continued

Sales Salaries
James C. Ferguson (Sales Manager)
Dewey W. Mann (Sales Representative)

Plant Wages
Anthony V. Bonno (Mixer Operator)
Norman A. Ryan (Electrician)
Thomas J. Sokowski (Supervisor)

FICA Taxes Payable—OASDI and FICA Taxes Payable—HI were credited for $524.75 and $122.74 respectively, the amounts deducted from employees' wages.

Employees SUTA Payable, Employees FIT Payable, Employees SIT Payable, Employees CIT Payable, and Union Dues Payable were credited for the total amount withheld for each kind of deduction from employees' wages. In subsequent payroll transactions, Group Insurance Premiums Collected will be credited for the amounts withheld from employees' wages for this type of deduction. Finally, Payroll Cash was credited for the sum of the net amounts paid all employees.

⑥ The payroll taxes for this pay were then recorded in the general journal (page 7–26) as follows:

Payroll Taxes	735.19	
FICA Taxes Payable—OASDI		524.75
FICA Taxes Payable—HI		122.72
FUTA Taxes Payable		16.32
SUTA Taxes Payable		71.40

Payroll Taxes was debited for the sum of the employer's FICA, FUTA, and SUTA taxes. The taxable earnings used in computing each of these payroll taxes was obtained from the appropriate column totals of the payroll register. The computation of the debit to Payroll Taxes was:

FICA—OASDI:	6.2% of $8,463.69 =	$524.75
FICA—HI:	1.45% of $8,463.69 =	122.72
FUTA:	.8% of $2,040.00 =	16.32
SUTA:	3.5% of $2,040.00 =	71.40
Total Payroll Taxes		$735.19

FICA Taxes Payable—OASDI was credited for $524.75, the amount of the liability for the employer's portion of the tax. FICA Taxes Payable—HI was credited for $122.72, the amount of the liability for the employer's share of this tax. FUTA Taxes Payable was credited for the amount of the tax on the employer for federal unemployment purposes ($16.32). SUTA Taxes Payable was credited for the amount of the contribution required of the employer under the state unemployment compensation law. This same amount, $71.40, was charged as part of the debit to Payroll Taxes.

⑦ The journal entries were posted to the proper ledger accounts (pages 7–35 to 7–42).

October 15

This is the day on which the deposits of FICA and FIT taxes and the City of Philadelphia income taxes for the September payrolls are due. However, in order to concentrate on fourth quarter payrolls, we will assume that the deposits and the appropriate entries were completed.

October 20

No. 2   On this date the Glo-Brite Paint Company must deposit the Pennsylvania state income taxes withheld from the October 9 payroll.

The deposit rule states that if the employer expects the aggregate amount withheld each quarter to be $1,000 or more, the employer must pay the withheld tax semimonthly. The tax, along with the deposit statement (Form PA 501R), must be remitted within three banking days after the close of the semimonthly periods ending on the 15th and the last day of the month.

① Prepare the journal entry to record the deposit of the taxes and post to the appropriate ledger accounts.

② Complete one of the Pennsylvania deposit statements (Form PA-501R) which appear on pages 7–52 to 7–54. The company's telephone number is (215) 555-9559.

October 23

No. 3   Prepare the payroll for the last pay period of October from Time Clerk's Reports Nos. 40 and 41.

The proper procedure in recording the payroll follows:

① Complete the payroll register.

Inasmuch as only a portion of the payroll register sheet was used in recording the October 9 payroll, the October 23 payroll should be recorded on the same sheet to save space. On the first blank ruled line after the October 9 payroll, insert "Payday October 23—For Period Ending October 17, 19—." On the following lines record the payroll information for the last pay date of October. When recording succeeding payrolls, continue to conserve space by recording two payrolls on each

Employee	Time Record							Time Worked	Time Lost
	S	**M**	**T**	**W**	**T**	**F**	**S**		
Bonno, A. V.		8	8	8	8	8	4	44 hrs.	. . .
Ford, C. L.		4	8	8	8	8		36 hrs.	4 hrs.*
Russell, V. A. . . .		8	8	8	8	8		40 hrs.	. . .
Ryan, N. A.		8	8	8	8	8		40 hrs.	. . .
Student		8	8	8	8	8		40 hrs.	. . .
Williams, R. V. . .		8	8	8	8	8		40 hrs.	. . .

TIME CLERK'S REPORT NO. 40
For the Week Ending October 10, 19—

*Time lost on account of death of relative; charged against annual personal leave; no deduction for time lost

separate payroll register sheet. In recording the payroll in actual practice, the payroll clerk might begin at the top of a new sheet.

The workers in the plant (Bonno and Ryan) are paid *time and a half* for any hours worked over eight each workday, and *twice* the regular hourly rate for work on Saturdays, Sundays, or holidays.

With this pay period, the *cumulative earnings* of several employees exceed the taxable income base set up by FUTA. This factor must be considered in preparing the payroll register and computing the employer's payroll taxes. Refer to each employee's earnings record to see the amount of cumulative earnings.

Also, be sure to deduct 30¢ premium for each $1,000 of group insurance carried by each employee.

② Make the entry transferring from Cash to Payroll Cash the net amount of the total payroll, and post.

③ Post the required information from the payroll register to each employee's earnings record.

④ Record in the journal the salaries, wages, taxes withheld, group insurance premiums collected, union dues withheld, and net amount paid, and post to the proper ledger accounts.

The entry required to record the October 23 payroll is the same as that to record the October 9 payroll, except it is necessary to record the liability for the amount withheld from the employees' wages to pay their part of the group insurance premium. The amount withheld should be recorded as a credit to Group Insurance Premiums Collected.

⑤ Record in the journal the employer's payroll taxes and the liabilities created; post to the appropriate ledger accounts.

November 4

No. 4 Deposit with the State of Pennsylvania the amount of state income taxes withheld from the October 23 payroll.

No. 5 Virginia Russell completed a new Form W-4, changing the number of withholding allowances to 2. Change Russell's earnings record (her marital status has not changed) and reflect this change in the November 6 pay.

	TIME CLERK'S REPORT NO. 41							
	For the Week Ending October 17, 19—							
Employee	**Time Record**						**Time Worked**	**Time Lost**
	S	M	T	W	T	F	S		
Bonno, A. V.		8	8	8	8	8		40 hrs.	. . .
Ford, C. L.		8	8	8	8	8		40 hrs.	. . .
Russell, V. A. . . .		8	8	8	8	8		40 hrs.	. . .
Ryan, N. A.		8	8	8	8	8	8	48 hrs.	. . .
Student		8	8	8	8	8		40 hrs.	. . .
Williams, R. V. . .		8	8	8	8	8		40 hrs.	. . .

No. 6   Thomas J. Sokowski completed a new Form W-4, showing his marital status changed to single and that the number of withholding allowances remains at 2. Change Sokowski's earnings record accordingly and reflect this change in the November 6 pay.

No. 7   Dewey Mann completed a new Form W-4, leaving his marital status as married but dropping the number of withholding allowances to 0. In addition, on Form W-4 he requests an extra $50 be taken out of each paycheck. Change Mann's earnings record accordingly and reflect these changes in the November 6 pay.

November 6

No. 8   Pay the treasurer of the union the amount of union dues withheld during the month of October.

No. 9   Prepare the payroll for the first pay period in November from Time Clerk's Reports Nos. 42 and 43 and record the paychecks issued to all employees. Record this payroll at the top of the second payroll register sheet.

   Note: Virginia Russell worked only 38 hours in the week ending October 24. Therefore, compute her pay for that week by multiplying 38 by $4.88 (her hourly rate). Ruth Williams worked only 39 hours in the week ending October 24. Therefore, compute her pay for that week by multiplying 39 by $7.13 (her hourly rate).

   Also, record the employer's payroll taxes.

November 13

No. 10   Because of her excessive tardiness and absenteeism, the company discharged Ruth V. Williams today. For the week ending November 7, she was late a total of six hours; and for this week, she missed one full day and was late two hours on another day. In lieu of two weeks' notice, Williams was given two full weeks' pay ($570.00). Along with her dismissal pay ($570.00), she was paid for the week ending November 7 (34 hours, or $242.42) and the days worked this current week (30 hours, or $213.90). The total pay for the two partial weeks is $456.32.

   ① Record a separate payroll register (on one line) to show Williams' total earnings, deductions, and net pay. The two weeks' dismissal pay is subject to all payroll taxes. Use the tax table for the biweekly payroll period for the total gross pay ($1,026.32) of Williams.

TIME CLERK'S REPORT NO. 42									
For the Week Ending October 24, 19—									
Employee	Time Record							Time Worked	Time Lost
	S	M	T	W	T	F	S		
Bonno, A. V.		8	8	8	8	8		40 hrs.	. . .
Ford, C. L.		8	8	8	8	8		40 hrs.	. . .
Russell, V. A. . . .		8	8	8	8	6		38 hrs.	2 hrs.*
Ryan, N. A.		8	8	8	8	8	1	41 hrs.	. . .
Student		8	8	8	8	8		40 hrs.	. . .
Williams, R. V. . .		8	8	8	7	8		39 hrs.	1 hr.**

*Time lost on account of auto accident; deduct 2 hours' pay.
**Time lost because of tardiness; deduct 1 hour's pay.

The deduction for group insurance premiums is $6.60. In the Time Record column make a note of Williams' discharge as of this date. Indicate the payroll check number used to prepare the final check for Williams. When posting to the earnings record, make a notation of Williams' discharge on this date.

② Prepare the journal entries to transfer the net cash and to record Williams' final pay and the employer's payroll taxes. Post to the ledger accounts.

③ Prepare a Wage and Tax Statement, Form W-2, which will be given to Williams with her final paycheck. Use the blank Form W-2 on page 7–60. Box "a" should be left blank since the Glo-Brite Paint Company does not use a control number to identify individual Forms W-2.

November 16

No. 11 Deposit with the City Bank the amount of FICA taxes and federal income taxes for the October payrolls. Since the company is subject to the monthly deposit rule, the deposit is due on the fifteenth of the following month. See the deposit requirements explained on pages 3–19 to 3–23. November 15 is a Sunday; therefore, the deposit is to be made on the next business day.

① Prepare the journal entry to record the deposit of the taxes and post to the appropriate ledger accounts.

② Complete the Federal Tax Deposit Coupon, Form 8109, to accompany the remittance, using one of the preinscribed forms on page 7–51. The company's telephone number is (215) 555-9559.

No. 12 Since the Glo-Brite Paint Company withholds the City of Philadelphia income tax, you must deposit the taxes with the Department of Revenue. The deposit rule that affects the Glo-Brite Paint Company states that if the withheld taxes are between $350 and $16,000 per month, the company must deposit the tax monthly by the 15th of the following month. The withheld taxes for the October payrolls were $850.40.

① Prepare the journal entry to record the deposit of the taxes and post to the appropriate ledger accounts.

② Complete one of the Philadelphia Employer's Return of Tax Withheld forms (Form W-1-5), which appear on pages 7–54 to 7–55.

Employee	Time Record							Time Worked	Time Lost
	S	M	T	W	T	F	S		
Bonno, A. V.		8	8	8	8	8		40 hrs.	. . .
Ford, C. L.		8	8	8	8	8		40 hrs.	. . .
Russell, V. A. . . .		8	8	8	8	8		40 hrs.	. . .
Ryan, N. A.		8	8	8	8	8		40 hrs.	. . .
Student		8	8	8	8	8		40 hrs.	. . .
Williams, R. V. . .		8	8	8	8	8		40 hrs.	. . .

TIME CLERK'S REPORT NO. 43
For the Week Ending October 31, 19—

November 17

No. 13 Prepare an employee's earnings record for Beth Anne Woods, a new employee who began work today, Tuesday. Woods is single and claims one withholding allowance. She is employed as a programmer at a monthly salary of $1,300. Address, 8102 Franklin Court, Philadelphia, PA 19105-0915. Telephone, 555-1128. Social Security No. 724-03-1587. She is eligible for group insurance coverage of $23,000 immediately, although her first deduction for group insurance will not be made until December 18.

> Department: Office.
> Weekly rate: $300.00.
> Hourly rate: $7.50.

November 18

No. 14 Deposit with the State of Pennsylvania the amount of state income taxes withheld from the November 6 and 13 (Ruth V. Williams) payrolls.

November 20

No. 15 Prepare the payroll for the last pay period of November from Time Clerk's Reports Nos. 44 and 45 and record the paychecks issued all employees. *Remember to deduct the premiums on the group insurance for each employee.* Also, record the employer's payroll taxes.

No. 16 Salary increases of $26 per month, effective for the two weeks covered in the December 4 payroll, are given to Catherine L. Ford and Virginia A. Russell. The group insurance coverage for Ford will remain at $18,000; for Russell, it will be increased to $16,000. Update the employees' earnings records accordingly. The new wage rates, effective for the December 4 payroll, are:

Employee	Weekly Rate	Hourly Rate
Ford, Catherine L.	$231.00	$5.78
Russell, Virginia A.	201.00	5.03

TIME CLERK'S REPORT NO. 44
For the Week Ending November 7, 19—

Employee	S	M	T	W	T	F	S	Time Worked	Time Lost
Bonno, A. V.		8	8	8	8	8		40 hrs.	...
Ford, C. L.		8	8	8	8	8		40 hrs.	...
Russell, V. A.		8	8	8	8	8		40 hrs.	...
Ryan, N. A.		8	8	8	8	8		40 hrs.	...
Student		8	8	8	8	8		40 hrs.	...
Williams, R. V. ...		6	8	7	7	6		34 hrs.	6 hrs.*

*Time lost because of tardiness; deduct 6 hours' pay.

November 30

No. 17 Prepare an employee's earnings record for Paul Winston Young, the president's nephew, who began work today. Young is single and claims one withholding allowance. He is training as a field sales representative in the city where the home office is located. His beginning salary is $1,000 per month. Address, 7936 Holmes Drive, Philadelphia, PA 19107-6107. Telephone, 555-2096. Social Security No. 432-07-6057. Young is eligible for group insurance coverage of $18,000.

> Department: Sales.
> Weekly rate: $230.77.
> Hourly rate: $5.77.

December 3

No. 18 Deposit with the State of Pennsylvania the amount of state income taxes withheld from the November 20 payroll.

December 4

No. 19 Prepare the payroll for the first pay period of December from Time Clerk's Reports Nos. 46 and 47 and record the paychecks issued all employees. Record this payroll at the top of the third payroll register sheet.

Note: Thursday, November 26, is a paid holiday for all workers.

Also, record the employer's payroll taxes.

No. 20 Anthony V. Bonno reports the birth of a son and completes an amended Form W-4, showing his total withholding allowances to be five. Change his earnings record accordingly, and implement the change in allowance status in the December 18 payroll.

No. 21 Both Anthony Bonno and Norman Ryan have been notified that their union dues will increase to $9 per pay starting with the last pay period of the year. Reflect these increases in the December 18 pay, and show the changes on their earnings records.

TIME CLERK'S REPORT NO. 45
For the Week Ending November 14, 19—

Employee	S	M	T	W	T	F	S	Time Worked	Time Lost
Bonno, A. V.	...	...	8	8	8			24 hrs.	...
Ford, C. L.	8	8	8	8	8			40 hrs.	...
Russell, V. A. . . .	8	8	8	8	8			40 hrs.	...
Ryan, N. A.	8	8	8	8	8	2		42 hrs.	...
Student	8	8	8	8	8			40 hrs.	...
Williams, R. V. . .	D	8	8	6	8			30 hrs.	10 hrs.*

*Time lost because of tardiness: deduct 2 hours' pay; and unexcused absence: deduct 8 hours' pay.

December 9

No. 22 Pay the treasurer of the union the amount of union dues withheld during the month of November.

December 11

No. 23 The payroll department was informed that Virginia A. Russell died in an automobile accident on her way home from work Thursday, December 10.

December 14

No. 24 ① Make a separate entry (on one line) in the payroll register to record the issuance of a check payable to the estate of Virginia A. Russell. This check covers Russell's work for the weeks ending December 5 and 12 ($361.96) plus her accrued vacation pay ($402.00).

Russell's final biweekly pay for time worked ($361.96) and the vacation pay ($402.00) are subject to FICA, FUTA, and SUTA taxes. Since Russell's cumulative earnings have surpassed the taxable earnings figures established by FUTA and SUTA, there will not be any unemployment tax on the employer; however, the earnings are subject to the employee's share of the SUTA tax. This final pay is not subject to withholding for FIT, SIT, or CIT purposes. The deduction for group insurance premiums is $4.80.

② Make a notation of Russell's death in the payroll register and on her earnings record.

③ Prepare journal entries to transfer the net pay and to record Russell's final pay and the employer's payroll taxes. Post to the ledger accounts.

④ Prepare a Wage and Tax Statement, Form W-2, which will be given to the executor of the estate along with the final paycheck. Report the final gross pay ($763.96) in Boxes 3 and 5, but not in Boxes 1, 17, and 20. Use the blank Form W-2 on page 7–60.

In addition, the unpaid wages and vacation pay must be reported on Form 1099-MISC. A Form 1096 must also be completed. These forms will be completed in February before their due date. (See Transaction Nos. 41 and 42.)

TIME CLERK'S REPORT NO. 46
For the Week Ending November 21, 19—

Employee	Time Record							Time Worked	Time Lost
	S	M	T	W	T	F	S		
Bonno, A. V.		8	8	8	8	8		40 hrs.	. . .
Ford, C. L.		8	8	8	8	8		40 hrs.	. . .
Russell, V. A.		8	8	8	8	8		40 hrs.	. . .
Ryan, N. A.		8	8	8	4	8		36 hrs.	4 hrs.*
Student		8	8	8	8	8		40 hrs.	. . .
Woods, B.A.		. . .	8	8	8	8		32 hrs.	. . .

*Time lost on account of personal business; deduct 4 hours' pay.

December 15

No. 25   Deposit with the City Bank the amount of FICA taxes and federal income taxes for the November payrolls.

No. 26   Deposit with the City of Philadelphia the amount of city income taxes withheld from the November payrolls.

December 18

No. 27   Deposit with the State of Pennsylvania the amount of state income taxes withheld from the December 4 payroll.

No. 28   Glo-Brite has been notified by the insurance company that there will be no premium charge for the month of December on the policy for Virginia Russell. Write a check on the regular cash account, payable to the estate of Virginia A. Russell, for the amount that was withheld for insurance from her December 14 pay.

No. 29   Prepare an employee's earnings record for Richard Lloyd Zimmerman, who was employed today as time clerk to take the place left vacant by the death of Virginia A. Russell last week. His beginning salary is $780 per month. Address, 900 South Clark Street, Philadelphia, PA 19195-6247. Telephone, 555-2104. Social Security No. 897-12-1502. Zimmerman is married and claims one withholding allowance. Zimmerman is eligible for group insurance coverage of $14,000, although no deduction for group insurance premiums will be made until the last payday in January.

Department: Office.
Weekly rate: $180.00.
Hourly rate: $4.50.

No. 30   In this pay, the president of the company, Joseph O'Neill, is paid his annual bonus. This does not affect O'Neill's insurance coverage which is based on regular pay. This year his bonus is $8,000. For withholding purposes, the bonus is considered a supplemental payment and is added to his gross pay, and the aggregate amount is taxed. To determine the federal income tax, use the *Table of Allowance Values* along with *Tax Table A.*

Effective with this pay, O'Neill completed a new Form W-4 changing his total withholding allowances to four. Previously, he had claimed

TIME CLERK'S REPORT NO. 47									
For the Week Ending November 28, 19—									
Employee	**Time Record**							**Time Worked**	**Time Lost**
	S	M	T	W	T	F	S		
Bonno, A. V.		8	8	8	PAID HOLIDAY	8	8	48 hrs.	. . .
Ford, C. L.		8	8	8		8		40 hrs.	. . .
Russell, V. A. . . .		8	8	8		8		40 hrs.	. . .
Ryan, N. A.		9	10	8		8		43 hrs.	. . .
Student		8	8	8		8		40 hrs.	. . .
Woods, B. A. . . .		8	8	8		8		40 hrs.	. . .

fewer allowances than he had been using on his tax return. Change his earnings record accordingly.

Prepare the payroll for the latter pay of December from Time Clerk's Reports Nos. 48 and 49 and record the paychecks issued all employees. Also, record the employer's payroll taxes.

Note: After posting the information for this last pay to the employees' earnings records, calculate and enter the quarterly and yearly totals on each earnings record.

NOTE: This completes the project insofar as recording the payroll transactions for the last quarter is concerned. The following additional transactions are given to illustrate different types of transactions arising in connection with the accounting for payrolls and payroll taxes. Record these transactions in the journal, but *do not* post to the ledger.

January 6

No. 31 Deposit with the State of Pennsylvania the amount of state income taxes withheld from the December 18 payroll.

January 8

No. 32 Pay the treasurer of the union the amount of union dues withheld during the month of December.

January 15

No. 33 Deposit with the City Bank the amount of FICA taxes and federal income taxes for the December payrolls.

Complete the Federal Tax Deposit Coupon, Form 8109, using one of the preinscribed forms on page 7–51.

No. 34 Deposit with the City of Philadelphia the amount of city income taxes withheld from the December payrolls.

February 1

No. 35 Prepare Form 941, Employer's Quarterly Federal Tax Return, with respect to wages paid during the last calendar quarter. Page 7–57 con-

TIME CLERK'S REPORT NO. 48
For the Week Ending December 5, 19—

Employee	S	M	T	W	T	F	S	Time Worked	Time Lost
Bonno, A. V.		8	8	8	8	8	4	44 hrs.	...
Ford, C. L.		8	8	8	8	8		40 hrs.	...
Russell, V. A.		8	8	8	8	8		40 hrs.	...
Ryan, N. A.		8	9	9	9	9		44 hrs.	...
Student		8	8	7	8	8		39 hrs.	1 hr.*
Woods, B. A.		8	8	8	8	8		40 hrs.	...
Young, P. W.		8	8	8	8	8		40 hrs.	...

*Time lost because of tardiness; deduct 1 hour's pay.

tains a blank Form 941. The information needed in preparing the return should be obtained from the ledger accounts, the payroll registers, the employees' earnings records, and the Federal Tax Deposit forms.

Form 941 and all forms that follow are to be signed by the president of the company, Joseph T. O'Neill.

No. 36 ① Complete Form 940-EZ, Employer's Annual Federal Unemployment (FUTA) Tax Return, using the blank form reproduced on page 7–58, and also Form 8109, Federal Tax Deposit Coupon, using the blank form reproduced on page 7–52. The information needed in preparing these forms can be obtained from the ledger accounts, the payroll registers, the employees' earnings records, and the following:

a. Contributions paid to the Pennsylvania unemployment fund for the year amount to $3,137.55. (This amount includes the employer's and the employees' contributions for the fourth quarter which will be determined and paid in Transaction No. 37.)
b. FUTA taxable wages for the first three quarters: $65,490.00
c. FUTA tax liability by quarter:

1st quarter—$272.71
2d quarter—$140.33
3d quarter—$110.88

d. All deposits for the first three quarters were made on the dates they were due.

Journalize the entry to record the deposit included with Form 8109.

No. 37 ① Prepare Form UC-2, Employer's Report for Unemployment Compensation—Fourth Quarter, using the blank form reproduced on page 7–59. In Pennsylvania, a credit week is any calendar week during the quarter in which the employee earned at least $50 (without regard to when paid). The telephone number of the company is (215) 555-9559. All other information needed in preparing the form can be obtained from the ledger accounts, the payroll registers, and the employees' earnings records.

② Journalize the entry to record the payment of the taxes for the fourth quarter.

No. 38 Complete Form W-2, Wage and Tax Statement, for each employee, using the blank statements reproduced on pages 7–61 to 7–64 and page 7–69. Use each employee's earnings record to obtain the information needed to complete the forms.

TIME CLERK'S REPORT NO. 49
For the Week Ending December 12, 19—

Employee	S	M	T	W	T	F	S	Time Worked	Time Lost
Bonno, A. V.		8	8	8	8	8	8	48 hrs.	. . .
Ford, C. L.		4	8	8	8	8		36 hrs.	4 hrs.*
Russell, V. A. . . .		8	8	8	8	D		32 hrs.	8 hrs.
Ryan, N. A.		10	8	8	9	8		43 hrs.	. . .
Student		4	8	8	8	8		36 hrs.	4 hrs.**
Woods, B. A. . . .		8	8	8	8	8		40 hrs.	. . .
Young, P. W. . . .		8	8	8	8	8		40 hrs.	. . .

*Time lost for dentist appointment; no deduction for this time lost.
**Time spent in training session; no deduction in pay.

No. 39 Complete Form W-3, Transmittal of Wage and Tax Statements, using the blank form reproduced on page 7–70. Use the information on Forms W-2 to complete this form.

No. 40 Complete Pennsylvania Form REV-1667 AS, W-2 Transmittal, using the blank form reproduced on page 7–70. Use the information on Forms W-2 to complete this report.

No. 41 Complete Form 1099-MISC, Miscellaneous Income, for the unpaid wages and vacation pay of Virginia A. Russell. The full amount of the December 14 payment must be reported in Box 3. Page 7–71 contains a blank form.

              Note: Wages paid after an employee dies were previously reported as nonemployee compensation in Box 7 on Form 1099-MISC. These wages are now to be reported as other income in Box 3, so that the IRS will not seek self-employment tax on such amounts.

No. 42 Complete Form 1096, Annual Summary and Transmittal of U.S. Information Returns, using the blank form on page 7–71. Use the information on Form 1099-MISC to complete this form.

No. 43 Prepare Form PA-W3R, Employer Quarterly Reconciliation Return of Income Tax Withheld, using the blank form on page 7–55. The telephone number of the company is (215) 555-9559.

No. 44 Prepare the Annual Reconciliation of Wage Tax for Philadelphia, using the blank form on page 7–56.

QUESTIONS ON THE PAYROLL PROJECT

1. The total payroll tax expense incurred by the employer on salaries and wages paid during the quarter ended December 31 was . . . . $ _____

2. The total payroll tax expense incurred by the employer on the salary of Joseph T. O'Neill during the fourth quarter was . . . . $ _____

3. The amount of the group insurance premiums collected from employees during the quarter ended December 31 was . . . . $ _____

4. O'Neill has decided to give all current employees (excluding himself) a bonus payment during January equal to 5% of their total gross pay for last year. Determine the total of this bonus payment. . . . . $ _____

5. On the financial statements prepared at the end of its first year of operations, the company must show an accurate picture of all expenses and all liabilities incurred. The last payday of the year was December 18. However, the payment to the employees on that day did not include the weeks ending December 19 and 26 and the four days (December 28-31) in the following week. These earnings will be reflected in the January payrolls. Two-column journal paper is provided for use in journalizing the following entry.

    Prepare the adjusting entry as of December 31 to record the salaries and wages that have accrued but remain unpaid as of the end of the year. When calculating the amount of the accrual for each hourly worker, assume each employee worked eight hours on each day during the period with no overtime. For each salaried worker, the accrual will amount to 14/10 of the worker's biweekly earnings, except for Zimmerman who worked only ten days.

    Each of the labor cost accounts should be debited for the appropriate amount of the accrual, and Salaries and Wages Payable should be credited for the total amount of the accrual. There is no liability for payroll taxes on the accrued salaries and wages until the workers are actually paid. Therefore, the company follows the practice of not accruing payroll taxes.

6. Also prepare the adjusting entry as of December 31 to record the accrued vacation pay as of the end of the year. Record the expense in a Vacation Benefits Expense account, and credit the appropriate liability account. Use the journal paper provided.

As of December 31, the vacation time earned but not used by each employee is listed below.

Bonno .... two weeks   Sokowski .... two weeks
Ferguson .... three weeks   Student .... two weeks
Ford .... two weeks   Woods .... none
Mann .... one week   Young .... none
O'Neill .... four weeks   Zimmerman ..... none
Ryan .... two weeks

JOURNAL   Page

	DATE	DESCRIPTION	POST. REF.	DEBIT	CREDIT	
1						1
2						2
3						3
4						4
5						5
6						6
7						7
8						8
9						9
10						10
11						11

ACCOUNTING RECORDS AND REPORTS

Contents

	DATE		DESCRIPTION	POST. REF.	DEBIT	CREDIT	
1	19— Oct.	9	Payroll Cash	12	6 4 6 0 69		1
2			Cash	11		6 4 6 0 69	2
3							3
4		9	Administrative Salaries	51	2 3 0 7 69		4
5			Office Salaries	52	1 7 1 0 00		5
6			Sales Salaries	53	2 1 5 0 00		6
7			Plant Wages	54	2 2 9 6 00		7
8			FICA Taxes Payable—OASDI	20.1		5 2 4 75	8
9			FICA Taxes Payable—HI	20.2		1 2 2 74	9
10			Employees SUTA Payable	23		1 2 72	10
11			Employees FIT Payable	24		6 7 0 00	11
12			Employees SIT Payable	25		2 3 6 99	12
13			Employees CIT Payable	26		4 1 9 80	13
14			Union Dues Payable	28		1 6 00	14
15			Payroll Cash	12		6 4 6 0 69	15
16							16
17		9	Payroll Taxes	56	7 3 5 19		17
18			FICA Taxes Payable—OASDI	20.1		5 2 4 75	18
19			FICA Taxes Payable—HI	20.2		1 2 2 72	19
20			FUTA Taxes Payable	21		1 6 32	20
21			SUTA Taxes Payable	22		7 1 40	21
22							22
23							23
24							24
25							25
26							26
27							27
28							28
29							29
30							30
31							31
32							32
33							33
34							34

JOURNAL

Page ____

	DATE	DESCRIPTION	POST. REF.	DEBIT	CREDIT	
1						1
2						2
3						3
4						4
5						5
6						6
7						7
8						8
9						9
10						10
11						11
12						12
13						13
14						14
15						15
16						16
17						17
18						18
19						19
20						20
21						21
22						22
23						23
24						24
25						25
26						26
27						27
28						28
29						29
30						30
31						31
32						32
33						33
34						34

	DATE	DESCRIPTION	POST. REF.	DEBIT	CREDIT	
1						1
2						2
3						3
4						4
5						5
6						6
7						7
8						8
9						9
10						10
11						11
12						12
13						13
14						14
15						15
16						16
17						17
18						18
19						19
20						20
21						21
22						22
23						23
24						24
25						25
26						26
27						27
28						28
29						29
30						30
31						31
32						32
33						33
34						34

JOURNAL

Page _____

	DATE		DESCRIPTION	POST. REF.	DEBIT	CREDIT	
1							1
2							2
3							3
4							4
5							5
6							6
7							7
8							8
9							9
10							10
11							11
12							12
13							13
14							14
15							15
16							16
17							17
18							18
19							19
20							20
21							21
22							22
23							23
24							24
25							25
26							26
27							27
28							28
29							29
30							30
31							31
32							32
33							33
34							34

JOURNAL   Page

	DATE		DESCRIPTION	POST. REF.	DEBIT	CREDIT	
1							1
2							2
3							3
4							4
5							5
6							6
7							7
8							8
9							9
10							10
11							11
12							12
13							13
14							14
15							15
16							16
17							17
18							18
19							19
20							20
21							21
22							22
23							23
24							24
25							25
26							26
27							27
28							28
29							29
30							30
31							31
32							32
33							33
34							34

	DATE		DESCRIPTION	POST. REF.	DEBIT	CREDIT	
1							1
2							2
3							3
4							4
5							5
6							6
7							7
8							8
9							9
10							10
11							11
12							12
13							13
14							14
15							15
16							16
17							17
18							18
19							19
20							20
21							21
22							22
23							23
24							24
25							25
26							26
27							27
28							28
29							29
30							30
31							31
32							32
33							33
34							34

JOURNAL   Page _____

	DATE	DESCRIPTION	POST. REF.	DEBIT	CREDIT	
1						1
2						2
3						3
4						4
5						5
6						6
7						7
8						8
9						9
10						10
11						11
12						12
13						13
14						14
15						15
16						16
17						17
18						18
19						19
20						20
21						21
22						22
23						23
24						24
25						25
26						26
27						27
28						28
29						29
30						30
31						31
32						32
33						33
34						34

JOURNAL

Page

	DATE	DESCRIPTION	POST. REF.	DEBIT	CREDIT	
1						1
2						2
3						3
4						4
5						5
6						6
7						7
8						8
9						9
10						10
11						11
12						12
13						13
14						14
15						15
16						16
17						17
18						18
19						19
20						20
21						21
22						22
23						23
24						24
25						25
26						26
27						27
28						28
29						29
30						30
31						31
32						32
33						33
34						34

JOURNAL

Page

	DATE		DESCRIPTION	POST. REF.	DEBIT	CREDIT	
1							1
2							2
3							3
4							4
5							5
6							6
7							7
8							8
9							9
10							10
11							11
12							12
13							13
14							14
15							15
16							16
17							17
18							18
19							19
20							20
21							21
22							22
23							23
24							24
25							25
26							26
27							27
28							28
29							29
30							30
31							31
32							32
33							33
34							34

GENERAL LEDGER

ACCOUNT **CASH**   ACCOUNT NO. 11

DATE		ITEM	POST. REF.	DEBIT	CREDIT	BALANCE	
						DEBIT	CREDIT
19— Oct.	1	*Balance*	√			8 9 8 4 6 33	
	9		J41		6 4 6 0 69	8 3 3 8 5 64	

ACCOUNT **PAYROLL CASH**   ACCOUNT NO. 12

DATE		ITEM	POST. REF.	DEBIT	CREDIT	BALANCE	
						DEBIT	CREDIT
19— Oct.	9		J41	6 4 6 0 69		6 4 6 0 69	
	9		J41		6 4 6 0 69	– – – –	– – – –

ACCOUNT **FICA TAXES PAYABLE—OASDI**   ACCOUNT NO. 20.1

DATE		ITEM	POST. REF.	DEBIT	CREDIT	BALANCE	
						DEBIT	CREDIT
19— Oct.	9		J41		5 2 4 75		5 2 4 75
	9		J41		5 2 4 75		1 0 4 9 50

ACCOUNT **FICA TAXES PAYABLE—HI**   ACCOUNT NO. 20.2

DATE		ITEM	POST. REF.	DEBIT	CREDIT	BALANCE	
						DEBIT	CREDIT
19— Oct.	9		J41		1 2 2 74		1 2 2 74
	9		J41		1 2 2 72		2 4 5 46

ACCOUNT **FUTA TAXES PAYABLE**   ACCOUNT NO. 21

DATE		ITEM	POST. REF.	DEBIT	CREDIT	BALANCE	
						DEBIT	CREDIT
19— Oct.	9		J41		1 6 32		1 6 32

ACCOUNT **SUTA TAXES PAYABLE**   ACCOUNT NO. 22

DATE		ITEM	POST. REF.	DEBIT	CREDIT	BALANCE	
						DEBIT	CREDIT
19— Oct.	9		J41		7 1 40		7 1 40

ACCOUNT **EMPLOYEES SUTA PAYABLE**   ACCOUNT NO. 23

| DATE | | ITEM | POST. REF. | DEBIT | CREDIT | BALANCE | |
						DEBIT	CREDIT
19— Oct.	9		J41		1 2 72		1 2 72

ACCOUNT **EMPLOYEES FIT PAYABLE**   ACCOUNT NO. 24

| DATE | | ITEM | POST. REF. | DEBIT | CREDIT | BALANCE | |
						DEBIT	CREDIT
19— Oct.	9		J41		6 7 0 00		6 7 0 00

ACCOUNT **EMPLOYEES SIT PAYABLE**   ACCOUNT NO. 25

| DATE | | ITEM | POST. REF. | DEBIT | CREDIT | BALANCE | |
						DEBIT	CREDIT
19— Oct.	9		J41		2 3 6 99		2 3 6 99

ACCOUNT **EMPLOYEES CIT PAYABLE**   ACCOUNT NO. 26

DATE	ITEM	POST. REF.	DEBIT	CREDIT	BALANCE	
					DEBIT	CREDIT
19— Oct. 9		J41		4 1 9 80		4 1 9 80

ACCOUNT **GROUP INSURANCE PREMIUMS COLLECTED**   ACCOUNT NO. 27

DATE	ITEM	POST. REF.	DEBIT	CREDIT	BALANCE	
					DEBIT	CREDIT

ACCOUNT **UNION DUES PAYABLE**   ACCOUNT NO. 28

DATE	ITEM	POST. REF.	DEBIT	CREDIT	BALANCE	
					DEBIT	CREDIT
19— Oct. 9		J41		1 6 00		1 6 00

ACCOUNT **ADMINISTRATIVE SALARIES**   ACCOUNT NO. 51

DATE		ITEM	POST. REF.	DEBIT	CREDIT	BALANCE	
						DEBIT	CREDIT
19—Oct.	1	*Balance*	√			4 2 6 9 2 27	
	9		J41	2 3 0 7 69		4 4 9 9 9 96	

ACCOUNT **OFFICE SALARIES**   ACCOUNT NO. 52

DATE		ITEM	POST. REF.	DEBIT	CREDIT	BALANCE	
						DEBIT	CREDIT
19—Oct.	1	*Balance*	√			2 8 3 5 0 00	
	9		J41	1 7 1 0 00		3 0 0 6 0 00	

ACCOUNT **SALES SALARIES**   ACCOUNT NO. 53

DATE		ITEM	POST. REF.	DEBIT	CREDIT	BALANCE	
						DEBIT	CREDIT
19—Oct.	1	*Balance*	√			2 8 5 2 5 00	
	9		J41	2 1 5 0 00		3 0 6 7 5 00	

ACCOUNT **PLANT WAGES**   ACCOUNT NO. 54

DATE		ITEM	POST. REF.	DEBIT	CREDIT	BALANCE	
						DEBIT	CREDIT
19—Oct.	1	Balance	√			4 2 6 5 7 30	
	9		J41	2 2 9 6 00		4 4 9 5 3 30	

ACCOUNT **PAYROLL TAXES**   ACCOUNT NO. 56

DATE		ITEM	POST. REF.	DEBIT	CREDIT	BALANCE	
						DEBIT	CREDIT
19—Oct.	1	Balance	√			1 3 9 0 6 21	
	9		J41	7 3 5 19		1 4 6 4 1 40	

EMPLOYEES' EARNINGS RECORDS

Employee Earnings Record — BONNO, Anthony Victor

DEPARTMENT	Plant
OCCUPATION	Mixer Operator
WORKS IN (STATE)	PA
S.S. ACCOUNT NO.	537-10-3481
SEX	M (X)
NAME—LAST	BONNO
FIRST	Anthony
MIDDLE	Victor
W/H ALLOW.	4
MARITAL STATUS	M
GROUP INSURANCE	$24,000—30¢/M
OTHER DEDUCTIONS INFORMATION — UNION DUES	$8 each pay
SALARY	$
WEEKLY RATE	$
HOURLY RATE	$ 7.65
OVERTIME RATE	$ 11.48

19__ PAYDAY	Reg. HRS	Reg. RATE	Reg. AMOUNT	OT HRS	OT RATE	OT AMOUNT	CUMULATIVE EARNINGS	FICA OASDI	FICA HI	SUTA	FIT	SIT	CIT	OTHER DEDUCTIONS	CK. NO.	NET PAID AMOUNT
YEAR-TO-DATE TOTAL			10293 40			1028 60	11322 00	701 96	164 17	16 98	310 00	317 02	561 66	216 80		9033 41
1 10/9	80	7 65	612 00				11934 00	37 94	8 87	92		17 14	30 36	8 00	672	508 77
2																
3																
4																
5																
6																
QUARTER TOTAL																
YEARLY TOTAL																

Employee Earnings Record — FERGUSON, James Claude

DEPARTMENT	Sales
OCCUPATION	Sales Manager
WORKS IN (STATE)	PA
S.S. ACCOUNT NO.	486-03-8645
SEX	M (X)
NAME—LAST	FERGUSON
FIRST	James
MIDDLE	Claude
W/H ALLOW.	5
MARITAL STATUS	M
GROUP INSURANCE	$49,000—30¢/M
OTHER DEDUCTIONS INFORMATION — UNION DUES	
SALARY	$ 32,500/yr.
WEEKLY RATE	$ 625.00
HOURLY RATE	$ 15.63
OVERTIME RATE	$

19__ PAYDAY	Reg. HRS	Reg. RATE	Reg. AMOUNT	OT HRS	OT RATE	OT AMOUNT	CUMULATIVE EARNINGS	FICA OASDI	FICA HI	SUTA	FIT	SIT	CIT	OTHER DEDUCTIONS	CK. NO.	NET PAID AMOUNT
YEAR-TO-DATE TOTAL			23125 00				23125 00	1433 75	335 31	34 69	1791 00	647 50	1147 00	132 30		17603 45
1 10/9	80		1250 00				24375 00	77 50	18 13	1 88	78 00	35 00	62 00		673	977 49
2																
3																
4																
5																
6																
QUARTER TOTAL																
YEARLY TOTAL																

Employee Payroll Record — FORD, Catherine Louise

DEPARTMENT	Office
OCCUPATION	Executive Secretary
WORKS IN (STATE)	PA
S.S. ACCOUNT NO.	213-09-4567
SEX	F (X)
NAME—LAST	FORD
FIRST	Catherine
MIDDLE	Louise
MARITAL STATUS	S
W/H ALLOW.	2
GROUP INSURANCE	$18,000—30¢/M
SALARY	$ 975/mo.
WEEKLY RATE	$ 225.00
HOURLY RATE	$ 5.63
OVERTIME RATE	$ 8.45

OTHER DEDUCTIONS INFORMATION — UNION DUES / OTHER

19— PAYDAY	REGULAR EARNINGS HRS.	REGULAR EARNINGS RATE	REGULAR EARNINGS AMOUNT	OVERTIME EARNINGS HRS.	OVERTIME EARNINGS RATE	OVERTIME EARNINGS AMOUNT	CUMULATIVE EARNINGS	FICA OASDI	FICA HI	SUTA	FIT	SIT	CIT	OTHER DEDUCTIONS	CK. NO.	NET PAID AMOUNT
YEAR-TO-DATE TOTAL			6300 00				63000 00	3906 0	91 35	9 45	439 00	176 40	312 48			4842 92
1 10/9	80		450 00				67500 0	27 90	6 53	68	24 00	12 60	22 32	37 80	674	355 97
2																
3																
4																
5																
6																
QUARTER TOTAL																
YEARLY TOTAL																

Employee Payroll Record — MANN, Dewey Wilson

DEPARTMENT	Sales
OCCUPATION	Sales Representative
WORKS IN (STATE)	PA
S.S. ACCOUNT NO.	282-37-9352
SEX	M (X)
NAME—LAST	MANN
FIRST	Dewey
MIDDLE	Wilson
MARITAL STATUS	M
W/H ALLOW.	4
GROUP INSURANCE	$35,000—30¢/M
SALARY	$ 1,950/mo.
WEEKLY RATE	$ 450.00
HOURLY RATE	$ 11.25
OVERTIME RATE	$

OTHER DEDUCTIONS INFORMATION — UNION DUES / OTHER

19— PAYDAY	REGULAR EARNINGS HRS.	REGULAR EARNINGS RATE	REGULAR EARNINGS AMOUNT	OVERTIME EARNINGS HRS.	OVERTIME EARNINGS RATE	OVERTIME EARNINGS AMOUNT	CUMULATIVE EARNINGS	FICA OASDI	FICA HI	SUTA	FIT	SIT	CIT	OTHER DEDUCTIONS	CK. NO.	NET PAID AMOUNT
YEAR-TO-DATE TOTAL			5400 00				54000 00	334 80	78 30	8 10	332 00	151 20	267 84			4196 26
1 10/9	80		900 00				63000 00	55 80	13 05	1 35	42 00	25 20	44 64	31 50	675	717 96
2																
3																
4																
5																
6																
QUARTER TOTAL																
YEARLY TOTAL																

Payroll Records

Employee 1

DEPARTMENT	Admin.
OCCUPATION	President
WORKS IN (STATE)	PA
SEX	M (X)
S.S. ACCOUNT NO.	897-04-1534
NAME—LAST	O'NEILL
FIRST	Joseph
MIDDLE	Tyler
MARITAL STATUS	M
W/H ALLOW.	3
GROUP INSURANCE	$90,000—30¢/M

SALARY	$ 60,000/yr.
WEEKLY RATE	$ 1,153.85
HOURLY RATE	$ 28.85
OVERTIME RATE	$

Earnings / Deductions

19__ PAYDAY	REGULAR EARNINGS HRS.	RATE	AMOUNT	OVERTIME EARNINGS HRS.	RATE	AMOUNT	CUMULATIVE EARNINGS	FICA OASDI	FICA HI	SUTA	FIT	SIT	CIT	OTHER DEDUCTIONS	NET PAID CK. NO.	AMOUNT
YEAR-TO-DATE TOTAL			426 9 2 27				426 9 2 27	26 4 6 92	6 1 9 04	6 4 04	6 1 1 6 00	1 1 9 5 38	2 1 1 7 54	2 0 2 50		297 3 0 85
1 10/9	80		23 0 7 69				449 9 9 96	1 4 3 08	3 3 46	3 46	3 1 4 00	6 4 62	1 1 4 46		676	16 3 4 61
2																
3																
4																
5																
6																
QUARTER TOTAL																
YEARLY TOTAL																

Employee 2

DEPARTMENT	Office
OCCUPATION	Time Clerk
WORKS IN (STATE)	PA
SEX	F (X)
S.S. ACCOUNT NO.	314-21-6337
NAME—LAST	RUSSELL
FIRST	Virginia
MIDDLE	Aloise
MARITAL STATUS	S
W/H ALLOW.	1
GROUP INSURANCE	$15,000—30¢/M

SALARY	$ 845/mo.
WEEKLY RATE	$ 195.00
HOURLY RATE	$ 4.88
OVERTIME RATE	$ 7.32

Earnings / Deductions

19__ PAYDAY	REGULAR EARNINGS HRS.	RATE	AMOUNT	OVERTIME EARNINGS HRS.	RATE	AMOUNT	CUMULATIVE EARNINGS	FICA OASDI	FICA HI	SUTA	FIT	SIT	CIT	OTHER DEDUCTIONS	NET PAID CK. NO.	AMOUNT
YEAR-TO-DATE TOTAL			62 4 0 00				62 4 0 00	3 8 6 88	9 0 48	9 36	4 4 2 00	1 7 4 72	3 0 9 44	3 1 50		47 9 5 62
1 10/9	80		3 9 0 00				66 3 0 00	2 4 18	5 66	59	3 0 00	1 0 92	1 9 34		677	2 9 9 31
2																
3																
4																
5																
6																
QUARTER TOTAL																
YEARLY TOTAL																

Payroll Ledger Card — RYAN, Norman Allen

DEPARTMENT	OCCUPATION	WORKS IN (STATE)	S.S. ACCOUNT NO.	SEX M/F	NAME—LAST	FIRST	MIDDLE
Plant	Electrician	PA	526-23-1223	M (X)	RYAN	Norman	Allen

W/H ALLOW.	MARITAL STATUS
4	M

GROUP INSURANCE: $31,000—30¢/M

OTHER DEDUCTIONS INFORMATION — UNION DUES: $8 each pay

SALARY: WEEKLY RATE $ ____ HOURLY RATE $9.80 OVERTIME RATE $14.70

19 __ PAYDAY	REGULAR EARNINGS HRS.	RATE	AMOUNT	OVERTIME EARNINGS HRS.	RATE	AMOUNT	CUMULATIVE EARNINGS	FICA OASDI	FICA HI	SUTA	FIT	SIT	CIT	OTHER DEDUCTIONS	CK. NO.	NET PAID AMOUNT
YEAR-TO-DATE TOTAL			132 87 50			13 97 80	146 85 30	910 49	212 94	22 03	870 00	411 19	728 34	235 70		112 94 61
1 10/9	80	9 80	784 00				154 69 30	48 61	11 37	1 18	24 00	21 95	38 89	8 00	678	630 00
2																
3																
4																
5																
6																
QUARTER TOTAL																
YEARLY TOTAL																

Payroll Ledger Card — SOKOWSKI, Thomas James

DEPARTMENT	OCCUPATION	WORKS IN (STATE)	S.S. ACCOUNT NO.	SEX M/F	NAME—LAST	FIRST	MIDDLE
Plant	Supervisor	PA	662-04-8832	M (X)	SOKOWSKI	Thomas	James

W/H ALLOW.	MARITAL STATUS
2	M

GROUP INSURANCE: $35,000—30¢/M

OTHER DEDUCTIONS INFORMATION — UNION DUES: ____

SALARY: WEEKLY RATE $450.00 HOURLY RATE $11.25 OVERTIME RATE $ ____

19 __ PAYDAY	REGULAR EARNINGS HRS.	RATE	AMOUNT	OVERTIME EARNINGS HRS.	RATE	AMOUNT	CUMULATIVE EARNINGS	FICA OASDI	FICA HI	SUTA	FIT	SIT	CIT	OTHER DEDUCTIONS	CK. NO.	NET PAID AMOUNT
YEAR-TO-DATE TOTAL			166 50 00				166 50 00	1032 30	241 43	24 98	1602 00	466 20	825 84	94 50		123 62 75
1 10/9	80		900 00				175 50 00	55 80	13 05	1 35	71 00	25 20	44 64		679	688 96
2																
3																
4																
5																
6																
QUARTER TOTAL																
YEARLY TOTAL																

Employee Payroll Record 1

DEPARTMENT	Office
OCCUPATION	Accounting Trainee
WORKS IN (STATE)	PA
NAME—LAST	
FIRST	
MIDDLE	
S.S. ACCOUNT NO.	
SEX	M / F
SALARY	$ 650/mo.
WEEKLY RATE	$ 150.00
HOURLY RATE	$ 3.75
OVERTIME RATE	$ 5.63
W/H ALLOW.	1
MARITAL STATUS	S
GROUP INSURANCE	$12,000—30¢/M

19__ PAYDAY	REGULAR HRS.	REGULAR RATE	REGULAR AMOUNT	OT HRS.	OT RATE	OT AMOUNT	CUMULATIVE EARNINGS	FICA OASDI	FICA HI	SUTA	FIT	SIT	CIT	OTHER DEDUCTIONS	CK. NO.	NET PAID AMOUNT
YEAR-TO-DATE TOTAL			5550 00				5550 00	344 10	80 48	8 33	409 00	155 40	275 28	32 40		4245 01
1 10/9	80		300 00				5850 00	18 60	4 35	45	16 00	8 40	14 88		680	237 32
2																
3																
4																
5																
6																
QUARTER TOTAL																
YEARLY TOTAL																

Employee Payroll Record 2

DEPARTMENT	Office
OCCUPATION	Programmer
WORKS IN (STATE)	PA
NAME—LAST	WILLIAMS
FIRST	Ruth
MIDDLE	Virginia
S.S. ACCOUNT NO.	518-30-6741
SEX	M / F X
SALARY	$ 1,235/mo.
WEEKLY RATE	$ 285.00
HOURLY RATE	$ 7.13
OVERTIME RATE	$ 10.70
W/H ALLOW.	0
MARITAL STATUS	S
GROUP INSURANCE	$22,000—30¢/M

19__ PAYDAY	REGULAR HRS.	REGULAR RATE	REGULAR AMOUNT	OT HRS.	OT RATE	OT AMOUNT	CUMULATIVE EARNINGS	FICA OASDI	FICA HI	SUTA	FIT	SIT	CIT	OTHER DEDUCTIONS	CK. NO.	NET PAID AMOUNT
YEAR-TO-DATE TOTAL			10260 00				10260 00	636 12	148 77	15 39	1306 00	287 28	508 86	59 40		7298 18
1 10/9	80		570 00				10830 00	35 34	8 27	86	71 00	15 96	28 27		681	410 30
2																
3																
4																
5																
6																
QUARTER TOTAL																
YEARLY TOTAL																

Left form:

DEPARTMENT | OCCUPATION | WORKS IN (STATE) | SEX M F | S.S. ACCOUNT NO. | NAME—LAST | FIRST | MIDDLE

OTHER DEDUCTIONS INFORMATION
GROUP INSURANCE
UNION DUES
OTHER

SALARY $
WEEKLY RATE $
HOURLY RATE $
OVERTIME RATE $

W/H ALLOW. | MARITAL STATUS

19 __ PAYDAY	REGULAR EARNINGS		OVERTIME EARNINGS			CUMULATIVE EARNINGS	DEDUCTIONS								NET PAID	
	HRS.	RATE	AMOUNT	HRS.	RATE	AMOUNT		FICA OASDI	FICA HI	SUTA	FIT	SIT	CIT	OTHER DEDUCTIONS	CK. NO.	AMOUNT
YEAR-TO-DATE TOTAL																
1																
2																
3																
4																
5																
6																
QUARTER TOTAL																
YEARLY TOTAL																

Right form:

DEPARTMENT | OCCUPATION | WORKS IN (STATE) | SEX M F | S.S. ACCOUNT NO. | NAME—LAST | FIRST | MIDDLE

OTHER DEDUCTIONS INFORMATION
GROUP INSURANCE
UNION DUES
OTHER

SALARY $
WEEKLY RATE $
HOURLY RATE $
OVERTIME RATE $

W/H ALLOW. | MARITAL STATUS

19 __ PAYDAY	REGULAR EARNINGS		OVERTIME EARNINGS			CUMULATIVE EARNINGS	DEDUCTIONS								NET PAID	
	HRS.	RATE	AMOUNT	HRS.	RATE	AMOUNT		FICA OASDI	FICA HI	SUTA	FIT	SIT	CIT	OTHER DEDUCTIONS	CK. NO.	AMOUNT
YEAR-TO-DATE TOTAL																
1																
2																
3																
4																
5																
6																
QUARTER TOTAL																
YEARLY TOTAL																

Left Form

DEPARTMENT | OCCUPATION | WORKS IN (STATE) | SEX M F | S.S. ACCOUNT NO. | NAME—LAST | FIRST | MIDDLE

OTHER DEDUCTIONS INFORMATION

GROUP INSURANCE | UNION DUES | OTHER

SALARY | WEEKLY RATE $ | HOURLY RATE $ | OVERTIME RATE $

W/H ALLOW. | MARITAL STATUS

19 ___ PAYDAY	REGULAR EARNINGS		OVERTIME EARNINGS			CUMULATIVE EARNINGS	DEDUCTIONS								NET PAID	
	HRS.	RATE	AMOUNT	HRS.	RATE	AMOUNT		FICA OASDI	HI	SUTA	FIT	SIT	CIT	OTHER DEDUCTIONS	CK. NO.	AMOUNT

YEAR-TO-DATE TOTAL
1
2
3
4
5
6
QUARTER TOTAL
YEARLY TOTAL

Right Form

DEPARTMENT | OCCUPATION | WORKS IN (STATE) | SEX M F | S.S. ACCOUNT NO. | NAME—LAST | FIRST | MIDDLE

OTHER DEDUCTIONS INFORMATION

GROUP INSURANCE | UNION DUES | OTHER

SALARY | WEEKLY RATE $ | HOURLY RATE $ | OVERTIME RATE $

W/H ALLOW. | MARITAL STATUS

19 ___ PAYDAY	REGULAR EARNINGS		OVERTIME EARNINGS			CUMULATIVE EARNINGS	DEDUCTIONS								NET PAID	
	HRS.	RATE	AMOUNT	HRS.	RATE	AMOUNT		FICA OASDI	HI	SUTA	FIT	SIT	CIT	OTHER DEDUCTIONS	CK. NO.	AMOUNT

YEAR-TO-DATE TOTAL
1
2
3
4
5
6
QUARTER TOTAL
YEARLY TOTAL

TRANSACTION NO. 11

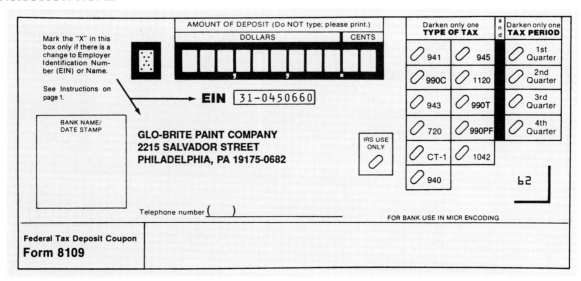

TRANSACTION NO. 25

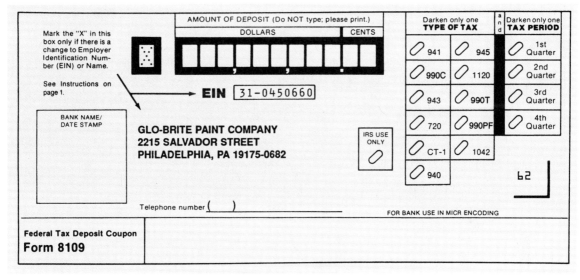

TRANSACTION NO. 33

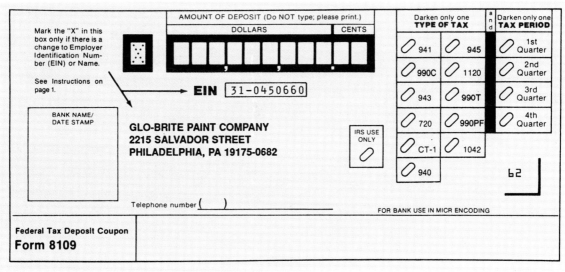

TRANSACTION NO. 36

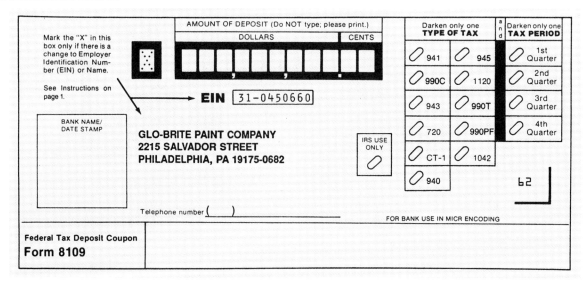

Mark the "X" in this box only if there is a change to Employer Identification Number (EIN) or Name.

See Instructions on page 1.

AMOUNT OF DEPOSIT (Do NOT type; please print.)

DOLLARS		CENTS

EIN 31-0450660

BANK NAME/ DATE STAMP

GLO-BRITE PAINT COMPANY
2215 SALVADOR STREET
PHILADELPHIA, PA 19175-0682

IRS USE ONLY

Telephone number (   )

Darken only one TYPE OF TAX		a n d	Darken only one TAX PERIOD
941	945		1st Quarter
990C	1120		2nd Quarter
943	990T		3rd Quarter
720	990PF		4th Quarter
CT-1	1042		
940			62

FOR BANK USE IN MICR ENCODING

Federal Tax Deposit Coupon
Form 8109

TRANSACTION NO. 2

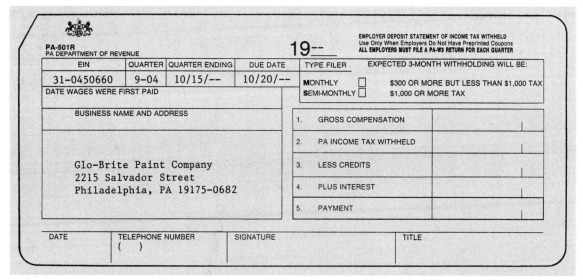

PA-501R
PA DEPARTMENT OF REVENUE

19--

EMPLOYER DEPOSIT STATEMENT OF INCOME TAX WITHHELD
Use Only When Employers Do Not Have Preprinted Coupons
ALL EMPLOYERS MUST FILE A PA-W3 RETURN FOR EACH QUARTER

EIN	QUARTER	QUARTER ENDING	DUE DATE	TYPE FILER	EXPECTED 3-MONTH WITHHOLDING WILL BE:
31-0450660	9-04	10/15/--	10/20/--	MONTHLY ☐	$300 OR MORE BUT LESS THAN $1,000 TAX
DATE WAGES WERE FIRST PAID				SEMI-MONTHLY ☐	$1,000 OR MORE TAX

BUSINESS NAME AND ADDRESS

Glo-Brite Paint Company
2215 Salvador Street
Philadelphia, PA 19175-0682

1.	GROSS COMPENSATION	
2.	PA INCOME TAX WITHHELD	
3.	LESS CREDITS	
4.	PLUS INTEREST	
5.	PAYMENT	

DATE	TELEPHONE NUMBER ( )	SIGNATURE	TITLE

TRANSACTION NO. 4

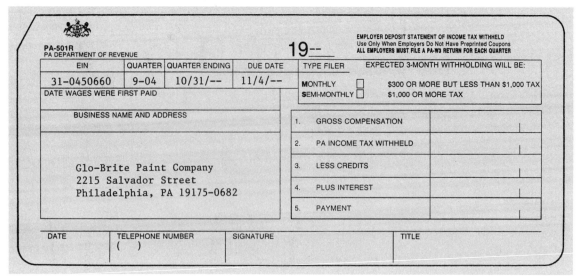

PA-501R
PA DEPARTMENT OF REVENUE

19--

EMPLOYER DEPOSIT STATEMENT OF INCOME TAX WITHHELD
Use Only When Employers Do Not Have Preprinted Coupons
ALL EMPLOYERS MUST FILE A PA-W3 RETURN FOR EACH QUARTER

EIN	QUARTER	QUARTER ENDING	DUE DATE	TYPE FILER	EXPECTED 3-MONTH WITHHOLDING WILL BE:
31-0450660	9-04	10/31/--	11/4/--	MONTHLY ☐	$300 OR MORE BUT LESS THAN $1,000 TAX
DATE WAGES WERE FIRST PAID				SEMI-MONTHLY ☐	$1,000 OR MORE TAX

BUSINESS NAME AND ADDRESS

Glo-Brite Paint Company
2215 Salvador Street
Philadelphia, PA 19175-0682

1.	GROSS COMPENSATION	
2.	PA INCOME TAX WITHHELD	
3.	LESS CREDITS	
4.	PLUS INTEREST	
5.	PAYMENT	

DATE	TELEPHONE NUMBER ( )	SIGNATURE	TITLE

TRANSACTION NO. 14

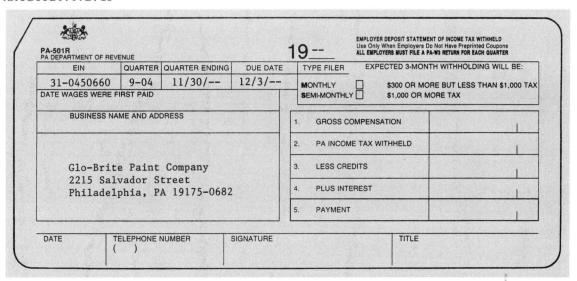

				EMPLOYER DEPOSIT STATEMENT OF INCOME TAX WITHHELD
			19--	Use Only When Employers Do Not Have Preprinted Coupons
PA-501R PA DEPARTMENT OF REVENUE				**ALL EMPLOYERS MUST FILE A PA-W3 RETURN FOR EACH QUARTER**

EIN	QUARTER	QUARTER ENDING	DUE DATE	TYPE FILER	EXPECTED 3-MONTH WITHHOLDING WILL BE:
31-0450660	9-04	11/15/--	11/18/--	MONTHLY ☐ SEMI-MONTHLY ☐	$300 OR MORE BUT LESS THAN $1,000 TAX $1,000 OR MORE TAX

DATE WAGES WERE FIRST PAID

BUSINESS NAME AND ADDRESS

Glo-Brite Paint Company
2215 Salvador Street
Philadelphia, PA 19175-0682

1. GROSS COMPENSATION
2. PA INCOME TAX WITHHELD
3. LESS CREDITS
4. PLUS INTEREST
5. PAYMENT

DATE	TELEPHONE NUMBER ( )	SIGNATURE	TITLE

TRANSACTION NO. 18

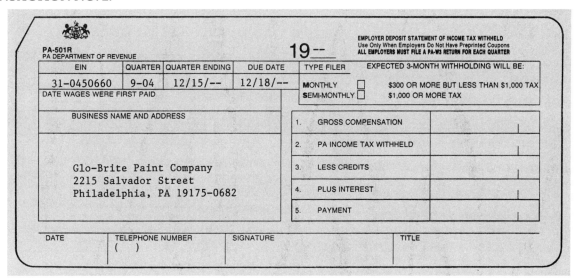

				EMPLOYER DEPOSIT STATEMENT OF INCOME TAX WITHHELD
			19--	Use Only When Employers Do Not Have Preprinted Coupons
PA-501R PA DEPARTMENT OF REVENUE				**ALL EMPLOYERS MUST FILE A PA-W3 RETURN FOR EACH QUARTER**

EIN	QUARTER	QUARTER ENDING	DUE DATE	TYPE FILER	EXPECTED 3-MONTH WITHHOLDING WILL BE:
31-0450660	9-04	11/30/--	12/3/--	MONTHLY ☐ SEMI-MONTHLY ☐	$300 OR MORE BUT LESS THAN $1,000 TAX $1,000 OR MORE TAX

DATE WAGES WERE FIRST PAID

BUSINESS NAME AND ADDRESS

Glo-Brite Paint Company
2215 Salvador Street
Philadelphia, PA 19175-0682

1. GROSS COMPENSATION
2. PA INCOME TAX WITHHELD
3. LESS CREDITS
4. PLUS INTEREST
5. PAYMENT

DATE	TELEPHONE NUMBER ( )	SIGNATURE	TITLE

TRANSACTION NO. 27

				EMPLOYER DEPOSIT STATEMENT OF INCOME TAX WITHHELD
			19--	Use Only When Employers Do Not Have Preprinted Coupons
PA-501R PA DEPARTMENT OF REVENUE				**ALL EMPLOYERS MUST FILE A PA-W3 RETURN FOR EACH QUARTER**

EIN	QUARTER	QUARTER ENDING	DUE DATE	TYPE FILER	EXPECTED 3-MONTH WITHHOLDING WILL BE:
31-0450660	9-04	12/15/--	12/18/--	MONTHLY ☐ SEMI-MONTHLY ☐	$300 OR MORE BUT LESS THAN $1,000 TAX $1,000 OR MORE TAX

DATE WAGES WERE FIRST PAID

BUSINESS NAME AND ADDRESS

Glo-Brite Paint Company
2215 Salvador Street
Philadelphia, PA 19175-0682

1. GROSS COMPENSATION
2. PA INCOME TAX WITHHELD
3. LESS CREDITS
4. PLUS INTEREST
5. PAYMENT

DATE	TELEPHONE NUMBER ( )	SIGNATURE	TITLE

TRANSACTION NO. 31

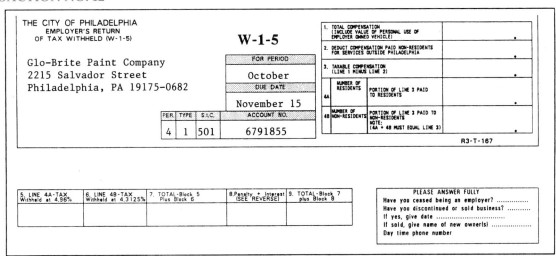

PA-501R				**19 --**	EMPLOYER DEPOSIT STATEMENT OF INCOME TAX WITHHELD
PA DEPARTMENT OF REVENUE					Use Only When Employers Do Not Have Preprinted Coupons
					ALL EMPLOYERS MUST FILE A PA-W3 RETURN FOR EACH QUARTER

EIN	QUARTER	QUARTER ENDING	DUE DATE	TYPE FILER	EXPECTED 3-MONTH WITHHOLDING WILL BE:
31-0450660	9-04	12/31/--	1/6/--	MONTHLY ☐	$300 OR MORE BUT LESS THAN $1,000 TAX
DATE WAGES WERE FIRST PAID				SEMI-MONTHLY ☐	$1,000 OR MORE TAX

BUSINESS NAME AND ADDRESS

Glo-Brite Paint Company
2215 Salvador Street
Philadelphia, PA 19175-0682

1.	GROSS COMPENSATION	
2.	PA INCOME TAX WITHHELD	
3.	LESS CREDITS	
4.	PLUS INTEREST	
5.	PAYMENT	

DATE	TELEPHONE NUMBER ( )	SIGNATURE	TITLE

TRANSACTION NO. 12

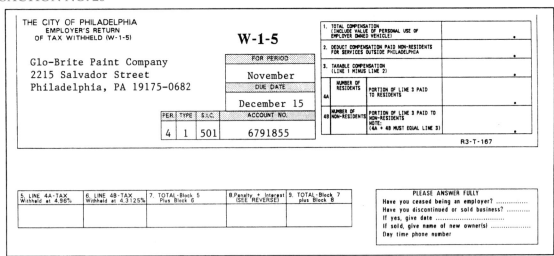

THE CITY OF PHILADELPHIA
EMPLOYER'S RETURN
OF TAX WITHHELD (W-1-5)

W-1-5

Glo-Brite Paint Company
2215 Salvador Street
Philadelphia, PA 19175-0682

FOR PERIOD
October
DUE DATE
November 15

PER.	TYPE	S.I.C.	ACCOUNT NO.
4	1	501	6791855

1. TOTAL COMPENSATION (INCLUDE VALUE OF PERSONAL USE OF EMPLOYER OWNED VEHICLE)	
2. DEDUCT COMPENSATION PAID NON-RESIDENTS FOR SERVICES OUTSIDE PHILADELPHIA	
3. TAXABLE COMPENSATION (LINE 1 MINUS LINE 2)	
4A NUMBER OF RESIDENTS / PORTION OF LINE 3 PAID TO RESIDENTS	
4B NUMBER OF NON-RESIDENTS / PORTION OF LINE 3 PAID TO NON-RESIDENTS NOTE: (4A + 4B MUST EQUAL LINE 3)	

R3-T-167

5. LINE 4A-TAX Withheld at 4.96%	6. LINE 4B-TAX Withheld at 4.3125%	7. TOTAL-Block 5 Plus Block 6	8. Penalty + Interest (SEE REVERSE)	9. TOTAL-Block 7 plus Block 8

PLEASE ANSWER FULLY
Have you ceased being an employer? ....
Have you discontinued or sold business? ....
If yes, give date ....
If sold, give name of new owner(s) ....
Day time phone number

TRANSACTION NO. 26

THE CITY OF PHILADELPHIA
EMPLOYER'S RETURN
OF TAX WITHHELD (W-1-5)

W-1-5

Glo-Brite Paint Company
2215 Salvador Street
Philadelphia, PA 19175-0682

FOR PERIOD
November
DUE DATE
December 15

PER.	TYPE	S.I.C.	ACCOUNT NO.
4	1	501	6791855

1. TOTAL COMPENSATION (INCLUDE VALUE OF PERSONAL USE OF EMPLOYER OWNED VEHICLE)	
2. DEDUCT COMPENSATION PAID NON-RESIDENTS FOR SERVICES OUTSIDE PHILADELPHIA	
3. TAXABLE COMPENSATION (LINE 1 MINUS LINE 2)	
4A NUMBER OF RESIDENTS / PORTION OF LINE 3 PAID TO RESIDENTS	
4B NUMBER OF NON-RESIDENTS / PORTION OF LINE 3 PAID TO NON-RESIDENTS NOTE: (4A + 4B MUST EQUAL LINE 3)	

R3-T-167

5. LINE 4A-TAX Withheld at 4.96%	6. LINE 4B-TAX Withheld at 4.3125%	7. TOTAL-Block 5 Plus Block 6	8. Penalty + Interest (SEE REVERSE)	9. TOTAL-Block 7 plus Block 8

PLEASE ANSWER FULLY
Have you ceased being an employer? ....
Have you discontinued or sold business? ....
If yes, give date ....
If sold, give name of new owner(s) ....
Day time phone number

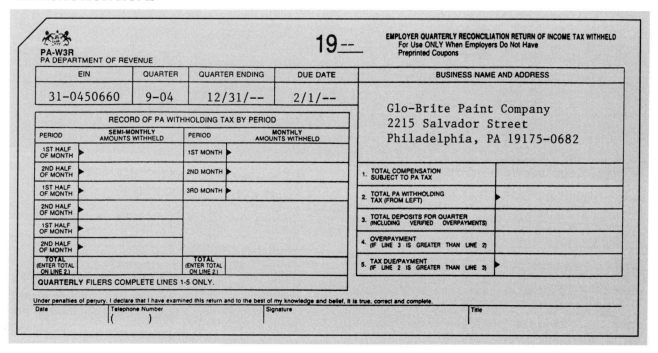

THE CITY OF PHILADELPHIA EMPLOYER'S RETURN OF TAX WITHHELD (W-1-5)	W-1-5	1. TOTAL COMPENSATION (INCLUDE VALUE OF PERSONAL USE OF EMPLOYER OWNED VEHICLE)		.
		2. DEDUCT COMPENSATION PAID NON-RESIDENTS FOR SERVICES OUTSIDE PHILADELPHIA		.

Glo-Brite Paint Company
2215 Salvador Street
Philadelphia, PA 19175-0682

FOR PERIOD
December

DUE DATE
January 15

PER.	TYPE	S.I.C.	ACCOUNT NO.
4	1	501	6791855

3. TAXABLE COMPENSATION (LINE 1 MINUS LINE 2)

4A NUMBER OF RESIDENTS — PORTION OF LINE 3 PAID TO RESIDENTS

4B NUMBER OF NON-RESIDENTS — PORTION OF LINE 3 PAID TO NON-RESIDENTS NOTE: (4A + 4B MUST EQUAL LINE 3)

R3-T-167

5. LINE 4A-TAX Withheld at 4.96%	6. LINE 4B-TAX Withheld at 4.3125%	7. TOTAL-Block 5 Plus Block 6	8. Penalty + Interest (SEE REVERSE)	9. TOTAL-Block 7 plus Block 8

PLEASE ANSWER FULLY
Have you ceased being an employer? ....
Have you discontinued or sold business? ....
If yes, give date ....
If sold, give name of new owner(s) ....
Day time phone number

PA-W3R
PA DEPARTMENT OF REVENUE

19--

EMPLOYER QUARTERLY RECONCILIATION RETURN OF INCOME TAX WITHHELD
For Use ONLY When Employers Do Not Have Preprinted Coupons

EIN	QUARTER	QUARTER ENDING	DUE DATE	BUSINESS NAME AND ADDRESS
31-0450660	9-04	12/31/--	2/1/--	

RECORD OF PA WITHHOLDING TAX BY PERIOD				Glo-Brite Paint Company 2215 Salvador Street Philadelphia, PA 19175-0682
PERIOD	SEMI-MONTHLY AMOUNTS WITHHELD	PERIOD	MONTHLY AMOUNTS WITHHELD	
1ST HALF OF MONTH		1ST MONTH		
2ND HALF OF MONTH		2ND MONTH		1. TOTAL COMPENSATION SUBJECT TO PA TAX
1ST HALF OF MONTH		3RD MONTH		2. TOTAL PA WITHHOLDING TAX (FROM LEFT)
2ND HALF OF MONTH				3. TOTAL DEPOSITS FOR QUARTER (INCLUDING VERIFIED OVERPAYMENTS)
1ST HALF OF MONTH				4. OVERPAYMENT (IF LINE 3 IS GREATER THAN LINE 2)
2ND HALF OF MONTH				5. TAX DUE/PAYMENT (IF LINE 2 IS GREATER THAN LINE 3)
TOTAL (ENTER TOTAL ON LINE 2)		TOTAL (ENTER TOTAL ON LINE 2)		

QUARTERLY FILERS COMPLETE LINES 1-5 ONLY.

Under penalties of perjury. I declare that I have examined this return and to the best of my knowledge and belief. It is true, correct and complete.

Date	Telephone Number ( )	Signature	Title

ANNUAL RECONCILIATION OF WAGE TAX

Due Date:
2/28/--

19 --

Print your numbers like this:

1	2	3	4	5	6	7	8	9	0

Glo-Brite Paint Company
2215 Salvador Street
Philadelphia, PA 19175-0682

Type
Tax   W

ACCOUNT NO.   6 7 9 1 8 5 5

Federal Identification Number

3 1 — 0 4 5 0 6 6 0

SEE INSTRUCTIONS ON BACK

DATE WAGES TERMINATED:
(IF APPLICABLE)   _____

Number of Residents   Number of Non-Residents

DATE BUSINESS TERMINATED:
(IF APPLICABLE)   _____

PREPARER'S DAYTIME PHONE :   _____

GROSS COMPENSATION PER W2'S ———→

1. Taxable Residents Compensation

2. Line 1 times .0496 (4.96%)

3. Taxable Non-Residents Compensation

4. Line 3 times .043125 (4.3125%)

5. Total Tax Due (Line 2 plus Line 4)

6. Tax Previously Paid For 19--

-------------------------------------DO NOT DETACH-------------------------------------

NAME:

ACCOUNT NO.

TYPE TAX: PERIOD: YEAR:

If Line 5 is Greater Than Line 6, Use Line 7

7. Tax Due (Line 5 Minus Line 6)
Make Check Payable To: City of Philadelphia

If line 5 is less than line 6, use line 8

8. Tax Overpaid (Line 6 Less Line 5)
        (SEE INSTRUCTIONS)

Signature:_____   Date _____

I certify that all amounts indicated as due the City of Philadelphia on this return were actually withheld from the gross compensation paid
by this taxpayer to its employees during the period(s) covered by this filing, and that I am authorized to so state.

TRANSACTION NO. 35

Form **941** — Employer's Quarterly Federal Tax Return

Department of the Treasury
Internal Revenue Service

4141

▶ See separate instructions for information on completing this return.
Please type or print.

OMB No. 1545-0029

Enter state code for state in which deposits made. ▶ □ (see page 2 of instructions).

Name (as distinguished from trade name)

Date quarter ended
DEC 31, 19--

Trade name, if any
GLO-BRITE PAINT COMPANY

Employer identification number
31-0450660

Address (number and street)
2215 SALVADOR ST.

City, state, and ZIP code
PHILADELPHIA, PA
19175-0682

| T |
| FF |
| FD |
| FP |
| I |
| T |

If address is different from prior return, check here ▶ □

IRS Use

Row: 1 1 1 1 1 1 1 1 1 1   2   3 3 3 3 3   4 4 4
Row: 5 5 5   6   7   8 8 8 8 8   9 9 9   10 10 10 10 10 10 10 10 10 10

If you do not have to file returns in the future, check here ▶ □ and enter date final wages paid ▶

If you are a seasonal employer, see **Seasonal employers** on page 2 and check here (see instructions) ▶ □

1 Number of employees (except household) employed in the pay period that includes March 12th ▶

2 Total wages and tips subject to withholding, plus other compensation	2
3 Total income tax withheld from wages, tips, and sick pay	3
4 Adjustment of withheld income tax for preceding quarters of calendar year	4
5 Adjusted total of income tax withheld (line 3 as adjusted by line 4—see instructions)	5
6a Taxable social security wages . $ × 12.4% (.124) =	6a
b Taxable social security tips . $ × 12.4% (.124) =	6b
7 Taxable Medicare wages and tips . $ × 2.9% (.029) =	7
8 Total social security and Medicare taxes (add lines 6a, 6b, and 7). Check here if wages are not subject to social security and/or Medicare tax ▶ □	8
9 Adjustment of social security and Medicare taxes (see instructions for required explanation) Sick Pay $_____ ± Fractions of Cents $_____ ± Other $_____ =	9
10 Adjusted total of social security and Medicare taxes (line 8 as adjusted by line 9—see instructions)	10
11 **Total taxes** (add lines 5 and 10)	11
12 Advance earned income credit (EIC) payments made to employees, if any	12
13 Net taxes (subtract line 12 from line 11). **This should equal line 17, column (d) below (or line D of Schedule B (Form 941))**	13
14 Total deposits for quarter, including overpayment applied from a prior quarter	14
15 Balance due (subtract line 14 from line 13). Pay to Internal Revenue Service	15

16 **Overpayment,** if line 14 is more than line 13, enter excess here ▶ $_____
and check if to be: □ Applied to next return OR □ Refunded.

- All filers: If line 13 is less than $500, you need not complete line 17 or Schedule B.
- Semiweekly depositors: Complete Schedule B and check here ▶ □
- Monthly depositors: Complete line 17, columns (a) through (d) and check here ▶ □

17 Monthly Summary of Federal Tax Liability.

(a) First month liability	(b) Second month liability	(c) Third month liability	(d) Total liability for quarter

Sign Here — Under penalties of perjury, I declare that I have examined this return, including accompanying schedules and statements, and to the best of my knowledge and belief, it is true, correct, and complete.

Signature ▶   Print Your Name and Title ▶   Date ▶

Form **941**

7–57

Form **940-EZ**		
Department of the Treasury Internal Revenue Service	**Employer's Annual Federal Unemployment (FUTA) Tax Return**	OMB No. 1545-1110 **19--**

		T	
		FF	
If incorrect, make any necessary changes. ►	Name (as distinguished from trade name) Calendar year 19--	FD	
	Trade name, if any GLO-BRITE PAINT COMPANY	FP	
	Address and ZIP code 2215 SALVADOR ST. PHILADELPHIA, PA 19175-0682	I	
	Employer identification number 31:0450660	T	

Follow the chart under **Who May Use Form 940-EZ** *on page 2. If you cannot use Form 940-EZ, you must use Form 940 instead.*

A Enter the amount of contributions paid to your state unemployment fund. (See instructions for line A on page 4.)► $ ....|....

B (1) Enter the name of the state where you have to pay contributions . . . . ► ....
    (2) Enter your state reporting number as shown on state unemployment tax return. ►

If you will not have to file returns in the future, check here (see **Who Must File**, on page 2) **complete, and sign the return** . . . . . . ► ☐
If this is an Amended Return check here . . . . ► ☐

Part I Taxable Wages and FUTA Tax

1	Total payments (including payments shown on lines 2 and 3) during the calendar year for services of employees	**1**	
			Amount paid
2	Exempt payments. (Explain all exempt payments, attaching additional sheets if necessary.) ► -- ---	**2**	
3	Payments for services of more than $7,000. Enter only amounts over the first $7,000 paid to each employee. Do not include any exempt payments from line 2. Do not use your state wage limitation. The $7,000 amount is the Federal wage base. Your state wage base may be different	**3**	
4	Total exempt payments (add lines 2 and 3)	**4**	
5	**Total taxable wages** (subtract line 4 from line 1) . . . . ►	**5**	
6	FUTA tax. Multiply the wages on line 5 by .008 and enter here. (If the result is over $100, also complete Part II.) .	**6**	
7	Total FUTA tax deposited for the year, including any overpayment applied from a prior year (from your records)	**7**	
8	**Amount you owe** (subtract line 7 from line 6). This should be $100 or less. Pay to "Internal Revenue Service". ►	**8**	
9	Overpayment (subtract line 6 from line 7). Check if it is to be: ☐ **Applied to next return, or** ☐Refunded ►	**9**	

Part II Record of Quarterly Federal Unemployment Tax Liability (Do not include state liability.) Complete only if line 6 is over $100.

Quarter	First (Jan. 1 – Mar. 31)	Second (Apr. 1 – June 30)	Third (July 1 – Sept. 30)	Fourth (Oct. 1 – Dec. 31)	Total for year
Liability for quarter	272.71	140.33	110.88		

Under penalties of perjury, I declare that I have examined this return, including accompanying schedules and statements, and, to the best of my knowledge and belief, it is true, correct, and complete, and that no part of any payment made to a state unemployment fund claimed as a credit was, or is to be, deducted from the payments to employees.

Signature ►   Title (Owner, etc.) ►   Date ►

Form **940-EZ**

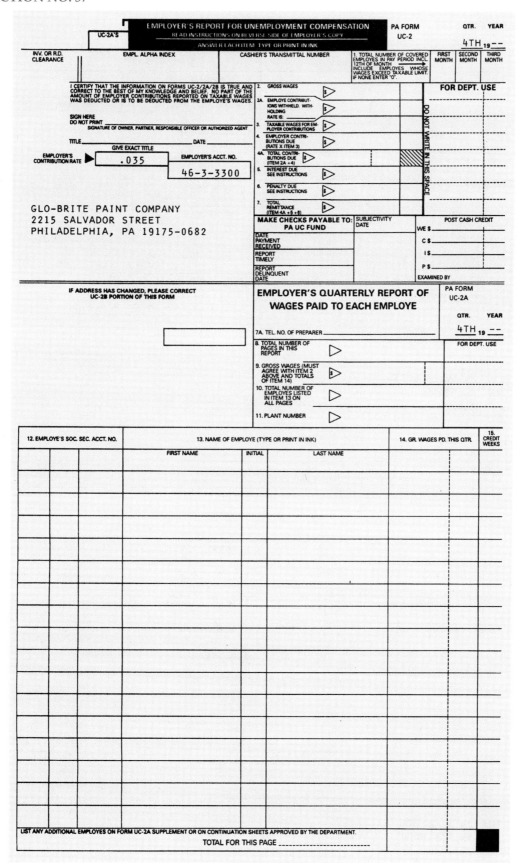

TRANSACTION NO. 10

a Control number	22222	Void ☐	For Official Use Only ► OMB No. 1545–0008		

b Employer's identification number		1 Wages, tips, other compensation	2 Federal income tax withheld

c Employer's name, address, and ZIP code	3 Social security wages	4 Social security tax withheld
	5 Medicare wages and tips	6 Medicare tax withheld
	7 Social security tips	8 Allocated tips

d Employee's social security number	9 Advance EIC payment	10 Dependent care benefits

e Employee's name (first, middle initial, last)	11 Nonqualified plans	12 Benefits included in box 1
	13 See Instrs. for box 13	14 Other

15 Statutory employee ☐	Deceased ☐	Pension plan ☐	Legal rep ☐	942 emp ☐	Subtotal ☐	Deferred compensation ☐

f Employee's address and ZIP code

16 State Employer's state I.D. No.	17 State wages, tips, etc.	18 State income tax	19 Locality name	20 Local wages, tips, etc.	21 Local income tax

Department of the Treasury—Internal Revenue Service

Form **W-2** **Wage and Tax Statement** **19—**
Copy A For Social Security Administration

TRANSACTION NO. 24

a Control number	22222	Void ☐	For Official Use Only ► OMB No. 1545–0008		

b Employer's identification number		1 Wages, tips, other compensation	2 Federal income tax withheld

c Employer's name, address, and ZIP code	3 Social security wages	4 Social security tax withheld
	5 Medicare wages and tips	6 Medicare tax withheld
	7 Social security tips	8 Allocated tips

d Employee's social security number	9 Advance EIC payment	10 Dependent care benefits

e Employee's name (first, middle initial, last)	11 Nonqualified plans	12 Benefits included in box 1
	13 See Instrs. for box 13	14 Other

15 Statutory employee ☐	Deceased ☐	Pension plan ☐	Legal rep ☐	942 emp ☐	Subtotal ☐	Deferred compensation ☐

f Employee's address and ZIP code

16 State Employer's state I.D. No.	17 State wages, tips, etc.	18 State income tax	19 Locality name	20 Local wages, tips, etc.	21 Local income tax

Department of the Treasury—Internal Revenue Service

Form **W-2** **Wage and Tax Statement** **19—**
Copy A For Social Security Administration

TRANSACTION NO. 38

a Control number	22222	Void ☐	For Official Use Only ► OMB No. 1545-0008	

b Employer's identification number		1 Wages, tips, other compensation	2 Federal income tax withheld
c Employer's name, address, and ZIP code		3 Social security wages	4 Social security tax withheld
		5 Medicare wages and tips	6 Medicare tax withheld
		7 Social security tips	8 Allocated tips
d Employee's social security number		9 Advance EIC payment	10 Dependent care benefits
e Employee's name (first, middle initial, last)		11 Nonqualified plans	12 Benefits included in box 1
		13 See Instrs. for box 13	14 Other

15 Statutory employee ☐ Deceased ☐ Pension plan ☐ Legal rep ☐ 942 emp ☐ Subtotal ☐ Deferred compensation ☐

f Employee's address and ZIP code

16 State Employer's state I.D. No.	17 State wages, tips, etc.	18 State income tax	19 Locality name	20 Local wages, tips, etc.	21 Local income tax

Department of the Treasury—Internal Revenue Service

Form W-2 Wage and Tax Statement 19—
Copy A For Social Security Administration

---

a Control number	22222	Void ☐	For Official Use Only ► OMB No. 1545-0008	

b Employer's identification number		1 Wages, tips, other compensation	2 Federal income tax withheld
c Employer's name, address, and ZIP code		3 Social security wages	4 Social security tax withheld
		5 Medicare wages and tips	6 Medicare tax withheld
		7 Social security tips	8 Allocated tips
d Employee's social security number		9 Advance EIC payment	10 Dependent care benefits
e Employee's name (first, middle initial, last)		11 Nonqualified plans	12 Benefits included in box 1
		13 See Instrs. for box 13	14 Other

15 Statutory employee ☐ Deceased ☐ Pension plan ☐ Legal rep ☐ 942 emp ☐ Subtotal ☐ Deferred compensation ☐

f Employee's address and ZIP code

16 State Employer's state I.D. No.	17 State wages, tips, etc.	18 State income tax	19 Locality name	20 Local wages, tips, etc.	21 Local income tax

Department of the Treasury—Internal Revenue Service

Form W-2 Wage and Tax Statement 19—
Copy A For Social Security Administration

a Control number	22222	Void ☐	For Official Use Only ▶ OMB No. 1545-0008		
b Employer's identification number				1 Wages, tips, other compensation	2 Federal income tax withheld
c Employer's name, address, and ZIP code				3 Social security wages	4 Social security tax withheld
				5 Medicare wages and tips	6 Medicare tax withheld
				7 Social security tips	8 Allocated tips
d Employee's social security number				9 Advance EIC payment	10 Dependent care benefits
e Employee's name (first, middle initial, last)				11 Nonqualified plans	12 Benefits included in box 1
				13 See Instrs. for box 13	14 Other

15 Statutory employee ☐	Deceased ☐	Pension plan ☐	Legal rep ☐	942 emp ☐	Subtotal ☐	Deferred compensation ☐

f Employee's address and ZIP code

16 State Employer's state I.D. No.	17 State wages, tips, etc.	18 State income tax	19 Locality name	20 Local wages, tips, etc.	21 Local income tax

Department of the Treasury—Internal Revenue Service

Form **W-2** **Wage and Tax Statement** **19—**

Copy A For Social Security Administration

a Control number	22222	Void ☐	For Official Use Only ▶ OMB No. 1545-0008		
b Employer's identification number				1 Wages, tips, other compensation	2 Federal income tax withheld
c Employer's name, address, and ZIP code				3 Social security wages	4 Social security tax withheld
				5 Medicare wages and tips	6 Medicare tax withheld
				7 Social security tips	8 Allocated tips
d Employee's social security number				9 Advance EIC payment	10 Dependent care benefits
e Employee's name (first, middle initial, last)				11 Nonqualified plans	12 Benefits included in box 1
				13 See Instrs. for box 13	14 Other

15 Statutory employee ☐	Deceased ☐	Pension plan ☐	Legal rep ☐	942 emp ☐	Subtotal ☐	Deferred compensation ☐

f Employee's address and ZIP code

16 State Employer's state I.D. No.	17 State wages, tips, etc.	18 State income tax	19 Locality name	20 Local wages, tips, etc.	21 Local income tax

Department of the Treasury—Internal Revenue Service

Form **W-2** **Wage and Tax Statement** **19—**

Copy A For Social Security Administration

a Control number	22222	Void ☐	For Official Use Only ▶ OMB No. 1545-0008		
b Employer's identification number				1 Wages, tips, other compensation	2 Federal income tax withheld
c Employer's name, address, and ZIP code				3 Social security wages	4 Social security tax withheld
				5 Medicare wages and tips	6 Medicare tax withheld
				7 Social security tips	8 Allocated tips
d Employee's social security number				9 Advance EIC payment	10 Dependent care benefits
e Employee's name (first, middle initial, last)				11 Nonqualified plans	12 Benefits included in box 1
				13 See Instrs. for box 13	14 Other

15 Statutory employee ☐	Deceased ☐	Pension plan ☐	Legal rep ☐	942 emp ☐	Subtotal ☐	Deferred compensation ☐

f Employee's address and ZIP code

16 State	Employer's state I.D. No.	17 State wages, tips, etc.	18 State income tax	19 Locality name	20 Local wages, tips, etc	21 Local income tax

Department of the Treasury—Internal Revenue Service

Form **W-2** **Wage and Tax Statement** **19—**
Copy A For Social Security Administration

---

a Control number	22222	Void ☐	For Official Use Only ▶ OMB No. 1545-0008		
b Employer's identification number				1 Wages, tips, other compensation	2 Federal income tax withheld
c Employer's name, address, and ZIP code				3 Social security wages	4 Social security tax withheld
				5 Medicare wages and tips	6 Medicare tax withheld
				7 Social security tips	8 Allocated tips
d Employee's social security number				9 Advance EIC payment	10 Dependent care benefits
e Employee's name (first, middle initial, last)				11 Nonqualified plans	12 Benefits included in box 1
				13 See Instrs. for box 13	14 Other

15 Statutory employee ☐	Deceased ☐	Pension plan ☐	Legal rep ☐	942 emp ☐	Subtotal ☐	Deferred compensation ☐

f Employee's address and ZIP code

16 State	Employer's state I.D. No.	17 State wages, tips, etc.	18 State income tax	19 Locality name	20 Local wages, tips, etc	21 Local income tax

Department of the Treasury—Internal Revenue Service

Form **W-2** **Wage and Tax Statement** **19—**
Copy A For Social Security Administration

a Control number	22222	Void ☐	For Official Use Only ▶ OMB No. 1545-0008		
b Employer's identification number				1 Wages, tips, other compensation	2 Federal income tax withheld
c Employer's name, address, and ZIP code				3 Social security wages	4 Social security tax withheld
				5 Medicare wages and tips	6 Medicare tax withheld
				7 Social security tips	8 Allocated tips
d Employee's social security number				9 Advance EIC payment	10 Dependent care benefits
e Employee's name (first, middle initial, last)				11 Nonqualified plans	12 Benefits included in box 1
				13 See Instrs. for box 13	14 Other

15 Statutory employee ☐	Deceased ☐	Pension plan ☐	Legal rep ☐	942 emp ☐	Subtotal ☐	Deferred compensation ☐

f Employee's address and ZIP code

16 State Employer's state I.D. No.	17 State wages, tips, etc.	18 State income tax	19 Locality name	20 Local wages, tips, etc.	21 Local income tax

Department of the Treasury—Internal Revenue Service

Form W-2 Wage and Tax Statement 19—

Copy A For Social Security Administration

a Control number	22222	Void ☐	For Official Use Only ▶ OMB No. 1545-0008		
b Employer's identification number				1 Wages, tips, other compensation	2 Federal income tax withheld
c Employer's name, address, and ZIP code				3 Social security wages	4 Social security tax withheld
				5 Medicare wages and tips	6 Medicare tax withheld
				7 Social security tips	8 Allocated tips
d Employee's social security number				9 Advance EIC payment	10 Dependent care benefits
e Employee's name (first, middle initial, last)				11 Nonqualified plans	12 Benefits included in box 1
				13 See Instrs. for box 13	14 Other

15 Statutory employee ☐	Deceased ☐	Pension plan ☐	Legal rep ☐	942 emp ☐	Subtotal ☐	Deferred compensation ☐

f Employee's address and ZIP code

16 State Employer's state I.D. No.	17 State wages, tips, etc.	18 State income tax	19 Locality name	20 Local wages, tips, etc.	21 Local income tax

Department of the Treasury—Internal Revenue Service

Form W-2 Wage and Tax Statement 19—

Copy A For Social Security Administration

a Control number	22222	Void ☐	For Official Use Only ▶ OMB No. 1545-0008		
b Employer's identification number			1 Wages, tips, other compensation		2 Federal income tax withheld
c Employer's name, address, and ZIP code			3 Social security wages		4 Social security tax withheld
			5 Medicare wages and tips		6 Medicare tax withheld
			7 Social security tips		8 Allocated tips
d Employee's social security number			9 Advance EIC payment		10 Dependent care benefits
e Employee's name (first, middle initial, last)			11 Nonqualified plans		12 Benefits included in box 1
			13 See Instrs. for box 13		14 Other

15 Statutory employee ☐	Deceased ☐	Pension plan ☐	Legal rep ☐	942 emp ☐	Subtotal ☐	Deferred compensation ☐

f Employee's address and ZIP code

16 State Employer's state I.D. No.	17 State wages, tips, etc.	18 State income tax	19 Locality name	20 Local wages, tips, etc.	21 Local income tax

Department of the Treasury—Internal Revenue Service

Form **W-2** **Wage and Tax Statement** **19—**

Copy A For Social Security Administration

---

a Control number	22222	Void ☐	For Official Use Only ▶ OMB No. 1545-0008		
b Employer's identification number			1 Wages, tips, other compensation		2 Federal income tax withheld
c Employer's name, address, and ZIP code			3 Social security wages		4 Social security tax withheld
			5 Medicare wages and tips		6 Medicare tax withheld
			7 Social security tips		8 Allocated tips
d Employee's social security number			9 Advance EIC payment		10 Dependent care benefits
e Employee's name (first, middle initial, last)			11 Nonqualified plans		12 Benefits included in box 1
			13 See Instrs. for box 13		14 Other

15 Statutory employee ☐	Deceased ☐	Pension plan ☐	Legal rep ☐	942 emp ☐	Subtotal ☐	Deferred compensation ☐

f Employee's address and ZIP code

16 State Employer's state I.D. No.	17 State wages, tips, etc.	18 State income tax	19 Locality name	20 Local wages, tips, etc.	21 Local income tax

Department of the Treasury—Internal Revenue Service

Form **W-2** **Wage and Tax Statement** **19—**

Copy A For Social Security Administration

a Control number				For Official Use Only ▶ OMB No. 1545-0008			
b **Kind of Payer** ▶	941 ☐	Military ☐	943 ☐	1 Wages, tips, other compensation		2 Federal income tax withheld	
	CT-1 ☐	942 ☐	Medicare govt. emp. ☐	3 Social security wages		4 Social security tax withheld	
c Total number of statements		d Establishment number		5 Medicare wages and tips		6 Medicare tax withheld	
e Employer's identification number				7 Social security tips		8 Allocated tips	
f Employer's name				9 Advance EIC payments		10 Dependent care benefits	
				11 Nonqualified plans		12 Deferred compensation	
				13 Adjusted total social security wages and tips			
				14 Adjusted total Medicare wages and tips			
g Employer's address and ZIP code				15 Income tax withheld by third-party payer			
h Other EIN used this year							
i Employer's state I.D. No.							

Under penalties of perjury, I declare that I have examined this return and accompanying documents, and, to the best of my knowledge and belief, they are true, correct, and complete.

Signature ▶   Title ▶   Date ▶

Telephone number ( )

Form **W-3** Transmittal of Wage and Tax Statements **19** --   Department of the Treasury
Internal Revenue Service

REV-1667 AS
PA DEPARTMENT OF REVENUE

19 --   **W-2 TRANSMITTAL**

EIN
31-0450660

DUE DATE
JANUARY 31. 19--

Section I   W-2 RECONCILIATION

1a Number of W-2 forms attached	
1b Number of W-2's reported on magnetic tape(s)	
1c Add 1a. and 1b. Enter total here.	
2 TOTAL COMPENSATION SUBJECT TO PA WITHHOLDING TAX	
3 PA INCOME TAX WITHHELD ▶	

FOR TAPE REPORTING

NUMBER OF TAPES	DENSITY:
TRACKS:	PARITY
ADDRESS TO WHICH TAPE(S) SHOULD BE RETURNED:	

Section II CORPORATE OFFICERS, PARTNERS OR PROPRIETOR
RESPONSIBLE FOR TAX RETURN INFORMATION

If preprinted, make necessary corrections. If blank, complete name(s) and SSN (s).

NAME: Joseph T. O'Neill
SOCIAL SECURITY NO.   897-04-1534
NAME:
SOCIAL SECURITY NO.

DO NOT SEND PAYMENT WITH THIS FORM.

Attach adding machine tape(s) or some acceptable listing of tax withheld as reported on accompanying paper W-2 form(s) to substantiate reported Pennsylvania Withholding Tax. This tape or listing applies only to paper W-2(s) **not** magnetic media reporting.

DATE	TELEPHONE ( )	SIGNATURE		TITLE

TRANSACTION NO. 41

9595 ☐ VOID ☐ CORRECTED

PAYER'S name, street address, city, state, and ZIP code	1 Rents $	OMB No. 1545-0115	**Miscellaneous Income**
	2 Royalties $	19--	
	3 Other income $		

PAYER'S Federal identification number	RECIPIENT'S identification number	4 Federal income tax withheld $	5 Fishing boat proceeds $	**Copy A**
RECIPIENT'S name		6 Medical and health care payments $	7 Nonemployee compensation $	**For Internal Revenue Service Center**
Street address (including apt. no.)		8 Substitute payments in lieu of dividends or interest $	9 Payer made direct sales of $5,000 or more of consumer products to a buyer (recipient) for resale ▶ ☐	**File with Form 1096.** For Paperwork Reduction Act Notice and instructions for completing this form,
City, state, and ZIP code		10 Crop insurance proceeds $	11 State income tax withheld $	see **Instructions for Forms 1099, 1098, 5498, and W-2G.**
Account number (optional)	2nd TIN Not. ☐	12 State/Payer's state number		

Form **1099-MISC**   Department of the Treasury - Internal Revenue Service

TRANSACTION NO. 42

Form **1096** Department of the Treasury Internal Revenue Service	**Annual Summary and Transmittal of U.S. Information Returns**	OMB No. 1545-0108 19--

A T T A C H I R S L A B E L H E R E

┌ FILER'S name

Street address (including room or suite number)

City, state, and ZIP code ┘

If you are not using a preprinted label, enter in box 1 or 2 below the identification number you used as the filer on the information returns being transmitted. Do not fill in both boxes 1 and 2.	Name of person to contact if the IRS needs more information Telephone number ( )	**For Official Use Only** ☐☐☐☐☐☐☐ ☐☐

1 Employer identification number	2 Social security number	3 Total number of forms	4 Federal income tax withheld $	5 Total amount reported with this Form 1096 $

Enter an "X" in only one box below to indicate the type of form being filed. | If this is your FINAL return, enter an "X" here . . ▶ ☐

W-2G 32	1098 81	1099-A 80	1099-B 79	1099-C 85	1099-DIV 91	1099-G 86	1099-INT 92	1099-MISC 95	1099-OID 96	1099-PATR 97	1099-R 98	1099-S 75	5498 28
☐	☐	☐	☐	☐	☐	☐	☐	☐	☐	☐	☐	☐	☐

Please return this entire page to the Internal Revenue Service. Photocopies are NOT acceptable.

Under penalties of perjury, I declare that I have examined this return and accompanying documents, and, to the best of my knowledge and belief, they are true, correct, and complete.

Signature ▶   Title ▶   Date ▶

Appendix

SOCIAL SECURITY BENEFITS

LEARNING OBJECTIVES

After studying this appendix, you should be able to:

1. Explain the factors used in computing the various kinds of social security benefits:

   a. Quarter of coverage
   b. Fully insured
   c. Currently insured
   d. Average monthly wage
   e. Primary insurance amount

2. Describe the different kinds of benefits provided under the social security system.

3. Describe the effect of working after retirement on social security benefits and taxation of benefits.

4. Identify the procedure to be followed in applying for social security benefits.

5. Explain the basic provisions of the three-part program of medical care for the aged and the needy.

This appendix covers the benefits related to the two programs of old-age, survivors and disability insurance, and health insurance for the aged and disabled. As the employees of a firm near retirement age, they may approach the payroll manager to find out what retirement benefits and hospital and medical benefits they are entitled to under social security. If workers become disabled or die, their families may turn to the payroll manager for information concerning their rights to disability or survivor benefits.

Social security benefits payable under the old-age, survivors, and disability program may be classified as:

1. Old-age or disability benefits paid to the worker.
2. Benefits for dependents of a retired or disabled worker.
3. Benefits for surviving family members of a deceased worker.
4. Lump-sum death benefits.

WHAT FACTORS ARE USED TO DETERMINE SOCIAL SECURITY BENEFITS?

Individuals and their families are eligible for most benefits if the person is "fully insured." If the person is only "currently insured," lump-sum benefits and certain survivor benefits are payable. To understand the method of computing the various benefits for individuals, their dependents, or their survivors requires knowledge of the following terms:

1. Quarter of coverage.
2. Fully insured.
3. Currently insured.
4. Primary insurance amount.
5. Average monthly wage.

Quarter of Coverage

A *quarter of coverage* is the minimum amount of wages or self-employment income with which individuals must be credited in a calendar quarter to receive credit toward being insured for that period. A calendar quarter is three consecutive months ending March 31, June 30, September 30, or December 31. Quarters of coverage determine whether *workers* (see Figure A–1) are fully insured, currently insured, or insured for disability benefits.

Fully Insured Individual

A *fully insured worker* needs between six and 40 quarters of coverage. The number of quarters needed depends on when the person reaches a specified age or dies. After earning 40 quarters of coverage (10 years), the worker is fully insured for life and does not need to be concerned about quarters of coverage.

Currently Insured Individual

Individuals are **currently insured** if they have at least six quarters of coverage during the 13-quarter period ending with (1) the quarter they died, or (2) the quarter in which they became entitled to old-age insurance benefits or disability benefits. The 13-quarter period does not have to be consecutive. Lump-sum and certain survivor benefits, not including retirement benefits, are payable if an individual is currently insured.

Wage-Earners	In 1995 workers receive one quarter of coverage, up to a maximum of four, for each $630 of earnings in the calendar year.
Self-Employed Persons	Net self-employment income must exceed $400 for the taxable year before any quarters can be credited with self-employment income. In 1995 a self-employed person is credited with one quarter of coverage for each calendar quarter in which $630 or more in self-employment income was allocated.
Farm Workers	Quarters of coverage are based on wages received during the calendar year, not during a calendar quarter. In 1995 farm workers receive one quarter of coverage, up to a maximum of four, for each $630 of earnings in the calendar year.

Figure A–1   *Classification of Workers*

Primary Insurance Amount

The **primary insurance amount** (PIA) is a person's monthly retirement or disability benefit and the base upon which monthly benefits of the worker's family and survivors are computed. Under the 1977 amendments to the Social Security Act, a formula determines the PIA of workers who reach 62, become disabled, or die. The PIA is determined from the worker's **average indexed monthly earnings**. **Indexing** adjusts the worker's average monthly earnings to reflect changes in wage levels up to the time of entitlement to benefits. Automatic increases in social security benefits are also made, based on the increase in the cost of living as measured by the Consumer Price Index.

WHAT BENEFITS ARE PROVIDED BY SOCIAL SECURITY?

Figure A–2 summarizes the kinds of benefits available and the qualifications needed by the insured worker or beneficiary to receive these benefits.

L E A R N I N G
O B J E C T I V E
2

Family Benefits

The monthly payments to members of a retired or a disabled worker's family and payments to the survivors of an insured worker are equal to a certain percentage of the worker's benefits, shown in Figure A–3.

Benefits for Aliens

If an alien is receiving benefits as a dependent or a survivor of an insured worker and has been outside the United States for six consecutive months, the benefits will be suspended. Exceptions exist for young children and beneficiaries who lived in the United States for at least five years and had a relationship with the worker which established eligibility for benefits. Benefits continue where international social security agreements are in force.

Old-Age or Disability Benefits	
Person to Receive Benefits	**Eligibility Requirements for Insured Individual**
Retired worker, age 62 or older.	Fully insured
Disabled worker (except one who is blind) under 65.	Fully insured and insured for disability
Benefits for Dependents of Retired or Disabled Workers	
Spouse, or divorced spouse, age 62 or older.	
Spouse, any age, if caring for child (except student age 18 or older) entitled to benefits.	
Unmarried child, grandchild, or great-grandchild if	Fully insured for old-age benefits or insured for disability benefits, whichever applies
a. under age 18 or	
b. under age 19 and a full-time elementary or secondary school student, or	
c. age 18 or older with a disability that began before age 22.	
Survivor Benefits	
Widow, widower, or divorced person, age 60 or older or age 50-59 and able to meet a special definition of disability.	
Widow, widower, or divorced parent of deceased worker's child, any age, caring for a young child entitled to benefits.	
Unmarried child, grandchild, or great-grandchild if child is	
a. under age 18	Either fully insured or currently insured
b. under age 19 and a full-time elementary or secondary school student, or	
c. age 18 or older with a disability that began before age 22.	
Dependent parents, 62 or older.	
Lump-Sum Death Payment	
Paid only, in priority to	
a. Worker's widow or widower living with worker at time of death	
b. Worker's widow or widower not living with but eligible on worker's earnings record, or	Either fully insured or currently insured
c. eligible surviving child.	

Figure A–2

Benefits for Prisoners

Persons confined in jail for a felony may not be paid benefits. Limited circumstances allow for benefits where the felon participates in an approved rehabilitation program. Benefits payable to a felon's spouse or children are not affected.

Benefits for the Self-Employed

Social security pays the same benefits to self-employed persons under the same conditions as wage earners and their dependents or survivors.

Benefits for Employees of Carriers

FICA exempts companies engaged as carriers and employees of carriers. The Railroad Retirement Tax Act sets up the provisions under which employees of

Relationship of Family Member to Worker	Percentage of Worker's Benefits to be Received
Wife, husband, divorced wife or husband	50% while worker is alive.
Child	50% while worker is alive; 75% if worker is dead.
Widow, widower or surviving divorced spouse	100% if full retirement age; 75% if caring for worker's child.
Dependent grandchild	50% if worker is alive; 75% if worker is dead; child's parents must be dead or disabled.
Dependent parent who outlives the worker	82½%; if both parents qualify, a total of 150% is received.

Figure A–3

carriers subject to the Interstate Commerce Act may retire and become eligible for annuities (benefits).

Special Minimum Benefit

Special provision is made for persons who have worked in jobs covered by social security for many years but at rather low earnings levels. These workers qualify for a special benefit higher than that available to them under the regular benefit computations. The special benefits payable under these provisions will be automatically adjusted for cost-of-living increases.

WHAT ARE REDUCED BENEFITS?

The full retirement age will be increased, starting in the year 2000, in gradual steps until it reaches age 67, and affects people born in 1938 and later. Figure A–4 shows the age to receive full social security benefits.

If a worker takes early retirement at age 62 (the earliest age to qualify), the benefits will be permanently reduced approximately 20%, based on the number of months the individual will receive checks before reaching full retirement age. If retirement starts at age 63, the reduction is about 13½%; at age 64 it is about 6⅔%. If you were born after 1937, you can still take your retirement benefits at age 62, but the reduction will be greater than people currently retiring. Eligible widows or widowers may receive reduced benefits as early as age 60. If

Figure A–4

Year of Birth	Full Retirement Age
1937 or earlier	65
1938	65 and 2 months
1939	65 and 4 months
1940	65 and 6 months
1941	65 and 8 months
1942	65 and 10 months
1943-1954	66
1955	66 and 2 months
1956	66 and 4 months
1957	66 and 6 months
1958	66 and 8 months
1959	66 and 10 months
1960 or later	67

the worker at any time received a reduced benefit, the widow or widower may not receive more than the greater of:

a. a benefit equal to the amount the worker would be getting if alive, or
b. 82.5% of the worker's PIA.

For widows or widowers whose spouse was not receiving a reduced benefit, the age-60 benefit will be 71.5% of the worker's PIA. If the widow or widower takes the benefit at age 62, it will be 82.9% of the worker's PIA. Severely disabled widows or widowers and surviving divorced spouses may receive reduced benefits at age 50, equal to 71.5% of the worker's unreduced benefit.

In 1945, 42 workers paid social security taxes for every beneficiary; today the ratio is about 3 to 1.

HOW DOES WORKING AFTER RETIREMENT AFFECT SOCIAL SECURITY BENEFITS ?

Individuals who continue to work after retirement must consider two implications on their social security benefits:

1. Reduced social security benefits.
2. Paying income tax on social security benefits.

Reduced Social Security Benefits

Individuals can continue to work and still receive retirement benefits if the earnings are under certain limits. These limits increase each year as average wages increase. The Social Security Administration provides a fact sheet, *How Work Affects Your Social Security Benefits (Pub. 05-10069),* that specifies the current amounts that may be earned without reducing benefits. For 1995, the following limits apply:

Under 65	$8,160
65 - 69	$11,280
70 and over	Unlimited

If earnings exceed the specified limit, some or all of the benefits will be offset by the earnings as summarized in Figure A–5.

Figure A–5 *Reduced Social Security Benefits*

If you are under 65	$1 in benefits is deducted for each $2 in earnings above the limit.
If you are 65-69	$1 in benefits is deducted for each $3 in earnings above the limit.
If you are 70	Earnings in or after the month you reach 70 will not affect benefits.

Under a special rule, a retired worker can receive full benefits for any month they are "retired," regardless of their yearly earnings. In the first year of retirement, benefits will not be lost for any month in which earnings are less than $680 (under 65) and $940 (age 65 through 69).

Taxable Benefits

A portion of a worker's social security benefits is included in taxable income for federal income tax purposes. The amount of benefits taxable is determined by a formula that relates to the worker's adjusted gross income (AGI). If income is more than the base amount, as much as 50% of social security benefits may be taxable. If income exceeds the adjusted base amount, as much as 85% of social security benefits may be taxable. (See Figure A–6). If an individual receives only social security benefits as income, these benefits are generally not taxable.

Figure A-6

Filing Status	Base Amount	Adjusted Base Amount
Married, filing jointly	$32,000	$44,000
Married, filing separately, living together anytime during the year	-0-	-0-
Married, filing separately, not living together	$25,000	$34,000
Single, head of household, qualified survivor	$25,000	$34,000

HOW DO YOU APPLY FOR SOCIAL SECURITY BENEFITS?

Workers can apply for social security benefits by telephone or by going to any Social Security office. Depending on the circumstances, documents that may be needed include:

L E A R N I N G
O B J E C T I V E
4

1. Social Security Number (SSN)
2. Birth Certificate
3. W-2 Forms or Self-Employment tax return for last year
4. Military Discharge Papers
5. Spouse's Birth Certificate and Social Security Number
6. Children's Birth Certificates and Social Security Numbers

Special application forms may be obtained from the nearest district office of the Social Security Administration. Applicants can receive assistance in preparing the forms, including notary services, at no charge.

Proof of Age

Applicants for benefits may be required to file a proof of age showing the date of birth. Acceptable records may include:

1. Public records of birth (birth certificate).
2. Church records of birth or baptism established or recorded before the age of 5.
3. Census Bureau notification of registration of birth.
4. Hospital birth record or certificate.
5. Foreign records of birth.
6. Physician's or midwife's birth record.
7. Certification, on approved form, of Bible or other family record.
8. Naturalization records.
9. Immigration papers.
10. Military records.
11. Passports.
12. School records.
13. Vaccination records.
14. Insurance policy.

15. Labor union or fraternal organization records.
16. Marriage records.
17. Other evidence of probative value, such as employment records and voting records.

Statement of Employer

The individual's wage record kept by the Social Security Administration may be several months in arrears. Therefore, employers may be requested to complete a **Statement of Employer, Form SSA-7011-F4** in order to bring an individual's wage record up-to-date. Employees may periodically check their social security accounts, using **Form SSA-7004-SM.**

WHAT IS MEDICARE?

LEARNING OBJECTIVE 5

Medicare is a three-part health insurance plan for people 65 or older. The first program, sometimes called Basic Medicare, Part A Medicare, or *the hospital insurance (HI) plan,* provides protections against the cost of certain hospital and related services. The second program, *the supplementary medical insurance benefits,* often referred to as supplementary, voluntary supplementary Medicare, the medical insurance program, or Part B Medicare, covers the cost of doctors' services and other items not covered under the basic plan. Monthly premiums are matched with contributions by the federal government to finance the program. The third program, called *Medicaid,* provides medical assistance to aged and needy persons by means of a joint federal-state program.

KEY TERMS

Average indexed monthly earnings
Currently insured
Fully insured
Hospital Insurance (HI) Plan
Indexing

Medicaid
Primary insurance amount (PIA)
Quarter of coverage
Social security benefits
Supplementary medical insurance plan

Appendix

COMPUTERIZED PAYROLL ACCOUNTING

LEARNING OBJECTIVES

1. Define the key terms associated with computerized payroll systems.

2. Operate the computer and payroll software using a keyboard or a mouse.

3. Perform system start-up procedures.

4. Add, change, and delete employees from the payroll.

5. Enter and correct payroll transactions.

6. Generate payroll and employer's payroll taxes journal entries.

7. Enter, correct, and find journal entries.

8. Display and/or print payroll reports.

9. Access Help information.

INTRODUCTION

Payroll is an application which lends itself well to the computer because of its repetitive procedures and calculations. Computerized payroll systems perform the same basic functions as those performed manually by payroll clerks. The important differences are the computer's speed, accuracy, reliability, and ability to easily generate reports.

In a computerized payroll system, the computer stores data for each employee such as the employee's name, address, social security number (SSN), marital status, number of withholding allowances, pay rate, and voluntary deductions. At the end of each pay period, the operator enters all payroll transaction data, such as regular and overtime hours for each employee, into the computer. The computer calculates all withholding taxes and other deductions and accumulates and updates the earnings and withholdings.

Before entering data for a new payroll period, the payroll transaction data from the previous payroll must be cleared. After payroll transactions for the new payroll period have been entered, a payroll report may be displayed to verify the information. While processing this report, the computer calculates the totals for salary expense, payroll taxes expense, and withholding liabilities (these totals appear in general journal format at the end of the payroll report). Next, these journal entries are integrated into the general ledger and posted. After the payroll report is displayed and verified for accuracy, and the journal entries posted, the journal report and general ledger reports are printed. At the end of the quarter, and at the end of the year, the taxable earnings report is displayed, from which the appropriate reports (i.e. quarterly reports and W-2 statements) may be prepared.

SOFTWARE PROGRAM OVERVIEW

The software you will be using makes use of a standard user interface that utilizes pull-down menus, movable overlapping windows, mouse support, list windows, and help windows. This standard interface resembles the interface used in many other software applications. Most of the techniques you will learn can be applied to many other software packages.

Using a Mouse

The Computerized Payroll Accounting software works with a mouse. If you have a mouse on your computer, the pointer will be displayed on your screen as a small rectangle (▮) or arrow (↗). The pointer moves on the screen as you move the mouse. The following functions can be performed with a mouse:

Point	Move the pointer to a specific location on the screen.
Click	Quickly press and release the left mouse button.
Drag	Press and hold down the left mouse button and move the mouse.
Point and Click.	Point to an object on the screen and click the mouse button ("clicking on the object"). For example, if directed to "click on" the Ok button, you should point to the Ok button and click the left mouse button.

Pull-Down Menus

One of the ways you can communicate with the computer is with a menu. A **Menu** is a list of commands. Figure B–1 shows the parts of the Computerized Payroll Accounting menu system.

- **Menu Bar.** The **Menu Bar** is the top line of the screen showing the menus available.

- **Menu Name.** Each of the words on the Menu Bar is the name of one of the pull down menus. If a menu name is "dimmed," it is not available.

- **Pull-Down Menu.** A Pull-Down Menu is a list of commands that appears immediately below the selected menu.

- **Menu Command.** The menu commands are the menu items such as New and Open Data File shown in the File menu in Figure B–1. They are referred to as commands because they command the computer to perform a particular action.

- **Quick Keys.** Each menu name and each menu command has a quick key associated with it. The quick keys appear on the screen either as a bright or underlined letter (within the menu or command name). The quick keys allow for easy menu or menu command selection.

- **Hot Keys.** Some menu options can be selected without pulling down a menu by simply pressing a key or a combination of keys. Frequently used menu commands (such as Print) can be quickly selected with Hot Keys. If a menu command has a Hot Key, it will be shown on the pull-down menu.

   Figure B–2 describes keyboard keys that you will find useful when working with the pull-down menus.

Selecting and Choosing Menus and Menu Commands

With the Computerized Payroll Accounting software, the terms **select** and **choose** have different meanings. When menus on the menu bar or menu commands are selected, they are highlighted. When a highlighted (or selected)

Figure B–1 *Pull-Down Menus*

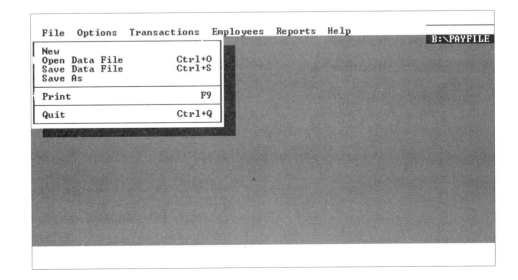

Key	Function
Alt	Use this key to transfer control to the Menu Bar to select a pull-down menu.
Esc	Use this key to release control from the Menu Bar or to remove any pull-down menu.
Down Arrow	Use this key to pull down a menu. Each time this key is pressed while a menu is pulled down, the highlight bar will move down to the next menu command. If the highlight bar is on the last command, it will wrap around to the first command.
Up Arrow	Use this key to move the highlight bar up to the previous command within a pull-down menu.
Right Arrow	This key selects the next menu.
Left Arrow	This key selects the previous menu.
Enter	Use this key to choose the currently highlighted menu or menu command.

Figure B–2   *Keys Used with Pull-Down Menus*

menu or command is chosen, the software will take the appropriate action. Dimmed commands are not available at the current time (you may need to select another command before using a dimmed command).

Using the Keyboard to Pull Down a Menu and Choose a Menu Command

1. **Press the Alt key.**
    When the Alt key is pressed, the first menu on the menu bar (File) is selected.
2. **Press the Left or Right Arrow key to select a menu.**
    As you move through the menus with the left and right arrow keys, any menus that are inactive (dimmed) are skipped.
3. **Press Enter to choose the selected menu.**
    The chosen menu will appear with the first menu command highlighted. If the File menu were chosen, the screen would appear as shown in Figure B–1.
4. Use the Up and Down Arrow keys to select the menu command, then press Enter to choose the command.
    Hint: If the menu command has a highlighted or underlined letter, you can choose a menu command by typing the letter that is highlighted or underlined. For example, to choose Open Data File, you would type **O**. These highlighted letters are called *Quick Keys* because they allow you to quickly select menu commands with the keyboard.

Using a Mouse to Pull Down a Menu and Choose a Menu Command

1. **Pull down the menu by pointing to the name of the menu on the menu bar and clicking the left mouse button.**
2. **Point to the menu command and click the left mouse button.**
    Hint: To move directly to a menu item, you can point to the menu name and drag the highlight bar down the menu until the menu command is highlighted, and then release the mouse button.

WINDOWS

You interact with the computer to perform payroll processing procedures through windows. A *window* is a rectangular area of the screen in which the software is communicating with the user. Often the screen contains only one window. At times, two or more overlapping windows appear on the screen. However, only one window is active at a time. The Computerized Payroll Accounting software uses windows to permit entry of data, to provide lists from which data may be selected, to present dialog messages, and to display reports.

Entering Data

As you enter data into the computer from the computer's keyboard, the data is displayed in a window. This process is called *data entry.* Figure B–3 shows the parts of a window used to key data.

Figure B–3   *Data Entry Window*

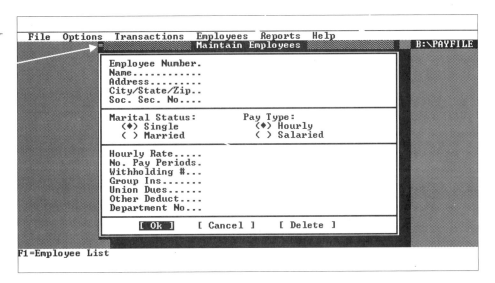

- **Window Title.** The title of the window.

- **Close Button.** The equal sign (=) in the upper left hand corner of the screen is the close button. Clicking on the close button with the mouse tells the computer to close the window. The window can be closed from the keyboard by pressing the Esc key.

- **Title Bar.** Any window with a wide title bar, like the one shown, can be moved with the mouse. To move a window, point to the title bar with the mouse, then click-and-drag the window where desired. As the window is dragged, an outlined image of the window follows your movements. When the mouse button is released, the window moves to where the outlined image was. The window will remain in its new location during your computer session and until the software is restarted. The contents of a window underneath a movable window may be viewed by clicking-and-holding the mouse button down while the mouse is pointing to the title bar.

- **Data Fields.** You use data fields to enter data or change (edit) previously entered data.

- **Option Buttons.** You can select only one option at a time. The selected option contains a diamond shaped character in parentheses (♦).

- **Command Buttons.** A command button initiates an immediate action. Choosing a command button is referred to as "pushing" the button.

Command buttons are located along the bottom of the windows. A command button is pushed by clicking on it with the mouse or by tabbing to it with the Tab key and pressing Enter. The default command button is always highlighted (selected). The default command button can be pushed from anywhere in the window by pressing Ctrl-Enter.

Data fields and buttons should be entered or selected in the normal tab sequence. The *tab sequence* is the logical sequence that the computer is expecting each data field and/or button to be entered. It is usually left-to-right and top-to-bottom. The Tab key moves the cursor to the next data field or button in the tab sequence. The Shift-Tab key moves the cursor to the previous data field or button in the tab sequence. Figure B–4 describes keys that you will find useful when working with data entry windows.

Figure B–4 *Keys Used with Data Entry Windows*

Key	Function
Tab	Use this key to move the cursor to the next data field or button in the tab sequence.
Shift-Tab	Strike the Tab key while holding down the Shift key to move the cursor backward to the previous data field or button in the tab sequence.
Enter	If the cursor is positioned to a command button, the command button will be executed. If the cursor is positioned to an option button, that option will be selected and the cursor will move to the next data field or button in the tab sequence. If the cursor is in a data field, the data will be accepted and the cursor will move to the next data field or button in the tab sequence.
Ctrl-Enter	Strike the Enter key while holding down the Ctrl key to select the action of the default (highlighted) command button regardless of the cursor location.
Home	Use the Home key to move the cursor to the first data field or button that appears in the data entry window.
Ctrl–Home	Strike the Home key while holding down the Ctrl key to move the cursor to the beginning of the **current data field.**
End	Use the End key to move the cursor to the last command button on the bottom (end) of the data entry window.
Ctrl-End	Strike the End key while holding down the Ctrl key to move the cursor to the end of the **current data field.**
Down Arrow	Use this key ($\downarrow$) to move down to the next data field or button. If the cursor is positioned to one of the command buttons at the bottom of the window, it will wrap around to the first data field/button.
Up Arrow	Use this key ($\uparrow$) to move up to the previous data field or button. If the cursor is located in the first data field/button, it will wrap around to the last button.
Right Arrow	Use this key ($\rightarrow$) to move one position to the right within the current data field.
Left Arrow	Use this key ($\leftarrow$) to move one position to the left within the current data field.
Insert	Use this key to toggle between insert and overstrike mode. When a data field is selected, it always defaults to the insert mode. When in insert mode, the cursor is displayed as a blinking underscore (_). When in overstrike mode, the cursor appears as a blinking square (■).
Backspace	Within a data field, use this key to erase the character immediately to the left of the cursor.
Delete	Within a data field, use this key to erase the character at the current cursor position.
Space Bar	Use this key to select the button the cursor is currently positioned on.
Esc	Use this key to close and remove the current window from the display screen.

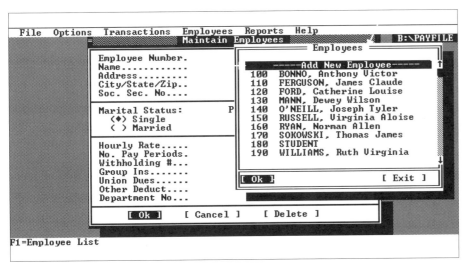

Figure B–5   *List Window*

Lists

A List window allows you to search and select items from lists. List windows are typically displayed on top of windows used to enter data. Figure B–5 shows an employee list window displayed on top of the Employees window.

When a list window is opened, no other menu commands can be chosen until the list window has been dismissed.

The *highlight bar* identifies the selected item in a list window. When a list window appears, the first item in the list is selected. The *scroll bar* is a bar on the right side of the list window that represents the range of items in the list window and is used in conjunction with the scroll box to view items that exist beyond the borders of the window. The *scroll box* indicates the relative position of the selected item within the range of items in the list.

Using the Keyboard to Select and Choose Employees from the List Window

1. Use the Up Arrow, Down Arrow, Page Up, Page Down, Home, and End keys to select the desired item from the list.
2. Press Enter to choose the selected item, or press Esc to cancel the list window.
   When an employee is chosen, the list window is closed and the employee's data is inserted into the data entry window.

Using a Mouse to Select and Choose Employees from the List Window

1. Use the mouse operations shown in Figure B–6 to select the desired employee.
2. Choose the selected employee by clicking on the Ok command button (click on the Exit command button to exit without choosing an employee).

Dialog Boxes

Dialog boxes provide informational and error messages. A decision from the user may be required. When a dialog box appears, one of the command buttons must be chosen before other menu commands can be selected. Figure B–7 shows the dialog box that will appear if the payroll system is ended before data has been saved.

Action	Mouse Operations
Scroll Up One Line	Click on the up arrow (↑) located at the top of the scroll bar to scroll upward (you may also click on the line immediately above the first item in the list window).
Scroll Down One Line	Click on the down arrow (↓) located at the bottom of the scroll bar to scroll downward (you may also click on the line immediately below the last item in the list window).
Scroll to Top	Click on the top of the scroll bar just below the up arrow.
Scroll to Bottom	Click on the bottom of the scroll bar just above the down arrow.
Scroll Anywhere	Click on the scroll bar at the relative position. For example, to scroll to the middle of the list, click on the middle of the scroll bar.

Figure B–6   *Mouse Operations*

Using the Keyboard to Select and Choose Command Buttons from a Dialog Box

1. **Use the Right and Left Arrow keys or the Tab and Shift-Tab keys to select the desired command button.**
2. **Press Enter to choose the selected (highlighted) command button.**

   If you have a mouse, click on the desired command button.

Reports

When a command is chosen from the Report menu or one of the Help commands is chosen, the corresponding information is displayed in a window so that it can be viewed and/or printed on an attached printer.

   Some reports have a **Selection Options** dialog window. You can restrict the data that appears on the report. For example, if the range of employees is 100 to

Figure B–7   *Dialog Window*

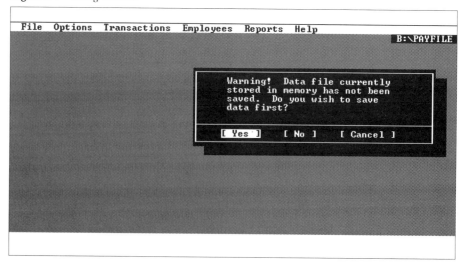

150, only employees with employee numbers from 100 through 150 will be printed.

After pushing the Ok command button, the selected report will appear in the scrollable Window as illustrated in Figure B–8. The report can be printed on an attached printer by either pulling down the File menu and choosing the Print command or by pressing the F9 key (the Hot Key for the Print command).

Figure B–8   *Report Window*

Using the Keyboard to Scroll Data in a Window

1.   **Use the Up Arrow, Down Arrow, Page Up, Page Down, Home, and End keys to view the data in the report window.**
2.   **Press Esc to close the window.**

Using a Mouse to Scroll Data in a Window

1.   **Use the mouse operations described in Figure B–6 to view the report.**
2.   **Close the window by clicking on the equal sign (=) in the upper left corner of the window.**

Printing the Contents of a Window

At any time while a report is displayed in a window, the contents of the window can be printed by pulling down the File menu and selecting the Print command. As a short cut, you can simply press the F9 function key. When the Print menu command is chosen, the Print Options data entry window shown in Figure B–9 will appear.

Figure B–10 describes each of the buttons and data fields on the Print Options data entry window.

START-UP PROCEDURES

To bring up the Computerized Payroll Accounting software, you must load a program called **PAYROLL.** The start-up procedure varies considerably, depending on the type of computer system you use. The procedure is different for

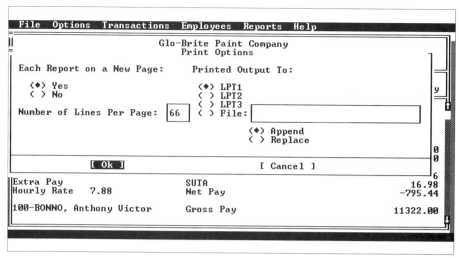

Figure B–9 *Print Options*

(1) a floppy disk system, (2) a hard disk system, (3) a workstation on a network, or (4) a hard disk system with a graphics user interface, such as Microsoft Windows[1] or IBM's OS/2.[2] Whatever the environment, the start-up is quite simple.

Figure B–10 *Data Fields and Buttons for Print Options Data Entry Window*

Button/Data Field	Explanation
Each Report on a New Page	If this option button is set to Yes, each report will be printed on a new page. If this button is set to No, the computer will space down several lines between reports, thus conserving paper.
Number of Lines per Page	This number represents the number of print lines that will fit on each page of paper. This option is necessary for a printer that feeds individual sheets of paper.
Printed Output to	If your computer has several printers attached, this option allows you to direct the output to a specific printer. To direct the report to a file, you must: (1) key the file name of the disk file that is to receive the output and (2) set the option buttons to indicate whether the output is to be added to the end of an existing file (Append) or a new file created (Replace). There are many uses for a file containing a printed report. For example, it could be printed later with the DOS Print command, or it could be merged into a word-processing document.
Ok	The Ok command button directs the computer to print the report. Once the report begins printing, it may be stopped by pressing the Esc key.
Cancel	The Cancel command button directs the computer to dismiss the Print Options data entry window and return to the Report Window.

---

[1] Microsoft and Windows are registered trademarks of Microsoft Corporation. Any reference to Microsoft or Windows refers to this footnote.

[2] IBM and OS/2 are registered trademarks of IBM Corporation. Any reference to IBM or OS/2 refers to this footnote.

Floppy Disk Based System Start-Up

1. At the Dos prompt (DOS version 2.0 or higher), set the default drive to the drive containing the Computerized Payroll Accounting software. For example, if you have the Computerized Payroll Accounting **program disk in Drive A, you would key "A:" (without the quotation marks). A>** will appear on your screen.
2. Key PAYROLL and press the Enter key.
3. After the program loads, a copyright window will appear. As indicated by the message at the bottom of the window: if the display is difficult to read, press the Ctrl+D keys to cause the computer to display a window that will permit you to force the computer to display its output as monochrome.

   If the computer you are using has a color graphics board, strike the Enter key to accept the Color option. (If using a mouse, click on the Color button.) If the computer you are using has a color graphics adapter board with a monochrome monitor, strike the Tab key to activate the MonoChrome button, then strike Enter. (If using a mouse, click on the MonoChrome button.)
4. From the Copyright window, strike the Esc key (if using a mouse, click on the Close button).
5. When the Menu Bar appears on an empty display screen, the Computerized Payroll Accounting software is ready to use.

Hard Disk Based System Start-Up

1. From the C> prompt (assuming your hard disk is Drive C), set the default drive and directory to the drive and directory containing the Computerized Payroll Accounting software.

   Hint: For example, if the software is stored on drive C in a directory called PAYACCT, you would:

   a. Key "C:" (without quotes) to set the default drive to Drive C.
   b. At the C> prompt, key "CD \PAYACCT" (without quotes) to set the default directory to PAYACCT.

2. Key PAYROLL and press the Enter key.
3. When the copyright window appears, follow the procedure described above, beginning with step number 3.

Network or Graphic User Interface

1. Because of the large number of networks available and because of the flexible program selection methods of the graphic user interfaces, it is not possible to provide step-by-step procedures for start-up. Your instructor will provide you with the necessary start-up procedures.
2. After start-up is completed, the copyright window will appear. Follow the procedure described above, beginning with step number 3.

OPERATING PROCEDURES

The payroll operating procedures consist of loading a payroll data file, preparing a new payroll, keying employee maintenance (additions, changes, and deletions), keying payroll transactions, and generating payroll reports and journal entries. At the end of the quarter and at the end of the year, the appropriate quarterly and yearly reports may be prepared from the information contained in the Taxable Earnings and general ledger reports.

File Menu

The pull-down File menu, shown in Figure B–11, consists of commands that handle all the Computerized Payroll Accounting input and output operations. Each of these commands are described below.

Figure B–11   *File Menu*

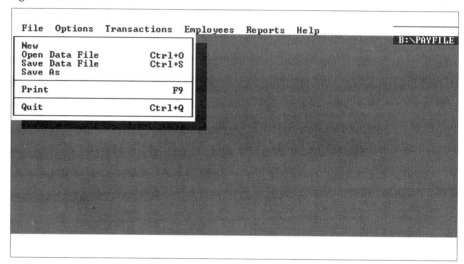

New. This menu command erases any existing data in the computer's memory and establishes empty payroll system files. The New menu command does **not** remove any data from disk.

Open Data File. Before stored data can be processed, it must be loaded from disk into the computer's memory with the Open Data File menu command.

1. **Choose the Open Data File menu command from the File menu.**
    The Open Data File data entry window will appear. If you have previously entered a Path and File name during this session, they will appear in the Path and File data fields. If not, the Path field will default to the current path and the File field will be blank.
2. **Key the path name to the drive and directory that contains the data file you wish to load.**
    If you are loading a template file (a file provided with the software), key the path to the drive and directory containing the template files (usually the same drive and directory containing the payroll software). If you are loading a previously saved data file, key the path to the drive and directory containing your data files.
    The path used depends on the configuration of your computer system and the location of the template files and data files.
3. **Key the file name you wish to load.**
    To view a list of files currently stored in the designated path, push the Directory button by clicking on it with the mouse or pressing the END key to move the cursor to the Directory button and press Enter.
4. **To load the file, push the Ok command button by clicking on it with the mouse or pressing Ctrl+Enter.**

Save Data File. The Save Data File command saves your data to disk so that you can continue a problem in a later session. The data will be saved to a file on disk with the path and filename currently displayed near the upper right corner of the screen.

1. **Choose the Save Data File command from the File menu.**
   Hint: Before you use the Save Data File command, check the current file name in the upper right corner of the screen to make certain you want to save with this path and name. If you wish to save your data with a path or filename different from the current path and file, use the Save As command.

Save As. The Save As command is the same as the Save Data File command except you save your data with a path and/or filename different from the path and filename shown in the upper right corner of the screen. This menu command is useful for making a *backup,* or copy of a data file. For example, you may want a backup of your data file before preparing for a new payroll period, or before clearing quarterly and yearly accumulators. To make a backup copy, load the data file you wish to backup and use the Save As command to save it with a different name.

1. **Choose the Save As menu command.**
2. **Key the path and file name under which you would like the data file saved.**
3. **Push the Ok button.**

Print. The purpose of the Print menu command is to print the report displayed in the Report Window. This process was described earlier under the Report Window section.

Quit. The Quit menu command is used to exit the accounting software. When the Quit command is chosen, the computer checks to see if the current data in its memory has been saved. If not, a dialog window will appear asking if you wish to save your data to disk.

Options Menu

The Options pull-down menu, shown in Figure B–12, contains commands that enable the user to specify general information about the company and computer problem to be solved. When the Options pull-down menu is selected from the Menu bar, the commands described in the following material will become available for execution.

Figure B–12   *Options Menu*

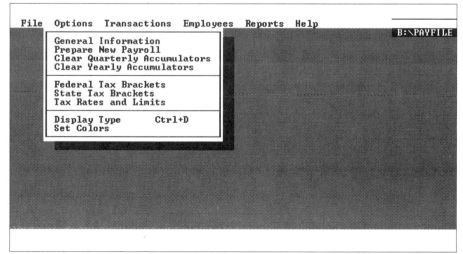

General Information Window. The purpose of the General Information window is to provide information to the payroll software for reference during execution. You are required to supply the Run Date (usually the pay-period date), your name, company name, and problem name. This information will be listed on each of your computer-generated reports.

1. **Choose the General Information command from the Options menu.**
   The General Information Window shown in Figure B–13 will appear.

Figure B–13 *General Information Window*

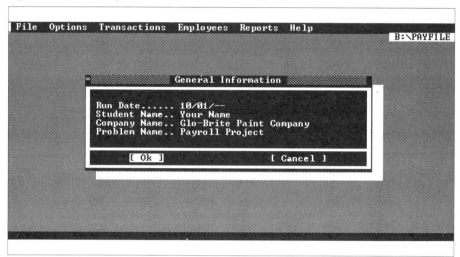

2. **Enter pay-period date in the Run Date field and your name in the Student Name field.**
   Note: The Company Name and Problem Name were entered when the data for this problem was created and stored to disk.
3. **Push the Ok button.**

Prepare New Payroll. The purpose of the Prepare New Payroll command is to erase the previous pay-period transactions data prior to keying the current pay-period data. You can correct the payroll transactions and reprint the payroll reports at any time until the Prepare New Payroll command is chosen to begin the next payroll period. If you do not select the Prepare New Payroll command before entering transactions for a new period, the computer assumes that you are correcting the transactions from the previous pay period rather than entering transactions for a new period. You must select Prepare New Payroll option before entering the current period's transactions.

1. **Choose Prepare New Payroll from the Options menu.**
2. **When the dialog window appears, push the Ok button.**

Clear Quarterly Accumulators. After printing and verifying the quarterly report and before processing the first payroll of the new quarter, you must instruct the computer to reset the quarterly accumulators to zero so that the next quarter's totals can be accumulated. When the Clear Quarterly Accumulators command is chosen, the current payroll data is also cleared.

1. **Choose Clear Quarterly Accumulators from the Options menu.**
2. **When the dialog window appears, push the Ok button.**

Clear Yearly Accumulators. After the W-2 statements are run and before the first payroll of the new year is run, the yearly accumulators must be reset to zero so that the totals for the next year can be accumulated. The Clear Yearly Accumulators option also clears the quarterly accumulators and the current payroll data.

1. **Choose Clear Yearly Accumulators from the Options menu.**
2. **When the dialog window appears, push the Ok button.**

Federal Tax Brackets, State Tax Brackets, Tax Rates and Limits. The Federal Tax Brackets command may be used to update the federal withholdings by referring to IRS Circular E (Employer's Tax Guide, Table 7 (Annual Payroll). The State Tax Brackets command may be used to change the state taxable rate percentage (and limit if necessary). The Tax Rates and Limits command may be used to update various tax rates, upper limits, and allowance amounts required by the software to calculate employee and employer payroll taxes.

You will not be required to use these commands to complete the payroll processing tasks in the student project. You should not change these rates when working the payroll problems. If the rates or percentages are changed, the calculated withholding amounts will no longer match the solutions provided to your instructor.

Display Type. The software checks the video card in your computer to determine whether you are using a monochrome or color monitor. In some cases monochrome monitors with graphics capability are mistakenly identified by the software as color monitors. The result is a "fuzzy" display that is difficult to read. If this occurs, you can choose the Set Display Type menu command and force the correct display type. When this command is selected, the Select Display type window will appear. Choose the display type desired by pushing either the "Color" or "Monochrome" command buttons.

If the software recognizes that you are using a computer with a monochrome monitor, or the Display Type has been set to monochrome, the Set Colors command will be dimmed and unavailable.

Set Colors. If you are using a color monitor, you may modify the colors that appear on the screen with the Set Colors Dialog window. Once set, color settings will remain in effect during your computer session and will be saved to disk along with your data.

1. **Push the Change button to change the colors.**
   A new, sample color combination will be displayed in the window boxes.
2. **Continue pushing the Change button until the color combination that you prefer appears.**
3. **Push the Ok button to record your selection.**

Transactions Menu

The pull-down Transactions menu, shown in Figure B–14, provides an Opening Balances command that may be used to enter the opening balance data when establishing a computerized payroll system, and a Payroll Transactions command that is used to enter payroll transaction data. When the Transactions menu is selected from the menu bar, the menu items described in this section will become available for execution.

Opening Balances. The Opening Balances command enables the user to enter, correct, and delete historical payroll data (quarter-to-date and year-to-date earnings and withholdings) that may be keyed into the computer in order to set up a new computerized payroll system. You will not be required to use this command to complete the project in this text.

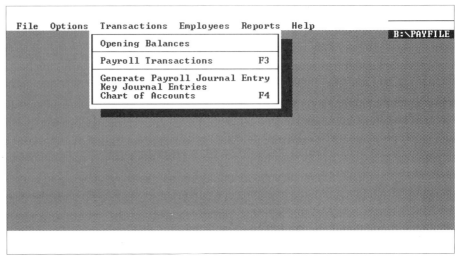

Figure B-14 *Transactions Menu*

Payroll Transactions. The purpose of the Payroll Transactions data entry window is to identify the employees to be paid for the current pay period, to key the hours worked for hourly employees, and to enter any extra pay. After a transaction is entered, the computer performs the payroll calculations and updates the employee's record. The transaction remains in memory until the computer is directed to prepare a new payroll.

1. **Choose the Payroll Transactions command from the Transactions menu.**
    When the Payroll Transactions command is chosen from the Transactions menu, the dialog window shown in Figure B–15 will appear.
2. **Push the Yes button to instruct the computer to deduct group insurance from the employees' pay for the current pay-period, or push the No button to instruct the computer not to deduct group insurance.**
    Note: The amount of group insurance that is deducted from each employee's pay check is stored by the computer in the employee's record. Figure B–16.

Figure B-15 *Deduct Group Insurance Dialog Window*

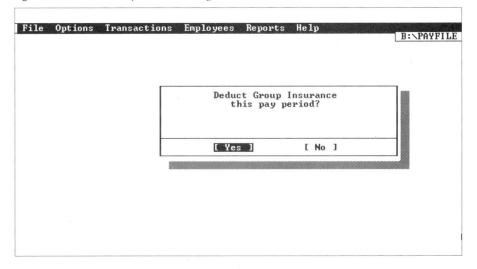

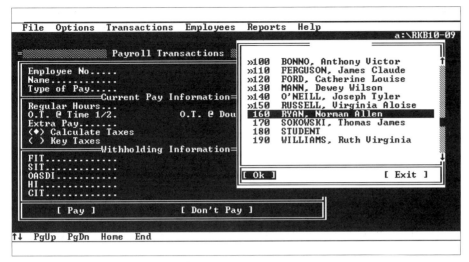

Figure B–16   *Payroll Transactions Window*

When the Deduct Group Insurance dialog window is dismissed, the Payroll Transactions window with an employee list window will appear, as shown in Figure B–16.

Notice: Employee numbers 100 through 150 have the symbol >> preceding their employee numbers in the list window. This indicates that payroll transaction data has already been entered and these employees are to be paid during the current pay-period.

Also note: After you have chosen the employee to pay, you may add a new employee to the payroll while keying payroll transactions by pressing the F2 hot key (or by pulling down the Employees menu and choosing the Maintain Employees command). The next section under the Employees menu covers the procedure to add a new employee.

3. **Choose the employee to be paid from the employee list window.**

   The list window will be dismissed and the Employee No., Name, and Type of Pay will be displayed as shown in Figure B–17.

   Note: To erase transaction data already entered and remove an employee from the pay status, select the employee, then push the Don't Pay button.

Figure B–17   *Payroll Transactions*

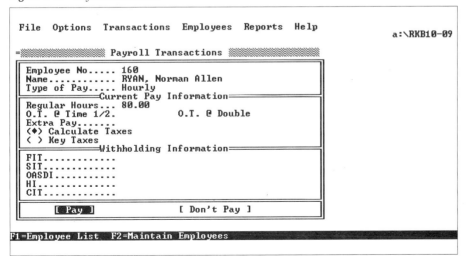

4. **Key the Current Pay Information. If the employee is paid Hourly, key the Regular and Overtime hours. (Key the overtime hours in the @ Time 1/2 field if you want the computer to calculate the overtime amount at one and one-half times the hourly rate. Key the overtime hours in the @ Double field if you want the computer to calculate the overtime amount at double the hourly rate.) If the employee is to be paid additional pay, key the Extra Pay.**

Leave the option button set to Calculate Taxes unless you wish to key the withholding tax information rather than have the computer calculate taxes.

5. **Push the Pay button.**

If you must change employee data that affects payroll calculations (marital status, pay type, pay rate, pay-periods per year, withholding allowances, or voluntary deductions), use this procedure: (1) select the employee from the list window, (2) eliminate the employee from being paid by pushing the Don't Pay button, (3) correct the employee's data using the Maintain Employees option, then (4) reenter the employee's payroll transaction data so the computer can recalculate the payroll information. Also, if the payroll journal entries have been generated and posted to the general ledger, you must perform this task again (see the Generate Payroll Journal Entry option that follows), and the computer will replace the incorrect entries.

Generate Payroll Journal Entry

The Generate Payroll Journal entry command automatically generates the current pay-period's payroll and employer's payroll taxes journal entries and posts them to the general ledger. The payroll journal entry includes: net amount of the total payroll transferred from cash to payroll cash, salaries, wages, taxes withheld, group insurance premiums collected, union dues withheld, and net amount paid. The payroll taxes journal entry includes: employer's payroll taxes and the liabilities created.

Journal entries generated by this command are corrected by first correcting whatever is wrong with the payroll that made the journal entries wrong. Then, regenerating the payroll journal entries. Once a new payroll period is started by choosing the Prepare New Payroll command, corrections can no longer be made and that payroll can no longer be run. At this point, you must revert to a backup.

Key Journal Entries

You use the General Journal window to key journal entries not automatically generated by the computerized payroll system (i.e. deposits of FICA taxes and federal income taxes, deposits with the state of Pennsylvania for the amount of state income taxes withheld, etc.). Figure B–18 illustrates a completed General Journal window showing an example of a journal entry to record the deposit of FICA taxes and federal income taxes. Notice that the last line of the screen contains a F4 "hot key". Pressing the F4 key calls up a chart of accounts list window that may be referenced, or from which accounts may be selected while keying journal entries.

The computer stores journal entries in date sequence. As you enter new journal entries, the computer will maintain the date sequence by inserting the new transaction into the journal file based on the transaction date.

Entering a Transaction in a General Journal Window

1. **Choose the Key Journal Entries command from the Transactions menu.**
When the Key Journal Entries command is chosen from the Transactions menu, the General Journal window shown in Figure B–18 will appear.

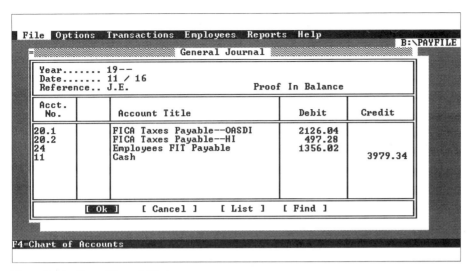

Figure B–18   *General Journal Window*

2. **Key the two-digit day of the month (or press Tab if it is correct as is).**
   If the month or year is incorrect, use the Shift+Tab keys to move to the Month or Year field.
3. **Key each of the data fields.**
   While the cursor is positioned at the Account Number field, you can press the F4 key to choose an account from a chart of accounts list window. Highlight the correct account and press Enter. The chosen account number will be inserted in the Account Number field.
4. **When the journal entry is complete, push the Ok button.**
   The Posting Summary window shown in Figure B–19 will appear. The purpose of this window is to show the journal entry in two-column format, giving you one last chance to verify the accuracy of your input and post the data.
5. **If the transaction is correct, push the Post button (push the Change button to return to the General Journal window and make changes).**

Changing or Deleting a Journal Entry

1. **Push the List command button near the bottom of the General Journal window.**

Figure B–19   *Posting Summary Window*

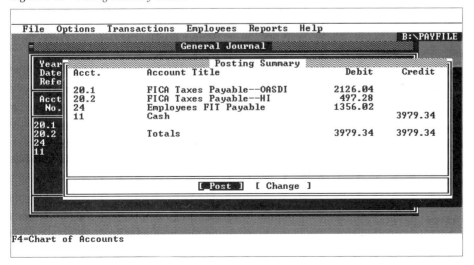

A list of general journal transactions will appear in a list window as shown in Figure B–20

Figure B–20 *Journal Entries List*

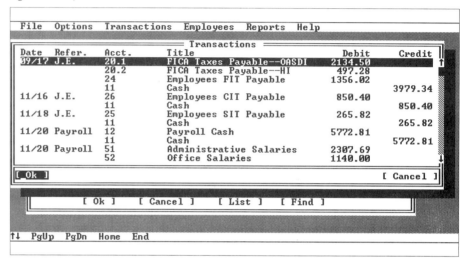

2. **Choose the transaction that you wish to change or delete.**
   The chosen transaction will be displayed in the General Journal window so that it may be changed or deleted.
3. **Key the corrections to the transaction and push the Ok button (or if you wish to delete the transaction, push the Delete command button).**

Finding a Journal Entry

1. **Push the Find command button.**
   The Find What? dialog window shown in Figure B–21 will appear.
2. **Key the date (month, day, and year), reference, or amount of the transaction you want to find and push the Ok command button.**
3. **If a matching transaction is found, it will be displayed in the General Journal window so that it may be changed or deleted.**

Figure B–21 *Find What? Dialog Window*

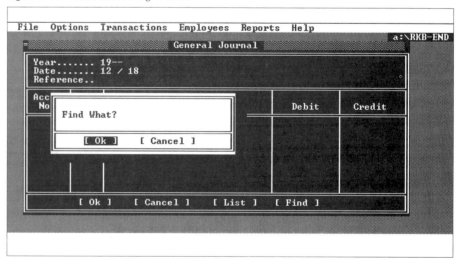

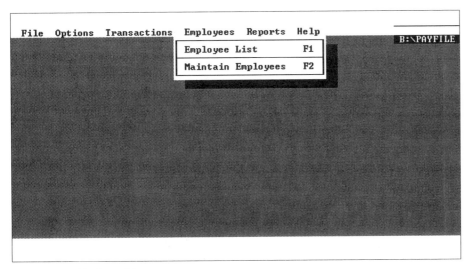

Figure B–22   *Employees Menu*

Chart of Accounts

The Chart of Accounts command (a list window showing the account numbers and titles of all the accounts in the general ledger) may be chosen whenever an account number or account title needs to be referenced, or from which accounts may be selected while keying journal entries.

Employees Menu

Whenever necessary, new employees must be added, data must be changed, and employees no longer employed must be deleted. The Employees menu, shown in Figure B–22, provides a command that lists all employees that currently exist in the computer and a command that enables the user to add, change, and delete employee records. When the Employees menu is selected from the Payroll menu bar, the two commands described in this section become available for execution.

1. **Choose the Maintain Employees command from the Employees menu.**
   Figure B–23 illustrates the Maintain Employees data entry window.

Figure B–23   *Maintain Employees Data Entry Window*

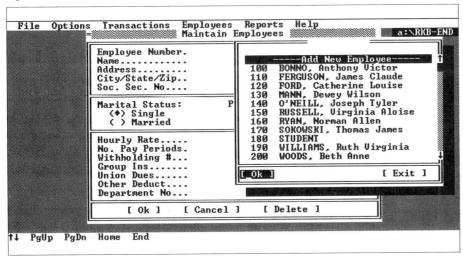

Adding a New Employee

1. Choose ——Add New Employee—— from the list window.
2. **Enter the employee data and set the Marital Status and Pay Type option buttons.'**
3. **Push the Ok button.**

Changing Employee Data

1. **Choose the employee you wish to change from the list window.**
    The list window will be dismissed and the data for the chosen employee will be displayed.
2. **Use the Tab key to position the cursor to the field you wish to change and rekey the correct data.**
3. **Push the Ok button.**

Deleting an Employee

1. **Choose the employee you wish to delete.**
2. **Push the delete button.**
    When the Delete Employee dialog window appears, push the Ok button.
    Note: You will not be allowed to delete an employee with cumulative earnings for the current year until after the Clear Yearly Accumulators command has been selected.

Reports Menu

The Reports menu, shown in Figure B–24, provides access to reports that are generated by the payroll system. Recall, the procedure to display and print the payroll reports was discussed in the Software Program Overview section earlier in this text. Once a report is displayed, it may be printed to an attached printer by choosing the Print command (in the File menu) or by pressing the F9 hot key. Each payroll report is described in the following section.

Payroll Report. The payroll report, which must be generated each pay period, actually contains two reports. The first report lists employee data with current, quarterly, and yearly earnings and withholdings. At the end of the payroll report is a second report, called the Payroll Summary that lists the total current quarterly and yearly earnings and withholdings.

Figure B–24   *Reports Menu*

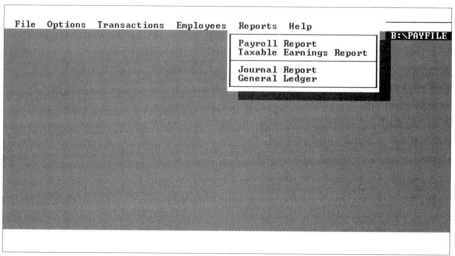

1. **Choose the Payroll Report command from the Reports menu.**
   The Selection Options dialog window will appear allowing you to select
   the employees that you wish to appear on the report.
   Hint: Use the F1 hot key to obtain a list window containing the numbers
   and names of all employees.
2. **Key the range of employees.**
3. **Push the Ok button.**

Taxable Earnings Report. The taxable earnings report contains the current,
quarterly, and yearly taxable OASDI, HI, SUTA, and FUTA earnings for each
employee, grand totals at the end of the report. Information contained in this
report can be used to help complete quarterly and year-end reporting.

1. **Choose the Taxable Earnings Report command from the Reports menu.**

Journal Report. As you have already learned, after each pay-period's transactions have been entered and verified for accuracy, the payroll journal entries are
generated and posted to the general ledger. The Journal Report lists the current
journal entries, as well as all the journal entries from the previous pay-periods
that have been posted.

1. **Choose the Journal Report command from the Reports menu.**
   The Selection Options dialog window will appear, allowing you to select
   the date range of the journal entries that you wish to appear on the report.
2. **Key the date range.**
3. **Push the Ok button.**

General Ledger. The General Ledger report lists each account, all the journal
entries posted to the account, and its current balance.

1. **Choose the General Ledger command from the Reports menu.**

Help Menu

Help windows have been provided as quick references when using the computerized payroll software to aid in the operation of the computer and software.
   The Help pull-down menu may be accessed at any time during program
execution. Operational information is provided in scrollable window displays.

1. **Choose the desired Help command from the Help pull-down menu.**
2. **Use the keyboard (or mouse if available) to scroll through the help information.**
3. **Press the Esc key (or click on the Close Box (=) located in the upper left
   corner of the help window) to dismiss the help window display.**
   Note: When a help window is dismissed, the computer returns to the point
   of interruption so processing may continue.

PAYROLL PROJECT

The payroll project that follows is the computerized version of the same project you completed manually in
Chapter 7 beginning on page 7–1 of this text. In this project you are employed by the Glo-Brite Paint Company as the person in the accounting department responsible for the Company's payroll processing, using
the computerized payroll system described in the preceding material.

Like the manual project in Chapter 7, you will assume that the payroll records, tax reports, and deposits have been completed and filed for the first three quarters of this year. Your work will involve the computer processing of the payrolls for the last quarter of the year and the completion of the last quarter and annual tax reports and forms. You may complete the required deposit, quarterly, yearly, etc. forms described in Chapter 7. If you have already completed these forms for the manual student project, check them as you progress through this project and make a note of any differences.

To help you get started, the first pay-period is provided as a tutorial problem that illustrates the principles and procedures required to process payroll transactions using the Computerized Payroll Accounting software. In subsequent pay-period processing, whenever a new operational procedure is used for the first time, additional instruction will be provided. Each of the step-by-step instructions below lists a task to be completed at the computer. If you need additional explanation for the task, a page reference is provided from the preceding material in this Appendix.

OCTOBER 9 PAYROLL

Step 1: **Remove the Student Project Audit Test found on page B–37. Answer the questions for the October 9 payroll as you complete processing for the pay-period.**

Step 2: **Start-up the Computerized Payroll Accounting software (Page B–9).**
At the DOS prompt, key PAYROLL (or follow the instructions provided by your instructor).

Step 3: **Load the opening balances template file, PAYFILE (Page B–12).**
Pull down the File menu and choose the Open Data File menu command. Key into the Path field the drive and directory containing the opening balance template file. Key a file name of PAYFILE and push the Ok button.

Step 4: **Set the run date to October 9 of the current year and enter your name (Page B–12).**
Choose the General Information command from the Options menu. Key October 9 of the current year (in the mm/dd/yy format) in the Run Date field, and key your name in the Student Name field. Verify that the Company Name field contains Glo-Brite Paint Company, and that the Problem Name field contains Payroll Project. If not, you may have loaded the wrong file. Then push the Ok button.

Step 5: **Enter employee maintenance data (Page B–14).**
Pull down the Employees menu and choose the Maintain Employees command. Select employee number 180 (Student) from the Employee List window. Key your name in the Name field and push the Ok command button.
Note: Do not change any of the other fields. If you do, your solutions will not be correct.

Step 6: **Prepare a new payroll (Page B–14).**
Pull down the Options menu, choose the Prepare New Payroll menu command. When the Prepare New Payroll dialog window appears, push the Ok button to erase any previous pay period transaction data that may be stored by the computer.

Step 7: **Key the payroll transactions (do not deduct Group Ins.) (Page B–16).**
Pull down the Transactions menu and choose the Payroll Transactions menu command. When the Deduct Group Insurance dialog box window appears, push the No command button. Key the following payroll transaction data (use the Calculate Taxes option):

Employees to Be Paid this Pay-Period:

Employee Number	Employee Name	Regular Hours	Overtime @ Time 1/2	Overtime @ Double
100	Bonno, Anthony Victor	80		
110	Ferguson, James Claude	(salaried)		
120	Ford, Catherine Louise	(salaried)		
130	Mann, Dewey Wilson	(salaried)		
140	O'Neill, Joseph Tyler	(salaried)		
150	Russell, Virginia Aloise	(salaried)		
160	Ryan, Norman Allen	80		
170	Sokowski, Thomas James	(salaried)		
180	Student (your name)	(salaried)		
190	Williams, Ruth Virginia	(salaried)		

Step 8: Display the Payroll Report (Page B–22).

Pull down the Reports menu and choose the Payroll Report menu command. When the Selection Options dialog window appears, key a range of employees from 100 to 190 (if not already specified). Figure B–25 shows the payroll report for Employee 100; Bonno, Anthony Victor, followed by the payroll summary.

Figure B–25 *Payroll Report*

```
   File   Options   Transactions   Employees   Reports   Help
==
||                      Glo-Brite Paint Company
||                           Payroll Report
||                             10/09/--
|
|                                          Current   Quarterly    Yearly
|
|100-BONNO, Anthony Victor      Gross Pay    612.00     612.00    11934.00
|694 Bristol Avenue             FIT                                 310.00
|Philadelphia, PA 19135-0617    SIT           17.14      17.14      334.16
|537-10-3481                    OASDI         37.94      37.94      739.90
|W/H Allow   4      Married     HI             8.87       8.87      173.04
|Department Plant               Group Ins.                          144.80
|Pay Periods 26                 Union Dues     8.00       8.00       80.00
|Reg. Hrs.     80.00            Other Ded.
|O.T. Hrs.                      CIT           30.36      30.36      592.02
|Extra Pay                      SUTA            .92        .92       17.90
|Hourly Rate     7.65           Net Pay      508.77     508.77     9542.18
|
|
|Payroll summary:               Gross Pay   8463.69    8463.69   150688.26
|                               FIT          663.07     663.07    14280.07
|                               SIT          236.99     236.99     4219.28
|                               OASDI        524.75     524.75     9342.67
|                               HI           122.74     122.74     2185.01
|                               Group Ins.                          929.70
|                               Union Dues    16.00      16.00      160.00
|                               Other Ded.
|                               CIT          419.80     419.80     7474.08
|                               SUTA          12.72      12.72      226.07
|                               Net Pay     6467.62    6467.62   111871.38
|
 ↑↓  PgUp  PgDn  Home   End   F9=Print   Esc=Close Window
```

Note: Throughout this project, some of the computer calculated withholding amounts (i.e. Federal Income Tax) will be slightly different than the amounts (from the tax tables) in the manual payroll project in Chapter 7. This occurs because the computer uses the annualized method to compute withholding taxes.

Step 9: Generate and post the Payroll Journal Entries (Page B–18).

Pull down the Transactions menu and choose the Generate Payroll Journal Entry command. When the dialog box window appears asking you to confirm that you want to generate the payroll journal entries for the 10/09/— payroll, push the Ok button. A second dialog box window will appear indicating that the journal entries have been posted to the general ledger; push the Ok button.

Step 10: **Display the Journal Report (Page B–23).**
Pull down the Reports menu, choose the Journal Report menu command, and display the October 9 payroll journal entries just generated and posted to the general ledger. Figure B–26 shows the report.

Figure B–26 *General Journal Report*

```
                      Glo-Brite Paint Company
                         General Journal
                            10/09/--

 Date   Refer.      Acct.  Title                      Debit      Credit

10/09  Payroll      12     Payroll Cash              6467.62
10/09  Payroll      11     Cash                                 6467.62

10/09  Payroll      51     Administrative Salaries   2307.69
10/09  Payroll      52     Office Salaries           1710.00
10/09  Payroll      53     Sales Salaries            2150.00
10/09  Payroll      54     Plant Wages               2296.00
10/09  Payroll      20.1   FICA Taxes Payable--OASDI             524.75
10/09  Payroll      20.2   FICA Taxes Payable--HI                122.74
10/09  Payroll      23     Employees SUTA Payable                 12.72
10/09  Payroll      24     Employees FIT Payable                 663.07
10/09  Payroll      25     Employees SIT Payable                 236.99
10/09  Payroll      26     Employees CIT Payable                 419.80
10/09  Payroll      28     Union Dues Payable                     16.00
10/09  Payroll      12     Payroll Cash                         6467.62

10/09  Payroll      56     Payroll Taxes              735.21
10/09  Payroll      20.1   FICA Taxes Payable--OASDI             524.75
10/09  Payroll      20.2   FICA Taxes Payable--HI                122.74
10/09  Payroll      21     FUTA Taxes Payable                     16.32
10/09  Payroll      22     SUTA Taxes Payable                     71.40
                                                     ---------  ---------
                           Totals                    15666.52   15666.52
                                                     ========   ========
```

Step 11: **Display the General Ledger report (Page B–23).**
Pull down the Reports menu, choose the General Ledger command, and display the general ledger as of the end of the October 9 payroll. Figure B–27 shows the report.

Step 12: **Use the Save As command to save data to disk with a file name of XXX10–09 (where XXX are your initials, and 10–09 is the pay-period date) (Page B–13).**
Pull down the File menu and choose the Save As menu command. Key the path to the drive and directory that contains your data files. Key a file name of XXX10–09 (where XXX are your initials and 10–09 represents month 10, day 09). Push the Ok button.

Step 13: **End the session (Page B–13).**
From the File menu, choose the Quit command.

OCTOBER 23 PAYROLL

The step-by-step instructions for completing the October 23 payroll (for the period ending October 17 are listed below.

Step 1: Answer the questions for the October 23 payroll on the Student Project Audit Test as you complete processing for the pay period.

Figure B–27   *General Ledger Report*

```
                        Glo-Brite Paint Company
                            General Ledger
                              10/09/--

Account          Journal   Date   Refer.      Debit      Credit    Balance

11-Cash
                 Op. Bal.  10/01  OP.BAL.    89846.33              89846.33Dr
                 General   10/09  Payroll                6467.62   83378.71Dr

12-Payroll Cash
                 General   10/09  Payroll     6467.62              6467.62Dr
                 General   10/09  Payroll                6467.62

20.1-FICA Taxes Payable--OASDI
                 General   10/09  Payroll                 524.75    524.75Cr
                 General   10/09  Payroll                 524.75   1049.50Cr

20.2-FICA Taxes Payable--HI
                 General   10/09  Payroll                 122.74    122.74Cr
                 General   10/09  Payroll                 122.74    245.48Cr

21-FUTA Taxes Payable
                 General   10/09  Payroll                  16.32     16.32Cr

22-SUTA Taxes Payable
                 General   10/09  Payroll                  71.40     71.40Cr

23-Employees SUTA Payable
                 General   10/09  Payroll                  12.72     12.72Cr

24-Employees FIT Payable
                 General   10/09  Payroll                 663.07    663.07Cr

25-Employees SIT Payable
                 General   10/09  Payroll                 236.99    236.99Cr

26-Employees CIT Payable
                 General   10/09  Payroll                 419.80    419.80Cr

27-Grp. Ins. Prem. Collected        ******* No Activity *******

28-Union Dues Payable
                 General   10/09  Payroll                  16.00     16.00Cr

29-Other Deduction Payable          ******* No Activity *******

51-Administrative Salaries
                 Op. Bal.  10/01  OP.BAL.    42692.27              42692.27Dr
                 General   10/09  Payroll     2307.69              44999.96Dr

52-Office Salaries
                 Op. Bal.  10/01  OP.BAL.    28350.00              28350.00Dr
                 General   10/09  Payroll     1710.00              30060.00Dr

53-Sales Salaries
                 Op. Bal.  10/01  OP.BAL.    28525.00              28525.00Dr
                 General   10/09  Payroll     2150.00              30675.00Dr

54-Plant Wages
                 Op. Bal.  10/01  OP.BAL.    42657.30              42657.30Dr
                 General   10/09  Payroll     2296.00              44953.30Dr

56-Payroll Taxes
                 Op. Bal.  10/01  OP.BAL.    13906.21              13906.21Dr
                 General   10/09  Payroll      735.21              14641.42Dr
```

Step 2: If you quit the software after processing the previous pay period, perform the following steps:

    a.   Start-up the Computerized Payroll Accounting software.

    b.   Load your file containing the last pay period data (XXX10–09).

Step 3: Set the run date to October 23 of the current year in the General Information data entry window.

Step 4: Enter and post the October 20 transaction required to record the deposit of the Pennsylvania state income taxes withheld from the October 9 payroll (Page B–18 to B–20).

Pull down the Transactions menu and choose the Key Journal Entry command. When the Journal Entries window appears, enter and post the transaction shown in Figure B–28.

Figure B–28 *Journal Entry to Record Deposit of October 9 State Income Taxes Withheld*

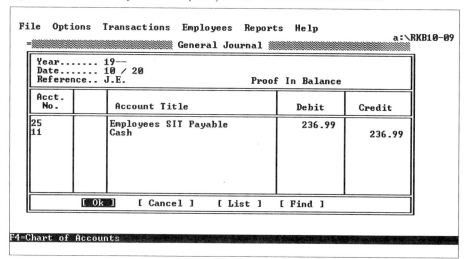

Step 5: Prepare a new payroll.

Pull down the Options menu and choose the Prepare New Payroll command. When the message window appears asking you to confirm your selection, push the Ok button.

Step 6: Enter the following payroll transactions (*do* deduct Group Ins.):

Employees to Be Paid this Pay-Period:

Employee Number	Employee Name	Regular Hours	Overtime @ Time 1/2	Overtime @ Double
100	Bonno, Anthony Victor	80		4
110	Ferguson, James Claude	(salaried)		
120	Ford, Catherine Louise	(salaried)		
130	Mann, Dewey Wilson	(salaried)		
140	O'Neill, Joseph Tyler	(salaried)		
150	Russell, Virginia Aloise	(salaried)		
160	Ryan, Norman Allen	80		8
170	Sokowski, Thomas James	(salaried)		
180	Student (your name)	(salaried)		
190	Williams, Ruth Virginia	(salaried)		

Step 7: Print or display a payroll report for all employees.

Step 8: Generate and post the Payroll Journal Entries.

Step 9: Display the Journal Report for 10/10/— through 10/23/—.

Step 10: Display the General Ledger report.

Step 11: Use the Save As command to save the October 23 payroll to disk with a file name of XXX10–23 (where XXX are your initials and 10–23 represents month 10, day 23).

Step 12: Proceed to the November 6 payroll. If necessary, end your payroll session.

NOVEMBER 6 PAYROLL

The step-by-step instructions for completing the November 6 payroll (for the period ending October 31) are listed below.

Step 1: Answer the questions for the November 6 payroll on the Student Project Audit Test as you complete processing for the pay-period.

Step 2: If you quit the software after processing the previous pay-period, perform the following steps:

a. Bring up the Computerized Payroll Accounting software.
b. Load your file containing the last pay-period data (XXX10–23).

Step 3: Set the run date to November 6 of the current year in the General Information data entry window.

Step 4: Enter and post the following transactions:
November 4: Deposited the Pennsylvania state income taxes withheld from the October 23 payroll.
November 6: Paid the treasurer of the union the amount of union dues withheld during the month of October.

243 09
32. – (28)

Step 5: Enter employee maintenance: (Page B–21)
Pull down the Employees menu and choose the Maintain Employees command. When the Maintain Employees window appears, enter the following maintenance data:
Change Virginia Russell's number of withholding allowances to 2.
Change Thomas J. Sokowski's marital status to Single (his number of withholding allowances remains at 2).
Change Dewey Mann's number of withholding allowances to 0.
Change Virginia Russell's salary amount to $380.44 this pay-period because she worked only 38 hours in the week ending October 24.
Change Ruth Williams salary amount to $563.07 this pay-period because she worked only 39 hours in the week ending October 24.

Step 6: Prepare a new payroll.

Step 7: Enter the following payroll transactions (*do not* deduct Group Ins):

Employees to Be Paid this Pay-Period:

Employee Number	Employee Name	Regular Hours	Overtime @ Time 1/2	Overtime @ Double
100	Bonno, Anthony Victor	80		
110	Ferguson, James Claude	(salaried)		
120	Ford, Catherine Louise	(salaried)		
130	Mann, Dewey Wilson	(salaried)		
140	O'Neill, Joseph Tyler	(salaried)		
150	Russell, Virginia Aloise	(salaried)		
160	Ryan, Norman Allen	80	1	
170	Sokowski, Thomas James	(salaried)		
180	Student (your name)	(salaried)		
190	Williams, Ruth Virginia	(salaried)		

Step 8: Add $50.00 to Dewey Mann's FIT as per his request.
Pull down the Transactions menu and choose the Payroll Transactions command. Select Dewey Mann (employee number 130) from the Employee list. When the data appears in the Payroll Transac-

tions window, set the Key Taxes option to On, tab to the FIT field and add $50.00 to the amount that appears there, then push the Pay button.

Step 9: Print or display a payroll report for all employees.

Step 10: Generate and post the Payroll Journal Entries.

Step 11: Display the Journal Report for 10/24/— through 11/06/—.

Step 12: Display the General Ledger report.

Step 13: Use the Save As command to save the November 6 payroll to disk with a file name of XXX11–06 (where XXX are your initials and 11–06 represents month 11, day 06).

Step 14: Proceed to the November 13 payroll. If necessary, end your payroll session.

NOVEMBER 13 PAYROLL

A special payroll needs to be run to process a discharged employee. (Ruth Williams has been discharged because of her excessive tardiness and absenteeism). The step-by-step instructions for completing the November 13 special payroll are listed below.

Step 1: Answer the questions for the November 13 payroll on the Student Project Audit Test as you complete processing for the pay-period.

Step 2: If you quit the software after processing the previous pay-period, perform the following steps:

    a.   Bring up the Computerized Payroll Accounting software.

    b.   Load your file containing the last pay-period data (XXX11–06).

Step 3: Set the run date to November 13 of the current year in the General Information data entry window.

Step 4: Enter the employee maintenance to change Ruth V. Williams' salary amount to $456.32 (for two partial weeks of work: $456.32) for her final pay.

Step 5: Prepare a new payroll.

Step 6: Pay Ruth V. Williams (via the payroll transactions menu option) for the two partial weeks of work entered in Step 4, plus enter 570.00 in the Extra Pay field for two full weeks' pay in lieu of two weeks' notice. (*Do* deduct Group Ins.).

Step 7: Print or display a payroll report for Ruth Williams (employee number 190).

Step 8: Generate and post the Payroll Journal Entries.

Step 9: Display the Journal Report for 11/07/— through 11/13/—.

Step 10: Display the General Ledger report.

Step 11: Use the Save As command to save the November 6 payroll to disk with a file name of XXX11–13 (where XXX are your initials and 11–13 represents month 11, day 13).

Step 12: Proceed to the November 20 payroll. If necessary, end your payroll session.

NOVEMBER 20 PAYROLL

The step-by-step instructions for completing the November 20 payroll (for the period ending November 14) follow.

Step 1: Answer the questions for the November 20 payroll on the Student Project Audit Test as you complete processing for the pay-period.

Step 2: If you quit the software after processing the previous pay-period, perform the following steps:

a. Bring up the Computerized Payroll Accounting software.
b. Load your file containing the last pay-period data (XXX11–13).

Step 3: Set the run date to November 20 of the current year in the General Information data entry window.

Step 4: Enter and post the following transactions:
November 16: Deposited with the City Bank, the amount of FICA *56 DR* taxes and federal income taxes for the October payrolls.
Hint: Display the General Ledger report to obtain these amounts from the FICA Taxes Payable—OASDI, FICA Taxes Payable—HI, and the Employees FIT payable account balances.
November 16: Deposited the City of Philadelphia employees withheld income tax ($850.40) with the Department of Revenue for the October payrolls (see the Employees CIT Payable account balance in the General Ledger report).
November 18: Deposited the Pennsylvania state income taxes withheld from the November 6 and 13 (Ruth V. Williams) payrolls. *265.82*

Step 5: Enter employee maintenance:
Change Virginia Russell's salary amount back to $390.00.
Add new employee: Employee number 200; WOODS, Beth Anne; 8102 Franklin Court, Philadelphia, PA 19105-0915; social security number, 724-03-1587; single, salaried, $600.00, number of pay periods per year, 26; withholding allowances, 1; group insurance $6.90; Department, 2 (Office).

Step 6: Prepare a new payroll.

Step 7: Enter the following payroll transactions (*do* deduct Group Ins.):

Employees to Be Paid this Pay-Period:

Employee Number	Employee Name	Regular Hours	Overtime @ Time 1/2	Overtime @ Double
100	Bonno, Anthony Victor	64		
110	Ferguson, James Claude	(salaried)		
120	Ford, Catherine Louise	(salaried)		
130	Mann, Dewey Wilson	(salaried)		
140	O'Neill, Joseph Tyler	(salaried)		
150	Russell, Virginia Aloise	(salaried)		
160	Ryan, Norman Allen	80		2
170	Sokowski, Thomas James	(salaried)		
180	Student (your name)	(salaried)		

Step 8: Add $50.00 to Dewey Mann's FIT as per his request.
Step 9: Print or display a payroll report for all employees.
Step 10: Generate and post the Payroll Journal Entries.
Step 11: Display the Journal Report for 11/14/— through 11/20/—.
Step 12: Display the General Ledger report.
Step 13: Use the Save As command to save the November 20 payroll to disk with a file name of XXX11–20 (where XXX are your initials and 11–20 represents month 11, day 20).
Step 14: Proceed to the December 4 payroll. If necessary, end your payroll session.

DECEMBER 4 PAYROLL

The step-by-step instructions for completing the December 4 payroll (for the week ending November 28) follow.

Step 1: Answer the questions for the December 4 payroll on the Student Project Audit Test as you complete processing for the pay period.

Step 2: If you quit the software after processing the previous pay period, perform the following steps:

a. Bring up the Computerized Payroll Accounting software.
b. Load your file containing the last pay period data (XXX11–20).

Step 3: Set the run date to December 4 of the current year in the General Information data entry window.

Step 4: Enter and post the following transaction:
December 3: Deposited the Pennsylvania state income taxes withheld from the November 20 payroll. 263.18

Step 5: Enter employee maintenance:
Change Catherine L. Ford's salary amount to $462.00.
Change Virginia Russell's salary amount to $402.00, and her Group Insurance deduction to $4.80.
Change Beth Wood's salary amount to $540.00 for her first payroll.
Add new employee: Employee number 210; YOUNG, Paul Winston; 7936 Holmes Drive, Philadelphia, PA 19107-6107; social security number, 432-07-6057; single, salaried, $461.54, number of pay-periods per year, 26; withholding allowances, 1; group insurance $5.40; Department, 3 (Sales).

Step 6: Prepare a new payroll.

Step 7: Enter the following payroll transactions (*do not* deduct Group Ins.):

Employees to Be Paid this Pay-Period:

Employee Number	Employee Name	Regular Hours	Overtime @ Time 1/2	Overtime @ Double
100	Bonno, Anthony Victor	80		8
110	Ferguson, James Claude	(salaried)		
120	Ford, Catherine Louise	(salaried)		
130	Mann, Dewey Wilson	(salaried)		
140	O'Neill, Joseph Tyler	(salaried)		
150	Russell, Virginia Aloise	(salaried)		
160	Ryan, Norman Allen	76	3	
170	Sokowski, Thomas James	(salaried)		
180	Student (your name)	(salaried)		
200	Woods, Beth Anne	(salaried)		

Step 8: Add $50.00 to Dewey Mann's FIT as per his request.
Step 9: Print or display a payroll report for all employees.
Step 10: Generate and post the Payroll Journal Entries.
Step 11: Display the Journal Report for 11/21/— through 12/04/—.
Step 12: Display the General Ledger report.
Step 13: Use the Save As command to save the December 4 payroll to disk with a file name of XXX12–04 (where XXX are your initials and 12–04 represents month 12, day 04).
Step 14: Proceed to the December 14 payroll. If necessary, end your payroll session.

DECEMBER 14

A special payroll needs to be run to process the death of an employee (Virginia A. Russell). The step-by-step instructions for completing the December 14 special payroll follow.

Step 1: Answer the questions for the December 14 payroll on the Student Project Audit Test as you complete processing for the pay period.

Step 2: If you quit the software after processing the previous pay period, perform the following steps:

   a.   Bring up the Computerized Payroll Accounting software.
   b.   Load your file containing the last pay period data (XXX12–04).

Step 3: Set the run date to December 14 of the current year in the General Information data entry window.

Step 4: Enter and post the following transaction:
December 9: Paid the treasurer of the union the amount of union *$32 (28) Debit* dues withheld during the month of November.

Step 5: Enter the employee maintenance:
Change Anthony V. Bonno's number of withholding allowances to 5, and change his Union Dues to $9.00.
Change Norman Ryan's Union Dues to $9.00.
Change Virginia A. Russell's salary amount to 361.96 (for two partial weeks of work).

Step 6: Prepare a new payroll.

Step 7: Pay Virginia A. Russell (pay will go to her estate), via the payroll transactions menu option, for the two partial weeks of work entered in Step 5, plus enter 402.00 in the Extra Pay field for her accrued vacation pay. (*do* deduct Group Ins).

Step 8: Remove the calculated withholding amounts for FIT, SIT, and CIT (final pay is not subject to these withholdings).
While still in the Payroll Transactions window, select Virginia A. Russell (employee number 150) from the Employee list. When the data appears in the Payroll Transactions window, set the Key Taxes option to On, set the FIT, SIT, and CIT fields to blank (or key a zero), then push the Pay button.

Step 9: Print or display a payroll report for Virginia A. Russell (employee number 150).

Step 10: Generate and post the Payroll Journal Entries.

Step 11: Display the Journal Report for 12/05/— through 12/14/—.

Step 12: Display the General Ledger report.

Step 13: Use the Save As command to save the December 14 special payroll to disk with a file name of XXX12–14 (where XXX are your initials and 12–14 represents month 12, day 14).

Step 14: Proceed to the December 18 payroll. If necessary, end your payroll session.

DECEMBER 18 PAYROLL

The step-by-step instructions for completing the December 18 payroll (for the week ending December 12) follow.

Step 1: Answer the questions for the December 18 payroll on the Student Project Audit Test as you complete processing for the pay period.

Step 2: If you quit the software after processing the previous pay period, perform the following steps:

   a.   Bring up the Computerized Payroll Accounting software.
   b.   Load your file containing the last pay period data (XXX12–14).

Step 3: Set the run date to December 18 of the current year in the General Information data entry window.

Step 4: Enter and post the following transactions:
December 15: Deposited with the City Bank, the amount of FICA *debit credit (56)* taxes and federal income taxes for the November payrolls.
December 15: Deposited the City of Philadelphia employees income tax withheld with the Department of Revenue from the November payrolls. *debit (25) credit (11)*

December 18: Deposited the Pennsylvania state income taxes withheld from the December 4 payroll.

December 18: Wrote check to Virginia Russell's estate from the regular cash account for the amount withheld from her December 14 pay for insurance.

Step 5: Enter employee maintenance:

Change Student (your) salary amount to $296.25 (loss of 1 hour).

Change Beth A. Woods salary amount to $600.00.

Add new employee: Employee number 220; ZIMMERMAN, Richard Lewis; 900 South Clark Street, Philadelphia, PA 19195-6247; social security number, 897-12-1502; married, salaried, $360.00, number of pay periods per year, 26; withholding allowances, 1; group insurance $4.20; Department, 2 (Office).

Step 6: Prepare a new payroll.

Step 7: Enter the following payroll transactions (*do* deduct Group Ins.):

Employees to Be Paid this Pay-Period:

Employee Number	Employee Name	Regular Hours	Overtime @ Time 1/2	Overtime @ Double
100	Bonno, Anthony Victor	80		12
110	Ferguson, James Claude	(salaried)		
120	Ford, Catherine Louise	(salaried)		
130	Mann, Dewey Wilson	(salaried)		
140	O'Neill, Joseph Tyler	(salaried + $4,000 extra pay)		
160	Ryan, Norman Allen	80	7	
170	Sokowski, Thomas James	(salaried)		
180	Student (your name)	(salaried)		
200	Woods, Beth Anne	(salaried)		
210	Young, Paul Winston	(salaried)		

Step 8: Add $50.00 to Dewey Mann's FIT as per his request.

Step 9: Print or display a payroll report for all employees.

Step 10: Generate and post the Payroll Journal Entries.

Step 11: Display the Journal Report for 12/15/— through 12/18/—.

Step 12: Display the General Ledger report.

Step 13: Use the Save As command to save the December 18 payroll to disk with a file name of XXX12–18 (where XXX are your initials and 12–18 represents month 12, day 18).

Step 14: This completes the project insofar as recording and processing the computerized payroll transactions for the last quarter is concerned. Proceed to the Optional Activities. End your payroll session.

OPTIONAL ACTIVITIES

This optional, clerical activity is provided to prepare the payroll file for the next calendar year, and to follow the manual student project in Chapter 7. The transactions have been included to illustrate different types of transactions arising in connection with the accounting for payrolls and payroll taxes. The information contained in the computerized Payroll reports may be referenced in order to complete the forms in this activity.

Step 1: Answer the questions for the additional transactions on the Student Project Audit Test as you complete the journal entries.

Step 2: If you quit the software after processing the previous pay period, perform the following steps:

a.   Bring up the Computerized Payroll Accounting software.
b.   Load your file containing the last pay period data (XXX12–18).

Step 3: Set the Run Date in the General Information window to January 1 of the next year.

Step 4: Clear the Yearly Accumulators.
Pull down the Options menu and choose the Clear Yearly Accumulators command. When the dialog window appears asking you to confirm your action, push the Ok button.

Step 5: Enter Employee maintenance:
Delete employee number 150 (Virginia A. Russell).
Delete employee number 190 (Ruth V. Williams).

Step 6: Use the Save As command to save the data to disk with a file name of XXX01–01 (where XXX are your initials and 01–01 represents month 1, day 01).
Note: This is the payroll file that will be used to begin processing for the new year.

Prepare the various quarter-end and year-end payroll tax forms, and make the accrual entries for the payroll at the end of the year.

Step 7: Load your file containing the last pay period data (XXX12–18).

Step 8: Set the run date to February 1 of the next year in the General Information data entry window.

Step 9: Use the information contained in the Computerized Payroll reports to complete the following forms—if not completed in the Student Project in Chapter 7. If completed in Chapter 7, check the forms and make a note of any differences. Refer to the February 1 narrative regarding the forms to be completed, on pages 7–20 to 7–22 in the manual student project in Chapter 7, if necessary.

a.   Form 941, Employer's Quarterly Federal Tax Return.
b.   Form 940-EZ, Employer's Annual Federal Unemployment (FUTA) Tax Return.
c.   Form UC-2, Employer's Report for Unemployment Compensation—Fourth Quarter.
d.   Form W-2, Wage and Tax Statement for each employee.
e.   Form W-3, Transmittal of Wage and Tax Statements.
f.   Pennsylvania form REV1667, W-2 Transmittal.
g.   Form 1099-MISC, Miscellaneous Income (for Virginia A. Russell).
h.   Form 1096, Annual Summary and Transmittal of U.S. Information Returns.
i.   Form PA-W3R, Employer Quarterly Reconciliation Return of Income Tax Withheld.
j.   Annual Reconciliation of Wage Tax for Philadelphia.

Step 10: Enter and post the following transactions:
January 6: deposited the Pennsylvania state income taxes withheld from the December 18 payroll.
January 8: paid the treasurer of the union the amount of union dues withheld during the month of December.
January 15: deposited with the City Bank, the amount of FICA taxes and federal income taxes for the December payrolls.
January 15: deposited the City of Philadelphia employees income tax withheld with the Department of Revenue from the December payrolls
February 1: deposited FUTA Taxes Payable for the quarter.
Hint: see the FUTA Taxes Payable account balance in the general ledger report.
February 1: paid the SUTA Taxes Payable and Employees SUTA Payable for the fourth quarter.

Hint: see the SUTA Taxes Payable and the Employees SUTA Payable account balances in the general ledger report.

Step 11: Display the Journal Report for January 1 of the next year through February 1 of the next year.

Step 12: Use the Save As command to save your data to disk with a file name of XXX-END (where XXX are your initials and END represents the payroll file containing the accrual entries at the end of the year).

Step 13: End your computer session.

STUDENT PROJECT AUDIT TEST

OPTIONAL ACTIVITIES: (Use the payroll file you saved under file name XXX–END to answer the following questions)

Journal Entries Report

1. What is the amount of the deposit for Pennsylvania state income taxes withheld from the December 18 payroll? ....   _____

2. What is the amount of Union Dues withheld during the month of December? ....   _____

3. What is the amount of FICA Taxes Payable—OASDI deposited from the December payrolls? ....   _____

4. What is the amount of the City of Philadelphia employees income tax deposited from the December payrolls? ....   _____

5. What is the amount of FUTA Taxes Payable deposited for the quarter? ...   _____

6. What is the amount of SUTA Taxes Payable and Employees SUTA Payable for the fourth quarter? ....   _____

Appendix

COMMERCIAL SOFTWARE FOR PREPARING PAYROLL

Even the smallest businesses can buy computer programs at an affordable cost that will satisfy their payroll preparation and reporting needs. Usually, the payroll software is part of an accounting package. These programs help the employer do the job faster and smarter than a manual system and less expensively than an outside payroll processing service.

Each package offers standard reports—from Payroll Registers to Payroll Tax Reports to Quarterly and Yearly Earnings Records. They can track vacation and sick-time and hiring anniversaries for annual reviews. They automatically distribute the gross pays to the appropriate general ledger accounts. With these programs, cafeteria plans and 401K plans can be easily monitored. All of these programs provide Tax Table Services that will update the rates and taxable limits annually.

To determine which program is best for your business, you must identify your needs and then evaluate the program's capabilities to satisfy your requirements. Some of these programs are designed for businesses with fewer than 20 employees while others can handle over 500 employees. Some can accommodate less than 10 payroll deductions; others over 30. Some cost less than $100; others more than $400. Many are available in a CD-ROM version. The leaders in the small business field include:

Checkmark Payroll *(Checkmark Software)*. A complete payroll system using a spreadsheet-type window for entering employee hours. This program handles salaried and hourly employees, overtime, double-time pay, and tracks sick and vacation pay. Automatically calculates federal, state, and local taxes. Data can be exported to Quicken, QuickBooks, Peachtree Accounting, and M.Y.O.B.

Cougar Mountain Software 9.5 *(Cougar Mountain Software)*. A complete accounting system including payroll. Payroll software features federal, state, and local tax updates, printing W-2's, 941, and checks, allows per-diem, contract, piece work, hourly and salary pay, and 22 user-defined benefits and deductions per employee. This program also supports 401 and cafeteria plans, and allows W-2's to be submitted on disk or magnetic media.

DacEasy 2.0 for Windows *(DacEasy, Inc.)*. A complete accounting and automated payroll processing system with interactive tutorials, a set-up checklist, paper-look-a-like screens and graphical help system. This software also allows invoice and statement faxing, one-key phone dialing, and tracks phone calls.

M.Y.O.B. 5.0 Small Business Accounting with Payroll *(Best!Ware)*. Instant accounting templates make this full-featured accounting program simple to get started. M.Y.O.B. Payroll performs automatic tax calculations and has unlimited wage categories.

One-Write Plus: Accounting with Payroll *(Nebs Inc.)*.

Painless Accounting *(Integra Software)*. A full featured accounting program using easy-to-follow screen formats and on-line help for every step. Complete payroll is included.

Peachtree Accounting for Windows *(Peachtree Software)*. A multi-user and network ready accounting program including: General Ledger, Invoicing, Inventory, Budgeting, Receivables, Payables, and Payroll.

Peachtree Complete Accounting 8.0 for DOS *(Peachtree Software)*. Powerful small business accounting system including: General Ledger, Budgeting, Payables, Invoicing, Inventory, Payroll, Purchasing, Job Costing, and Fixed Assets.

Peachtree First Accounting *(Peachtree Software)*. An accounting program for first time users. The program offers Navigational Aids and SmartGuides to walk the user through most common tasks. Users can invoice customers, manage receivables, pay vendors, pay employees, and track job costs.

Power $ales Basics *(Syntax Retail Systems)*. A POS and accounting software system that not only handles sales, receivables, inventory, and purchasing, but can also process payroll and job costing through an Accounting Manager add on.

QuickBooks *(Intuit)*. This program uses familiar on-screen forms to perform invoicing, receivables, payables, financial reports and also writes checks. QuickPay adds a complete payroll program to the QuickBooks system.

Simply Accounting *(Computer Associates)*. An entry-level accounting program that supports both accrual and cash basis accounting. The program offers pre-formatted financial statements, management reports, and multiple payroll options.

TAX TABLE
A

TABLE OF ALLOWANCE VALUES

Payroll period	One withholding allowance
Weekly	$ 48.08
Biweekly	96.15
Semimonthly	104.17
Monthly	208.33
Quarterly	625.00
Semiannually	1,250.00
Annually	2,500.00
Daily or miscellaneous (each day of .. the payroll period)	9.62

Tables for Percentage Method of Withholding
(For Wages Paid in 1995)

TABLE 1—WEEKLY Payroll Period

(a) SINGLE person (including head of household)—

If the amount of wages (after subtracting withholding allowances) is:

The amount of income tax to withhold is:

Not over $50. . . . . $0

Over—	But not over—		of excess over—
$50	—$476 . . .	15%	—$50
$476	—$999 . . .	$63.90 plus 28%	—$476
$999	—$2,295 . .	$210.34 plus 31%	—$999
$2,295	—$4,960 . .	$612.10 plus 36%	—$2,295
$4,960 .	. . . . .	$1,571.50 plus 39.6%	—$4,960

(b) MARRIED person—

If the amount of wages (after subtracting withholding allowances) is:

The amount of income tax to withhold is:

Not over $123 . . . . $0

Over—	But not over—		of excess over—
$123	—$828 . . .	15%	—$123
$828	—$1,664 . .	$105.75 plus 28%	—$828
$1,664	—$2,839 . .	$339.83 plus 31%	—$1,664
$2,839	—$5,011 . .	$704.08 plus 36%	—$2,839
$5,011	. . . . . .	$1,486.00 plus 39.6%	—$5,011

TABLE 2—BIWEEKLY Payroll Period

(a) SINGLE person (including head of household)—

If the amount of wages (after subtracting withholding allowances) is:

The amount of income tax to withhold is:

Not over $100 . . . . $0

Over—	But not over—		of excess over—
$100	—$952 . . .	15%	—$100
$952	—$1,998 . .	$127.80 plus 28%	—$952
$1,998	—$4,590 . .	$420.68 plus 31%	—$1,998
$4,590	—$9,919 . .	$1,224.20 plus 36%	—$4,590
$9,919 .	. . . . .	$3,142.64 plus 39.6%	—$9,919

(b) MARRIED person—

If the amount of wages (after subtracting withholding allowances) is:

The amount of income tax to withhold is:

Not over $246 . . . . $0

Over—	But not over—		of excess over—
$246	—$1,656 . .	15%	—$246
$1,656	—$3,329 . .	$211.50 plus 28%	—$1,656
$3,329	—$5,679 . .	$679.94 plus 31%	—$3,329
$5,679	—$10,021 .	$1,408.44 plus 36%	—$5,679
$10,021 .	. . . . .	$2,971.56 plus 39.6%	—$10,021

TABLE 3—SEMIMONTHLY Payroll Period

(a) SINGLE person (including head of household)—

If the amount of wages (after subtracting withholding allowances) is:

The amount of income tax to withhold is:

Not over $108 . . . . $0

Over—	But not over—		of excess over—
$108	—$1,031 . .	15%	—$108
$1,031	—$2,165 . .	$138.45 plus 28%	—$1,031
$2,165	—$4,973 . .	$455.97 plus 31%	—$2,165
$4,973	—$10,746 . .	$1,326.45 plus 36%	—$4,973
$10,746	. . . . .	$3,404.73 plus 39.6%	—$10,746

(b) MARRIED person—

If the amount of wages (after subtracting withholding allowances) is:

The amount of income tax to withhold is:

Not over $267 . . . . $0

Over—	But not over—		of excess over—
$267	—$1,794 . .	15%	—$267
$1,794	—$3,606 . .	$229.05 plus 28%	—$1,794
$3,606	—$6,152 . .	$736.41 plus 31%	—$3,606
$6,152	—$10,856 .	$1,525.67 plus 36%	—$6,152
$10,856 .	. . . . .	$3,219.11 plus 39.6%	—$10,856

TABLE 4—MONTHLY Payroll Period

(a) SINGLE person (including head of household)—

If the amount of wages (after subtracting withholding allowances) is:

The amount of income tax to withhold is:

Not over $217 . . . . $0

Over—	But not over—		of excess over—
$217	—$2,063 . .	15%	—$217
$2,063	—$4,329 . .	$276.90 plus 28%	—$2,063
$4,329	—$9,946 . .	$911.38 plus 31%	—$4,329
$9,946	—$21,492 . .	$2,652.65 plus 36%	—$9,946
$21,492	. . . . .	$6,809.21 plus 39.6%	—$21,492

(b) MARRIED person—

If the amount of wages (after subtracting withholding allowances) is:

The amount of income tax to withhold is:

Not over $533 . . . . $0

Over—	But not over—		of excess over—
$533	—$3,588 . .	15%	—$533
$3,588	—$7,213 . .	$458.25 plus 28%	—$3,588
$7,213	—$12,304 .	$1,473.25 plus 31%	—$7,213
$12,304	—$21,713 .	$3,051.46 plus 36%	—$12,304
$21,713 .	. . . . .	$6,438.70 plus 39.6%	—$21,713

TABLE 5—QUARTERLY Payroll Period

(a) SINGLE person (including head of household)—			(b) MARRIED person—		
If the amount of wages (after subtracting withholding allowances) is:		The amount of income tax to withhold is:	If the amount of wages (after subtracting withholding allowances) is:		The amount of income tax to withhold is:
Not over $650		$0	Not over $1,600		$0
Over—	But not over—	of excess over—	Over—	But not over—	of excess over—
$650	—$6,188 . .	15% —$650	$1,600	—$10,763 . .	15% —$1,600
$6,188	—$12,988 . .	$830.70 plus 28% —$6,188	$10,763	—$21,638 . .	$1,374.45 plus 28% —$10,763
$12,988	—$29,838 . .	$2,734.70 plus 31% —$12,988	$21,638	—$36,913 . .	$4,419.45 plus 31% —$21,638
$29,838	—$64,475 . .	$7,958.20 plus 36% —$29,838	$36,913	—$65,138 . .	$9,154.70 plus 36% —$36,913
$64,475	. . . . . .	$20,427.52 plus 39.6%—$64,475	$65,138.	. . . . . .	$19,315.70 plus 39.6%—$65,138

TABLE 6—SEMIANNUAL Payroll Period

(a) SINGLE person (including head of household)—			(b) MARRIED person—		
If the amount of wages (after subtracting withholding allowances) is:		The amount of income tax to withhold is:	If the amount of wages (after subtracting withholding allowances) is:		The amount of income tax to withhold is:
Not over $1,300 . . .		$0	Not over $3,200		$0
Over—	But not over—	of excess over—	Over—	But not over—	of excess over—
$1,300	—$12,375 . .	15% —$1,300	$3,200	—$21,525 . .	15% —$3,200
$12,375	—$25,975 . .	$1,661.25 plus 28% —$12,375	$21,525	—$43,275 . .	$2,748.75 plus 28% —$21,525
$25,975	—$59,675 . .	$5,469.25 plus 31% —$25,975	$43,275	—$73,825 . .	$8,838.75 plus 31% —$43,275
$59,675	—$128,950. .	$15,916.25 plus 36% —$59,675	$73,825	—$130,275 . .	$18,309.25 plus 36% —$73,825
$128,950	. . . . . .	$40,855.25 plus 39.6%—$128,950	$130,275	. . . . . .	$38,631.25 plus 39.6%—$130,275

TABLE 7—ANNUAL Payroll Period

(a) SINGLE person (including head of household)—			(b) MARRIED person—		
If the amount of wages (after subtracting withholding allowances) is:		The amount of income tax to withhold is:	If the amount of wages (after subtracting withholding allowances) is:		The amount of income tax to withhold is:
Not over $2,600 . . .		$0	Not over $6,400		$0
Over—	But not over—	of excess over—	Over—	But not over—	of excess over—
$2,600	—$24,750 . .	15% —$2,600	$6,400	—$43,050 . .	15% —$6,400
$24,750	—$51,950 . .	$3,322.50 plus 28% —$24,750	$43,050	—$86,550 . .	$5,497.50 plus 28% —$43,050
$51,950	—$119,350. .	$10,938.50 plus 31% —$51,950	$86,550	—$147,650 . .	$17,677.50 plus 31% —$86,550
$119,350	—$257,900. .	$31,832.50 plus 36% —$119,350	$147,650	—$260,550 . .	$36,618.50 plus 36% —$147,650
$257,900	. . . . . .	$81,710.50 plus 39.6%—$257,900	$260,550	. . . . . .	$77,262.50 plus 39.6%—$260,550

TABLE 8—DAILY or MISCELLANEOUS Payroll Period

(a) SINGLE person (including head of household)—			(b) MARRIED person—		
If the amount of wages (after subtracting withholding allowances) divided by the number of days in the payroll period is:		The amount of income tax to withhold per day is:	If the amount of wages (after subtracting withholding allowances) divided by the number of days in the payroll period is:		The amount of income tax to withhold per day is:
Not over $10.00 . . .		$0	Not over $24.60		$0
Over—	But not over—	of excess over—	Over—	But not over—	of excess over—
$10.00	—$95.20 . .	15% —$10.00	$24.60	—$165.60 . .	15% —$24.60
$95.20	—$199.80 . .	$12.78 plus 28% —$95.20	$165.60	—$332.90 . .	$21.15 plus 28% —$165.60
$199.80	—$459.00 . .	$42.07 plus 31% —$199.80	$332.90	—$567.90 . .	$67.99 plus 31% —$332.90
$459.00	—$991.90 . .	$122.42 plus 36% —$459.00	$567.90	—$1,002.10 . .	$140.84 plus 36% —$567.90
$991.90	. . . . . .	$314.26 plus 39.6% —$991.90	$1,002.10	. . . . . .	$297.15 plus 39.6% —$1,002.10

TAX TABLE
B

WAGE-BRACKET WITHHOLDING TABLES

SINGLE Persons—WEEKLY Payroll Period
(For Wages Paid in 1995)

If the wages are—		And the number of withholding allowances claimed is—										
At least	But less than	0	1	2	3	4	5	6	7	8	9	10
		The amount of income tax to be withheld is—										
$50	$55	0	0	0	0	0	0	0	0	0	0	0
55	60	1	0	0	0	0	0	0	0	0	0	0
60	65	2	0	0	0	0	0	0	0	0	0	0
65	70	2	0	0	0	0	0	0	0	0	0	0
70	75	3	0	0	0	0	0	0	0	0	0	0
75	80	4	0	0	0	0	0	0	0	0	0	0
80	85	5	0	0	0	0	0	0	0	0	0	0
85	90	5	0	0	0	0	0	0	0	0	0	0
90	95	6	0	0	0	0	0	0	0	0	0	0
95	100	7	0	0	0	0	0	0	0	0	0	0
100	105	8	1	0	0	0	0	0	0	0	0	0
105	110	8	1	0	0	0	0	0	0	0	0	0
110	115	9	2	0	0	0	0	0	0	0	0	0
115	120	10	3	0	0	0	0	0	0	0	0	0
120	125	11	3	0	0	0	0	0	0	0	0	0
125	130	11	4	0	0	0	0	0	0	0	0	0
130	135	12	5	0	0	0	0	0	0	0	0	0
135	140	13	6	0	0	0	0	0	0	0	0	0
140	145	14	6	0	0	0	0	0	0	0	0	0
145	150	14	7	0	0	0	0	0	0	0	0	0
150	155	15	8	1	0	0	0	0	0	0	0	0
155	160	16	9	2	0	0	0	0	0	0	0	0
160	165	17	9	2	0	0	0	0	0	0	0	0
165	170	17	10	3	0	0	0	0	0	0	0	0
170	175	18	11	4	0	0	0	0	0	0	0	0
175	180	19	12	5	0	0	0	0	0	0	0	0
180	185	20	12	5	0	0	0	0	0	0	0	0
185	190	20	13	6	0	0	0	0	0	0	0	0
190	195	21	14	7	0	0	0	0	0	0	0	0
195	200	22	15	8	1	0	0	0	0	0	0	0
200	210	23	16	9	2	0	0	0	0	0	0	0
210	220	25	17	10	3	0	0	0	0	0	0	0
220	230	26	19	12	5	0	0	0	0	0	0	0
230	240	28	20	13	6	0	0	0	0	0	0	0
240	250	29	22	15	8	1	0	0	0	0	0	0
250	260	31	23	16	9	2	0	0	0	0	0	0
260	270	32	25	18	11	4	0	0	0	0	0	0
270	280	34	26	19	12	5	0	0	0	0	0	0
280	290	35	28	21	14	7	0	0	0	0	0	0
290	300	37	29	22	15	8	1	0	0	0	0	0
300	310	38	31	24	17	10	2	0	0	0	0	0
310	320	40	32	25	18	11	4	0	0	0	0	0
320	330	41	34	27	20	13	5	0	0	0	0	0
330	340	43	35	28	21	14	7	0	0	0	0	0
340	350	44	37	30	23	16	8	1	0	0	0	0
350	360	46	38	31	24	17	10	3	0	0	0	0
360	370	47	40	33	26	19	11	4	0	0	0	0
370	380	49	41	34	27	20	13	6	0	0	0	0
380	390	50	43	36	29	22	14	7	0	0	0	0
390	400	52	44	37	30	23	16	9	2	0	0	0
400	410	53	46	39	32	25	17	10	3	0	0	0
410	420	55	47	40	33	26	19	12	5	0	0	0
420	430	56	49	42	35	28	20	13	6	0	0	0
430	440	58	50	43	36	29	22	15	8	1	0	0
440	450	59	52	45	38	31	23	16	9	2	0	0
450	460	61	53	46	39	32	25	18	11	4	0	0
460	470	62	55	48	41	34	26	19	12	5	0	0
470	480	64	56	49	42	35	28	21	14	7	0	0
480	490	66	58	51	44	37	29	22	15	8	1	0
490	500	69	59	52	45	38	31	24	17	10	2	0
500	510	72	61	54	47	40	32	25	18	11	4	0
510	520	75	62	55	48	41	34	27	20	13	5	0
520	530	78	64	57	50	43	35	28	21	14	7	0
530	540	80	66	58	51	44	37	30	23	16	8	1
540	550	83	69	60	53	46	38	31	24	17	10	3
550	560	86	72	61	54	47	40	33	26	19	11	4
560	570	89	75	63	56	49	41	34	27	20	13	6
570	580	92	78	65	57	50	43	36	29	22	14	7
580	590	94	81	68	59	52	44	37	30	23	16	9
590	600	97	84	70	60	53	46	39	32	24	17	10

SINGLE Persons—WEEKLY Payroll Period
(For Wages Paid in 1995)

If the wages are—		And the number of withholding allowances claimed is—										
At least	But less than	0	1	2	3	4	5	6	7	8	9	10
		The amount of income tax to be withheld is—										
$600	$610	100	87	73	62	54	47	40	33	26	18	11
610	620	103	89	76	63	56	49	41	34	27	20	13
620	630	106	92	78	65	57	50	43	36	28	21	14
630	640	108	95	82	68	59	52	44	37	30	23	16
640	650	111	98	84	71	60	53	46	39	32	24	17
650	660	114	101	87	74	62	55	47	40	33	26	19
660	670	117	103	90	76	63	58	49	42	35	27	20
670	680	120	106	93	79	66	59	50	43	36	29	22
680	690	122	109	96	82	69	61	52	45	38	30	23
690	700	125	112	98	85	71	63	53	46	39	32	25
700	710	128	115	101	88	74	64	55	48	41	33	26
710	720	131	117	104	90	77	66	56	49	42	35	28
720	730	134	120	107	93	80	67	58	51	44	36	29
730	740	136	123	110	96	83	70	59	52	45	38	31
740	750	139	126	112	99	85	72	61	54	47	39	32
750	760	142	129	115	102	88	75	62	55	48	41	34
760	770	145	131	118	104	91	78	64	57	50	42	35
770	780	148	134	121	107	94	80	67	58	51	44	37
780	790	150	137	124	110	97	83	70	60	53	45	38
790	800	153	140	126	113	99	86	72	61	54	47	40
800	810	156	143	129	116	102	89	75	63	56	48	41
810	820	159	145	132	118	105	92	78	65	57	50	43
820	830	162	148	135	121	108	94	81	67	59	51	44
830	840	164	151	138	124	111	97	83	70	60	53	46
840	850	167	154	140	127	113	100	86	73	62	54	47
850	860	170	157	143	130	116	103	89	76	63	56	49
860	870	173	159	146	132	119	106	92	79	65	57	50
870	880	176	162	149	135	122	108	95	81	68	59	52
880	890	178	165	152	138	125	111	98	84	71	60	53
890	900	181	168	154	141	127	114	100	87	74	62	55
900	910	184	171	157	144	130	117	103	90	76	63	56
910	920	187	173	160	146	133	120	106	93	79	66	58
920	930	190	176	163	149	136	122	109	95	82	68	59
930	940	192	179	166	152	139	125	112	98	85	71	61
940	950	195	182	168	155	141	128	114	101	88	74	62
950	960	198	185	171	157	144	131	117	103	90	76	64
960	970	201	188	174	160	147	134	120	107	93	80	66
970	980	204	191	177	163	150	136	123	109	96	82	69
980	990	206	194	180	166	153	139	125	112	99	85	72
990	1,000	209	196	182	169	155	142	128	114	102	88	75
1,000	1,010	212	199	185	172	158	145	131	118	104	91	77
1,010	1,020	215	201	188	174	161	148	134	121	107	94	80
1,020	1,030	218	204	191	177	164	150	137	123	109	96	83
1,030	1,040	222	207	194	180	167	153	140	126	112	99	86
1,040	1,050	225	210	196	183	169	156	142	129	115	102	89
1,050	1,060	228	213	199	186	172	159	145	132	118	105	91
1,060	1,070	231	216	202	188	175	161	148	135	121	108	94
1,070	1,080	234	219	204	191	178	164	151	137	124	110	97
1,080	1,090	237	222	207	194	181	167	154	140	127	113	100
1,090	1,100	240	225	210	196	183	169	156	143	130	116	103
1,100	1,110	243	228	213	199	186	172	159	145	132	119	105
1,110	1,120	246	231	216	201	189	176	162	148	135	122	108
1,120	1,130	249	235	220	205	192	178	165	151	138	124	111
1,130	1,140	253	238	223	208	195	181	168	154	141	127	114
1,140	1,150	256	241	226	211	197	184	170	157	144	130	117
1,150	1,160	259	244	229	214	200	187	173	160	146	133	119
1,160	1,170	262	247	232	217	203	190	176	163	149	136	122
1,170	1,180	265	250	235	220	206	192	179	165	152	138	125
1,180	1,190	268	253	238	223	209	195	182	168	155	141	128
1,190	1,200	271	256	241	226	211	198	184	171	158	144	131
1,200	1,210	274	259	244	229	215	201	187	174	160	147	133
1,210	1,220	277	262	247	233	218	204	190	177	163	150	136
1,220	1,230	280	266	251	236	221	206	193	179	166	152	139
1,230	1,240	284	269	254	239	224	209	196	182	169	155	142
1,240	1,250	287	272	257	242	227	212	198	185	172	158	145
$1,250 and over		Use Table 1(a) for a SINGLE person										

WAGE-BRACKET WITHHOLDING TABLES

MARRIED Persons—WEEKLY Payroll Period
(For Wages Paid in 1995)

If the wages are—		And the number of withholding allowances claimed is—										
At least	But less than	0	1	2	3	4	5	6	7	8	9	10
		The amount of income tax to be withheld is—										
$0	$125	0	0	0	0	0	0	0	0	0	0	0
125	130	1	0	0	0	0	0	0	0	0	0	0
130	135	1	0	0	0	0	0	0	0	0	0	0
135	140	2	0	0	0	0	0	0	0	0	0	0
140	145	3	0	0	0	0	0	0	0	0	0	0
145	150	4	0	0	0	0	0	0	0	0	0	0
150	155	4	0	0	0	0	0	0	0	0	0	0
155	160	5	0	0	0	0	0	0	0	0	0	0
160	165	6	0	0	0	0	0	0	0	0	0	0
165	170	7	0	0	0	0	0	0	0	0	0	0
170	175	7	0	0	0	0	0	0	0	0	0	0
175	180	8	1	0	0	0	0	0	0	0	0	0
180	185	9	2	0	0	0	0	0	0	0	0	0
185	190	10	2	0	0	0	0	0	0	0	0	0
190	195	10	3	0	0	0	0	0	0	0	0	0
195	200	11	4	0	0	0	0	0	0	0	0	0
200	210	12	5	0	0	0	0	0	0	0	0	0
210	220	14	6	0	0	0	0	0	0	0	0	0
220	230	15	8	1	0	0	0	0	0	0	0	0
230	240	17	9	2	0	0	0	0	0	0	0	0
240	250	18	11	4	0	0	0	0	0	0	0	0
250	260	20	12	5	0	0	0	0	0	0	0	0
260	270	21	14	7	0	0	0	0	0	0	0	0
270	280	23	15	8	1	0	0	0	0	0	0	0
280	290	24	17	10	3	0	0	0	0	0	0	0
290	300	26	18	11	4	0	0	0	0	0	0	0
300	310	27	20	13	6	0	0	0	0	0	0	0
310	320	29	21	14	7	0	0	0	0	0	0	0
320	330	30	23	16	9	1	0	0	0	0	0	0
330	340	32	24	17	10	3	0	0	0	0	0	0
340	350	33	26	19	12	4	0	0	0	0	0	0
350	360	35	27	20	13	6	0	0	0	0	0	0
360	370	36	29	22	15	7	0	0	0	0	0	0
370	380	38	30	23	16	9	2	0	0	0	0	0
380	390	39	32	25	18	10	3	0	0	0	0	0
390	400	41	33	26	19	12	5	0	0	0	0	0
400	410	42	35	28	21	13	6	0	0	0	0	0
410	420	44	36	29	22	15	8	0	0	0	0	0
420	430	45	38	31	24	16	9	2	0	0	0	0
430	440	47	39	32	25	18	11	3	0	0	0	0
440	450	48	41	34	27	19	12	5	0	0	0	0
450	460	50	42	35	28	21	14	6	0	0	0	0
460	470	51	44	37	30	22	15	8	1	0	0	0
470	480	53	45	38	31	24	17	9	2	0	0	0
480	490	54	47	40	33	25	18	11	4	0	0	0
490	500	56	48	41	34	27	20	12	5	0	0	0
500	510	57	50	43	36	28	21	14	7	0	0	0
510	520	59	51	44	37	30	23	15	8	1	0	0
520	530	60	53	46	39	31	24	17	10	2	0	0
530	540	62	54	47	40	33	26	18	11	4	0	0
540	550	63	56	49	42	34	27	20	13	5	0	0
550	560	65	57	50	43	36	29	21	14	7	0	0
560	570	66	59	52	45	37	30	23	16	8	1	0
570	580	68	60	53	46	39	32	24	17	10	3	0
580	590	69	62	55	48	40	33	26	19	11	4	0
590	600	71	63	56	49	42	35	27	20	13	6	0
600	610	72	65	58	51	43	36	29	22	14	7	0
610	620	74	66	59	52	45	38	30	23	16	9	2
620	630	75	68	61	54	46	39	32	25	17	10	3
630	640	77	69	62	55	48	41	33	26	19	12	5
640	650	78	71	64	57	49	42	35	28	20	13	6
650	660	80	72	65	58	51	44	36	29	22	15	8
660	670	81	74	67	60	52	45	38	31	23	16	9
670	680	83	75	68	61	54	47	39	32	25	18	11
680	690	84	77	70	63	55	48	41	34	26	19	12
690	700	86	78	71	64	57	50	42	35	28	21	14
700	710	87	80	73	66	58	51	44	37	29	22	15
710	720	89	81	74	67	60	53	45	38	31	24	17
720	730	90	83	76	69	61	54	47	40	32	25	18
730	740	92	84	77	70	63	56	48	41	34	27	20

MARRIED Persons—WEEKLY Payroll Period
(For Wages Paid in 1995)

If the wages are—		And the number of withholding allowances claimed is—										
At least	But less than	0	1	2	3	4	5	6	7	8	9	10
		The amount of income tax to be withheld is—										
$740	$750	93	86	79	72	64	57	50	43	36	28	21
750	760	95	88	80	73	66	59	52	44	37	31	23
760	770	96	89	82	75	67	60	53	46	39	31	24
770	780	98	91	83	76	69	62	55	47	40	33	26
780	790	99	92	85	78	70	63	56	49	42	34	27
790	800	101	94	86	79	72	65	58	50	43	36	29
800	810	102	95	88	81	73	66	59	52	45	37	30
810	820	104	97	89	82	75	68	61	53	46	39	32
820	830	105	98	91	84	76	69	62	55	48	40	33
830	840	108	100	92	85	78	71	64	56	49	42	35
840	850	111	101	94	87	79	72	65	58	50	43	36
850	860	113	103	95	88	81	74	67	59	52	45	37
860	870	116	104	97	90	82	75	68	61	53	46	39
870	880	119	106	98	91	84	77	69	62	55	48	40
880	890	122	108	100	93	85	78	71	64	56	49	42
890	900	125	111	101	94	87	80	72	65	58	51	43
900	910	127	114	103	96	88	81	74	67	59	52	45
910	920	130	117	104	97	90	83	75	68	61	54	46
920	930	133	119	106	99	91	84	77	69	62	55	48
930	940	136	122	109	100	93	86	78	71	64	57	49
940	950	139	125	112	102	94	87	80	73	65	58	51
950	960	141	128	115	103	96	89	81	74	67	60	53
960	970	144	131	118	105	97	90	83	76	68	61	54
970	980	147	134	120	107	99	92	84	77	70	63	56
980	990	150	137	123	110	100	93	86	79	71	64	57
990	1,000	153	140	126	113	102	95	87	80	73	66	59
1,000	1,010	155	142	129	115	103	96	89	82	74	67	60
1,010	1,020	158	145	132	118	105	98	90	83	76	69	62
1,020	1,030	161	148	134	121	108	99	92	85	77	70	63
1,030	1,040	164	151	137	124	110	101	93	86	79	72	65
1,040	1,050	167	154	140	127	113	102	95	88	80	73	66
1,050	1,060	169	156	143	129	116	104	96	89	82	75	68
1,060	1,070	172	159	146	132	119	105	98	91	83	76	69
1,070	1,080	175	162	148	135	122	108	99	92	85	78	71
1,080	1,090	178	165	151	138	124	111	101	94	86	79	72
1,090	1,100	181	168	154	141	127	114	102	95	88	80	73
1,100	1,110	183	170	157	143	130	116	104	97	89	82	75
1,110	1,120	186	173	160	146	133	119	105	98	91	84	77
1,120	1,130	189	176	162	149	136	122	109	100	92	85	78
1,130	1,140	192	179	165	152	138	125	111	101	94	87	80
1,140	1,150	195	182	168	155	141	128	114	103	95	88	81
1,150	1,160	197	184	171	157	144	130	117	104	97	90	83
1,160	1,170	200	187	174	160	147	133	120	106	98	91	84
1,170	1,180	203	190	176	163	150	136	123	109	100	93	86
1,180	1,190	206	193	179	166	152	139	125	112	101	94	87
1,190	1,200	209	196	182	169	155	142	128	115	103	96	89
1,200	1,210	211	198	185	171	158	144	131	118	104	97	90
1,210	1,220	214	201	188	174	161	147	134	120	107	99	92
1,220	1,230	217	204	190	177	164	150	137	123	110	100	93
1,230	1,240	220	207	193	180	166	153	139	126	113	102	95
1,240	1,250	223	210	196	183	169	156	142	129	115	103	96
1,250	1,260	225	212	199	185	172	158	145	132	118	105	98
1,260	1,270	228	215	202	188	175	161	148	134	121	107	99
1,270	1,280	231	218	204	191	178	164	151	137	124	110	101
1,280	1,290	234	221	207	194	180	167	153	140	127	113	102
1,290	1,300	237	224	210	197	183	170	156	143	129	116	104
1,300	1,310	239	226	213	199	186	172	159	146	132	119	105
1,310	1,320	242	229	216	202	189	175	162	148	135	121	108
1,320	1,330	245	232	218	205	192	178	165	151	138	124	111
1,330	1,340	248	235	221	208	194	181	167	154	141	127	114
1,340	1,350	251	238	224	211	197	184	170	157	143	130	116
1,350	1,360	253	240	227	213	200	186	173	160	146	133	119
1,360	1,370	256	243	230	216	203	189	176	162	149	135	122
1,370	1,380	259	246	232	219	206	192	179	165	152	138	125
1,380	1,390	262	249	235	222	208	195	181	168	155	141	128

$1,390 and over — Use Table 1(b) for a MARRIED person

WAGE-BRACKET WITHHOLDING TABLES

SINGLE Persons—BIWEEKLY Payroll Period
(For Wages Paid in 1995)

If the wages are—		And the number of withholding allowances claimed is—										
At least	But less than	0	1	2	3	4	5	6	7	8	9	10
		The amount of income tax to be withheld is—										
$0	$105	0	0	0	0	0	0	0	0	0	0	0
105	110	1	0	0	0	0	0	0	0	0	0	0
110	115	2	0	0	0	0	0	0	0	0	0	0
115	120	3	0	0	0	0	0	0	0	0	0	0
120	125	3	0	0	0	0	0	0	0	0	0	0
125	130	4	0	0	0	0	0	0	0	0	0	0
130	135	5	0	0	0	0	0	0	0	0	0	0
135	140	6	0	0	0	0	0	0	0	0	0	0
140	145	6	0	0	0	0	0	0	0	0	0	0
145	150	7	0	0	0	0	0	0	0	0	0	0
150	155	8	0	0	0	0	0	0	0	0	0	0
155	160	9	0	0	0	0	0	0	0	0	0	0
160	165	10	0	0	0	0	0	0	0	0	0	0
165	170	10	0	0	0	0	0	0	0	0	0	0
170	175	11	0	0	0	0	0	0	0	0	0	0
175	180	12	0	0	0	0	0	0	0	0	0	0
180	185	13	0	0	0	0	0	0	0	0	0	0
185	190	14	0	0	0	0	0	0	0	0	0	0
190	195	14	0	0	0	0	0	0	0	0	0	0
195	200	15	0	0	0	0	0	0	0	0	0	0
200	205	15	1	0	0	0	0	0	0	0	0	0
205	210	16	2	0	0	0	0	0	0	0	0	0
210	215	17	2	0	0	0	0	0	0	0	0	0
215	220	18	3	0	0	0	0	0	0	0	0	0
220	225	18	4	0	0	0	0	0	0	0	0	0
225	230	19	5	0	0	0	0	0	0	0	0	0
230	235	20	5	0	0	0	0	0	0	0	0	0
235	240	21	6	0	0	0	0	0	0	0	0	0
240	245	21	7	0	0	0	0	0	0	0	0	0
245	250	22	8	0	0	0	0	0	0	0	0	0
250	260	23	9	0	0	0	0	0	0	0	0	0
260	270	25	10	0	0	0	0	0	0	0	0	0
270	280	26	12	0	0	0	0	0	0	0	0	0
280	290	28	13	0	0	0	0	0	0	0	0	0
290	300	29	15	1	0	0	0	0	0	0	0	0
300	310	31	16	2	0	0	0	0	0	0	0	0
310	320	32	18	3	0	0	0	0	0	0	0	0
320	330	34	19	5	0	0	0	0	0	0	0	0
330	340	35	21	6	0	0	0	0	0	0	0	0
340	350	37	22	8	0	0	0	0	0	0	0	0
350	360	38	24	9	0	0	0	0	0	0	0	0
360	370	40	25	11	0	0	0	0	0	0	0	0
370	380	41	27	12	0	0	0	0	0	0	0	0
380	390	43	28	14	0	0	0	0	0	0	0	0
390	400	44	30	15	1	0	0	0	0	0	0	0
400	410	46	31	17	2	0	0	0	0	0	0	0
410	420	47	33	18	4	0	0	0	0	0	0	0
420	430	49	34	20	5	0	0	0	0	0	0	0
430	440	50	36	21	7	0	0	0	0	0	0	0
440	450	52	37	23	8	0	0	0	0	0	0	0
450	460	53	39	24	10	0	0	0	0	0	0	0
460	470	55	40	26	11	0	0	0	0	0	0	0
470	480	56	42	27	13	0	0	0	0	0	0	0
480	490	58	43	29	14	0	0	0	0	0	0	0
490	500	59	45	30	16	2	0	0	0	0	0	0
500	520	62	47	33	18	4	0	0	0	0	0	0
520	540	65	50	36	21	7	0	0	0	0	0	0
540	560	68	53	39	24	10	0	0	0	0	0	0
560	580	71	56	42	27	13	0	0	0	0	0	0
580	600	74	59	45	30	16	1	0	0	0	0	0
600	620	77	62	48	33	19	4	0	0	0	0	0
620	640	80	65	51	36	22	7	0	0	0	0	0
640	660	83	68	54	39	25	10	0	0	0	0	0
660	680	86	71	57	42	28	13	0	0	0	0	0
680	700	89	74	60	45	31	16	2	0	0	0	0
700	720	92	77	63	48	34	19	5	0	0	0	0
720	740	95	80	66	51	37	22	8	0	0	0	0
740	760	98	83	69	54	40	25	11	0	0	0	0
760	780	101	86	72	57	43	28	14	0	0	0	0
780	800	104	89	75	60	46	31	17	3	0	0	0

SINGLE Persons—BIWEEKLY Payroll Period
(For Wages Paid in 1995)

If the wages are—		And the number of withholding allowances claimed is—										
At least	But less than	0	1	2	3	4	5	6	7	8	9	10
		The amount of income tax to be withheld is—										
$800	$820	107	92	78	63	49	34	20	6	0	0	0
820	840	110	95	81	66	52	37	23	9	0	0	0
840	860	113	98	84	69	55	40	26	12	0	0	0
860	880	116	101	87	72	58	43	29	15	3	0	0
880	900	119	104	90	75	61	46	32	18	6	0	0
900	920	122	107	93	78	64	49	35	21	6	0	0
920	940	125	110	96	81	67	52	38	24	9	0	0
940	960	128	113	99	84	70	55	41	27	12	0	0
960	980	133	116	102	87	73	58	44	30	15	1	0
980	1,000	138	119	105	90	76	61	47	33	18	4	0
1,000	1,020	144	122	108	93	79	64	50	36	21	7	0
1,020	1,040	150	125	111	96	82	67	53	39	24	10	0
1,040	1,060	155	128	114	99	85	70	56	42	27	13	0
1,060	1,080	161	134	117	102	88	73	59	45	30	16	2
1,080	1,100	166	140	120	105	91	76	62	48	33	19	5
1,100	1,120	172	145	123	108	94	79	65	51	36	22	7
1,120	1,140	178	151	129	111	97	82	68	54	39	25	10
1,140	1,160	183	156	135	114	100	85	71	57	42	28	13
1,160	1,180	189	162	141	117	103	88	74	60	45	31	16
1,180	1,200	194	168	146	120	106	91	77	63	48	34	19
1,200	1,220	200	173	152	123	109	94	80	66	51	37	22
1,220	1,240	206	179	157	126	112	97	83	69	54	40	25
1,240	1,260	211	184	163	130	115	100	86	72	57	43	28
1,260	1,280	217	190	169	136	118	103	89	75	60	46	31
1,280	1,300	222	196	174	142	121	106	92	78	63	49	34
1,300	1,320	228	201	180	147	124	109	95	81	66	52	37
1,320	1,340	234	207	185	153	127	112	98	84	69	55	40
1,340	1,360	239	212	191	158	132	115	101	87	72	58	43
1,360	1,380	245	218	197	164	137	118	104	90	75	61	46
1,380	1,400	250	224	202	170	143	121	107	93	78	64	49
1,400	1,420	256	229	208	175	148	124	110	96	81	67	52
1,420	1,440	262	235	213	181	154	127	113	99	84	70	55
1,440	1,460	267	240	219	186	160	133	116	102	87	73	58
1,460	1,480	273	246	225	192	165	138	119	105	90	76	61
1,480	1,500	278	252	230	198	171	144	122	108	93	79	64
1,500	1,520	284	257	236	203	176	149	125	111	96	82	67
1,520	1,540	290	263	242	209	182	155	128	114	99	85	70
1,540	1,560	295	268	247	214	188	161	134	117	102	88	73
1,560	1,580	301	274	253	220	193	166	139	120	105	91	76
1,580	1,600	306	280	259	226	199	172	145	123	108	94	79
1,600	1,620	312	285	258	231	204	177	151	126	111	97	82
1,620	1,640	318	291	264	237	210	183	156	129	114	100	85
1,640	1,660	323	296	269	242	216	189	162	135	117	103	88
1,660	1,680	329	302	275	248	221	194	167	140	120	106	91
1,680	1,700	334	308	281	254	227	200	173	146	123	109	94
1,700	1,720	340	313	286	259	232	205	179	152	126	112	97
1,720	1,740	346	319	292	265	238	211	184	157	130	115	100
1,740	1,760	351	324	297	270	244	217	190	163	136	118	103
1,760	1,780	357	330	303	276	249	222	195	168	141	121	106
1,780	1,800	362	336	309	282	255	228	201	174	147	124	109
1,800	1,820	368	341	314	287	260	233	207	180	153	127	112
1,820	1,840	374	347	320	293	266	239	212	185	158	131	115
1,840	1,860	379	352	325	298	272	245	218	191	164	137	118
1,860	1,880	385	358	331	304	277	250	223	196	169	142	121
1,880	1,900	390	364	337	310	283	256	229	202	175	148	124
1,900	1,920	396	369	342	315	288	261	235	208	181	154	127
1,920	1,940	402	375	348	321	294	267	241	213	186	159	132
1,940	1,960	407	380	353	326	300	273	246	219	192	165	138
1,960	1,980	413	386	359	332	305	278	251	224	197	171	144
1,980	2,000	418	392	365	338	311	284	257	230	203	176	149
2,000	2,020	424	397	370	343	316	289	263	236	209	182	155
2,020	2,040	431	403	376	349	322	295	268	241	214	187	160
2,040	2,060	437	408	381	354	328	301	274	247	220	193	166
2,060	2,080	443	414	387	360	333	306	279	252	225	199	172
2,080	2,100	449	420	393	366	339	312	285	258	231	204	177
$2,100 and over		Use Table 2(a) for a **SINGLE** person										

WAGE-BRACKET WITHHOLDING TABLES

MARRIED Persons—BIWEEKLY Payroll Period
(For Wages Paid in 1995)

If the wages are—		And the number of withholding allowances claimed is—										
At least	But less than	0	1	2	3	4	5	6	7	8	9	10
		The amount of income tax to be withheld is—										
$0	$250	0	0	0	0	0	0	0	0	0	0	0
250	260	1	0	0	0	0	0	0	0	0	0	0
260	270	3	0	0	0	0	0	0	0	0	0	0
270	280	4	0	0	0	0	0	0	0	0	0	0
280	290	6	0	0	0	0	0	0	0	0	0	0
290	300	7	0	0	0	0	0	0	0	0	0	0
300	310	9	0	0	0	0	0	0	0	0	0	0
310	320	10	0	0	0	0	0	0	0	0	0	0
320	330	12	0	0	0	0	0	0	0	0	0	0
330	340	13	0	0	0	0	0	0	0	0	0	0
340	350	15	0	0	0	0	0	0	0	0	0	0
350	360	16	2	0	0	0	0	0	0	0	0	0
360	370	18	3	0	0	0	0	0	0	0	0	0
370	380	19	5	0	0	0	0	0	0	0	0	0
380	390	21	6	0	0	0	0	0	0	0	0	0
390	400	22	8	0	0	0	0	0	0	0	0	0
400	410	24	9	0	0	0	0	0	0	0	0	0
410	420	25	11	0	0	0	0	0	0	0	0	0
420	430	27	12	0	0	0	0	0	0	0	0	0
430	440	28	14	0	0	0	0	0	0	0	0	0
440	450	30	15	1	0	0	0	0	0	0	0	0
450	460	31	17	2	0	0	0	0	0	0	0	0
460	470	33	18	4	0	0	0	0	0	0	0	0
470	480	34	20	5	0	0	0	0	0	0	0	0
480	490	36	21	7	0	0	0	0	0	0	0	0
490	500	37	23	8	0	0	0	0	0	0	0	0
500	520	40	25	10	0	0	0	0	0	0	0	0
520	540	43	28	13	0	0	0	0	0	0	0	0
540	560	46	31	16	2	0	0	0	0	0	0	0
560	580	49	34	19	5	0	0	0	0	0	0	0
580	600	52	37	22	8	0	0	0	0	0	0	0
600	620	55	40	25	11	0	0	0	0	0	0	0
620	640	58	43	28	14	0	0	0	0	0	0	0
640	660	61	46	31	17	3	0	0	0	0	0	0
660	680	64	49	34	20	6	0	0	0	0	0	0
680	700	67	52	37	23	9	0	0	0	0	0	0
700	720	70	55	40	26	12	0	0	0	0	0	0
720	740	73	58	43	29	15	0	0	0	0	0	0
740	760	76	61	46	32	18	3	0	0	0	0	0
760	780	79	64	49	35	21	6	0	0	0	0	0
780	800	82	67	52	38	24	9	0	0	0	0	0
800	820	85	70	55	41	27	12	0	0	0	0	0
820	840	88	73	58	44	30	15	1	0	0	0	0
840	860	91	76	61	47	33	18	4	0	0	0	0
860	880	94	79	64	50	36	21	7	0	0	0	0
880	900	97	82	67	53	39	24	10	0	0	0	0
900	920	100	85	70	56	42	27	13	0	0	0	0
920	940	103	88	73	59	45	30	16	1	0	0	0
940	960	106	91	76	62	48	33	19	4	0	0	0
960	980	109	94	79	65	51	36	22	7	0	0	0
980	1,000	112	97	82	68	54	39	25	10	0	0	0
1,000	1,020	115	100	85	71	57	42	28	13	0	0	0
1,020	1,040	118	103	88	74	60	45	31	16	2	0	0
1,040	1,060	121	106	91	77	63	48	34	19	5	0	0
1,060	1,080	124	109	94	80	66	51	37	22	8	0	0
1,080	1,100	127	112	97	83	69	54	40	25	11	0	0
1,100	1,120	130	115	100	86	72	57	43	28	14	0	0
1,120	1,140	133	118	103	89	75	60	46	31	17	2	0
1,140	1,160	136	121	106	92	78	63	49	34	20	5	0
1,160	1,180	139	124	109	95	81	66	52	37	23	8	0
1,180	1,200	142	127	112	98	84	69	55	40	26	11	0
1,200	1,220	145	130	115	101	87	72	58	43	29	14	0
1,220	1,240	148	133	118	104	90	75	61	46	32	17	3
1,240	1,260	151	136	121	107	93	78	64	49	35	20	6
1,260	1,280	154	139	124	110	96	81	67	52	38	23	9
1,280	1,300	157	142	127	113	99	84	70	55	41	26	12
1,300	1,320	160	145	130	116	102	87	73	58	44	29	15
1,320	1,340	163	148	133	119	105	90	76	61	47	32	18
1,340	1,360	166	151	136	122	108	93	79	64	50	35	21
1,360	1,380	169	154	139	125	111	96	82	67	53	38	24

MARRIED Persons—BIWEEKLY Payroll Period
(For Wages Paid in 1995)

If the wages are—		And the number of withholding allowances claimed is—										
At least	But less than	0	1	2	3	4	5	6	7	8	9	10
		The amount of income tax to be withheld is—										
$1,380	$1,400	172	157	143	128	114	99	85	71	56	42	27
1,400	1,420	175	160	146	131	117	102	88	74	59	45	30
1,420	1,440	178	163	149	134	120	105	91	77	62	48	33
1,440	1,460	181	166	152	137	123	108	94	80	65	51	36
1,460	1,480	184	169	155	140	126	111	97	83	68	54	39
1,480	1,500	187	172	158	143	129	114	100	86	71	57	42
1,500	1,520	190	175	161	146	132	117	103	89	74	60	45
1,520	1,540	193	178	164	149	135	120	106	92	77	63	48
1,540	1,560	196	181	167	152	138	123	109	95	80	66	51
1,560	1,580	199	184	170	155	141	126	112	98	83	69	54
1,580	1,600	202	187	173	158	144	129	115	101	86	72	57
1,600	1,620	205	190	176	161	147	132	118	104	89	75	60
1,620	1,640	208	193	179	164	150	135	121	107	92	78	63
1,640	1,660	211	196	182	167	153	138	124	110	95	81	66
1,660	1,680	215	199	185	170	156	141	127	113	98	84	69
1,680	1,700	221	202	188	173	159	144	130	116	101	87	72
1,700	1,720	227	205	191	176	162	147	133	119	104	90	75
1,720	1,740	232	208	194	179	165	150	136	122	107	93	78
1,740	1,760	238	211	197	182	168	153	139	125	110	96	81
1,760	1,780	243	217	200	185	171	156	142	128	113	99	84
1,780	1,800	249	222	203	188	174	159	145	131	116	102	87
1,800	1,820	255	228	206	191	177	162	148	134	119	105	90
1,820	1,840	260	233	209	194	180	165	151	137	122	108	93
1,840	1,860	266	239	212	197	183	168	154	140	125	111	96
1,860	1,880	271	245	218	200	186	171	157	143	128	114	99
1,880	1,900	277	250	223	203	189	174	160	146	131	117	102
1,900	1,920	283	256	229	206	192	177	163	149	134	120	105
1,920	1,940	288	261	234	209	195	180	166	152	137	123	108
1,940	1,960	294	267	240	213	198	183	169	155	140	126	111
1,960	1,980	299	273	246	219	201	186	172	158	143	129	114
1,980	2,000	305	278	251	224	204	189	175	161	146	132	117
2,000	2,020	311	284	257	230	207	192	178	164	149	135	120
2,020	2,040	316	289	262	235	210	195	181	167	152	138	123
2,040	2,060	322	295	268	241	214	198	184	170	155	141	126
2,060	2,080	327	301	274	247	220	201	187	173	158	144	129
2,080	2,100	333	306	279	252	225	204	190	176	161	147	132
2,100	2,120	339	312	285	258	231	207	193	179	164	150	135
2,120	2,140	344	317	290	263	237	210	196	182	167	153	138
2,140	2,160	350	323	296	269	242	215	199	185	170	156	141
2,160	2,180	355	329	302	275	248	221	202	188	173	159	144
2,180	2,200	361	334	307	280	253	226	205	191	176	162	147
2,200	2,220	367	340	313	286	259	232	208	194	179	165	150
2,220	2,240	372	345	318	291	265	238	211	197	182	168	153
2,240	2,260	378	351	324	297	270	243	216	200	185	171	156
2,260	2,280	383	357	330	303	276	249	222	203	188	174	159
2,280	2,300	389	362	335	308	281	254	227	206	191	177	162
2,300	2,320	395	368	341	314	287	260	233	209	194	180	165
2,320	2,340	400	373	346	319	293	266	239	212	197	183	168
2,340	2,360	406	379	352	325	298	271	244	217	200	186	171
2,360	2,380	411	385	358	331	304	277	250	223	203	189	174
2,380	2,400	417	390	363	336	309	282	255	229	206	192	177
2,400	2,420	423	396	369	342	315	288	261	234	209	195	180
2,420	2,440	428	401	374	347	321	294	267	240	213	198	183
2,440	2,460	434	407	380	353	326	299	272	245	218	201	186
2,460	2,480	439	413	386	359	332	305	278	251	224	204	189
2,480	2,500	445	418	391	364	337	310	283	257	230	207	192
2,500	2,520	451	424	397	370	343	316	289	262	235	210	195
2,520	2,540	456	429	402	375	349	322	295	268	241	214	198
2,540	2,560	462	435	408	381	354	327	300	273	246	219	201
2,560	2,580	467	441	414	387	360	333	306	279	252	225	204
2,580	2,600	473	446	419	392	365	338	311	285	258	231	207
2,600	2,620	479	452	425	398	371	344	317	290	263	236	210
2,620	2,640	484	457	430	403	377	350	323	296	269	242	215
2,640	2,660	490	463	436	409	382	355	328	301	274	248	221
2,660	2,680	495	469	442	415	388	361	334	307	280	253	226
$2,680 and over		Use Table 2(b) for a MARRIED person										

WAGE-BRACKET WITHHOLDING TABLES

SINGLE Persons—SEMIMONTHLY Payroll Period
(For Wages Paid in 1995)

If the wages are—		And the number of withholding allowances claimed is—										
At least	But less than	0	1	2	3	4	5	6	7	8	9	10
		The amount of income tax to be withheld is—										
$0	$110	0	0	0	0	0	0	0	0	0	0	0
110	115	1	0	0	0	0	0	0	0	0	0	0
115	120	1	0	0	0	0	0	0	0	0	0	0
120	125	2	0	0	0	0	0	0	0	0	0	0
125	130	3	0	0	0	0	0	0	0	0	0	0
130	135	4	0	0	0	0	0	0	0	0	0	0
135	140	4	0	0	0	0	0	0	0	0	0	0
140	145	5	0	0	0	0	0	0	0	0	0	0
145	150	6	0	0	0	0	0	0	0	0	0	0
150	155	7	0	0	0	0	0	0	0	0	0	0
155	160	7	0	0	0	0	0	0	0	0	0	0
160	165	8	0	0	0	0	0	0	0	0	0	0
165	170	9	0	0	0	0	0	0	0	0	0	0
170	175	10	0	0	0	0	0	0	0	0	0	0
175	180	10	0	0	0	0	0	0	0	0	0	0
180	185	11	0	0	0	0	0	0	0	0	0	0
185	190	12	0	0	0	0	0	0	0	0	0	0
190	195	13	0	0	0	0	0	0	0	0	0	0
195	200	13	0	0	0	0	0	0	0	0	0	0
200	205	14	0	0	0	0	0	0	0	0	0	0
205	210	15	0	0	0	0	0	0	0	0	0	0
210	215	16	0	0	0	0	0	0	0	0	0	0
215	220	16	1	0	0	0	0	0	0	0	0	0
220	225	17	2	0	0	0	0	0	0	0	0	0
225	230	18	2	0	0	0	0	0	0	0	0	0
230	235	19	3	0	0	0	0	0	0	0	0	0
235	240	19	4	0	0	0	0	0	0	0	0	0
240	245	20	5	0	0	0	0	0	0	0	0	0
245	250	21	5	0	0	0	0	0	0	0	0	0
250	260	22	6	0	0	0	0	0	0	0	0	0
260	270	24	8	0	0	0	0	0	0	0	0	0
270	280	25	9	0	0	0	0	0	0	0	0	0
280	290	27	11	0	0	0	0	0	0	0	0	0
290	300	28	12	0	0	0	0	0	0	0	0	0
300	310	30	14	0	0	0	0	0	0	0	0	0
310	320	31	15	0	0	0	0	0	0	0	0	0
320	330	33	17	1	0	0	0	0	0	0	0	0
330	340	34	18	2	0	0	0	0	0	0	0	0
340	350	36	20	4	0	0	0	0	0	0	0	0
350	360	37	21	5	0	0	0	0	0	0	0	0
360	370	39	23	7	0	0	0	0	0	0	0	0
370	380	40	24	8	0	0	0	0	0	0	0	0
380	390	42	26	10	0	0	0	0	0	0	0	0
390	400	43	27	11	0	0	0	0	0	0	0	0
400	410	45	29	13	0	0	0	0	0	0	0	0
410	420	46	30	15	1	0	0	0	0	0	0	0
420	430	48	32	16	2	0	0	0	0	0	0	0
430	440	49	33	18	4	0	0	0	0	0	0	0
440	450	51	35	19	5	0	0	0	0	0	0	0
450	460	52	36	21	6	0	0	0	0	0	0	0
460	470	54	38	22	8	0	0	0	0	0	0	0
470	480	55	39	24	9	0	0	0	0	0	0	0
480	490	57	41	25	10	0	0	0	0	0	0	0
490	500	58	42	27	12	0	0	0	0	0	0	0
500	520	60	45	29	13	0	0	0	0	0	0	0
520	540	63	48	32	16	1	0	0	0	0	0	0
540	560	66	51	35	19	4	0	0	0	0	0	0
560	580	69	54	38	22	7	0	0	0	0	0	0
580	600	72	57	41	25	10	0	0	0	0	0	0
600	620	75	60	44	28	13	0	0	0	0	0	0
620	640	78	63	47	31	16	0	0	0	0	0	0
640	660	81	66	50	34	19	3	0	0	0	0	0
660	680	84	69	53	37	22	6	0	0	0	0	0
680	700	87	72	56	40	25	9	0	0	0	0	0
700	720	90	75	59	43	28	12	0	0	0	0	0
720	740	93	78	62	46	31	15	0	0	0	0	0
740	760	96	81	65	49	34	18	3	0	0	0	0
760	780	99	84	68	52	37	21	6	0	0	0	0
780	800	102	87	71	55	40	24	9	0	0	0	0
800	820	105	90	74	58	43	27	12	0	0	0	0

SINGLE Persons—SEMIMONTHLY Payroll Period
(For Wages Paid in 1995)

If the wages are—		And the number of withholding allowances claimed is—										
At least	But less than	0	1	2	3	4	5	6	7	8	9	10
		The amount of income tax to be withheld is—										
$820	$840	108	93	77	61	46	30	15	0	0	0	0
840	860	111	96	80	64	49	33	18	2	0	0	0
860	880	114	99	83	67	52	36	21	5	0	0	0
880	900	117	102	86	70	55	39	24	8	0	0	0
900	920	120	105	89	73	58	42	27	11	0	0	0
920	940	123	108	92	76	61	45	30	14	0	0	0
940	960	126	111	95	79	64	48	33	17	1	0	0
960	980	129	114	98	82	67	51	36	20	4	0	0
980	1,000	132	117	101	85	70	54	39	23	7	0	0
1,000	1,020	135	120	104	88	73	57	42	26	10	0	0
1,020	1,040	138	123	107	91	76	60	45	29	13	0	0
1,040	1,060	144	126	110	94	79	63	48	32	16	1	0
1,060	1,080	149	129	113	97	82	66	51	35	19	4	0
1,080	1,100	155	132	116	100	85	69	54	38	22	7	0
1,100	1,120	160	135	119	103	88	72	57	41	25	10	0
1,120	1,140	166	138	122	106	91	75	60	44	28	13	0
1,140	1,160	172	143	125	109	94	78	63	47	31	16	0
1,160	1,180	177	148	128	112	97	81	66	50	34	19	3
1,180	1,200	183	154	131	115	100	84	69	53	37	22	6
1,200	1,220	188	159	134	118	103	87	72	56	40	25	9
1,220	1,240	194	165	137	121	106	90	75	59	43	28	12
1,240	1,260	200	171	141	124	109	93	78	62	46	31	15
1,260	1,280	205	176	147	127	112	96	81	65	49	34	18
1,280	1,300	211	182	153	130	115	99	84	68	52	37	21
1,300	1,320	216	187	158	133	118	102	87	71	55	40	24
1,320	1,340	222	193	164	136	121	105	90	74	58	43	27
1,340	1,360	228	199	169	140	124	108	93	77	61	46	30
1,360	1,380	233	204	175	146	127	111	96	80	64	49	33
1,380	1,400	239	210	181	151	130	114	99	83	67	52	36
1,400	1,420	244	215	186	157	133	117	102	86	70	55	39
1,420	1,440	250	221	192	163	136	120	105	89	73	58	42
1,440	1,460	256	227	197	168	139	123	108	92	76	61	45
1,460	1,480	261	232	203	174	145	126	111	95	79	64	48
1,480	1,500	267	238	209	179	150	129	114	98	82	67	51
1,500	1,520	272	243	214	185	156	132	117	101	85	70	54
1,520	1,540	278	249	220	191	161	135	120	104	88	73	57
1,540	1,560	284	255	225	196	167	138	123	107	91	76	60
1,560	1,580	289	260	231	202	173	143	126	110	94	79	63
1,580	1,600	295	266	237	207	178	149	129	113	97	82	66
1,600	1,620	300	271	242	213	184	155	132	116	100	85	69
1,620	1,640	306	277	248	219	189	160	135	119	103	88	72
1,640	1,660	312	283	253	224	195	166	138	122	106	91	75
1,660	1,680	317	288	259	230	201	171	142	125	109	94	78
1,680	1,700	323	294	265	235	206	177	148	128	112	97	81
1,700	1,720	328	299	270	241	212	183	153	131	115	100	84
1,720	1,740	334	305	276	247	217	188	159	134	118	103	87
1,740	1,760	340	311	281	252	223	194	165	137	121	106	90
1,760	1,780	345	316	287	258	229	199	170	141	124	109	93
1,780	1,800	351	322	293	263	234	205	176	147	127	112	96
1,800	1,820	356	327	298	269	240	211	181	152	130	115	99
1,820	1,840	362	333	304	275	245	216	187	158	133	118	102
1,840	1,860	368	339	309	280	251	222	193	164	136	121	105
1,860	1,880	373	344	315	286	257	227	198	169	140	124	108
1,880	1,900	379	350	321	291	262	233	204	175	146	127	111
1,900	1,920	384	355	326	297	268	239	209	180	151	130	114
1,920	1,940	390	361	332	303	273	244	215	186	157	133	117
1,940	1,960	396	367	337	308	279	250	221	192	162	136	120
1,960	1,980	401	372	343	314	285	255	226	197	168	139	123
1,980	2,000	407	378	349	319	290	261	232	203	174	145	126
2,000	2,020	412	383	354	325	296	267	237	208	179	150	129
2,020	2,040	418	389	360	331	301	272	243	214	185	156	132
2,040	2,060	424	395	365	336	307	278	249	220	190	161	135
2,060	2,080	429	400	371	342	313	283	254	225	196	167	138
2,080	2,100	435	406	377	347	318	289	260	231	202	172	143
2,100	2,120	440	411	382	353	324	295	265	236	207	178	149
$2,120 and over		Use Table 3(a) for a SINGLE person										

WAGE-BRACKET WITHHOLDING TABLES

MARRIED Persons—SEMIMONTHLY Payroll Period
(For Wages Paid in 1995)

If the wages are—		And the number of withholding allowances claimed is—										
At least	But less than	0	1	2	3	4	5	6	7	8	9	10
		The amount of income tax to be withheld is—										
$90	$270	0	0	0	0	0	0	0	0	0	0	0
270	280	1	0	0	0	0	0	0	0	0	0	0
280	290	3	0	0	0	0	0	0	0	0	0	0
290	300	4	0	0	0	0	0	0	0	0	0	0
300	310	6	0	0	0	0	0	0	0	0	0	0
310	320	7	0	0	0	0	0	0	0	0	0	0
320	330	9	0	0	0	0	0	0	0	0	0	0
330	340	10	1	0	0	0	0	0	0	0	0	0
340	350	12	2	0	0	0	0	0	0	0	0	0
350	360	13	4	0	0	0	0	0	0	0	0	0
360	370	15	5	0	0	0	0	0	0	0	0	0
370	380	16	7	0	0	0	0	0	0	0	0	0
380	390	18	8	0	0	0	0	0	0	0	0	0
390	400	19	10	0	0	0	0	0	0	0	0	0
400	410	21	11	0	0	0	0	0	0	0	0	0
410	420	22	13	0	0	0	0	0	0	0	0	0
420	430	24	14	0	0	0	0	0	0	0	0	0
430	440	25	16	0	0	0	0	0	0	0	0	0
440	450	27	17	0	0	0	0	0	0	0	0	0
450	460	28	19	0	0	0	0	0	0	0	0	0
460	470	30	21	0	0	0	0	0	0	0	0	0
470	480	31	24	0	0	0	0	0	0	0	0	0
480	490	33	27	2	0	0	0	0	0	0	0	0
490	500	34	30	3	0	0	0	0	0	0	0	0
500	520	37	33	5	0	0	0	0	0	0	0	0
520	540	40	36	8	0	0	0	0	0	0	0	0
540	560	43	39	11	0	0	0	0	0	0	0	0
560	580	46	42	14	2	0	0	0	0	0	0	0
580	600	49	45	17	5	0	0	0	0	0	0	0
600	620	52	48	20	8	0	0	0	0	0	0	0
620	640	55	51	23	11	0	0	0	0	0	0	0
640	660	58	54	26	14	0	0	0	0	0	0	0
660	680	61	57	29	17	0	0	0	0	0	0	0
680	700	64	60	32	20	1	0	0	0	0	0	0
700	720	67	63	35	23	4	0	0	0	0	0	0
720	740	70	66	38	26	7	0	0	0	0	0	0
740	760	73	69	41	29	10	0	0	0	0	0	0
760	780	76	72	44	32	13	0	0	0	0	0	0
780	800	79	75	47	35	16	0	0	0	0	0	0
800	820	82	78	50	38	19	1	0	0	0	0	0
820	840	85	81	53	41	22	6	0	0	0	0	0
840	860	88	84	56	44	25	9	0	0	0	0	0
860	880	91	87	59	47	28	12	0	0	0	0	0
880	900	94	90	62	50	31	15	0	0	0	0	0
900	920	97	93	65	53	34	18	3	0	0	0	0
920	940	100	96	68	56	37	21	6	0	0	0	0
940	960	103	99	71	59	40	24	9	0	0	0	0
960	980	106	102	74	62	43	27	12	0	0	0	0
980	1,000	109	105	77	65	46	30	15	0	0	0	0
1,000	1,020	112	108	80	68	49	33	18	2	0	0	0
1,020	1,040	115	111	83	71	52	36	21	5	0	0	0
1,040	1,060	118	114	86	74	55	39	24	8	0	0	0
1,060	1,080	121	117	89	77	58	42	27	11	0	0	0
1,080	1,100	124	120	92	80	61	45	30	14	0	0	0
1,100	1,120	127	123	95	83	64	48	33	17	2	0	0
1,120	1,140	130	126	98	86	67	51	36	20	5	0	0
1,140	1,160	133	129	101	89	70	54	39	23	8	0	0
1,160	1,180	136	132	104	92	73	57	42	26	11	0	0
1,180	1,200	139	135	107	95	76	60	45	29	14	0	0
1,200	1,220	142	138	110	98	79	63	48	32	17	1	0
1,220	1,240	145	141	113	101	82	66	51	35	20	4	0
1,240	1,260	148	144	116	104	85	69	54	38	23	7	0
1,260	1,280	151	147	119	107	88	72	57	41	26	10	0
1,280	1,300	154	150	122	110	91	75	60	44	29	13	0
1,300	1,320	157	153	125	113	94	78	63	47	32	16	3
1,320	1,340	160	144	128	113	97	81	66	50	35	19	3
1,340	1,360	163	147	131	116	100	84	69	53	38	22	6
1,360	1,380	166	150	134	119	103	87	72	56	41	25	9
1,380	1,400	169	153	137	122	106	90	75	59	44	28	12
1,400	1,420	172	156	140	125	109	93	78	62	47	31	15

MARRIED Persons—SEMIMONTHLY Payroll Period
(For Wages Paid in 1995)

If the wages are—		And the number of withholding allowances claimed is—										
At least	But less than	0	1	2	3	4	5	6	7	8	9	10
		The amount of income tax to be withheld is—										
$1,420	$1,440	175	159	143	128	112	96	81	65	50	34	18
1,440	1,460	178	162	146	131	115	99	84	68	53	37	21
1,460	1,480	181	165	149	134	118	102	87	71	56	40	24
1,480	1,500	184	168	152	137	121	105	90	74	59	43	27
1,500	1,520	187	171	155	140	124	108	93	77	62	46	30
1,520	1,540	190	174	158	143	127	111	96	80	65	49	33
1,540	1,560	193	177	161	146	130	114	99	83	68	52	36
1,560	1,580	196	180	164	149	133	117	102	86	71	55	39
1,580	1,600	199	183	167	152	136	120	105	89	74	58	42
1,600	1,620	202	186	170	155	139	123	108	92	77	61	45
1,620	1,640	205	189	173	158	142	126	111	95	80	64	48
1,640	1,660	208	192	176	161	145	129	114	98	83	67	51
1,660	1,680	211	195	179	164	148	132	117	101	86	70	54
1,680	1,700	214	198	182	167	151	135	120	104	89	73	57
1,700	1,720	217	201	185	170	154	138	123	107	92	76	60
1,720	1,740	220	204	188	173	157	141	126	110	95	79	63
1,740	1,760	223	207	191	176	160	144	129	113	98	82	66
1,760	1,780	226	210	194	179	163	147	132	116	101	85	69
1,780	1,800	229	213	197	182	166	150	135	119	104	88	72
1,800	1,820	234	216	200	185	169	153	138	122	107	91	75
1,820	1,840	239	219	203	188	172	156	141	125	110	94	78
1,840	1,860	245	222	206	191	175	159	144	128	113	97	81
1,860	1,880	250	225	209	194	178	162	147	131	116	100	84
1,880	1,900	256	228	212	197	181	165	150	134	119	103	87
1,900	1,920	262	232	215	200	184	168	153	137	122	106	90
1,920	1,940	267	238	218	203	187	171	156	140	125	109	93
1,940	1,960	273	244	221	206	190	174	159	143	128	112	96
1,960	1,980	278	249	224	209	193	177	162	146	131	115	99
1,980	2,000	284	255	227	212	196	180	165	149	134	118	102
2,000	2,020	290	260	231	215	199	183	168	152	137	121	105
2,020	2,040	295	266	237	218	202	186	171	155	140	124	108
2,040	2,060	301	272	242	221	205	189	174	158	143	127	111
2,060	2,080	306	277	248	224	208	192	177	161	146	130	114
2,080	2,100	312	283	254	227	211	195	180	164	149	133	117
2,100	2,120	318	288	259	230	214	198	183	167	152	136	120
2,120	2,140	323	294	265	236	217	201	186	170	155	139	123
2,140	2,160	329	300	270	241	220	204	189	173	158	142	126
2,160	2,180	334	305	276	247	223	207	192	176	161	145	129
2,180	2,200	340	311	282	253	226	210	195	179	164	148	132
2,200	2,220	346	316	287	258	229	213	198	182	167	151	135
2,220	2,240	351	322	293	264	235	216	201	185	170	154	138
2,240	2,260	357	328	298	269	240	219	204	188	173	157	141
2,260	2,280	362	333	304	275	246	222	207	191	176	160	144
2,280	2,300	368	339	310	281	252	225	210	194	179	163	147
2,300	2,320	374	344	315	286	257	228	213	197	182	166	150
2,320	2,340	379	350	321	292	263	233	216	200	185	169	153
2,340	2,360	385	356	326	298	268	239	219	203	188	172	156
2,360	2,380	390	361	332	303	274	245	222	206	191	175	159
2,380	2,400	396	367	338	309	279	250	225	209	194	178	162
2,400	2,420	402	372	343	314	285	256	228	212	197	181	165
2,420	2,440	407	378	349	320	291	261	232	215	200	184	168
2,440	2,460	413	384	354	325	296	267	238	218	203	187	171
2,460	2,480	418	389	360	331	302	273	243	221	206	190	174
2,480	2,500	424	395	366	337	307	278	249	224	209	193	177
2,500	2,520	430	400	371	342	313	284	255	227	212	196	180
2,520	2,540	435	406	377	348	319	289	260	231	215	199	183
2,540	2,560	441	412	382	353	324	295	266	237	218	202	186
2,560	2,580	446	417	388	359	330	301	271	242	221	205	189
2,580	2,600	452	423	394	365	335	306	277	248	224	208	192
2,600	2,620	458	428	399	370	341	312	283	253	227	211	195
2,620	2,640	463	434	405	376	347	317	288	259	230	214	198
2,640	2,660	469	440	410	381	352	323	294	265	235	217	201
2,660	2,680	474	445	416	387	358	329	299	270	241	220	204
2,680	2,700	480	451	422	393	363	334	305	276	247	223	207
2,700	2,720	486	456	427	398	369	340	311	281	252	226	210
$2,720 and over		Use Table 3(b) for a **MARRIED** person										

WAGE-BRACKET WITHHOLDING TABLES

SINGLE Persons—MONTHLY Payroll Period
(For Wages Paid in 1995)

If the wages are—		And the number of withholding allowances claimed is—										
At least	But less than	0	1	2	3	4	5	6	7	8	9	10
		The amount of income tax to be withheld is—										
$0	$220	0	0	0	0	0	0	0	0	0	0	0
220	240	1	0	0	0	0	0	0	0	0	0	0
240	250	3	0	0	0	0	0	0	0	0	0	0
250	260	4	0	0	0	0	0	0	0	0	0	0
260	270	6	0	0	0	0	0	0	0	0	0	0
270	280	7	0	0	0	0	0	0	0	0	0	0
280	290	9	0	0	0	0	0	0	0	0	0	0
290	300	10	0	0	0	0	0	0	0	0	0	0
300	320	12	0	0	0	0	0	0	0	0	0	0
320	340	14	0	0	0	0	0	0	0	0	0	0
340	360	17	0	0	0	0	0	0	0	0	0	0
360	380	20	0	0	0	0	0	0	0	0	0	0
380	400	23	0	0	0	0	0	0	0	0	0	0
400	420	26	0	0	0	0	0	0	0	0	0	0
420	440	29	2	0	0	0	0	0	0	0	0	0
440	460	32	5	0	0	0	0	0	0	0	0	0
460	480	35	8	0	0	0	0	0	0	0	0	0
480	500	38	11	0	0	0	0	0	0	0	0	0
500	520	41	14	0	0	0	0	0	0	0	0	0
520	540	44	17	0	0	0	0	0	0	0	0	0
540	560	47	20	0	0	0	0	0	0	0	0	0
560	580	50	23	0	0	0	0	0	0	0	0	0
580	600	53	26	0	0	0	0	0	0	0	0	0
600	640	56	29	0	0	0	0	0	0	0	0	0
640	680	61	35	4	0	0	0	0	0	0	0	0
680	720	67	41	10	0	0	0	0	0	0	0	0
720	760	73	47	16	0	0	0	0	0	0	0	0
760	800	79	53	22	0	0	0	0	0	0	0	0
800	840	85	59	28	0	0	0	0	0	0	0	0
840	880	91	65	34	3	0	0	0	0	0	0	0
880	920	97	71	40	9	0	0	0	0	0	0	0
920	960	103	77	46	15	0	0	0	0	0	0	0
960	1,000	109	83	52	21	0	0	0	0	0	0	0
1,000	1,040	115	89	58	27	0	0	0	0	0	0	0
1,040	1,080	121	95	64	33	2	0	0	0	0	0	0
1,080	1,120	127	101	70	39	8	0	0	0	0	0	0
1,120	1,160	133	107	76	45	14	0	0	0	0	0	0
1,160	1,200	139	113	82	51	20	0	0	0	0	0	0
1,200	1,240	145	119	88	57	26	0	0	0	0	0	0
1,240	1,280	151	125	94	63	32	0	0	0	0	0	0
1,280	1,320	157	131	100	69	38	6	0	0	0	0	0
1,320	1,360	163	137	106	75	44	12	0	0	0	0	0
1,360	1,400	169	143	112	81	50	18	0	0	0	0	0
1,400	1,440	175	149	118	87	56	24	0	0	0	0	0
1,440	1,480	181	155	124	93	62	30	0	0	0	0	0
1,480	1,520	187	161	130	99	68	36	5	0	0	0	0
1,520	1,560	193	167	136	105	74	42	11	0	0	0	0
1,560	1,600	199	173	142	111	80	48	17	0	0	0	0
1,600	1,640	205	179	148	117	86	54	23	0	0	0	0
1,640	1,680	211	185	154	123	92	60	29	0	0	0	0
1,680	1,720	217	191	160	129	98	66	35	4	0	0	0
1,720	1,760	223	197	166	135	104	72	41	10	0	0	0
1,760	1,800	229	203	172	141	110	78	47	16	0	0	0
1,800	1,840	235	209	178	147	116	84	53	22	0	0	0
1,840	1,880	241	215	184	153	122	90	59	28	0	0	0
1,880	1,920	247	221	190	159	128	96	65	34	3	0	0
1,920	1,960	253	227	196	165	134	102	71	40	9	0	0
1,960	2,000	259	233	202	171	140	108	77	46	15	0	0
2,000	2,040	265	239	208	177	146	114	83	52	21	0	0
2,040	2,080	271	245	214	183	152	120	89	58	27	0	0
2,080	2,120	277	251	220	189	158	126	95	64	33	1	0
2,120	2,160	287	257	226	195	164	132	101	70	39	7	0
2,160	2,200	299	263	232	201	170	138	107	76	45	13	0
2,200	2,240	310	269	238	207	176	144	113	82	51	19	0
2,240	2,280	321	275	244	213	182	150	119	88	57	25	0
2,280	2,320	332	285	250	219	188	156	125	94	63	31	0
2,320	2,360	343	296	256	225	194	162	131	100	69	37	6
2,360	2,400	355	307	262	231	200	168	137	106	75	43	12
2,400	2,440	377	319	268	237	206	174	143	112	81	49	18

SINGLE Persons—MONTHLY Payroll Period
(For Wages Paid in 1995)

If the wages are—		And the number of withholding allowances claimed is—										
At least	But less than	0	1	2	3	4	5	6	7	8	9	10
		The amount of income tax to be withheld is—										
$2,440	$2,480	388	330	274	243	212	180	149	118	87	55	24
2,480	2,520	399	341	283	249	218	186	155	124	93	61	30
2,520	2,560	411	352	294	255	224	192	161	130	99	67	36
2,560	2,600	422	363	305	261	230	198	167	136	105	73	42
2,600	2,640	433	375	316	267	236	204	173	142	111	79	48
2,640	2,680	444	386	328	273	242	210	179	148	117	85	54
2,680	2,720	455	397	339	280	248	216	185	154	123	91	60
2,720	2,760	467	408	350	292	254	222	191	160	129	97	66
2,760	2,800	478	419	361	303	260	228	197	166	135	103	72
2,800	2,840	489	431	372	314	266	234	203	172	141	109	78
2,840	2,880	500	442	384	325	272	240	209	178	147	115	84
2,880	2,920	511	453	395	336	278	246	215	184	153	121	90
2,920	2,960	523	464	406	348	289	252	221	190	159	127	96
2,960	3,000	534	475	417	359	300	258	227	196	165	133	102
3,000	3,040	545	487	428	370	312	264	233	202	171	139	108
3,040	3,080	556	498	440	381	323	270	239	208	177	145	114
3,080	3,120	567	509	451	392	334	276	245	214	183	151	120
3,120	3,160	579	520	462	404	345	287	251	220	189	157	126
3,160	3,200	590	531	473	415	356	298	257	226	195	163	132
3,200	3,240	601	543	484	426	368	309	263	232	201	169	138
3,240	3,280	612	554	496	437	379	321	269	238	207	175	144
3,280	3,320	623	565	507	448	390	332	275	244	213	181	150
3,320	3,360	635	576	518	460	401	343	285	250	219	187	156
3,360	3,400	646	587	529	471	412	354	296	256	225	193	162
3,400	3,440	657	599	540	482	424	365	307	262	231	199	168
3,440	3,480	668	610	552	493	435	377	318	268	237	205	174
3,480	3,520	679	621	563	504	446	388	329	274	243	211	180
3,520	3,560	691	632	574	516	457	399	341	280	249	217	186
3,560	3,600	702	643	585	527	468	410	352	293	255	223	192
3,600	3,640	713	655	596	538	480	421	363	305	261	229	198
3,640	3,680	724	666	608	549	491	433	374	316	267	235	204
3,680	3,720	735	677	619	560	502	444	385	327	273	241	210
3,720	3,760	747	688	630	572	513	455	397	338	280	247	216
3,760	3,800	758	699	641	583	524	466	408	349	291	253	222
3,800	3,840	769	711	652	594	536	477	419	361	302	259	228
3,840	3,880	780	722	664	605	547	489	430	372	314	265	234
3,880	3,920	791	733	675	616	558	500	441	383	325	271	240
3,920	3,960	803	744	686	628	569	511	453	394	336	278	246
3,960	4,000	814	755	697	639	580	522	464	405	347	289	252
4,000	4,040	825	767	708	650	592	533	475	417	358	300	258
4,040	4,080	836	778	720	661	603	545	486	428	370	311	264
4,080	4,120	847	789	731	672	614	556	497	439	381	322	270
4,120	4,160	859	800	742	684	625	567	509	450	392	334	276
4,160	4,200	870	811	753	695	636	578	520	461	403	345	286
4,200	4,240	881	823	764	706	648	589	531	473	414	356	298
4,240	4,280	892	834	776	717	659	601	542	484	426	367	309
4,280	4,320	903	845	787	728	670	612	553	495	437	378	320
4,320	4,360	915	856	798	740	681	623	565	506	448	390	331
4,360	4,400	927	867	809	751	692	634	576	517	459	401	342
4,400	4,440	940	879	820	762	704	645	587	529	470	412	354
4,440	4,480	952	890	832	773	715	657	598	540	482	423	365
4,480	4,520	965	901	843	784	726	668	609	551	493	434	376
4,520	4,560	977	912	854	796	737	679	621	562	504	446	387
4,560	4,600	989	925	865	807	748	690	632	573	515	457	398
4,600	4,640	1,002	937	876	818	760	701	643	585	526	468	410
4,640	4,680	1,014	950	888	829	771	713	654	596	538	479	421
4,680	4,720	1,027	962	899	840	782	724	665	607	549	490	432
4,720	4,760	1,039	974	910	852	793	735	677	618	560	502	443
4,760	4,800	1,051	987	921	863	804	746	688	629	571	513	454
4,800	4,840	1,064	999	935	874	816	757	699	641	582	524	466
4,840	4,880	1,076	1,012	947	885	827	769	710	652	594	535	477
4,880	4,920	1,089	1,024	959	896	838	780	721	663	605	546	488
4,920	4,960	1,101	1,036	972	908	849	791	733	674	616	558	499
4,960	5,000	1,113	1,049	984	920	860	802	744	685	627	569	510
5,000	5,040	1,126	1,061	997	932	872	813	755	697	638	580	522
$5,040 and over		Use Table 4(a) for a SINGLE person										

WAGE-BRACKET WITHHOLDING TABLES

MARRIED Persons—MONTHLY Payroll Period
(For Wages Paid in 1995)

If the wages are— At least	But less than	And the number of withholding allowances claimed is— 0	1	2	3	4	5	6	7	8	9	10
		The amount of income tax to be withheld is—										
$50	$540	0	0	0	0	0	0	0	0	0	0	0
540	560	3	0	0	0	0	0	0	0	0	0	0
560	580	6	0	0	0	0	0	0	0	0	0	0
580	600	9	0	0	0	0	0	0	0	0	0	0
600	640	13	0	0	0	0	0	0	0	0	0	0
640	680	19	0	0	0	0	0	0	0	0	0	0
680	720	25	0	0	0	0	0	0	0	0	0	0
720	760	31	0	0	0	0	0	0	0	0	0	0
760	800	37	6	0	0	0	0	0	0	0	0	0
800	840	43	12	0	0	0	0	0	0	0	0	0
840	880	49	18	0	0	0	0	0	0	0	0	0
880	920	55	24	0	0	0	0	0	0	0	0	0
920	960	61	30	0	0	0	0	0	0	0	0	0
960	1,000	67	36	5	0	0	0	0	0	0	0	0
1,000	1,040	73	42	11	0	0	0	0	0	0	0	0
1,040	1,080	79	48	17	0	0	0	0	0	0	0	0
1,080	1,120	85	54	23	0	0	0	0	0	0	0	0
1,120	1,160	91	60	29	0	0	0	0	0	0	0	0
1,160	1,200	97	66	35	3	0	0	0	0	0	0	0
1,200	1,240	103	72	41	9	0	0	0	0	0	0	0
1,240	1,280	109	78	47	15	0	0	0	0	0	0	0
1,280	1,320	115	84	53	21	0	0	0	0	0	0	0
1,320	1,360	121	90	59	27	0	0	0	0	0	0	0
1,360	1,400	127	96	65	33	2	0	0	0	0	0	0
1,400	1,440	133	102	71	39	8	0	0	0	0	0	0
1,440	1,480	139	108	77	45	14	0	0	0	0	0	0
1,480	1,520	145	114	83	51	20	0	0	0	0	0	0
1,520	1,560	151	120	89	57	26	0	0	0	0	0	0
1,560	1,600	157	126	95	63	32	1	0	0	0	0	0
1,600	1,640	163	132	101	69	38	7	0	0	0	0	0
1,640	1,680	169	138	107	75	44	13	0	0	0	0	0
1,680	1,720	175	144	113	81	50	19	0	0	0	0	0
1,720	1,760	181	150	119	87	56	25	0	0	0	0	0
1,760	1,800	187	156	125	93	62	31	0	0	0	0	0
1,800	1,840	193	162	131	99	68	37	6	0	0	0	0
1,840	1,880	199	168	137	105	74	43	12	0	0	0	0
1,880	1,920	205	174	143	111	80	49	18	0	0	0	0
1,920	1,960	211	180	149	117	86	55	24	0	0	0	0
1,960	2,000	217	186	155	123	92	61	30	0	0	0	0
2,000	2,040	223	192	161	129	98	67	36	4	0	0	0
2,040	2,080	229	198	167	135	104	73	42	10	0	0	0
2,080	2,120	235	204	173	141	110	79	48	16	0	0	0
2,120	2,160	241	210	179	147	116	85	54	22	0	0	0
2,160	2,200	247	216	185	153	122	91	60	28	0	0	0
2,200	2,240	253	222	191	159	128	97	66	34	3	0	0
2,240	2,280	259	228	197	165	134	103	72	40	9	0	0
2,280	2,320	265	234	203	171	140	109	78	46	15	0	0
2,320	2,360	271	240	209	177	146	115	84	52	21	0	0
2,360	2,400	277	246	215	183	152	121	90	58	27	0	0
2,400	2,440	283	252	221	189	158	127	96	64	33	2	0
2,440	2,480	289	258	227	195	164	133	102	70	39	8	0
2,480	2,520	295	264	233	201	170	139	108	76	45	14	0
2,520	2,560	301	270	239	207	176	145	114	82	51	20	0
2,560	2,600	307	276	245	213	182	151	120	88	57	26	0
2,600	2,640	313	282	251	219	188	157	126	94	63	32	1
2,640	2,680	319	288	257	225	194	163	132	100	69	38	7
2,680	2,720	325	294	263	231	200	169	138	106	75	44	13
2,720	2,760	331	300	269	237	206	175	144	112	81	50	19
2,760	2,800	337	306	275	243	212	181	150	118	87	56	25
2,800	2,840	343	312	281	249	218	187	156	124	93	62	31
2,840	2,880	349	318	287	255	224	193	162	130	99	68	37
2,880	2,920	355	324	293	261	230	199	168	136	105	74	43
2,920	2,960	361	330	299	267	236	205	174	142	111	80	49
2,960	3,000	367	336	305	273	242	211	180	148	117	86	55
3,000	3,040	373	342	311	279	248	217	186	154	123	92	61
3,040	3,080	379	348	317	285	254	223	192	160	129	98	67
3,080	3,120	385	354	323	291	260	229	198	166	135	104	73
3,120	3,160	391	360	329	297	266	235	204	172	141	110	79
3,160	3,200	397	366	335	303	272	241	210	178	147	116	85
3,200	3,240	403	372	341	309	278	247	216	184	153	122	91

MARRIED Persons—MONTHLY Payroll Period
(For Wages Paid in 1995)

If the wages are— At least	But less than	And the number of withholding allowances claimed is— 0	1	2	3	4	5	6	7	8	9	10
		The amount of income tax to be withheld is—										
$3,240	$3,280	409	378	347	315	284	253	222	190	159	128	97
3,280	3,320	415	384	353	321	290	259	228	196	165	134	103
3,320	3,360	421	390	359	327	296	265	234	202	171	140	109
3,360	3,400	427	396	365	333	302	271	240	208	177	146	115
3,400	3,440	433	402	371	339	308	277	246	214	183	152	121
3,440	3,480	439	408	377	345	314	283	252	220	189	158	127
3,480	3,520	445	414	383	351	320	289	258	226	195	164	133
3,520	3,560	451	420	389	357	326	295	264	232	201	170	139
3,560	3,600	457	426	395	363	332	301	270	238	207	176	145
3,600	3,640	467	432	401	369	338	307	276	244	213	182	151
3,640	3,680	478	438	407	375	344	313	282	250	219	188	157
3,680	3,720	490	444	413	381	350	319	288	256	225	194	163
3,720	3,760	501	450	419	387	356	325	294	262	231	200	169
3,760	3,800	512	456	425	393	362	331	300	268	237	206	175
3,800	3,840	523	465	431	399	368	337	306	274	243	212	181
3,840	3,880	534	476	437	405	374	343	312	280	249	218	187
3,880	3,920	546	487	443	411	380	349	318	286	255	224	193
3,920	3,960	557	498	449	417	386	355	324	292	261	230	199
3,960	4,000	568	510	455	423	392	361	330	298	267	236	205
4,000	4,040	579	521	463	429	398	367	336	304	273	242	211
4,040	4,080	590	532	474	435	404	373	342	310	279	248	217
4,080	4,120	602	543	485	441	410	379	348	316	285	254	223
4,120	4,160	613	554	496	447	416	385	354	322	291	260	229
4,160	4,200	624	566	507	453	422	391	360	328	297	266	235
4,200	4,240	635	577	519	460	428	397	366	334	303	272	241
4,240	4,280	646	588	530	471	434	403	372	340	309	278	247
4,280	4,320	658	599	541	483	440	409	378	346	315	284	253
4,320	4,360	668	610	552	494	446	415	384	352	321	290	259
4,360	4,400	680	622	563	505	452	421	390	358	327	296	265
4,400	4,440	691	633	575	516	458	427	396	364	333	302	271
4,440	4,480	702	644	586	527	469	433	402	370	339	308	277
4,480	4,520	714	655	597	539	480	439	408	376	345	314	283
4,520	4,560	725	666	608	550	491	445	414	382	351	320	289
4,560	4,600	736	678	619	561	503	451	420	388	357	326	295
4,600	4,640	747	689	631	572	514	457	426	394	363	332	301
4,640	4,680	758	700	642	583	525	467	432	400	369	338	307
4,680	4,720	770	711	653	595	536	478	438	406	375	344	313
4,720	4,760	781	722	664	606	547	489	444	412	381	350	319
4,760	4,800	792	734	675	617	559	500	450	418	387	356	325
4,800	4,840	803	745	687	628	570	512	456	424	393	362	331
4,840	4,880	814	756	698	639	581	523	464	430	399	368	337
4,880	4,920	826	767	709	651	592	534	476	436	405	374	343
4,920	4,960	837	778	720	662	603	545	487	442	411	380	349
4,960	5,000	848	790	731	673	615	556	498	448	417	386	355
5,000	5,040	859	801	743	684	626	568	509	454	423	392	361
5,040	5,080	870	812	754	695	637	579	520	462	429	398	367
5,080	5,120	882	823	765	707	648	590	532	473	435	404	373
5,120	5,160	893	834	776	718	659	601	543	484	441	410	379
5,160	5,200	904	846	787	729	671	612	554	496	447	416	385
5,200	5,240	915	857	799	740	682	624	565	507	453	422	391
5,240	5,280	926	868	810	751	693	635	576	518	460	428	397
5,280	5,320	938	879	821	763	704	646	588	529	471	434	403
5,320	5,360	949	890	832	774	715	657	599	540	482	440	409
5,360	5,400	960	902	843	785	727	668	610	552	493	446	415
5,400	5,440	971	913	855	796	738	680	621	563	505	452	421
5,440	5,480	982	924	866	807	749	691	632	574	516	458	427
5,480	5,520	994	935	877	819	760	702	644	585	527	469	433
5,520	5,560	1,005	946	888	830	771	713	655	596	538	480	439
5,560	5,600	1,016	958	899	841	783	724	666	608	549	491	445
5,600	5,640	1,027	969	911	852	794	736	677	619	561	502	451
5,640	5,680	1,038	980	922	863	805	747	688	630	572	513	457
5,680	5,720	1,050	991	933	875	816	758	700	641	583	525	466
5,720	5,760	1,061	1,002	944	886	827	769	711	652	594	536	477
5,760	5,800	1,072	1,014	955	897	839	780	722	664	605	547	489
5,800	5,840	1,083	1,025	967	908	850	792	733	675	617	558	500
$5,840 and over		Use Table 4(b) for a MARRIED person										

T–14

WAGE-BRACKET WITHHOLDING TABLES

SINGLE Persons—DAILY OR MISCELLANEOUS Payroll Period
(For Wages Paid in 1995)

If the wages are—		And the number of withholding allowances claimed is—										
At least	But less than	0	1	2	3	4	5	6	7	8	9	10
		The amount of income tax to be withheld is—										
$0	$12	0	0	0	0	0	0	0	0	0	0	0
12	15	1	0	0	0	0	0	0	0	0	0	0
15	18	1	0	0	0	0	0	0	0	0	0	0
18	21	1	0	0	0	0	0	0	0	0	0	0
21	24	2	1	0	0	0	0	0	0	0	0	0
24	27	2	1	0	0	0	0	0	0	0	0	0
27	30	3	2	0	0	0	0	0	0	0	0	0
30	33	3	2	1	0	0	0	0	0	0	0	0
33	36	4	2	1	0	0	0	0	0	0	0	0
36	39	4	3	1	0	0	0	0	0	0	0	0
39	42	4	3	2	1	0	0	0	0	0	0	0
42	45	5	4	2	1	0	0	0	0	0	0	0
45	48	5	4	3	1	1	0	0	0	0	0	0
48	51	6	4	3	2	1	0	0	0	0	0	0
51	54	6	5	3	2	1	0	0	0	0	0	0
54	57	7	5	4	2	1	0	0	0	0	0	0
57	60	7	6	4	3	2	1	0	0	0	0	0
60	63	8	6	5	3	2	1	0	0	0	0	0
63	66	8	7	5	4	2	1	0	0	0	0	0
66	69	9	7	6	4	3	1	1	0	0	0	0
69	72	9	8	6	5	3	2	1	0	0	0	0
72	75	10	8	7	5	4	2	1	0	0	0	0
75	78	10	9	7	6	4	3	1	0	0	0	0
78	81	10	9	8	6	5	3	2	1	0	0	0
81	84	11	9	8	7	5	4	2	1	0	0	0
84	87	11	10	8	7	6	4	3	1	0	0	0
87	90	12	10	9	8	6	5	3	2	0	0	0
90	93	12	11	9	8	7	5	4	2	1	0	0
93	96	13	11	10	9	7	6	4	3	1	0	0
96	99	13	12	10	9	8	6	5	3	2	0	0
99	102	14	12	11	9	8	7	5	4	2	1	0
102	105	15	13	11	10	8	7	6	4	3	1	0
105	108	16	14	12	10	9	7	6	5	3	2	0
108	111	17	15	13	11	9	8	7	5	4	2	1
111	114	18	16	14	12	10	8	7	6	4	3	1
114	117	18	16	15	13	11	9	8	6	5	3	2
117	120	19	17	15	13	11	10	8	7	5	4	2
120	123	20	18	16	14	12	10	9	7	6	4	3
123	126	21	19	17	15	13	11	9	8	6	5	3
126	129	22	19	18	16	14	12	10	8	7	5	4
129	132	23	20	17	15	15	13	11	9	7	6	4
132	135	24	21	18	16	16	14	12	10	8	6	5
135	138	25	22	19	17	17	15	13	11	9	7	5
138	141	26	23	20	18	17	16	14	12	10	8	6
141	144	27	24	21	19	18	17	15	13	11	8	7
144	147	27	24	22	19	16	14	12	10	8	7	6
147	150	28	25	23	20	17	14	13	11	9	8	7
150	153	29	26	24	21	18	15	13	12	10	9	8
153	156	30	27	25	22	19	16	14	13	11	9	8
156	159	31	28	26	23	20	17	15	13	12	10	9
159	162	31	28	26	23	20	18	15	13	12	10	9
162	165	32	30	27	24	21	19	16	14	12	11	9
165	168	33	30	28	25	22	20	17	15	13	11	10
168	171	34	31	29	26	23	21	18	16	14	12	11
171	174	34	32	29	26	24	21	18	16	14	12	11
174	177	35	33	30	27	24	22	19	16	14	12	12
177	180	36	34	31	28	26	23	20	18	15	13	12
180	183	37	35	32	29	26	24	21	19	16	14	13
183	186	38	35	33	30	27	25	22	19	17	15	14
186	189	39	36	33	31	28	25	22	20	17	15	14
189	192	39	37	34	31	29	26	23	21	18	15	13
192	195	40	38	35	32	30	27	24	21	19	16	14
195	198	41	38	36	33	30	28	25	22	20	17	15
198	201	42	39	36	34	31	29	26	23	20	18	15
201	204	43	40	37	35	32	29	27	24	21	19	16
204	207	44	41	38	36	33	30	28	25	22	19	17
207	210	45	42	39	36	34	31	28	26	23	20	18
210	213	46	43	40	37	35	32	29	26	24	21	19
213	216	47	44	41	38	35	33	30	27	25	22	19
216	219	48	45	42	39	36	34	31	28	25	23	20

SINGLE Persons—DAILY OR MISCELLANEOUS Payroll Period
(For Wages Paid in 1995)

If the wages are—		And the number of withholding allowances claimed is—										
At least	But less than	0	1	2	3	4	5	6	7	8	9	10
		The amount of income tax to be withheld is—										
$219	$222	48	46	43	40	37	34	32	29	26	24	21
222	225	49	46	43	41	38	35	33	30	27	24	22
225	228	50	47	44	41	39	36	33	31	28	25	23
228	231	51	48	45	42	40	37	34	32	29	26	23
231	234	52	49	46	43	40	38	35	33	30	27	24
234	237	53	50	47	44	41	39	36	33	31	28	25
237	240	54	51	48	45	42	39	37	34	32	29	26
240	243	55	52	49	46	43	40	38	35	33	30	27
243	246	56	53	50	47	44	41	38	36	33	31	28
246	249	57	54	51	48	45	42	39	37	34	32	29
249	252	58	55	52	49	46	43	40	37	35	32	29
252	255	59	56	53	50	47	44	41	38	36	33	30
255	258	60	57	54	51	48	45	42	39	37	34	31
258	261	61	58	55	52	48	46	43	40	38	35	32
261	264	62	59	56	53	50	47	44	41	38	36	33
264	267	62	59	57	53	51	48	45	42	39	36	34
267	270	63	60	57	54	52	48	46	43	40	37	34
270	273	64	61	58	55	52	49	46	43	41	38	35
273	276	65	62	59	56	53	50	47	44	41	39	36
276	279	66	63	60	57	54	51	48	45	42	39	37
279	282	67	64	61	58	55	52	49	46	43	40	38
282	285	68	65	62	59	56	53	50	47	44	41	39
285	288	69	66	62	60	57	54	51	47	45	42	39
288	291	70	67	63	61	58	55	51	49	46	43	40
291	294	71	68	64	62	59	56	52	50	47	44	41
294	297	72	69	66	63	60	57	54	51	48	45	42
297	300	73	70	67	64	61	58	55	52	49	46	43
300	303	74	71	68	65	62	59	56	53	50	47	44
303	306	75	72	68	66	63	60	57	54	51	48	45
306	309	75	73	69	67	64	61	58	55	52	49	46
309	312	76	74	70	68	65	61	59	56	53	50	47
312	315	77	74	71	68	66	62	60	57	54	51	48
315	318	78	75	72	69	67	63	61	58	55	52	48
318	321	79	76	73	70	68	64	62	59	56	53	49
321	324	80	77	74	71	68	65	62	60	57	54	50
324	327	81	78	75	72	69	66	63	60	57	54	51
327	330	82	79	76	73	70	67	64	61	58	55	52
330	333	83	80	77	74	71	68	65	62	59	56	53
333	336	84	81	78	75	72	68	66	63	60	57	54
336	339	85	82	79	76	73	69	67	64	61	58	55
339	341	86	83	80	77	74	71	68	65	62	59	56
341	343	86	84	81	78	74	72	68	65	62	59	57
343	345	87	84	82	78	75	72	69	66	63	60	57
345	347	88	85	82	79	76	73	70	67	64	61	58
347	349	88	85	83	79	76	73	70	67	64	61	58
349	351	89	86	83	80	77	74	71	68	65	62	59
351	353	89	86	84	80	77	74	71	68	65	62	59
353	355	90	87	84	81	78	75	72	69	66	63	60
355	357	91	88	85	82	79	76	73	70	67	64	61
357	359	91	88	85	82	79	76	73	70	67	64	61
359	361	92	89	86	83	80	77	74	71	68	65	62
361	363	92	89	86	83	80	77	74	71	68	65	62
363	365	93	90	87	84	81	78	75	72	69	66	63
365	367	94	91	88	85	82	79	76	73	70	67	64
367	369	94	91	88	85	82	79	76	73	70	67	64
369	371	95	92	89	86	83	80	77	74	71	68	65
371	373	95	92	89	86	83	80	77	74	71	68	66
373	375	96	93	90	87	84	81	78	75	72	69	67
375	377	97	94	91	88	85	82	79	76	73	70	68
377	379	97	94	91	88	85	82	79	76	73	70	68
379	381	98	95	92	89	86	83	80	77	74	71	68
381	383	98	95	92	89	86	83	80	77	74	71	69
383	385	99	96	93	90	87	84	81	78	75	72	70
385	387	100	97	94	91	88	85	82	79	76	73	71
387	389	100	97	94	91	88	86	83	80	77	74	71
$389 and over		Use Table 8(a) for a SINGLE person										

T–15

WAGE-BRACKET WITHHOLDING TABLES

MARRIED Persons—DAILY OR MISCELLANEOUS Payroll Period
(For Wages Paid in 1995)

If the wages are—		And the number of withholding allowances claimed is—										
At least	But less than	0	1	2	3	4	5	6	7	8	9	10
		The amount of income tax to be withheld is—										
$27	$30	0	0	0	0	0	0	0	0	0	0	0
30	33	0	0	0	0	0	0	0	0	0	0	0
33	36	1	0	0	0	0	0	0	0	0	0	0
36	39	1	0	0	0	0	0	0	0	0	0	0
39	42	2	1	0	0	0	0	0	0	0	0	0
42	45	3	1	0	0	0	0	0	0	0	0	0
45	48	3	2	0	0	0	0	0	0	0	0	0
48	51	3	2	1	0	0	0	0	0	0	0	0
51	54	4	3	1	0	0	0	0	0	0	0	0
54	57	5	3	2	0	0	0	0	0	0	0	0
57	60	5	4	2	0	0	0	0	0	0	0	0
60	63	6	4	3	1	0	0	0	0	0	0	0
63	66	6	5	3	1	0	0	0	0	0	0	0
66	69	7	5	4	2	0	0	0	0	0	0	0
69	72	7	5	4	3	1	0	0	0	0	0	0
72	75	8	6	4	3	1	0	0	0	0	0	0
75	78	8	6	5	3	2	0	0	0	0	0	0
78	81	9	7	5	4	2	0	0	0	0	0	0
81	84	9	7	6	4	3	1	0	0	0	0	0
84	87	9	8	6	5	3	1	0	0	0	0	0
87	90	10	8	7	5	4	2	0	0	0	0	0
90	93	10	9	7	6	4	2	0	0	0	0	0
93	96	10	9	8	6	5	3	1	0	0	0	0
96	99	11	9	8	7	5	3	1	0	0	0	0
99	102	11	10	8	7	6	4	2	0	0	0	0
102	105	12	10	9	7	6	4	2	0	0	0	0
105	108	12	11	9	8	7	5	3	1	0	0	0
108	111	12	11	10	8	7	5	3	1	0	0	0
111	114	13	12	10	9	7	6	4	2	0	0	0
114	117	14	12	11	9	8	6	4	2	0	0	0
117	120	14	13	11	10	8	7	5	3	1	0	0
120	123	14	13	12	10	9	7	5	3	1	0	0
123	126	15	14	12	11	9	8	6	4	2	0	0
126	129	15	14	13	11	10	8	6	4	2	0	0
129	132	16	14	13	12	10	9	7	5	3	1	0
132	135	16	15	13	12	11	9	7	5	3	1	0
135	138	17	15	14	13	11	10	8	6	4	2	0
138	141	17	16	14	13	12	10	8	6	4	2	0
141	144	18	16	15	13	12	11	9	7	5	3	1
144	147	18	17	15	14	13	11	9	7	5	3	1
147	150	19	17	16	14	13	12	10	8	6	4	2
150	153	19	18	16	15	14	12	10	8	6	4	2
153	156	19	18	17	15	14	13	11	9	7	5	3
156	159	20	18	17	16	14	13	11	9	7	5	3
159	162	20	19	17	16	15	13	12	10	8	6	4
162	165	21	19	18	17	15	14	12	10	8	6	4
165	168	21	20	18	17	16	14	13	11	9	7	5
168	171	22	20	19	17	16	15	13	11	9	7	5
171	174	23	21	19	18	17	15	14	12	10	8	6
174	177	24	21	20	18	17	16	14	12	10	8	6
177	180	25	22	20	19	18	16	15	13	11	9	7
180	183	26	23	21	19	18	17	15	13	11	9	7
183	186	26	24	22	20	19	17	16	14	12	10	8
186	189	27	25	22	20	19	18	16	14	12	10	8
189	192	28	26	23	21	20	19	17	15	13	11	9
192	195	29	26	24	21	20	19	17	15	13	11	9
195	198	30	27	25	22	21	20	18	16	14	12	10
198	201	31	28	26	23	22	20	18	16	14	12	10
201	204	31	29	26	23	22	21	19	17	15	13	11
204	207	32	30	27	24	23	22	19	17	15	13	11
207	210	33	30	28	25	24	22	20	18	16	14	12
210	213	34	31	29	26	25	23	20	18	16	14	12
213	216	35	32	30	27	26	24	21	19	17	15	13
216	219	36	33	30	28	27	25	22	20	18	16	14
219	222	37	34	31	28	28	26	23	21	18	16	15
222	225	38	35	32	30	29	26	24	21	19	17	16
225	228	38	36	33	30	29	27	24	22	19	17	16
228	231	39	36	34	31	30	28	25	22	20	18	17
231	234	40	37	34	32	31	29	26	23	20	18	17

MARRIED Persons—DAILY OR MISCELLANEOUS Payroll Period
(For Wages Paid in 1995)

If the wages are—		And the number of withholding allowances claimed is—										
At least	But less than	0	1	2	3	4	5	6	7	8	9	10
		The amount of income tax to be withheld is—										
$234	$237	41	38	35	33	30	27	25	22	20	19	17
237	240	42	39	36	33	31	28	25	23	21	19	18
240	243	42	40	37	34	32	29	26	24	22	20	18
243	246	43	41	38	35	32	30	27	24	22	20	18
246	249	44	41	39	36	33	31	28	25	23	20	19
249	252	45	42	40	37	34	32	29	26	23	21	19
252	255	46	43	40	38	35	32	30	27	24	22	20
255	258	47	44	41	39	36	33	30	28	25	22	20
258	261	47	45	42	39	37	34	31	29	26	23	21
261	264	48	46	43	40	38	35	32	29	27	24	21
264	267	49	46	44	41	38	36	33	30	28	25	22
267	270	50	47	45	42	39	37	34	31	28	26	23
270	273	51	48	45	43	40	37	35	32	29	27	24
273	276	51	49	46	43	41	38	35	33	30	27	25
276	279	52	50	47	44	42	39	36	34	31	28	26
279	282	53	51	48	45	43	40	37	34	32	29	26
282	285	54	51	49	46	43	41	38	35	33	30	27
285	288	55	52	50	47	44	42	39	36	33	31	28
288	291	56	53	50	48	45	43	40	37	34	32	29
291	294	57	54	51	49	46	43	41	38	35	32	30
294	297	58	55	52	49	47	44	41	39	36	33	31
297	300	58	55	53	50	48	45	42	40	37	34	31
300	303	59	56	54	51	48	46	43	40	38	35	32
303	306	60	57	55	52	49	47	44	41	39	36	33
306	309	61	58	55	53	50	47	45	42	39	37	34
309	312	62	59	56	54	51	48	46	43	40	37	35
312	315	63	60	57	54	52	49	46	44	41	38	36
315	318	63	61	58	55	53	50	47	45	42	39	36
318	321	64	62	59	56	53	51	48	45	43	40	37
321	324	65	62	60	57	54	52	49	46	44	41	38
324	327	66	63	61	58	55	52	50	47	44	42	39
327	330	67	64	61	59	56	53	51	48	45	43	40
330	333	68	65	62	60	57	54	51	49	46	44	41
333	336	68	66	63	60	58	55	52	49	47	44	42
336	339	69	67	64	61	59	56	53	50	48	45	42
339	341	70	67	65	62	59	57	54	51	48	46	43
341	343	71	68	65	62	60	57	54	52	49	46	44
343	345	72	68	66	63	60	58	55	52	50	47	44
345	347	72	69	66	64	61	58	56	53	50	48	45
347	349	73	70	67	64	61	59	56	53	51	48	45
349	351	73	70	67	65	62	59	57	54	51	49	46
351	353	74	71	68	65	63	60	57	55	52	49	47
353	355	75	72	69	66	64	61	58	56	53	50	48
355	357	76	72	69	67	64	62	59	56	54	51	48
357	359	76	73	70	67	65	62	59	57	54	51	49
359	361	76	73	71	68	65	63	60	57	54	52	49
361	363	77	74	71	68	66	63	61	58	55	53	50
363	365	78	75	72	69	66	64	61	58	56	53	51
365	367	78	75	72	70	67	65	62	59	56	54	51
367	369	79	76	73	70	67	65	62	59	57	54	52
369	371	79	77	73	71	68	66	63	60	57	55	52
371	373	80	77	74	72	69	66	64	61	58	55	53
373	375	80	78	75	72	69	67	64	61	59	56	53
375	377	81	78	75	73	70	67	65	62	59	57	54
377	379	82	79	76	73	70	68	65	62	60	57	54
379	381	83	80	77	74	71	68	66	63	60	57	55
381	383	83	80	77	74	72	69	66	63	61	58	55
383	385	84	81	78	75	72	70	67	64	61	59	56
385	387	85	81	78	76	73	70	67	65	62	59	56
387	389	85	82	79	76	74	71	68	65	63	60	57
389	391	86	83	80	77	74	71	69	66	63	60	58
391	393	86	83	80	77	75	72	69	66	64	61	58
393	395	87	84	81	78	75	73	70	67	64	62	59
395	397	88	84	82	79	76	73	70	67	65	62	59
397	399	88	85	82	79	76	74	71	68	65	62	59

$399 and over   Use Table 8(b) for a **MARRIED** person

ANSWERS TO SELF-STUDY QUIZZES

Self-Study Quiz 2–1

2. False. Live-in domestic workers do not have to be paid overtime.
4. False. Individual employee coverage is not affected by the work of fellow employees.

Self-Study Quiz 2–2

1. $60
2. $20 $170 ($4.25 × 40 hours)
         −90 weekly wage
         −60 tip credit claimed by employer
         $20

Self-Study Quiz 2–3

	Hourly Rate	Overtime Rate
1.	$13.13	$19.70
2.	$11.15	$16.73
3.	$16.73	$25.10
4.	$9.23	$13.85

Self-Study Quiz 2–4

1. $200.00
2. $4.35 ($200 ÷ 46)
3. $2.18 ($4.35 × .50)
4. $13.08 ($2.18 × 6)
5. $213.08

Self-Study Quiz 3–1

1. Yes. Full-time life insurance salespersons are covered as statutory employees for social security, Medicare, and FUTA tax purposes.

2. Maybe. Hoyas is considered a technical service specialist. If the company has a business arrangement with each of its clients, the determination of whether Hoyas is an employee of the company is controlled by the 20-factor test for common-law employees. If Hoyas fails to meet the qualifications of this test, she may be treated as an independent contractor. Ordinarily, there is a relief provision which allows an employer who reasonably believes and treats an individual as an independent contractor can be relieved of having to pay employment taxes on that individual. This provision is not available for technical service employees. Therefore, the company must make an accurate determination of Hoyas' status.
3. Yes. It does not matter what position Hernadez holds in the company if he is receiving wages for services he provides as an employee of the corporation.
4. Yes. Children under 18 employed by a parent (sole proprietorship) or by a partnership consisting of only parents are excluded from social security and Medicare taxes. Since the company is a corporation, Sarah cannot be excluded from coverage.
5. No. Schuck offers his services to the general public and is considered an independent contractor.

Self-Study Quiz 3–2

1. No. The gift certificates are of nominal value.
2. Yes. Personal use of a company vehicle for non-business related activities constitutes a taxable fringe benefit.
3. No. An employer may contribute to an SEP set up by or on behalf of its employees. The employer's contributions are exempt from FICA taxes if reason to believe exists that employees will be entitled to deduct the employer contributions for federal income tax purposes.
4. No. Generally, employers do not have to include in wages or withhold on the value of payment made for job-related training for their employees.
5. Yes. Payments by employers for involuntary separation of an employee from the employer's service are taxable under FICA.

Self-Study Quiz 3–3

Employee	OASDI	HI
Mary Britton	13.95	3.26
Bob Yold	18.60	4.35
Martin Rold	10.85	2.54
Maria Aldo	62.00	14.50
Gil Hammerstien	136.40	31.90
Totals	241.80	56.55
Employer's taxes (based on $3,900 gross wages)	241.80	56.55

Gil Hammerstien will earn an annual salary of $114,400, which exceeds the wage base for OASDI taxes.

On the 29th weekly payday, Hammerstien will have cumulative wages of $61,600 (for the first 28 paydays).

When the payment is made on the 29th payday, Hammerstien will exceed the wage base for OASDI taxes:
Cumulative wages $61,600
Current wage payment 2,200
$63,800

Self-Study Quiz 3–4

1. $48,800 ($900 per week × 52 = $46,800 + $2,000 bonus).
2. $66,800 ($48,800 + $18,000)
3. $14,200 (Taxable wage base $63,000 – 48,800)

Self-Study Quiz 3–5

1. Braxton should deposit its taxes by the following Wednesday.
2. During the first calendar year for a new business, the company is a monthly depositor. However, if during the year it has an undeposited tax liability of $100,000 (which triggers the one-banking-day rule), the company becomes a semiweekly depositor for the remainder of the year.
3. The additional taxes are not accumulated with the previous liability of $105,000. The company should follow the semiweekly deposit rules and deposit the $20,000 by Friday.

Self-Study Quiz 4–1

✓   a. Meals provided to employees for the convenience of the employer on the employer's premises.
___   b. Bonuses to managers and supervisors are considered compensation for services rendered as employees and are subject to withholding.
✓   c. The use of on-site athletic facilities by employees are considered a nontaxable fringe benefit.
✓   d. Advances for business expenses reasonably expected to be incurred.
___   e. Sick pay is subject to withholding.
___   f. Memberships in social or country clubs is a taxable fringe benefit and is subject to withholding.
✓   g. No-additional-cost meals provided to employees at an employer-operated eating establishment.

Self-Study Quiz 4–2

1. The payroll manager should inform Kyle that the company cannot reimburse her for any overwithholding that may have occurred prior to her submitting a new W-4. The only circumstances that allow the employer to reimburse an employee for overwithholding is if the employer failed to put a new W-4 into effect that resulted in overwithholding.
2. The payroll manager must inform Bradley that an employee may claim exemption from withholding for only one tax year at a time. The exemption must be claimed each year by February 15. If a new certificate is not filed, the employer must withhold at the single rate with zero withholding allowances.
3. Volmer may claim seven personal allowances, as identified on the personal allowance worksheet accompanying Form W-4:

    a. One allowance for himself.
    b. One allowance for his spouse.
    c. One allowance for being married, having one job, and his spouse not working.
    d. One allowance for each dependent child (total of 3).
    e. One allowance for child care expenses of at least $1,500.

Self-Study Quiz 4–3

Step 1—Round gross wages: **$1,100**
Step 2—Multiply the number of allowances by the weekly allowance amount: **$3 \times \$48.08 = \$144.24$**
Step 3—Subtract the value of the allowances from the gross pay: **$\$1,100 - \$144.24 = \$955.76$**
Step 4—Compute the tax from the percentage tax table for WEEKLY MARRIED person:
     Over $828 But not over $1,664 . . . . $105.75 plus 28% of excess over $828
     $\$955.76 - \$828.00 = \$127.76 \times 28\% = \$35.77$ **Total tax to be withheld: $105.75 + $35.77 = $141.52**

Self-Study Quiz 4–4

Employee	Tax
Lamb	$135
Nurin	$111
Hogan	$ 43
Vick	$508.39
Marks	$118

Self-Study Quiz 4–5

Method A: $28\% \times \$500 = \$140$
Method B: Tax previously withheld on semimonthly wage of $1,450 = $146
                Tax on wage and bonus ($1,950): $221
                Less tax previously withheld: 146
                Withholding on bonus: $ 75

Self-Study Quiz 4–6

1. According to Figure 4–13, Brewer is entitled to an advance EIC payment of $7 per week.
2. The Gregory company can treat the EIC payments as if the company has paid the total amount of income taxes withheld, and can use any remaining amounts against its deposit of social security taxes. The company must, however, make a deposit for the amount of employment taxes (employees' income taxes, social security taxes, and employer's social security taxes) that exceeds the amount of the EIC payments.

Self-Study Quiz 4–7

1. The company should report the total amount deducted from each employee in Box 14 of Form W-4. This box is to provide "other" information the company wants to give the employees. The company should label the amount as "union dues" in Box 14.
2. If an employee leaves the service of the employer, the employer may furnish Form W-2 any time after employment ends. If the employee requests Form W-2, the employer should give it to them within 30 days of the request or final wage payment, whichever is later. If there is a reasonable expectation that the employees may be re-hired before the end of the year, the employer may delay providing Form W-2 until January following the close of the calendar year.
3. If Form W-2 has been destroyed or lost, employers are authorized to furnish substitute copies to the employee. Trident should provide a substitute form to Becker. The form should be clearly marked "Reissued Statement", and the company should not send the substitute statement to the Social Security Administration.

Self-Study Quiz 5–1

4.1% of $188,000 =	$ 7,708	SUTA tax
6.2% of $188,000 =	11,656	Gross FUTA tax
4.1% of $188,000 = $7,708		Credit for SUTA tax paid
1.3% of $188,000 = 2,444	10,152	Additional credit to get to 5.4%
0.8% of $188,000	$ 1,504	Net FUTA tax

Self-Study Quiz 5–2

From the Summary of State Laws (Figure 5–1), the taxable wages in Colorado is $10,000. However, the company receives a credit of $6,000 against this limit because of unemployment taxes paid to Arizona on John's wages in that state. Therefore, the calculation is:

John's wages in Colorado	$26,000
Over taxable limit	16,000
Colorado's SUTA wage limit	10,000
Credit for wages taxed in Arizona	6,000
John's taxable wages in Colorado	4,000
Moss' SUTA tax rate in Colorado	× 2.9%
Amount of the company's SUTA tax in Colorado	$116

Self-Study Quiz 5–3

1st Quarter—$22,000 × .008 = $176.00 due on 4/30/96
2nd Quarter—$24,000 × .008 = $192.00 due on 7/31/96
3rd Quarter—$12,000 × .008 = $96.00 no deposit due
4th Quarter—$10,000 × .008 = $80.00 + $96.00 = $176.00 due on 1/31/97

Self-Study Quiz 6–1

January 22	Salary Expense	95,190.00	
	FICA Taxes Payable—OASDI		5,901.78
	FICA Taxes Payable—HI		1,380.26
	Employees FIT Payable		14,270.00
	Employee SIT Payable		1,427.85
	SUTA Taxes Payable		951.90
	Salaries Payable (Cash)		71,258.21

Self-Study Quiz 6–2

January 22	Payroll Taxes	11,042.05	
	FICA Taxes Payable—OASDI		5,901.78
	FICA Taxes Payable—HI		1,380.26
	FUTA Taxes Payable		761.52
	SUTA Taxes Payable		2,998.49

GLOSSARY

Affirmative action plan a formal plan that prescribes a specific program to eliminate, limit, or prevent discriminatory treatment on the basis of race, ethnic group, and sex.

Annualizing wages method of determining amount of income taxes to be withheld by multiplying the wages for one payroll period by the number of periods in the year, determining the annual amount of withholding required on the total wages, and dividing the annual withholding by the number of payroll periods.

Application form personnel record which gives the applicant an opportunity to provide complete information as to personal qualifications, training, and experience.

Average indexed monthly earnings a worker's average monthly earnings, updated to reflect changes in wage levels.

Backup withholding amount of income tax withheld by payers of taxable interest, dividends, and certain other payments made to payees who have failed to furnish the payers with correct identification numbers.

Biweekly every two weeks.

Business expense cost of operating a business that is deductible by the employer for federal income tax purposes.

Change in payroll rate form document that notifies the proper departments of a change in the employee's rate of remuneration.

Check-off system withholding of union dues from employees' wages by the employer.

Commission stated percentage of revenue paid an employee who transacts a piece of business or performs a service.

Common-law relationship the state existing when the employer has the right to control both what work will be done and how it will be done.

Constructively paid wages remunerations that are credited to the account of, or set apart for, an employee so that they may be drawn upon at any time, even though they are not actually possessed by the employee.

Continental system method of recording time on time cards in which the day is divided into one 24-hour period, with time running from 12 midnight to 12 midnight.

Contribution report quarterly tax return filed with the state by the employer that provides a summary of the wages paid during the period and shows the computation of the tax or contribution.

Cumulative withholding method of determining income taxes to be withheld by adding wages for a particular payroll period to total wages already paid during the year, dividing the aggregate by the number of payroll periods to which it pertains, computing the tax on the average amount of wages, subtracting the amount of tax already withheld during preceding payroll periods, and deducting any excess tax from current payment of wages.

Currently insured criterion used to determine eligibility for social security benefits; persons must have at least six quarters of coverage during the 13-quarter period ending with (1) the quarter in which they died, or (2) the quarter in which they became entitled to old-age insurance benefits or most recently became entitled to disability benefits.

Dependency allowance an additional weekly benefit paid to unemployed workers with dependents.

Disability benefits payments to employees who are absent from their jobs because of illness, accident, or disease not arising out of their employment.

Dismissal payments amounts paid by employers to workers who have been separated from employment; also known as *payments in lieu of notice, separation pay,* or *terminal leave pay.*

Disposable earnings the earnings remaining after withholding for income taxes and for other amounts required by law.

Domestic service services of a household nature performed in or about a private home of the person who employs the domestic.

Earned income credit (EIC) reduction in federal income taxes mostly for workers who have dependent children and maintain a household.

Educational assistance the expenses that an employer pays for an employee's education, such as tuition, fees, and payments for books, supplies, and equipment.

Electronic funds transfer system (EFTS) system whereby the employer transfers employees' net pays to employees' bank accounts with electronic equipment rather than issuing paychecks.

Employee any individual performing services for an employer in the legal relationship of employer and employee.

Employee history record continuous record of the relationship between the employer and the employee.

Employee's earnings record payroll record for each employee that is used to provide complete information about the accumulated earnings of each employee.

Employer any person or organization who employs one or more individuals for the performance of services, unless such services or employment are specifically excepted by law.

Employment any service performed by employees for their employer, regardless of the citizenship or residence of either.

Enterprise coverage applied to determine if employees of an enterprise are covered under the provisions of the FLSA. The test criteria are: at least two employees engaged in interstate commerce and an annual gross sales volume of at least $500,000.

Executive order regulation issued by the federal government that bans, in employment on government contracts, discrimination based on race, color, religion, sex, or national origin.

Exempt employee worker exempt from some, or all, of the FLSA requirements such as minimum wages, equal pay, and overtime pay.

Experience rating method by which employer contribution payments may be adjusted because of a favorable employment record; also known as *merit rating.*

Fair employment legislation laws that deal with discrimination on the basis of age, race, color, religion, sex, or national origin as a condition of employment.

Form W-2, Wage and Tax Statement form used by the employer to report the amount of wages paid each worker in the course of the trade or business of the employer.

Fully insured criterion used to determine eligibility for most retirement and disability benefits; generally, a worker needs between six and 40 quarters of coverage.

Garnishment legal or equitable procedure by means of which a portion of the wages of any person must be withheld for payment of a debt.

Gross earnings total regular earnings and total overtime earnings, also known as *gross pay*.

Group insurance life insurance program for employees at a low cost.

Hiring notice form that is sent to the Payroll Department so that new employees are properly added to the payroll.

Hospital Insurance (HI) Plan program of medical care that provides protection against costs of certain hospital and related services; also known as Basic Medicare or Part A Medicare.

Human resources system those procedures and methods related to recruiting, selecting, orienting, training, and terminating personnel.

Immediate credit item a check or other instrument of payment for which immediate credit is given the payee by the receiving bank in accordance with its check-collection schedule.

Income tax levy on the earnings of most employees that is deducted from their gross pay.

Independent contractor a person who follows an independent trade, business, or profession where services are offered to the public.

Indexing updating, or adjusting a dollar amount over any particular time period (such as a calendar year) to reflect changes in wage levels that have occurred since a predetermined base time period.

Individual-account plan supplemental unemployment benefits plan in which the employer's contributions are paid into a separate trust for each employee.

Individual employee coverage applied to determine if the FLSA covers an employee. The test is that the employee either engages in interstate commerce or produces goods for such commerce.

Individual retirement account (IRA) employee's pension plan which is established and funded by the individual employee.

Information return form upon which an employer reports compensation paid to individuals who are not employees.

Interstate employee an individual who works in more than one state.

Investigative consumer report study done by a consumer reporting agency on a job applicant or current employee concerning the individual's character, general reputation, and mode of living.

Job cost card time card prepared for each job in process, showing the time spent by each employee on that particular job.

Journal entry a transaction recorded in the accounting system of a business.

Lookback period the block of time, consisting of four quarters beginning July of the second preceding year and ending June 30 of the prior year, used to determine if an employer is a monthly or a semiweekly depositor.

Medicaid program of medical assistance provided to aged and needy persons by means of a joint federal-state program.

Merit rating see experience rating.

Monthly depositor one who reported employment taxes of $50,000 or less for the four quarters in the lookback period.

Negative-balance employers those whose reserve accounts have been charged for more benefits paid out than contributions paid into the fund.

Partial unemployment employment by the individual's regular employer on a reduced scale because of lack of work.

Partial unemployment notice form completed by employer and given to partially unemployed workers so that supplemental unemployment benefits may be obtained.

Payroll accounting system those procedures and methods related to the disbursement of pay to employees.

Payroll journal book of original entry used for recording each payroll transaction and as the source for posting to appropriate general ledger accounts.

Payroll register multicolumn form used to assemble and summarize the data needed at the end of each payroll period. It lists all employees who earned remuneration, the amount of remuneration, the deductions, and the net amount paid.

Percentage method method of determining amount of income taxes to be withheld using Table of Allowance Values and Percentage Method Withholding Table.

Person an entity defined by law as an individual, a trust or estate, a partnership, or a corporation.

Personal allowance a deduction allowed in computing taxable income; also known as a personal exemption.

Piece-rate system compensation plan under which workers are paid according to their output (units or pieces produced).

Pooled-fund laws unemployment insurance system wherein the cost of unemployment benefits is spread among all employers in a particular state.

Pooled-fund plan supplemental unemployment benefits plan financed by employers' contributions into a general fund; also known as the *auto* or *Ford-type plan*.

Positive-balance employers those who have built up a balance in their reserve accounts (contributions paid in less benefits charged).

Prehire inquiries questions asked in the employment interview and on application forms, resumes of experience or education required of an applicant, and any kind of written testing.

Primary insurance amount (PIA) a person's monthly retirement or disability benefit, which is the base upon which monthly benefits of the worker's family and survivors are computed.

Principal activities those tasks employees must perform for the employer.

Profit-sharing plan compensation plan in which employer shares with employees a portion of the profits of the business.

Quarter of coverage criterion used to determine if workers are fully insured, currently insured, or insured for disability benefits; the minimum amount of wages or self-employment income with which individuals must be credited in a calendar quarter if they are to receive credit toward being insured for that period.

Quarterly averaging of wages method of determining amount of income taxes to be withheld by estimating the employee's average wages for the calendar quarter, computing an average payment, and withholding an amount based on the average payment.

Reciprocal agreement arrangement entered into by two or more states whereby the resident of one state working in another state will not be subject to the withholding of income taxes by the state in which the person is employed if that state has entered into a similar agreement with the employee's resident state.

Reciprocal arrangements agreements between states to provide unemployment insurance coverage and payment of benefits to interstate workers.

Reference inquiry form document used by the employer to investigate the references given on the application blank by the job applicant.

Requisition for personnel document submitted by a department head to the Human Resources Department asking for additional or replacement employees.

Reserve-ratio formula experience-rating plan used in most states, based on: Contributions less Benefits Paid ÷ Average Payroll.

Safe harbor rule rule that determines if an employer has satisfied the deposit obligations by (a) having no shortfall that exceeds the greater of $100 or 2% of the amount of employment taxes required to be deposited and (b) having deposited the shortfall on or before the shortfall make-up date.

Salary remuneration paid on a monthly, biweekly, semimonthly, or yearly basis.

Self-employment income the net earnings derived by individuals from a business or profession carried on as a sole proprietorship or as a partnership.

Semimonthly twice a month.

Semiweekly depositor one who reported employment taxes of more than $50,000 for the four quarters in the lookback period.

Separation report report that provides a wage and employment record of the separated employee and the reason for leaving.

Shortfall the excess of the amount of employment taxes required to be deposited over the amount deposited on or before the last date prescribed for the deposit.

Sick pay any payment made to individuals because of their personal injury or sickness that does not constitute wages.

Simplified employee pension (SEP) plan formal plan by means of which employers may make contributions to individual retirement accounts on behalf of their employees.

Social security benefits payments made under Title II of the Social Security Act to retired workers, their spouses, children and parents, as well as widows, widowers, and some divorced persons; also known as OASDI benefits and Title II benefits.

Special withholding allowance allowance claimed by employees so that wages which are below the level subject to the income tax will not be subject to withholding.

Standard deduction an amount of money used to reduce an individual's adjusted gross income in computing taxable income.

Status report initial statement filed by new employers with their state unemployment office, which determines their liability to make contributions into the state unemployment compensation fund.

Supplemental unemployment benefits private supplementation of state unemployment compensation benefits to employees during periods of layoff.

Supplemental wage payments additional compensation such as vacation pay, bonuses, and commissions paid to employees.

Supplementary medical insurance plan program of voluntary medical care for aged and disabled designed to cover costs of doctors' services and other items and services not covered under the basic program; also known as supplementary or voluntary Medicare or Part B Medicare.

Taxable wage base the maximum amount of wages during a calendar year that is subject to a particular tax, such as FICA.

Time card form on which employee's time worked is recorded manually by the worker or automatically by a time clock.

Time sheet form that indicates an employee's time of arrival and time of departure.

Tip gift or gratuity given by a customer in recognition of service performed for him or her.

Tipped employee one engaged in an occupation in which tips of more than $30 a month are customarily and regularly received.

Title XII advances funds borrowed from the federal government by states who, due to financial difficulties, cannot pay their unemployment compensation benefits.

Unemployment compensation benefits payments made to workers who are temporarily unemployed.

Unemployment insurance a federal-state program that provides economic security for workers during periods of temporary unemployment.

Unemployment insurance taxes the source of funds at the state level which are used to provide benefits for unemployed workers.

Vesting the process of conveying to employees the right to share in a retirement fund in the event they are terminated before the normal retirement age.

Voluntary contributions payments deliberately made by employers to their state funds in order to qualify for a lower unemployment compensation tax rate.

Wage remuneration paid on an hourly, weekly, or piecework basis.

Wage and tax statement statement furnished by employers to their employees informing them of the wages paid during the calendar year and the amount of taxes withheld from those wages.

Wage information report statement filed by the employer, usually with the quarterly contribution report, which lists employee names, social security numbers, taxable wages, taxable tips, state in which worker was employed during the reported quarter, and employer's federal account number.

Wage-bracket method method of determining amount of income taxes to be withheld by reading amount from tables provided by the IRS, which take into consideration length of payroll period, gross earnings, marital status, and number of withholding allowances claimed.

Wages total compensation paid to employees for services, such as wages, salaries, commissions, or bonuses, including the fair market value of noncash property.

Workers' compensation insurance protection provided employees and their dependents against losses due to injury or death incurred during employment.

Workweek fixed and regularly recurring period of 168 hours—7 consecutive 24-hour periods.